CADOGANguides

BRITTANY

'An air of mystery remains along much of the Breton shore, in the endless confusion of its headlands and indented estuaries, and in the drama of reefs and rocks, which in places such as Paimpol and Penmarc'h look as if a shower of meteorites has rained down on the sea.'

Philippe Barbour

About the Guide

The full-colour introduction gives the author's overview of the region, together with suggested itineraries and a regional 'where to go' map and feature to help you plan your trip.

Illuminating and entertaining cultural chapters on local history, food, drink and everyday life give you a rich flavour of the region.

Planning Your Trip starts with the basics of when to go, getting there and getting around, coupled with other useful information, including a section for disabled travellers. The Practical A–Z deals with all the essential information and contact details that you may need while you are away.

The regional chapters are the core of the book, guiding you with Cadogan's trademark verve to the sights and activities you can enjoy around Brittany. They are arranged in a loose touring order, and the author's top 'Don't Miss' ⭐ sights are highlighted at the start of each chapter.

A language and pronunciation guide, a glossary of Breton words and a comprehensive index can be found at the end of the book.

Although everything we list in this guide is personally recommended, our authors inevitably have their own favourite places to eat and stay. Whenever you see this Author's Choice ★ icon beside a listing, you will know that it is a little bit out of the ordinary.

Hotel Price Guide (*see also* p.72)

Luxury	€€€€€	€230 and above
Very Expensive	€€€€	€150–230
Expensive	€€€	€100–150
Moderate	€€	€60–100
Inexpensive	€	under €60

Restaurant Price Guide (*see also* p.77)

Very Expensive	€€€€	€50 and above
Expensive	€€€	€35–50
Moderate	€€	€20–35
Inexpensive	€	€20 and under

About the Author

Philippe Barbour is both Petit Breton and Grand Breton, being half-Breton and half-British. He is passionate about Brittany, and explored virtually every one of its creeks, chapels and boulders to present you with the best of the region in this guide. He has written several other books for Cadogan, including guides to the Loire and to the Rhône-Alpes, and is co-author of the Cadogan Guide to France.

4th edition published 2009

Above: Gorgeous Port St-Goustan in the Morbihan saw Benjamin Franklin land in France

less well known, such as the staggeringly beautiful Bay of St-Brieuc not far east of the fabulous pink rocks of the Côte de Granit Rose.

You really need to head far inland to find truly tranquil corners in the region in high summer. Travel up any of the ever so many crooked, delightful Breton rivers and you quickly leave the pounding ocean for quieter, wooded banks. These estuaries are sometimes known as 'abers' or 'avens'. The most renowned is that of Pont-Aven, made so famous by the shockingly colourful art of Paul Gauguin and Emile Bernard. Up the estuaries, you come to large historic towns, with their old quays tucked well out of sight from invaders, such as Morlaix, one of the best hide-outs for Breton corsairs, or Quimper, internationally known for its pottery.

After the defensive chain of estuary towns, you can then go in search of peaceful Breton countryside, perhaps following the rivers right up to their sources. You might track the Blavet, for instance, a splendid river that supplies the gorgeous Lac de Guerlédan in the heart of Brittany. Chapels and villages of granite or schist hide among the ridges and boulder-strewn landscapes of the Breton interior. Some of the rocks were turned into Neolithic monuments. The chapels most often display naïve statues of the Breton saints. The much-celebrated elaborate calvaries of the province are mainly a feature of the Finistère in the west. In fact, the further west you go in Brittany, the more typically Breton the region looks.

Breton culture thrives, right in the centre of Brittany and right by the shore. Breton dance, Breton bagpipe music and the *pardons*, the pious pilgrimages when local saints are taken out of their humid churches for an annual airing, are still going strong. Go and join in these and other celebrations, as well as lazing on those gorgeous beaches or feeling the wind in your hair as you walk or sail around the sensational Breton coast.

01 INTRODUCING BRITTANY

Brittany's magnificently varied shores can be intensely exhilarating or extremely calming depending on how you decide to spend your time here... Seagulls bark at you as you walk along a dramatic coastal path, the winds threatening to blow you off that treacherous rocky promontory. Sea foam flies against a Breton lighthouse as you sail by. Waves roar into beaches fully exposed to the Atlantic more noisily than motorway traffic, or lap as gently as a caress in the more protected bays. Barnacles scratch the soles of your feet as you scramble across extraordinary rocks, while gelatinous algae creepily stroke your legs as you swim along, creating mythical sea monsters in your mind. Relaxing on one of Brittany's hundreds of magical sandy beaches, translucent sand-hoppers or playful children tickle you out of your reveries as you lie daydreaming on warm sands. At a restaurant terrace with sea views, you wash down piles of crêpes or platters of seafood with country cider or a tingling Muscadet.

An air of mystery remains along much of the Breton shore, in the endless confusion of its headlands and indented estuaries, and in the drama of reefs and rocks, which in places such as Paimpol and Penmarc'h look as if a shower of meteorites has rained down on the sea. Yet much of the Breton coast and all the islands are now fought over by tourists. Such is the high regard in which the Breton resorts are held that, in a recent survey of tour operators asking them which they considered the finest beaches in the world, La Baule in Brittany was voted second. There are numerous more wonderful major resorts to me. Seeking out a quieter corner along the coast in high summer isn't easy, but I have given good coverage in the touring chapters to places by the sea that are comparatively

Top: A lone fisherman braves the elements, Pointe de la Torche, Finistère

Above: The boats often seem calmer than the crowds at Pont-Aven, Finistère

Below: Notre-Dame de la Joie chapel stands on the southwestern tip of Cornouaille, Finistère

Brittany's Top Ten Sights

1. On the Rance River, three exceptional Breton towns battling it out for your attention: St-Malo, Dinard and Dinan.

2. The ruggedly beautiful Cap Fréhel promontory, plus neighbouring Fort La Latte, Brittany's most unforgettable castle.

3. The Côte de Granit Rose, boasting the most extraordinary and amusing rocks in France.

4. The Bay of Morlaix, choc-a-block with delights, and a trio of extraordinary ports: Roscoff, St-Pol-de-Léon and Morlaix.

5. The Monts d'Arrée, with unspoilt villages and chapels scattered across their atmospheric hills (and the most famous church enclosures in Brittany down below in the Elorn Valley).

6. The Baie de Douarnenez, magically calm, its northern flank protected from the raging Atlantic by the Presqu'île de Crozon and the most impressive cliffs in Brittany .

7. The gently seductive Southern Cornouaille coast from Pont-l'Abbé to art-crazed Pont-Aven.

8. The Blavet Valley, offering enchantments around every corner.

9. The Golfe du Morbihan, vertically challenged, but with mesmerizing horizons. Neolithic men adored the place and the great Carnac lies just a bit west.

10. It's impossible to single out the one best island off the Breton coast, so read on for the author's particular favourites.

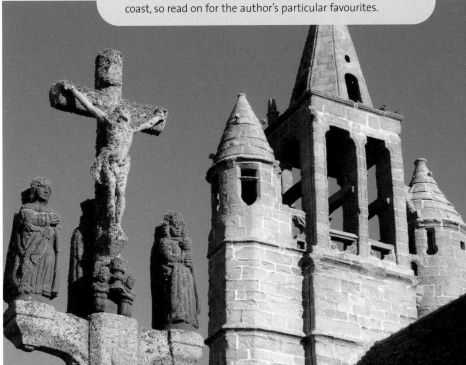

Where to Go

I've explored the whole length of Brittany's shores for this guide, from the deep calm of the Bay of the Mont St-Michel, around the rough Atlantic shores and calmer bays, to the beaches beyond the Loire estuary. All along the Breton coast, the vestiges of Neolithic civilization, the remnants of fortifications, the memories of colonial times and the scars of Nazi occupation mingle with spectacular beaches, bays and ports. The place names, from St-Malo round to the Pointe de St-Gildas, recall the religious men who crossed the Channel in the Dark Ages to set up communities on this Armorican peninsula, turning it into Brittany. These men were turned into the semi-legendary Breton saints never recognized by the Catholic Church. I've covered inland Brittany with equal zeal – with so many atmospheric towns, villages, museums, churches and natural attractions, don't ignore it.

For the touring chapters, I've divided Brittany up according to its four official French administrative *départements*: the Ille-et-Vilaine, the Côtes d'Armor, the Finistère and the Morbihan. I've also included highlights of a fifth, the Loire Atlantique, most of which was traditionally a part of Brittany, with its main town, Nantes, the last capital of the independent medieval duchy.

The **Ille-et-Vilaine** in the northeast of the region may only have a tiny stretch of Breton shoreline, but it's packed with an amazing number of highlights, St-Malo and Dinard vying for the main attention. To the west, the string of resorts gives way to the drama of Cap Fréhel and Fort La Latte, while to the east, gorgeous Cancale overlooks the Baie du Mont St-Michel – Brittany claims a large chunk of that great bay. Inland, lines of gritty castles and picturesque villages may detain you on your way to the Breton capital, Rennes, a buzzing, youthful city. Attractions close to it include Merlin's Forest of Paimpont (or should I say Brocéliande?) and the purple Vilaine Valley, while out east, the Breton frontier is marked by the hugely impressive fortresses of Fougères and Vitré.

The **Côtes d'Armor** boasts the most colourful stretches of Breton coast, especially along the Côte de Granit Rose, with its exceptionally spectacular rockscapes and resorts. Dinan and Tréguier are this *département*'s two grandest historic stops, understandably touristy. Moving inland, a semi-circle of attractive, but less well-known towns, Lamballe, Moncontour, Quintin and Guingamp, surround the *département*'s capital, St-Brieuc. Further south, you enter deliciously rural parts, and can hunt down the Lac de Guerlédan, a beautiful lake at the very heart of Brittany.

With dramatic coasts along three of its four sides, the **Finistère** out west is the very essence of Brittany. Towering lighthouses guard against the most dangerous rocks; ports and beaches find highly picturesque spots in which to shelter. There are vibrant estuary

Above: Brittany's historic inland towns and villages prove as enchanting as the coastal ports and resorts; here, Quimper, capital of Cornouaille, Finistère, with the striking twin spires of its cathedral

Chapter Divisions

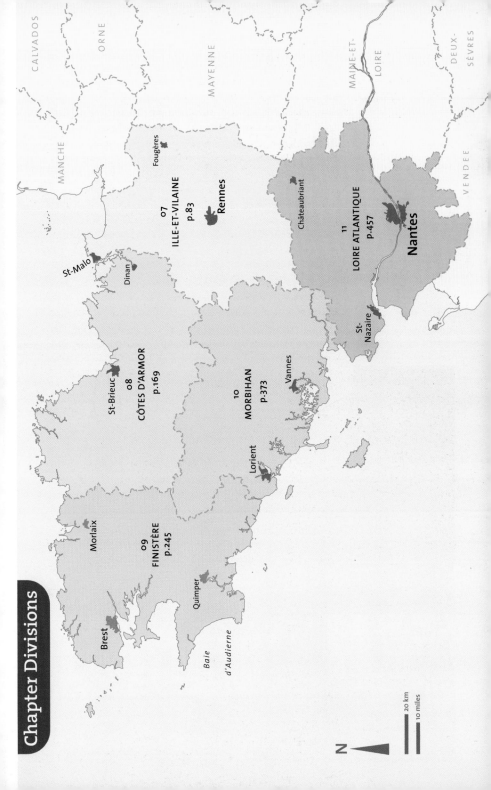

07
ILLE-ET-VILAINE
p.83
Rennes

Fougères
St-Malo
Dinan

08
CÔTES D'ARMOR
p.169
St-Brieuc

Morlaix

09
FINISTÈRE
p.245

Brest

Quimper

Baie
d'Audierne

Lorient

10
MORBIHAN
p.373
Vannes

11
LOIRE ATLANTIQUE
p.457
Nantes

Châteaubriant

St-
Nazaire

CALVADOS
ORNE
MANCHE
MAYENNE
MAINE-ET-
LOIRE
DEUX-
SÈVRES
VENDÉE

N

20 km
10 miles

Below: Rennes, capital of the Ille-et-Vilaine and of the whole of Brittany, is full of glamorous squares

towns to enjoy here, such as Morlaix and Quimper, but the best-known river-bank settlement is Pont-Aven, where Gauguin was famously inspired. There are calmer corners to discover as well, for example in the great bays of Brest and Douarnenez, or following the Breton calvary trails inland through the atmospheric hills of the Monts d'Arrée and Montagnes Noires.

The **Morbihan** is the place to go for the most famous concentration of Neolithic sights in Europe, with Carnac at the centre of the prehistoric action. It's not the only important Neolithic sight – several others are scattered around the splendidly mysterious inland sea known as the Golfe du Morbihan. A tail of land, the Quiberon peninsula, sticks out from the mainland. This leads you to the place where ferries depart for Belle-Ile, Brittany's largest island, a stunning holiday destination in its own right. Pretty villages and sights are scattered about inland Morbihan, most notably along the Blavet and Oust Rivers.

The **Loire Atlantique** may no longer be a part of Brittany officially, but historically, it was. Nantes, former Breton capital, is a happening place today, especially given the massive renovation of the Ile de Nantes and the creation of the awesome Machines de l'Ile. Out along the coast, you'll find plenty of traditional Breton ports and resorts north of the Loire, while to the south, Pornic is a last outpost of Brittany.

Above: The exhilaratingly rocky sea route to the islands beyond Morlaix, Finistère

Island Hopping

Islands abound off the Breton coast. Some are joined to the mainland by sandy walkways that appear miraculously at low tide, offering you the possibility of a joyous if brief voyage of discovery on foot. Others are only reachable by ferry. Below, we focus on the most gorgeous among the latter.

1 Bréhat, a gem of geology.
2 Belle-Ile – as the name implies, this, the largest of Brittany's islands, is very beautiful all round.
3 Houat and Hoëdic, little pearls just off Belle-Ile.
4 Big old Groix, more down to earth than neighbouring Belle-Ile, but none the worse for that.
5 Batz above Roscoff, preserving its authentic feel too.
6 The name of Ouessant, or Ushant, has long put fear into sailors, but visitors have a ball exploring its wild side.
7 Sein, long thought to be a stepping stone to eternity, lying off France's Land's End.
8 Les Glénan, giving you a tiny taste of the Caribbean off the southern Finistère coast.
9 L'Ile aux Moines, in the midst of the Golfe du Morbihan, makes for a truly delightful day out.
10 The impressive Sept Iles above Perros-Guirec are a bird reserve, but on certain days you're allowed to step briefly onto one.
11 Plus, to spend an exceptional night or two on a scarcely inhabited island, see about the possibility of staying on either L'Ile Millau or L'Ile de Quémenès – find out about these in our touring chapters.

The Best of Inland Brittany in a Fortnight

If you have less time, just do the northern half or the southern half of this itinerary.

Day 1 Entering inland Brittany from the east, you pass through the **Breton Marches**, former frontier lands once guarded by vast fortresses. The two very best castles stand at **Fougères** and **Vitré**, both charming historic towns.

Day 2 **Rennes**, capital of Brittany, cultured and studenty, boasts a mix of amazing timber-frame houses and grand granite squares, plus a whole exciting new quarter, including the revamped Musée de Bretagne.

Day 3 Follow the purple road down the **Vilaine** from Rennes and you come upon some surprising sights, the best of which are the little-known Neolithic monuments of St-Just.

Day 4 The **Forêt de Paimpont** west of Rennes is also known as the Forêt de Brocéliande, the setting of many a tale of Merlin in Breton Arthurian legend.

Day 5 North of Rennes, the clutch of castles is filled with meaning in Breton culture. Choose between **Montmuran**, **Combourg** and **La Bourbansais**. And pay a visit to bookish **Bécherel**, the Breton Hay-on-Wye.

Day 6 North again, dominating the Rance River, **Dinan** will stop you in its tracks with its tremendous ramparts, behind which lies a splendid historic city.

Day 7 Less well known, but full of charm, is the string of smaller historic towns forming a ring inland from St-Brieuc. Choose between **Lamballe**, with a stud farm devoted to Breton horses right in the centre, highly picturesque **Moncontour**, the weaving-rich **Quintin**, or **Guingamp**, deeply Breton in feel.

Day 8 The **Lac de Guerlédan** might be called the heart of Brittany, and it's utterly delightful, its wooded, indented shores resembling the Breton coast in some ways. Although created by the building of a modern dam, the lake is surrounded by adorable historic sights, including old churches, and an Ancien Régime forge as pretty as any château.

Day 9 In the **countryside between Morlaix and Brest** stands one of the most famous strings of Breton churches, often with elaborate calvaries and parish enclosures, the trail well-marked.

Day 10 The **Monts d'Arrée** hills dividing northern and southern Finistère are peppered with enchanting villages and churches.

Day 11 Moving to the southern half of the Finistère, around the wooded slopes of the **Montagnes Noires**, the towns and villages are proud of their strong Breton traditions. The bucolic **Aulne River** doubles as the Canal de Nantes à Brest here.

Day 12 Northwest Morbihan. The **Blavet Valley** between Pontivy and Hennebont is utterly enchanting. Choose from a selection of very sweet little tourist sights you can visit scattered along its unspoilt length.

Day 13 Northeast Morbihan. Here, the château and town of **Josselin**, on the Oust River, is perhaps the most fascinating of a bunch of extraordinary tourist villages, although it has very stiff competition from exquisite **Rochefort-en-Terre** and from **La Gacilly**, the fief of herbal cosmetics pioneer Yves Rocher.

Day 14 Medieval capital of Brittany, banished postwar to become capital of the new Pays de la Loire region, **Nantes** is an intriguing city set beside France's greatest river. It has been undergoing a huge makeover in the first decade of the 21st century.

Above left: A dramatic cobbled street at Dinan, Côtes d'Armor

Below left: Breton church art can be impressively naive, as at St-Aignan church, Lac de Guerlédan

Above: Grieving over the dead Christ in a typical time-worn calvary scene, Brasparts, Finistère

Right: The Château de Josselin reflected in the Canal de Nantes à Brest, Morbihan

01 | Introduction | The Best of Inland Brittany in a Fortnight

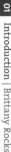

Above: A rock like a giant skull oversees the beach at Trégastel, Côtes d'Armor

Below: The Phare d'Eckmühl reflected in rock pools at the Pointe de Penmarc'h, Finistère

Brittany Rocks

Brittany is the land of rocks and boulders *par excellence*. You'll encounter them in profusion not just along the coast, but inland, too. Nature has played extraordinary tricks with its granite creations here. Along the Côte de Granit Rose, the most famous, colourful and extraordinarily shaped rocks in Brittany have to be seen to be believed, adopting their strange shapes and acrobatic poses. But all around Brittany, you'll find rocks that will fill you with awe, or spark your imagination with their intriguing forms. Here are some of the natural rocky highlights, including the odd lighthouse overseeing them.

1 The wildly eccentric pink and orange rock formations at Trégastel and Ploumanach on the Côte de Granit Rose.
2 The Sillon de Talbert sticking its improbably long, pebbly finger into the sea.
3 Cap Fréhel, its lighthouse set amidst the moorlands around its sensational promontory.
4 The cliffs around Plouha, the tallest in Brittany.
5 The Ile Vierge lighthouse rising far above the vicious rocks surrounding it.
6 The Mont-Dol, overlooking the Bay of Mont St-Michel in a dramatic spot where St Michael is said to have fought Satan.
7 The sensationally competing headlands of the Presqu'île de Crozon.
8 Chaucer made one of his *Canterbury Tales* revolve around the 'grisly feendly rokkes blake' of the Pointe de Penmarc'h, now guarded by the Phare d'Eckmühl.
9 Huelgoat's giant moss-covered boulders, associated with Celtic gods and giants.
10 The artistically inspiring 'stepping stones' of Pont-Aven.

Breton Culture Marked by Stone

Down the centuries, the inhabitants of the region have put the local stone to remarkable use, too, most memorably in the Neolithic millennia, with their *dolmen* ('stone table') tombs and *menhirs* ('standing stones'), and in medieval and Renaissance times, with the building of castles, churches and outdoor calvaries in distinctively Breton style. Here follow some man-made rocky highlights.

1 The amazing, mysterious Neolithic stones of Carnac and the Golfe du Morbihan.

2 Europe's largest Neolithic tomb, at Barnenez, overseeing the Bay of Morlaix.

3 Merlin's links with the Neolithic stones of the Forêt de Paimpont.

4 The most gorgeously decorated Neolithic tomb in Brittany, on the island of Gavrinis.

5 The more secretive Neolithic monuments of St-Just, standing in splendid isolation.

6 Tréguier cathedral, with its many towers and the tomb of Brittany's most important medieval saint, Yves.

7 The calvary trail across the Elorn Valley and Monts d'Arrée.

8 Fort La Latte, the most awesome of Brittany's coastal castles.

9 The Château de Josselin reflected in the Oust.

10 Fougères castle, a mighty eastern outpost.

11 The Château de Nantes, recently scrubbed clean to house a major new museum.

Top: The mighty Château de Fougères on Brittany's eastern frontier, Ille-et-Vilaine

Above: One of Carnac's hundreds of intriguing, moody standing stones, Morbihan

Best Ports

In our recent tourist times, the distinction has become increasingly blurred in Brittany between what's a port and what's a resort. All the ports chosen below now have a double vocation as resorts. In addition, even if they may not make it onto conventional lists of Breton highlights, your Cadogan *Brittany* author has a soft spot for the former military harbours of Brest, Lorient, and St-Nazaire, converting their poisoned war legacies with great panache, and making the most of their stunning locations.

Above: Erquy, in the Côtes d'Armor, doubles admirably as both port and resort

Below: Shellfish doesn't come fresher than this

1 St-Malo, a sensational place at which to arrive in Brittany.
2 Overlooking the Baie du Mont St-Michel is gorgeous Cancale, now almost as devoted to tourists as to the cultivation of oysters and mussels.
3 Roscoff, perhaps beating St-Malo in the stakes for France's most attractive ferry port.
4 Douarnenez's string of wonderfully contrasting ports.
5 Old wooden fishing boats dying by the jetty at Camaret.
6 Audierne, which offers a lovely Breton haven away from the battering Atlantic.
7 The family of Pays Bigouden ports from St-Guénolé to Loctudy are all bursting with gritty atmosphere.
8 Concarneau, with its walled island city, its artistic legacy and its fine beaches.
9 Port-Louis and Lorient, not only for their colonial legacy, but also the funky recent addition of the Cité de la Voile.
10 Le Croisic, overlooking the salt marshes of Guérande.

Brittany isn't just about tradition, although the traditional is irresitible here...

Right: St-Malo's rampart cannon are now purely decorative, Ille-et-Vilaine

Below middle: Peace at Kérity harbour, Finistère

Bottom right: The enchanting strait between Loctudy and L'Ile-Tudy, Finistère

Below left: The Cité de la Voile's groundbreaking sailing centre, Morbihan

Best Resorts

The competition is stiff. Here are some top contenders, counting great beaches among their many assets. As for Breton beaches generally, there are so many hundreds of beautiful ones around the region, we'll leave you to select your top ten in whichever area you plump for – whether you be on the north, west or south coast, you'll be spoilt for breathtaking choices.

1 Dinard, the *grande dame* of Breton seaside resorts, with fabulous coastal paths passing below palatial villas.

2 Erquy, a very cheerful holiday spot, with the gorgeous sands of Sables-d'Or-les-Pins just around the corner.

3 Perros-Guirec, stretching round a magnificent headland.

4 Locquirec and Carantec, chic sister resorts each set on their own exclusive peninsula near Roscoff.

5 Morgat, in a laid-back location on the exhilarating Crozon peninsula.

6 Enchanting Bénodet and Ste-Marine, facing each other across the estuary of the Odet, popularly referred to in Brittany as the prettiest river in France.

7 Carnac: not just about the hundreds of standing stones, while nearby La Trinité-sur-Mer attracts the finest yachtsmen.

8 Quiberon, for a handful of good reasons, even if it's a bit of a mess.

9 La Baule, not Breton in character, but with beach and seaside facilities that are hard to beat.

10 Pornic may lie south of the Loire, but it boasts many enchanting Breton attractions.

Top: La Baule in the Loire Atlantique offers all the joys of a beach holiday along its great arc of sand

Above: Perros-Guirec presents a plethora of attractions in the Côtes d'Armor

CONTENTS

Contents

Maps and Plans

Reference

History, Art and Architecture

O2

History

Stepping into a Fog of Celtic Romance

Breton history has been dogged by the thickest fog of romance and it looks unlikely this will ever entirely lift. Even if serious historians have been trying to find more trustworthy paths through it, many don't care to follow. Misinterpretations and misrepresentations have abounded, and some have stuck. Let's start with a few major examples.

For ages, the widely scattered remains of a great neolithic society on the Armorican peninsula (as Brittany is also somewhat technically known) were incorrectly regarded as vestiges of a much later Celtic civilization. Moving swiftly on, certain nationalistic Bretons created a nostalgic view of the Middle Ages in Brittany, portraying this as a golden age of independence – small matter that in that period, the vast majority of rural Bretons had no choices in their subjugated lives, as politics then were dominated by aristocratic feudal ties of service, marriage and warring that jumped regional frontiers when convenient. As to Brittany after its union with France under the Ancien Régime, all too little mention has been made in general history books of the slave trade in which many Breton merchants were deeply involved. A rapid chronological guide follows through Brittany's hotly debated history.

Fiery Prehistory, Neolithic Society and Gaulish Armorica

The first remains of human ancestors found on the Armorican peninsula have been dated to the middle of the Paleolithic Age, a dauntingly long and distant period stretching from c. 700,000 BC to 10,000 BC. Most excitingly in archaeology, prehistoric finds made at Menez Dregan in the Finistère in 1998 shattered scientists' views on how long ago our ancestors discovered the use of fire, almost doubling estimates from 250,000 years ago to 465,000 years ago, very roughly speaking. If correct, these count, to date, as one of the oldest known traces of fire made by our ancestors anywhere in the world, although some argue about the validity of the finds.

As the last ice age ended some 10,000 or so years ago, and Europe started to warm up again, a few Mesolithic hunter-gatherers were established on the Armorican peninsula. Modest traces of them have been discovered, notably skeletons covered with shell necklaces and antlers on islands off Quiberon. Mesolithic communities appear to have been rapidly supplanted by neolithic agricultural settlers.

Brittany's neolithic period is considered to have lasted longer than our Christian era, from 5000 BC to 2000 BC. These neolithic people had acquired the skills of agriculture once thought to have been developed in the Middle East, although recently academics have argued that they were invented quite separately here. The people cleared land for farming, reared cattle and grew cereals. They also developed stone tools, pottery and weaving. It's quite possible that some sailed large distances to trade. A complex system of beliefs evolved, along with hierarchical social structures.

These people are best known to us through their mysterious menhirs or standing stones, and their grand tombs. Two thousand years and more before the great pyramids went up in Egypt, neolithic men in Armorica were already constructing vast burial monuments, which aren't unique to Brittany, but are particularly numerous and spectacular here. To discover more about the neolithic inhabitants, visit the museums at Carnac, Vannes and Penmarc'h, as well as the many neolithic sights signalled in our touring chapters.

As a tourist, you'll find few remains of civilization dating from between 2000 BC and the Roman conquest of 57 BC in Brittany. Although it was traditionally thought that there was a large Celtic influx this far west in the latter half of the 1st millennium BC, some recent historians think it may be more a case of Celtic influences gradually infiltrating the communities already well established here.

No traces of significant pre-Roman communities have been found in the province, except at Alet, St-Malo's precursor. However, towards the end of the pre-Roman period, evidence of strong trading ties with southern Britain emerge. Culturally, the Armorican peoples appear to have been close to other western European tribes, with a similar mythology and language as well as shared tribal and place names.

Caesar and a few other classical writers give us rare glimpses of Celtic Gaulish culture as they saw it. They identified two privileged groups, the nobles and the druids, who lorded it over a virtually enslaved populace. The druids seem to have been enormously respected, deciding on legal matters, being exempt from military service and taxes, and officiating at religious ceremonies and sacrifices. They passed on learning orally, as their religion prohibited them from committing their knowledge to writing. Caesar claims they also believed in magic and an afterlife.

Roman Conquest and Enslavement, Prosperity and Christianity

Caesar's troops had little trouble conquering Gaul, the Armorican peninsula included. Even if no one had a magic potion to help, the region's tribes did soon take part in revolts, perhaps particularly anxious that the Romans were going to take away their lucrative trade with southern Britain. Caesar, in *The Conquest of Gaul*, tells of a stroke of luck in the campaign to beat and punish them, when the skilled sailors of the Veneti tribe (in what is now the Morbihan) were becalmed at the critical moment.

Under the Roman Empire, in the 1st and 2nd centuries AD, economic prosperity grew substantially, as did the first major Armorican towns, Gallo-Roman tribal centres. But the Romans didn't bring only good things; a sad sign used to stand by a small segment of Roman road by the Vilaine River, recalling: 'The Romans had this road built by their slaves, the Gauls.' The Romanization of Armorica was particularly strong in the urban areas, and while major villas did go up in the countryside, the mass of country folk probably saw life change little, sticking to many pre-Roman ways.

Christianity caught on slowly. Before the Roman Empire's official adoption of the religion, Christians were often persecuted. One tale of horror tells how, in AD 304, Donatien and Rogatien, sons of a governor of Nantes, were tortured and beheaded for their beliefs. Under 10 years later, however, the Emperor Constantine elevated Christianity to the position of exclusive imperial religion. Early bishoprics were set up at Nantes and Rennes. When Christianity turned from persecuted to persecutor, the rural peoples would put up some resistance to its intolerance of old beliefs.

The Dark Ages and the Creation Myths of Brittany, Little Britain

Swirling mists of disorientating legend obscure any clear view of how the Armorican peninsula turned into Brittany, or little Britain, you might say, during the Dark Ages. The extremely hazy picture is of a large number of strongly Christian immigrants fleeing from Ireland and the so-called Celtic fringes of western Britain, particularly south Wales, to impose themselves on the natives, profoundly influencing the culture of the region. The stories of saintly miracle men leading this exodus (*see* 'Stone Boats and Slain Dragons', p.41) are much more immediately entertaining than what may actually have happened.

Credible recent historians have proposed a complex variety of reasons why Britons settled on the Armorican peninsula. They estimate that the emigrations took place over several centuries, lasting up to the early 7th century, and probably commencing before the collapse of the Roman Empire. Certain historians reckon that violent Irish pirates and Irish incursions into western Britain from the late 3rd century caused an early panic emigration. Some British mercenaries called upon to serve the Empire in trying to help stop the advance of tribes from eastern Europe may also have settled in France's far west afterwards. However, the most significant factor is generally considered to have been the pressure put on western Britons by the Angle and Saxon invasions of Britain, causing many to migrate south.

One oft-quoted source on the subject of the Britons' emigration, Gildas, wrote angrily and poetically in the mid-6th century of the way his people had yielded too meekly to the Angles and Saxons in the previous century. The first known instance of the Armorican peninsula being referred to as Brittany, or rather Britannia, comes from the Byzantine historian Procopius; writing in the same period as Gildas, he seems to imply that the region was heavily colonized by then. Legends telling of the heroic creation of a British state spanning both sides of the Channel would flourish from this time. They would be most famously peddled by the 12th-century writer Geoffrey of Monmouth, in his unreliable *History of the Kings of Britain*.

What's sure is that zealous Christian leaders looking for new challenges and conquests played a very important part in the region's change to Brittany. Irish monks may have been the first to try to work their religious magic on the Armorican peninsula. Charismatic Welsh Christian leaders certainly had a major effect in spreading the word of the Celtic Church. Seven of these early Welsh evangelizers became known as the **founding saints of Brittany**. Most of the host of Breton saints who followed were probably well educated and able to negotiate a good deal for themselves and their followers when they landed, and the communities they established certainly appear to have included members who could spin a good yarn... The papal-controlled Church of Rome would eventually impose its authority on western Brittany, but a distinctly different Celtic Christianity would last in the region up until the 9th century and beyond.

There is a pretty notion that the Dark Ages Celtic immigrants were simply warmly received by the natives, without any complications. Events were doubtless nowhere near that innocent. What seems likely is that the people firmly settled in the peninsula at the end of the Roman Empire found themselves increasingly pressured by British immigrants establishing themselves in particular in northern and western Armorica. Then there were the **Frankish** settlers moving in from the east with which to contend. The areas around Rennes, Nantes and Vannes, which contained rich agricultural lands and mineral deposits, in fact came under the rule of Frankish nobles in the 6th century.

The most feared Breton leader to emerge in the period was Waroc, who took on the Franks of the Vannetais and won after a cunning campaign; this extended Breton frontiers eastwards. That spectacularly unreliable but entertaining historian from the period, Bishop Gregory of Tours, related some gruesome tales of those times. The Vilaine River, and in the north the Couesnon River, perhaps acted as a kind of boundary between Bretons and Franks.

The Short-lived 'Kingdom of Brittany'

After the deposition in AD 751 of the Merovingian dynasty by **Pépin le Bref**, the first of the Carolingian Franks, warring flared up on the Breton borders, and Pépin's troops even sacked Vannes. The Carolingian Empire created the March of Brittany, a protective border zone covering the areas around Rennes and Nantes, but failed to establish its authority in Brittany; instead, through its antagonism, it probably helped to unite the Bretons. Fighting having proved frustrating, the Carolingian emperor and son of Charlemagne, **Louis le Pieux**, tried diplomacy in the 820s. This worked initially, and some talented Breton figures soon rose high in the imperial ranks.

Nomenoë (or Nominoë), a native Breton, was given the honour of becoming imperial *missus*, giving him control of military, civil, judicial and, unusually, ecclesiastical power over much of Brittany. While Louis le Pieux reigned, Nomenoë remained loyal. But in the disintegration of the empire that followed Louis's death, Nomenoë and his son Erispoë made a break for independence. **Charles le Chauve** (the Bald), new king of the Franks, tried to intervene with almost disastrous consequences – his troops were routed by Nomenoë's at the **Battle of Ballon** (near Redon by the Vilaine) in 845, and for a few days some thought that Charles himself had been killed.

Viking raids were a major threat by this time. It seems that Nomenoë managed to bribe these unwelcome newcomers into going and looking for booty elsewhere. Nomenoë took control of the Church across Brittany, replacing the bishops at Alet, Dol-de-Bretagne, St-Pol-de-Léon, Quimper and Vannes with Bretons of his own choice. When Nomenoë died in 851, Charles the Bald thought he might be able to defeat **Erispoë**; but he was again deeply humiliated, this time in 851, at the **Battle of Jengland-Beslé** (also by the Vilaine River).

Erispoë capitalized on Charles the Bald's weak position; he would accept peace only in return for territories on the fringes of Brittany, the counties of Rennes, Nantes and the area of Retz south of the Loire. Erispoë's gains would profoundly change the Breton boundaries, to last pretty much unchanged through to the 1960s. Erispoë also demanded suitably grand recognition, and became the first non-Carolingian to be given the title of ruler of a kingdom in the Holy Roman Empire. Brittany became the Regnum Britanniae. In 856, the year before he was violently assassinated by his cousin, Erispoë even saw his daughter married to Charles le Chauve's eventual successor as king of the Franks, Louis le Bégayeur (the Stammerer).

Salaun (or Salomon), Erispoë's lethal cousin, went on to become the most successful of all Breton leaders in terms of the territories that he acquired. Charles the Bald conceded a piece of Anjou and then handed him the whole Cotentin (or Cherbourg) peninsula in gratitude for helping to defeat a common enemy. In exchange, Salaun seems to have integrated Brittany more fully into the Carolingian system, both administratively and religiously. He moved the centre of Breton political affairs further east, where it has remained ever since.

Breton ecclesiastical and cultural life in the early 9th century shared in the so-called Carolingian Renaissance. Importantly, though, in Brittany, a passion for the great Celtic Christian evangelizing immigrants of earlier centuries was kept alive. These ancient leaders were venerated in a spate of largely fabricated biographies, which would continue to be churned out in the ensuing centuries.

Vicious Vikings, Breton Dukes and the Counts Next Door

The viciousness of the **Viking raids** on Brittany got dramatically worse in the early 10th century. As some Norsemen began settling into cohesive communities, many counts across Brittany felt forced to flee to Britain, as did the very king of the Franks, the well-named Louis d'Outremer (Overseas Louis). There is only evidence of one count in Brittany staying and successfully resisting the Norman takeover at this period, **Berengar of Rennes**. The Breton hero of the period, though, is **Alain Barbetorte** (Twisted Beard), Count of Cornouaille (or southwest Brittany), who came back from Britain in 936 to take on and oust the unwelcome settlers. After this traumatic break in Breton and Carolingian history, ducal Brittany emerged.

Alain Barbetorte and the leaders of Brittany who followed him were, more modestly than their predecessors, titled Duces Britonum. The **Breton dukes** of this early feudal period proved unable to wield the same power as their predecessors. The territorial gains Salaun had made were lost. Over the next few centuries, Brittany's ducal rulers would find themselves more and more pressurized and influenced by the **increasing might of the neighbouring regions, first Normandy and then Anjou**. These two expanded into substantial European powers for a time, while the Capetian kings of France ruled over a much weakened kingdom based around Paris and Orléans. Brittany couldn't compete with its strongly led neighbours, particularly because the Breton dukes found it impossible to unite the Breton counts below them.

Brittany around 950 was divided into **nine dioceses** that would last until the Revolution, the bishops based at Alet, Dol-de-Bretagne, Rennes, St-Brieuc, Tréguier, St-Pol-de-Léon, Quimper, Vannes and Nantes. These religious centres formed the nucleus for Brittany's important early medieval towns. The founding of feudal *castellanies*, based around a castle, with a priory close by, led to the establishment of other significant medieval towns, such as Fougères, Vitré, Dinan and Josselin.

Conan I, Count of Rennes, and his successors assumed the role of dukes of Brittany between around 970 and 1066. Under **Duke Conan II** (ruler from 1040 to 1066), the duke's uncle and former guardian, Eudes, started a messy civil war in Brittany. The counts of Cornouaille also acted very independently during this time. In fact, **Hoël of Cornouaille** assumed the title of duke in 1066, as Duke Conan II left no direct heir.

Breton nobles played a significant part in the Norman conquest of England in 1066 and were rewarded with English estates. One Breton and English nobleman, **Raoul de Gaël**, proved, however, to be a particularly tricky thorn in William the Conqueror's side; the Norman attacked Dol-de-Bretagne in 1076, but failed to take it, as illustrated on the Bayeux tapestry. But Duke Hoël's son and successor **Duke Alain IV** would marry first into the Normandy ruling family, then into the Angevin one. His second wife, Duchess Ermengarde, greatly influenced the reign of her son, the next Breton duke, **Conan III**.

Religious foundations mushroomed up in Brittany in the 11th and 12th centuries, in particular in the east; they brought greater links with the main ecclesiastical movements in France, but many Bretons still clung doggedly to old ways, particularly in the west. Superstition and magic apparently flourished, even among parish priests and monks. These strands of alternative belief remained strong in rural Brittany down to modern times. In the western half of the province, the Breton language thrived, too, but the feudal systems that had been adopted faster in eastern, Gallo-speaking Brittany were gradually reinforced. By the late 12th century, Brittany consisted of around 40 major *castellanies* under which lay another important level of local lordships, *seigneureries*.

Plantagenet and Capetian Intervention and Domination

Angevin **Henri II Plantagenêt**, who also became King Henry II of England, imposed his will of steel on the Breton peninsula in the second half of the 12th century. He controlled **Duke Conan IV**, who was much put upon by the feuding factions within his province, and so became a kind of puppet duke. In 1166, King Henry II arranged for Constance, a daughter of Conan IV, to be betrothed to his fourth son, Geoffrey. He then decided he would rule Brittany directly until Geoffrey came of age.

Angevin administration was imposed on Brittany and feudal obligations were much more rigidly defined; these changes were to remain influential down the Middle Ages. Henry II had no truck with dissenters; the castles at Rennes, Fougères, Bécherel and Léhon were among those destroyed on the king's orders when the nobles there displeased him. Surprisingly, early medieval Brittany had been scarcely involved in sea trade, but thanks to Angevin links with Aquitaine and England, Breton ports developed rapidly. Breton shipping merchants flourished and many Breton vessels carried Bordeaux wine to England.

Henry II's son and successor, **Richard the Lionheart**, would maintain an iron grip on Brittany. This caused the frustrated **Duke Geoffrey** to side with the Capetian **French king, Philippe Auguste**. Geoffrey's life was cut short when he was killed in an accident, and when King Richard died in 1199, **Duke Arthur** of Brittany had a strong claim to the English throne as grandson of Henry II, but Richard's brother John inherited. Arthur paid homage to Philippe Auguste and from this time on until the end of the feudal system, the kings of France remained the immediate suzerains of the Breton dukes. The wily King John, however, managed to capture Arthur and is reckoned to have had him killed – this treachery features large in Shakespeare's *King John*, although the Bard is never to be relied on as an historical source. What is certain is that Philippe Auguste did successfully seize most of King John's lands in France at the start of the 13th century.

The inheritance of the Breton duchy fell to Alix, half-sister of Duke Arthur; she was married to **Pierre de Dreux**, a Capetian relative of Philippe Auguste. Pierre tried to cut his vassals down to size and to diminish the Church's holdings in Brittany (hence his nickname, **Mauclerc**, 'Bad to Clerics'). He swiftly became enormously unpopular, but did manage for a time to control many of the warring factions within the province, also fighting back opportunist neighbours. He entered into alliances both with other awkward French princes to defy the French king, and with King Henry III of England. In 1230, rebel Breton nobles called on **King Louis IX**'s assistance against Mauclerc, and in 1234 the Breton duke had to yield to the French crown. He was forced to give up the dukedom to his son Jean as soon as the latter came of age. This he did in 1237.

Like father, like son. **Duke Jean I** not only angered the French king; he also found himself excommunicated by the pope. He succeeded, though, in subduing the many Breton lordly families, who detested him, and enjoyed the longest reign of any Breton duke – an impressive 49 years. **Duke Jean II**, who succeeded in 1286 and ruled until 1305, benefited from his father's successes. All in all, the 13th century saw the position of the Breton dukes much strengthened, but in the early part of the 14th century the French crown put pressure on the duchy, making heavier demands for troops and taxes. Brittany would soon be split in two by a terrible war of succession that followed **Duke Jean III**'s death in 1341 without any legitimate heir.

The Breton War of Succession, 1341 to 1365

The question of Breton succession became another bone of contention between the kingdoms of France and England, and would play out like a subplot to the early Hundred Years War. Breton law stated that Duke Jean III's nearest descendant should inherit, be that person a man or a woman. The most obvious heir was **Jeanne de Penthièvre**, a niece of his. She had been married to a nobleman with French royal connections, **Charles**, son of Guy, **Count of Blois**, and nephew of **Philippe VI** – the first Valois king of France. The latter had successfully defended his right to inherit the French throne in 1328 against the claim of **King Edward III of England**, but this had led Edward to go to war with France; it was the outbreak of the Hundred Years War.

Back in Brittany, Jeanne de Penthièvre and Charles de Blois had a rival for the Breton duchy. He was **Jean de Montfort**, son of Duke Arthur II of Brittany (who had preceded Duke Jean III) by the latter's second marriage; he was also Jeanne de Penthièvre's half-uncle. Philippe VI decided who should inherit and, unsurprisingly, declared in favour of Jeanne de Penthièvre and Charles de Blois. Edward III, in defiance, offered the Honour of Richmond, the English estates traditionally granted to the dukes of Brittany by the English crown, to Jean de Montfort. With such favourable backing, de Montfort called upon supporters to rally round him and the Breton War of Succession began. Some absurdly basic interpretations of this war make it sound as though the English simply arrived as an invading enemy force, the French supporting the Bretons, which was far from the case. Close family ties bound most of the powerful lords of northern Brittany to the Penthièvre cause. Jean de Montfort found followers among the disgruntled lesser nobles, notably in the Breton-speaking west. It seems that many Breton towns and ports readily supported de Montfort because of the importance of their trading ties with English territories.

Early on, Jean de Montfort was captured. But his feisty wife, **Jeanne de Flandres**, remained free and furious, heading a resistance movement. In response, several English armies arrived in Brittany in 1342, and the English-backed de Montfortists secured the ports in the west and south of the province. A truce was called in 1343, and Edward III returned to England with Jeanne de Flandres, leaving lieutenants in charge of the section of Brittany under their control. Traitors to the de Penthièvre cause in Vannes allowed the de Montfortists into that city, which became the centre of de Montfortist administration for the remainder of the war.

In 1345, Jean de Montfort, on parole in Paris, ran off to England and payed homage to Edward III; new troops were gathered for him there. De Montfort headed off to Brittany, only to die promptly from an infected wound. So the English lieutenants were effectively left to run the de Montfortist campaign until 1362, when finally de Montfort's heir, his son, also called Jean, came of age. Meanwhile, Charles de Blois had been captured in 1347 and taken as a prisoner to England; Jeanne de Penthièvre took up the cause.

However, with the campaigns of the Hundred Years War spreading into several parts of France, and with the terrifying scourge of the Black Death devastating the country in 1348 and 1349, the action was halted for a time. When fighting resumed, the military leaders spread terror through the countryside. **Bertrand du Guesclin** is the one most remembered, an extraordinarily powerful Breton knight, but a highly ambiguous figure in Breton history, as he in fact headed off to war for the French monarchy. Nationalistic French school history books long portrayed him as a national hero, fighting off the English. As we've shown, the conflicts around France and Brittany were more complex than that. What is sure is that the common Breton people suffered terribly through this protracted conflict. Many Breton towns built fortified walls to try to protect themselves during the warring.

By March 1353, it appeared that King Edward III might be ready to accept Charles de Blois as the new duke. But the matter wasn't settled and by 1356 Henry of Lancaster was taking the **young Jean de Montfort** over to Brittany to lay siege to Rennes. Charles de Blois lost the next round of the bout and was forced to pay huge ransoms. The volatile situation continued into the 1360s. Sir John Chandos was besieging **Auray** in 1364 when a much larger army led by Charles de Blois and du Guesclin came to meet the enemy. De Blois made a terrible tactical blunder and attacked from an unfavourable position. He was killed and his army defeated; Jeanne de Penthièvre conceded defeat. Du Guesclin was captured, but the English sportingly and unwisely let him go. By the **Treaty of Guérande** of 1365, the young Jean de Montfort was declared **Duke Jean IV of Brittany**.

The de Montfort Dukes, 1365 to 1491

The de Montfort dukes and their administrations would foster a keen sense of Breton identity at the expense of both the French and the English. However, Duke Jean IV's reign almost got off to a disastrous start when he became embroiled in the greater Anglo–French conflict in 1369. The French king **Charles V** attacked Brittany and Jean IV had to flee to England. Briefly it looked as if his duchy would be forcibly joined to France. The king missed his opportunity, however, by alienating the de Penthièvre party; so angered were they that in an extraordinary move, they called on Jean IV to return to Brittany. Du Guesclin had become leader of the French armies by this time and could have stopped Jean IV from landing had he wished. He made no effort to do so – perhaps his loyalties were divided on that occasion. Jean IV regained his ducal authority, and after Charles V's death, the second Treaty of Guérande of 1381 brought peace between Brittany and France.

In the period of the de Montfortist dukes a kind of semi-independent Breton nationhood was fostered. The ducal administration became a dogged defender of Breton interests, and tax revenues increased, helping to pay for an army. The ducal household grew in number, as did courtly pomp.

Cleverly building up its international status, the duchy was represented side by side with sovereign states through the 15th century. Even the Breton Church carried on independently from the French one. In 1460, the University of Nantes was founded with papal blessing, an important symbol of intellectual independence for Brittany. Many Breton histories would be written in the period of the de Montfort dukes, emphasizing Brittany's strong, independent roots. However, some leading Bretons opted for plum positions in French royal circles, with the greater wealth and influence that arena offered. Another phenomenal Breton warrior lord, **Olivier de Clisson**, succeeded du Guesclin as head of the French army after an extraordinary volte-face (see p.498).

Yet all was not harmonious within Brittany itself. **Duke Jean V** (ruler of Brittany, 1399–1442), after the humiliation of being held prisoner briefly by Breton cousins, confiscated and redistributed his captors' lands. With the second half of the Hundred Years War in full swing, he first supported the Anglo–Burgundian alliance against the weak **King Charles VII** of France, but then signed a treaty with the last. The Breton duke managed to steer Brittany clear of the worst fighting, however. Duke François I, who succeeded Duke Jean V, continued to support the French side, as did the short-lived Breton dukes who followed, Pierre II and Arthur III.

With the advent of **King Louis XI** in 1461, **Duke François II** of Brittany was faced with a much tougher, expansionist French monarch. As François had no male heirs, Louis XI made preparations to secure Brittany, enticing Breton courtiers to his side with extravagant rewards. François had many Breton border towns heavily fortified, but the days of the Breton duchy were numbered.

Marshal Rieux was one powerful Breton who bitterly resented the influence some non-Breton councillors had acquired in Brittany's court under François II. After King Louis XI's death, he allied himself with the regents acting on behalf of the young **King Charles VIII** of France. A French army entered Brittany in 1487 and besieged the ducal capital of Nantes. Rieux actually then changed sides and helped push back the French a first time, but the Valois forces were on the offensive. At the decisive **Battle of St-Aubin-du-Cormier** on 28 July 1488, the French defeated the Breton army. The Treaty of Le Verger, a humiliating peace, was signed in neighbouring Anjou. François II died within weeks, leaving his young daughter, **Anne de Bretagne**, as his successor.

Though the 15th century has often been referred to as a golden age for Brittany, a good half of the Breton population are reckoned to have still been living at subsistence level. At least Brittany escaped most of the atrocities of the second half of the Hundred Years War that lasted from 1415 to 1453 and so devastated some other French regions. Alcoholism, crime, prostitution and leprosy, though, were rife in Breton towns, although such religious figures as **Vincent Ferrier** tried to harangue the populace into leading virtuous lives. On the positive side, Breton textile manufacturing was growing into a hugely prosperous enterprise for the region, fine houses and churches the result for the wealthy communities concerned.

Anne de Bretagne's Hand Unites Brittany with France

After Duke François II's death, an international diplomatic skirmish ensued to gain Anne de Bretagne's hand in marriage. In December 1490, the Holy Roman Emperor Maximilian's envoy even came to Brittany and placed his bare leg on Anne's bed, thus symbolizing an extremely prestigious marriage by proxy. However, Anne and her advisers agreed, under an immense amount of French royal pressure, that the young duchess should accept the hand of the young King Charles VIII of France. Their marriage in 1491 spelt the end of the semi-independent duchy of Brittany.

Anne de Bretagne is often portrayed in popular Breton history in a quasi-saintly light; you'll find her image depicted across Brittany, and her name mentioned in reverential tones on many a guided tour. Actually, she seems to have been a pragmatic politician intent on defending her own interests, as well as an extremely extravagant figure. Anne and Charles didn't produce a male heir before the king accidentally killed himself in 1498, fatally bumping his head on a doorway in their Loire château at Amboise.

Anne's marriage contract forced her to marry his successor, **King Louis XII**. With her new husband, Anne did acquire more freedom to run Breton affairs, until her death in 1514. François d'Angoulême, Anne's son-in-law, became Louis XII's successor as **King François I**. He stepped in rapidly after Anne's death and appointed his own administrators to run Brittany. From this stage on, Brittany was politically dictated to by central French rule. The **Act of Union between Brittany and France**, signed by the Estates of Brittany and the king in Vannes in 1532, did supposedly grant Brittany some special privileges, although the monarchy could easily ignore them.

Brittany has often been portrayed as inward-looking and backward, yet this was often far from the case. Breton fishing fleets set out from the very beginning of the 16th century for the great cod-fishing banks off Newfoundland – some Breton stories claim they even began exploring North America before Columbus. The gruelling long-distance cod trade would last centuries, many Breton ports deeply involved in it. The most famous Breton sailor at this time was **Jacques Cartier** (see box, p.102). While the Breton nobles and merchants successfully exploited trading opportunities overseas, the mass of the rural population remained wretched and rooted in its old ways.

The **Breton Parlement**, an important regional law court run by aristocrats, rather than a parliament with wider-reaching powers, was created in 1554 under King **Henri II**. It would last a little over 200 years, until the Revolution. The French kings would be represented in Brittany through this period by a powerful, royal-appointed governor or *intendant*.

French Religious Wars and Colonial Wars with Britain

In the second half of the 16th century, tensions between the newly formed Protestant Christians and the Catholics boiled over into the hideous French **Wars of Religion**, and Brittany, as elsewhere, was torn between the warring factions. Protestantism had caught on strongly in eastern and southern Brittany, notably in the territories of the mighty **Rohan family** based at Josselin. The **Duc de Mercœur**, governor of Brittany towards the end of the century, became the savage ultra-Catholic leader in the province. Spanish and English troops became involved on opposing sides in the bloody conflict, and in these barbarous times warlords swept around creating hell on earth.

King **Henri IV** of France's famed **Edict of Nantes** of 1598 brought most of the fighting to an end, granting religious rights to Protestants as well as Catholics. In the **Counter-Reformation** of the 17th century, however, the Catholic Church and Jesuits in particular took a very firm grip of Breton religious life, and in 1685 the Edict of Nantes protecting Protestants was revoked by King Louis XIV. The power of the Catholic Church in Brittany has continued right through to recent times.

The largest Breton ports assumed considerable importance in the Ancien Régime's **empire-building** of the 17th and 18th centuries. Sailors set forth from them on adventures of exploration, colonization and slave trading, as well as on naval expeditions. The great shipbuilders could make the most of the iron-making industry that had taken off in eastern and central Brittany. The very names of certain ports reflected the colonial aspirations of the French monarchy, such as Port-Louis and L'Orient. You can get personal glimpses of Breton life in the late 17th century by reading Mme de Sévigné's vivid letters (*see also* box, p.146) written during her visits to her provincial château and to Rennes, where, in 1675, she witnessed the crushing of a major Breton revolt against crippling new royal taxes in the **Révolte du Papier Timbré**, seen by some as early revolutionary rumblings.

The western European **battle for colonies** was vicious, with endless fighting in the pursuit of exotic, and highly profitable, riches. St-Malo became a massively wealthy French city at the close of the 17th century, both through international trade and its corsairs. Corsairs, sometimes nicknamed 'pirates with a permit', were often immensely successful in their raids and added greatly to the tensions at sea.

In the 18th century, the **slave trade** reached staggering proportions in Brittany. Shipping magnates at Nantes benefited greatly; they organized almost half of all French slaving expeditions. St-Malo and Lorient shipowners were also significant players in this profoundly insalubrious business. In the mid-18th century, colonial conflicts and wars between France and Britain succeeded each other, most significantly the **Seven Years War** of 1756 to 1763. In 1758, the British landed near St-Malo, but the expedition was a failure and the governor of Brittany, the Duc d'Aiguillon, led his troops to crush the stranded rearguard at St-Cast-le-Guildo. The French struck a medal to celebrate the 'battle'; the British referred to it simply as an 'action' or an 'affair'. The next year, however, the British navy wiped out a good portion of the French fleet at the **Battle of Quiberon Bay**, and France would soon lose much of its extensive empire to Britain.

The Breton Parlement came increasingly into conflict with the extravagant French monarchy towards the end of the 18th century. In 1762, Breton nobleman Louis-

René de Caradeuc de La Chalotais led a move to expel the overpowerful, much-resented Jesuits from Brittany. This brought the regional Parlement into conflict with King Louis XV himself. Such was the level of protest by Breton aristocrats that the king had to climb down. The days of the French monarchy were numbered anyway.

The Chouannerie Fights the French Revolution

Most Bretons were living a pretty wretched existence when the **French Revolution** exploded. Not that the Revolution was particularly popular in large sections of Brittany. Furthermore, over three-quarters of the Breton clergy refused to swear the civil oath as the state demanded. Support for the persecuted Church, added to enforced conscription and a strong contingent of angry expatriate noblemen, led to a widespread counter-Revolutionary guerrilla movement in the province, known as the **Chouannerie**. It would not be successful.

General Hoche's name is equated with the bloody repression of the Chouannerie by **Republican forces**. In 1795, an émigré invasion in the Bay of Quiberon turned into a disaster for the Chouannerie, while anti-Revolutionary Vendéens coming up from south of the Loire were crushed at Savenay by the river. At Nantes, the Republican Jean-Baptiste Carrier organized particularly horrific drownings of anti-Revolutionaries in the Loire. The Chouan leaders are still regarded as heroes by some Bretons; several little museums specifically commemorate them. The Revolutionary authorities came to look upon Brittany, now divided into its five geographical *départements*, as an awkward, counter-revolutionary, deeply reactionary province.

Painful Progress through to the 20th-Century Wars

A chaos of endlessly changing French governments followed on after the traumatizing Revolution and Napoleonic follies. Brittany was neglected, exploited and denigrated by many 19th-century French governments. However, the armed forces and the navy continued to recruit Bretons in large numbers. The major Breton canals, one linking the north and south coasts, the other connecting Nantes and Brest, were vast engineering projects for their time, but water transport would rapidly be superseded by rail, tracks being laid from the middle of the century. In the course of the 18th and 19th centuries, the ocean-going ships had grown considerably in size, until many of the large Breton ports that had been built protectively down river estuaries could no longer receive these vessels. St-Nazaire, by the mouth of the Atlantic, would grow out of nothing to become one of the great shipbuilding ports of France. Around the coast, massive lighthouses went up to warn boats away from Brittany's reefs, although in past times, certain coastal communities had been accused of trying to wreck ships with misleading fires.

Before the end of the 19th century, the Breton population exceeded the 3 million mark. As mass industrialization developed, fish-canning and various other sea-related enterprises took off, for example at Douarnenez, Concarneau and Quiberon. Many people from the poor rural communities moved into the new industrial towns. The railway, and the peace that was achieved in the so-called Belle Epoque between the Franco–Prussian War of 1870–71 and the outbreak of the First World

War in 1914, enabled the first Breton resorts to blossom. Aristocrats, and even European royalty, flocked to Dinard in the first instance, while Breton fishermen continued to head out on terrifying expeditions and inland, Breton peasant families shared their gruel from a single pot set in the middle of the kitchen table. A growing number of intellectuals and artists were, however, realizing the strengths and the enormous appeal of Breton culture. **Breton nationalism** also began to gain some popularity, and political and cultural groups such as the Gorsedd, the Bleun Brug and the Breton Nationalist Party were formed.

Statistics put the number of Bretons who died in the **First World War** at between 200,000 and 250,000 – a huge proportion of the total population. It was felt that French military commanders had used Bretons as cannon fodder all too easily. It's perhaps not surprising, then, that Breton nationalism increased in strength, as the French government continued to enforce a policy stopping the speaking of Breton, let alone its teaching, in schools.

Detached from these issues, property developers went ahead with building further glamorous Breton resorts between the two wars. Gritty Douarnenez, by contrast, elected France's first Communist mayor in 1921, and France's first female councillor in 1924, although the law forbade her from serving. Douarnenez also saw some of the biggest Breton strikes in the 1920s.

In the **Second World War**, as France was overrun by the Nazis, some Bretons immediately took up de Gaulle's call to fight to free France from abroad, most memorably the men of the tiny island of Sein. Some Bretons stayed and joined Resistance units in the territory. Many others, however, were forced to work for the Nazis or collaborated with them. Some of the Breton nationalist movements fantasized that through Nazism they would find an opportunity to assert Breton independence. A large number of Bretons, though, were simply downtrodden by occupation; the feelings of division and bitterness from this period still run deep for those who experienced it.

The Germans forced prisoners to help build portions of an Atlantic wall of defences. Most infamously, the Nazis built up huge submarine bases at Brest, Lorient and St-Nazaire. From here, the dreaded U-Boat submarine fleets set out to destroy the vital convoys between North America and Britain in the battle for the Atlantic. Trying to halt activities in the strategic ports the Germans had developed, the Allied bombers smashed several Breton coastal ports to smithereens. While most of Brittany was liberated in summer 1944, pockets of Nazi resistance held out right up until May 1945, notably around the submarine bases and St-Malo.

Brittany Recovers its Pride

The annihilated Breton ports were quite swiftly reconstructed, though countless German blockhouses have been left exposed along Brittany's sides as war scars – you may spot their eerie presence all along the coast. A renewed sense of **regionalism** began to develop in France after the Second World War, only this time supported by central government. From the 1950s, the Conseils Généraux of the *départements* were given much greater powers over social and economic affairs, while gradually the Breton language became more accepted in the region's schools, although by then many Bretons had stopped speaking in their native tongue even at home. In the shake-up of the French regions, the Loire Atlantique with its capital, Nantes, was removed from administrative Brittany. Culturally however, much of the Loire Atlantique remains a part of the old province. The official Région Bretagne today still only numbers some 3 million inhabitants; add the Loire Atlantique and that increases by a million.

Since the war, various small **Breton nationalist groups** such as the clandestine ARB (the Breton Revolutionary Army) and the FLB (the Breton Liberation Front) have occasionally carried out relatively minor acts of terror, but there has been little support for such violence or for these groups' visions of independence among the majority of Bretons.

Other Bretons have thrown themselves into working towards the **economic development** of the province. The creation of powerful agricultural cooperatives in postwar Brittany led to commercial success and, thanks to lateral thinking, the launch of Brittany Ferries. But with the speed of advances in agriculture, rural Brittany began to empty. *Remembrement*, the government policy of eradicating old field-divides to form larger, more efficient plots, has radically altered the look of many parts of the Breton countryside that had remained unaltered for centuries.

Farming has become an increasingly beleaguered profession. Fishing has also been badly affected by recent cuts, as has the navy. The **protests** have been loud, and sometimes very messy. In 1994, after a fishermen's demonstration in Rennes, the historic Breton Parlement building was burnt down by a stray firework. The seas, though, have also been associated with Breton glory in the last few decades, notably through exceptional **yachting feats**. A string of legendary names in the sailing world have followed each other from Brittany, including Eric Tabarly and Olivier de Kersauzon.

Tourism has become a hugely successful modern 'industry' in Brittany, of course, though some in this field have disregarded the consequences for their region's **environment** – sections of the coast have been much altered by holiday developments and second homes, although all around the peninsula you can still find wild, unspoilt stretches of coast aplenty. Other major environmental concerns include the actions of the farmers, most noticeably in the Côtes d'Armor, the largest pork-producing département in France, where pig farmers have been blamed for polluting the soil, although they are by no means singlehandedly responsible for the problem.

Many Bretons, however, have campaigned against nuclear energy in a country that has otherwise meekly accepted the French government's enormous reliance on this controversial source of power. Yet they could do little against a series of oil tanker disasters in the 1960s and 1970s, most notoriously that involving the *Amoco Cadiz*, which carried in black tides of oil over long stretches of the north Breton shore. More recently, the oil tanker *Erika* broke into two south of the Finistère peninsula in 1999, and more than 300,000 birds perished in the muck. The coastline does recover quite rapidly from these man-made catastrophes, luckily, and the French government has now taken vigorous steps to discourage rogue tankers, with huge fines for illegal tank emptying near the French coast.

At the start of the 21st century, many traditional Breton activities have been badly squeezed. The naval forces, the fishing fleets, the Breton canneries, all have experienced dramatic decline in the last decade. On the positive side, some ports have managed to hold their own with specialist fishing, and several have created shiny new marinas, the very latest opening at Brest and Roscoff.

While the last lighthouse-keepers have been sent packing from their staggering watchtowers along the coast, many of these endangered engineering marvels have been opened to the public. Of course, these lighthouses were built to warn shipping off Brittany's innumerable rocks, but rocks mean seaweed, and algae are proving to be amazing plants, not just being used in the culinary and cosmetic industries, but also showing the potential to become an extraordinarily significant biofuel.

Brittany is at the forefront in many technological fields, including marine research. On top of that, it continues to produce some of the finest yachts in the world, as well as some of the greatest yachtsmen – Francis Joyon is the latest Breton hero of the high seas, having recently smashed Ellen McArthur's solo round-the-world sailing record. Brittany may be seen as attractively traditional by most tourists, but the region has long had a cutting-edge, forward-looking side.

At the same time as the Breton language has fast died out (*see* 'A Dying Language in Black Dog Shit', p.46), the championing of **Breton culture** has been greatly encouraged. Breton events have thrived in the past few decades and a large number of Bretons still derive an enormous amount of joy from their traditions.

Brittany hasn't stood still either where tourism is concerned. The choice of activities for holiday-makers has never been greater, and even in greyer summers, the Breton museums, aquaria, thalassotherapy centres, Breton games halls and cultural centres that have mushroomed in recent times will entertain you. Brittany remains a huge favourite with the French and the Brits. In short, it's fair to say that in these tourist times, France's most magical province continues to cast its spell.

Art and Architecture

Breton Building Blocks: from Pink Granite to Mottled Schist

Think of Brittany and it conjures up many powerful visual images: neolithic dolmens and menhirs; lichen-covered chapels topped by their openwork steeples; weather-eroded calvary sculptures; towering Breton *coiffes* that look like lighthouses of lace; and brilliant Gauguin paintings from around Pont-Aven.

Gauguin's vibrant blocks of colour stand in strong contrast to the subdued grey tones of the stone mainly associated with Breton architecture – **granite**. This grainy stone was often used in the building of towns, villages, churches and chapels. Some of the region's granite, especially on the north coast, takes on surprisingly bright hues, the rock impregnated millions of years ago with pink and orange elements.

Yet only around a third of the region's surface is made up of this stone. The rest consists mainly of types of **schist** or shale, which also give off surprising dashes of colour, from tinges of browns and oranges to blues and even greens. The castles of eastern Brittany, such as Fougères, Vitré and Châteaubriant, show off schist's distinctive mottled effects, while the architecture around the Fôret de Paimpont has striking patches of purple schist to it. Bright white limestone, associated with Loire Valley architecture, only puts in an appearance in the very south of Brittany.

Slate counts among the types of shale found in Brittany, and most Breton houses are roofed with black rectangles of it that turn shades of silver and blue in the sunshine. Most of the **thatch** that preceded the slate has disappeared, except in small pockets, notably the Brière, today the most densely thatched part of France. Brittany's **whitewashed houses**, in particular along the coasts and down the river estuaries, help give the region its immediately recognizable and friendly look. In the Breton ports, you will often find brighter scenes, with more diverse colours, while splendid **timberframe facades** have been preserved in many of the main towns.

From Numerous Neolithic Remains to Rare Romanesque Ones

You often don't have to venture far from a Breton beach to discover some of the earliest architectural achievements of western Europe. **Neolithic tombs, dolmens and menhirs** are scattered around the Breton countryside almost as liberally as churches and chapels. Carnac is far and away the most famous area for Breton neolithic culture. But around the whole of the Golfe du Morbihan you'll find a mass of fascinating neolithic sites, especially those at Erdeven, Locmariaquer, Arzon and Gavrinis. Beyond the Golfe du Morbihan, the most imposing vestiges of Armorican neolithic culture are to be found at Barnenez, La Roche-aux-Fées and St-Just.

In contrast, few visual signs remain of the cultures of the Armorican peninsula from the end of the neolithic period to the early Middle Ages. That's a big gap of some 3,000 years. You may chance upon the odd **Iron Age** promontory fort or grooved column. A few vestiges of Gallo-Roman Armorica do remain, such as small sections of ancient walls and seaside villas, while the most moving little vestige of Gallo–Roman art is concealed in a tiny chapel in Langon. Very disappointingly, virtually no traces have been found of the religious foundations and communities established by the Breton immigrants of the Dark Ages, though the excellent Musée Thomas Dobrée in Nantes does include some Dark Ages finds. St-Philbert-de-Grand-Lieu abbey stands apart for the well-preserved remains of its Carolingian church.

After the destruction wrought by the Vikings, **Romanesque** architecture developed in the 11th and 12th centuries. Few Breton Romanesque buildings have survived intact, but many Breton churches have retained portions of Romanesque structures. Churches at Dinan, Daoulas, Landévennec, Loctudy, Quimperlé, St-Gildas-de-Rhuys and Redon count among those with the finest vestiges. Dol-de-Bretagne's main street has the rare distinction of having preserved some Romanesque houses.

Breton Churches – Stern, Colourful and Awkward

If some visitors come to Brittany in search of neolithic remains, many more are in search of Breton countryside churches. The further west you travel, the more pronounced the Breton look and culture become; it is in the western Breton church enclosures that you come across the elaborate outdoor calvaries, covered with sculptures telling the story of Christ's Passion, while the ossuary, where the bones of the dead were collected, may show a figure of the mocking **Breton Grim Reaper**, *l'Ankou*, one of the most inescapable and haunting figures in regional culture and folk tales. Calvary, ossuary, a large side porch with statues of the apostles lined up, a gateway for the dead, and a low surrounding stone wall – these make up a typical Breton *enclos paroissial* or parish enclosure. The most impressive calvaries are those of Tronoën, Pleyben, Plougastel-Daoulas, Guimiliau, St-Thégonnec, St-Herbot, Plougonven, Kergrist-Moëlou and Pestivien.

All nine Breton cathedrals except Rennes show how the **Gothic style** was embraced in the region. One of the first attempts at Gothic in Brittany was carried out in St-Malo's cathedral in the 12th century, and many new monastic establishments or buildings were erected in the God-glorifying, light-filled style in the 13th century. The most famous stands just over the Normandy border, the Merveille of the Mont St-Michel. The Breton cathedrals are, architecturally, rather eccentric. Tréguier's has a nave in which virtually every column is different, while Quimper's has a kink in it, and between its spires, instead of a religious statue rides the figure of legendary Breton king Gradlon. Other significant Gothic buildings, including those at Beauport, Léhon, Boquen and St-Mathieu, have not fared as well, though they remain awe-inspiring.

After the first few decades of the 15th century, a new Gothic style spread across Brittany, **Flamboyant Gothic**, and lasted a relatively long time. The decorative joy of window tracery in the shape of flames, trefoils, quatrefoils, tears or hearts, the ornate brackets of the accolade arches, the wild panoply of stone figures and monsters flying out from gables and corners, all make the style so very appealing. Some of the Breton Gothic openwork church towers rose to vertiginous heights, quite out of proportion with the buildings they soared above. Marvel, for example, at the competing spires of St-Pol-de-Léon.

Flamboyant Gothic would be tamed across most of France in the 16th century by the rigid, harmonious, symmetrical discipline of the **Renaissance style**, but in Brittany the new form found it hard to establish itself. In Breton religious architecture you'll rarely come across a completely Renaissance church or building. Rather, an addition, such as a tower or porch, might be built in the Renaissance style, with its characteristic decorative motifs derived from antiquity, such as triangular pediments, domes and shells.

Moving into the **Ancien Régime**, after the 16th-century Reformation and through the 17th century, the Catholic Church hit back with the **Counter-Reformation**. Huge new monasteries and convents went up in the major towns. In the parishes, in order to dazzle worshippers, colourful, elaborate decoration was commissioned for the church interiors. Highly carved baptistries, pulpits, set-piece Entombment scenes and the like proliferated. Showy sacristies were often tacked on to churches, and ornate altarpieces, or retables, became a particularly common feature of Breton churches; those of eastern Ille-et-Vilaine and of the western Finistère are particularly extravagant.

Dark Breton granite and schist can look dour on a dull day, but go inside Breton churches and chapels and you may sometimes be surprised by the highly coloured, even gaudy-looking pieces of decoration. There, you'll most likely find an over-elaborate 17th-century retable smothered with figures of saints. The stringbeams, intricately carved in many cases and once vibrantly painted, may also be worth looking up for. If stained-glass windows are relatively common, few wall paintings have survived. A few Breton churches have retained their naïve 15th-century painted ceilings, however, such as Châtelaudren, St-Gonéry, Kermaria-in-Isquit and Kernascléden, and another half dozen or so have preserved their delightful Gothic rood screens, notably Le Folgoët, St-Fiacre, Kerfons, Locmaria and Loc-Envel. Numerous churches hold collections of statues of Breton saints. There may even be the odd *ex voto* of a ship, donated by sailors thanking the Lord or their patron saint for saving them from drowning at sea. Breton church decoration often has a naïve, almost crude look. Breton art can only rarely be described as refined, and can even have a touch of unintentional comic charm: when you see a statue such as the one of St Thélo at the abbey of Daoulas, where the religious man seems to be squashing the deer he rides on, it's hard to resist a smile.

The best areas for traditional Breton churches and chapels include: in the Finistère, around the Elorn Valley, along the Aulne Valley and through the Cap Sizun and Pays Bigouden; in the Côtes d'Armor, in the western Goëlo, south and west of Guingamp or around the Lac de Guerlédan; and in the Morbihan, around Pontivy and Le Faouët.

Breton Secular Architecture

Brittany's rural art and architecture have great charm, but its historic towns are deeply appealing too, with plenty of architecture worth visiting. Notable are the **nine cathedral cities** (*see* p.24). Towns were heavily fortified in the Middle Ages, and awesome fortifications still ring historic St-Malo and Dinan. Guérande has an extraordinarily well-preserved set of ramparts, as does Concarneau. Other towns that have retained impressive parts of their defensive medieval walls include Quimper, Hennebont and Vannes.

The Breton dukes had several **châteaux** built around their territories. Substantial ones survive at Suscinio, Dinan, Vannes and Nantes, for instance. Fort La Latte, though, is the most spectacular of the coastal castles dating back to medieval times. You can visit further major Breton medieval castles (many in ruins) at Josselin, Combourg, Montmuran, Châteaubriant, La Hunaudaye, Tonquédec and Clisson, among others. At the mighty castles of Fougères and Vitré, when visiting them, you get a good lesson in the developing styles of military architecture through the Middle Ages. One of the most glorious and comical examples of the Renaissance in Brittany is the Château de Châteaubriant. The châteaux of Kerjean and La Bourbansais count among further well-known examples, while the Château de Goulaine follows the fashions of the Loire Valley.

The Breton coast continued to be heavily and dramatically fortified during the Ancien Régime. You can now enter many Ancien Régime **forts** unchallenged; the spiky creations of Port-Louis or Belle-Ile make stunning architecture, and Port-Louis's contains a good museum on French colonial history. Vauban's and Garangeau's defensive works, notably around St-Malo, are text-book stuff.

Brittany's grandiose, Parisian-looking **Parlement** went up in Rennes in the first half of the 17th century. As overseas commerce and the slave trade grew in the second half of that century, Breton merchants grew richer. Brittany's major colonial **trading cities**, St-Malo, Nantes and Lorient, expanded rapidly. Increasingly wealthy merchants ordered sturdy **granite houses**, even in small country towns such as the gorgeous Locronan, Quintin, Rochefort-en-Terre and Guerlesquin.

Gauguin, Nazis and Le Corbusier – the Past Two Centuries

Perhaps the most remarkable feature of 19th-century architecture in Brittany is the plethora of mighty **lighthouses** built out to sea. The villa of La Garenne Lemot near Clisson and the Palais Briau close to Varades are interesting one-offs of the period, while in the new tourist resorts, a plethora of sumptuous and eccentric villas sprouted up, most remarkably at Dinard and La Baule.

Yet the 19th century is perhaps most interesting for the **fine arts**. Treasures confiscated at the Revolution, plus additional donations, led to the opening of substantial museums in Rennes and Nantes. By the second half of the 19th century, Brittany was attracting foreign artists in good number, and Gauguin and Emile Bernard created a new vision in western European art at Pont-Aven (*see* box, p.367). The main fine arts museums of Brittany, at Rennes, Nantes, Quimper and Brest, all have representative works by the leading lights of the **Pont-Aven School**, while the Pont-Aven museum puts on fascinating exhibitions. There are other fine arts museums at Vannes, and, on a smaller scale, at Le Faouët, Lamballe, Dinan and Fougères. The Quimper pottery tradition clearly shows how that city's ceramicists began catering for the first tourists' desire for Breton quaintness as early as the 1870s, depicting Breton peasant figures on their wares.

For those who tire of the cutely picturesque side of Brittany, Brest, Lorient and St-Nazaire, rebuilt in uncompromisingly modern style after the war bombings, have a gritty attraction that up until recently had been unfairly dismissed out of hand. For an unusual experience, you can also see inside the U-Boat installations at Lorient and St-Nazaire. Or you can always look out for the countless Nazi blockhouses along the coast. They may be repulsive carbuncles, but they stand as testament to Brittany's Second World War suffering.

The most famous experiment in modern architecture and modern living in Brittany came with Le Corbusier's design in the 1950s of the Maison Radieuse in Rezé, south of Nantes. Other big cities, such as Brest, Rennes and now Lorient, with its brand-new Cité de la Voile, have been encouraging contemporary design.

Contemporary art even gets a good airing in Brittany, in particular in some of the fine arts museums, Nantes' above all. The Château de Kerguéhennec puts on splendid shows in the countryside, as does Le Dourven, or more modestly, the chapels around Pontivy or the Cap Sizun. As to the village of Bazouges-la-Pérouse, it has allowed a colony of cutting-edge artists to take over in high season.

The proliferation of **museums commemorating local Breton life** in the 19th century and the first half of the 20th century are certainly worth visiting, but often with these museums it feels as if traditional Breton culture has been tidied up into cluttered old homes serving as storage cupboards for the Breton past. It is an issue for some that much Breton culture has been reduced to quaint curiosity, but at least since the 1960s **Breton music and dance** have undergone a revival. Traditional Breton bands, called *bagadou*, fight it out in numerous musical competitions, while anyone can join in the dancing at the traditional *festou noz*, lively evening festivals. And bagpipes fill the air each year in the first fortnight in August, for the largest gathering of modern-day Celts at the Festival Interceltique in Lorient, one of the largest of a huge number of festivals put on in the region (*see* 'Calendar of Events', p.65).

Topics

03

Nutty Theories on the Neolithic

You never know when you might need a menhir.

Obélix

The odd plausible attempt has been made to try to explain the purpose of the neolithic alignments and innumerable single menhirs or standing stones scattered all across Brittany. One of the more sensible lines of enquiry speculates as to whether the rows of standing stones were erected as some kind of seasonal solar calendar connected with religious rites. Although the precise meanings of the alignments and menhirs remain a mystery, they have inspired some very entertaining and ludicrous notions, especially the most famous alignments of all – those of Carnac.

Nutty theories advanced about Carnac's lines of menhirs include claims that the structures were built for a massive fish-drying enterprise, or that these standing stones were the basic columns for a vast marketplace. Lawyers might favour the suggestion that the rows are vast symbolic legal documents. One further potty argument says that the lines of menhirs were solid posts erected by a Roman army to set up camp below. As to the Celtic Christian legend of St Cornély, it suggests a different role for the Romans regarding these alignments – when the legionnaires tried to capture and persecute the religious Cornély, the story goes that he literally petrified them, or turned them to stone.

Some have argued that the stone rows recognize heroes who fell in prehistoric battles. A certain Hirmenech even claimed specifically that it was warriors from Homer's Trojan Wars who were brought here for burial. Another suggestion is that the alignments were built as an elaborate device to guard against invaders from the sea. It was also said, tongue in cheek, that after the end of the last war, when the Americans arrived to liberate this part of Brittany, some of them thought the menhirs had been planted by the Nazis as anti-tank defences. Those with a futuristic bent might prefer to explore the explanation that the alignments are landing signals for extraterrestrials.

A few people have wondered whether it might have been the Egyptians or the Phoenicians who erected the menhirs of Brittany. Breton legends have concocted a few other stories about the neolithic monuments. The two traditional favourites were that they were put up by Breton fairies, the *korrigans*, or by galumphing giants – Gargantua is even associated with a few of Brittany's standing stones. The Dracontia theory, meanwhile, sees the menhir alignments as the temples of dragons or serpents.

Christian moralizers have sometimes espoused the idea that the monuments were wicked people who had been turned to stone by way of punishment by a vengeful God. The Almighty, for example, was apparently angered by a group of girls who went dancing rather than turning up to church on Sunday at Les Demoiselles de Langon, and by a band of debauched monks who indulged in some un-Christian rituals at Le Jardin aux Moines in the forest of Paimpont. As to the alignment on the side of the Montagne St-Michel-de-Brasparts, it's said that evil revellers at a wedding banquet, in their wild state, stopped the priest from going to give the last rites to a dying man and were duly dealt with by God.

The Christian Church certainly didn't like these menhirs at all; some resemble uncomfortably that greatly mystifying taboo in Christian societies, the male erection. A fair number of menhirs were Christianized by priests, a simple cross plonked on top of them. Menhirs may well have symbolized fertility originally; although the standing stones of the Breton alignments tend not to be carefully shaped, the isolated menhirs dotted around Brittany are often much more convincingly phallic. It's said that some infertile couples would go to touch a menhir, or to rub themselves against one, or even to slide down one where possible. It's even claimed that desperate couples went to make love in the shadow of a menhir to see if that would bring them joy.

Some people have just been far too frivolous about the possible purposes of the alignments, claiming sporting reasons for planting so many thousands of painfully heavy rocks in the ground. The alignments could, some of these factions argue, have formed solid arenas, or racing tracks, or have constituted the framework for a complex game played out in a labyrinth. And though you may be one of those who leaves Brittany unmoved by the region's neolithic sites, one particularly unobservant physicist by the name of Deslandes was more blasé still – he simply reckoned that the standing stones were a natural phenomenon, not put up by anyone at all.

Stone Boats and Slain Dragons – the Breton Saints

Crossing the seas in stone boats, religious men from Ireland, Wales and Cornwall emigrated to the Armorican peninsula in the Dark Ages, fighting dragons and serpents when they arrived. Or so legends of the Breton saints have it. The Celtic Christians who converted the peninsula into Brittany were certainly fired with missionary zeal. How peaceful or not this crusading immigration was, it's hard to say. The simplistic picture is that the new arrivals were warmly received by their Gaulish Celtic cousins from pre-Roman times, the natives of Armorica. Not all seems to have been plain sailing, however.

In several Breton saints' stories, the new Christian evangelizers are not always greeted with open arms. Some of these tales claim that the pinkish rocks of the north Breton shore are tinted that way from the blood of persecuted British immigrants. And when one Irish religious man known as Ké, or Quay, landed in Brittany in the Bay of St-Brieuc he was supposedly beaten with gorse by the Armorican women who spotted him arriving. He fell to the ground and was knocked out, but on the very spot where he hit his head a fountain of water sprang up and revived him. Ste Noyale was not so lucky when she ventured across the Channel... on tree leaves, in the 6th century. She was captured by an evil chieftain, Nizall, who had her decapitated for rejecting his advances; she simply picked up her head and continued on her journey. Several other Breton saints wisely began by settling on an uninhabited island first and then progressed on to the mainland.

Legends of Breton saints of the Dark Ages exist all along the Breton coastline. Detailed maps of Brittany reveal just how many places have been named after the

Dark Ages British immigrants, from St-Malo in the northeast, right round the Breton coast to the Pointe de St-Gildas south of the Loire by Pornic. Some of the names should be distinctly familiar to those living in southwest England and Wales. The Breton saints also appear to have covered every patch of inland Brittany, leaving no stone unturned in their efforts to convert the pagan peninsula to Christianity.

Who were the Breton Celtic saints? Irish religious figures appear to have been among the first to settle, perhaps in the 5th century or before. The Breton saints Ronan, Ké, Efflam and Aaron (who beat Malo to St-Malo) count among the best-known Irish religious men to have made the Armorican peninsula their home, but many of them remain relatively obscure figures.

However, it was a group of particularly influential Welsh religious men of the 6th century who came to be regarded as the founding fathers of Celtic Christian Brittany. The great abbey of Llantwit Major, or Llanilltud Fawr, in South Glamorgan is said to have supplied a couple of the seven founding fathers of Brittany. Illtud, the creator of Llantwit Major, wasn't one of them, but several Breton places carry his name and he possibly visited Brittany to deliver famine supplies. A couple of his disciples did become Breton founding fathers; Samson settled at Dol-de-Bretagne, while St Pol Aurelian travelled via Cornwall and Ouessant to create religious foundations at Batz-sur-Mer and, more famously, St-Pol-de-Léon.

Other Welsh founding fathers of Celtic Christian Brittany include Brieuc (hence St-Brieuc), and Tugdual (also known as Tudwal or Tual), patron saint of Tréguier. St Patern, patron saint of Vannes and another of the Breton founding fathers, also came from Wales, where he had set up the influential abbey of Llanbadarn Fawr in Dyfed.

The other two Breton founding fathers are St Malo and St Corentin. It is pretty obvious where Malo (or Maclou, or MacLow, very possibly of Scottish origin) settled in Brittany. St Corentin may have come from Cornwall, or at least been of Cornish descent. The best-known story ascribed to him is that he fed himself from a single fish, from which he would cut a slice each day. He would then return the fish to the water for it to regenerate. He plays a pivotal role in the great Breton legend of King Gradlon and the drowned city of Ys (*see* box, p.324).

Another particularly important Breton saint who ranks up there with these seven founding fathers is Gildas. He became an extremely influential figure across Celtic Christian circles and corresponded with and visited Irish monasteries. He wrote a famous 6th-century text, *De excidio Britanniae*, portraying the rulers and clergy of Britain as a decadent lot who only had themselves to blame for the victories of the Anglo-Saxons. Later in life he went to Brittany, founding a famous monastery at St-Gildas-de-Rhuys and seemingly influencing a large area of southern Brittany.

The saints' tales were written down on both sides of the Channel, the Welsh ones and the Breton ones elaborating different versions of stories that had been passed down the centuries. For example, Brittany's legends claim that the man whom Bretons call Divy, the great Welsh saint Dewi (known as David in English), was born in far western Brittany after his mother Non or Nonna had moved to the Armorican peninsula. Some Breton saints' lives even tell of religious men going from Brittany to Celtic lands to the north. For example, St Thégonnec and St Nonna (a man, not to be confused with Nonna, mother of Dewi) are said to have travelled to Ireland to become bishops of Armagh.

The main sources for the lives of these Breton saints were recorded by monks. The earliest surviving ones date from around the 9th century, but the tradition of writing these Celtic hagiographies lasted several centuries more. They are extremely unreliable. The scribes often resorted to invention, or muddled together several influential figures. Yet the Breton saints remained revered, their stories long the best-known ones in Breton communities after those of the Bible. In the 17th century, Albert Le Grand of Morlaix played a crucial role in collating the Breton saints' stories in his book *La Vie des saints bretons*. This became one of the most influential and most widely read books in Brittany, which would have been the staple text along with the Bible in poor country homes up to the Second World War.

Go into any Breton church or chapel and there's a good chance that you'll come face to face with a statue of a local Breton saint. Although most of the saints may date back to the Dark Ages, the statues you'll see were mainly carved in the late medieval period or later. These statues remain venerated by many confirmed Breton Catholics to this day, particularly in the *pardons*, the Breton local pilgrimage processions, when the statues of the Breton saints are given a good airing, carried around the countryside, pilgrims chanting Catholic prayers behind them.

Each saint has a more or less murky history linking him or her with miracles and healing powers. There's a long tradition of *saints guérisseurs*, healing saints. St Cado, for example, was supposed to help the hard of hearing. St Jacut was among the many invoked for epilepsy or any behaviour considered mad. A large number of saints were prayed to by young women hoping for a good marriage. The tradition at Perros-Guirec was for young hopefuls to stick a pin in Guirec's nose. Not only was the statue's nose deformed by this superstition, it disappeared completely.

Many Breton saints are closely linked with particular animals. Cattle were of particular importance in Breton rural communities. St Cornély is represented along with cows at Carnac. At St-Herbot, locks of animal hair were laid out on a special altar at the annual *pardon*, and in the deeply rural chapel of Notre-Dame de Restudo in the Côtes d'Armor, horse hooves still cover one of the walls of a side chapel. A number of saints are linked with deer, such as Elorn, Edern and Thélo. As to St Hervé, he was born blind, all the better to see into men's characters, the story goes, and went through Brittany guided by a tamed wolf. Innumerable saints are linked with springs in the countryside. Strong saintly ties with water, fertility, cattle and deer are all thought to have links with pre-Christian Armorican and Celtic beliefs, and some of the *pardons*, such as the famous one at Locronan, may well follow sacred tracks laid out before Christian times.

The Breton saints of the Dark Ages are not recognized by the Catholic Church of Rome; they have not been canonized. The Catholic Church viewed these saints as part of the dubious traditions of the Celtic Christian Church, which it wanted to suppress. Despite this, a few major medieval religious figures in Brittany did receive approval from the Church of Rome. A 13th-century bishop of St-Brieuc, Guillaume Pinchon, was the first officially recognized by the papacy. Another exceptional 13th-century Breton religious figure, Yves, defender of the poor, is much better remembered and revered. He was canonized soon after his death, and you'll often see St Yves portrayed in churches across Brittany. Surprisingly, the Christian warrior Charles de Blois, who fought unsuccessfully for the Penthièvres in the Breton War of Succession in the 14th century, was made into a saint, though his canonization only dates from very recently. Vincent Ferrier, a 15th-century Spanish preacher who went on an important mission through Brittany, also made the grade for the Church of Rome.

Many mainstream Catholic saints such as St Michael and his dragon are popular in Brittany. So too are St Roch and St Sebastian, who were frequently prayed to in times of plague. But most popular of the lot are the Virgin and her mother, St Anne. This Marian tradition was strong across France but thrived in the region – St Anne is regarded as the patron saint of Brittany. However, the story that claims she spent some of her life at Ste-Anne-la-Palud in the Finistère is exceptionally far-fetched, even by Breton standards. Arguably the most venerated religious site in modern Brittany is Ste-Anne-d'Auray, in the Morbihan. Even Pope John-Paul II visited on his trip to France in 1996.

The Web of Breton Arthurian Legend

The main centre of Breton Arthurian action is the legendary Forêt de Brocéliande, also known as the Forêt de Paimpont, west of Rennes. But how and when did the link between Brocéliande in particular and Arthurian romance start? No one seems sure. Talk is of roots in a cross-Channel resistance campaign against Dark Ages invaders, or even of much older links with pre-Roman Celtic ritual.

The passion for Arthurian legends certainly flowered in early medieval times. A claim made at the Château de Comper suggests that Raoul I de Gaël Montfort, one of the proprietors of the Forêt de Paimpont in the 11th century, took part in the Norman conquest of England and that during this time he became deeply enthusiastic about the Arthurian tales he heard there. Once back in Brittany, he may have started encouraging storytellers to set Arthurian episodes in his Brocéliande. There is much discord, however, among devotees of Arthurian legends as to the precise locations of Arthurian sites. The biggest killjoys even claim that Paimpont Forest is not Brocéliande.

The Breton Arthurian plots here revolve around four main figures. Merlin the magician comes first. Then there is Viviane, with whom he falls passionately and fatefully in love. Morgane la Fée, the bitter half-sister of King Arthur, also features frighteningly large, while Lancelot du Lac is said to have been brought up at Comper. King Arthur and the knights of his Round Table tend to stay on the periphery, though various tales talk of him and his knights coming to end their lives in Brittany. The Breton word for apples, *avalou*, sounds remarkably close to the name of Avalon, the mythical island where Arthur goes to die, or at least to sleep until he and his men should be called upon to rescue the two Bretagnes (Britain and Brittany) once again. Brittany's Ile d'Aval is a contender for Avalon.

King Arthur is supposed to have learnt of the existence of the Holy Grail preserving drops of blood from Christ's crucifixion from Merlin. But before that, in Breton Arthurian tales, Merlin supposedly travels to Brittany to ask the Breton chiefs to join Arthur in fighting the Anglo-Saxons. On his way back he passes through the forest of Brocéliande, the name thought to derive from Barc'h Hélan, the empire of the druids. In the forest, Merlin meets Viviane at the Fontaine de Barenton on 21 June, date of the summer solstice, and falls madly for her. Despite the fate he foresees for himself, he can do nothing to resist his feelings for her. The beautiful lady is sometimes described as the daughter of the local lord, Dyonas, owner of half the forest of Brocéliande, who had his castle at Comper. On one of the Fontaine de Barenton's stones known as Merlin's Step, the enchanter is himself enchanted. He cannot leave Viviane until she has promised him her love; in exchange she demands that Merlin pass on to her his knowledge and his powers.

Merlin returns to Britain, where Arthur's great Christian army has gathered to fight the enemy who have advanced to Salisbury Plain. The Arthurian troops win a hard-fought battle and Arthur is declared *roi des deux Bretagnes*, king of the two Britains. Arthur and Guinevere tie the knot, and after the wedding Merlin returns to Brocéliande, where the wiley Viviane cajoles him into revealing more and more of his secrets to her. Viviane's aim is to learn such mastery of magic from Merlin that she will eventually be able to force him to stay with her forever. Merlin, through his magical powers, conjures up the most beautiful castle for Viviane, not *by* the lake of Comper, but *in* it. She finds a baby by the waters, the child of Ban of Brittany and Queen Helen in Breton Arthurian tales. The boy is named Lancelot, and Viviane takes him to live in her underwater, invisible palace. From this time on, she calls herself the Lady of the Lake and the boy becomes known as Lancelot du Lac.

Merlin has work to do elsewhere, notably in setting up the quest for the Holy Grail. Returning to Arthur's court, the magician appears in several playful guises before announcing the quest. He explains that only one man can find the Holy Grail, but that the name of this knight will remain undisclosed until the chalice is recovered, leaving all to strive for it. The son of Lancelot du Lac, Galahad, proves to be the chosen one.

Several important Arthurian side-stories involving Lancelot and Morgane la Fée are set in Brocéliande. Lancelot is portrayed as the most noble of the knights of the Round Table. When Guinevere is kidnapped by the 'king of the country from which no one returns', Lancelot manages to defy the impossible-sounding odds. Having released Guinevere, the two become lovers. Guinevere tells Lancelot of her passion for him on the Bridge of Secrets, which one tourist leaflet in Brocéliande rather unromantically situates 'on the road from Plélan to Ploërmel'. Morgane la Fée, in Breton Mor Guen (White Sea), is a wicked magician who resorts to terrible action when her lover Guyomart proves unfaithful to her. She imprisons him in her hide-out in the forest of Brocéliande, the Val Sans Retour, or Valley of No Return. This valley becomes a trap for all unfaithful knights, but Lancelot, in his unshakeable love for Guinevere, proves capable of overcoming Morgane's wiles.

Arthur, meanwhile, has been mortally wounded in battle due to the treachery of one of his own sons, Mordred. The dying king goes off to the island of Avalon. But it does not seem that he actually dies. Rather, fairies heal his wounds and keep him in a deep sleep to await his resurrection for when Britain should once again be in dire trouble. As to Merlin, he will be trapped by Viviane in the forest of Brocéliande, forever ensnared in the Tombeau de Merlin. But there is a story that says that Arthur will in time come to Merlin's rescue; then the Celts of Wales, Cornwall and Brittany will unite and rise up to find new glory after a desolate period of servitude. In the meantime, Arthurian legends have grown into a vast, confusing literary labyrinth and have provided countless tourist trails through the forest of Brocéliande.

A Dying Language in Black Dog Shit

The Breton language died out rapidly in the 20th century. Small groups are still trying to keep it alive, but while it once had to be defended against persecution, now the battle is with indifference. Unlike with Welsh, to which Breton is so closely related, the generational language chain has been well and truly broken in Brittany.

If the future of the language looks doubtful, its origins remain extremely obscure. It seems that in the immediate pre-Roman period, the Late Iron Age, Armoricans spoke a kind of Celtic. It would have been a language shared with other Celtic-influenced communities, or a closely related dialect. This would probably have been spoken over large portions of Europe, including across the precursor of France, Roman Gaul. Similar tribal and place names either side of the Channel in that period are taken to indicate how close the languages and cultures were.

With the Roman conquest of Gaul came the Roman language. But in far-flung corners of the Roman Empire such as the Armorican peninsula, while Latin was probably largely adopted in the new towns, the learning of the conquerors' tongue may well have been extremely slow and faltering in the countryside. And one of the major effects of the waves of emigration from the British Isles in the Dark Ages is most probably that it strengthened the region's Celtic dialects.

The Breton language is most closely associated with western Brittany, or Basse Bretagne. Eastern Brittany, or Haute Bretagne, was much less affected by it. Neither historic capital of Brittany, Nantes or Rennes, was ever a mainly Breton-speaking city. The boundaries of the language probably spread to their widest limits under the so-called Breton kings of the second half of the 9th century. This seems to be reflected in the spread of Breton place names, which are packed particularly densely along the northern and western coastal strips of Brittany. There is, though, a pocket of Breton names as far south as Guérande, close to the Loire.

The Ligne Loth is the name that is sometimes given to the historically shifting language divide cutting north to south across Brittany, showing the frontier of the Breton-speaking communities changing through time. From its most easterly position in the 9th century, this line regressed westwards until the mid-17th century, when the language divide roughly cut down through the middle of the Côtes d'Armor and the Morbihan.

Many leading Breton lords of the Middle Ages may well have been trilingual, speaking French in their connections with foreign courts, being familiar with Latin in official and religious circles, and understanding the Breton used in their home territories. Although Breton was widely spoken in western Brittany, it was not written down all that often; it was more an oral than a literary language. Fragments of texts written in Breton have survived from the Middle Ages, but the remains are meagre. One of the first printed books in Brittany was, however, the *Catholicon*, a trilingual dictionary dealing with French, Latin and Breton.

Among ordinary western Bretons, Breton was the common language through the Middle Ages and the Ancien Régime, but the Revolutionary authorities had little time for the practical fact that in Brittany many ordinary people spoke Breton as their first or only language. French was the sole language that French revolutionary *Liberté* allowed. It would take further concerted efforts from the centralizing French governments of the 19th century and first half of the 20th century to suppress the Breton language. Schooling became compulsory in France, but only in French. The use of a regional language, even if it was your mother tongue, was made to appear shameful and backward through the educational system. French, in contrast, was championed as the language of civilization and progress. It was compulsory in the civil service and the armed forces. Breton parents, increasingly ashamed of Breton, encouraged their children to learn French, which they felt would give them more opportunities in life.

Through the 19th century, Breton language and culture did find their defenders. In 1805 an Académie Celtique was founded, one of whose members, Jean-François Le Gonidec, worked at establishing a Breton grammar and preparing a new Breton dictionary. In the 1830s, Hersart de la Villemarqué published his first edition of the *Barzaz Breiz*, an influential collection of Breton songs. The next decade saw the founding of the Association Bretonne, with economic and historical goals, while the bishop of Quimper of the time, Monseigneur Graverand, started up an influential missionary periodical in Breton, the *Lizeri Breurriez ar Feiz*. Leading Church figures continued to act as defenders of the region's language. Although the teaching of Breton language and history was pushed aside in schools, and the Association Bretonne was suspended through the 1860s, an increasing number of Celtic magazines came into existence. And in the late 19th century, academic chairs were created in Celtic culture.

The late 19th century saw further efforts to write down traditional Breton tales and legends, to record the long Breton oral tradition. It is probable, given the large Breton population at the end of the 19th century and in the early 20th century, that that was actually the period in history in which there were the most Breton speakers.

Tensions grew again between central government and defenders of Breton language and culture at the start of the 20th century, as the Combes government was both against the clergy and against the Breton language. Not content with Breton being forbidden in schools, it wanted to forbid Breton in the churches. This was a surefire way of creating animosity in deeply religious Brittany. One Abbot Perrot led the founding of *Bleun Brug*, a Breton Catholic organization created to defend Breton language and religion. The Parti Nationaliste Breton came into existence in 1911; this radical party called for Brittany's total separation from France and for Breton to become the sole national language of Brittany.

The First World War had a strong impact on the Breton language, not just in causing the death of so many young Breton men – it also spread the use of French across the province. After the war, Breton was suppressed in schools with renewed vigour. The shaming of pupils caught speaking Breton became more widespread. In certain schools, the first child heard using their mother tongue might even be handed a symbolic object, possibly a cow, to indicate their shame; when the next child was caught speaking Breton, the symbol of shame would be passed on.

The Breton nationalist movements that had grown up in the first half of the 20th century became closely associated with the growth of Fascism. Such was the paranoia about this in central government that the Breton language came to be seen as a potential danger, and the speaking of Breton on the telephone was banned in the Finistère in 1939. After the Second World War, spoken Breton continued to decline at an alarming rate. Yet most Bretons seemed uninterested, and practical action to protect the language took a long time coming. Breton has not survived the 20th century like Welsh or Irish Gaelic, and was never made compulsory in Breton schools.

It's only a hardcore of Bretons that has continued to show interest in the Breton language, but central French government has become increasingly sensitive to the issue, if rather late in the day. The 1951 Loi Deixonne allowed the optional teaching of minority languages in French schools, although no measures were taken to train teachers in specialist language instruction. Despite Breton becoming an official school subject right to final exams in 1965, very few Bretons took up the option.

In the 1970s, though, the creation of private Breton-speaking schools, the Diwan establishments, was a step forward. Most of them were set up in the Finistère. They have struggled to stay alive, so small are the numbers that attend, but government support has now put them on a firmer financial footing.

No accurate census of Breton-speakers has ever been carried out, but a recent estimate reckoned that there were around 300,000 Breton speakers today, although how many are passive listeners is unclear. The typical Breton speaker today is a farmer or retired person, living in the Côtes d'Armor or Finistère.

Language is, of course, much more than just a language. It expresses and defines ways of thinking, and is intimately linked with the history of communities and with

Breton Sayings

On growing up obediently: *Al lestr na zent ked ouz ar stur/Ouz ar garreg a zento sur.* (The ship that does not obey the helm/Will surely have to obey the reef.)

On getting in the potential mother-in-law's good books: *A ziwar moue ar gazeg/ E vez paked an eubeulez.* (It's by the mare's mane/That you catch the filly.)

On marriage taming the wilder male elements: *Evid reiza ar bleizi/Ez eo red o dimezi.* (To get wolves to settle down/They have to be married.)

A warming culinary Breton expression on love-making: *Pa'h a ar billig war an tan/Eh a an daou en unan.* (When the crêpe-making pan [the man] is placed on the fire [the woman]/The two become one.)

A traditional comparison between women and the sea: *Evid ar mor beza treitour/Treitourroh ar merhed.* (The sea may be fickle/Women are much more so.)

On traditional male and female roles: *Er forniou-red, er milinou/E vez kleved ar heloiou/Er poullou hag er zanaillou/E vez kleved ar marvaillou.* (At the ovens and the mills/You hear the news/At the wash place and in the attics/You hear gossip.)

A justification of the social hierarchy and the different expectations of life for rich and poor: *Mad eo lêz dous, mad eo lêz trenk/Ha mad da beb hini goûd chom en e renk.* (Sweet milk is good, bitter milk is good/And it is good for everyone to keep in their rank.)

An apparent warning against speculating that might be extended to life generally: *Ar pez a zeu gand ar mare lano/Gand ar mare a dre er mêz a yelo.* (What the sea brings in at high tide/It takes away at low tide.)

their imaginations. The death of a language also means the death of a significant part of a culture. Languages are inventive and playful, and with their loss much creativity disappears. The Bretons have been caricatured as being stern and dour by French people who couldn't understand their language. But having a look at traditional Breton idioms, you can see how colourful and humorous Bretons can be.

A cousin and I once asked our grandmother, brought up Breton-speaking, to teach us some Breton. She is a dignified former schoolteacher who would never dream of saying a swearword in French. But she had a little giggle as she told us some of the popular Breton expressions she and her schoolfriends used to enjoy using. It was something of a shock when she came up with the first one, *kor ki du*. What did that mean, we innocently asked. 'Black dog shit,' she said calmly in French. 'But you must understand that Breton was much more earthy than French,' she explained. And the phrase did seem particularly appropriate in expressing the present state of the Breton language.

In Breton bookshops you can seek out books of Breton phrases translated into French. *Proverbes et Dictons de Basse Bretagne,* for example, collects sayings in the Breton tongue. Most of the sayings in this book offer familiar words of wisdom, but they often use examples from the immediate natural and animal world. Some have a particularly Breton flavour, and can make an entertaining first introduction to the Breton language. A few sound very much more obscure than they would have done a generation or two ago, and of course some are far from politically correct. In the box opposite is a small selection of sayings to set you thinking about the Breton language.

A Footnote on Astérix and Bécassine

Internationally, the most famous figures to have emerged from Brittany are Astérix and Obélix. But they are not portrayed as Bretons, of course, being Gauls from well before the time of the Dark Ages emigrations to Armorica from Britain. What comes as a bit of a shock is that their names are derived from the language of their would-be oppressors – the words asterisk and obelisk come from ancient Mediterranean languages.

Astérix and Obélix's adventures are supposed to take place in 50 BC, just after the Roman conquest of Gaul. In fact, their encounters with Visigoths, Vikings and the like take them into different time periods. Time is concertinaed in these cartoons. Even feminist issues have put in an appearance, as have modern-day stars, thinly disguised under the make-up of caricatural drawing.

Unfortunately for the real Armorican Gauls, there were no successful pockets of resistance against the Romans, no invincible villagers, and no magic potion – despite the claims made by some Breton makers of old-style beer, or *cervoise*, that such beer was the Gauls' secret weapon. One Armorican tribe, the Veneti, did, however, play an important part in a widespread Gaulish uprising against Caesar. Caesar himself gave a classic account of the sea battle that ensued and of how he enslaved the defeated enemy. This story is a far cry from the scenario in Astérix, where the brilliant villagers persecute the much put-upon flabby Roman legions.

A few fanatics have tried to pinpoint the true location of the fictional village of Astérixian legend. It is clear that the village lies on the northern, Channel coast, not on the southern coast of the Veneti; just look at the view you're shown through the magnifying glass in the introduction to each new adventure. The *département* of the Côtes d'Armor puts in strong claims for the magic village. Le Yaudet, with its Iron Age fort overlooking the Léguer estuary, has been suggested, but the place is built on a cramped height, while the cartoon evidence clearly shows Astérix's and Obélix's village on flattish ground, by a wide beach. The Bay of Erquy, featured in some Astérix competitions, looks more the part. Perhaps you and your children could seek out your own ideal location for Astérix's village.

Brittany did spawn an earlier cartoon icon. In 1905 the character Bécassine, more correctly known as Annaïk Labornez, was born. A farmer's daughter from a remote corner of the Finistère, she goes to Paris to become the *domestique* of the Marquise de Grand'Air. Twenty-three adventures follow of the naïve Breton servant girl faced with the big city. For some time to French girls what Tintin was to French boys, her crass and sometimes cruelly mocking misadventures upset quite a number of Bretons, touching on sensitive subjects, and the series is now even studied as a source by social historians looking at the way Bretons were viewed by other French people.

Food and Drink

04

Food

... a thin, black buckwheat pancake is the national meal – only the Bretons can comprehend its miserable culinary attractions.

Balzac, *Les Chouans*

How wrong Balzac was. **Breton crêpes** (or *galettes*, as the savoury variety tend to be called in eastern Brittany) are appreciated far and wide now. And the Breton crêpe is now regarded as the aristocrat of the pancake world, not a miserable thing. Extremely thin and delicate, it bears no relation to the thick and stodgy pancakes many of us are familiar with at home. There is an art to making a good Breton crêpe, which, along with the choice of fillings and décor, is why some crêperies are much better than others. You'll find crêperies in every corner of Brittany and they are generally reliably cheap places to eat.

In the mid-19th century, when Balzac came to Brittany, ordinary Breton cooking would, however, have been truly monotonous. *Bouillie*, or gruel, and potatoes were the mainstay of the peasant diet at the time. Chestnuts, *châtaignes*, were gathered as a poor man's food, and *soupe au lait*, milk soup with bread dunked in it, was a popular dish. Meats, vegetables and fruit would have been seasonal treats. Crêpes might have been made once a week; they would certainly not have come with fancy fillings.

Nowadays you can order crêpes stuffed with an increasingly imaginative variety of ingredients, for example all manner of Breton meats or seafood. Savoury crêpes were traditionally made with *blé noir* or *sarrasin*, buckwheat. Sweet crêpes are now made with more ordinary wheat called *froment*. In some crêperies you will even be able to see the *crêpière* in action, making her crêpes. The traditional drinks to accompany crêpes are cider or a milk drink, either *lait ribot* (the residue from butter-making, which is also sometimes used as a kind of filling – to some tongues sour milk), or *gros lait* (curd, made using rennet from a calf's stomach). Crêpe stalls in town are good places to buy a snack, and for the serious crêpe enthusiast, the town of Gourin in central Morbihan even hosts a crêpe festival (*see* p.391).

The other main types of food visitors immediately associate with Brittany are **fish and seafood**. You'll find a plethora of the stuff on offer in port markets or shops every day of the week except Monday, as the fishermen take a day of rest. Do go to see the *criée*, the professionals' fish auction market, or visit a *poissonnerie*, a fishmonger's, in a coastal town.

In restaurants, **shellfish** often feature in Breton starters or *hors d'œuvres*, and are frequently served in their shells; the exceptions are the posher places. Otherwise, you'll most often be expected to peel your own langoustines or prawns, crack open your own crab, or winkle out your own whelks. You may even have to split open clams with a dangerously sharp knife. If you have problems with any of this, ask for help. Oysters and clams are often served raw, or *cru*, as are a few other types of shellfish. The most elaborate way in which to try Breton shellfish is by ordering a *plateau de fruits de mer*, a seafood platter. Such a platter tends to be quite expensive and quite copious. Bretons can be serious gluttons when they go out to a restaurant, and they'll often tuck in to such a *plateau* as a mere starter. Beginners are probably best advised to stick to one as a main course.

Different sections of the Breton coastline are associated with different catches. The ports of the Pays Bigouden are renowned for their langoustines (sometimes translated as Dublin Bay prawns), generally simply cooked in saltwater and then served with a rich home-made mayonnaise. Langoustines are widely available in summer. Oysters are especially associated with Cancale in northern Brittany and with the Morbihan coast in southern Brittany, although Belon in the Finistère is synonymous with a particularly fine type, too. Oysters are generally served raw in Brittany, either with lemon to squeeze over them, or with a vinegar sauce, to which chopped shallots are added. You can eat oysters all year round. Mussels thrive in particular in the waters of the Bay of the Mont St-Michel and the Bay of St-Brieuc in northern Brittany, and at the mouth of the Vilaine River in southern Brittany. Going out to see the forest of wooden posts, the *bouchots*, on which they grow in the Bay of Mont St-Michel, for example, makes for a memorable outing. The most common way for mussels to be served is *à la marinière*, in a light white wine sauce with plenty of onions and parsley added. *Coquilles St-Jacques*, scallops, flourish in the Bay of St-Brieuc, and the Rade de Brest also provides good conditions for them. They are fished during the winter months. *Pétoncles* are baby scallops, often known as queen scallops.

Crab is commonplace in Brittany. You can try several different varieties, such as *araignées* (spider crabs), *dormeurs* or *tourteaux* (common crabs) and *étrilles* or *crabes cerises* – the last have a velvety texture, hence the English name of velvet crabs. Although most people in North America and Britain may not be familiar with these as edible crabs, they're considered to have a deliciously subtle taste in Brittany. Shrimps make another popular starter, either *crevettes roses* or the smaller *crevettes grises*; the latter can be eaten whole. The *grises* also have a certain spiciness and can be used to make a *bisque*, a shellfish soup. Lobster, which can feature in a *bisque* too, is expensive, but restaurants across Brittany serve it and it is still regarded as the most refined of seafoods. *Homard* is the blue-black, enormous-pincered variety. *Langouste* is spiny lobster or rock lobster.

Other shells you may find on menus include *palourdes* or *praires* (clams), often stuffed with garlic butter but perhaps the finest sea shells to eat raw, with their natural nutty and citrus flavours. *Coques* are cockles, *bigorneaux* winkles and *bulots* whelks, the last being large and fatty, and once considered the poor man's shellfish. *Oursins* (sea urchins) are much rarer, and *ormeaux*, the magnificent-tasting ormers or abalones, are virtually never seen any more.

On to **fish** in Brittany. *Cotriade*, which is the Breton answer to the Mediterranean *bouillabaisse*, is a good place to start. It's a Breton sailors' soup, traditionally made from the leftovers of the catch. It might include whiting, cod, haddock, hake, richer mackerel and eel, even some mussels or other shellfish; potatoes add substance. As Breton cuisine has become more refined, chefs have tried all manner of combinations in their *nouvelles cotriades*.

There are some 30 types of fish commonly sold from Breton ports. Certain ones are highly prized, such as *St-Pierre* (John Dory), *bar* (sea bass), *daurade* (sea bream), *rouget* (red mullet), turbot and sole. Other fish such as sardines, mackerel, whiting, pollock, coley, lemon sole and tuna are quite common. Eel can be delicate, although conger eel is definitely not for the faint-stomached. *Cabillaud*, fresh cod, is distinguished from *morue*, salt cod. In the second half of the 19th century, tinned fish became a speciality in Brittany, and a major industry. There are still canning factories in ports such as Douarnenez, Concarneau and Quiberon, where fish is prepared using traditional methods. Often the fish are canned in a white wine and shallot sauce, although the manufacturers are experimenting more these days, even adding whisky to some sauces. Breton fish soups have a good reputation. The use of *algues*, seaweed, in Breton cuisine is a more recent affair, and *salicornes*, or samphire, which are grown in the Breton salt pans, are another speciality being experimented with in cuisine.

In terms of **meat**, Brittany is known in France for its pork. You can try all manner of Breton *saucissons* (the French equivalent of salami), some with garlic, some covered in pepper. Breton *andouille* uses unmentionable bits of pork to form a sausage much appreciated in the province, Guémené-sur-Scorff being the capital of this delicacy. *Boudin noir*, black pudding, is popular, as are hams and pork pâtés. Cattle are numerous in eastern Brittany, and the town of Châteaubriant is famed for the thick grilled fillet steak named after it. The lambs that graze in the salty fields of Ouessant or the Bay of Mont St-Michel are regarded as being especially tasty but will only feature on a menu in the places where they are reared. It may come as a relief to some of you that Breton horse meat is no longer so popular. The Brière and Nantes are known for duck; Canard Nantais is a classic of the former Breton capital, served with *petits pois*. Free-range chickens are reared in good number around Janzé, also in eastern Brittany. One very traditional dish that has come back into fashion in restaurants is *kig-ar-farz*, which simply means meat and pudding in Breton. Here the many elements are cooked together, the meat, vegetables and pudding added to the broth. The pudding is savoury, made from buckwheat or wheat, sometimes with raisins, and is dropped in a tight bag into the broth to cook.

Breton butter, quite strongly salty, is considered to be a gastronomic treat in itself. It's used both in the preparation of meats and of cakes. Guérande is strongly associated with **Breton salt**, as the stuff is still produced in its salt pans in the old-fashioned way. Crossing the Marais Salants of Guérande on a bright summer day you may see packets of salt piled on kitchen chairs in front of homes, on sale to passers-by. The *fleur de sel* is the best type of salt.

The sandy Breton soil has proved excellent for growing a wide variety of **vegetables**. The north shore is renowned for its artichokes, cauliflowers and onions. It was from Roscoff that the Johnny onion-sellers set off to conquer the British market. Brittany also produces fine potatoes, shallots, leeks and chicory. Dried beans were once a staple in the province, *cocos de Paimpol* still quite popular; now green beans are produced in large quantity. Garlic stalls are common around the Bay of the Mont St-Michel. The sauce *à l'armoricaine* so popular across Brittany is made with garlic, tomatoes and olive oil. You'll see large quantities of maize being grown, but the vast majority is destined for animal feed.

Moving on to sweet matters, the main **fruit** associated with Brittany is the apple. Brittany is serious cider-drinking territory (*see* opposite). Fouesnant is particularly reputed for its cherries, while the farmers of Plougastel-Daoulas, a peninsula just south of Brest, have built their fortunes on fine strawberries. In the Nantes region, melons grow well.

Butter is the main ingredient in **Breton cakes and biscuits**. In fact, the most traditional of Breton cakes, *kouign aman*, is served dripping with the stuff, which explains its Breton name, meaning 'cake-butter'. *Gâteau breton* is another highly buttery recipe, producing a denser, heavier Breton butter cake that should melt in the mouth. Some towns, notably Pleyben and Pont-Aven, are well known for their *galettes*, here meaning butter biscuits, not a type of crêpe. In fact Pont-Aven is almost as famous in France for its biscuits as for its artists. Nantes developed into a major biscuit producer in the 18th century, when biscuits formed an important part of ships' provisions. The town is closely associated with the major Breton biscuit manufacturer Lu. *Crêpes dentelles* were invented in Quimper in the late 19th century. These are superbly crunchy but frustratingly flaky wafer biscuits made of ultra-thin layers wrapped round and round. Returning to more substantial old-style Breton puddings, you'll find *far*, a heavy eggy pudding with dried fruit in the batter, served in most places. Apples feature in many a Breton pudding too, of course.

Drink

Cider, Apple Alcohols, Muscadet and Other Breton Brews

Cider has long been the traditional Breton alcoholic drink. Some cider-producing areas of the province have even pressed for and obtained their own *appellation d'origine contrôlée* (AOC), a label that guarantees authentic, well-monitored, high-quality local production, as with French wines. Look out too for the terms *cidre fermier* or *cidre traditionnel* on the label, signs that the cider has been made either on smallholdings or traditionally. Cider is produced across most of the province; you'll even find several cider-themed museums dotted around Brittany. If you're offered a *kir breton* it'll be cider mixed with blackberry or blackcurrant liqueur.

Lambig, the Breton equivalent of Normandy Calvados, only much rarer, is an extremely well-kept secret. Its distinctive appley dryness varies according to the distiller. Fine de Bretagne is a Lambig that has been aged for six years or more. Brittany also produces an alcoholic apple apéritif, *pommeau*, worth giving a try.

Vines did used to be cultivated around Brittany in medieval times, before cider took over. Now wine is only made in any quantity in the Loire Atlantique. The famous wine name of that *département* is **Muscadet**, which is, appropriately enough, the most common wine served with Breton fish and seafood. Its zingy, crisp, fresh taste can stand up to the strong flavours of the sea. The best wine-making area of Muscadet lies just to the southeast of Nantes, the Muscadet de Sèvre et Maine (*see* p.497). Muscadet-sur-Lie is a class above your average Muscadet. The Loire Atlantique produces other white wines, such as the rather lesser Gros Plant and the rare Malvoisie of the Coteaux d'Ancenis. Otherwise, the Coteaux d'Ancenis produce a range of largely red wines.

The beer (*bière*) on sale is often from one of the run-of-the-mill big brands from Alsace, Belgium or Germany; draft beer (*pression*) is cheaper than bottled. Ask if there are any local beers on offer. A number of small-scale breweries keep up the tradition of Breton **cervoise**, the name the Gauls gave to the brew – it's what Astérix and his friends order in the French version of the comic. **Chouchen** is mead, a sweet alcoholic drink made from honey; producers claim it to be the oldest alcoholic drink in Brittany.

Soft Drinks and Water

Mineral water (*eau minérale*) comes either sparkling (*gazeuse* or *pétillante*) or still (*non-gazeuse* or *plate*). The best-known Breton water bottled at source is **Plancoët**. The usual international corporate soft drinks are available as well as a variety of bottled **fruit juices** (*jus de fruits*). Some bars also do the refreshing freshly squeezed lemon and orange juices known as *citron pressé* or *orange pressée*, served with plenty of chilled water. Some French people are fond of sweet **fruit cordials**, for example red *grenadine*, milky-coloured *sirop d'orgeat*, or ghastly green *menthe*. If lemonade is mixed with them, they become *diabolos*. Many Bretons dislike their **tap water**, and buy bottled water to drink at home. *Eau potable* means drinkable water in French; *non potable* means it is not fit for consumption.

Restaurant Basics

Eating Hours

The Bretons tend to eat quite early in restaurants, at 12 noon or 12.30 for lunch, and generally start their evening meal between 7.30 and 8.30pm. Breton meals can go on for a very long time, especially if you're beginning with the challenge of a large seafood platter. Many restaurants do a good-value lunchtime menu. Call at least a day in advance to book a table at restaurants that have a well-established reputation, or that are well located; out of season, phone ahead to check whether or not a restaurant is open. With *fermes-auberges* (*see* p.73) and other specialist types of restaurant, you have to call in advance to be served.

Restaurant Menus and Wine

Restaurants should post their menus outside the entrance, but you may want to check that they accept credit cards at the start of the meal – a certain number don't take plastic. Most restaurants, unless they're very small, will normally offer a choice of set-price menus with two to five or even more courses.

A full French restaurant meal normally begins with an apéritif that is served with little savoury snacks known as *amuses-bouche* or *amuses-gueule* (*gueule* is a rather vulgar word for a mouth). The *hors d'œuvre* are the starters; the *entrées* or *plats/pièces de résistance* or *plats principaux* are the main courses. (Note that if you order a side salad, it will normally come before or after the main course.) *Les fromages*, cheeses, in France are served prior to the *desserts*, the puddings. You could finish a meal with a *digestif* or a cup of coffee, tea, or a *tisane*, a herbal tea. Drinks to end a meal are often accompanied by *petits fours* or chocolates.

More ordinary meals consist of a starter, a main course and either cheese or pudding. A *plat du jour*, sometimes also referred to as the *plat du marché*, is the day's special, which could be eaten by itself. A *menu dégustation* is a selection of the chef's or the region's specialities. Eating *à la carte* will always be much more expensive than opting for a set menu.

Menus in cheaper restaurants sometimes include a bottle or a carafe of house wine in the price (denoted by the words *vin compris*). Wine in French restaurants tends to be on the expensive side, though the house wine can be good value. French families often splash out on a reasonable bottle when eating out; however, some places now serve *le vin au verre*, wine by the glass. By law, service should be automatically included in the price of set menus nowadays, but you may wish to add a small tip if you're happy with your meal and service.

Markets and Picnic Food

In small towns, the market day is *the* event of the week, though most of them finish up by around noon. Once you've sorted the parking problem, you should be able to find all sorts of local farm produce, the freshest fish, and piles of seafood. In big towns you can also find more established daily covered markets, *les Halles*. Other good sources for picnic food are *boulangeries* (selling bread, but also tarts and pastries often), *charcuteries* (selling meat specialities, especially pork), *traiteurs* (delicatessens, selling a diversity of elaborate prepared dishes) and *pâtisseries*.

Cafés and Bars

The French café isn't only a place to drink, but for many people also a home from home; you can sit for hours over one drink and shouldn't feel hurried by the staff. Prices for drinks are listed on the *tarif des consommations*; they go up according to whether you're served at the bar (*le comptoir*), at a table inside the café (*en salle*) or outside (*en terrasse*). Cafés often serve croissants, baguettes, *croque-monsieurs* (toasted ham and cheese sandwiches) and maybe French pastries, and can make for an atmospheric and cheap setting for the first meal of the day, or for lunch.

French coffee is strong and black, and if you order *un café* you'll get a very small *express*. For more than these few drops of caffeine, ask for *un grand café*; coffee with milk is *un café crème*. The French tend to order *café au lait*, a small amount of coffee topped up with a large quantity of hot milk, at breakfast. Decaffeinated coffee is usually abbreviated to *un déca*. *Un thé* is most likely a teabag in a cup of hot water; you'll probably have to specify *thé au lait* (tea with milk) or *thé au citron* (tea with lemon) to get any frills. *Chocolat chaud*, hot chocolate, is popular among children. Popular *infusions* or *tisanes*, or herbal teas, include: camomille, *menthe* (mint), *tilleul* (lime or linden blossom) and *verveine* (verbena).

French Menu Vocabulary

Starters/Soups
(*Hors d'œuvre/Soupes*)

assiette assortie plate of mixed cold hors d'œuvre
bisque shellfish soup
bouillon broth
charcuterie mixed cold meats
cotriade Breton mixed fish soup
crudités raw vegetable platter
potage thick vegetable soup
velouté thick smooth soup

Fish/Shellfish
(*Poissons/Coquillages*)

aiglefin little haddock
alose shad
anchois anchovy
anguille eel
araignée spider crab
bar sea bass
barbue brill
baudroie anglerfish
belon flat oyster
beurre blanc sauce of shallots and wine vinegar whisked with butter

bigorneau winkle
blanchailles whitebait
brème bream
brochet pike
bulot whelk
cabillaud cod
calmar squid
carrelet plaice
colin hake
congre conger eel
coque cockle
coquillages shellfish
coquille St-Jacques scallop
crabe cerise velvet crab
crevette grise shrimp
crevette rose prawn
darne slice or steak of fish
daurade sea bream
dormeur common crab
écrevisse freshwater crayfish
éperlan smelt
escabèche fish fried, marinated
  and served cold
escargot snail
espadon swordfish
esturgeon sturgeon
étrille velvet crab
flétan halibut
friture deep-fried fish
fruits de mer seafood
gambas giant prawn
gigot de mer a large fish cooked whole
grondin red gurnard
hareng herring
homard Atlantic (Norway) lobster
huître oyster
lamproie lamprey
langouste spiny Mediterranean lobster
langoustine Dublin Bay prawn or scampi
lieu pollack or coley
limande lemon sole
lotte monkfish
loup (de mer) sea bass
maquereau mackerel
matelote d'anguilles eels in a wine sauce
merlan whiting
merlus hake
morue salt cod
moule mussel
omble chevalier char
ormeau ormer or abalone
oursin sea urchin
palourde clam
pêche du jour catch of the day
pétoncle queen scallop or baby scallop
poulpe octopus
praire small clam
raie skate

rouget red mullet
roussette dogfish
St-Pierre John Dory
sandre zander or pikeperch
saumon salmon
sole (meunière) sole (with butter, lemon
  and parsley)
telline tiny clam
thon tuna
tourteau common crab
truite trout
truite saumonée salmon trout
vieille wrasse

Meat and Poultry (Viandes et Volailles)

agneau (de pré-salé) lamb (grazed in fields
  by the sea)
aileron chicken wing
andouille pigs' intestine sausage
andouillette chitterling (tripe) sausage
autruche ostrich
bifteck beefsteak
blanc breast or white meat
blanquette stew of white meat, thickened with
  egg yolk
bœuf beef
boudin blanc sausage of white meat
boudin noir black pudding
brochette meat (or fish) on a skewer
caille quail
canard, caneton duck, duckling
carré crown roast
cassoulet haricot bean stew with sausage, duck,
  goose, etc.
cervelle brains
chapon capon
Châteaubriant porterhouse steak
cheval horsemeat
chevreau kid
chevreuil venison
civet meat (usually game) stew, in wine
  and blood sauce
cœur heart
confit meat cooked and preserved in its
  own fat
contre-filet sirloin steak
côte, côtelette chop, cutlet
cou d'oie farci goose neck stuffed with pork,
  foie gras and truffles
crépinette small sausage
cuisse thigh or leg
cuisses de grenouilles frogs' legs
dinde, dindon turkey
entrecôte ribsteak
épaule shoulder
estouffade a meat stew marinated,
  fried and then braised
faisan pheasant

faux-filet sirloin
foie liver
foie gras fattened goose or duck liver
frais de veau calf testicles
fricadelle meatball
gésier gizzard
gibier game
gigot leg of lamb
graisse, gras fat
grillade grilled meat, often a mixed grill
jambon ham
jarret knuckle
langue tongue
lapereau young rabbit
lapin rabbit
lard (lardons) bacon (diced bacon)
lièvre hare
maigret/magret (de canard)
  breast (of duck)
manchon duck or goose wing
marcassin young wild boar
merguez spicy red sausage of North African
  origin
mouton mutton
museau muzzle
navarin lamb stew with root vegetables
noix de veau (agneau) topside of veal (lamb)
oie goose
os bone
perdreau, perdrix partridge
petit gris little grey snail
petit salé salt pork
pieds trotters
pintade guinea fowl
plat-de-côtes short ribs or rib chops
porc pork
pot au feu meat and vegetables cooked
  in stock
poulet chicken
poussin baby chicken
quenelle very light poached dumplings
  made of fish, fowl or meat and bound
  with egg
queue de bœuf oxtail
rillettes a coarse type of pâté
ris (de veau) sweetbreads (veal)
rognon kidney
rosbif roast beef
rôti roast
sanglier wild boar
saucisse sausage
saucisson salami-like sausage
selle (d'agneau) saddle (of lamb)
steak tartare raw minced beef, often topped
  with a raw egg yolk
suprême de volaille fillet of chicken breast
  and wing
taureau bull's meat

tête (de veau) (calf's) head, brawn
tournedos thick round slices of beef fillet
travers de porc spare ribs
tripes tripe
veau veal
venaison venison

Vegetables, Herbs, etc. (Légumes, Herbes, etc.)

ail garlic
aneth dill
anis anis
artichaut artichoke
asperge asparagus
aubergine aubergine (eggplant)
avocat avocado
basilic basil
betterave beetroot
blé noir buckwheat
blette Swiss chard
cannelle cinnamon
céleri (-rave) celery (celeriac)
cèpe ceps, wild boletus mushroom
champignon mushroom
chanterelle wild yellow mushroom
chicorée curly endive
chou cabbage
chou-fleur cauliflower
choucroute sauerkraut
ciboulette chive
citrouille pumpkin
cœur de palmier heart of palm
concombre cucumber
cornichon gherkin
cresson watercress
échalote shallot
endive chicory (endive)
épinards spinach
estragon tarragon
fenouil fennel
fève broad (fava) bean
flageolet white bean
fleur de courgette courgette blossom
frites chips (French fries)
froment type of wheat used for sweet crêpes
galipette large round mushroom
genièvre juniper
gingembre ginger
haricot (rouge, blanc) (kidney, white) bean
haricot vert green (French) bean
jardinière mixed vegetables
laitue lettuce
laurier bay leaf
macédoine diced vegetables
(épis de) maïs sweetcorn (on the cob)
marjolaine marjoram
menthe mint
mesclun salad of various leaves
morille morel mushroom

navet turnip
oignon onion
oseille sorrel
panais parsnip
persil parsley
petits pois small peas
pied bleu wood blewits (type of mushroom)
piment pimento
pissenlits dandelion greens
poireau leek
pois chiche chickpea
pois mange-tout sugar pea, mangetout
poivron sweet pepper (capsicum)
pomme de terre potato
potiron pumpkin
primeurs young vegetables
radis radish
romarin rosemary
roquette rocket
safran saffron
salade verte green salad
salicorne samphire (small, fleshy plant that thrives in salt pans)
salsifis salsify
sarriette savory
sarrasin buckwheat
sauge sage
seigle rye
serpolet wild thyme
truffe truffle

Fruit and Nuts (*Fruits et Noix*)

abricot apricot
amande almond
ananas pineapple
banane banana
bigarreau red and yellow cherry
brugnon nectarine
cacahouète peanut
cassis blackcurrant
cerise cherry
citron lemon
citron vert lime
(*noix de*) *coco* coconut
coing quince
datte date
fraise (*des bois*) (wild) strawberry
framboise raspberry
fruit de la passion passion fruit
grenade pomegranate
griotte morello cherry
groseille redcurrant
mandarine tangerine
mangue mango
marron chestnut
mirabelle mirabelle plum
mûre (*sauvage*) mulberry, blackberry
myrtille bilberry
noisette hazelnut

noix walnut
noix de cajou cashew
pamplemousse grapefruit
pastèque watermelon
pêche (*blanche*) (white) peach
pignon pinenut
pistache pistachio
poire pear
pomme apple
prune plum
pruneau prune
raisin/raisin sec grape/raisin
reine-claude greengage plum

Desserts

Bavarois mousse or custard in a mould
bombe ice-cream dessert in a round mould
brioche light sweet yeast bread
charlotte sponge fingers and custard cream dessert
chausson turnover
clafoutis batter fruit cake
compote stewed fruit
corbeille de fruits basket of fruit
coupe ice cream: a scoop or in cup
crème anglaise thin egg custard
crème caramel vanilla custard with caramel sauce
crème Chantilly sweet whipped cream
crème fraîche slightly sour cream
crème pâtissière thick egg custard
crêpe dentelle thin, crunchy Breton biscuit
far filling Breton eggy flan of batter and dried fruit
galette butter biscuit or pancake
gâteau cake
gâteau Breton dense Breton butter cake
gaufre waffle
génoise rich sponge cake
glace ice cream
kouign aman crisp Breton pudding dripping with butter
macaron macaroon
madeleine sponge cake
miel honey
mignardise petits fours (see below)
œufs à la neige floating island/meringue on a bed of custard
pain d'épice gingerbread
parfait rich frozen mousse
petits fours tiny cakes and pastries
profiteroles choux pastry balls, often filled with cream, *crème pâtissière* or ice cream, and covered with chocolate
sablé shortbread
savarin a filled cake, shaped like a ring
tarte, tartelette tart, little tart
truffe chocolate truffle
pâte à chou choux pastry

fouace (or *fouée*) dough ball that puffs up
  when cooked
fourchette fork
huile (*d'olive*) oil (olive)
lait milk
menu set menu
moutarde mustard
nouilles noodles
pain bread
œuf egg
poivre pepper
riz rice
sel salt
service compris/non compris
  service included/not included
sucre sugar
vinaigre vinegar

Drinks (Boissons)
bière (*pression*) (draught) beer
(*demi*) *bouteille* (half) bottle
brut very dry
café coffee
café au lait white coffee
café express espresso coffee
café filtre filter coffee
chocolat chaud hot chocolate
chouchen mead
cidre cider
citron pressé fresh lemon juice
demi a third of a litre
doux sweet (wine)
eau water
  gazeuse sparkling
  minérale mineral
  plate still
eau-de-vie brandy
eau potable drinking water
glaçon ice cube
infusion/tisane herbal tea
  camomille camomile
  menthe mint
  tilleul linden blossom
  verveine verbena
jus juice
lait milk
moelleux semi-dry
mousseux sparkling (wine)
orange pressée fresh orange juice
pichet pitcher
pression draught
sec dry
thé tea
verre glass
vin (*blanc/mousseux/rosé/rouge*)
  (white/sparkling/rosé/red) wine

Cheese (Fromage)
(*fromage de*) *brebis* sheep's cheese

chèvre goat's cheese
doux mild
(*plateau de*) *fromage* (board) cheese
fromage blanc yoghurty cream cheese
fromage frais a bit like sour cream
fromage sec general name for hard cheeses
fort strong

Cooking Terms and Sauces
à point medium (steak)
aigre-doux sweet and sour
aiguillette thin slice
à l'anglaise boiled
à l'armoricaine sauce with brandy, white wine,
  shallots, tomatoes, garlic and
  cayenne pepper
à la marinière light white wine sauce with
  onions and parsley
au feu de bois cooked over a wood fire
au four baked
barquette pastry boat
beignet fritter
béarnaise sauce of egg yolks, shallots and white
  wine
bien cuit well-done (steak)
bleu very rare (steak)
bordelaise red wine, bone marrow and
  shallot sauce
broche roasted on a spit
chaud hot
cru raw
cuit cooked
émincé thinly sliced
en croûte cooked in a pastry crust
en papillote baked in buttered paper
épice spice
farci stuffed
feuilleté flaky pastry
flambé set aflame with alcohol
fleur de sel the finest salt crystals
fourré stuffed
frais, fraîche fresh
frappé with crushed ice
frit fried
froid cold
fumé smoked
galantine cooked food served in
  cold jelly
galette savoury pancake
garni with vegetables
(*au*) *gratin* topped with melted cheese
  and breadcrumbs
haché minced
marmite casserole
médaillon round piece
mijoté simmered
pané breaded
pâte pastry or pasta
pâte brisée shortcrust pastry

pâte feuilletée flaky or puff pastry
paupiette rolled and filled thin slices of
  fish or meat
pavé slab
poché poached
salé salted, spicy
saignant rare (steak)
sucré sweet
timbale pie cooked in a
  dome-shaped mould
tranche slice
vapeur steamed
vinaigrette oil and vinegar dressing

Miscellaneous
addition bill (check)
baguette long loaf of bread
beurre butter
carte menu
confiture jam
couteau knife
crème cream
cuillère spoon
formule/menu set menu
fouace (or *fouée*) dough ball that puffs up
  when cooked
fourchette fork
huile (*d'olive*) oil (olive)
lait milk
menu set menu
moutarde mustard
nouilles noodles
pain bread
œuf egg
poivre pepper
riz rice
sel salt
service compris/non compris
  service included/not included
sucre sugar

vinaigre vinegar

Drinks (Boissons)
bière (*pression*) (draught) beer
(*demi*) *bouteille* (half) bottle
brut very dry
café coffee
café au lait white coffee
café express espresso coffee
café filtre filter coffee
chocolat chaud hot chocolate
chouchen mead
cidre cider
citron pressé fresh lemon juice
demi a third of a litre
doux sweet (wine)
eau water
  gazeuse sparkling
  minérale mineral
  plate still
eau-de-vie brandy
eau potable drinking water
glaçon ice cube
infusion/tisane herbal tea
  camomille camomile
  menthe mint
  tilleul linden blossom
  verveine verbena
jus juice
lait milk
moelleux semi-dry
mousseux sparkling (wine)
orange pressée fresh orange juice
pichet pitcher
pression draught
sec dry
thé tea
verre glass
vin (*blanc/mousseux/rosé/rouge*)
  (white/sparkling/rosé/red) wine

Planning
Your Trip

05

When to Go

Climate

Breton weather is not reliable, but it is generally mild. It very rarely snows, and it doesn't tend to get too hot even in the height of summer. The coast is often windy; enormous white clouds rush across the Breton skies on many a day of the year. Although Brittany is not as rainy as the cliché would have you believe, always bring a raincoat and something to keep your head warm.

Mid-July to mid-August is the most consistent period for Breton sunshine, but also the high point of the Breton tourist season, when you'll be packed like sardines on the beaches of the most popular resorts. The first half of July and the last half of August can be almost as warm and sunny, and tends to be rather less crowded. May and June, and September and October, can be delightful or disappointing, depending on your luck with the weather. May can be surprisingly busy, as the French have a series of long weekends off in that month, but the countryside looks at its best then. In September, kids will be back in class and you can have large stretches of the coast to yourself. November to March is the best time to see fierce waves crashing against cliffs or jumping over jetties. In autumn and winter, fog and mist will obscure your sea views from time to time. The granite and schist of Breton architecture can look particularly dark in the winter months, but the popular whitewashed houses keep up their bright appearance from afar. April is often particularly cheerful because of the Easter holidays and the colours and foliage returning to the countryside.

Outside the main holiday seasons, many of the houses in the Breton resorts are closed up, though more recently hotels have been encouraged to stay open for at least ten months of the year.

Major Breton Festivals and *Pardons*

In summer, countless Breton communities organize a *fest noz*, a traditional night festival involving Breton music and dancing, and usually a lot of cider or other alcohol. *Bagadou*, when traditional Breton bands lock

Average Temperature Chart in °C

Jan	Feb	Mar	April	May	June
9.3	8.6	11.1	17.1	16.0	22.7

July	Aug	Sept	Oct	Nov	Dec
25.1	24.1	21.2	16.5	12.1	9.3

in lively musical competition, are fairly numerous too. *Pardons*, by contrast, are serious, sober religious ceremonies, held during the course of the day; they are local pilgrimages, when the saint or saints and the banners of the local church are taken out for a walk with the pilgrims. Virtually every community church and chapel has its *pardon*. Tourists are welcome but must be respectful.

See also 'National Holidays', p.79.

Tourist Information

For general tourist information on France in your own country, contact the relevant French Government tourist office, though it will not be able to supply you with anything like the detailed information you get from the *département* and local tourist bodies in France. French Government tourist offices are listed below.

For details of France-based tourist information, *see* p.80.

French Government Tourist Offices

UK: Lincoln House, 300 High Holborn, London WC1V 7JH, **t** 09068 244 123 (60p/min), *www.uk.franceguide.com/*.

Ireland: 30 Upper Merion Street, Dublin 2, **t** (01) 662 9345, *www.ie.franceguide.com*.

USA: 825 Third Avenue, 29th Floor, New York, NY 10022, **t** (514) 288 1904; 205 North Michigan Avenue, Suite 3770, Chicago, IL 60601, **t** (312) 327 0290; 9454 Wilshire Boulevard, Suite 210, Beverly Hills, CA 90212, **t** (310) 271 6665; nationwide info, **t** (900) 990 0040, *www.us.franceguide.com*.

Canada: 1800 Avenue McGill College, Suite 101, Montréal, Quebec H3A 3J6, **t** (514) 288 2026, *www.ca.franceguide.com*.

Australia: Level 13, 25 Bligh Street, Sydney, NSW 2000, **t** (2) 9231 5244, *www.au.franceguide.com*.

South Africa: 3rd Floor, Village Walk Office Tower, cnr Maude and Rivonia, Sandton, **t** (11) 523 8292, *www.za.franceguide.com*.

Calendar of Events

The dates of some festivals can change so if you are making a special trip, check first with the local tourist office.

May

3rd Sun Tréguier *Pardon de St Yves*
Trinity Sun Rumengol *Pardon*

June

late June/early July Nantes *Quinzaine Celtique* music festival

July

1st six days Rennes *Tombées de la Nuit* open-air entertainments
Nantes *Aux Heures d'Eté* culture festival (runs until mid-August)
1st Sun Quimper *Pardon de Ty Mamm Doué*
mid-July Dinan *Fête des Remparts* historic street festival
Landerneau *Festival Kann al Loar* music and maritime festival
2nd week Pont-l'Abbé *Fête des Brodeuses* folk festival
Quimperlé *Festival Musiques Mosaïques*
2nd week (every six years, next one 2013) Locronan *Pardon de la Grande Troménie*
3rd Sun Paimpol *Fête des Terre-Neuvas et des Islandais* folklore festival
3rd week Quimper *Festival de Cornouaille* culture festival
Vannes *Fêtes Historiques*
Fouesnant *Fête des Pommiers* local cider festival

25–26 July Ste-Anne d'Auray *Pardon*
late July–early Aug Concarneau *Festival International de la Baie* world music and dance festival
Vannes *Festival de Jazz*

August

through most of Aug Quimper *Semaines Musicales*
early Aug Lamballe *Fête Folklorique des Ajoncs d'Or*
Pont-Aven *Fête des Fleurs d'Ajonc*
1st fortnight St-Malo *Festival Couleurs Jazz*, Lorient *Festival Interceltique*
Plomodiern *Festival Folklorique du Ménez-Hom*
St-Lyphard *Fête de la Tourbe* local culture festival
Vannes *Fêtes d'Arvor* culture festival
Lizio *Fête des Artisans d'Art* craft festival
Perros-Guirec *Fête des Hortensias* Celtic music and culture festival
15 Aug Ste-Marie-du-Ménez-Hom *Pardon*
2nd fortnight Guingamp *Festival de la Danse Bretonne et la Fête de la St-Loup*
Moncontour *Fête Médiévale*
2nd Sun after 15 Aug Ste-Anne-la-Palud *Pardon*

September–December

1st Sun Le Folgoët *Pardon*
Sun nearest 29 Sept Mont St-Michel *Fête de la St-Michel d'automne (classical and religious music)*
Early Dec Rennes *Les Transmusicales* international rock festival

Embassies and Consulates

UK: 58 Knightsbridge, London SW1X 7JT, t (020) 7073 1000, *www.ambafrance-uk.org*; 21 Cromwell Rd, London SW7 2EN, t (020) 7073 1200, *www.consulfrance-londres.org* (for visas); 11 Randolph Crescent, Edinburgh EH3 7TT, t (0131) 225 7954, *www.consulfrance-edimbourg.org*.

Ireland: 36 Ailesbury Rd, Ballsbridge, Dublin 4, t (01) 277 5000, *www.ambafrance.ie*.

USA: 4101 Reservoir Rd NW, Washington, DC 200007, t (202) 944 6000, *www.ambafrance-us.org*; 934 5th Ave, New York NY 10021, t (212) 606 3600, *www.consulfrance-newyork.org*. There are also French consulates in Chicago,

Los Angeles, Atlanta, Boston, Houston, Miami, New Orleans and San Francisco.

Canada: 42 Sussex Drive, Ottawa, ON K1M 2C9, t (613) 789 1795, *www.ambafrance-ca.org*. There are also consulates in Toronto, Montréal, Quebec City, Vancouver and Moncton.

Australia: 6 Perth Ave, Yarralumla, ACT 2600, Canberra, t (02) 6216 0100, *www.ambafrance-au.org*. The French consulate is based in Sydney, t (02) 9268 2400.

New Zealand: Rural Bank Building, 13th Floor, 34–42 Manners St, PO Box 11-343, Wellington, t (4) 384 2555, *www.ambafrance-nz.org*.

South Africa: 250 Melk St, Nieuw Muckleneuk, Pretoria 0181, t (12) 425 1600, *www.ambafrance-rsa.org*. There are French consulates in Johannesburg and Cape Town.

Entry Formalities

Passports and Visas

Holders of EU, US, Canadian, Australian and New Zealand passports don't need a visa to enter France for stays of up to three months, but everyone else should check the requirements. Apply for a visa at the nearest French consulate in your home country. The most convenient visa to get is the *visa de circulation*, allowing for multiple stays of three months over a five-year period. If you plan to stay longer than three months in France (and, except for EU citizens, this includes people who come from a country whose citizens don't need to get a visa to enter France for shorter stays) French law states that you must get a *carte de séjour*. For information, contact the nearest French consulate in your home country.

Customs

EU citizens over the age of 17 do not have to declare goods imported into France for personal use if they have paid duty on them in the country of origin. In theory, you can buy as much as you like, provided you can prove the purchase is for your own use. In practice, customs will be more likely to ask questions if you buy in bulk, e.g. more than 3,200 cigarettes or 400 cigarillos, 200 cigars or 3kg of tobacco; plus 10 litres of spirits, 90 litres of wine and 110 litres of beer. Travellers caught importing any of the above for resale will have the goods and their vehicle seized, and could face up to seven years' imprisonment.

Travellers from **outside the EU** must pay duty on goods worth more than €175 that they import into France.

Travellers from the USA are allowed to bring home, duty-free, goods to the value of $800, including 200 cigarettes or 100 cigars; plus one litre of alcohol. For more information, call the US Customs Service. You're not allowed to bring back absinthe or Cuban cigars. Canadians can bring home $750 worth of goods after each absence of seven days, which can include some tobacco and alcoholic products.

French Customs, *www.douane.gouv.fr*.

UK Customs, t 0845 010 9000, *www.hmce.gov.uk*.

US Customs, t (202) 354 1000, *www.customs.gov*.

Canadian Customs, *www.cbsa.gc.ca*.

Disabled Travellers

In recent years, tourism facilities for the disabled across France have really moved on and a large number of disabled people visit France each year.

Every *département* in Brittany can now provide details on those tourist places that have been awarded the *Tourisme et Handicap* label. The recommendations provide details for four main types of handicap: auditory, mental, mobility and visual. Visit *www.bretagne-accessible.com* and *www.voyage-handicap.fr* for region-specific information, or consult the *Guide de la Bretagne Accessible*, written by a wheelchair user.

The **APF** (*Association des Paralysés de France*), 17 Boulevard Auguste Blanqui, 75013 Paris, t 01 40 78 69 00, *www.apf.asso.fr*, has a branch in every French *département*. It publishes *Où Ferons-Nous Etape? (Where Shall We Stay?)*. The French railway company, the **SNCF**, publishes a pamphlet, *Guide Pratique du Voyageur à Mobilité Réduite*, covering travel by train for disabled people – contact Rail Europe (*see* p.70). Contact **Gîtes de France** (*www.gites-de-france-bretagne.com*) for *gîtes* suitable for disabled guests.

RADAR (Royal Association for Disability and Rehabilitation), 12 City Forum, 250 City Road, London EC1V 8AF, t (020) 7250 3222, *www.radar.org.uk*, publishes *There and Back*, a travel guide for disabled people.

In the USA, **Mobility International USA**, PO Box 10767, Eugene, OR 97403, t (503) 343 1248, provides information on exchange programmes and volunteer service. **The Society for the Advancement of Travel for the Handicapped**, 347 Fifth Avenue, Suite 610, New York, NY 10016, t (212) 447 7284, *www.sath.org*, provides travel and access information. The Travel Information Service of the MossRehab Hospital, Philadelphia, offers advice for disabled travellers, t (215) 456 9900, *www.mossresourcenet.org*.

Insurance and EHIC cards

Make sure you're covered before you leave. The E111 forms for EU nationals have been replaced by the **European Health Insurance Card** (EHIC) that will give the bearer access to the state health-care scheme and public hospitals in all EU countries. Like the old system, the card is available for UK residents for free at post offices. Unlike the E111 forms, however, you'll need to apply for a card for every member of the family (you'll need passports and national insurance numbers). The EHIC must be renewed regularly. The NHS website, *www.nhs.uk/healthcarefrance* provides information on claiming refunds.

The French health service will only reimburse up to 75–80% of costs, so even with an EHIC consider taking out private medical insurance. **If you have private medical insurance**, check that you're clear about conditions and procedures to follow before you leave home. Citizens of non-EU countries should check that they have adequate insurance for any medical expenses, and the cost of returning home. Australia has a reciprocal health-care scheme with France, but New Zealand, Canada and the USA do not. If you already have health insurance, a student card or a credit card, you may be entitled to some medical cover abroad.

General Insurance

Consider taking out a general travel insurance policy, **covering theft and losses and offering a 100% medical refund**. Check it covers repatriation for the worst cases. Make sure you have **extra cover for sporting accidents** if you feel that's necessary. You might also verify cover in the case of strikes, always a possibility in French services.

Money and Banks

To check on the latest euro exchange rates, log on to *www.xe.com/ucc*.

You can take as much currency as you like into France, but by law you're only allowed to take out €750 in cash.

Travellers' cheques and Eurocheques, though a safe way of carrying money, aren't always accepted, as French banks charge an absurd fee to cash them.

The major **credit cards** are widely accepted throughout France, but you should verify whether this is the case in rural areas. A fair number of restaurants don't accept payment by credit cards. Some shops and restaurants don't accept payment by credit cards for amounts below €15–20. Before leaving home, find out from your bank which bank tellers (*guichets automatiques*) to use in France if you want to get out money in that way. International Giro cheques are exchangeable at any French post office.

Banks are generally open 8.30–12.30 and 1.30–4. Most close on Saturday or Monday as well as on Sunday. They are closed on national holidays.

Exchange rates vary and nearly all banks take a commission. *Bureaux de change* that do nothing but exchange money and hotels and train stations usually have the worst rates or charge the heftiest commission.

Getting There

By Air

From the UK, Ireland and Paris

The three major airports in Brittany are at Rennes, Nantes and Brest.

At the time of writing there is considerable instability in the airline industry; at present, the following flights are in operation: **Flybe** flies to Rennes from Manchester, Glasgow, Southampton and Exeter with summer-only flights from Newcastle, Edinburgh and Belfast. There are also flights to Brest from Dublin and Luton, and to Nantes from Bournemouth, Dublin, Liverpool, East Midlands and Stansted plus summer-only flights from Shannon. **Aer Lingus** flies between Dublin and Rennes, while **Aer Arran** operates between Nantes and Cork, and from Cardiff or Cork to Brest. The smaller airport at Dinan receives **Ryanair** flights from Bristol, Birmingham, East Midlands and Stansted, as well as **Aurigny** flights from the Channel Islands. Lorient Bretagne Sud, near Ploemeur, has flights to Galway, Cork, Waterford and Kerry with **Aer Arran**.

To fly to Brittany from elsewhere, including the USA and Canada, you have to change at one of the Paris airports, though there is a summer flight from Montréal to Nantes with **Air Transit**. Most flights from Paris to Brittany (about 1hr), are by **Air France**. Flights go either from Orly-Ouest or Roissy-Charles-de-Gaulle,

Airline Carriers

UK and Ireland

Aer Arran, t 0818 210 210, *www.aerarran.com*.

Aer Lingus, t 0818 365 000, *www.aerlingus.com*.

Air France, UK t 0871 66 33 777,
www.airfrance.co.uk.

British Airways, t 08444 93 07 87,
www.britishairways.com.

FlyBe, (UK) t 08717 00 20 00 (10p/min),
(Ireland) t 1392 268 500, *www.flybe.com*.

Ryanair, (UK) t 08712 46 00 00 (10p/min),
(Ireland) t 0818 30 30 30, *www.ryanair.com*.

USA and Canada

Air Canada, (Canada and USA) t 1 888 247 2262,
www.aircanada.ca.

Air France, (USA) t 800 237 2747, *www.
airfrance.com*, (Canada) t 800 667 2747,
www.airfrance.ca.

Air Transit, *www.airtransit.com*.

Aurigny, t 0871 871 0717, *www.aurigny.com*.

British Airways, t 800 AIRWAYS, *www.ba.com*.

Delta Airlines, US t 800 221 1212,
www.delta.com.

Northwest Airlines, US t 800 225 2525, t 800
328 2298 (hearing impaired), *www.nwa.com*.

United Airlines, US t 800 538 2929, t 800 323
0170 (TDD), *www.united.com*.

Discounts and Youth Fares

UK and Ireland

Budget Travel, 134 Lower Baggot St, Dublin 2,
t (01) 631 1111, *www.budgettravel.ie*.

Club Travel, 30 Lower Abbey St, Dublin 1,
t (01) 570 719 880 (€1.70/min),
www.clubtravel.ie.

STA, 52 Grosvenor Gardens, Victoria, London
SW1W 0AG, t 0871 468 0649, *www.statravel.
co.uk*. With 45 branches throughout the UK.

Trailfinders, 194 Kensington High St, London
W8 7RG, t (020) 7938 3939; 4–5 Dawson St,
Dublin 2, t (01) 677 7888, *www.trailfinders.co.uk*;
plus branches in other major UK cities.

United Travel, 12 Clonkeen Rd, Deansgrange,
Blackrock, Co. Dublin, t (01) 219 0600,
www.unitedtravel.ie.

USA and Canada

Airhitch, 481 Eighth Ave, Suite 1771, New York,
NY 10001-1820, t (212) 247 4482 or t 877
AIRHITCH, *www.airhitch.org*.

Last Minute Club, 1300 Don Mills Rd, Toronto,
Ontario M3B 2W6, t (416) 441 2582.

STA, t 800 781 4040, *www.statravel.com*. With
branches at most universities and at 30 3rd
Avenue, New York, NY 10003, t (212) 473 6100,
and 920 Westwood Boulevard, Los Angeles, CA
90024, t (310) 824 1574.

Travel Cuts, 187 College St, Toronto, Ontario
M5T 1P7, t 888 FLY CUTS (toll free) or t (416)
979 2406, *www.travelcuts.com*. Canada's
largest student agency; branches at most
universities.

Internet Travel Sites

UK and Ireland

www.aboutflights.co.uk (t 0870 330 7311)

www.cheapflights.co.uk

www.expedia.co.uk

www.flyaow.com

www.lastminute.com

www.majortravel.co.uk

www.opodo.co.uk

www.orbitz.com (also US/Canada)

www.sky-tours.co.uk

www.traveljungle.co.uk

www.travellersweb.com

www.travelocity.com (also US/Canada)

USA and Canada

www.eurovacations.com

www.expedia.com

www.flights.com

www.priceline.com (bid for tickets)

www.smartertravel.com

www.traveldiscounts.com

to Rennes, Nantes, Brest, Quimper-
Cornouaille and Lorient Bretagne Sud.

From North America

During off-peak periods, you should be able
to get a scheduled economy flight to Paris
from the USA for around $600–700. Tickets
can be booked through **Air France**, **British
Airways**, **Northwest Airlines** or **Delta Airlines**.

Check the Sunday-paper travel sections for
the latest deals, or look up US cheap-flight
websites such as *www.priceline.com* (to bid
on flights) or *www.expedia.com*.

By Car

There are three particular important points
to note when driving in France. First, drive on

the right-hand side of the road. Second, watch out for *priorité à droite*, an archaic and cunning system whereby traffic coming from streets to your right, unless halted by a stop sign and/or a thick white line, automatically has right of way over you. Third, French motorists rarely respect pedestrian crossings.

If you're involved in an **accident**, consult your insurance papers. The procedure is to fill out and sign a *constat amiable*. If your French isn't sufficient, try to find someone to translate, so you don't incriminate yourself.

A strong campaign against **drink-driving** and **speeding** has been going for some time in France, and police traps are often set up after French Sunday lunch. Try not to drink any alcohol if you're driving; the permissible levels of alcohol in the blood correspond to only a very small amount of alcohol at a meal. **Fines** for drink-driving can be huge, and like the fines for speeding are payable on the spot. Often, French drivers warn about the presence of police traps by flashing their lights. It is illegal to use a mobile phone while driving (though seeing French drivers, you wouldn't believe it); if caught, French police enforce their law much more rigorously than their UK counterparts.

Petrol (*essence*) is expensive in France, especially on motorways. Stations can be few and far between in rural areas, and they often shut at lunchtimes, during the night and on Sunday afternoons. Unleaded is called *sans plomb*, and diesel is often referred to as *gazole* or *gasoil*. If an attendant helps you, they may expect a small tip.

In Brittany, apart from the A84 heading north out of Rennes towards Caen, there are no motorways as such, only dual carriageways (divided highways) which do not have tolls. They are frequently referred to as *voies express*. The speed limits are: 130km/80mph on motorways; 110km/69mph on dual carriageways; 90km/55mph on other roads; and 50km/30mph in urban areas.

The word for a breakdown is *une panne*. To break down is *tomber en panne*. If you break down on major roads or motorways, use the orange emergency phones to contact rescue services or the police. If you're a member of a motoring club affiliated to the Touring Club de France, ring them; if not, ring the police, **t** 17.

Channel Crossings

Brittany Ferries, **t** 0871 244 0439, *www.brittanyferries.com*. The best choice of ferries to all parts of the Brittany coast: Plymouth–Roscoff, Cork–Roscoff, Poole–Cherbourg, Portsmouth–Cherbourg, St-Malo or Caen. A major new luxury mini-cruise vessel, the *Armorique*, launches in 2009, crossing from Britain to Brittany.

Condor Ferries, **t** 0845 609 1024, *www.condorferries.co.uk*. High-speed ferries (Weymouth and Poole to St-Malo, Portsmouth to Cherbourg).

hdferries, **t** 0844 576 8831, *www.hdferries.co.uk*. Operate between the Channel Islands and Brittany.

Hoverspeed, **t** 0870 240 8070, *www.hoverspeed.co.uk*. Dover–Calais, Dover–Ostend and Newhaven–Dieppe.

LD Lines, *www.ldline.co.uk*. Operates a service between Portsmouth and Le Havre.

Norfolkline, *www.norfolkline.com*. Services between Dover and Dunkerque, for car passengers only.

P&O, **t** 08716 64 56 45, *www.poferries.com*. Services between Dover and Calais.

SeaFrance, **t** 08705 711 711, *www.seafrance.com*. Dover–Calais ferries.

Transmanche, *www.transmancheferries.com*. Services between Dieppe and Newhaven.

Eurotunnel, **t** 08705 353 535, *www.eurotunnel.com*. Trains travelling from near Folkestone to near Calais.

By Coach

Eurolines, **t** 08717 81 81 81, *www.eurolines.co.uk*, runs coaches from the UK to Rennes and Nantes.

By Sea

St-Malo and Roscoff are the main ferry ports in northern Brittany. For a full list of operators at the time of writing, *see* box, above.

By Train

To get quickly from Britain to Brittany by train and avoid changing in Paris, take the **Eurostar**, **t** 08705 186 186 *www.eurostar.com*, to Lille in northern France, roughly a 1hr 40min journey from London. From Lille, you can reach the following Breton destinations: Rennes (*c.* 4hrs); Nantes (*c.* 4hrs); Redon (*c.* 4hrs); Vannes (*c.* 5hrs); Auray (a little over

Discount Rail Fares

The earlier you book the more likely you are to get a cheap ticket, but you can't book more than 60 days before your return date or the date of your journey if it is single. If you are travelling on Eurostar you can book 90 days ahead. For booking from abroad, *see* below.

Discount schemes change all the time. If you buy a return or circular ticket and travel at least 200km within 2 months, you get a 25% discount. You have to depart in a *période bleue* (off-peak: Monday 10am to Friday noon, Friday midnight to Sunday 3pm, and outside holidays).

Carte 12–25 Young people aged 12–25, travelling frequently by train, can purchase this card; it's good for a year and gives 50% discount on travel begun in blue periods.

Carte Découverte 12–25 Young people are eligible for a 25% discount if they buy their ticket in advance and begin travel in a *période bleue*.

Carte Enfant+ This is issued in the name of a child aged 4–12, and allows the child and up to four people a 50% discount on TGVs and other trains when starting in a *période bleue*. It is valid for 1 year and allows a discount on Avis car hire.

Carte Senior People over 60 can purchase a *carte senior*, valid for a year, offering 50% off blue period travel and 25% at other times. It allows a discount on Avis car hire.

Découverte à Deux If two people (related or not) are making a return trip together, they are eligible for a 25% discount in 1st or 2nd class for journeys begun in blue periods. It also entitles you to a discount if you hire an Avis car from a station.

Découverte Enfant+ This is free, issued in the name of a child aged 4–12, and allows a 25% discount for up to four others on trains departing in a *période bleue*. Again, there's a discount on Avis car hire.

Senior Découverte Eligibility for 25% off the journey for those over 60, travelling in a *période bleue*. Discount on Avis car hire.

5hrs); Lorient (*c*. 5hrs); Quimperlé (*c*. 5hrs); Rosporden (*c*. 6hrs); and Quimper (*c*. 6hrs). Check with Eurostar about connections and waiting times at Lille.

French trains are run by the nationalized SNCF company. The French rail network is gradually opening up to competition, so look out for developments. From Paris, the SNCF's excellent **TGVs** (*trains à grande vitesse –*

French high-speed trains) leave the capital for Brittany from the Gare Montparnasse. (The Eurostar from London arrives in Paris at the Gare du Nord.) There are three main TGV lines through Brittany. The northern line goes to Brest via Rennes, a southern line serves Quimper via Rennes, and the yet more southerly service goes as far as Le Croisic, via Nantes. The TGV journeys from Paris to Rennes last a little over 2hrs. Those to Nantes likewise. The TGVs to Brest take around 4hrs 20mins, those to Quimper a minimum of 4hrs 10mins. Le Croisic is only some 3hrs away from the French capital by TGV. St-Brieuc, Guingamp and Morlaix in northern Brittany, and Vannes, Auray and Lorient in southern Brittany, are well served by the TGVs along the way to Brest or Quimper. The occasional TGV stops at Lamballe, Plouaret-Trégor and Landerneau in northern Brittany, and at Redon, Quimperlé and Rosporden in southern Brittany. Other Breton stops include Ancenis, St-Nazaire and La Baule.

If you are starting your train journey in France, you *have* to **stamp your ticket yourself** in one of the orange machines by the platform entrances or you may be fined. For details and advance reservations of train travel in France, contact **Rail Europe** at: 1 Lower Regent St, London SW1Y 4XT, t 0844 84 84 064, *www.raileurope.co.uk*, or Westchester One, 44 S. Broadway, 11th Floor, White Plains, NY 10601, (US) t 888 382 7245, (Canada) t 800 361 7245, *www.raileurope.com*.

Getting Around

By Air

You can fly to the island of Ouessant from Brest-Guipavas with **Finist'Air, t** 02 98 84 64 87, *www.finistair.fr*.

By Bus

Each French *département* is run by a *Conseil Général* which, among other duties, oversees public transport in the area. The websites of the different Conseils Généraux give up-to-date information on transport across the area; we give the relevant internet links at the start of each touring chapter.

The extent of services on the French bus network varies between *départements*, though it can take you to many more rural spots than the trains. In larger towns, buses normally leave from the *gare routière* ('road station') as opposed to the *gare* (railway station). Tourist offices should hold accurate information on local public transport.

By Car

See 'Getting There By Car', p.68. The main Breton roads, all crossing the region east–west, are: along the **northern coastal strip**, the N176 followed by the N12, taking you from near the Mont St-Michel to Brest; along the **southern coastal strip**, the N165 linking Nantes and Quimper – the busiest road in Brittany during the summer holidays; for the **centre** of Brittany, the N164, which is joined to Rennes by the N12, and ending up near the Crozon peninsula.

By Train

SNCF nationwide information number, t 36 35 (€0.34/min), from abroad **t** 892 35 35 35).

The TGV lines from Paris (*see* 'Getting There By Train', opposite) are generally excellent. Beyond that, Brittany has a network of much slower trains serving further destinations, especially towns on the coast. The train service does not serve inland Brittany well. (The local bus network is more extensive; see above.) Prices on the SNCF are reasonable, and discounts are available (*see* opposite).

Make sure to *composter votre billet*, or date-stamp your ticket, in one of the orange machines located by the platform entrances, otherwise you will be liable to a fine. Not all stations have left luggage facilities.

By Bicycle

Before taking your bike by air to France, check whether the bike needs to be boxed and whether it is included as part of your total baggage weight. Certain trains (with a bicycle symbol indicated on the timetable) carry bikes for free, otherwise you can dismantle and pack your cycle (max size 120x90cm); check before booking.

The main towns always seem to have at least one shop that hires out bikes – local tourist offices have lists. You can also hire bikes from most SNCF stations in larger

towns, and then drop the bike back off at a different station, as long as you specify where you'll drop it when you hire the bike. *Vélo* is the common colloquial word for a bicycle and a *vélo tout terrain*, or *VTT*, is a mountain bike. Be prepared to pay a fairly hefty deposit on a good bike and/or to supply your credit card number. You may want to enquire about insurance against theft.

The major development recently is the creation of a special network of cycling paths around Brittany called **Véloroutes**. These new trails, which are gradually being extended across the region, offer cyclists excellent routes around Brittany, both along the coast and inland, steering them away from major roads, often making them use adapted disused railway lines, river towpaths and the **Voies Vertes** network (*see* 'On Foot', below).

Get maps and cycling information from the **Fédération Française de Cyclotourisme**, 12 rue Louis Bertrand, 94207 Ivry-sur-Seine, **t** 01 56 20 88 88, *www.ffct.org.uk*, or in Britain from the **Cyclists Touring Club**, Parklands, Railton Rd, Guildford, Surrey GU2 9JX, **t** (01483) 238 337, *www.ctc.org.uk*. *See* also the list of specialist tour operators on p.74. Also note that it is now compulsory for cyclists to wear a reflective yellow jacket outside the cities and if visibility is poor.

On Foot

You can walk almost all the way round the Breton coast by following the region's coastal paths. Breton coastal paths are commonly and unromantically known as *Sentiers des Douaniers*, or Customs Officers' Paths. The main coastal path is also known as the Sentier Côtier, the Sentier du Littoral or the Grande Randonnée (GR) 34.

The **Grandes Randonnées** are a national network of walking paths through France. Apart from GR34, many other Grandes Randonnées go through Brittany: GR3, GR347, GR380, GR37, GR38 and GR39. They are marked with white and red signs. *Gîtes d'étapes* are simple, cheap shelters with bunk beds and rudimentary kitchen facilities set along the GRs. You can buy detailed but expensive guides, Topoguides, to the individual *Grande Randonnée* tracks; contact the **Fédération Française de la Randonnée**

Pédestre, 64 rue du Dessous des Berges, 75013 Paris, **t** 01 44 89 93 90, *www.ffrandonee.fr*. Smaller walking paths known as GRPs are marked with yellow and red signs, and are planned to offer a week of walking. PRs are even smaller, marked in yellow, or sometimes with thematic symbols, and are meant to last anything from an hour up to a day. Signposts along these French walking paths mark destinations in time rather than distance.

There are two other special walking paths that are worth pointing out. The **E5 European path** leaves from the Pointe du Raz, which is one of the westernmost tips of the Finistère, to take you on foot to Venice. The revived 500km **Tro Breizh** or Tro Breiz ('Tour of Brittany' in Breton, *see www.trobreiz.com*) was the traditional Breton medieval pilgrimage; it stops at the seven cathedrals dedicated to the Breton saints who are regarded as the founders of the Celtic Christian Brittany of the Dark Ages (*see* p.42).

Les Voies Vertes are a whole new network of special paths conceived for walkers, although sometimes to be shared with cyclists, roller-skaters and horse-riders, that have been developed across Brittany in the last few years, with work still ongoing to extend them further. Special provision is made for disabled users. You can find out more on Les Voies Vertes on the main regional tourist website, *www.tourisme bretagne.com*, or via the organization dedicated to walking in Brittany, **Rando-Breizh**, **t** 02 99 27 03 20, *www.randobreizh.com*, giving specific maps and details on lodgings – on which the **Rando Plumes** are often excellent, cheap but character-filled places specially geared to walkers along the routes. Look out too for the development of **Relais-Rando** along the ways, to offer further specialist facilities.

Where to Stay

Hotels

Please note that in high season many hotels will only offer half board or full board, not the room by itself. This may suit you for a day or two, but you may find such an imposition a bit restrictive for a longer period.

The French authorities star-grade hotels by their facilities rather than by charm or location, as in most countries in Europe. Stars go from the luxurious 4 (sometimes with an L added to underline exceptional luxuriousness) to a basic single star. One-star hotel rooms are pretty basic and may not have their own WC, bathroom or television, but some offer the occasional pleasant surprise. There are even some hotels without any stars at all. Most of these are bottom of the range and cheap, but a few may simply not have registered and may be quite smart.

Single rooms are relatively rare and usually two-thirds the price of a double. If there are a few of you travelling together and looking for a cheap option, some hotels have triples or quads that can be good value. Hotel breakfasts can be expensive, so check on the price and ask whether it's optional. If it seems too much, a local bar may be better.

Don't confuse **umbrella organizations** such as **Relais & Châteaux**, **Châteaux et Hôtels de France** and **Logis de France** with the chain hotels. Such organizations gather together generally independent hotels to promote themselves more effectively and to maintain standards. **Relais & Châteaux** hotels (*www.relaischateux.com*) are top of the range, generally extremely beautiful and luxurious, with gourmet cuisine. **Châteaux et Hôtels de France** (*www.chateuxhotels.com*) have a greater variety of hotels full of character, some expensive, some surprisingly good value. Their guidebook includes a number of private châteaux receiving guests, which is the speciality of **Bienvenue au Château** (*www.bienvenue-chateau*). These wonderful historic places can be very expensive, but while many are extremely well run, others are not quite so well geared to tourists. That said, the welcome is often delightfully personal, and most owners are clearly in love with their home. *Logis de France* is a much larger organization, its aver-

Hotel Price Categories

Note: all prices listed here and elsewhere in this book are for a double room with bath/shower in high season.

luxury	€€€€€	Over €230
very expensive	€€€€	€150–230
expensive	€€€	€100–150
moderate	€€	€65–100
inexpensive	€	Under €65

agely priced hotels signalled by a green and yellow sign with a fireplace depicted in the middle. Some *Logis de France* are good value, a few are excellent, and some are dowdy and unpleasant, so the sign shouldn't be taken as a guarantee of quality. Take a look inside first if unsure. You can get a copy of their free guide at member hotels, which are rated 1, 2 or 3 chimneys, or see *www.logis-de-france.fr*.

Bed and Breakfast and *Fermes-auberges*

Bed and breakfast is known as *chambre d'hôte* in France. B&Bs vary in quality and are officially graded accordingly. By choosing a *chambre d'hôte*, as well as avoiding too many other tourists, you may get the chance to chat with your hosts. Generally, a *chambre d'hôte* offers good value, with breakfast included. Guests do not get the same facilities and services as in a hotel, but B&Bs tend to be much more peaceful and personal. Bear in mind when planning your trip that some prohibit single-night bookings over the busy summer period. Most tourist offices can provide you with a handy-sized directory of *chambres d'hôtes* in the Brittany region.

Table d'hôte is when a *chambre d'hôte* address offers the possibility of an evening meal, which is generally shared with the proprietors, who may in some cases speak some English. You have to let your hosts know in advance if you want to eat with them. *Table d'hôte* is relatively expensive, but it is a very good way to meet French people.

Fermes-auberges, farms-turned-inns, are also good value. Good traditional country cooking using almost nothing but local farm produce is their strong point. Local tourist offices have lists of *fermes-auberges* in their area.

Youth Hostels and *Gîtes d'Etape*

Most large towns have a youth hostel (*auberge de jeunesse*) offering dormitory accommodation and breakfast for around €8–12 a night. Check out the wide range of possibilities in Brittany on *www.fuaj.org*.

To get into a youth hostel you need a Youth Hostel Association membership card. The regulations say that you should get this in your home country (in the UK see *www.yha.org.uk*; in the USA *www.hiusa.org*; in Canada *www.hihostels.ca*; and in Australia *www.yha.com.au*), but you can almost always buy one on the spot, or buy international Welcome Stamps. Many youth hostels have kitchen facilities, or can provide cheap meals.

Youth hostels are the best deal for people who are travelling on their own. For those travelling together, a 1-star hotel can be as cheap. One negative side to youth hostels is that they're often out of the centre of town, and in summer you need to arrive early to be sure of getting a room. It's worth calling ahead to see if you can reserve a place.

A *gîte d'étape* is a simple shelter with bunk beds (no bedding) and a basic self-catering kitchen, set up by a village along walking paths or scenic bike routes. Such accommodation should cost around €7 a night.

Camping

Camping is very popular, especially among the French themselves, and there's at least one *camping municipal* in every French parish; it is often an inexpensive, no-frills site. Other camp sites are graded with stars like hotels, from 4-star luxury to 1-star basics. At the top of the range you can expect lots of trees and grass, maybe an individually hedged plot, hot showers, a pool, sports facilities, a grocer's, a bar and/or a restaurant. Prices for the top of the range are similar to 1-star hotels. The tourist bodies for the individual *départements* can send you a full list of their camp sites, while local tourist offices should be able to supply you with details on those in their specific area. Camp sites by beaches are numerous in Brittany, but they get very busy in the height of summer. If you want to camp in the countryside, it's essential to ask permission from the landowner first. There are specialist guides to camping in France in which the camp sites are graded.

Gîtes de France and Other Self-Catering Accommodation

Brittany offers a huge range of self-catering options in each of its *départements*, from farm cottages to history-laden châteaux and fancy villas, or even canal boats (*www.gites-de-france-bretagne.com*). Each *département*

Specialist Tour Operators

As well as the details that follow here, it is well worth exploring the holiday breaks offered by the various *départements*. The regional tourist board also offers tours, short breaks, spa and thalassotherapy, golf, horse-riding and nature holidays. Take a look at *www.brittany-best-breaks.com* for details.

In the UK

Breton Bikes, t 296 248 672, *www.bretonbikes.com*. Family-run company offering campsite-, hotel- and gîte-based cycling holidays.

Canvas Holidays, t 0870 192 1154, *www.canvasholidays.com*. Camping and mobile home holidays.

Cresta Holidays, t 0870 238 7711, *www.crestaholidays.com*. Flights and hotels.

Crown Blue Line, t 468 94 52 72, *www.crownblueline.com*. Canal holidays from Messac in eastern Brittany to Dinan and Nantes, or west along the canal from Nantes to Brest.

Siblu Holidays, t 08719 11 22 88, *www.siblu.com*. Camping and mobile homes at a holiday park in Pont Aven, Finistère.

Your Golf Holidays, t 01277 824 100, *www.yourgolfholidays.com*. Golf breaks.

In the USA

Backroads, 801 Cedar Street, Berkeley, CA 94710-1800, t (510) 527 1555, *www.backroads.com*. Five- to nine-day cycling and walking holidays.

Self-catering

In the UK

See also below.

Allez France, Cutter House, 1560 Parkway, Whiteley, Fareham PO15 7AG, t 0845 330 2059 (bookings only), *www.allezfrance.com*.

Brittany Ferries Holidays, Millbay Docks, Plymouth PL1 3EW, t 08712 44 07 44, *www.brittanyferries.com*.

Brittany Travel, t 08452 30 13 80, *www.brittany.co.uk*.

Chez Nous, Spring Mill, Earby, Barnoldswick, Lancs BB94 0AA, t 0870 197 1000, *www.cheznous.com*.

The Individual Travellers Company, Spring Mill, Earby, Barnoldswick, Lancs BB94 0AA, t 08456 04 38 77, *www.indiv-travellers.com*.

Interhome, Gemini House, 10–18 Putney Hill, London SW15 6AY, t (020) 8780 6633, *www.interhome.co.uk*.

VFB Holidays, Dowty House, Anson Business Park, Cheltenham Rd East, Gloucester GL2 9QU, t (01242) 716 840, *www.vfbholidays.co.uk*.

In the USA

Home Away, 3801 S. Capital of Texas Highway, Suite 150, Austin, TX 78704, t (512) 493 0382, *www.homeaway.com*.

Villas of the World, PO Box 1800, Sag Harbour, New York 11963, t 631 725 9308, *www.villasoftheworld.com*.

now has a dedicated service, offering holiday packages and short breaks.

If you want a place near the beaches in the holiday season, book early. The *Fédération Nationale des Gîtes de France* is a French Government service that gives out information on inexpensive accommodation by the week. Lists with photos covering *gîtes* by *département* are available from French Government tourist offices and most local tourist offices. Prices range from €200 to €1,000 a week for four people, depending on the time of year you go as well as facilities. You'll almost always have to begin your stay on a Saturday. The tourist bodies for the indi-

vidual French *départements*, the CDTs, have listings specifically for their county – contact the relevant CDT for further details (*see* p.80).

The UK Sunday papers are full of self-catering accommodation direct from private owners, as are websites such as *www.frenchconnections.co.uk*. Or contact one of the specialist firms listed in the Sunday papers or above. The accommodation the latter offer is nearly always more comfortable and costly than a *gîte*, but the discounts that holiday firms get you on ferries, plane tickets or car rentals can make up for the price difference. For *gîtes* for disabled people, *see* p.66.

Practical A–Z

06

Conversions: Imperial–Metric

Length (multiply by)
Inches to centimetres: 2.54
Centimetres to inches: 0.39
Feet to metres: 0.3
Metres to feet: 3.28
Yards to metres: 0.91
Metres to yards: 1.09
Miles to kilometres: 1.61
Kilometres to miles: 0.62

Area (multiply by)
Inches square to centimetres square: 6.45
Centimetres square to inches square: 0.15
Feet square to metres square: 0.09
Metres square to feet square: 10.76
Miles square to kilometres square: 2.59
Kilometres square to miles square: 0.39
Acres to hectares: 0.40
Hectares to acres: 2.47

Weight (multiply by)
Ounces to grams: 28.35
Grammes to ounces: 0.035
Pounds to kilograms: 0.45
Kilograms to pounds: 2.2
Stones to kilograms: 6.35
Kilograms to stones: 0.16
Tons (UK) to kilograms: 1,016
Kilograms to tons (UK): 0.0009
1 UK ton (2,240lbs) = 1.12 US tonnes (2,000lbs)

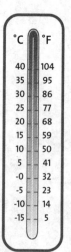

Volume (multiply by)
Pints (UK) to litres: 0.57
Litres to pints (UK): 1.76
Quarts (UK) to litres: 1.13
Litres to quarts (UK): 0.88
Gallons (UK) to litres: 4.55
Litres to gallons (UK): 0.22
1 UK pint/quart/gallon =
1.2 US pints/quarts/
gallons

Temperature
Celsius to Fahrenheit:
multiply by 1.8 then
add 32

Fahrenheit to Celsius:
subtract 32 then multiply
by 0.55

°C	°F
40	104
35	95
30	86
25	77
20	68
15	59
10	50
5	41
-0	32
-5	23
-10	14
-15	5

France Information

Time Differences
Country: + 1hr GMT; + 6hrs EST
Daylight saving from last weekend in March to end of October

Dialling Codes
Note: omit first zero of area code
France country code: 33
To France from: UK, Ireland, New Zealand 00 / USA, Canada 011 / Australia 0011 then dial 33 and then the number without the initial zero
From France to: UK 00 44; Ireland 00 353; USA, Canada 001; Australia 00 61; New Zealand 00 64 then the number without the initial zero
Directory enquiries: 118 000
International directory enquiries: 118 700

Emergency Numbers
Police: 17
Ambulance: 15
Fire: 18

Embassy Numbers in France
UK: 01 44 51 31 00; **Ireland:** 01 44 17 67 00
USA: 01 43 12 22 22; **Canada:** 01 44 43 29 00
Australia: 01 40 59 33 00; **NZ:** 01 45 01 43 43

Shoe Sizes
Europe	UK	USA
35	2½ / 3	4
36	3 / 3½	4½ / 5
37	4	5½ / 6
38	5	6½
39	5½ / 6	7 / 7½
40	6 / 6½	8 / 8½
41	7	9 / 9½
42	8	9½ / 10
43	9	10½
44	9½ / 10	11
45	10½	12
46	11	12½ / 13

Women's Clothing
Europe	UK	USA
34	6	2
36	8	4
38	10	6
40	12	8
42	14	10
44	16	12

Beaches

The Breton coastline measures more than 1,000km. By law, the French coast up to 3m in from the highest tidal point remains public property and only one or two sections of the Breton coastline are inaccessible – within military zones or in protected bird reserves.

The north Breton (Channel) shore tends to have slightly calmer beaches than the western and southern coasts exposed to the Atlantic, though an indented shoreline with countless protected bays makes for notable exceptions. On the north side of Brittany, the deep, flat bays are greatly affected by the tides; the sea can disappear into the distance and then rush back in surprisingly fast – be careful. Local tourist offices and the local press have the times of the daily tides.

Some Breton beaches are dangerous for swimming. *Baignade interdite* means bathing is forbidden. The French term indicating that a beach has a lifeguard is *baignade surveillée*. Flags indicate instructions on bathing: green flags mean that swimming is permitted and that a lifeguard is watching the shore (*Baignade autorisée et surveillée*); orange flags mean that swimming is not advised, but that there is a lifeguard on duty (*Baignade surveillée mais déconseillée*); red flags mean that swimming is forbidden and that there is no lifeguard (*Baignade interdite*).

Generally, the Breton beaches get a clean bill of health. For up-to-date info, the state and regional environmental authorities produce regular leaflets, the latest being *L'état des Plages* (2007). See *www.bretagne-environnement.org* for further information. The quality of the water is divided into four categories, from A (good) to D (poor).

Topless bathing is accepted everywhere, though naturism is only allowed on specific beaches. French Government tourist offices can supply information on specialist naturist holidays in France, and you can contact local tourist offices to find out where beaches are situated. Most such beaches are gay-friendly.

Crime and the Police

Outside cities, the term for a policeman in France is *gendarme*; a *gendarmerie* is a police station. Within city structures, it's *agents de police/poste de police*. Report thefts to *gendarmeries* or *postes de police*. Be warned that this can be a frustrating bureaucratic exercise, particularly if you don't speak French – be patient but firm. Theft from cars is a problem across France. Try not to leave valuables in your car, even in the boot. If your passport is stolen, contact the police and your relevant consulate for emergency travel documents. Holiday homes, as anywhere in France, are targets for burglary. You need to get an official piece of paper from the *gendarmerie* to put in an insurance claim.

By law, the police in France can stop anyone anywhere and demand presentation of official identification. If you are stopped on the road, you're expected to have your official car documents. Speeding fines are payable on the spot and breathalyser tests are common.

Eating Out

By law, **service** should be included in the price of set menus, marked by *service compris* or *s.c.* Many people still leave a tip if they are happy with their meal and the service. If you eat *à la carte*, add a tip of around 10%.

The **restaurants recommended in this guide** mostly serve French or Breton food. In towns especially, you'll find a fair number of ethnic restaurants, including Moroccan, Tunisian, Algerian, Vietnamese and Italian.

Crêpes are relatively cheap, unless you eat a dozen, and the more exotic the filling, the more expensive the crêpe. **Vegetarians** will find crêperies one of the best options.

Emergencies and Health

Emergencies

ambulance (SAMU national emergency organization), **t** 15;
police and **ambulance**, **t** 17;
fire brigade (*pompiers*), **t** 18.

Restaurant Price Categories

Prices quoted throughout the book are for an average two-course à la carte meal without wine, for one person.

very expensive	€€€€	Over €60
expensive	€€€	€35–60
moderate	€€	€20–35
inexpensive	€	Under €20

In a medical emergency (*un cas d'urgence médicale*), take the person concerned to the local hospital – note that *hôtel-dieu* is sometimes used in place of the word *hôpital*, or the phrase *centre hospitalier*. You can also call the local **SOS Médecins**. If you can't consult a phone book, the internet or Minitel, dial **t** 118 000 for directory enquiries to ask for help.

Local newspapers should give details of doctors on call (*de service*) and should also give the addresses of chemists (*pharmacies*) open for night duty. Note that pharmacists in France are trained in first aid.

Health

Pharmacists should have details of local doctors (*docteurs* or *médecins*) who speak English, if that's necessary.

For information on **insurance** and **EHIC cards**, *see* p.66.

Internet Facilities

As you would expect, public internet and email facilities are usually limited to the larger towns. Generally, you pay a charge at internet bars or Médiacap centres. Local libraries sometimes offer free facilities, but you may have to book in advance. Tourist offices may also have access points.

Leisure and Sports

The best way to get information on special activities and sports is by contacting either the CDT for the relevant *département* (*see* p.80) or the local tourist office. The French term used for leisure activities is *loisirs*.

Breton Traditions

The Finistère is the most obvious *département* in which to learn something about Breton culture, including **Breton language, dancing, music, embroidery and crêpe-making**; try Ti Ar Vro in Quimper, **t** 02 98 90 69 20, *www.tiavro.org*. In the Loire Atlantique, for all manner of Breton cultural courses, contact the **Agence Culturelle Bretonne**, **t** 02 51 84 16 07, *www.a.b.c.free.fr*.

Water Sports, Sailing, Boat Trips

Active water sports: you can get lists with contact details from the Breton CDTs or local

Breton Coastal and Estuary Marinas

Arzal-Camoël, **t** 02 99 90 05 86
Bénodet, **t** 02 98 57 05 78
Binic, **t** 02 96 73 61 86
Brest Moulin Blanc, **t** 02 98 02 20 02
Camaret-sur-Mer, **t** 02 98 27 89 31
Concarneau, **t** 02 98 97 57 96
Crozon-Morgat, **t** 02 98 27 01 97
Douarnenez Tréboul, **t** 02 98 74 02 56
La Trinité-sur-Mer, **t** 02 97 55 71 49
Le Croisic, **t** 02 40 23 10 95
Le Crouesty, **t** 02 97 53 73 33
Le Pouliguen, **t** 02 40 11 97 97
Loctudy, **t** 02 98 87 51 36
Lorient Bassin à Flot, **t** 02 97 21 10 14
Lorient Kernével, **t** 02 97 65 48 25
Paimpol, **t** 02 96 20 47 65
Perros-Guirec, **t** 02 96 49 80 50
Pornic, **t** 02 40 82 05 40
Pornichet, **t** 02 40 61 03 20
Port Daouët at Pléneuf-Val-André, **t** 02 96 72 82 85
Port La Forêt-Fousnant, **t** 02 98 56 98 45
Quiberon Port Haliguen, **t** 02 97 50 20 56
St-Malo Bas-Sablons, **t** 02 99 81 71 34
St-Malo Port Vauban, **t** 02 99 56 51 91
St-Quay-Portrieux, **t** 02 96 70 81 30
Ste-Marine, **t** 02 98 56 38 72
Tréguier, **t** 02 96 92 42 37
Vannes, Port La Rabine, **t** 02 97 54 16 08

tourist offices on the following: diving (*la plongée*), sailing (*la voile*), sand yachting (*char à voile*), canoeing (sometimes on the sea) and windsurfing (*la planche à voile*). *Centres/ bases/clubs/cercles nautiques* or *écoles de mer* will generally offer courses in sailing and other water sports. The term for a yacht harbour or marina is a *port de plaisance*.

A large number of Breton ports now offer **boat trips out to sea, to Breton islands, or along Breton estuaries**, either in old-style boats (generically known as *vieux gréements*) or in modern vessels. The CDTs and local tourist offices should have listings.

Major Breton islands you can visit by boat and stay on include: on the northern Breton coast, the Ile de Bréhat and the Ile de Batz; on the western coast, Molène, Ouessant (Ushant) and Sein; on the southern coast, Les Glénans, Groix, Belle-Ile, Houat and Hoëdic. You can enjoy boat trips around the Golfe du Morbihan, landing on the Ile d'Arz, the Ile aux Moines or the Ile de Gavrinis. You can visit but not stay on many other Breton islands.

Thalassotherapy

The term covers a wide variety of seawater treatments, which are for beauty or medical purposes. Increasingly promoted as well-being retreats, these centres have done something to revive an off-season life in traditionally 'summertime' tourist resorts. The CDTs and local tourist offices will have listings but, as a guide, St-Malo, Roscoff, Douarnenez, Bénodet, Quiberon, Carnac, La Baule and Pornichet have the best-known centres.

General Sports

You can get lists with contact details from the Breton CDTs or local tourist offices on canoeing, cycling (le vélo), fishing (la pêche), golf, horse-riding (l'équitation), swimming in public pools, tennis, walking (la randonnée) and more. In some cases, the CDTs produce an annual brochure on several or all of these sports, or they may advise you to contact the relevant sporting body in the département.

Regional Parks

There are two French natural regional parks in Brittany: the Parc Régional Naturel d'Armorique, covering a swathe of central Finistère (see p.299); and the much smaller peat marshes of the Parc Régional Naturel de la Brière in the Loire Atlantique (see p.471).

Environment and Ornithology

The best centres dedicated to Brittany's natural environment include the Maison de la Baie du Mont-St-Michel at Le Vivier-sur-Mer (see p.116), the Maison de la Baie de St-Brieuc at Hillion (see p.194), and the Maison de la Baie d'Audierne west of Pont-l'Abbé (see p.348). The guided walks are particularly good. There are a few other Maisons du Littoral around the Breton coast, for example on the Côte de Granit Rose.

Bird reserves are dotted around the coast, notably at the Baie du Mont-St-Michel, the islands off Cancale, the Cap Fréhel, the Sept-Iles off Perros-Guirec, the Baie de Morlaix, the Molène or Ouessant archipelago, the Cap Sizun, the Glénan islands, the eastern Golfe du Morbihan and Belle-Ile.

Other important places for bird-watching in Brittany are the Brière and the Lac de

National Holidays

On French national holidays, known as jours fériés, banks, shops, businesses and most museums close, though hotels and restaurants stay open. Dates to remember are as follows:

1 Jan New Year's Day (le jour de l'an)
Easter Sunday le dimanche de Pâques
Easter Monday le lundi de Pâques
1 May Labour Day (la Fête du Travail)
8 May Victory in Europe Day (la Fête de la Libération)
Ascension Day
Whitsun/Pentecost, plus the following Monday la Pentecôte, le Lundi de Pentecôte
14 July Bastille Day (celebrating the start of the French Revolution)
15 August Assumption (Assomption)
Early Nov All Saints' Day (la Toussaint)
11 Nov Armistice Day (l'Armistice)
Christmas Day Noël

Grand-Lieu. Some Breton bird reserves are situated on inaccessible islands. An exciting way to appreciate bird life in Brittany is to go on the boat tour around the Sept-Iles from Perros-Guirec (see p.231).

Opening Hours

Opening times for many French museums and sights are quite restricted. The majority are reliably open 10am–12 and 2–5 or 6pm, but these times are somewhat deceptive: it's advisable to arrive a good hour before any stated closing time to avoid being disappointed. A growing number of museums and sights are starting to become more flexible about their opening hours. The further you get away from the main tourist season, the more restricted opening times tend to be. All publicly owned museums close on Tuesdays.

Breton churches in the countryside are not always easy to visit. Rural communities are particularly concerned about theft, so they tend to keep churches locked. Local tourist offices should be able to help you (as well as providing details on special guided tours of rural Brittany), and opening times are often posted on church doors. In some rural areas, there may be a notice telling you where you can get the key from. Don't hesitate to go and ask for la clef, though you may have to leave your car keys in exchange.

Religion

Times of Catholic mass, *la messe*, can be found at tourist offices or on a board at the entrance to the smaller towns and villages. Protestant churches are *temples*.

Shopping

Shops in France normally open at 9 or 10am. Many shops in smaller towns and in villages close for lunch, normally 12–2pm or later. Closing time at the end of the day is generally 7pm. In many towns, Sunday morning is a busy shopping period. However, most shops close on Sunday afternoons and Mondays (except some grocers and supermarkets). Breton specialities to look out for include:

Clothes: stripy fishermen's jumpers (also in children's sizes); embroidered aprons or waistcoats; fishermen's hats (*casquettes*); lace shawls; clogs, called *sabots*.

Food: fish soups and traditional canned fish; *saucisson* (salami) or *andouille* (pigs' intestine sausage); biscuits, cakes and crêpes; cider and *lambig* (see p.55).

Luxury goods: Quimper pottery; Breton lace, which is known as *picot*.

VAT is *TVA* in French. Value added tax on many goods in France is 19.6%. If you are from outside the EU and are making major purchases to take home, it is worth asking whether TVA is deductible for export.

Students

Students with the relevant international student card can benefit from considerable reductions on flights, trains and admissions to museums, concerts and more. Agencies specializing in student and youth travel can help you apply for a card if you are entitled to one, as well as advise you on the best deals. Try STA (for your nearest branch, see *www.statravel.com*). Note that *tarifs jeunes* (for the under-25s, student or otherwise) are available on most means of public transport.

Telephones and Post

Telephones and Faxes

Virtually all French telephone and fax numbers now have 10 digits, the first being a 0. If you are telephoning or faxing France from abroad, first dial the international code, t 00 33, then remove the first 0 and dial the nine digits that follow it.

To telephone from a public telephone booth, you often need a **telephone card**, or *télécarte*, available at newspaper kiosks or tobacconists as well as at the post office, or you may be able to use your credit card. You can telephone from a metered booth in many post offices and then pay at the counter.

On the internet, *www.pagesjaunes.fr* is the French Yellow Pages *www.pagesblanches.fr* is the residential equivalent. To look up a number at a post office you may have to use the Minitel electronic directory.

Postal Services

French post boxes are yellow, marked with a blue bird. Post offices are called *La Poste*, *Le Bureau de Poste* or the *PTT*. Offices in cities are open Mon–Fri 8am–7pm, and Sat 8am–12 noon. In smaller towns and in villages, post offices may only open at 9am, are likely to close for lunch from 12 noon to 2pm, and may close as early as 4.30 or 5pm.

CRT and CDTs

Comité Régional du Tourisme de Bretagne: 1 Rue Raoul Ponchon, 35069 Rennes Cedex, t 02 99 28 44 30, *www.tourismebretagne.com*.

CDT Ille-et-Vilaine: 5 Rue de Pré Bolté, B.P. 60149, 35101 Rennes Cedex 3, t 02 99 78 47 40, *www.bretagne35.com*.

CDT Côtes d'Armor: 7 Rue St-Benoît, B.P. 4620, 22046 St-Brieuc Cedex 2, t 02 96 62 72 01, *www.cotesdarmor.com*.

CDT Finistère: 4 Rue du 19 Mars 1962, B.P. 1419, 29018 Quimper, t 02 98 76 25 64, *www.finistere tourisme.com*.

CDT Morbihan: PIBS, Allée Nicholas Le Blanc, B.P. 408, 56010 Vannes Cedex, t 08 25 13 56 56, *www.morbihan.com*.

CDT Loire Atlantique: 11 Rue du Chateau l'Eruadière, C.S. 40698, Nantes, Cedex, t 02 51 72 95 40, *www.loire-atlantique-tourisme.com*.

Stamps can be bought at newspaper kiosks and tobacconists as well as at post offices.

Toilets or Rest Rooms

Public toilets in Brittany are generally appalling, although there are signs of improvements. Visitors should be warned that the hole-in-the-ground lavatory is still surprisingly common.

On Breton main roads it makes sense to head straight for the (free) service station facilities, and it's wise to keep a stock of emergency toilet paper on you at all times. There are some public toilets for which you have to pay, either to get into – those funky modern oval-shaped street facilities – or to get out of, when there's a toilet caretaker (you should leave a small tip).

Tourist Information

France is divided up geographically and administratively into *départements*, each with its central tourist information service, the **Comité Départemental du Tourisme** or **CDT**. These are a mine of information, as are local tourist offices. Larger local tourist offices are Offices du Tourisme; smaller ones are misleadingly known as Syndicats d'Initiative.

Another level of official tourist information providers between the CDTs and the local tourist offices, the **Pays d'Accueil Touristique**, often offer excellent tourist booklets and information for their area. You can call or write to Pays d'Accueil, but they don't have offices. Addresses for the Pays d'Accueil Touristique and many local tourist offices are given in the touring chapters. In many cases, their websites are worth checking out for links to local services and hotels, *chambres d'hôte*, etc.

There is also an official regional tourist service based in Rennes, the Comité Régional du Tourisme de Bretagne (CRT Bretagne), as well as the CRT Loire Atlantique in Nantes, although this cannot provide as useful and specific information as the CDTs, the Pays d'Accueil Touristique or the local tourist offices. It does however, help make inter-esting guidebooks to Brittany, in French, often published by Ouest-France.

For general tourist information on France in your own country, contact the relevant French Government tourist office, though it will not be able to supply you with anything like the detailed information you get from the *département* and local tourist bodies in France.

Visiting Museums, Sights and Towns

The opening times for museums and sights are included in the text where possible, though these can change (if just the month is given, the place is open the whole of that month). Almost all museums and sights charge an admission fee.

Please note that the opening times for many French museums and sights are quite restricted. The majority are reliably open between 10am and 12 noon and between 2pm and 5 or 6pm, but bear in mind that these times are somewhat deceptive: it's advisable to arrive a good hour before any closing time stated to avoid being disappointed. Guided tours, where they're available or compulsory, normally start on the hour. A growing number of museums and sights are starting to become more flexible about their opening hours, many even doing away with the sacred provincial 2-hour lunch break. The further you get away from the main tourist season, the more restricted opening times tend to be. Virtually all French sights are closed on Christmas Day and New Year's Day, and many close on 1 May and All Saints' at the beginning of November (*see* 'National Holidays', p.79). All publicly owned museums close on Tuesdays.

Breton churches in the countryside are not always easy to visit. Rural communities are particularly concerned about theft these days, so they tend to keep their churches locked. Local tourist offices should be able to tell you at what times local churches are open, and opening times are also often posted on church doors. In some rural areas, there may be a notice telling you where you can get the key from. Don't hesitate to go and ask for *la clef*, though occasionally you may have to leave your own car keys or some official document in exchange. It's a good idea to take binoculars to look at some of the ornate stringbeams and stained-glass windows. Tourist offices should have details on special guided tours of rural Breton chapels by local experts.

Cultural tours of historic Breton towns are also organized regularly in holiday times via the tourist offices. Depending on the guide, they can be fascinating. Many Breton towns have a *petit train touristique* that takes you round some of the highlights (if you can cope with the naffness of it all).

Ille-et-Vilaine

The Ille-et-Vilaine (or Haute-Bretagne – Upper, and Eastern, Brittany) is scarcely Breton at all, some western Bretons argue. It was only Breton-speaking for a short period; much of the architecture and many of the churches don't look typically Breton; Rennes, though Brittany's vibrant capital, was built in good part for aristocratic provincial parliamentarians hardly in touch with the majority of the poor Breton people; and the St-Malo merchants who made a killing through sea voyages remained aloof and independent in their haughty walled city, or their country *malouinières*.

Yet the Vilaine Valley crossing the *département did* serve as a border between ancient Brittany and the Franks to the east. And it was close to Redon on the Vilaine that Nomenoë grabbed Breton independence in the 9th century. Even if the Breton language receded westwards, Breton place names at least have stuck up to the Vilaine, and Breton legends and traditions linger. On top of that, although the Ille-et-Vilaine may only have a very short stretch of Brittany's vast seashore, what a staggering one it is.

07

Don't miss

1 A rogueish town – and its prim sister
St-Malo and Dinard
pp.87 and 108

2 An otherworldly site
Mont St-Michel p.113

3 The capital of Brittany
Rennes p.148

4 Valleys and forests
The Vilaine Valley and Merlin's Forest p.160

5 A forgotten neolithic trail
St-Just p.164

See map overleaf

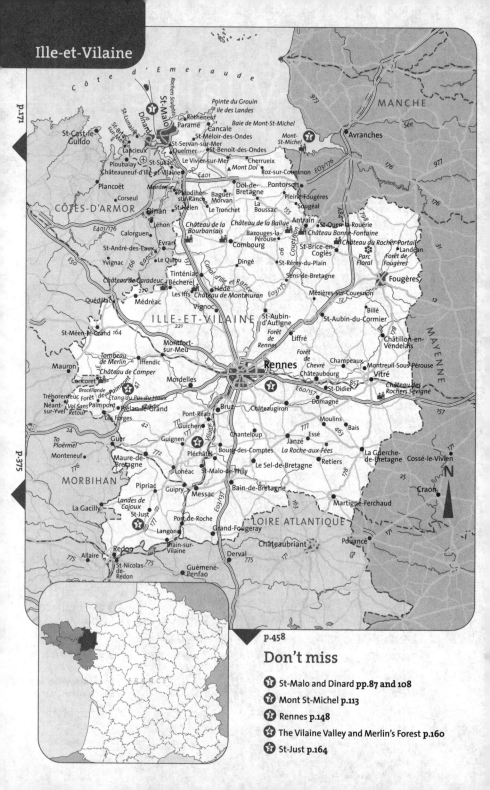

Ille-et-Vilaine

Côte d'Emeraude

MANCHE

St-Malo
Dinard
St-Lunaire
St-Briac-sur-Mer
St-Cast-le-Guildo
Lancieux
Ploubalay
St-Suliac
Châteauneuf-d'Ille-et-Vilaine
Plancoët
Corseul
CÔTES-D'ARMOR
Mordreuc
Plouer-sur-Rance
St-Hélen
Léhon
Dinan
Calorguen
St-André-des-Eaux
Yvignac
Le Quiou
Évran
Quédillac
Médréac
Bécherel
Les Iffs
Hédé
Tinténiac
Vignoc
ILLE-ET-VILAINE
St-Méen-le-Grand
Montfort-sur-Meu
Tombeau de Merlin
Iffendic
Mauron
Château de Comper
Concoret
Brocéliande
Tréhorenteuc
Forêt de Paimpont
Néant-sur-Yvel
Val Sans Retour
Les Forges
Mordelles
Étang du Pas du Houx
Plélan-le-Grand
Paimpont
Guer
Guignen
Guichen
Pont-Réan
Bruz
Monteneuf
Maure-de-Bretagne
Lohéac
Pléchâtel
St-Malo-de-Phily
Pipriac
Messac
Guipry
MORBIHAN
La Gacilly
Landes de Cojoux
St-Just
Langon
Pont-de-Roche
Redon
Allaire
St-Nicolas-de-Redon
Brain-sur-Vilaine
Guémené-Penfao
Derval

Pointe du Grouin
Île des Landes
Rothéneuf
Paramé
Cancale
St-Méloir-des-Ondes
St-Servan-sur-Mer
Quelmer
St-Benoît-des-Ondes
Le Vivier-sur-Mer
Cherrueix
Mont Dol
Roz-sur-Couesnon
Baie de Mont-St-Michel
Mont-St-Michel
Avranches
Dol-de-Bretagne
Baguer-Morvan
La Boussac
Le Tronchet
Pleine-Fougères
Sougéal
Pontorson
Pleudihen-sur-Rance
Combourg
Château de la Bourbansais
Château de la Ballue
Bazouges-la-Pérouse
Antrain
St-Quen-la-Rouërie
Château Bonne-Fontaine
Château du Rocher-Portail
Landean
St-Brice-en-Coglès
Dingé
St-Rémy-du-Plain
Parc Floral
Forêt de Fougères
Sens-de-Bretagne
Fougères
Château de Caradeuc
Château de Montmuran
Mézières-sur-Couesnon
Billé
St-Aubin-d'Aubigné
St-Aubin-du-Cormier
Liffré
Forêt de Rennes
Châtillon-en-Vendelais
Champeaux
Forêt de Chevré
Montreuil-Sous-Pérouse
Rennes
Châteaubourg
Vitré
St-Didier
Château des Rochers Sévigné
Chavagne
Domagné
Châteaugiron
Moulins
Bais
Chanteloup
Essé
Janzé
La Roche-aux-Fées
Retiers
La Guerche-de-Bretagne
Cossé-le-Vivien
Bourg-des-Comptes
Le Sel-de-Bretagne
Martigné-Ferchaud
Craon
Bain-de-Bretagne
MAYENNE
LOIRE ATLANTIQUE
Grand-Fougeray
Châteaubriant
Pouancé

p.458

Don't miss

Getting around the Ille-et-Vilaine

For precise, up-to-date information on public transport by **bus** in the Ille-et-Vilaine, go to website of the Ille-et-Vilaine Conseil Général (the equivalent of an English county council), *www.ille-et-vilaine.fr*, or straight to its specialist transport website, *www.illenoo-services.fr*.

ⓘ **Comité Départemental du Tourisme de Haute-Bretagne Ille-et-Vilaine**
t 02 99 78 47 40, www.bretagne35.com; a good starting point for tourist information across the region, but also consult the more local town and country tourist offices. It has its own holiday service, Loisirs Accueil Haute-Bretagne Ille-et-Vilaine, proposing short breaks or weekends away (see www.haute-bretagne-resa.com).

The Ille-et-Vilaine's short but sensational fragment of coastline runs from just west of the holy mount of the Mont St-Michel to a little way west of Dinard, that much younger, primmer sister of the great and gritty Breton sea adventurers' city, St-Malo. This section of the Côte d'Emeraude (the Emerald Coast), as the shore is called here, is enviably beautiful.

The daytime mirages and evening sunsets across the Bay of the Mont St-Michel make for some of the most mesmerizing images by which to remember Brittany. OK, the holy mount officially stands in Normandy – as the popular saying puts it:

The Couesnon in a moment of folly
Put the Mont St-Michel in Normandy

indicating that the regional divide between Normandy and Brittany here has traditionally been the Couesnon River. We've been charitable and found a place for the heavenly sight in this chapter. However, Brittany has little to be jealous about – much of the spectacular Bay of the Mont St-Michel lies within the Breton border.

St-Malo, with its ruthless merchants and privateers, used to attract naval attacks from Britain. Now both it and Dinard compete for the British tourist hordes, the one with its ferry port, the other with its airport. Both have great beaches looking onto gorgeous rock-strewn seascapes. In contrast, the town of Rennes may seem a less obvious tourist destination, but the capital of not just the Ille-et-Vilaine but the whole of Brittany proves to be a happening, cultured city, with grand squares and acrobatic displays of high-rise historic timberframe buildings, plus a new quarter that includes the funkily redone Musée de Bretagne celebrating the entire region's culture.

Between the coast and Rennes, châteaux liberally dot the countryside, while the mighty fortresses of Fougères and Vitré still show off their strength on Brittany's eastern flank. As to Combourg, the Ille-et-Vilaine's best-known castle, it's linked with gushing French Romantic writer, François-René de Chateaubriand. The Route Chateaubriand is an association of sights with connections to the figure that might encourage you to discover the interior of the *département*.

The most enticing literary location in the area, though, is Merlin's forest, officially called Paimpont, better known in legend as

Brocéliande. In its landscapes of curious purple stones, small neolithic vestiges have been blown out of all proportions into fantasy locations for Arthurian legend. The most famous example of neolithic architecture in the Ille-et-Vilaine is La Roche-aux-Fées, but St-Just, down the quietly gorgeous Vilaine Valley from Rennes, counts among the most magical, if unsung, prehistoric sites in Brittany.

St-Malo and the Clos Poulet

Our touring chapters start with the fireworks of St-Malo, a stunning maritime and military city, its splendid walled old town surrounded on all sides by water, its peppering of islands just out to sea fortified down the centuries to keep English invaders at bay. Now, you'll be glad to know, the English are, generally speaking, warmly welcomed in this once-feared place, which today also doubles as a ferry port and beach resort.

The Clos Poulet, the stocky, wider promontory on which St-Malo is located, is full of interesting tourist sights, including the home of Jacques Cartier, the Breton who played such an important role in

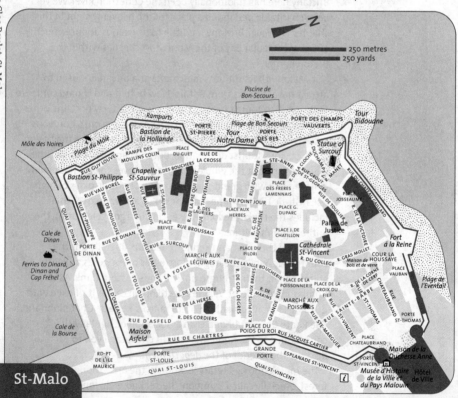

St-Malo

Getting to and around St-Malo

Condor Ferries (St-Malo enquiries, **t** 02 99 40 78 10) runs fast ferries to St-Malo from Poole (4hrs 35mins) and Weymouth (5hrs 15mins), with brief stops on the Channel Islands. Brittany Ferries (St-Malo enquiries, **t** 02 99 40 64 41) offers services between Portsmouth and St-Malo (average travel time 10hrs 45mins). HD Ferries operates fast catamarans to and from the Channel Islands.

The nearest **airport** is Dinard-Pleurtuit just across the Rance estuary, **t** 08 25 08 35 09, serviced by flights from London-Stansted, Bristol, Birmingham and East Midlands (Nottingham) with Ryanair, and from Guernsey by Aurigny.

By **train**, St-Malo is served by two (three in summer) TGVs a day from Paris (3 hrs), *www.tgv.com*. Ordinary trains connect St-Malo to Rennes.

For **bus** services, the central *gare routière* is on Esplanade St-Vincent outside Porte St-Vincent. To explore the area by coach, Les Courriers Bretons (*www.lescourriersbretons.fr*, **t** 02 99 19 70 80), and the Compagnie Armoricaine de Transport (*www.cat29.fr*, **t** 02 98 44 53 24) offer services to a variety of destinations.

'discovering' Canada. The later, mighty Malouin merchants built their country houses, or *malouinières*, across this area.

St-Malo

⭐ St-Malo

Le rocher ('the rock') is the surprisingly plain way by which the inhabitants of St-Malo, the Malouins, refer to their magnificently arrogant walled old city, or *ville intra-muros*. But most of the city you see isn't actually old. In 1944, during the Second World War, the town was reduced almost entirely to rubble by Allied bombings attempting to dislodge the Germans holed up here; the air attacks destroyed 80 per cent of the buildings within the old ramparts. In June 1971, a stone cross was placed at the top of the cathedral of St-Vincent to symbolize the completion of St-Malo's long reconstruction. It has re-emerged as a great and cheerful city.

History

St-Malo has one of the most spectacular, fiery and controversial histories of any French city.

From Aleth to St-Malo

Ignore St-Malo for a moment. The very early action took place to the west, at Aleth, or Alet, which arose to guard the entrance to the estuary of the Rance River; the Celtic Coriosolitae built a port here, active by the 1st century BC. These men traded with southern Britain and with the Channel Islands, and erected a substantial promontory fort, one of the very few major pre-Roman settlements to have been found in Brittany.

With the Roman conquest of Gaul, the main Coriosolitae town became Corseul, inland up the Rance. Towards the end of the Roman Empire, as tribes from the east moved into Gaul, Aleth became an important fortified Gallo-Roman site, a few fragments of which remain, and the first cathedral was built.

Thanks to the subsequent arrival of immigrants from across the Channel, this Christian centre thrived. Although Irish pioneers Aaron and Brendan got here a little before him, the man who most left his mark was called Malo (or was it Maclou, or MacLow?), arriving from Britain in the 6th century. Malo became bishop and worker of miracles, his name eventually given to the main rock north of Aleth. Aleth continued to be a lively centre until the Vikings came to lay waste to it, although the ruins of the 10th-century cathedral are still easily visible there.

In the ensuing centuries, attention moved from Aleth to St-Malo's rock, only joined to the mainland by a strip of sand, people perhaps encouraged to move to its safety due to Viking raids. The man considered the principal developer of medieval St-Malo is Jean de Chatillon. Elected bishop in 1143, he took on the power of the Benedictine monks on the rock, sent them packing, and transferred the bishopric here, ordering a new cathedral, and having the whole place defended by solid ramparts. Great mastiffs were brought from England to guard the city, and the tradition of these terrifying beasts being let out at night to roam the strands would continue up to the 18th century.

In 1230, the then duke of Brittany gave the port a great number of trading privileges. That same year, troops of King Henry III of England landed in St-Malo, sent on an expedition to Brittany. However, under the French king Louis IX, or Saint Louis, St-Malo crews took part in the defeat of the English fleet down by Bayonne.

Internally, the religious and secular authorities would often take opposing sides in the course of St-Malo's history. The extremely divisive Breton War of Succession split the city; the bishopric supported the French-backed candidate, the town the English-backed one. The latter side eventually won in the bloody conflict when Jean de Montfort became Duke Jean IV of Brittany. But he would incur the wrath of the Malouins.

Ni Français, ni Breton: Malouin suis

'Neither French, nor Breton, but Malouin' ran a popular motto, reflecting St-Malo's citizens' proud independence. The town cultivated this independent streak down the centuries, and became something of a defiant city state. Duke Jean IV of Brittany, seeing his ducal treasury depleted, tried to cash in on the city's wealth, and the townsmen revolted. In the 1370s, backed by substantial English troops, Jean IV tried to gain control of St-Malo. It held out from June until November. The French king, Charles V, keenly supported the Malouins' uprising, sending his great Breton commander, Bertrand du Guesclin, to dislodge the English.

The French in turn attempted to impose their authority. Charles V was foolish enough to try prematurely to declare Brittany's union with the French kingdom in 1379, and many of the Breton lords united to call back Duke Jean IV. But the effective leader of St-Malo then, Bishop Josselin de Rohan, proclaimed that the town recognized no overlord except the Pope. The angry duke laid siege to St-Malo again and had the sturdy Tour Solidor built on the Rance to the south of Aleth in 1382, to hold a garrison. In the second year of the siege, the bishop called upon the Avignon pope, Clement VII, to intervene. The papal legate persuaded the Malouins to give in to the duke, but two years later, the Malouins simply turfed out his officers. The citizens survived the next siege, and this time took the defiant step of calling on the next king of France, Charles VI, to be their overlord. Charles VI granted the rebel city important privileges, not levying any duties on its commerce.

In the second half of the Hundred Years War, the Malouin merchants didn't fare too badly, prospering in part from pillaging English ships. Such ruthless means of supplementing their business were to become a trademark of the tough Malouins over many centuries. Following English raids on the Breton coasts, in 1403 Malouin forces sacked Plymouth. Two years later they targeted Yarmouth.

The Malouin ships' captains were often daring; in 1425, they defied the English siege of the Mont St-Michel, managing to take supplies to the island. King Charles VII of France thanked the city by giving its merchants special trading rights with other French ports. Duke Jean V of Brittany had also become close to the French king, and the latter handed over the lordship of St-Malo to him. Jean V soon had to submit to the English, though. In 1427, he was forced to make peace with King Henry VI of England, who demanded rights of entry into St-Malo.

Duke François II succeeded Jean V and expanded St-Malo's ducal fortress. With the Wars of the Roses raging in England, Henry Tudor (the future King Henry VII) came to take refuge in St-Malo's cathedral, causing the English king to declare war on François II. Then it was the turn of the acquisitive French king to do likewise. In this conflict, the Malouins supported the Breton duke for once. But French forces under the commander La Trémouïlle marched on St-Malo, having beaten the Breton troops at the decisive Battle of St-Aubin-du-Cormier in 1488. The French cannon managed to breach the walls and the Malouins gave in quickly to a demand for 12,000 gold *écus*.

Once Anne de Bretagne, the last Breton duchess, had then been forced into marriage to the French king, Charles VIII, work began on another enormous tower for the ducal château. The Malouin authorities were displeased and told Anne so. She dismissed the complaints, and the tower became known as the Quic en Groign, after a phrase that Anne de Bretagne had engraved on it: *Quic en groign, ainsi sera, c'est mon plaisir* ('Whoever may complain, this is how it will be – such is my pleasure').

According to Anne's marriage contract, Brittany was supposed to remain largely autonomous, keeping its privileges and freedoms. But Charles VIII couldn't resist taking command of such a rich corner of Brittany, and declared himself master of St-Malo. The Malouins don't appear to have complained overmuch, as he gave them good terms, promising fewer taxes and a larger share of booty from captured ships.

St-Malo's Revered Sailors and Breakaway Republic

Jacques Cartier is the most famous 16th-century Malouin and the most famous French explorer of that century – *see* box, p.102. Like many boys from St-Malo, he first took to the seas on gruelling fishing expeditions off Newfoundland. Later, he suggested expeditions of his own, leading to the founding of Canada.

Cartier died of the plague in 1557, just before the period dominated by the terrible French Wars of Religion. The night of the horrific St Bartholomew's Day massacre in 1572, when fanatical Catholics butchered Huguenots around France, the Catholic Malouins spared the enemy in their midst, and left the Huguenots to flee to England and to Holland, but the city did go on to support the fanatically Catholic *Ligue*. Much more deadly for the townsfolk was a terrible bout of plague that struck in 1583 – some estimates reckon it wiped out half the population.

When the French king, Henri III, had Henri Duc de Guise, the leader of the *Ligue*, assassinated in the royal castle of Blois on the Loire in 1588, the Malouins reacted with anger. In March 1590, the royal governor was assassinated, and the leader of the attack, Picot de la Gicquelais, led the cry '*Vive la République*' – St-Malo effectively became a republic from that time up to December 1594, only relenting after Henri III's successor, Henri IV, had renounced the Huguenot faith.

Whatever the terribly negative moral judgements that can be made on St-Malo's rapacious shipowners, ships' captains and corsairs seen from today's perspective, many of the leading Malouins were spectacularly successful through the 17th and 18th centuries, and were often involved in extraordinary expeditions as well as outrageous acts.

Jean-Baptiste Colbert, that tirelessly enterprising minister under King Louis XIV, took an understandable interest in St-Malo, intent on building up a French fleet to match the English and the Dutch, and on reorganizing the French colonies. In 1655, it was decided that the crew for the king's Western Fleet should be made up entirely of Malouins, as they were such tried and tested sailors. In 1660, Colbert founded an Ecole d'Hydrographie in town to train naval officers, and it's still going strong.

Most significantly, Colbert founded the French Compagnie des Indes trading company in 1664, following previous abortive attempts at organizing French colonial commerce. But with Colbert's death and other difficulties, the company found itself in trouble. The minister Louis de Pontchartrain realized that the Malouin shipowners were important partners to get on board to rescue the situation. He invited 'the gentlemen of St-Malo, the most capable in the realm of supporting such a grand enterprise as the commerce with the Indies', to take on its running. This they did, and for 15 years all the trade from the French Indies ended up at St-Malo. Some 40 Malouin families built hugely successful trading empires around the world, controlling a large slice of French colonial trade.

Colonial Wars and the Corsairs of St-Malo, an Idolized Scourge

Malouin corsairs also made a killing in the latter part of the 17th century. Corsairs aren't to be confused with plain pirates, although they are humorously nicknamed 'pirates with a permit'. They were officially given *lettres de course* by the royal administration to go 'coursing' after the enemy, hence their name. The mere threat of boarding was often enough to make the enemy capitulate. Between 1688 and 1697, Malouin corsairs captured a staggering number of foreign commercial vessels.

Angry British and Dutch merchants called upon their governments to attack St-Malo itself. The English mounted attacks on the city in the 1690s. After the Battle of La Hogue in 1692, 21 French vessels took refuge down the Rance to avoid destruction. The next year, in November, more cunning plots were thought up

The English Infernal Machine

It seemed the massive English bombardment of St-Malo of 1693 had come to an end after three terrible days. But the English were planning a still deadlier finale to put an end to the scourge of St-Malo. Under cover of night, they launched an unmanned, black-sailed ship towards St-Malo, packed with an enormous amount of explosives: an estimated 25 tonnes of gunpowder and some 600 huge bombs, with petrol, sulphur and straw placed on top. The idea was that this infernal machine should be carried by the tide to hit St-Malo's main rock and there blow up, destroying much of the city. The English calculations didn't work out, however, and the black ship hit another rock, 400 metres from the city. The massive explosion was supposedly heard as far away as Granville on the Normandy coast. Bits of metal rained down on the roofs of St-Malo and most of the city's windows were blown out, but the damage was otherwise limited.

by the English. Their vessels came bearing white flags, and the Malouin look-outs mistook them for a French squadron from Brest. It was actually a British force under John Benbow, drawing surreptitiously into St-Malo's waters. British cannon then bombarded the city for three whole days. Although fires broke out in St-Malo, the English eventually appeared to have given up. But they had one more trick up their sleeve (*see* box, below).

The British returned two years later, supported by Dutch ships. They launched over 1,500 missiles on the city over three days. Once again St-Malo survived the onslaught, the townspeople putting out many of the fires with sand.

After the shock and the close shave, during the 1690s, the islands just off St-Malo would be strongly fortified. The great French military engineer Vauban planned the considerable number of military installations involved, but it was a subordinate of his, Siméon de Garengeau, who actually oversaw their construction. La Conchée is a particularly admired feat of engineering, making the most of the natural shape of that particular rocky island.

Slaves, Revolution, Cod and War

The start of the 18th century was perhaps the most lucrative period for the big St-Malo merchants, who built their country retreats, the *malouinières*, as the town expanded. The 18th century was also the major slave-trading period for France, and St-Malo saw the mounting of 216 slave-trading expeditions across the century. However, mid-18th-century colonial wars made 'honest' trade much harder, and the corsairs would come back into their own. The Malouin merchants were increasingly crippled by Louis XV's chaos of conflicts. Many went bankrupt.

Come the time of revolutions, St-Malo became one of the French ports where volunteers for the American War of Independence set

Duguay-Trouin, Corsair Extraordinaire

The most notorious and successful of St-Malo's corsairs during the Ancien Régime was René Duguay-Trouin. Originally destined for the priesthood, he proved equally as excited by women as by war. As he put it in his memoirs, 'Mars and Venus were my two ruling passions.' By the age of 18, such was Duguay-Trouin's skill in taking enemy vessels that he was given command of his own ship. For three years, he wrought havoc in the Irish Sea.

In 1694, his vessel was caught in a trap by six English ships and he was taken to Portsmouth as a prisoner. The story goes that having seduced an English rose, he managed to escape. His continued triumphs led to his presentation at the French royal court, and at the age of 24 he was elevated to the rank of captain of a frigate in the French navy. In the papers conferring nobility on him, Duguay-Trouin's achievements were lovingly noted: he had taken more than 300 merchant vessels and 20 enemy warships and corsairs' vessels. His most outrageous act was seizing Rio de Janeiro from the Portuguese in 1711 and ruining the enemy fleet there. He was made lieutenant general in 1728, and long afterwards would end up with the posthumous honour of having his remains moved into St-Malo's cathedral.

off to fight the British. Their resources much depleted, the town's merchants did though manage to drum up 360,000 francs for the Revolutionary authorities. They didn't show enough zeal to satisfy Le Carpentier, however. This fanatical figure under the Terror changed the name of the city to Port Malo and had an inventory drawn up of each family's belongings. Protesters were imprisoned. St-Malo's great political Romantic, François-René de Chateaubriand (*see* box, p.132), headed off during the Revolution as members of his family lost their heads. With the fall of Robespierre and Le Carpentier, St-Malo became a stronghold for anti-Revolutionaries. The Napoleonic period brought some relief to its fortunes, but blockades made trade extremely hard.

Time was up for the corsairs and slave-traders as the 19th century progressed. Cod fishing in distant waters became the main occupation for St-Malo through most of the century. The first railway line reached town in 1864, while a radical change in Anglo–French relations brought a very different breed of Englishman from centuries past – the peaceable tourist. Then St-Malo's little sister Dinard would blossom.

But the first half of the 20th century also brought disastrous German warfare. The St-Malo cod-fishing fleet was seriously depleted in the First World War. Still, in the period between the wars, the port remained a substantial destination of long-distance fishermen. The main story recounted about St-Malo in the Second World War is of the city's destruction as Germans and Allies battled it out to the last. The Nazis surrendered on the mainland on 17 August 1944, but a hardcore of German troops resisted on the Ile Cézembre until 9 September.

The city helped put this harrowing period behind it with its determined rebuilding programme in granite of the walled old town and developed into a thriving holiday spot. It has managed to maintain a fair number of its shipbuilding and sea trading activities as well as creating vibrant festivals to celebrate its

One More Malouin Makes his Fortune out of Misfortune

St-Malo did have one last 'hero' of a corsair at the end of the 18th century and start of the 19th. He was Robert Surcouf, who built up a dazzling career and fortune in very little time, partly through slave-trading, but in the main from the most daring of corsair raids. His first extraordinary feat was typical of the man: in 1795, he captured the British ship *Triton* with its 150-man crew and 30 cannon, while it's said he was in charge of a mere 19 sailors manning just four cannon. The capture in 1800 of the British ship, the Kent, featured as his greatest accomplishment – the vessel was returning from Brazil, filled with treasure.

By his late 20s, at the start of the 19th century, Surcouf had made a fortune large enough for him to retire. Napoleon, full of admiration for the man, offered him an important naval post, but Surcouf preferred to keep his independence and accepted a title of baron instead. Surcouf also became the first Malouin captain to receive the Légion d'Honneur, the French order of merit created by Boney.

preeminent position on the seas. Its citizens may still be proud of their city, but they take a more jocular view of themselves, transforming their old saying to read: '*Malouin suis, Breton peut-être, Français s'il en reste*', roughly translated as, 'Definitely Malouin, maybe Breton too, and a bit French if there's anything left over.'

A Tour of the Walled City

> *That's where I was brought up, companion of the waves and the wind.*
> Chateaubriand, *Mémoires d'outre-tombe*
> *A crown of stone placed on the waves.*
> Flaubert
> *... a real sea bird's nest ...*
> Maurice de Guérin
> *... basically, it's a prison ...*
> Stendhal

Taking on the Ramparts

St-Malo's marvellous walled city looks both noble and defensively aloof as you arrive. The many-storeyed mansion blocks built in austere grey granite peer haughtily over the imposing **ramparts**. As the tide goes out, the most inviting golden-sanded beaches spread out at their feet. To appreciate the seascapes from the walled city and to peek indiscreetly into grand Malouin apartments, take a walk up on the glorious broad ramparts. You can follow these almost all the way around the old town; they make for the most wonderful promenade.

Start from beside the massive castle towers. Once up on the ramparts above the **Porte St-Vincent** gateway, you can look out to the *bassins à flot*, St-Malo's extensive protected inner harbours. The views this side are industrial. By contrast, within the walls, the elongated **Place Chateaubriand** at your feet is full of cafés and bustling crowds, the most engagingly lively part of the old town, and also one of its few spacious-feeling corners. Before the city was enlarged to cover this area in 1708, there used to be a beach here, the Anse de Bonne Mer, and it was from this spot that Jacques Cartier set sail on his famed expedition to Canada in 1534.

Continue along the ramparts to the **Grande Porte** above **Place du Poids du Roi**. Below lies the area in which the corsairs came to find work in times of war, drafted in inns with colourful names. The gate itself is the oldest entrance into the city, with enormous twin drum towers dating from the 15th century. These house the Association du Cotre Corsaire, which saw to the construction of a replica of corsair extraordinaire Surcouf's ship, the *Renard*.

The **southwestern ramparts** are pierced in the centre by the **Porte de Dinan**. Outside this gate, the little **ferry boats cross to Dinard**, on a wonderful short trip over the Rance estuary. The *vedettes* run longer tours, inland to Dinan, and out to Cap Fréhel (see p.185). The tentacle of the **Môle des Noires**, a long, thin jetty, sticks out into the sea, with wonderful views opening out as you reach its tip.

St-Malo's fine central beaches start below the **Bastion St-Philippe**, marking the southern corner of the city, but the sands only reveal themselves as the tide recedes. The **Plage du Môle** lies at the foot of the ramparts between the Bastion St-Philippe and the **Bastion de la Hollande**. Up on the lawn perched on high, a dramatic statue of Jacques Cartier stands out prominently. Cannon point out to sea, but with purely decorative intent these days.

On one end of the Bastion de la Hollande, the **Porte St-Pierre** allows you to go down the ramp, past the **sailing school**, to the **Plage de Bon Secours**, a splendid urban beach, the sun umbrellas of the Bar du Soleil providing much-appreciated shade on bright days. Although the waters withdraw a long way at low tide, this beach is provided with a brilliant swimming pool, the **Piscine de Bon Secours**, filled with sea water. When the tide is out, it makes for a magical walk to go on to the island of Grand Bé, the location of Chateaubriand's tomb, or to the Petit Bé.

Below the Bastion de la Hollande seek out the kennel in which the terrifying night guards of St-Malo were once housed; 24 mastiffs would be let loose to patrol the beaches once the nightly curfew had sounded. They were done away with in 1770, after a tragic accident in which a naval officer was mauled to death.

Back up on the ramparts, at the Tour Notre Dame, you can get down to the other end of the beach of Bon Secours via the **Porte des Bés**. Up on the triangular **Champs Vauverts**, with its **Jardin du Cavalier**, a statue of the corsair Surcouf cuts a dashing figure. Just set back from here, the **Maison du Québec**, set in cute little old stone buildings, provides all manner of information on Canada, and hosts Canadian cultural events, including concerts and cinema. Close by, the impressive **Tour Bidouane** dates from the 15th century. With extremely thick-walled chambers on many levels, it's now used for **temporary exhibitions**, artistic or historical. The **Chapelle St-Sauveur** offers a larger venue for such exhibitions, too.

Continuing along the northern ramparts, views open out onto further alluring islands. The tour of the ramparts ends at the **Porte St-Thomas**, where you can get out on to the rockier beach, the **Plage de l'Eventail**, a large natural paddling pool left in place when the tide is out. This is the spot where Chateaubriand most enjoyed playing as a child. The account in his memoirs of his pre-revolutionary boyhood reads more like Tom Sawyer than the great Romantic. The description of impoverished aristocratic hooligans brawling on the seashore is particularly entertaining. Nowadays, the great shimmering sands of Paramé, St-Malo's seaside resort, stretch away to the east. Enjoy the scene from the simple café down by the beach.

Sights and Museums Within the City Walls

Down from the ramparts, the streets within St-Malo's walls can seem quite dark and overbearing. The height of the granite mansion blocks shows this was something of a high-rise city for the 18th century. The builders generally constructed short streets and used curves to break the force of the winds. So instead of vistas, you get the feeling you're entering a disorientating labyrinth. Sadly, due to the war bombs, most of the buildings are postwar reconstructions. Perhaps the most evocative way to imagine historic St-Malo is to think of the corsairs who brought such wild life to these streets under the Ancien Régime. On their return from successful raids they would be greeted as heroes. Then they would often tour the town, getting appallingly drunk. God forbid that any British tourists should emulate them today.

If you're interested in shopping, then start with **Rue St-Vincent**, smart boutiques competing for your attention, including some selling Breton stripy jumpers or all manner of marine objects. Passing below the cathedral choir, it comes as a surprise to find a long-established sweet shop specializing in buttery Breton toffees stuck to the back of the church. Around here, explore the **little squares** whose names, such as **Place de la Poissonnerie**, **Place aux Herbes** and **Marché aux Légumes**, indicate the specific traders whose stalls once dominated these quarters. Around the last of the three mentioned, you'll find a number of popular cafés. Heading down the city's southern slope, **Rue Broussais** and **Rue de Dinan** form the other half of the somewhat wiggling main shopping axis through town.

If history is more your bag, follow a discreet but well-signposted and numbered **historical trail** from **Place Chateaubriand**. It takes you almost immediately to the façade of the house where our Romantic hero was born in 1768, the 17th-century **Hôtel de la Gicquelais**, on **Rue Chateaubriand**. Close to Chateaubriand's first home, the **Maison de la Duchesse Anne** probably never saw the duchess, but it does have a certain 15th-century grandeur, with its stairtower and sculpted corner figures. The trail leads to another distinctive, old-style building, the **Maison de Bois et de Verre**, the House of Wood and Glass. This is now home to the **Maison Internationale des Poètes et des Ecrivains**, a venue for highly popular recitals of poetry and traditional song, small-scale art exhibitions, and lively street theatre evenings in summer. Check out their programme.

Maison Internationale des Poètes et des Ecrivains *www.mipe.asso.fr/ malo, t 02 99 40 28 7; open Tues–Sat 2–6 for exhibitions*

The trail then takes you to the highest point on the Rock, going past the grand 17th-century entrance to the posh school of St-Malo, close to a ruined cloister in the Ecole Hydrographique's grounds, and on to the plain little chapel to the rather forgotten St Aaron.

Musée d'Histoire in the Château de St-Malo

Musée d'Histoire in the Château de St-Malo
www.ville-saint-malo.fr, t 02 99 40 71 57; open April–Sept daily, Oct–March Tues–Sun, 10–12.30 and 2–6

Opposite vibrant Place Chateaubriand, the massive, impressively bulky Château de St-Malo is home to the town hall, but the city's decaying old main museum is also locked away in here. The town council has voted to build a brand-new maritime museum in the coming years, to present the rich collections on that theme quite separately, while the general history of St-Malo will be presented here in more modern fashion.

For the moment, the Musée d'Histoire looks dark, dismal and rather dead, but you can follow many interesting themes inside. The first gloomy chamber evokes the Malouins' maritime history, with a panel indicating the far-flung corners of the earth to which they sailed. Ships' models, guns and the odd colonial object are displayed. Another room features a huge wooden prow carved as a dandy corsair's head. Ecclesiastical mementoes from the area fill a further room, while yet another charts the dreadful destruction of St-Malo in the Second World War, followed by its reconstruction. An upper room is devoted to St-Malo's remarkable clutch of 19th-century writers and intellectuals, Chateaubriand depicted in windswept pose in a famous work of 1807 by Girodet.

A huge adjoining castle tower forms a further part of the museum. There, one level concentrates on the Malouin tradition of fishing in Newfoundland, with maps, icy paintings and models all combining to give a good picture of the trade. On another level, pipes carved with mermaids and grotesques vie for attention with coiffes placed on silly wooden faces and other bits and pieces of past Clos Poulet culture. The top floor displays a mixed bag of paintings of St-Malo, including Paul Signac's cheering *Le Pardon des Terre-Neuvas* of 1928.

Cathédrale St-Vincent

The cathedral rises close to the heart of town, with a series of spacious squares in front of it allowing you to view its facade and steeple from a distance. In the square immediately in front of the facade, the odd art gallery displays marine paintings and sculptures. The sharp, soaring spire signals St-Malo from far out to sea, and acts as a useful seamark. But the edifice didn't always look like this – the building was partially destroyed in the Second World War. Photos in a side chapel show the extent of the devastation. The nave and its vaulting, along with most of the choir, did survive the bombs. All the original stained-glass windows fell out, though, hence the modern

07 Ille-et-Vilaine | St-Malo and the Clos Poulet: St-Malo

figurative series in the nave telling of major episodes in St-Malo's history, and the slightly sickly coloured contemporary ones in the choir in which pinks and yellows dominate.

A major Romanesque church was begun here in the 12th century by Benedictine monks, on the site of an earlier, much more modest building. After the influential bishop Jean de Chatillon had the Benedictines turfed out, work on the nave continued, but the construction of the ceiling shows how the new, early Gothic style was employed, using deep ribbed vaults. The 13th-century choir was influenced by Norman techniques, and even the stone came from Caen in Normandy. Its quirky end wall contains a fine rose window.

One or two fine statues of the Virgin show her importance to the community here, but St-Malo's cathedral seems dedicated almost as much to Jacques Cartier's glory as to God's; the Malouin explorer is practically sanctified inside. Along the aisle, a plaque in the floor declares: 'Jacques Cartier kneeled here to receive the benediction of the bishop of St-Malo before his departure for the discovery of Canada.' Look out too for stained glass representing him, and for his tomb.

La Demeure de Corsaire or L'Hôtel d'Asfeld

La Demeure de Corsaire or L'Hôtel d'Asfeld
www.demeure-de-corsaire.com, t 02 99 56 09 40; open for guided tours Feb–Nov Tues–Sun 2.30–6.30, July and Aug daily 10–12 and 2.30–6.30

You'll get the best picture of the life of the wealthy St-Malo merchants of the Ancien Régime by visiting this building, one of the very few original 18th-century mansions to have survived the war. It stands in the southeastern corner of town, close to the Porte St-Louis. In this house, voyages were planned, exotic produce stored and commercial deals struck. Family life went on here too – that of just one family. François-Auguste Magon, for whom this grand townhouse was built, had by the age of 45 amassed an immense fortune as director of the French East India Company. The Magons were one of the most successful of all St-Malo's trading dynasties. 'Shake any bush and a Magon will fall out of it', the Malouins used to joke.

The 70-room building, built in 1725, is now divided up into flats, but one of the tenants organizes lively guided tours round parts of the house. A couple of the reception rooms stand quite empty except when the odd amateur painting exhibition is put on. There are many hidden passageways behind the walls. The visit ends in the cellars, occupied by a wine merchant – the conditions are excellent for keeping bottles. At the period the Magons lived here, spices and tea would have been stored down here.

The Magon family only spent around three months a year in their town house. François-Auguste also owned one of the most delightful *malouinières* in the countryside, **La Chipaudière**, where he and his family enjoyed much more space and cleaner air. A branch of the Magon family still owns that property, and its gardens can be visited – *see* p.106.

Today, Peter Meazey, a wonderfully enthusiastic Welshman who has fallen for Brittany, leads lively summer evening tours (lasting c.1hr 30mins) around town in L'Invitation au Voyage. Dressed in period costume, he evokes the Ancien Régime when St-Malo merchants were frantically busy oganizing all manner of expeditions. Your guide explains how these were carried out.

The Islands around the Ville Intra-Muros

When the tide goes out it uncovers a beach of the finest sand. Then it is possible to walk all the way round the nest where I was born. Rocks lie scattered around, some close by, some far out to sea, some turned into forts, others uninhabited – Fort-Royal, La Conchée, Cézembre and Le Grand Bé, the latter where my grave will be.
Chateaubriand, *Mémoires d'outre-tombe*

Ant trails of tourists head out from the *ville intra-muros* for the islands made accessible when the tide goes out, making the most of an opportunity for an extraordinary walk. Looking back on the walled city from the sands, St-Malo makes a stunning picture.

Many French people go to the **Grand Bé** expressly to see **Chateaubriand's tomb**, a place of Byronic proportions to them. With a simple granite cross on a simple base, it looks out towards the Channel. The **Fort du Petit Bé** can be visited, too, at low tide, or you can head out to it by boat. This well-preserved fortification has recently opened to tourists, and has been evocatively kitted out with cannon, as well as presenting an exhibition on the tides.

Fort du Petit Bé
www.petit-be.com,
t 06 08 27 51 20; tours,
times depending
on tides

The **Fort National** is also splendidly located. At low tide, you pick your way through small rocks to arrive at the sharp layers of its fortifications. Before 1689, this islet not only served as the location for a lighthouse: during the time the St-Malo authorities had the right to administer justice, it was also where people condemned to death were executed. In 1689, its conversion into a fort began, its defences bringing clearly to mind brutal times and military campaigns.

Fort National
www.fortnational
.com, t 02 99 85 34 33;
tours, times depending
on tides

With such big forts, with their layers upon layers of defences, it can come as a bit of a disappointment to see the diminutive size of the building at the heart, but the effect is of diminishing Russian dolls. The place was fitted out to hold a reasonably sized garrison, with two water tanks and gunpowder rooms built into the rock below. On the tour, you're taken down into these dark underground chambers. The Fort National has never been taken by force, to date.

The **Ile de Cézembre** makes for a tempting excursion by sea (boats leave from in front of the Porte de Dinan, summer only) on sunny days, but be warned that it can be a harsh place, lacking practically any shade. Breton monks retreated here from the 6th century on. Local legend has it that young women from St-Malo would go out to Cézembre on a pilgrimage to St Brendan's oratory. There they would pray for his help in finding a lizard with three tails – a curious and rather unlikely sign that they would get married within the year. You're not supposed to wander off from the blindingly white sands, as German mines may still be lurking under the surface of Cézembre.

Market Days in St-Malo

St-Malo Intra-muros: Tuesday and Friday

Festivals in St-Malo

Major sailing races often start or finish in St-Malo, but the place also hosts many festivals that don't move from dry land.

Etonnants Voyageurs is a reputed international travel-writing festival held in May.

Folklores du Monde, in mid-July, celebrates folklore from around the world.

Fête du Nautisme held mid-May.

Le Solidor en Peinture is an artists' gathering at the end of June;

Le Solidor Métiers d'Art, a gathering of craftspeople, is held in mid-Sept.

Festival de Musique Sacrée caters for classical music lovers from mid-July to mid-Aug.

Promenades Littéraires, a programme of literary walks, runs in July and Aug.

La Route du Rock is a major rock festival that takes place over the mid-August holiday.

Quai des Bulles is the second biggest cartoon festival in France, held end of Oct.

Where to Stay

⭐ **France et Chateaubriand** ➤➤

ⓘ **St-Malo** ➤
Esplanade St-Vincent;
t 08 25 13 52 00,
www.saint-malo-
tourisme.com

St-Malo Intra-Muros ✉ 35412
It's usually vibrant within the old city's historic walls, but if you prefer a greater choice of sea views, see Paramé below, or if you want a nice place right by the ferry terminal, *see* St-Servan.

***de la Cité, 26 Rue Ste-Barbe, t 02 99 40 55 40, *www.hotelcite.com* (€€€€€–€€). Appealing decor reflecting the spirit of Ancien Régime St-Malo. Some of the nice rooms have a sea view.

***Elizabeth, 2 Rue des Cordiers, t 02 99 56 24 98, *www.st-malo-hotel-elizabeth.com* (€€€–€€). Its rare late-16th-century façade conceals stylish rooms; further comfortable rooms are in a more recent section.

***Central, 6 Grande Rue, t 02 99 40 87 70, *www.hotel-central-st-malo.com* (€€€–€€). The rooms are larger than most here, the decorations varied. Fishing paraphernalia and seafood dominate in the restaurant (€€).

***Le Louvre, 2 Rue des Marins, t 02 99 40 86 62, *www.hoteldulouvre-saintmalo.com* (€€€–€€). So well renovated recently that it gained an extra star. The rooms are soberly modern, some spacious enough to cater to large families.

**France et Chateaubriand, Place Chateaubriand, t 02 99 56 66 52, *www.hotel.fr.chateaubriand.com* (€€€–€€). At the centre of the action on the busiest square, great if you like liveliness and crowds, who are drawn to its irresistible café terrace. Some rooms benefit from sea views.

**L'Univers, Place Chateaubriand, t 02 99 40 89 52, *www.hotel-univers-saintmalo.com* (€€). Neighbour and rival of the above, with well cared for rooms (but no sea views), plus a good restaurant, as well as the Bar de l'Univers.

⭐ Le San Pedro >

Le San Pedro, 1 Rue Ste-Anne, **t 02 99 40 88 57, *hotelsanpedro@ wanadoo.fr* (€€–€). A charming small hotel with sweet little rooms, tucked away in a great location just behind the ramparts leading to the Plage de Bon Secours, with a couple of tempting restaurants opposite. *Closed mid-Nov–Feb.*

⭐ La Duchesse Anne >>

Le Croiseur, 2 Place de la Poissonnerie, **t 02 99 40 80 40, *hotel.le.croiseur@free.fr* (€€–€). This place has stylishly contemporary rooms at reasonable price, plus a bar. *Closed mid-Nov–mid-Jan.*

⭐ Le Chalut >>

Le Nautilus, 9 Rue de la Corne de Cerf, **t 02 99 40 42 27, *www. lenautilus.com* (€). A cheerful address, with brightly decorated rooms. As there's a loud bar attached, it draws a younger crowd.

du Palais, 8 Rue Toullier, **t 02 99 40 07 30, *www.hoteldupalais-saint malo.com* (€). If you prefer a peaceful option, this pleasant hotel in a quiet area up the hill should fit the bill.

Porte St-Pierre, 2 Place du Guet, **t 02 99 40 91 27, *www.hotel-porte stpierre.com* (€€). This is an old-style Logis de France good for young families, in a great location close to a beach, boasting some rooms with sea views. Traditional restaurant (€€€–€€). *Closed mid-Nov–Jan.*

You can find a variety of cheap options well outside the ramparts and the city centre, close to the railway station, but the area isn't particularly charming.

Eating Out in St-Malo

Delaunay, 6 Rue Sainte-Barbe, **t** 02 99 40 92 46 (€€€). A well-established, fairly formal restaurant renowned for very fresh dishes and fine use of the excellent local vegetables. *Closed Sun and Mon out of season.*

La Duchesse Anne, by Porte St-Vincent, **t** 02 99 40 85 33 (€€€). A Malouin classic with extravagant decorations, set within the thick town ramparts. *Closed Wed and Mon eve, and Sun eve out of season.*

Le Chalut, 8 Rue de la Corne de Cerf, **t** 02 99 56 71 58 (€€€–€€). A posh restaurant offering superb fresh fish dishes. *Closed Mon and Tues.*

Crêperie du Corps de Garde, 3 Montée Notre-Dame, **t** 02 99 40 91 46 (€). In a great setting up in an old observation post on the ramparts, a good, friendly crêperie with fabulous terrace.

Crêperie Brigantine, 13 Rue de Dinan, **t** 02 99 56 82 82 (€). One of the more charming crêperies down in town, its walls covered with photos of classic sailing ships.

Rue Jacques Cartier has a string of very touristy restaurants on one side, covering Breton favourites, including seafood. Top dog along here is **L'Ancrage**, **t** 02 99 40 15 97 (€€–€).

East of St-Malo

Paramé, St-Malo's seaside resort, stretches east of the *ville intra-muros* behind a glorious arc of sand, although this beach vanishes completely at high tide. Paramé is now very built up and hugely popular in summer, with a great number of hotels lining the shore, looking out to sea. The busy road hemmed in by the suburban clutter just behind the coast leads to Jacques Cartier's manor.

Musée-Manoir Jacques Cartier or Manoir de Limoëlou

www.musée-jacques-cartier.com, **t** 02 99 40 97 73; open July and Aug daily 10–11.30 and 2.30–6; June and Sept Mon–Sat 10–11.30 and 2.30–6; Oct–May tours Mon–Sat at 10 and 3

Musée-Manoir Jacques Cartier or Manoir de Limoëlou

Jacques Cartier, born in the walled city of St-Malo in 1491, bought this little country home on the back of his adventures, notably his 'discovery' of Canada in 1534 to 1535 (*see* box, p.102). There isn't a great deal to see inside – lifestyles were relatively simple in the

Jacques Cartier and the French Connection with Canada

Life was tough for a young man growing up in St-Malo. From the age of 11, Cartier was sent on cod-fishing expeditions to Newfoundland. Shortly after getting married to the daughter of the constable of St-Malo, he leapt at the opportunity, in the early 1520s, of joining the navigator Giovanni da Verrazzano on a royal-backed voyage of discovery, to seek a westerly route from France to Asia via North America. Cartier had many skills for the period: he could read and write, as well as having a detailed knowledge of navigation. Although after a year of sailing up and down the American coast the expedition proved a flop, Cartier had been bitten by the bug of exploration.

Gathering funds for a voyage of his own proved no easy matter, and such adventures into uncharted territory clearly carried huge risks. But the Malouin showed indomitable persistence. His father-in-law's high office and contacts helped his cause. In 1532, King François I had gone to the nearby Mont St-Michel on pilgrimage. Cartier gained a royal audience, the royal seal of approval for his voyage and 6,000 livres to pay for it. The mission, according to Cartier's own memoirs, was rather vague, but the aim deeply material, rather than elevating: 'to discover certain islands where it is said that a large quantity of gold and other riches are to be found'. He left St-Malo in 1534, and it took him a mere 19 days to reach what he called the Détroit de Belle Ile. Heading a short way into the continent, he met some Iroquois Indians and brought back two sons of their chieftain to present to François I.

The next year he left on another royal-backed trip, departing with three ships from the Tour Solidor on the Rance. This time the crossing to the Détroit de Belle Ile lasted 40 days and he took back the two Indians. On 10 August 1535, they reached the estuary of a great river. It was the feast day of St Lawrence – so the river got its European name. The ships travelled inland down the estuary and Cartier dropped off the Indians at the place that would one day become Quebec City. He planted a cross there before travelling further upriver, planting another cross on the spot that would develop into Montréal.

The third important Cartier voyage took place in 1541. By this time, François I was intent on securing French royal possession of any foreign land that French sailors discovered. However, Cartier was not noble, and it required an aristocrat to be able to lay claim officially to colonial lands. On this expedition, Cartier was supposed to go as the explorer, Lord Roberval as the colonizer. But the impatient Cartier was ready to set sail 10 months before Roberval and left well before his superior. The Indians he met this time talked of another kingdom and a sea three moons away. Cartier must have thought that he was going to find glory; he reckoned that this was the fabled northwest passage to the Orient and even went as far as naming one turbulent stretch of river the Rapides de la Chine. He also thought he had discovered diamonds and precious stones. The cold weather coming in and the increasing hostility of the natives caused Cartier to return home. On the way back he crossed paths with Roberval.

Rather than being greeted triumphantly, Cartier found himself out of favour with the king. He had disobeyed his superior. He hadn't managed to discover a way to China. And he had returned with fool's gold and dud diamonds. But he had found what would prove a very important route to the Great Lakes, and new territories for the French colonizers. He took the Native American Indian word for 'little village' and gave it to the immense new lands he had come across – Canada.

16th century. However, on the guided tour you learn the story of Cartier's life. A short slide show with commentary in the first room helps put his achievements in the context of French exploration and colonial expansion more generally. Only fleeting attention is paid to the Native Americans who helped Cartier.

After his voyages, Cartier settled at Limoëlou. For a person whose life had such an impact on the history of the New World, the interior of his Old World manor is fairly basic. He enlarged it to make it into a comfortable family home with a smart stairtower. In the 19th century, a further extension was added. David MacDonald Stewart, a Canadian tobacco tycoon turned philanthropist, bought the farm from a local man in the 1970s, and it was turned into this museum to Cartier's memory. The rooms inside are furnished to look like the ones Cartier might have known. The tour ends with a second slide show explaining Cartier's Canadian voyages.

The Rochers Sculptés of Rothéneuf

The Rochers
Sculptés of
Rothéneuf
t 02 99 56 23 95;
open daily Easter–
Sept 9–7.30; rest of
year 10–5

These extensive, sculpted coastal rocks are very bizarre indeed. The crude, chaotic carvings were seemingly undertaken as therapy for a sickness-struck priest, the Abbé Fouré, who worked on them for some 25 years through the late 19th century. His characters are like cartoon figures in stone, telling the confusing story of the legendary Rothéneuf pirate family, their retinue, and their battles. The story's action apparently unfolds between the 16th century, when the Rothéneufs established their supremacy, and the Revolution, after which pirates from the Channel Islands wrought havoc on the family. The carnage attracted sleeping monsters from the bottom of the sea, who rose up to devour the bodies, including that of the last Rothéneuf. Beyond the Rochers Sculptés, the **Havre de Rothéneuf** provides a haven of calm, with fine, clean beaches.

Towards the Pointe du Grouin

The **Anse du Guesclin** with its long, sandy beach and its rock pools may look like an idyllic holiday spot now, but the island, cut off by high tides, has been fortified since the early Middle Ages. The ramparts date from 1757, put up to guard against attack by the British. This bay inspired the poet Théophile Briant and the poetic French singer Leo Ferré. The latter even came to live in the Fort du Guesclin for a time in the 1960s, accompanied by his pet monkey Pépée. The French author Colette particularly loved this stretch of Brittany's Emerald Coast, too (*see* box, below).

Continuing east, a handful of further dark rocky headlands stretch their rough fingers out into the sea before the Pointe du Grouin. A number of sandy beaches lie in the protected bays between them. The **Chapelle du Verger**, which overlooks the largest, contains a variety of *ex votos* of boats hanging from the ceiling; they were donated by fishermen who went off to Newfoundland and managed to make it back from the brink of disaster. From this spot, their wives would come and watch the fleet heading west on its way off to those dreaded expeditions.

07 Ille-et-Vilaine | St-Malo and the Clos Poulet: East of St-Malo

Erotic Orangeade

Colette, one of the most sensual writers in French literature, came frequently to stay on the coast between Cancale and St-Malo, at Roz-Ven east of the Pointe du Meinga. She set one of her most evocative and erotic books here, *Le Blé en herbe* (Corn on the Blade), a tale of a pure childhood summer friendship changing radically in nature as two adolescents discover their sexuality. Her prose is at its most caressing in *Le Blé en herbe*, and reading this book on a winter's day, you'll immediately be transported to summer on the north Breton coast, from the very first paragraph when Vinca goes off fishing in rock pools in her *'espadrilles racornies par le sel'* ('espadrilles curled by salt'). Be warned though that this is no innocent tale; Colette still has the power to shock even today.

Market Days East of St-Malo

Paramé: Wednesday and Saturday

Where to Stay and Eat East of St-Malo

(★) Le Beaufort >>

(★) Le Villefromoy >>

Towards Paramé and Rothéneuf ✉ 35400

Many smart hotels look out onto the great arc of a beach leading east from the walled city.

****Grand Hôtel des Thermes, 100 Blvd Hébert, t 02 99 40 75 00, www.thalassotherapie.com (€€€€€–€€€). The grandest option on the seafront, a big hotel with a thalassotherapy centre, pool and gym. Many of the spacious rooms have great views. Very elaborate dishes are served in its Art Deco dining room, but the cheapest menu isn't bad value. Closed middle part of Jan.

***Alba, 17 Rue des Dunes, t 02 99 40 37 18, www.hotelalba.com (€€€–€€). A delightful seaside hotel redone in very stylish manner, a few of its elegant rooms with terraces.

***Le Beaufort, 25 Chaussée du Sillon, t 02 99 40 99 99, www.hotel-beaufort.com (€€€€–€€). Another charming option, closer to the old city. Several of its rooms boast a private terrace looking out to sea.

***La Villefromoy, 7 Blvd Hébert, t 02 99 40 92 20, www.villefromoy.fr (€€€€–€€). The two villas making up this hotel have some delightful rooms. Closed mid-Nov–mid-Dec and early Jan–early Feb.

**Les Charmettes, 64 Blvd Hébert, t 02 99 56 07 31, www.hotel-les-charmettes.com (€€). Well located; a neat option with just a few rooms looking out to sea.

South of St-Malo

St-Malo's ferry port lies south of the old town. South beyond that you come to **Aleth-St-Servan**. Aleth has kept plenty of character of its own. On the St-Malo side, the **Bas Sablons** has a great, old-fashioned-looking beach. The area also has a big **marina**. The views onto St-Malo *intra-muros* make it worth a visit in itself.

On the tip of Aleth, the ruined 18th-century **fort** was originally built by English troops when they briefly occupied this point of land in 1758. This was also the location of the pre-Roman Celtic town. The Nazis turned it into a stronghold and now it's a camp site. The **Mémorial 1939–1945**, in a German blockhouse actually in the camp site, recalls St-Malo under Nazi occupation, and its liberation. Take a walk along the Promenade de la Corniche to appreciate the setting. Heading down from the tip, you pass by the ruins of Aleth's grand 10th-century cathedral.

Turn the corner to the west, and the awesome 14th-century **Tour Solidor** comes into view, a great medieval guard over the Rance. The **Musée International du Long-Cours Cap-Hornier** inside could tell the story of centuries of perilous voyages round Cape Horn in more exciting manner, but for the moment this remains an old-fashioned museum. The history of the feared sea route, undertaken by many brave to foolhardy Malouin sailors, is charted roughly chronologically floor by floor. On the ground floor, you're shown the limits of the world as it was known to western

Mémorial 1939–1945
www.st-malo.fr,
t 02 99 82 41 74; tours
July–Aug daily 10.15 and
11am, 2, 3, 4 and 5pm;
April–June and Sept
Tues–Sun 2.30, 3.15 and
4.30; Oct Tues–Sun 3.15
and 4pm for tours

The Musée International du Long-Cours Cap-Hornier
www.st-malo.fr,
t 02 99 40 71 58; open
April–Sept daily,
Oct–March Tues–Sun
10–12 and 2–6

Europeans from 1400 to 1600, and you can trace the various paths that were taken by the most significant explorers.

Of the great 18th-century navigators featured passing round the savage cape, you may be faintly familiar with Louis Antoine de Bougainville; the gorgeously gaudy bougainvillea plant was named after him, as was the largest of the Solomon Islands. He colonized the Falkland Islands for France – for a long time they were known as the Iles Malouines – and then saw to their transfer to Spain, hence the Spanish and Argentinian name for them, Las Malvinas. He took part in the American War of Independence against Britain, and Napoleon awarded him the Légion d'Honneur.

Old texts, maps, models of boats, photos of natives and the odd exotic object picked up on voyages make up the rest of the rather meagre débris meant to help build up a picture of further dramatic voyages. On one floor, paintings depict the huge waves that batter the cape, said to suffer storms on 300 days of the year. Out on the battlements, you can take in Dinard and St-Malo.

Grand Aquarium
www.aquarium-st-malo.com, t 02 99 21 19 00; open daily July and Aug 9.30–8 (mid-July–mid-Aug until 10pm); April–June and Sept 10–7; Oct–Mar 10–6; closed 3 weeks Jan

In St-Malo's southern suburbs, the **Grand Aquarium** is the city's massive out-of-town fish-gazing complex. You have to get through offputting layers of mass commercialization to reach its eight major aquaria, but they turn out to be very intelligently presented. They're also air-conditioned and dimly lit, making the place an attractive option on blinding hot summer days as well as rainy ones. The most sensational room is the *anneau*, a large ring of an aquarium – you can stand in the middle and feel as if you're caught in the midst of a shoal, watching the fish turn in endless circles.

Malouinières and the Rance Estuary

The great Malouin merchants of the Ancien Régime grew massively wealthy but kept a restrained appearance to their houses. As well as their sober mansions in town, they also built country retreats, known as *malouinières*, between the 1660s and the late 18th century. More than 100 survive, scattered around the Clos Poulet. They were most densely situated nearer to the city, as the merchants wanted to remain within comfortable distance of the port. Decoration was kept to a minimum on the outside even of the *malouinières* – in fact, many of them look pretty dour at first sight, not showy or flamboyant, but neat and practical, and they're normally hidden behind long stone walls. The merchant families enjoyed coming out into the country to find peace away from the stresses of their harrowing trading... and from the terrible stench of Ancien Régime St-Malo in summer.

Château du Bos
t 02 99 81 40 11

Perhaps the best-known *malouinière*, the very elegant 18th-century **Château du Bos**, was built for a branch of the Magon family on the back of vast profits from corsair expeditions. It has charming panelled rooms, and delectable grounds sloping down to the Rance. Recently it has been undergoing major restoration, so check in advance to see if it has reopened.

Château de Montmarin
t 02 99 88 58 79, www.domaine-de-montmarin.com; gardens only, April–Oct Sun–Fri 2–6

The exceptional *malouinière* of the Château de Montmarin was one of the last ones to be built, and it looks much more ornate and fancy than most. Unusually, it stands on the west bank of the Rance, just outside the Clos Poulet. Here, you really feel the exoticism that the Malouin sea voyages brought home. An impressive steep rockery garden has been laid out down by the river, where you can see the remnants of an old shipbuilding yard.

La Chipaudière
t 02 99 81 61 41, garden tours daily July–10 Aug 4pm, May, June and Sept by appointment

Parc de la Briantais
t 02 99 81 83 42; open daily July–Aug 9–7, Mar–June and Sept–Oct 2–6, Nov–Feb 2–5

Le Puits Sauvage
open for tours, June and Sept w/e, July–Aug daily 2–6

La Ville Bague
www.la-ville-bague.com, t 02 99 00 87; tours May–Sept Thurs–Tues 2.30 and 4pm

Recently, several further grand *malouinières* have opened their gardens to the public. For more on the Magon family of La Chipaudière, read about the Hôtel d'Asfeld in St-Malo above. You can also visit the Parc de la Briantais, its gardens, designed by the renowned Bühler, cascading down to the sea. Le Puits Sauvage is a more modest *malouinière*, but its owners have the distinction of being descendants of the original family that ordered the place. As well as having extensive gardens known for their orchard and vegetables, it conceals some interesting quirky features, including an exceptional collection of cacti and a horse pool.

La Ville Bague is a particularly beautiful *malouinière*. The pigeon house, chapel and outer walls date from the 17th century, but the main house was rebuilt in the early 18th century, and contains a wealth of antiques.

Exploring the Rance's east bank below St-Malo takes you to many further charming spots. The indented bays off the wide estuary were once exploited with salt pans and by tidal mills, traces of which you can still see. Birds of many species are attracted to the marshy areas.

Don't miss the very attractive Rance-side village of St-Suliac, with its pretty houses of speckled stone. The Breton saint, Suliac, founded a priory here in the 6th century. He features in a relatively recent statue added to the church's north porch, shown slaying a three-headed dragon which was supposedly terrorizing the area. You can see the saint's tomb and relics within. A separate oratory overlooks one side of the village, built to the Virgin by Newfoundland fishermen in thanks for bringing them back safely from a late-19th-century expedition. The village's sloping main street leads down to a long, peaceful riverside front, although in the tourist season, the sailing school brings an injection of life, as the protected estuary is a good place for beginners. Night fishing for sand eels in the Rance remains a popular local pastime.

Fort de St-Père-Marc-en-Poulet
t 02 99 58 34 40

Close to the village of Châteauneuf d'Ille-et-Vilaine lies the semi-ruined Fort de St-Père-Marc-en-Poulet. Normally, forts show off their mighty defences to intimidate the enemy, but this huge one (covering roughly the same area as St-Malo *intra-muros*) hides out in the countryside. It was built in 1777 to help protect the Clos Poulet from the English, who also tried to take St-Malo by land, and has remained virtually intact. German prisoners of war were kept here in the First World War, while the Nazis stored arms here in the Second. Up to 1985 the French army still used it as a munitions base, until the local parish bought it and tidied it up. Artists have been encouraged to exhibit here (Easter–Sept), and major concerts are occasionally put on in these curious surrounds.

Market Days South of St-Malo

St-Servan: Tuesday and Friday
Rocabey: Monday, Thursday and Saturday

Where to Stay and Eat South of St-Malo

(★) Le Saint-Placide >>

St-Servan ✉ 35400
This is the best area if you want to be close to the ferry terminal, and it has charm.

(★) Le Valmarin >

***Le Valmarin, 7 Rue Jean XXIII, **t** 02 99 81 94 76, *levalmarin@wanadoo.fr* (€€€–€€). A gracious, historic *malouinière* set its own shaded grounds, with stylish rooms, some very spacious, and old-style décor. *Closed Jan.*

***Korrigane, 39 Rue Le Pomellec, **t** 02 99 81 65 85, *www.st-malo-hotel-korrigane.com* (€€€). There's a *belle époque* feel to this smart 19th-century home with period furniture and its own garden, and extremely comfortable rooms.

(★) Château de Bonaban >>

***Manoir du Cunningham, 9 Place Monseigneur Duchesne, **t** 02 99 21 33 33, *www.st-malo-hotel-cunningham.com* (€€€€–€€€). A Normandy-style plush timberframe address, with the advantage that many of its rooms look out to sea. *Closed mid-Nov–mid-March.*

(★) L'Ascott >

***L'Ascott, 35 Rue du Chapitre, **t** 02 99 8189 93, *www.ascotthotel.com* (€€€–€€). Offers smart rooms in a lovely villa with garden set a bit away from the centre.

La Rance, 15 Quai Sébastopol, **t 02 99 81 78 63, *www.larancehotel.com* (€€). Close to the Tour Solidor, this small, traditional hotel has rooms overlooking the beautiful Rance estuary. *Closed mid-Nov–early Feb.*

L'Aleth, 2 Rue des Hauts-Sablons, **t 02 99 21 33 33, *www.st-malo-hotel-cunningham.com* (€). Cheerful, good-value option, some rooms with sea views. It has a bar.

Le Saint-Placide, 6 Place du Poncel, **t** 02 99 81 70 73 (€€). A cosy establishment on a leafy square a few steps from the sea, offering lovely variations on classic Breton dishes.

L'Atre, Esplanade du Commandant Menguy, **t** 02 99 81 68 39 (€€€–€€). In lovely location by the beach, a popular little restaurant much appreciated for its delightful dishes, served in minimalist surrounds. *Closed Wed, and early Jan–early Feb.*

Le Bulot, 13 Quai Sébastopol, **t** 02 99 81 07 11 (€€). Tiny restaurant with lovely terrace, great for a very pleasing meal. *Closed Sun eve.*

La Gouesnière ✉ 35350

***Château de Bonaban, 1 Rue Rapheal Folligné, **t** 02 99 58 24 50, *www.chateaudebonaban.com* (castle rooms €€€€€–€€€; manor rooms €€). This spectacular 17th-century château sits on a hill with views, above its hamlet south of La Gouesnière, in the centre of the Clos Poulet. The rooms in the castle are absolutely sumptuous, but there are cheaper ones at the coach house. The restaurant (€€€–€€; *closed Wed*) offers grand dining.

Dinard and the Coast to St-Briac-sur-Mer

Although very different in feel and history, and although separated from each other by the broad Rance estuary, Dinard and St-Malo are very close. The most joyous way of travelling to and fro between the two is by the little ferries that link them, although you also get fine views along the Rance going by road, crossing the estuary via its ground-breaking tidal electricity dam.

At Dinard, the gorgeous beaches and winding coastal paths watched over by grand villas are the highlights. They continue into St-Lunaire and St-Briac-sur-Mer, practically merged into one now. The rocky islands scattered so picturesquely just out to sea, with colourful sails weaving in and out of them, make this one of the most pleasing stretches of coast in Brittany. Royalty, aristocracy and artists once flocked to Dinard. The British and American connections are deep rooted and an English-speaking community still thrives here.

Dinard

✪ Dinard

We have one Mrs Faber to thank for Dinard. She settled here in the 1850s, on a near-virgin coast, and was soon joined by a few British and American families. The trend was set for holidays in this beautiful location. By the turn of the century, Dinard had developed into one of the most fashionable resorts in the world. European royals swanned around town, as did the ultra-wealthy from many continents, together with the likes of the home-grown Cognac-Hennessey family. These visitors built palatial villas along the rocky cliffs above the protected beaches – 400 are now listed historic buildings. The place attracted artists, too, notably Picasso, who painted a few of his most wildly exuberant pictures here during the course of two summers; to go by them, you might think he wasn't too impressed by the women he saw at Dinard, or that the sea air quite turned his head – these were certainly some of his most deliberately provocative and grotesque images of what don't look like members of a fairer sex, but deformed female monsters. Dinard may have lost some of its lustre and its power to attract the glitterati, but it remains a charming resort.

A Tour of Dinard

The main tourist attention focuses on the **Plage de l'Ecluse** and its promenade, but this isn't the finest part of the town. Several of the grand buildings that once watched over this beach have been truncated or destroyed. There is action aplenty, though, with the

Getting to Dinard

Dinard has a small **airport** linked to London Stansted, Birmingham, Bristol and East Midlands (Nottingham) by low-cost Ryanair flights (*see* p.67).

casino (containing a fine restaurant with fabulous views), the swimming pools, and the beach itself, backed by lines of changing booths. In summer, fresh blue and white striped changing tents are set up on the sands.

Place M. Joffre is where everything collides, roughly halfway along the beach. Hotels, restaurants and stalls cluster around the square. A statue paying homage to Alfred Hitchcock blew down in recent times, but Dinard still holds an annual festival of British cinema (in October). In front of the square, towards the sea, you may spot one or two of the ten panels scattered along Dinard's coast, telling of its history and famous visitors.

From the Plage de l'Ecluse, you look out onto the splendid, eccentric neo-Gothic villas of the Pointe du Moulinet to the east and the Pointe de la Malouine to the west. Islands lie out to sea, notably the Ile de Cézembre. Whether you walk east or west, the coastal path is fabulous. The tourist office can provide interesting free English brochures written by experts on aspects of Dinard to appreciate on either walk. It can also give you details on the excellent **sporting facilities**, including four sailing schools on different beaches, and clubs for kayaking, diving, or horse-riding.

Head round the **Pointe du Moulinet** and St-Malo comes stunningly into view. Beyond one of the landing stages for the ferry service to St-Malo is the **Promenade du Clair de Lune**; on July and August evenings (from 9.30pm) the exotic plants along here are lit up in gaudy colours, and recorded music is piped into the air, the theme changing each night, from classical to jazz, to traditional Breton. The path leads down to the wonderfully well-protected **Plage du Prieuré**, with charming restaurants set around it. There are now two **companies running boat-trips across to St-Malo**, April to October, from this side of town, the **Compagnie Corsaire** and **Les Vedettes de St-Malo**.

Climb steep Rue Faber to reach the neo-Gothic **British–American church of St Bartholomew**; with its small palm garden, it provides a pretty haven in the summer and is a reminder, all year, of English ways, with its embroidered kneelers and flower-arranging rota.

Further back from the beaches, the **Villa Eugénie** stands out with its four corner towers, one of the grandest of all Dinard's grand holiday homes. It was built in 1868 and carries the name of Napoleon III's capricious wife. Rumour had it that the imperial family was set to spend the summer here and officially inaugurate the resort. The excitement was short-lived; the story goes that the preposterously fussy couple fell out over a dog the empress wanted to bring with her but that the emperor couldn't abide – what's certain is that things weren't going well in the marriage. Eugénie never came to Dinard, flouncing off to make Biarritz all the rage instead. The villa has been undergoing a major make-over to be reborn as a **Centre d'Interprétation du Patrimoine**. When this opens, you'll be able to learn in detail here about how the resort and its villas grew up.

Back at the main Plage de l'Ecluse, the coastal path leading west round the **Pointe de la Malouine** to St-Enogat makes for the most unforgettable of all Dinard's walks. The narrow path takes you under rocks and grand villas to beautiful sandy beaches. The views out to sea, the waters strewn with reefs and sails, are superlative.

Head southeast to the Rance and from close to the dam, you can embark on an enjoyable cruise down the stunningly indented **Rance estuary** with **Les Croisières Chateaubriand**. You can even eat onboard the company's smart, wood-clad boat.

Les Croisières Chateaubriand
t 02 99 46 44 40, www.chateaubriand. com; lunch and dinner possible

The road over the **Rance** is built on top of a ground-breaking **dam**, about which you can learn at the visitor centre of the **EDF-Usine Marémotrice de la Rance**.

EDF-Usine Marémotrice de la Rance
t 02 99 16 37 14, www.edf.fr/html/en/ decouvertes/voyage/ usine/retour-usine.html; open July–Aug daily 10–6, April–June and Sept daily 10–1 and 2–6, Oct Fri–Sun 10–1 and 2–6; other school holidays Wed–Sun 10–1 and 2–6

There have been tidal mills here since the 12th century, but in the 1960s, a unique tidal power plant was constructed to make the most of the exceptionally strong tidal surge. Its turbines derive enough energy from the waters to provide electricity to 250,000 households. Interactive displays and a film tell you more about this renewable energy, and the efforts that have been made to preserve the local ecosystem since the dam started operating in 1967.

St-Lunaire

Continuing west along the coast, Debussy was apparently inspired to compose at St-Lunaire, giving some indication of the magic of this place. The resort attracted artists and speculators aplenty in the late 19th century. In fact it was a massively wealthy Haitian, Scylla Laraque, who decided to create this resort from scratch, ordering the building of the grandiose block of the Grand Hôtel that still dominates the main beach.

For the truly smart Belle Epoque set that Laraque wished to attract, his architects also designed a series of extravagant villas by the **Pointe du Décollé**, west of the Grand Hôtel beach. The rocky point has been marred by modern restaurants, but the views in either direction are worth the detour. The old **church of St-Lunaire** doesn't go back as far as the 6th century, when Lunaire hit the shore (see box, opposite), but it has preserved its 11th-century Romanesque nave. Look out for St Lunaire's supposed tomb, a Gallo-Roman sarcophagus with a 14th-century effigy on top.

How a Saint Cuts His Way Through Fog

As the name of the resort of St-Lunaire indicates, a Breton saint got here well before the property developers and holiday villas. The religious man supposedly landed in the 6th century; being a saint, however, it had to be by slightly unorthodox means. The legend goes that dense fog greeted Lunaire as he approached the Armorican coast with his 70 or so companions. Impatient to find land on which to settle, he took out his sword and literally cut through the fog; the horizon suddenly opened up before him. You're supposed to be able to make out his sandal marks where he stepped on to dry land among the rocks of the Pointe du Décollé.

St-Lunaire has four **beaches** in all. The small ones to the east are well sheltered, while the large Plage de Longchamp to the west attracts windsurfers. At the western tip of this beach you come to the **Pointe de la Garde-Guérin**. The moorland here plunges dramatically into the sea. From this spot, in 1758, the local guards witnessed the landing of some 10,000 English troops in the Anse de la Fosse. This army had been sent on an expedition to destroy that British *bête noire*, St-Malo. The campaign ended with the disastrous English defeat at St-Cast.

Dinard golf course, one of the oldest and most famous in France in fact straddles St-Lunaire and St-Briac. Created from 1887 to 1892 and spectacularly located above the sea, it has long attracted wealthy Brits and Americans. The Germans mined it most inconsiderately in the Second World War, but it has long since regained its renown. The dunes of the **Plage du Port-Hue** below are well protected. The beach looks out to the islands of Dame-Jouanne and Agot.

St-Briac-sur-Mer

The coast all around St-Briac is cluttered with villas, while the village itself looks on to the Frémur estuary. The delightful **estuary beaches** here are provided with beach huts, and otherworldly rockscapes emerge at low tide in front of them. In the old fishermen's village, go in search of the odd stone-carved mackerel on the **church**. Mackerel, when they came into local waters, announced the arrival of spring and were considered a sign of good fortune. The church's ornate granite belltower displays the arms of a local noble family, the Pontbriands. Inside, the Irish saint Briac, who is said to have founded a religious community here in the Dark Ages, is depicted in the modern stained-glass windows.

Painters were attracted to St-Briac when it developed into a resort at the end of the 19th century. In the 1880s, Auguste Renoir, Emile Bernard and Paul Signac all came. The last introduced Henri Rivière to the village; Rivière then executed a series of much-loved woodcuts, inspired by Japanese models, depicting scenes from this part of the Breton coast.

de la Vallée »

(i) Dinard >
2 Blvd Féart,
t *02 99 46 94 12,*
www.ot-dinard.com

Printania »

**Reine
Hortense >**

Didier Méril

Market Days in and around Dinard

Dinard: Tuesday
St-Enogat: Wednesday in July and Aug
St-Lunaire: Sunday April–Sept
St-Briac: Friday all year; Monday July and Aug

Where to Stay and Eat in and around Dinard

Dinard ✉ 35800

****Grand Hôtel Barrière**, 46 Ave George V, **t** 02 99 88 26 26, *www.lucienbarriere.com* (€€€€). A large, fashionable establishment high above the Rance promenade, looking across to St-Malo. Rooms are elegant, with all mod cons. There are two restaurants, the 333 Café (€), with generous terrace, open for light lunches only, and Le Blue B (€€€€) open dinner only. Pool and cocktail bar. *Closed late Nov–mid-March.*

***Reine Hortense**, 19 Rue de la Malouine, **t** 02 99 46 54 31, *www.villa-reine-hortense.com* (€€€€€–€€€€). A grand old villa perched just above the beach, with refined rooms named after queens, to put you in the spirit. Many have sea views.

***Roche-Corneille**, 4 Rue Georges Clemenceau, **t** 02 99 46 14 47, *www.dinard-hotel-roche-corneille.com* (€€€€–€€). Elegant rooms, but without sea views, in another of Dinard's fine listed villas. The restaurant (€€€–€€; dinner only; *closed Mon, and mid-Nov–March, exc main hols*) serves classic dishes.

***Novotel Thalassa**, Ave Château Hébert, **t** 02 99 16 78 10, *www.novotel dinard.com* (€€€€–€€€). A monster of a health-break hotel with splendid sea views from above the rocks at the western end of the beach of St-Enogat west of Dinard. Indoor heated seawater pool, saunas, jacuzzis

and gym. The restaurant (€€€–€€) offers both gourmet and dieters' fare. Attached to the establishment, **Les Villas de la Falaise**, **t** 02 99 16 78 00, offer more personalized, attractive seaside rooms.

*****Emeraude Plage**, 1 Blvd Albert 1er, **t** 02 99 46 15 79, *www.hotel emeraudeplage.com* (€€€€€–€€; the top price is for deluxe seafront rooms). This welcoming hotel close to the central beach has been completely renovated. The lovely rooms on each floor follow a different decorative theme.

***de la Vallée**, 6 Ave Georges V, **t** 02 99 46 94 00, *www.hoteldela vallee* (€€€–€€). In an enchanting location beside the sea, this hotel has been totally revamped, gaining a third star. Some of its crisp rooms have fabulous views. The restaurant (€€€), serving seafood and other dishes, is excellent.

Printania, 5 Ave Georges V, **t** 02 99 46 13 07, *www.printaniahotel.com* (€€€). A wonderful, old-fashioned hotel lapped by the waves. Many rooms here have fine views towards St-Malo, although some may be in need of a bit of attention. The restaurant has traditional Breton decorations and offers traditional fare. *Closed mid-Nov to mid-March.*

Le Balmoral, 26 Rue du Maréchal Leclerc, **t** 02 99 46 16 97, *www.hotels-balmoral.com* (€€). This hotel in the heart of town has undergone a complete makeover recently thanks to the young couple who run it. The rooms are excellent, mixing modern and traditional touches, and with air-conditioning. Some have balconies.

L'Hôtel du Parc des Tourelles, 20 Ave Edouard VII, **t** 02 99 46 11 39, *www.hotelduparc.org* (€€). Not glamorous, but with a touch of old-fashioned charm.

Didier Méril, 1 Place du Général de Gaulle, **t** 02 99 46 95 74, *www.restaurant-didier-meril.com* (€€€€–€€). This beautifully located place looking onto Plage du Prieuré has six lovely rooms, some with splendid sea views, but it's best-known for its restaurant (€€€€–€€), which has all the ingredients for a fabulous seaside meal. *Closed mid-Nov–mid-Dec.*

Some of Dinard's best restaurants are at the hotels listed above, including the excellent Didier Méril.

L'Escale à Corto, 12 Ave George V, **t** 02 99 46 78 57 (€€). An atmospheric seafood restaurant near the sea. *Closed lunch and Mon eve.*

La Gonelle, 5 Ave Georges V, **t** 02 99 16 40 47 (€€€–€€). Tempting waterside oyster and seafood bar with lovely terrace. *Closed winter.*

La Passerelle du Clair de Lune, Promenade du Clair de Lune, **t** 02 99 16 96 37 (€€€–€€). With another beautiful waterside terrace, serving more diverse world cuisine. *Closed Sun eve, Mon and Tues lunch, plus Jan.*

du Roy, 9 Blvd Féart, **t** 02 99 46 10 57 (€). The classic large, busy, central Dinard crêperie.

Le Dauphin, 5 Bld Féart, **t** 02 99 46 76 83 (€). A simple, good-value crêperie.

Saint-Lunaire ✉ 35800

Le Décollé, 1 Pointe du Décollé, **t** 02 99 46 01 70 (€€€–€). This restaurant has great views to accompany the good seafood, best savoured on the wonderful terrace. *Closed Mon and Tues exc July–Aug, and mid-Nov–Jan.*

Pleurtuit ✉ 35730

★★★Le Manoir de la Rance, Château de Jouvente, 7km south of Dinard down the Rance, **t** 02 99 88 53 76, *www.chateauxhotels.com* (€€€€–€€). A 19th-century manor with beautiful views onto the estuary, private gardens and large rooms.

Le Jersey Lillie, 51 Rue de la Cale de Jouvente, **t** 02 99 88 51 80, *www.jerseylilliejouvente.com* (€€–€). In a delightful riverside spot below the Manoir de la Rance, many rooms enjoying the views. It's a lovely spot to eat, too.

St-Briac ✉ 35800

Hotel de la Houle, 14 Boulevard de la Houle, **t** 02 99 88 32 17, *www.hoteldelahoule.com* (€€€–€). Great atmosphere, with its ornately decorated rooms, the more luxurious ones in the main house, the simpler ones in the annexe. *Closed Nov–Feb.*

Le Moulin de Rochegoude B&B, **t** 02 99 88 03 10 or 06 25 80 15 87, *www.lemoulinderochegoude.fr* (€€€). An 18th-century mill on the Frémur estuary, with four big, stylish rooms.

Les Copains d'Abord, 7 Grande Rue, **t** 02 99 88 04 44 (€€€). Fine cuisine you can enjoy on the terrace.

ⓘ **St-Briac ≫**
49 Grande Rue,
***t** 02 99 88 32 47,*
www.saint-briac.com

ⓘ **St-Lunaire ≫**
Blvd du Général de Gaulle, ***t** 02 99 46 31 09,*
www.saint-lunaire.com

The Bay of the Mont St-Michel

📍 **Mont St-Michel**

The greater part of the fabulous Baie du Mont St-Michel lies within Breton territory, although the wondrous island monastery in the east stands just within Normandy. Forget the regional boundaries – we cover both bay and mount in the following touring sections. The whole Bay of the Mont St-Michel is one of those places of rare beauty classified as a world heritage site by UNESCO. It's completely flat, which is why the monastery appears all the more imposing, visible from such long distances.

Cancale

Cancale greets the morning sun in its stunning location, looking right across the Bay of the Mont St-Michel from its western cliffside seat. Part port, part resort, its name is synonymous with

Getting to and around the Bay of Mont St-Michel

If you don't have a car, you can use the **bus** services from St-Malo to explore this region (*see* St-Malo, p.87, for coach company details).

oysters in northern Brittany. In front of the **Port de la Houle**, oysters packed tight into their bags grow until they're big enough to be eaten by the tourists packed tight as sardines in the resort's very many restaurants. Cancale is a victim of its own success in the main holiday period. The problem is exacerbated because the portside simply consists of a narrow strip of houses backing on to the cliffs. But once settled among the crowds, gazing past the flat-bottomed oyster boats and across the vast bay, it's hard not to be enchanted by the glory of the site. On good days, you may just be able to make out the Mont St-Michel, a speck on the horizon. The youthful race down to the beach to swim, sail or kayak from here.

The easiest way to get closer to the oysters beyond the restaurant plate is by visiting the small oyster stalls set up in a wonderfully picturesque waterside location under the little lighthouse on the northern jetty. Or there's Chez Mazo, a specialist oyster shop the other, southern end of the port, open 7/7. Then again, on the sloping one-way road down to the harbour from the south of Cancale you can visit the **Ferme Marine**. The tour of this oyster farm gives you a quite detailed insight into the history of Cancale's oysters, including the French court's profitable predilection for them, and how the supposedly aphrodisiac shellfish are reared today.

Ferme Marine
www.ferme-marine.com, t 02 99 89 69 99; open mid-Feb–June and mid-Sept–Oct Mon–Fri, tours in French at 3pm; July–mid-Sept daily, tours in French at 1 and 3pm, in English at 2pm

In the times when the oyster-fishing season was firmly set, the first day of the new season was a time of great excitement in Cancale. The light local bisquines sailing boats that the local fishermen used from the 19th century onwards would rush out to sea to drag up oysters in their nets. Today, a limited number of visitors can go on trips on a *bisquine, La Cancalaise,* that still operates. You have to join its **association** first, however, which costs around 60 euros.

La Cancalaise association
t 02 99 89 77 87

The main livelihood for the men of Cancale came for a long time from joining the fishing fleets that went off for many months to catch cod off Newfoundland. The Cancalaises, the women of the port, gained a reputation for being tough creatures, as they had to run their own communities for much of the year and to deal with the all too frequent tragic news of deaths at sea. They are honoured in a quite cleverly combined sculpture and fountain in the **upper town**, a pleasant place, if eclipsed by the glamour of the port today.

Jeanne Jugan, born into a typical Cancale fishing family, would create the charitable order of the Petites Soeurs des Pauvres to look after the elderly without means of support. Her order spread around the world, and in 1982 she was beatified by the pope. The **Maison Natale de Jeanne Jugan** in the upper town has been turned into a museum to her memory, interesting too for its 18th-century furniture.

Maison Natale de Jeanne Jugan
open by appointment,
t 02 23 15 14 22

Many shipowners built their smart houses on Cancale's heights in the 18th century. The curvaceous-roofed church dedicated to St Méen, the possible founder of the original village, has been converted into the **Musée des Arts et Traditions Populaires**. Here, the harrowing fishing expeditions to Newfoundland are recalled, as well as other old Cancale customs.

Musée des Arts et Traditions Populaires
t 02 99 89 79 32; open July and Aug Mon 2.30–6.30, Tues–Sun 10–12 and 2.30–6.30; June and Sept Fri–Mon 2.30–6.30

Two rocks lie out to sea just to the north of Cancale, the **Rocher de Cancale** and the **Ile des Rimains**, the latter fortified after Cancale came under bombardment by the British fleet in 1779. Seek out the pretty little bays before the Pointe du Grouin. Just before this dramatic headland, **Port-Mer** boasts one of the first properly sandy beaches along Brittany's north coast. Sitting at one of the bars and restaurants here, you can admire the grandeur of the Bay of the Mont St-Michel.

From the rocky **Pointe du Grouin**, you get spectacular views both east and west. This headland closes off the Bay of the Mont St-Michel on its western side. **L'Ile des Landes**, with its scaly dragon's back, adds mystery to the foreground as you look across towards Normandy. It's been turned into a bird reserve by the Breton Society for the Protection of the Natural Environment (the SEPNB), which has adapted a Nazi bunker on the mainland into an information centre. Great cormorants particularly appreciate the Ile des Landes, and you may manage to spot the colony of dolphins that comes fishing for mackerel off the point in summer. When the tide is out, you can climb down to the grotto that looks out onto the Iles des Landes and the **Herpin lighthouse** out to sea.

From Cancale to Cherrueix

Descend from Cancale to a string of bay-side communities between **St-Méloir-des-Ondes** and **Le Vivier-sur-Mer**, and quite a culinary stretch of coast. The road hugs the flat, rather bleak edge of the bay. The many **windmills** along the way have stopped turning, being transformed to other uses, one for example serving as an art gallery, another as a beer shop. The fertile fields just behind the coast produce a wealth of vegetables, roadside stalls selling the produce, including tresses of garlic. The vast mudflats revealed across the bay at low tide have also proved highly productive, for rearing oysters and mussels, again for sale in many roadside outlets. This is not a stretch of coast for beaches or swimming, but **Hirel** has a small stretch of sand.

Not many visitors know, or even notice, that the Breton side of the Bay of the Mont St-Michel boasts an extraordinary forest – of wooden posts, or **bouchots**, on which the mussels are cultivated. Taking a tractor out onto the muddy sands at low tide and then walking through the thick gunge among the hundreds of thousands of wooden pillars makes for an unforgettable experience (*see* below). The best place to sign up for such a tour is the **Maison de la Baie du Mont St-Michel at Le Vivier-sur-Mer**. As well as offering information on the bay, they put on walking tours into the western, Breton part, and the guides can speak English.

From **Cherrueix** you can also take a highly enjoyable tractor ride with **Le Train Marin** out into the bay to see this amazing sandscape where the mussels really grow on trees. Again, an expert guide leads you on a fascinating walk. Cherrueix is the nearest Breton coastal community to the Mont St-Michel, although it still lies some 30km from the magical sight by road. From the village's protective seawall, you can make out the mount very clearly on good days. The **windmill** here has been converted to create the **Maison du Terroir** (*opens 2009*), explaining all the produce that comes from these exceptional fertile lands. The little 17th-century chapel of Ste-Anne stands isolated on the dyke east of the long-drawn-out village. From the chapel, keen walkers can follow the GR34 path across the polders to the mount. Just up the slope from the coast, at **Roz-sur-Couesnon** on the Breton–Norman border, the **Maison des Polders** tells the story of how men conquered these marshy lands. This new museum is set in a splendid, renovated manor typical of these parts.

Maison de la Baie du Mont St-Michel at Le Vivier-sur-Mer
t 02 99 48 84 38,
www.maison-baie.com;
tours available in school hols and at weekends, but the centre itself is open year-round

Le Train Marin
t 02 99 48 84 88,
www.train-marin.com

The Bay's Measurements, Mussels and Other Vital Statistics

Can you picture 50,000 very muddy football pitches laid out side by side? That is apparently how many could be fitted into the 25,000 hectares of the Baie du Mont St-Michel. Geographically, the bay stretches from the Pointe du Grouin above Cancale to the Pointe de Champeaux in Normandy. The waters withdraw as much as 25 kilometres with big tides. The bay has the fastest-moving tides in Europe, coming in at around 9 kph. Every year tragedies occur because some people don't heed the warnings about these treacherous waters.

What marine life might you see on a trip into the bay? Certainly artificially grown mussels galore. The flat oysters, the *plates*, are native to the area, but now the much more viable concave *creuses* are shipped in from far afield. Cockles, razorshells or razorclams, green crabs, orange sponges, and red and green sea lettuce are all common. You may come across transparent langoustines wriggling in the mud, or even lobsters in their earliest stages.

Foreign invaders, shells called *crépidules*, are all too prolific, causing a big problem now. As well as gulls, you can spot teal, sandpipers and crested lapwing; in winter thousands of geese stop in the bay.

Farmers have been exploiting the bay for a long time, as well as protecting themselves from it. The first dykes date as far back as the 12th century, built to guard the fishing villages on the water's edge and the agricultural lands behind. On a tractor tour taking you several kilometres out into the bay, you're shown some of the old fishing methods, using fences made out of interlocking branches. Then the mussel-farming is explained. It began here in 1954. The families who started this trade have planted a staggering 300 kilometres or so of wooden pillars in the mud.

Moules de bouchot is a description you'll see on many restaurant menus in Brittany, generally taken as a sign of good-quality mussels. A *bouchot* is, in fact, technically, 110 posts planted in a line 100 metres long. The mussels are brought up first in the Charente-Maritime on France's western Atlantic coast. The *naissains*, or spats, are transported here after a few months and attach themselves to the oak supports. They dine on plankton and are left to mature undisturbed for 14 to 22 months. They're only harvested once they've grown to 3.5cm or more. Leviathans, part-tractor, part-boat, drive out into the bay to pick the mussels with their monstrous claws. Up to 15,000 tonnes can be harvested each year. The mussels from the bay are highly regarded and local farmers were recompensed with the granting of *appellation d'origine contrôlée* status for their produce in 2006, a prestigious indicator of quality.

To Mont-Dol and Dol-de-Bretagne

I dwell among scorpions, surrounded by a double wall of bestiality and perfidy.

Baudry of Bourgueil, Archbishop of Dol from 1107 to 1130

South from Le Vivier-sur-Mer, the additional startling granite hill emerging from the flat landscape is the **Mont Dol**, once an island surrounded by sand and sea like the Mont St-Michel, but now stranded on dry land. Go to the top for fantastic views. The landscapes at its feet are peacefully bucolic, but picnickers and photographers take over the summit in summer. Palaeolithic remains of mammoths, deer and other creatures were found in digs here, while 19th-century Christianity left its mark more obviously – a tall white Virgin stands at the top of the narrow-staired tower, which visitors fight to climb for a marginally better view.

In the Footsteps of Satan and St Michael

The tale goes that St Michael was called upon to fight Satan on the Mont-Dol. The marks of their legendary struggle can supposedly be seen in some of the rocks... if you have a good imagination – the devil's claws, the devil's seat and the devil's hole are among the evocative names they've been given. There's also the imprint of St Michael's foot, left behind when he took an almighty leap back onto the Mont St-Michel after his victory. The chapel on the Mont Dol contains a stained-glass window in honour of survivors of the First World War who made a special pilgrimage here.

Dol-de-Bretagne looks like an innocent little tourist and shopping town now, so it's hard to imagine this place as the den of debauchery described by Baudry of Bourgueil. It became the seat of one of the first set of Breton cathedrals founded when British immigrants came across the Channel in the Dark Ages to settle and spread Celtic Christianity (*see* box, opposite).

Breton tradition maintains that it was in Dol that Nomenoë had himself crowned the first Breton king in 850. Serious historians now say there's no firm evidence that this crowning took place, but Nomenoë's choice of new Breton bishops is attested, a move that secured the Breton Church a good degree of independence, for a time.

Dol remained a significant religious centre right up to the Revolution, and the town's merchants profited, as you can see from the medieval buildings along the main street. The cathedral was an important halt on the **Tro Breizh**, the major pilgrimage route around the cathedrals of the seven founding Celtic Christian saints of Brittany. At the end of Dol's long line of bishops, Monseigneur de Hercé was shot during the Revolution, and in 1801 the city lost its bishopric for good.

So close to the border with Normandy, Dol suffered wave after wave of sieges in the Middle Ages. William the Conqueror, Duke of Normandy as well as King of England, had a go at it three times without success, the Bretons here backed by the might of the French Carolingians. King John of England's troops burned down the Romanesque cathedral in 1204. Much later, the Catholic, royalist, anti-Revolutionary Chouans put up a fierce resistance to the Republican army in Dol.

As its cliff edge indicates, Dol once stood right by the sea. Some historians claim that the waves still lapped at the city's feet as late as the 10th century. Now it overlooks the Marais de Dol, the marshlands reclaimed when the water retreated. Dol's severe, miserable hulk of a **cathedral of St-Samson** sulks to one side of town, looking out mournfully over the Marais. The building, set in rather barren surrounds, looks so defensive that it doesn't even come as much of a surprise to find what look like crenellations on the north side of the choir. The main façade is unprepossessing, with virtually no decoration. However, one ugly gargoyle stands

A Welsh Samson Leaves his Mark on Dol

Dol's Christian seeds were sown, it's said, by a 6th-century Welshman called Samson. Something of his life is supposedly known from an 11th-century manuscript that survived down the centuries. According to the story, the young Samson was sent to the great south Welsh abbey of Llantwit Major, run by Illtut. Educated in the ways of the Celtic Church, he fast acquired enviable knowledge, to the extent that Illtut's nephews became so jealous of him that he was forced to leave.

Samson went on to become the very model of a Celtic Christian missionary, travelling far and wide to spread the gospel. He first went to Caldey Island in Wales, where he became abbot. Then he crossed to Ireland and reformed a monastery there. After that, he spent a period as a hermit living close to the Severn River, before taking on the position of abbot in a nearby monastery.

The restless evangelizer continued on to Cornwall. There he settled for a longer period. His disciples included Austell, Mewan and Winnow, important figures in the Cornish Church, while one of the Isles of Scilly is named after him. Like many other Welsh evangelizers of the time, his ceaseless quest took him on to Brittany. The Breton side of this Samson's story has it that he was donated land by the local lord of Dol-de-Bretagne by way of thanks for curing the nobleman's wife of leprosy and exorcizing demons that had been plaguing the man's daughter.

out, said by the townspeople to be a likeness of the detested King John, whose men destroyed the previous cathedral.

On the south side, a Flamboyant Gothic porch sticks out incongruously, covered with white panels carved with low-relief sculptures that were only added in the early 19th century. The smaller neighbouring porch dates from the 13th and 14th centuries; its central column is decorated with hearts, in a playful pun on the name of one bishop, Etienne Coeuret – *coeur* being the French for heart.

As you enter the cathedral, striking 13th-century stained glass adds colour to the distant apse – the edifice is almost 100 metres in length. The nave's pillars are typical of Norman Gothic style. The choir was completed around 1280. The stained glass in its main window, the oldest such glass to have survived in Brittany, is admirable, if much restored. Try to see the ornate 14th-century choir stalls with their carved heads. In the transept, the sumptuous tomb of Bishop Thomas James counts as one of the earliest Renaissance-style works to be found in Brittany, but it was executed by Italians working in the Loire Valley.

Médiévalys
www.medievalys.com,
t 02 99 48 35 30; open
all year, daily 10–7

Playing on Dol's medieval legacy, **Médiévalys** by the cathedral offers a lively look at the Middle Ages, re-creating a period interior, and covering how the mighty cathedrals were constructed. There's also a section dealing with the Knights Templars, who became hugely wealthy and powerful through crusading and banking, until they got their comeuppance.

The **Grande Rue des Stuarts**, by contrast with the cathedral, looks cheerful, lined with some surprisingly old and quirky medieval houses. Look out for characteristic arches of the Romanesque period, now turned into delightful shopfronts. Victor Hugo compared this main street to a wide river fed by the little streams of its sidestreets. A new **Centre Culturel** opened in 2008, putting on

Away with the Fairies – the Allée Couverte de la Maison-es-Feins

As they can, a fairy's herd of cows caused damage to the fields of a local farmer. By way of apology, the fairy offered him a loaf that would never run out and never go stale, as long as he didn't reveal how he'd come by it. After enjoying the advantages of this magic gift for many years, the farmer let slip the secret, and the bread turned to stone. Some loaf! The tomb measures around 11 metres in length and is covered by seven weighty stones. It was probably made around 2500 BC. Pairs of breasts, considered a sign that an Earth Mother was worshipped here, were carved in relief in the granite chamber at the entrance, although many have been mutilated.

a monthly programme of concerts, plays and folklore events, so check what's on. The cinema caters to English speakers, showing a number of films in the original English-language version.

Just south of town, the **Menhir de Champ-Dolent** is one of the most impressive neolithic standing stones in Brittany, its pinkish granite form rising to almost 10 metres. Legend claims that this rock fell from the skies to separate two feuding brothers engaged in bloody battle. The menhir is slowly sinking into the ground; when the stone disappears, the world will end, so the typical Breton conclusion goes.

Musée de la Paysannerie
t 02 99 48 04 04;
open July and Aug
daily 10–7

Southwest of Dol and east of Baguer-Morvan, the Musée de la Paysannerie recalls the rural Breton life of the past, with displays of traditional crafts and old agricultural implements.

A bit further southwest, the **Abbaye du Tronchet** presents a bucolic picture of 17th-century monasticism, but the place is now in large part a hotel (see p.122). Just beyond, the **Forêt du Mesnil** makes for a deeply shaded, dark setting for the **Allée Couverte de la Maison-es-Feins or Tressé**, a neolithic tomb whose existence used to be attributed to fairies (*see* box, above).

Market Days around the Bay of Mont St-Michel

Cancale: Sunday; oyster market daily
St-Méloir-des-Ondes: Thursday
Dol-de-Bretagne: Saturday

Where to Stay and Eat around the Bay of Mont St-Michel

Cancale ✉ 35260

⭐ **Le Querrien** >>

ⓘ **Cancale**
44 Rue du Port,
t 02 99 89 63 72,
www.cancale-
tourisme.fr

⭐ **Maisons de Bricourt** >

****Maisons de Bricourt**, 1 rue Duguesclin, **t** 02 99 89 64 76, *www.maisons-de-bricourt.com* (€€€€€–€€€). One of France's greatest, most exciting chefs, Olivier Roellinger, has opened several exquisite establishments in and around Cancale over the years. His fabulous restaurant (€€€€) is at 1 Rue Duguesclin, where he cooks up a storm with his amazing inventive concoctions mixing spices with the finest ingredients. Nearby Les Rimains has just a few exclusive rooms in an enchanting setting high above the sea – see the Château de Richeux opposite for the other rooms and restaurant. *Closed mid-Dec–mid-March.*

***Le Querrien**, 7 Quai Duguay-Trouin, **t** 02 99 89 64 56, *www.le-querrien.com* (€€€–€€). One of the best of the many hotels lined up behind the quays, the majority of its attractive rooms benefiting from sea views. The nautical décor in the restaurant (€€–€) makes for a lively backdrop to the good menus.

***Le Continental**, 4 Quai A. Thomas, **t** 02 99 89 60 16, *www.hotel-cancale.com* (€€€–€€). Looking over to

★ Château Richeux >>

★ Le Grand Large >

the port, many of its comfortable rooms with sea views, the good restaurant (€€€–€) with a terrace extending out from the front to make the most of the location. *Closed mid Jan–mid Feb.*

**Le Grand Large, 4 Quai Cartier, t 02 99 89 82 90, *www.hotelgrand large.com* (€€–€). In an adorable house under the cliff on the southern end of the quays, with some charming rooms, many with sea views. The restaurant (€€€) is in a light-filled modern building closer to the water.

Le Surcouf, 7 Quai Gambetta, t 02 99 89 61 75 (€€€). Among the many seafood restaurants along Cancale's quays, this appealing address is well known for its excellent dishes. *Closed Wed and Thurs exc July and Aug.*

★ La Hamelinais B&B >>

Côté Mer, Route de la Corniche, t 02 99 89 66 08, *www.restaurant-cotemer.fr* (€€€€–€€). With a conservatory dining room with views on to the southern part of Cancale's port, though the delicious seafood specialities and platters will distract you from the views. *Closed low season Sun eve and Wed.*

Ty Breiz, 13 Quai Gambetta, t 02 99 89 60 26 (€€–€). Good, simple seafood dishes served on the port-side terrace or in the deeply rustic interior. *Closed Tues eve and Wed, and mid Nov–mid Feb.*

The choice of tempting restaurants with terraces along Cancale's quays is exceptional, so there are many other good places to try.

ⓘ Dol-de-Bretagne/Pays de la Baie du Mont St-Michel >>
3 Grande Rue des Stuarts, t 02 99 48 15 37, www.pays-de-dol.com

★ Hotel de la Pointe du Grouin >

Around Cancale

**Hôtel de la Pointe du Grouin, t 02 99 89 60 55, *www.hotelpointedu grouin.com* (€€€–€€). In a location to die for, on the headland looking across the Bay of Mont St-Michel. The dining room shares the romantic views. *Closed Tues and Thurs lunch out of season.*

**Le Châtellier, 1km west of Cancale along the main inland D355 road towards St-Malo, t 02 99 89 81 84, *www.hotelchatellier.com* (€€–€). A converted family farm resembling a comfortable modern Breton home, run by a charming couple.

There are lots of B&Bs just off the coastal road south from Cancale.

St-Méloir-des-Ondes ✉ 35350
****Château Richeux, Le Point du Jour, t 02 99 89 64 76, *www.maisons-de-bricourt.com* (€€€€€–€€€€). Olivier Roellinger's (*see* Maisons de Bricourt, left) other luxurious rooms are set in this stunning country villa *c.*6km south of Cancale. It's a magical house, its glorious rooms packed with comforts, and benefiting from splendid views across the Bay of Mont St-Michel. Here, the stylish restaurant Le Bistrot Marin Le Coquillage (€€€€–€€), run by a protégé of Roellinger's, offers delicious dishes. *Closed early Jan–early Feb.*

Cherrueix ✉ 35120
La Hamelinais B&B, t 02 99 48 95 26 (€). A lovely farmhouse offering old-fashioned comforts and garden with orchard.

Manoir La Pichardière B&B, 172 La Pichardière, t 02 99 48 83 82 (€€). Neat rooms around a peaceful former farmyard, close to the Chapelle Ste-Anne.

Mont Dol ✉ 35120
La Roche B&B, t 02 99 48 01 65 (€). Decent B&B rooms just below the Mont Dol.

Roz-sur-Couesnon ✉ 35610
Polder Teisserenc de Bort B&B, St Georges de Grehaigne, t 02 99 80 27 57 (€€). A guesthouse with superb views out on to the Bay of the Mont St-Michel.

Dol-de-Bretagne ✉ 35120
**Grand Hotel de la Gare, 21 Avenue Aristide Biand, t 02 99 48 00, *hoteldelagaredoldebretagne@orange.fr* (€). A simple, cheap hotel with refurbished rooms.

La Grabotais, 4 Rue Ceinte, t 02 99 48 19 89, *www.lagrabotais.com* (€€–€). This restaurant occupies an historic timberframe house, serving fish specialities and some meats grilled on a wood fire. *Closed Mon.*

Le Saint Samson, 21 rue Ceinte, t 02 99 48 40 55 (€). Reasonably priced traditional cuisine and crêpes in a central location with terrace.

⭐ Le Mesnil des Bois B&B >>

Baguer-Morvan ✉ 35120

Manoir de Launay-Blot B&B, south of Baguer-Morvan, **t** 02 99 48 07 48, *www.launay-blot.com* (€€). Appealing rooms in a charming if slightly unkempt 17th-century setting. *Table d'hôte* possible.

Le Tronchet ✉ 35540

***Hostellerie Abbatiale, **t** 02 99 58 98 21, *www.abbatiale.com* (€€). An attractive, sprawling hotel in former abbey buildings in the countryside. Hotel guests get special rates at the golf course of St-Malo–Le Tronchet right beside it, and the traditional restaurant (€€–€) has views onto the greens. *Closed mid-Nov–Feb.*

Le Mesnil des Bois B&B, **t** 02 99 58 97 12, *www.le-mesnil-des-bois.com* (€€€–€€). This lovely country manor was once the property of St-Malo corsair Robert Surcouf. Now it's a very welcoming haven with a handful of stylish rooms. *Closed mid-Nov–Feb.*

Mont St-Michel

Slip across the Breton frontier to visit the breathtaking Mont St-Michel, just in Normandy. A visit here can be uplifting or hellish, depending on the crowds when you go, but the power of the Church could scarcely be more awesomely or more appealingly presented. What a glorious piece of Christian propaganda the mount makes. You can read so many symbols into its very appearance. From a distance, even its triangular shape evokes the Holy Trinity. The very narrow strip of sand joining the rock to the mainland recalls the straight and narrow path Jesus talked of leading to the kingdom of heaven. And that human-defying steeple pointing so sharply to the skies appears like a timeless reminder to think to paradise... even if it only dates from the 19th century.

The Mont St-Michel has two major problems. The first is the number of visitors who come each year, some three million. The second is that the bay around it has been silting up. That is why nowadays only the biggest tides actually carry the sea water right up to the mount's ramparts. The elevation of the natural causeway and the canalization of the Couesnon (the main river flowing out into the bay) in the 19th century added significantly to the problem. A massive project has gradually been coming into effect over the last few years, to re-establish the Mont St-Michel as an island. One of the most obvious major changes is set to come with the destruction of the causeway, to be replaced by a pedestrian and rail bridge. For details, see *www.projetmontsaintmichel.fr*.

History

Actually, two extraordinary islands rise from the bay, the Mont St-Michel and the Ile Tombelaine. A dramatic geological tale tells how these rocks came to be so isolated here – it seems a major geological shift swallowed up the forested lands around them after the end of the last Ice Age. These sensational islands have had a magnetic effect on men ever since.

Neolithic people erected a monument on top of the Mont St-Michel. Much later, in the 6th century, hermits settled on the island. Two chapels were built, one to St Etienne, the other to St Symphorien. Then, in the early 8th century, Aubert, bishop of the nearby town of Avranches, had a vision that would transform the rock's destiny, turning it into one of France's greatest monasteries and one of the most significant pilgrimage sights in Europe.

One night in 708, so the story goes, St Michael swooped down into Aubert's dreams and instructed him to build a church in his honour on the mount. Aubert was at first unconvinced by his visionary visitor, but received several further insistent messages from the militant saint, and responded.

Aubert commissioned a copy of the grotto on Mount Gargano, a place in Italy where St Michael had also supposedly put in an appearance. Pilgrims started to come to the grotto and the rock became known as the Mont St-Michel. After his death, Aubert's supposed skull ended up in the church of St-Gervais in Avranches; the story goes that the hole in the cranium was caused by St Michael aggressively badgering Aubert with his prodding finger – St Michael has always appeared as one of the most violent enforcers of the Christian message.

The religious buildings would develop and be added to through the medieval period. From 867 to 933 at least, the Mont St-Michel was officially the possession of Breton lords. However, Duke Richard I of Normandy came to impose Norman ownership. In 966, a band of Benedictine monks from the Seine were sent to the mount to take control of St Michael's sanctuary. This became the first Benedictine foundation in western Normandy. The spiritual sight grew in importance under the Benedictines and it was decided to construct a much more substantial monastery.

The Romanesque abbey went up roughly from the start of the 11th century to the mid 12th. Donations of lands from nobles and of money from visiting pilgrims gave the place considerable wealth. It became a celebrated school of learning as well as a renowned centre for producing illuminated manuscripts. Robert de Tombelaine and Anastase the Venetian counted among the most revered scholars of their day, working on the mount in the 11th century. In that period, a first collection of stories of miracles connected with the mount was compiled here. A whole network of pilgrimage routes to the holy place evolved, known as the *chemins montais*.

It was in the second half of the 12th century, under Robert de Torigni, abbot from 1154 to 1186, that the abbey knew its greatest period. With Torigni, who was close to Plantagenet King Henry II, the number of monks reached its peak of 60. Such was the prolific production of manuscripts in this period that the Mont St-Michel became known as the Cité des Livres, the City of Books. The town of Avranches still conserves many of the abbey's manuscripts.

The mount also became a strategic and symbolic stronghold in the Middle Ages. At the start of the 13th century, King Philippe Auguste of France decided to win back Normandy from the English monarchy. Breton soldiers fighting for his cause set fire to part of the abbey, destroying much of it. After his victories, the repentant Philippe Auguste donated a huge sum for a magnificent new building on the north side of the abbey church. This Merveille, or Wonder, as the new block became known, counts as the greatest architectural achievement on the mount. From the mid-13th century through to the start of the 16th, further administrative and residential buildings went up around the church.

The impressive ring of ramparts dates in the main from the 15th century, built to defend the rock from English assailants in the Hundred Years War. The enemy never managed to take the mount, and once the war over, visitors came to thank St Michael for delivering them from the evil scourge of the English. They also gave money to pay for the rebuilding of the choir end of the church, destroyed during that war.

Practically all the French kings came to the Mont St-Michel on pilgrimage. However, abbey life was radically altered during the early 16th century, when the royal administration took over control of the appointment of abbots in France under the system of the *commende*. These posts became lucrative preferments for absentee lords, and some of these *abbés commendataires* scarcely came here at all. Monastic life and scholarship suffered dramatically.

During the bloody French Wars of Religion, the iconoclastic Huguenots, or Protestants, tried to attack the abbey, but many of them were massacred. With the installation of the Maurist Benedictine order in 1622, religious life regained some momentum, but only 10 monks occupied the abbey towards the end of the 18th century. With the Revolution, the situation only got worse. The monks were expelled and replaced by prisoners. At least this demeaning function kept the abbey buildings from crumbling entirely.

During the course of the 19th century, people interested in protecting French culture, including Victor Hugo, protested at this sacrilegious use of the abbey. Under Napoleon III, in 1863, the place was freed from its role as a prison and the restorers moved in in force. The architect Edouard Corroyer, who made some wonderful cross-section drawings of the mount, was one of the principal planners of the repairs, working on the place between 1872 and 1888. The splendid neo-Gothic spire, which was built in 1897, was

the work of Victor Petigrand. The sparkling, gilded statue of St
Michael topping the spire was executed by Emmanuel Frémiet.
Some Benedictine monks were allowed back to the abbey in recent
times, but they have been replaced by the Monastic Fraternity of
Jerusalem, who continue to receive guests on religious retreats.
UNESCO has, unsurprisingly, included the Mont St-Michel on its list
of World Heritage Sites.

Up the Mont St-Michel and a Tour of the Abbey

The entrance to this heavenly site proves heavily military. Once
you've walked through the massive rampart gates, a couple of
enormous cannon greet you. These were taken from the English in
the course of the Hundred Years War. Look upwards and your gaze
will be struck by the extraordinary gilded figure of St Michael
flying at vertiginous height way above you. The arduous, crowded
climb up the one street to the abbey then begins, the route lined
with very touristy shops and restaurants.

The Abbey

The Abbey
*www.abbaye-
montsaintmichel.com,*
t 02 33 89 80 00;
*open May–Aug 9–7,
Sept–April 9.30–6.
Service in the abbey
church Tues–Sat
at 12.15, Sun at 11.30*

You can visit the abbey by yourself or on a guided tour, in English
or in French. As to the *tour-conférence*, it offers a splendid, more
detailed, more energetic tour in French, and sometimes in English.

Such a tempting gem viewed from afar, the abbey looks austere
and forbidding close up. Don't expect many decorative frills here;
the builders were clearly asked to avoid distractions for the monks.
The buildings are awe-inspiring though. They were made from
granite quarried locally and on the Iles Chausey, islands to the
north off the Normandy coast.

Entering the abbey, at the top of the first impressive flights of
steps, you come to a smallish room with useful **models** showing
how the place developed down the centuries. You then go out onto
the spacious **terrace** in front of the church. You can enjoy
spectacular views from here, both of the abbey, with its sheer
stone sides plunging down the rock, and of the great sands that
surround the mount. To the north, you get good views of the
other substantial rock stranded in the sands of the bay, the
Ile Tombelaine.

In 1776, a storm destroyed the western end of the Romanesque
nave of the vast **abbey church**, hence the truncated form fronted
by a classical façade. As you walk through the door, all you see for a
second is a thin Gothic window in the distance. Then the light of
the tall Gothic choir with its lancet shapes draws your attention.
But most of the church dates from the earlier, Romanesque period.
Much has been restored inside, but the nave's south aisle is
original 11th century.

The Romanesque construction was of great size, height and daring for its time, provided with three levels, the top one with good-sized windows. The way the edifice was built right on the pinnacle of the mount is extraordinary. The crossing of the church was placed on the very top of the rock, while the rest was supported by four doubly useful lower chapels, or crypts. The choir is late Gothic, started in the 1440s, but with little decorative sculptural detail, and just the odd Renaissance element added on later. The **flying buttresses** supporting the exterior of the choir make a quite a sight.

A couple of the crypts are only open to those who follow the *tour-conférence*. A dizzying walk takes you down a spiral staircase to the **Crypte des Gros Piliers**. This dates from the same Gothic period as the choir above. You reach the second crypt, the **Crypte des 30 Cierges**, via a very narrow corridor. Here it feels like you're really reaching into the rock. Traditionally, 30 monks would come down here, each carrying a candle, to pray to the Virgin, hence the name. The statue of the Virgin isn't original, but the large, strange figure with its oversized head and timid smirk is one of the rare effigies you'll see on a tour of the abbey.

The delicately vaulted Romanesque **promenoir** leads you round to **Notre-Dame Sous Terre** (Our Lady Under Ground), in fact a pre-Romanesque building from the mid-10th century, the oldest surviving part of the abbey. This could be the spot where Bishop Aubert had the first sanctuary to St Michael built in the 8th century. Beyond this underground chapel is the area where the monks' infirmary used to be. Here, an enormous wheel was installed to shift great blocks of stone up the sharp incline of the rockface. The spectacular machine would have been set in motion and driven by men running within the wheel like hamsters. The last crypt you can visit is the **Chapelle St-Martin**, the twin of the Crypte des 30 Cierges, which has kept its pleasing 11th-century volumes. It served as the chapel of the dead.

In addition to the church and its crypts, there was the **monastery** that grew up alongside. Most of the Romanesque one was destroyed in fighting, but the new monastery, or **Merveille**, that Philippe Auguste substantially financed is a work of staggering brilliance. Rising up the north side of the rock, it basically consists of two major rooms on each of its three floors. On the top level, the cloister stands open to the skies. The delicate reddish columns were made from English Purbeck stone. You can spot the very few original ones, slightly eaten away by time. The staggered layout of the columns reflects an unusual stylistic theme in the Merveille's architecture.

The long **refectory** next to the cloister is beautifully lit, but there are no direct views out from here. Instead, the diagonal line is used to make the light come in subtly and indirectly. The room would have been colourful in the medieval period, and you can easily hear how musical the acoustics are. It's here that the monks would eat, listening to readings from biblical or saintly works.

On the next level down, you come to two vast rooms. The **salle des hôtes**, under the refectory, was where noble and prestigious pilgrims would have been received. They would also have eaten and slept here. Guests would first have been led to the side chapel of the great room, to take part in prayers of purification.

The room next door, referred to as the **salle des chevaliers**, is thought to have served in its time both as the abbey's chapterhouse and as its scriptorium, known also as a *chauffoir*. The ornate manuscripts would have been prepared here. The windows provided a consistent light for the copying and colouring work, while the vast fireplaces helped warm not just the monks' hands but also the ink.

On the Merveille's lowest level, the ordinary people would have been received in the **aumônière**. Next door was the dark and massive **cellar**, used to store the mountains of provisions needed by the abbey and its pilgrims. A copy of Frémiet's statue of St Michael is displayed here; from so close up, he looks particularly mean and menacing.

At night, the abbey is gloriously lit up. In high season it opens its doors after nightfall for a deeply atmospheric **Balade Nocturne** (*July–Aug, plus sometimes in Sept*), when you can explore the place to the sound of music. Works of art are also displayed along the route. With far fewer people around, the vast abbey can feel distinctly eerie and Gothick.

Other Tourist Sights on and around the Mount

Most of these sights inevitably lie along the **Grande Rue**, the main street that snakes up to the abbey entrance. Tucked into the rock to one side of it stands the **church of St-Pierre**, the other serious religious stop on the mount. In fact, the rockface puts in an appearance behind the rows of benches. This charming building dates from the 15th and 16th centuries, with many decorative items of religious devotion added in the 19th. Joan of Arc stands at the entrance, and in the side chapel a bizarre, bejewelled, metal-covered 19th-century St Michael looks stoical as he slays the dragon.

Back outside, take the arch under the apse for the quiet cemetery. From here, you might either adopt the little-known higher route back up to the abbey or the westerly one – the Mont St-Michel isn't quite a one-street village, it turns out.

The abbey can seem very cold and empty to children, and a tour of it long. The multi-media **Archéoscope** along the Grande Rue

Archéoscope
www.au-mont-saint-michel.com, t 02 33 89 01 85; open July–Aug 9–6.30, Feb–June and Sept–mid-Nov 9–5.30

07 Ille-et-Vilaine | Mont St-Michel

offers them an appealing introduction, using a slick 20-minute presentation to explain how and why the abbey was built. Smoke, lights and videos bombard the senses. The commentary is only in French, but the splendid film footage, taken from a helicopter, is easy for all to appreciate.

Musée Historique
www.lemontsaintmic hel.info; open daily 9–6

By contrast, the **Musée Historique**, close to the stairs at the entrance to the abbey, is archaic, with a few very amusing elements, the most absurd being a tableau of the mount made from fragments of postage stamps. The tour here ends with a short recorded historical commentary in a cavernous room full of waxworks. You emerge in the midst of a souvenir shop.

Maison de Tiphaine
open daily 9–6

The **Maison de Tiphaine** is claimed to have been built by the Breton and French warrior Bertrand du Guesclin (*see* box, p.134) for his wife Tiphaine to stay in while he was off warring. The tall, narrow house has a certain dilapidated charm, and it can sometimes provide a quieter corner in the chaos of the mount.

Musée de la Mer et de l'Ecologie
open daily 9–6

In the miniature-storeyed **Musée de la Mer et de l'Ecologie** (close to the bottom of the Grande Rue), English-speaking visitors are given a taped commentary to listen to via headphones. Most of the displays are of model ships and boats, but the succinct films explain the tides in the bay and its natural habitat, the problem of silting and possible solutions. The place also gives advice on walking across the bay. The museum ends in another souvenir shop.

Alligator Bay
www.alligator-bay.com, t 02 33 68 11 18; open April–Sept daily 10–7, Oct–Nov and Feb–March daily 2–6, Dec–Jan only weekends and school hols 2–6

If the heavenly sight and all its attractions or walks around the bay fail to move your children, perhaps **Alligator Bay** at Beauvoir immediately south might float their boat, with its many alligators and giant turtles – but they're not from Brittany, you'll be surprised to hear.

Activities on and around Mont St-Michel

ⓘ Mont St-Michel >
t 02 33 60 14 30, www.ot-montsaint michel.com

Maisons de la Baie Information Centres: The official Maisons de la Baie, at four locations around the Bay of Mont St-Michel, offer all manner of information about the natural environment and outings. The Maison at **Genêts** (t 02 33 89 64 00) is the place to find out about walks across the sands to Mont St-Michel, and that at **Courtils** (t 02 33 58 47 87) has an excellent interactive exhibition on the history and ecology of the bay. There's another Maison at Vains west of Avranches, while the one in Brittany, at Le Vivier, features on p.116. Their collective websites are *www.baie-mont-saint-michel.fr* and *www. maison-baie.com*.

Several other expert organizations and individuals provide specialist guided walks (the programmes usually going April–Oct). **No one should try any walks in the bay without an expert guide.** Reliable guides include those you can contact at:

Chemins de la Baie, 14 Place des Halles, Genêts, t 02 33 89 80 88, *www.cheminsdelabaie.com*.

Maison du Guide, 1 Rue Montoise, Genêts, t 02 33 70 83 49, *www.decouvertebaie.com*. A big range of walks, including night walks, and crossings on horseback.

Didier Lavadoux, 36 Grande Rue, Genêts, t 02 33 70 84 19, **m** 06 75 08

84 69, *www.traversee-baie.com*. An expert naturalist who specializes in nature rambles.

To see the Mont St-Michel from a plane, call **t** 02 33 58 02 91; from a microlight, **t** 02 33 48 67 48. For sports enthusiasts, there's an annual marathon around the Bay of the Mont St-Michel in May, *www.montsaintmichel-marathon.com*

Where to Stay and Eat on Mont St-Michel

On the Mount ✉ 50116

You pay a high price to stay here, and you need to book ages in advance to stay in high season.

***La Mère Poulard, t 02 33 89 68 68, *www.mere-poulard.com* (€€€€€–€€€). The famous name here, which has received many celebrities. The location at the entrance to the mount is great, and the rooms are very pretty, a few with sea views, but prices reach sky-high, so you might be happy simply to sample the famous fluffy omelettes produced in its swish restaurant or a

calvados in the piano bar, although there are menus (€€€€–€€€) too.

***Auberge Saint-Pierre, t 02 33 60 14 03, *www.auberge-saint-pierre.fr* (€€€€–€€). Comfy little rooms in the historic part, more spacious ones in the newer bit, with some great views. There's a choice of kitsch dining rooms, plus a fabulous terrace, at the restaurant.

***La Croix Blanche, t 02 33 60 14 04, *www.hotel-la-croix-blanche.com* (€€€€–€€). The rooms are less inspiring inside, but the views are incredible. Restaurant/crêperie.

**Le Mouton Blanc, t 02 33 60 14 08, *www.lemoutonblanc.fr* (€€€–€€). Some slightly less pricey rooms, scattered in several buildings, and two restaurants, one in a 14th-century building.

La Vieille Auberge, t 02 33 60 14 34, *www.lavieilleauberge-montsaint michel.com* (€€€–€€). Rooms with terraces and a sea view, and a lunchtime brasserie.

La Sirène, t 02 33 60 08 60 (€). A good, popular option for crêpes.

Châteaux between St-Malo and Rennes

You may not associate Brittany with châteaux, but like most French regions, it has its fair share of them. Here they tend towards the dark and moody, but they prove interesting places, laden with history. Between the Bay of the Mont St-Michel and Rennes, there are two lines of châteaux to visit, set close to pretty, quirky villages; the first string goes from Antrain to La Bourbansais, the second from Hédé to St-Méen.

Bazouges-la-Pérouse and the Château de la Ballue

Château de Bonne Fontaine
t 02 99 98 31 13, www. bonnefontaine.com; open Easter–Oct daily 2–6

On our tour of châteaux and villages, you might start with an enjoyable stroll round the smart, peaceful grounds of the **Château de Bonne Fontaine** beside Antrain.

The steeple of **Bazouges-la-Pérouse** signals this wacky village for many miles around. Simple houses snail up the hillside towards the church. On the flat top of the hill, the streets are set out in a grid pattern. **Avant-garde artists** have been encouraged to take up residence here in summer. Several traditional houses have been turned into galleries, the former little private school into an

Getting around between St-Malo and Rennes

A **bus** links St-Méen-le-Grand with Rennes. Transports Armor Express, **t** 02 99 26 16 00, runs buses from Rennes to Dinard, via Bécherel. Combourg lies on a **train** line linking Rennes with Dol-de-Bretagne, St-Malo and Dinard.

exhibition space. A number of the trendy painters who base themselves temporarily in this surprisingly cutting-edge backwater are well known in Paris, several contributing to the thriving French cartoon magazine scene. The old people, the main year-round inhabitants of Bazouges-la-Pérouse, often help out these seasonal artists by keeping the galleries open when they go off travelling.

The exceptional size of the **church** is explained by the fact that two medieval religious edifices here were rolled into one in the 19th century. Inside, the most notable features include the carved baptismal fonts from the 13th century, one engraved with gorgeous animals symbolizing the evangelists, and the 16th-century stained glass near the entrance, depicting the life of Christ.

Château de la Ballue
www.laballue.com,
t 02 99 97 47 86;
garden open mid-
Mar–Oct 10.30–6.30,
château for concerts
and exhibitions

The **Château de la Ballue** just northeast also hosts **modern art exhibitions**. The château was one of three built in the Ille-et-Vilaine for Gilles Ruellan, a self-made man. Born to innkeepers in Antrain, he joined the Protestant forces supporting Henri de Navarre against the fanatical Catholics in the French Wars of Religion. Such was his success that he was richly rewarded by Henri when the latter became king of France. Appointed a tax collector, Ruellan amassed the wealth to build his string of châteaux. This pretty little 17th-century home boasts delightfully playful, Baroque-inspired formal **gardens** with glorious views.

Château de Combourg

Château de Combourg
www.combourg.net,
t 02 99 73 22 95; park
open April–Oct daily
9–12 and 2–6; château
open for 45-minute
tours 2–5.30;
Mar and Nov by
appointment only

... secret passages and stairs, prison cells and dungeons, a labyrinth of galleries, some covered, others open, walled-up underground tunnels which disappeared off no one knew where; all around, silence, darkness and the stony appearance of the place...
François-René de Chateaubriand in his *Mémoires d'outre-tombe*

To appreciate a visit to the somewhat daunting Château de Combourg, it helps to know something of the life of its most famous inhabitant, the great French Romantic writer and politician, François-René de Chateaubriand (*see* box, p.132). As to the history of the place, the first fortification here goes back to the 11th century, when Ginguené, a bishop of Dol, decided to strengthen control of his lands. The château then passed into military hands. Through to the 13th century, it was periodically besieged and battered in warring between Brittany and neighbouring Normandy.

The castle you now see dates in the main from the 14th and 15th centuries. The look is forbiddingly military still. During the Breton War of Succession, the lords here supported the French claimant to the dukedom, Charles de Blois. Later, Jean de Coetquen of Combourg fought against the fanatical Catholic side of the Ligue during the French Wars of Religion, and his descendants remained powerful military figures into the 18th century. The Maréchal de Duras became lord of the castle in the mid-18th century but decided to sell it. In 1761, it was bought, along with the title, by René-Auguste de Chateaubriand, father of the famed writer.

The tall, sheer castle walls rise up in hostility as you approach, a defensive tower guarding each corner. Above the main entrance, the coat of arms with *fleurs de lys* recalls a medieval lord of Châteaubriant (a stronghold in southern Brittany – see p.460) who went off to serve the French king in the crusades. 'My blood colours the banner of France', the motto reads gorily. Chateaubriand's eldest brother, Jean-Baptiste, inherited the castle from his father in 1786 but was guillotined in 1794. Eventually the property was handed back to Jean-Baptiste's son, but was left to fall into ruin.

The neo-Gothic interiors therefore date from after Chateaubriand's time, but the memory of Chateaubriand the writer is preserved inside. The chapel is where his mother spent much of her time, praying for a change to her husband's terrifying, tyrannical moods, but on a happier note, it also witnessed the double marriage of two of Chateaubriand's beloved sisters.

Along with a massive tapestry on the central staircase, you can see a Venetian chest portraying battle scenes, apparently a wedding gift from when Chateaubriand married Céleste Buisson de la Vigne. The *salle des gardes* so eerily depicted by the Romantic writer was converted into two rather brighter rooms later in the 19th century. The salon walls were covered with rich wall paintings of lions, palms and crusaders. A portrait of Malesherbes, a major liberal Ancien Régime politician close to Chateaubriand, and a couple of 15th-century paintings, are to be admired.

Up one tower, you can view the Romantic's deathbed, his desk and some other battered pieces related to his life. There's also a copy of Girodet's famous moody portrait of him and an engraving portraying Juliette Récamier, whose passionate friendship was so important in later life. The guides speak of a superstitious tradition in the 14th century of placing a live black cat or a stillborn child in a castle's walls to ward off evil spirits; the screaming cat skeleton on display was apparently found embedded in a wall here during 19th-century restoration work.

The château lies in what the French call an English-style park, which you can walk round. Also wander along the prettyish main street of the little **town** at its feet, perhaps on a guided tour in

France's Most Miserable Romantic

Chateaubriand, France's most famous Romantic writer and prime contender as the nation's most miserable memorialist, described in brilliant detail the dark and dour Château de Combourg, where he spent a little of his deeply unhappy childhood. Reading the opening sections of Chateaubriand's cheerfully titled autobiography, *Mémoires d'outre-tombe* (Memoirs from Beyond the Grave), you're given a vivid depiction of Combourg, as well as of St-Malo, where the writer was born in 1768.

Chateaubriand has been seen by some French people as a hero, but heavily criticized by others for his conservative political and Christian views... he had his reasons, living through the Revolution, in which members of his family lost their heads, and then through the disillusionment of Napoleon's reign. Few readers today have the patience to plough through the hundreds of pages charting his adventures and depressions, but his stirring style can carry you away like a whirlwind.

He had a fascinating life, embarking on a great journey through North America in the course of the Revolutionary turmoil, becoming a political journalist and ambassador, and writing heady, challenging fiction that tests the limits of Christian morality. His most famous creative works, *Atala* and *René* (mercifully much shorter than his memoirs, more the length of short stories), are set along the Mississippi. They drip with descriptions of nature and details of Native American Indians eating bear ham and sacred dog, but they also reflect upon the moral and religious outlooks separating the civilizations of Europe and America.

After America, Chateaubriand went to live in exile in London for a period, suffering bitter poverty. He went on to champion the cause of Christianity, which had suffered such persecution, censorship and denigration during the French Revolution. In his *Génie du Christianisme*, he put forward his reasons for continuing to believe, and his Christian ideals pervade his fiction. He also had grandiose political aspirations, which were never entirely fulfilled, although he held some important posts, including several as French ambassador.

English, or get diverted into the wine shop specializing in organic wines and bottles from small producers. The best views of the castle are to be had from the far side of the atmospheric **lake** right beside the town.

Château de la Bourbansais

Château de la Bourbansais
www.labourbansais. com, t 02 99 69 40 48; zoo and garden open April–Sept 10–7, château tours at 11.15am, 2, 3, 4 and 5pm

The park of La Bourbansais (outside the village of Pleugueneuc just east of the dual carriageway between St-Malo and Rennes) looks elegant enough, but the château is more beautiful still in its speckled stone. The perspective to the main façade has a remarkably planned symmetry, with two dovecotes, followed by two mansarded outbuildings, then the two side wings to the castle leading in to two corner towers, each topped by a delightfully domed, bell-shaped roof. All this is a sure sign that this château dates from after the arrival of Renaissance architecture in France. It was started in the late 16th century for the Breton parliamentarian Jean du Breil. Jacques Androuet du Cerceau, an architect famed for his bird's-eye drawings of the period's royal châteaux, designed the main façade. Descendants of the same family have lived here since its completion.

You can visit a series of small salons on the ground floor. Originally, these spaces simply served as cellars and as a buffer against the dampness of the marshy location. But then windows were pierced in the walls and the rooms were kitted out with gorgeous Ancien Régime panelling, tapestries and decoration. The panelling was the masterpiece of the carpenter Mancelle, done in refined Louis XVI style. Republican troops passed this way in 1793, intent on setting fire to the château. Mancelle's son had become the château-keeper while the proprietors were away. He couldn't bear to see the pride of his father's life destroyed, so he appeased the revolutionary vandals by offering them a drink from the château cellars; he got them so merry that they left without harming the interiors.

In the little **zoo** attached to the château, deer are among the animals protected; somewhat ironically, on the other side of the château, you can also admire a pack of hunting hounds.

Châteaux and Villages from Hédé to Bécherel

Hédé, 20 kilometres northwest of Rennes, stands high above the valley through which the **Canal d'Ille et Rance** runs. With this extraordinary 19th-century engineering project, the two rivers, and hence the Breton Channel coast and the Breton Atlantic coast, were joined together almost at the widest point across the province.

Now, a new **Voie Verte** offers a hiking and cycling track linking Rennes to St-Malo via the banks of the canal, avoiding cars along its length. Take a look from the towpath below Hédé at the amazing sight of 11 close-packed **locks**. The **Maison du Canal d'Ille et Rance** here commemorates the construction of the canal and recalls the trading boats that once employed this waterway. **Hédé** itself is a quietly attractive place, with its ruined castle and its Romanesque church. At **Tinténiac**, just north along the canal, another little museum, the **Musée de l'Outil et des Métiers** remembers the old crafts that were so important before the age of the tractor.

The village of **Les Iffs** is a bucolic backwater with a surprisingly richly decorated **church**, **St-Ouen**, dating from the 14th century. Keys are available from the wary lady behind the village bar, who will demand a car key or passport in return. The stained glass is the main attraction inside. Nine windows here date from the Renaissance, their illustrations executed by the workshop of Michel Bayonne of Rennes. As well as New Testament and saintly figures (including Breton lawyer St Yves – see box, p.225), the local lords feature in their finery. Outside the village, the 15th-century **Fontaine St-Fiacre** is a rare example of the covered fountains which are so common in western Brittany. It used to be called upon to provide miraculous rain in periods of drought – the local priest would lead a procession to dip his cross in its waters, and if the locals' prayers were heard, a storm would soon follow.

Maison du Canal d'Ille et Rance
www.maisonducanal-chez-alice.fr, t 02 99 45 48 90; open July and Aug daily 10.30–12.30 and 1.30–6; May–June and Sept–Oct Wed–Mon 2–6; Nov–April Wed and Sun 2–6

Musée de l'Outil et des Métiers
t 02 99 23 09 30; open July–Sept Mon–Sat 10–12 and 2.30–6, Sun 2.30–6

Château de Montmuran
www.chateau-montmuran.com, t 02 99 45 88 88; open June–Sept Sun–Fri 2–6

On the guided tour of the **Château de Montmuran** just north of the village, Bertrand du Guesclin, the viciously ambitious 14th-century Breton warrior who went on to become leader of the French armies, plays the starring role (*see* box, below).

The high ridge on which the château was built, with its glorious views northwards, has been fortified since at least the 11th century. The oldest surviving parts date back to the 12th and 13th centuries. You enter via a rare surviving medieval drawbridge. Spot a couple of comical hump-backed medieval figures in stone seemingly struggling to hold up the massive weight on either side of the drawbridge. As to the splendid entrance *châtelet*, one tower is 14th century, the other 15th. One of the most peculiar features of the architecture is the chapel, placed above the vaulted passageway into the courtyard. Once you reach the courtyard, the splendid

Bertrand du Guesclin, Brittany's Most Famous Warrior

Bertrand du Guesclin came into the world in 1321 at the Château de la Motte-Broons near Dinan, the first child of a minor Breton noble family. Something of a runt, portraits depict him as being notably ugly. With nine siblings born after him, he had to learn how to fend for himself from an early age, although the claim that he had an army at the age of 12 is to be taken with a pinch of salt. The story goes that he became an uncontrollable delinquent, leading a band of local peasants into terrible mischief. At the age of 17, he entered a jousting tournament in Rennes, where he distinguished himself memorably (*see* box, p.150).

In the Breton War of Succession, du Guesclin decided to fight for Charles de Blois, the contender backed by the French monarchy. With the private army he amassed, he terrorized the enemy. He's supposed to have come to the Château de Montmuran in 1354 for a grand feast, while English troops lay close by at Bécherel. Suspecting that the enemy might attack during the festivities, he posted archers on the road to the castle, and surprised the assailants with an unexpected reception party. The tale goes that he was immediately honoured for his actions by being knighted at the château.

Du Guesclin was involved in another joust of major chivalric significance in Dinan (*see* box, p.175). One romantic strand to his story tells of how a bright young woman of that town, Tiphaine Raguenel, was so impressed by his performance that she was easily wooed by him and they got married. In 1360, du Guesclin was made governor of Pontorson, just south of the Mont St-Michel. On the holy mount itself he built a safe home for Tiphaine while he went off warring around France and Europe.

In western Brittany during campaigning in 1363, du Guesclin took many strongholds, but also organized an abortive expedition across the Channel from St-Pol-de-Léon. Then in 1364 came the disaster of the Battle of Auray. Charles de Blois was killed, bringing an end to the Breton War of Succession. Although Charles's troops were led by du Guesclin, some say that he had been against the action. He was imprisoned, the French side purportedly paying 100,000 crowns for his release.

Du Guesclin then went off to war for the French king on a much wider scale, becoming a major player in the Hundred Years War, but remaining something of an ambivalent figure in Brittany, as he became so closely linked with the French monarchy; such was his success that he reached the very pinnacle of the French military, being appointed Connétable de France – basically, commander in chief of the French armies – in 1370.

After Tiphaine's death, du Guesclin married his second wife at the Château de Montmuran in 1374. Jeanne de Laval was a mere 17, her husband 53. An idealized 19th-century depiction of them can be seen in Montmuran's chapel. Du Guesclin battled on to the very end of his life. He was still out warring when he died, in 1380, in the Massif Central. His will stated that he wished to be buried at Dinan and so his heart was taken there. In a very rare honour, his skeleton was buried with the Capetian kings of France, in their family mausoleum at St-Denis outside Paris.

views are offset by the massed banks of outstanding 200 year-old lime trees.

You only see a few rooms inside but they are full of curiosities, including a model of the full medieval fort and a 15th-century hot water and hot air system. Most unexpected of all is a carved chest said to date back to Carolingian times. The tour finishes with a climb up the *châtelet*, not for those who suffer from vertigo.

Bécherel and Around

The attractive hilltop village of **Bécherel** draws attention to itself from afar. This was a fortified spot as far back as Gallo-Roman times. Its excellent location overlooking the surrounding countryside was then chosen as an obvious site for a fort by Alain de Dinan in the 12th century. The Plantagenets grabbed hold of it later that century, and King Henry II Plantagenet had the whole village fortified, only for his son, Geoffrey, to besiege it and burn it down. In the Breton War of Succession, English troops supporting the claim of Jean de Montfort took control of the place. Repeatedly attacked, one siege lasted 18 months.

A few meagre traces remain of the castle, plus small portions of five out of nine towers that once protected the village. You can get a fine sense, though, of the hill's defensive advantages from the garden at the top of the village, reached by navigating a labyrinthine network of alleyways. The grand houses below are explained by the success of the linen made here and exported to parts of Europe from the 16th to the 18th centuries.

Since 1989, Bécherel has found a new direction, developing into Brittany's answer to very literary Hay-on-Wye in Wales. The place has been successfully colonized by second-hand **bookshops** and book-related businesses, giving it a cultivated feel, with a wry sense of humour, to be seen in the very shop names, such as La Vache qui lit (as opposed to La Vache qui rit, indicating a serious literary cow rather than a laughing one). Get a full list of the dozen and more bookshops from the tourist office. Thanks to its new vocation, the village has become a small but significant eastern outpost of the dwindling Breton-speaking culture; and English-speakers are catered for, most of the shops having a selection of titles in English. Two of the shops double as tea shops, or try the crêperie. There's a **book market** on the first Sunday of every month, while Bécherel **book festival** takes place on Easter weekend. The big plan now is for the former village hall to be turned into **La Maison du Livre** (opening c.2010), with a permanent exhibition on book-making, and all manner of facilities for book lovers.

To the west of Bécherel lie the gardens of the **Château de Caradeuc**, a place built in 1723 for Anne-Nicolas de Caradeuc, a member of the Breton Parlement. His son Louis-René famously

Château de Caradeuc
www.chateaux-france.com/caradeuc,
t *02 99 66 77 76;*
open Easter–June and Sept–Oct Sat–Sun 2–6, July–Aug daily 12–6

stood up to the royal-appointed governor of Brittany, the Duc d'Aiguillon, in the 1760s. At that time, the Breton authorities wanted to expel the over-powerful religious and teaching order of the Jesuits from Brittany and voted for their removal, against royal policy. King Louis XV had Caradeuc imprisoned for a time as one of the leaders of this insubordination, although the monarch was later forced into a humiliating climb-down. Surprisingly, given the clash, a colossal white statue of Louis XVI stands out among the outrageous ornaments scattered around the château's sweet gardens.

St-Méen-le-Grand

The Dark Ages saint, Méen, has been upstaged in recent times by a new hero at **St-Méen** (some way further west). **Louison Bobet** was the son of a local *boulanger* who was sent out to deliver fresh *baguettes* by bike at breakneck speed from an early age – the perfect training for a figure who would become a French cycling legend. He became the first man to win the Tour de France three times in a row, back in the 1950s. The town has created a small museum devoted to him. Louison Bobet is doubly famous in Brittany for having brought *thalassothérapie* to the region; he opened the first seawater therapy centre in Quiberon in 1963.

Musée Louison Bobet
open Oct–June Wed–Mon 2–5

At the **abbey of St-Méen**, learn about the town's other saintly figure. Méen, or Mewen, came over from Britain in the 6th century, and at one point was sent into the Breton interior to settle a dispute between two rival lords. On the way, he met Kaduon, who offered him land. Having sorted out the dispute, he took up Kaduon's offer and founded a monastery here. In a side chapel, worn frescoes recall the story.

ⓘ **Bazouges-la-Pérouse >>**
2 Place de l'Hôtel de Ville, t 02 99 97 40 94, www.bazouges.com

★ **Château de la Ballue B&B >>**

Market Days between St-Malo and Rennes

Bécherel: Saturday
Hédé: Tuesday
Tinténiac: Wednesday
Combourg: Monday
Bazouges-la-Pérouse: Thursday
Antrain: Tuesday

Where to Stay and Eat between St-Malo and Rennes

St-Ouen-la-Rouërie ✉ 35460

Château des Blosses B&B, t 02 99 98 36 16, *lesblosses@hotmail.com* (€€€). A little 19th-century château set in spacious grounds, with comfortable rooms, hunting trophies on the walls, *table d'hôte*, and a swing-golf course.

Bazouges-la-Pérouse ✉ 35560

Château de la Ballue B&B, t 02 99 97 47 86, *www.la-ballue.com* (€€€€–€€€). In an enchanting little castle with beautiful gardens (*see* p.130) in the countryside outside Bazouges. Spacious, elegantly done-up rooms with uplifting views, though the corner bathrooms are a little strange. *Table d'hôte* available.

St-Rémy-du-Plain ✉ 35560

La Haye d'Irée B&B, 15km south of Bazouges-la-Pérouse down D90, **t 02 99 73 62 07,** *www.chateaubreton.com* (€€€–€€). Very elegant rooms in an 18th-century granite Breton manor with views of the surrounding countryside, a heated pool and lovely grounds. *Table d'hôte* (€€). *Closed Nov–March.*

Combourg and Around ✉ 35270

Château du Grand Val B&B, t 02 99 73 19 08, *www.grandval.nu* (€€€–€€). A stunningly updated 18th-century castle in delightful countryside 3km from Combourg, offering B&B rooms among many other possibilities.

***Le Château**, 1 Place Chateaubriand, t 02 99 73 00 38, *www.hoteldu chateau.com* (€€–€). A grand, well-positioned town house, many rooms giving onto the garden. The restaurant (€€€€–€; *closed Mon lunch, Sat lunch, and Sun eve exc July–Aug*) proposes creative cuisine, although classic Chateaubriand steak is a speciality. There's a terrace looking down to the lake.

****Hôtel du Lac**, 2 Place Chateaubriand, t 02 99 73 05 65, *www.hotel-restaurant-du-lac.com* (€€). Comfortable, modern rooms by the atmospheric lake. There's also an airy dining room and a garden for barbecues on summer evenings.

L'Ecrivain, 1 Place St Gilduin, t 02 99 73 01 61, *www.restaurantlecrivain.com* (€€€). Refined food. *Closed Sun and Wed eve in low season, Thurs all year.*

Crêperie Moustache, 11 Place Albert Parent, t 02 99 73 06 54 (€). A wonderfully named and well-regarded crêperie.

St-Pierre-de-Plesguen ✉ 35720

Le Petit Moulin du Rouvre B&B, t 02 99 73 85 84, *www.aumoulin durouvre.com* (€€). In a delightful waterside location a bit north of La Bourbansais, this address offers a few cosy rooms at the former watermill, and an array of beautifully located, stylish contemporary tree-houses around the grounds. *Table d'hôte* (€€).

Le Pont Ricoul, t 02 99 73 92 65, *www.pontricoul.com* (€). Smart suites at bargain prices, one in a waterside former washhouse, the other in the main stone house. *Table d'hôte.*

Pleugueneuc ✉ 35720

Le Lézard Tranquille B&B, Les Cours Verdiers, at entrance to the Château de la Bourbansais park, t 02 99 69 40 36, *www.lelezardtranquille.fr* (€). Spacious rooms and a summer terrace.

Hédé ✉ 35630

La Vieille Auberge, Ancienne N137, Le Perray, Bazouges-sous-Hédé, t 02 99 45 46 25, *www.lavieilleauberge35.fr* (€€€). Good local cuisine is served at this 17th-century mill by a lake, with a cosy dining room and a terrace. *Closed Sun eve, Mon and 2wks Aug–Sept.*

Quédillac ✉ 35290

****Relais de la Rance**, 6 Rue de Rennes, t 02 99 06 20 20, *relaisdela rance@21s.fr* (€€–€). A well-reputed establishment in typical 19th-century granite buildings in the middle of this village between St-Méen and Médréac. Good traditional restaurant (€€€€–€). *Closed mid-Dec–mid-Jan.*

Bécherel ✉ 35190

Le Logis de la Filanderie B&B, 3 Rue de la Filanderie, t 02 99 66 73 17, *www.la-filanderie.com* (€€). Cosy rooms in a lovely house in the centre, with garden and country views. Friendly English-speaking host.

Mme Goar B&B, 1 Porte Bertault, t 02 99 66 71 10, *guillemette.goar@free.fr* (€€). Run by a bookbinder, with rooms in an 18th-century setting.

Vignoc ✉ 35630

Château de la Villouyère, just south of Vignoc (a few km south of Hédé along the N137), t 02 99 69 80 69, *www. lavillouyere.com* (€€). Lodgings in the former home of Admiral Jean Toussaint de la Motte Picquet, with elegant, symmetrical forms dating from the 18th century.

Iffendic ✉ 35750

Château du Pin B&B, t 02 99 09 34 05, *www.chateaudupin-bretagne.com* (€€€). Elegant rooms themed around writers from Victor Hugo to Marguerite Yourcenar in a charming manor. *Table d'hôte* on offer.

ⓘ **Combourg >**
Maison de la Lanterne, t 02 99 73 13 93, www.combourg.org

★ **Le Château >**

ⓘ **Bécherel >>**
8 Place Alexandre Jéhanin, t 02 99 66 75 23, www.becherel.com

★ **Château du Pin B&B >>**

Brittany's Northern Marches

The Breton Marches form Brittany's frontier with France. Breton boundaries changed a fair degree through history, but on the map, you can follow a clear arc of defensive eastern towns, from Dinan and Dol in the north, via Fougères, Vitré, La Guerche-de-Bretagne and Châteaubriant in the centre, down to Ancenis, Clisson and Guérande on or not far from the Loire. Here we cover the areas around Fougères and Vitré, two startling historic towns that boast a couple of the country's mightiest medieval forts.

Fougères and its Forests

Surprisingly, Fougères' castle doesn't stand on the town's substantial hill, but down beside the river below, a rare choice for medieval planners. In a rather wooden description, Victor Hugo once compared Fougères to a great big spoon. The castle he saw as the spoon itself, the steep old ramp of a street leading up the hill as the spoon's handle. For the best view of the château down in the Nançon Valley, climb to the rather grand upper town. Visitors often miss this so-called Bourg Neuf, but it's packed with fine historic monuments.

History

Fougères castle was the centre of feudal power games through the Middle Ages. Around it, tanners and weavers built up their prosperity. In fact, the traders' impressive belfry, built in 1387 up on the hilltop, is the earliest of its type in Brittany, a symbol of the early power they achieved.

The Duc de Mercoeur, the fanatical Catholic leader in Brittany during the 16th-century French Wars of Religion, caused chaos and bloodshed in the region by occupying Fougères until King Henri IV had renounced Protestantism. A series of fires then wiped out much of the town centre in the 18th century, so the great architect Jacques Gabriel, among others, helped redesign the place. Linen- and sail-making brought wealth to Fougères' merchants through

Balzac's Vision of a Brutal Breton Uprising

'*Nous sommes diables contre diables* (We are devils fighting devils)', one of the leading Chouans declares in *Les Chouans, ou la Bretagne en 1799*, published in 1829 and regarded by many critics as Balzac's first major work. It gives a dramatic and damning picture of French society scarred by the Revolution and the Napoleonic era. The terrible turmoil in the Marches of Brittany at the close of the 18th century is the main subject of the novel, although the serious topic is somewhat undermined by a love story that develops at the same time. A clog filled with the hot blood of a Breton traitor who has had his head chopped off like an animal by former comrades counts among the most savage acts described in this rip-roaring, filmic read recalling terrible times in these parts.

Getting to and around Brittany's Northern Marches

Vitré is the best-connected town for **rail** travel. It lies on the line from Paris to Rennes, and TGV rapid trains from Paris very occasionally stop at Vitré, taking under 2 hours.

the Ancien Régime. Fine cut glass became another speciality; the odd leading perfume brands still have their bottles made here.

Fougères and its area became one of the most significant centres of the Chouannerie, the anti-Republican, pro-Catholic, pro-royalist uprising in which so many Bretons fought against the French Revolution. Hugo, whose great muse, Juliette Drouet, was born in Fougères, largely set his now forgotten *Quatre-Vingt-Treize*, reflecting these events, in and around Fougères. The more memorable novel describing the anti-Revolutionary uprising here is Balzac's *Les Chouans* (*see* box, opposite). As to Romantic writer Chateaubriand, whose family was decimated by the Revolution, he wrote of an extraordinarily terrible incident at Fougères involving his sister, but this wasn't fiction, this was the real thing. A **promenade en littérature** helps you retrace all these violent literary happenings.

Touring Fougères

Begin a tour of Fougères up among the well-planned streets and squares of the **Bourg Neuf**, on **Place Aristide Briand**. On this square stands a house that belonged to Armand Tuffin, Marquis de la Rouërie, who fought for George Washington in the American War of Independence before coming back to wage war against the French Revolution. His birthplace was later transformed into the magistrates' court.

Above Place Aristide Briand lies sweet **Place du Théâtre** with its ornate late-19th-century town theatre. From here, **Rue de la Pinterie** can take you swiftly and extremely steeply down the hillside to the castle, but stay up in the Bourg Neuf to explore more sights or to shop. Head along the grandiose, mainly 18th-century **Rue Nationale**, off which you can easily spot the 14th-century **belfry**, which also served as a watchtower. Back on Rue Nationale, a medallion marks the façade of the house where Chateaubriand came frequently to visit one of his sisters.

Along Rue Nationale you'll find the **Musée Emmanuel de la Villéon**. The rare late-Gothic house it occupies makes a charming setting for a beautiful little collection of paintings by Emmanuel de la Villéon, born in Fougères in 1858. He subsequently spent little time here, but did paint many scenes of Breton peasants and Breton landscapes. Down the road, the **Atelier Musée de l'Horlogerie** traces the evolution of time measurement in modern fashion, but also functions as a workshop, allowing you to see a watchmaker in action.

Musée Emmanuel de la Villéon
open daily June–Sept; rest of year Sat, Sun and school hols

Atelier Musée de l'Horlogerie
t 02 99 99 40 98; open mid-June–Aug Mon–Sat 9–12.30 and 2–7, Sun 2–6.30; Sept–mid-June Tues– Sat 9–12 and 2–7

07 Ille-et-Vilaine | Brittany's Northern Marches: Fougères and its Forests

Big dragon gargoyles try to spit down on people passing below the substantial Gothic **church of St-Léonard** at the end of Rue Nationale. The interior has some fine 12th-century stained glass, with one medallion, depicting scenes from the life of St Benedict, said to be the oldest piece of stained glass in Brittany, although it was originally made for the royal abbey of St-Denis outside Paris. If you don't suffer from vertigo, take the somewhat alarming stairs up the 17th-century **belltower** for views down on the town, including Fougères's castle, the quarried cliffs beyond standing out. Beside the church, the **Place aux Arbres public garden** provides a delightful spot to rest, and to look down on the lower town. A path meanders down from here towards the château.

Don't miss the **Bourg Vieil**, or historic lower town, beyond the castle's walls. Tanners and dyers once made great use of the river's waters. Washhouses still line the fast-flowing stream, its bright green watergrasses combed by the current. The timberframe houses give atmosphere to the quarter, which has been pedestrianized in recent times. **Place du Marchix**, the old market square, looks particularly colourful. Off Rue des Tanneurs, the oldest house to have survived in Fougères, the **Maison de Savigny**, hosts a variety of exhibitions during the summer months. Off Rue Lusignan, a path leads up the wooded **Butte de Bigot**, from which you can get another good view down onto the castle.

Opposite the castle's vast walls and moat, the **church of St-Sulpice** is packed with engrossing features and art, inside and out. Fervent Catholics go to pray to the statue of Notre-Dame des Marais within. This probably dates from the 14th century (though it now sports an 18th-century head), but the story goes that it was irreligiously thrown into the castle moat by King Henry II Plantagenet's troops, only to be dredged up again around 1300, miraculously saved, they say.

Fougères Castle

This magnificent debris of the Middle Ages... adorned with its square and rounded towers, each one large enough to put up a whole regiment.

Balzac, *Les Chouans*

Fougères Castle
t 02 99 99 79 59; open daily 9.30–12.30 and 2–6.30; tours at 10, 11, 12, 2, 3, 4 and 5pm, some in English

Now an immense empty shell, the Château de Fougères still makes a spectacular display with its great lengths of walls and its mass of towers – 13 have survived. All the machicolations and loopholes, plus the conical slate roofs, make the place look a perfect picture of medieval defence, even if most of the inner buildings have disappeared.

An initial fort went up on this site early in the 11th century. In a struggle for regional supremacy in the next century, Duke Conan IV of Brittany submitted to the mighty Angevin, King Henry II Plantagenet of England. But one Breton vassal of Conan's, Raoul II de Fougères, then defied Plantagenet power. Henry II's troops destroyed Fougères's castle in 1166; Raoul II set about rebuilding it on a much greater scale.

The castle in fact offers as an excellent illustration of advances in military fortifications across the medieval centuries. The square towers date from the late 12th or early 13th centuries; the round ones (allowing better views of the enemy on all sides and resisting projectiles better) are mainly from the 13th or 14th centuries; the horseshoe-shaped ones went up in the 15th century, built to resist new artillery fire.

Once across the moat with its row of watermill wheels, you have to penetrate several protective layers to reach the heart of these massive medieval fortifications. The Tour de la Haye St-Hilaire leads you into the first restricted trap of a courtyard, l'Avancée. Then the Tour de Coëtlogon takes you through a second line of ramparts into the main *basse cour*, where daily château life would have taken place. Only traces of the chapel and the lord's quarters remain here. Up on a hillock within the fort, a third ring of defences protected the Réduit; this was the last refuge from invaders.

Although it's often described as a Breton frontier castle, for much of the medieval period the Château de Fougères was a pawn in the much more complex and local power games of feudal times. The various lords of Fougères frequently showed conflicting loyalties as to which overlord to support. For such an impregnable-looking structure, the place has a pretty ignominious track record – sometimes sieges, sometimes ruses caused the castle to be taken.

For example, in the later stages of the Hundred Years War, Surienne, a Spaniard working for the English, swiped the château by stealth one night in 1449, and he and his men pillaged Fougères. Duke François II of Brittany had to come and lay siege to the rebellious Spaniard, who gave up when plague struck within the castle. After this, the duke had the two anti-artillery towers called Françoise and Tourasse erected. To little avail. Soon La Trémouïlle was attacking Fougères in the name of the French king. He took the castle within a week, just before the Battle of St-Aubin-du-Cormier, which sealed the fate of an independent Breton duchy. The enormous castle served little over the following centuries.

An exciting new lease of life is being brought back to the castle from 2009 with the creation of sound and light shows in many of the towers, the scenes helping retell the history of the Breton Marches. You can also walk along long stretches of the ramparts. In addition, temporary sculpture exhibitions are often displayed within the fort, adding an enjoyable artistic note.

Attractions Radiating Out From Fougères

Parc Floral de Haute Bretagne at the Château de la Foltière
www.parcfloral bretagne.com, t 02 99 95 48 32; open July–Aug daily 10.30–6.30, April–June and Sept 10–12 and 2–6, Mar and Oct–Nov 2–5.30

Set in a countryside of gorgeous towering beeches a dozen kilometres northwest of Fougères, the **Parc Floral de Haute Bretagne at the Château de la Foltière** was recently created from nothing, virtually overnight. The magic has been wrought by Alain Jouno, an engineer who fell in love with the property when he saw it in an abandoned state and bought it in 1995. He has done phenomenal work, giving the place a new spirit. The series of separately inspired gardens are set in a landscaped park, by a 19th-century country house rather in the style of a *malouinière* (*see* p.105). The various gardens each have a clear theme, reflected in their names, such as the Persian Garden, the City of Antiquity, the Valley of the Kings, the Vale of Poets, or the Blue Lagoon... These titles may sound a bit clichéd, but the care put into creating each set piece is admirable. Each year, new sections are created, including in 2009 a garden appealing to the senses for the visually impaired.

Ferme de Chênedet
www.chenedet.loisirs. com, t 02 99 97 35 46

For an alternative excursion, the **Ferme de Chênedet**, at Landéan, northeast of Fougères through the Forêt de Fougères, offers outdoor activities year-round, notably horse-riding and mountain-biking.

West of Fougères towards Rennes, you can follow the picturesque **Couesnon Valley** to the town of **St-Aubin-du-Cormier**, known in Brittany as the site of the battle in 1488 in which the last duke of Brittany's troops were defeated for the final time. Some six thousand Bretons are said to have died in the terrible, fateful encounter. English, German and Spanish mercenaries had fought alongside them, but all those who survived were expelled after this defeat. The duke's heiress Anne would have to ask King Charles VIII of France's permission to marry; he himself would soon insist that she be wedded to him, and hence Brittany to France. The French dismantled the castle here; only a few sad fragments remain, a symbol of the ducal disaster.

Vitré and its Pays

Its fabulously turreted triangular castle makes Vitré most memorable, but the town's splendid historic houses leave almost as much of an impression on visitors.

History

Vitré once lay provocatively far east on the Breton border with France, like an outpost to protect Rennes. The history of its major ruling families illustrates just how divided loyalties were for many nobles living on feudal frontiers – their allegiance vacillated between the Breton dukes and the kings of France.

The first fort went up in the 11th century, the count of Rennes calling upon the then trusted family here to help establish firm defences for the border and for Breton autonomy. The triangular château took shape in the 13th century, and the town was surrounded by walls. However, 1251 saw a vital change in Vitré's ownership. The baron of the time passed away, leaving Vitré to his daughter, who married the baron of Laval in the neighbouring province of Maine. For centuries to come, Vitré was ruled over by a line of Lavals, who owed allegiance to the French king. Fruitful marriages added estates to the family's possessions, so that the Lavals became just about the most powerful family in Haute Bretagne, as the eastern half of Brittany is known.

Brittany's independence was fast drawing to an end by the second half of the 15th century. But one famous Vitréen, Pierre Landais, served the last Breton duke, François II, in memorable fashion. The most powerful merchant the town ever knew, Landais became treasurer of Brittany and the duke's principal counsellor, but his underhand politicking led to serious ducal displeasure, and he was executed in Nantes in 1485. Though further massive fortifications had been added to Vitré in the last duke's time, in the final campaign by the French, Vitré put up no serious resistance.

The wealth of Vitré's merchants through the 15th and 16th centuries is still very evident today in the extravagant town houses they had built on the fortunes they made exporting the local cloth far afield. However, in the second half of the 16th century, the town was rocked by the French Wars of Religion. By inheritance, the town had come into a branch of the Coligny family, staunch Protestants. Catholic troops came to lay siege to the stronghold for five months one year, but were unsuccessful. In the 17th century, Vitré became the property of another mighty French family, the La Trémouïlles, but they neglected the castle, which fell into disrepair.

Touring Vitré

Château de Vitré
*open May–Sept
Wed–Mon 10–12.45 and
2–6; Oct–April
Wed–Mon 10–12.15 and
2–5.30, closed Sun am*

The main interest in visiting the **Château de Vitré** today lies in getting a closer glimpse of its tremendous architecture. You're encouraged to clamber up and down bits of the ramparts, as the Vitré museum is scattered around various parts of the castle. The Tour St-Laurent tower contains fine fragments of old stone carvings and decorative finials from Vitré houses, while the Tour de l'Argenterie conceals a bizarre collection of preserved animals. A room in the Tour de l'Oratoire displays religious objects. Down in the castle courtyard, the fine detail on the Renaissance oratory includes a very curious row of breasts.

Historic **Vitré** outside the castle walls has retained its **medieval street plan**, with just a few 19th-century arteries added, and many of the solid town ramparts have remained in good shape. Leaving **Place du Château**, head up to **Place Notre-Dame**. At the top of this sloping square, the broad façade of the **church** dominates the scene. With Gothic pinnacles looking sparkling new, it also boasts richly carved Renaissance doors. Inside, the furnishings are neo-Gothic. Down in one of the bottom corners of the square, a little passageway takes you under two town houses that serve as a bridge and leads out to the **town ramparts**.

Back up by the church of Notre Dame, heading up along **Rue Notre Dame**, you pass some delightful timberframe houses and the magnificent Hôtel Ringues de la Troussannais, a 16th-century mansion set back in its own little courtyard. Its delightful French Renaissance details include putti standing on top of the windows. You then come to a string of further pretty squares; from here you might head back into the old town from Place de la République via a different route. **Rue de la Borderie** is a main shopping street that leads in the right direction. Arcaded **Rue Poterie** and **Rue Sévigné** are worth seeking out, too, while **Rue Baudrairie** (*baudroyeurs* were leather workers) has the best display of timberframe houses in town. **Rue d'En Bas** leading off Rue Baudrairie does vie for attention with it though.

Musée St-Nicolas
open same hours as Château de Vitré

Rue du Bas Val descends sharply past the château's foundations to the St-Nicolas quarter. The **Musée St-Nicolas** lies in this lower part of town, beyond the washhouses on the Vilaine River. It celebrates sacred art, having taken over the enormous former chapel of Vitré's historic hospital. A few very worn frescoes can still be made out on its tall walls, but pale into insignificance compared with the Church wealth displayed in the reliquary crosses, chalices and other ritual paraphernalia. One of the oldest pieces is a remarkable 15th-century reliquary box covered with roughly cut precious stones.

Around Vitré

Musée de la Faucillonnaie
open same hours as Château de Vitré

Well signposted north out of Vitré, the **Musée de la Faucillonnaie** at **Montreuil-sous-Pérouse** recalls the more comfortable side of country life in centuries past. This is not one of those desperately cluttered country museums that attempts to demonstrate with a thousand and one objects how poor and unmaterialistic previous times were; here, just a small but carefully chosen number of items is displayed in the rooms of this plain-fronted manor. Evocative paintings of the Vitré area add to the atmosphere.

The little village of **Champeaux** less than 10 kilometres northwest of Vitré has a delightful collection of light, mottled stone houses set around a green. Before being turned into villagers' houses, the buildings were the homes of canons serving the collegiate **church of St Mary Magdalene**, set up and paid for by the wealthy local Espinay family from 1432. The main attraction inside is the decoration in the choir end. The Renaissance stained glass shows remarkable finesse.

Château des Rochers Sévigné

I go for a wander along these pleasant alleys. I have a lackey who follows me. I have books. I move from one spot to another and vary the course of my walks. A book of devotion, another on history, one switches – that makes things entertaining. One dreams a little of God, of providence, of the soul, of the future. Finally, at 8 o'clock I hear a bell. It is supper time.

Madame de Sévigné writing to her daughter in 1689

Château des Rochers Sévigné
Open same hours as Château de Vitré

The prettily freckled Château des Rochers Sévigné under 10 kilometres south of Vitré was the Breton country retreat of the 17th-century society figure Mme de Sévigné, whose private correspondence, published by her family in the early 18th century, reveals so much about her times as well as her temperament. Her Breton country house still hides coyly behind a walled garden, just the odd tower emerging as you arrive. Mme de Sévigné's spirit wafts over the place, much more tellingly than the few badly aged mementoes of her you're shown in the château.

Mme de Sévigné paid some attention to Les Rochers, notably seeing to the addition of the octagonal chapel. The painting here of an exquisite Annunciation to the Virgin is attributed to Guido Reni. The ground floor displays in the main building include various published editions of the marquise's letters, and a few battered personal possessions of hers. Among several portraits on the first floor, the full-length one of Mme de Sévigné at the time of her marriage stands out. She appears dauntingly mature for her age. Her granddaughter Pauline de Grignan, Marquise de Simiane, is

07 Ille-et-Vilaine | Brittany's Northern Marches: Vitré and its Pays

Hot Chocolate and Politics from Perceptive Mme de Sévigné

Marie de Rabutin-Chantal was 18 when she married Henri de Sévigné in 1644. Les Rochers had been in her husband's family since the early 15th century, but had been largely reconstructed in the 17th century. The couple spent some happy times here at the beginning of their marriage, but after only six years of wedlock the roguish husband was killed in a duel over '*la belle Lolo*', described as a lady of easy virtue. Mme de Sévigné came to mourn here. She never remarried, living on until 1696.

Mme de Sévigné didn't spend huge amounts of time at Les Rochers, but the place meant a great deal to her. She found solitude here away from a hectic social life. She also came to collect the rents from her estates to help pay for her partying and her trips. Her correspondence was mainly with her beloved daughter, who had married a Provençal lord, and whose letters she seemed to live for more than for anything else at times. In her depictions, political events were treated as swiftly as her social life, her state of mind and her health, and were considered alongside such weighty matters as her up-and-down relationship with drinking chocolate.

portrayed as more of a vacuous, rosy-cheeked stereotype of her era. This granddaughter is the person who decided to have her grandmother's correspondence published, though she burned some letters that she considered too uncomplimentary to the family.

South from Vitré

The small, quiet Marches town of **La Guerche-de-Bretagne** has retained its lovely arcaded streets, although its château has long gone. The town was given ramparts in the 13th century, the same period that the **collegiate church of Notre-Dame** first went up. Only the choir remains from that time, along with a defensive-looking, stocky slate tower. A towering neo-Gothic spire was added to the west front in the 19th century. The interior contains a row of rich stained-glass windows, some mutilated in the Wars of Religion, but still showing vivid figures. However, the most striking art is reserved for the shocking choir stalls, carved in part with Gothic monstrosities, in part with Renaissance grotesques.

West of La Guerche, the **Dolmen de la Roche aux Fées** counts among the most impressive neolithic tombs in Brittany. This one is thought, very vaguely, to date from between 3000 BC and 2500 BC. It differs a good deal from the style of dolmens found further west in Brittany, its form linked more closely with the Loire Valley. The opening, which leads into a sort of antechamber, is aligned with the rising sun of the winter solstice. The scale is so large that you can stand up quite comfortably in the main gallery. The structure would originally have been covered with a mound of stones and earth, but this has completely disappeared. On many Wednesday evenings in July and August, you can join an atmospheric guided walk, **La Balade des Fées**, taking you through the local legends.

Musée Louis Raison
t 02 99 00 06 80;
open Mon–Fri 9–12 and 2–6, Sat and Sun 2–6

Southwest from Vitré, at **Domagné**, the Musée Louis Raison recalls old cider-making ways in this, one of the biggest cider-apple growing corners left in Brittany. Opened by Louis Raison, who has one of the largest cider-making businesses in the region, it offers free tastings.

Southwest again, at the village of **Châteaugiron**, a charming main street curves up to the daunting, bulging towers of the **château**. Its sheer size gives an indication of Châteaugiron's former importance as an outpost of Rennes. The barons based here were once powerful in the Breton duchy, several receiving the title of chamberlain to the duke through inheritance. In 1472, the then duke of Brittany signed a joint treaty with the English king here in a vain attempt to keep out the French. There's little to see inside the château today, but the enormous separate 13th-century keep houses the tourist office and local exhibitions.

Market Days in the Northern Marches

Fougères: Saturday

Vitré: Monday and Saturday

St-Aubin-du-Cormier: Thursday

Châteaugiron: Thursday

La Guerche-de-Bretagne: Tuesday (since 1121)

Marché de l'Aumaillerie, La Selle-en-Luitré: Friday (one of the biggest cattle markets in Europe)

Where to Stay and Eat in the Northern Marches

Fougères ✉ 35300

**Les Voyageurs, 10 Place Gambetta, t 02 99 99 08 20, *www.hotel-fougeres.fr* (€). A neat and tidy choice, with brightly refurbished rooms. The restaurant (€€€€; *closed Sat and Sun eves*) serves good traditional local fare.

**Le Balzac, 15 Rue Nationale, t 02 99 99 42 46, *www.balzachotel.com* (€). A simple but nice option well placed in the upper town, its rooms redone. Balzac wrote his famous novel *Les Chouans* here (*see* box, p.138).

Les Vins et une Fourchette, 1 Rue de la Fourchette, t 02 99 94 55 88 (€€). A little old butcher's shop near the castle entrance, with delightfully decorated little dining rooms in which to enjoy really tasty dishes. *Closed Sun and Tues eves.*

Le Médiéval, 2 Place Raoul II, t 02 99 94 92 59 (€€–€). In the appealing pedestrian area at the foot of the castle, this warm, welcoming, pretty restaurant offers good cuisine plus a tempting terrace.

Haute-Sève, 37 Blvd Jean Jaurès, t 02 99 94 23 39 (€€). Behind its appealing timberframe front, a good-value stop for excellent fresh cuisine. *Closed Sun eve and Mon, and mid-July–mid-Aug.*

Le Chatellier 35133

Château de la Foltière B&B, *www.parcfloralbretagne.com*, t 02 99

95 48 32 (€€€€). With a splendid handful of spacious, elegant rooms looking out onto the fabulous gardens (*see* p.142).

St-Brice-en-Coglès ✉ 35460

**Le Lion d'Or, 6–8 Rue Chateaubriand, t 02 99 98 61 44, *www.hotel-leliondor.fr* (€€). An old coaching inn in a village c.15km northwest of Fougères, with decent, redone rooms and a really warm restaurant (€€€–€).

Le Manoir de la Branche B&B, t 02 99 97 77 95, *www.manoirdela branche.com* (€€€€–€€). Exceptionally beautiful, tastefully decorated rooms in a gorgeous 15th-century home. *Table d'hôte* served by the great fireplace.

Vitré ✉ 35500

**du Château, 5 Rue Rallon, t 02 99 74 58 59, *hotel-du-chateau2@wanadoo.fr* (€€). Pleasant basic hotel with recently redone rooms. Ask for one on the upper floors for a view of the castle ramparts.

**Le Minotel, 47 Rue Poterie, t 02 99 75 11 11, *www.leminotel.fr* (€). A hotel in a beautiful renovated building in the historic centre. The modernized rooms are in 'golf club chic' style.

Fauchers B&B, 2 Chemin des Tertres Noirs, t 02 99 75 08 69 (€). A welcoming B&B in a characterful old house down the hill near to the Musée St-Nicolas.

Taverne de l'Ecu, 12 Rue de la Baudrairie, t 02 99 75 11 09, *www.tavernedelecu.fr* (€€€). A restaurant in a 15th-century inn, serving hearty specialities in a medieval-style room. *Closed low season Sun and Tues eves and Wed.*

Le Petit Pressoir, 20 Rue de Paris, t 02 99 74 79 79, *lepetitpressoir35@ wanadoo.fr* (€€). A friendly address at which to enjoy good family cooking. *Closed Sun eve and Mon.*

Le Pichet, 17 Blvd de Laval, t 02 99 75 24 09, *www.lepichet.fr* (€€). For creative modern Breton cuisine, a little way east of the centre, served either in the bright dining room or the pretty garden.

ⓘ **Pays d'Accueil Touristique des Portes de Bretagne** *www.pays-des-portes-de-bretagne.com*

ⓘ **Pays d'Accueil Touristique de Fougères** *www.bretagne-fougeres.com*

ⓘ **Fougères >** *2 Rue Nationale, t 02 99 94 12 20, www.ot-fougeres.fr*

ⓘ **Vitré >>** *Place St-Yves, t 02 99 75 04 46, www.ot-vitre.fr*

★ **Château de la Foltière B&B >**

⊕ Château des Tesnières B&B

Torcé 35370

Château des Tesnières B&B, **t** 02 99 49 65 02, *www.chateaudestesnieres.com* (€€€€–€€€). This fantastic 19th-century Loire-style castle stands c.10km southwest of Vitré. The extremely gracious rooms have been wonderfully decorated. *Closed Dec–Jan.*

St-Didier ⊠ 35220

⊕ La Guerche-de-Bretagne >>
30 Rue du Guesclin,
t 02 99 96 30 78, otsi.
laguerche@wanadoo.fr

★★★Pen'Roc, La Peinière, just north of St-Didier, **t** 02 99 00 33 02, *www.penroc.fr* (€€€–€€). Smart contemporary rooms, some with terraces, plus the benefits of a pool, an exercise room and a sauna. Stylish seafood dishes are served either in the modern dining room or on the pretty patio (€€).

Châteaubourg ⊠ 35220

★★★Ar Milin, 30 Rue de Paris, **t** 02 99 00 30 91, *www.armilin.com* (€€€–€€).

Pretty little rooms, some set in a former flour mill on the River Vilaine, the grounds peppered with contemporary art. In the elegant restaurant (€€€€), grilled meats among the chef's specialities.

Châteaugiron ⊠ 35410

La Loriette, 2 Boulevard Pierre et Julien Gourdel, **t** 02 99 37 41 35 (€€). For lovingly prepared Breton cuisine in a traditional setting.

La Guerche-de-Bretagne ⊠ 35130

★★La Calèche, 16 Ave du Général Leclerc, **t** 02 99 96 21 63, *www. lacaleche.com* (€). Spacious, comfortable rooms and a bright restaurant (€€–€) where you can enjoy good copious cuisine. *Closed Fri and Sun eves and Mon, and most Aug.*

Rennes

⊕ Rennes

Brittany's capital never lacks vitality, not surprisingly, with up to 60,000 students and researchers milling around its wonderful old streets and with its masses of bookshops, bars and bistrots. The historic centre boasts both grand thoroughfares leading to straight-laced squares, and quirkier corners crammed with timberframe houses that seem to lean drunkenly against each other.

Most of the action takes place north of the Vilaine, but a funky new cultural centre, Les Champs Libres, has just gone up south of the old quays and includes the new Musée de Bretagne celebrating Breton culture. The city has long been proud of its fine arts museum, theatres and many concert venues, not forgetting the Breton Parlement, restored after it burned down – following a typically rowdy Breton fishermen's protest that got out of hand. Rennes brings out the wild side in some. Numerous students have even been adopting northern European binge-drinking habits, particularly on Thursday evenings, but this is also a city with a very healthy cultural programme to satisfy many tastes.

History

Rennes developed where the Ille River meets the Vilaine, at a crossing of trading routes in the Celtic era. The Riedones, who were one of five main tribes of the Armorican peninsula, settled here. Under Roman rule, this main settlement of theirs became known as Condate, meaning confluence. There's virtually nothing visible in Rennes from Gallo-Roman times, let alone Celtic ones, but the

Getting to and around Rennes

Rennes-St Jacques **airport** (**t** 02 99 29 00 00, *www.rennes.aeroport.fr*) is serviced by Flybe flights from Southampton, Edinburgh, Newcastle, Belfast and Dublin. Rennes is just 2 hours from Paris by TGV train (direct trains twice an hour at peak times). The **bus** station (**t** 02 99 30 87 80) is close to the railway station. Rennes also benefits from a **metro** service (**t** 08 11 55 55 35, *www.star.fr*) and a pick-up and drop-off **bicycle** system (buy cards at the Mairie on Place de la Mairie, **t** 02 23 62 10 10, or online at *www.rennes.fr*).

Musée de Bretagne displays interesting vestiges of these civilizations. A huge number of Roman coins was discovered in the Vilaine, thought to have been offerings to the water gods.

The town became the seat of an early bishopric with the arrival of Christianity in the peninsula. In Carolingian times, perhaps in response to Breton incursions across the Vilaine, the Franks set up their buffer zone in the Breton Marches, the county of Rennes forming part of this defensive system. But in the 9th century, successful Breton leaders won the territory. From this time, religious institutions multiplied in the area; in the 11th and 12th

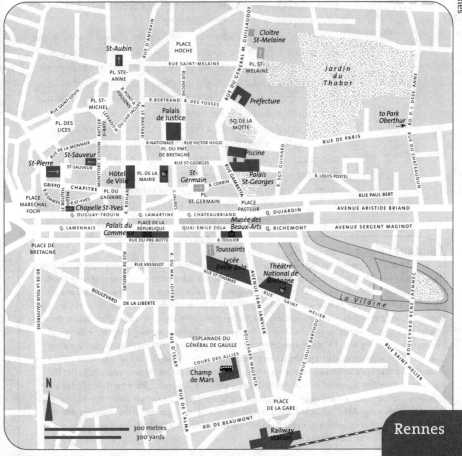

Rennes

Du Guesclin Jousts His Way Into His Father's Heart

The best-known story in Rennes from the period of the Breton War of Succession and the Hundred Years War is of the young warrior Bertrand du Guesclin's appearance on the scene. Shunned by his family as an ugly misfit, at 17 he supposedly came to a Rennes tournament to prove himself. On Place des Lices he demonstrated his unmatched skill in jousting. Appearing as an anonymous contender, he remained unbeatable, until it was time to face his father in the joust – he bowed out, revealing his true identity. His dubious dad was finally able to accept his odd son with pride. Du Guesclin would become the most important knight on the French side in the first part of the Hundred Years War. In 1356, he even played an instrumental part in seizing Rennes for France. (*See also* box, p.134.)

centuries, they mushroomed. St Melaine played a major role in helping to spread monasticism across the duchy, while St-Georges became the first significant nunnery in Brittany.

Links between Brittany and England were strengthened by the Bretons' part in the Norman conquest. Conan IV of Rennes, for example, was confirmed in his succession to the earldom of Richmond by Plantagenet King Henry II of England. Henry II later came to tear down castles in the Breton Marches, including Rennes'. But in the ensuing centuries, the city confirmed its pre-eminent position in the Breton duchy.

Thirteen provincial Parlements were set up around France in the Ancien Régime, and a royal decision was taken in 1561 that the Parlement de Bretagne should settle in Rennes. The mainly noble Breton parliamentarians, who met twice a year, exercised quite some control over regional politics and justice, and benefited from their position, as did Rennes, where they built sumptuous town houses. In the 17th century, a grand parliament house was also built. This Parlement incorporated the highest court in Brittany and became a provincial body increasingly at odds with the royal authorities and their representatives, the governors.

Among the most traumatic times for Rennes, and Brittany, in the Ancien Régime was when the royal administration attempted to impose a crippling tax on official documents in 1675. This led to the

Brittany's Biggest Tax Revolt

Witnessing Brittany's most significant revolt of the Ancien Régime, Mme de Sévigné wrote of 5,000 soldiers arriving in Brittany's capital to impose the royal will: 'A tax of 100,000 écus has been levied on the merchants; and if this money is not raised within 24 hours the amount will be doubled and the soldiers will be able to go into action to demand it. The families in one of the main streets in town have been chased out of their houses and banished, while others have been forbidden from taking them in on punishment of death. So you could see all these wretched people, among them the elderly and women with newly born children, wandering in tears through the outskirts of town, not knowing where to go, without food or a place to sleep. A violin player who had started up a dance mocking the stamped paper tax was broken on the wheel the day before yesterday. He was quartered after his death, and the four pieces of his body were displayed around the town... Sixty merchants have been arrested. Tomorrow the hangings begin. This province offers a good example to the others, above all that governors should be respected, not insulted, and that it is dangerous to throw stones into their gardens.' As part of its punishment for its involvement, Rennes saw the Parlement moved to Vannes for 15 years – a major blow to the city.

Révolte du Papier Timbré across Brittany. The uprising was violently crushed by the royal troops, especially in Rennes.

In towns packed with timber houses, fire was always a major risk. In 1720, a drunken carpenter started one off that destroyed much of the old centre of town. The terrible conflagration lasted a week, and hundreds of the finest houses went up in smoke. It was decided that the new town centre would be built almost entirely using stone façades. Even if wonderful pockets of timberframe buildings remained, a much more carefully planned city structure emerged, with wider streets and grand vistas. Rennes also gained a university in the 18th century.

You can see many important 19th-century additions to the town on a tour of Rennes, including the Lycée Emile Zola, where Jewish scapegoat Alfred Dreyfus underwent his second painful trial, most of the town's citizens apparently indifferent to his plight.

In the Second World War, Rennes did suffer damage from bombings, but not on the scale of the Breton naval bases, and it was one of the very first major towns in France to be liberated, on 4 August 1944. Since those painful times, Rennes has been very much looking forwards. Led by strong socialist mayors, it also became home for a time to some high-profile exiles, including the Portuguese politician Mario Soares, and the great Czech writer Milan Kundera.

Culture has been high on the city's agenda, but so too have been hi-tech industries requiring high-level researchers. The new industries have settled in the specialist Atalante research quarters growing up around the city's edges, putting Rennes at the forefront of developments in new technologies in France. But in the fanciest new development in the centre of town, Les Champs Libres, an important place has been given to the Espace des Sciences alongside the new Musée de Bretagne, the latter boldly attempting to cover the whole region's history and culture.

The Vilaine Quays and Southern City Centre

The most splendid streets and squares of old Rennes lie just north of the Vilaine, but in recent times, attention has been turning more and more to the south of the river. Even if the Vilaine River was canalized and rather drearily covered up in the 19th century, the straight lines of the **quays** still form a very clear divide between the northern and southern halves of the centre, the odd grand historic building standing out along the route, including the fine arts museum, the Musée des Beaux-Arts (*see* p.153). Shops, restaurants and bars congregate along the western quays. One of the most striking, grandiose post offices in France, the **Palais du Commerce**, dominates **Place de la République**. This area, spreading over where the Vilaine passes underground, has been given a recent make-over, brightened up with comfortable benches set around outdoor flower stalls, making it a popular place to meet.

A bit to the south, there are a few charming historic streets to discover. Along **Rue du Pré-Botté**, the successful newspaper *Ouest-France* and its predecessor *Ouest-Eclair* used to be produced in the impressive printworks. *Ouest-France*, today the largest regional daily in France, also publishes a very extensive book list, specializing in titles on French culture and tourism. The company's head office has a **Ouest-France bookshop** with a wide choice of titles on Brittany and a spot where you can consult the local paper. **Rue Vasselot** is the most enticing steet nearby, with its timberframe houses and string of lively restaurants and bars.

One of the main reasons why the Rennais would head south of the Vilaine in the past, beyond using the railway station, was to attend a cultural event at either the major, revamped **Théâtre National de Bretagne** (known as the TNB) or at the **Maison de la Culture**, which cuts its figure of eight along Rue Saint-Hélier. These places help Rennes offer a rich, year-round cultural programme.

Almost opposite these venues stands the **Lycée Emile Zola**, a very grand school indeed, designed in the 19th century by town architect Jean-Baptiste Martenot. This place is famous in late-19th-century French history for hosting the **second trial of Alfred Dreyfus**, the Jewish French army officer falsely accused of spying in the mid-1890s. The persecuted Dreyfus wasn't cleared, unfortunately, although the many conservative Catholic Rennais were untroubled – it would take Major Henry's admission of forgery and a third, civilian trial in 1906 to clear Dreyfus's name. The substantial, striking **All Saints church** rises behind the school.

The most exciting redevelopment in central Rennes over the last few years has been happening around **Esplanade du Général de Gaulle**, past **Les Halles**, the covered market, and close to the railway station. A major new **multiplex cinema** has opened here, while **Le Liberté** has been conceived as the latest, state-of-the-art concert and entertainment venue. The major permanent new cultural draw close by is the funky Les Champs Libres centre.

Musée de Bretagne in Les Champs Libres

Musée de Bretagne in Les Champs Libres
www.leschampslibres. fr, t 02 23 40 66 00; open Tues 12–9, Wed–Fri 12–7, weekends 2–7; closed Mon

This flagship building for contemporary Rennes was designed by renowned French architect Christian de Portzamparc. His task was to include three cultural institutions under the one roof: the main town library, a science centre, and a museum dedicated to the whole of Brittany. He has clearly reflected the different functions in the architecture, the town library set in an upturned glass pyramid, the science centre incorporated into a slate-clad meteorite, while the Musée de Bretagne draws a figure of eight around these two. These interlocking parts help explain the deliberately clashing looks of the place. In parts, the exterior walls are clad with great slabs of purple Breton stone, while a vast mirrored section up top reflects the area's roofs.

Visit the **Musée de Bretagne** for a serious introduction to Breton history and culture in these trendy new surrounds – the history of Rennes is covered separately, in a beautiful converted Gothic chapel next to the tourist office. With half a million years of Breton ancestors to cover (the recent digs at the archaeological site of Menez Dregan in the Finistère have revealed some of the earliest traces of fire made by man's ancestors anwhere in the world), it's inevitable that the overview has to be fairly cursory. The approach is chronological, by period, the presentation slick, but one issue is that all the displays feel a bit like they've simply been set down in a vast lobby. Plus there's no natural lighting in this section of the building.

Neolithic times are quite well covered, and the Roman period, as ever, left a reasonable number of artefacts, but little material evidence has ever been found of the crucial arrival of immigrants from western Britain through the Dark Ages, or of the subsequent Viking raids of the 9th and 10th centuries. Once you get to the medieval sections, there's much more material. Under the Ancien Régime, as the French monarchy took much greater control of the province, the creation of major regional institutions, including the Parlement de Bretagne, is clearly charted. Further sections rush you through regional history from the Revolution to the Second World War. One of the best features of the new presentations is the booths where a small number of visitors can sit and watch short videos on various themes, or even, in one corner, listen to old Breton legends, recorded in both French and Breton languages.

Read our History chapter at the start of this guidebook to fill in some of the rather large gaps and omissions: for instance, while the retrial of Alfred Dreyfus in Rennes is extensively covered, the slave trade from which so many Breton merchants made a killing in the 18th century is virtually ignored, bar one model of a slaving vessel – go to the Château de Nantes (*see* p.484) for much better coverage of that painful issue. Major temporary cultural exhibitions will take place at Les Champs Libres down the years – one of the first ones concentrated on the importance of Arthurian legends in Brittany and beyond.

Musée des Beaux-Arts
www.mbar.org, t 02 23 62 17 45; open Wed–Sun 10–12 and 2–6

Musée des Beaux-Arts

Back up on the Vilaine quays stands the grandiose fine arts museum. It's thanks to the plunderings of private and foreign collections during the Revolution and the Napoleonic Empire that Rennes so rapidly acquired its collections. The Marquis de Robien had amassed a phenomenal art collection before the end of the Ancien Régime; when his son ran off at the Revolution, the city felt free to 'adopt' the family treasures, almost all 17th-century works, over half from northern European schools. This collection was added to early in the 19th century by a handout from all the Revolutionary and foreign booty gathered at the Louvre. The most famous painting Rennes thus acquired is Georges de La Tour's *Le Nouveau-né*, a work depicting a newborn baby with exceptional glowing tenderness, although the lot also included Rubens' terrifying *Tiger Hunt*. Violence appears as a noticeably frequent theme in the collections, although a few paintings stand out for their gentler tone, for instance the Chardin still lifes.

The major French schools of the 19th century are also represented, such as Orientalism. With the works from the end of that century, you come to paintings with more Breton subject matter. Among the post-Impressionists, look out for a couple of Pont-Aven School pictures here – Paul Sérusier's *Solitude*, which depicts a deeply melancholic coiffed girl in a countryside of Breton boulders, and Emile Bernard's strikingly beautiful *L'Arbre jaune*. Intriguing Breton pieces by Loiseau, Maufra and Moret also stand out, but most original of all is Georges Lacombe's highly stylized wave painting, *Marine bleue, effet de vagues*. Picasso's *Baigneuse*, painted at the Breton resort of Dinard, can still shock with the distorted geometry of the woman's body and the provocative simplicity of its forms. Probing still deeper into the subconscious is *L'Inspiration*, an aqueous work by the great Breton Surrealist Yves Tanguy. The contemporary art collections are also worth perusing, several important Breton figures represented in the selection. (Look up all the works on the museum's marvellous website.)

Historic Quarters North of the Vilaine

On the north side of the quays, turn up **Rue Georges Dottin** to enter the **oldest quarter** to have survived the 1720 fire, full of timberframed atmosphere and multicoloured cobblestones. At the corner of **Rue St-Yves** stands the delightful, light-stoned Gothic **Chapelle St-Yves**, looking slightly wonky on the outside, but tall, solid and airy within. Now attached to the tourist office, it serves as an exhibition space, with an appealing presentation of Rennes' history, together with a video on the painstaking work to reconstruct the Parlement de Bretagne.

The curve of **Rue des Dames** heading towards the cathedral front reveals where part of the former town ramparts used to lie. **Rue**

Griffon and **Rue du Chapitre** are lined with many fine 16th-century houses, some revived to their original shockingly bright colours. Set back from the street, the **Hôtel de Blossac** looks more sober and grand than the rest.

St-Sauveur and the Cathedral

At the eastern end of Rue du Chapitre, the straight line formed by **Rue Montfort**, **Rue Clisson** and **Rallier du Baty** constitutes one of the grand shopping axes in Rennes, connecting Place du Calvaire to Place St-Michel. Go up as far as the **church of St-Sauveur**, soberly classical on the outside, still drawing many traditional Catholics inside. The interior contains a splendid organ, an absurdly ornate baldaquin over the choir, a unique metallic pulpit, and a painting showing Rennes in flames, in the terrible fire of 1720. **Rue St-Sauveur** is lined with some tremendous timberframe houses and leads into **Rue de la Psalette**, which conceals a secretive series of further wonderful timberframe façades, ending with the gilded, scrolled monsters on the house on the corner with the Rue du Chapitre. You find yourself at the back of the cathedral here.

The **Cathédrale St-Pierre** was built on the site of a Gallo-Roman temple, but the oldest part of the church now standing only goes back as far as 1560. The edifice took more than a century to complete. The architecture behind the façade was started in the late 18th century on the plans of architect Mathurin Crucy. Two colonnades of brown-veined stone glisten along the nave. The side aisles take the form of spacious walks. Decoration overwhelms the interior; much of the wall painting and the gilding was added in the course of the 19th century. The wall paintings depict the saints most revered in the different parts of Brittany, their names usefully written below them. Look out for the fine depictions of Christ's stations of the cross placed higher up. Follow the life story of the Virgin in the exceptionally ornate gilded 15th-century reredos from Flanders in one side chapel; the wealth of Gothic detail overwhelms at first glance. A much simpler but exquisite terracotta statue of the Virgin and Child has been placed in the nave recently.

Rennes's Grand Squares

West of the cathedral front, a neglected side street (off Rue de la Monnaie) leads to the **Portes Mordelaises**, once the grandest town entrance, now sadly sidelined. **Place des Lices**, generally cited as Rennes's most spectacular square, surrounded as it is by timberframe façades (although the competition is stiff), stands just north of Rue de la Monnaie. Its soaring, beam-patterned buildings date from surprisingly late, from the mid-17th century, providing a contrast with the sober classical style more in vogue at the time. Two stylish steel and brick 19th-century market halls occupy the centre of the square. These were designed by Jean-Baptiste Martenot, the most influential Rennes architect of the 19th century.

Leave the square by the northeast corner and you come to the restaurant- and bar-crowded **Place St-Michel**, one of the liveliest and prettiest meeting places in town, its terraces absolutely buzzing on warm evenings. A hop and a skip east, **Place du Champ Jacquet** is overseen by an amazing line of timberframe houses that appear to prop each other up, and look down on a statue of Leperdit, portrayed as a heroic mayor of Rennes during the Revolution. **Place Ste-Anne**, just north, counts among the busiest social hubs of old Rennes, teeming with students and tourists in the evenings, several of its sides packed with restaurants whose terraces spill out generously. The strangely truncated **church of St-Aubin** towers over the square. To the left of the church, **Rue St-Malo** has an edgier feel, and acts as a magnet for the trendy and slightly alternative. All sorts of ethnic restaurants line its way.

Return to the corner watchtower at the meeting of Rue du Champ Jacquet and **Rue Le Bastard**. Despite the curious name, this last street actually turns out to be one of the most respectable and chic avenues in town, leading down to the most central of the town squares, **Place de la Mairie**. The playful architecture gives a light touch to this spacious square, with its carousel. The central section of the town hall, topped by its ornate belfry, was given a concave front, while opposite, the theatre was given a convex auditorium. Much more sober and serious, **Place du Parlement de Bretagne** is dominated on one side by the former home of the parliament of Brittany, still the home of the highest law court in the region.

Parlement de Bretagne

Parlement de Bretagne
Guided tours only via the tourist office, so sign up there. Visits last 1h 30mins

It took the disaster of the burning down of the **Parlement de Bretagne** in 1994 for the Bretons, and the Rennais in particular, to appreciate fully the importance of the highly symbolic building that still stamps its authority on the heart of Brittany's capital. Of course, the place was a daunting presence in centuries past, run by and mainly in the interests of the province's aristocrats through the Ancien Régime. Although set up by a centralizing French monarchy, the Breton noblemen who met here did hold quite some sway over regional policies. This role came to an abrupt end at the Revolution, but the place continued to exercise its other main function, as the main court of the province, afterwards, and still does to this day.

In 1994, during a fishermen's protest march through town, a flare was set off that quietly lodged itself in the top of the Parlement, but later burst into flames that same night. The roofs were burnt to a cinder, but the fire service saved the rest of the building, even if its sumptuously decorated chambers were waterlogged. The restoration work was meticulously done and lasted 10 years, although the judges and lawyers moved back in much more quickly than the artwork. One positive thing to come out of the fire is that it was decided that visitors should be given much more regular access to the interiors.

The classical building went up in the 17th century, the facade modelled by Salomon de Brosse, who designed Paris's Palais du Luxembourg. The chambers around the upper floor were given the most elaborate decors, paintings incorporated into coffered ceilings, tapestries framed around the walls. The Breton nobles originally asked the monarchy for money to help with the decoration; this wasn't forthcoming, but the crown did grant them the right to levy taxes on wine and cider to pay for the heady allegorical extravaganza.

They didn't commission naive Breton artists here; you're treated to the most fashionable Parisian period styles inside. Most of the pieces, including the canvases for the ceilings, were executed in Paris, and shipped here by waterways. Louis XIV's official leading artist for a time, Charles Hérard, was at first in charge of the project, even executing three gilded trompe-l'oeil figures himself, but it was his pupil Noël Coypel who took over the bulk of the painting for the Grand' Chambre, eclipsing his master, who fell out of favour as Le Brun took his place. The allegorical figures, executed between 1655 and 1665, are superbly done, with some exquisite figures and scenes full of drama representing Justice at work. One particularly memorable one shows Fraud, a sexually ambivalent figure, being unmasked.

After Coypel's elevating finesse, the quality of the painting can't compete in the other chambers. At the end of the 17th century, Jean Jouvenet was commissioned to bring religion more evidently into the picture in the Conseil de la Grand' Chambre, but his touch is less certain. In further rooms, certain 19th-century artists really went overboard, notably Jobbé Duval, whose work verged on the pornographic.

The tapestries fared worse than the paintings in the fire, and an additional accident led to half of them going up in flames in a storage warehouse. Just one is back in place, a huge 20th-century piece representing the death of medieval warrior du Guesclin, a fitting subject for the ambivalent Parlement, as although he was a Breton, du Guesclin fought for the king of France. All the restoration work has cost a fortune, but there isn't talk of putting a tax on the wine or cider in Rennes today to pay for it.

East towards St-Melaine and the Jardin du Thabor

On the corner of **Rue St-Georges**, look out for the gorgeous carving at the entrance to the Maison de la Coiffure, including, comically enough, an amazing figure in a wig. The street is packed with atmospheric crêperies and other eateries. Art galleries and antique shops are the specialities along **Rue Victor Hugo**, north parallel to Rue St-Georges.

South from Rue St-Georges, you come to **Place St-Germain** around the **Eglise St-Germain**. This towering Flamboyant Gothic church was built for the wealthy town haberdashers, its façade completed in the mid-16th century. It's a bit of a botched building, but with some charming features and some towering stained-glass windows. A few cafés and restaurants are distributed around the ajdoining squares, visibly patched up after the war.

At the back of the church, Rue Corbin leads east to **Rue Gambetta**. It's hard to miss the bulk of the **Palais Abbatial St-Georges** with its formal gardens sloping towards the river; the scale and grandeur of its 17th-century façade give a good notion of the former wealth of this religious institution. Most irreverently, the site of the former abbey church up Rue Gambetta is now occupied by a colourfully ornamented 1920s swimming pool, a cheerful piece of architecture with an appealing purpose.

A string of streets climb north from Rue Gambetta to the Thabor gardens. Substantial old town houses and grand civic buildings line the way via the Contour de la Motte and Rue du Général Guillaudot. A statue of the Virgin lords it over the **church of St-Melaine**, standing proud on her copper tower. The façade below drips with Baroque decoration; look out for a whole row of fine, full putti faces. The founder of the monastery is represented facing St Benedict. The simple Romanesque interior contrasts surprisingly with this elaborate exterior. To the north of the church, the abbot's palace, with its cloister, displays further 17th-century grandeur.

The Benedictines' garden was long ago transformed into Rennes's elegant main **public garden**, the **Jardin du Thabor**. Some of Rennes's most exclusive 19th-century town houses lie on the sides of these extensive gardens. With shaded alleys of trees, formal French parterres, statues and topiary, a bandstand and a children's carousel, plus an outdoor table-football table that you can play on if you bring your own ball, this garden is where many Rennais come for a stroll or to play. North and east of the Jardin du Thabor, the modern university buildings and campuses stretch out.

Outside the centre, fans of contemporary art might check out **Le Bon Accueil** to the north. The Site Experimental de Pratiques Artistiques (SEPA), an 'artistic laboratory', opened in 1998 to provide a work and resource space for gifted young local artists.

Le Bon Accueil
74 Canal St-Martin,
t 02 99 59 22 76,
www.lebonaccueil.org,
open Tues–Sat 2–7

Ecomusée du Pays de Rennes, La Bintinais
www.ecomuse-rennes-metropole.fr; open April–Sept Tues–Fri 9–6, Sat 2–6, Sun 2–7; Oct–Mar Tues–Fri 9–12 and 2–6, Sat 2–6, Sun 2–7

ⓘ **Rennes >>**
11 Rue St-Yves, t 02 99 67 11 11, www.tourisme-rennes.com

★ **Lecoq Gadby >>**

★ **Auberge St-Sauveur >>**

Heading out to the southern edge of town, the towerblocks almost come up to touch the **Ecomusée du Pays de Rennes, La Bintinais** a substantial showcase of a Rennes farm-turned-museum of rural life. Cider-apple trees grow here, including rare varieties, and several rare breeds of cattle and even Breton chickens are kept in very clean conditions. The place also sells honey from its bees. Interesting temporary exhibitions are held in the converted farm buildings.

Market Days in Rennes

Place des Lices: Saturday

Les Halles, Place Commeurec (south of the Palais du Commerce). The city's daily, bustling permanent covered market, with attractive stalls in 1920s architecture.

Festivals in Rennes

Tombées de la Nuit, t 02 99 32 56 56, *www.lestombeesdelanuit.com*. Cultural festival which practically takes over the whole of the centre of Rennes at the start of July.

Les Transmusicales, t 02 99 31 12 10, *www.lestrans.com*. A major French rock festival held in the first or second week of December. Many successful French artists have launched their careers here.

Rock 'n' Solex, t 02 23 23 86 12, *www.rocknsolex.fr*. A left-field contemporary music festival that has been run by students for 40 years in late May and early June.

Jazz à l'Ouest, *www.jazzalouest.com*. A yearly programme of jazz at MJC Brequigny in the Villejean university district northwest of the centre, culminating in the second week of Nov. Information from the **Ferme de la Harpe**, Avenue Charles-Tillon, **t** 02 99 59 45 38.

Le Grand Soufflet, mid-October, **t** 02 99 22 27 30. An annual accordion festival with music concerts and informal performances in bars.

In July and August there's a programme of free **organ concerts** in the main churches.

Where to Stay in Rennes

Rennes ✉ 35000

****Lecoq Gadby, 156 Rue d'Antrain, **t** 02 99 38 05 55, *www.lecoq-gadby.com* (€€€€). A good 15-minute walk north of the centre, this very smart address in the residential quarters has been extending the number of its rooms, and the range of the luxuries it offers, which include pool, court, spa and beauty treatments. It has a luxurious gourmet restaurant, La Coquerie (€€€–€€).

***Mercure Pré Botté, Rue Paul Louis Courrier, **t** 02 99 78 82 20, *www.accorhotels.com* (€€€€). Chain hotel, but located in the cleverly converted former print works of Ouest-Eclair, predecessor of regional leader Ouest-France. Though centrally located, it benefits from being on the quieter, southern side of the Vilaine quays.

des Lices, 7 Place des Lices, **t 02 99 79 14 81, *www.hotel-des-lices.com* (€€–€). With some rooms looking over the spectacular square.

Nemours, 5 Rue de Nemours, **t 02 99 78 26 26, *www.hotelnemours.com* (€€). A good option, pristinely renovated, within close proximity of Place de la République.

Eating Out in Rennes

Auberge St-Sauveur, 6 Rue St-Sauveur, **t** 02 99 79 32 56 (€€€). For a very fine classic French meal in one of the original timberframe houses that escaped the 1720 fire. *Closed Mon and Sat lunch, Sun, and 3wks Aug–Sept*.

Auberge du Chat Pitre, 18 Rue du Chapitre, **t** 02 99 30 36 36 (€€). A 15th-century timberframe house where waiters in medieval costume serve the dishes. *Open eves only.*

Café Breton, 14 Rue Nantaise, t 02 99 30 74 95 (€€). Refined food in an atmosphere reminiscent of a Parisian bistrot. *Closed Sat and Sun eve.*

Ar Pillig, 10 Rue d'Argentré (near Quai Lamennais), t 02 99 79 53 89 (€). Outstanding central crêperie with fascinating décor by Breton artists.

Crêperie Ste-Anne, Place Ste-Anne, t 02 99 79 22 72 (€). Choice of eating in the irresistible timberframe house, or on the terrace on this lively square. *Closed Sun.*

You'll find a wide choice of traditional Breton options and classic cafés and French restaurants along Rue St-Georges and around Place St-Michel and Place Ste-Anne. To see and be seen, the Italian restaurant Picca on Place de la Mairie boasts a glamorous terrace. Rue St-Malo, up from Place Ste-Anne, has a wide choice of inexpensive ethnic restaurants.

The Forêt de Paimpont and Vilaine Valley

✪ The Vilaine Valley and Merlin's Forest

Wandering around the old streets of Rennes, you may notice the variety of colours of the cobbles beneath your feet. Many are shades of purple. Much of this stone comes from the southwestern corner of the Ille-et-Vilaine we focus on here, giving it a distinctive look. The Forêt de Paimpont west of the Breton capital has gained an international reputation among fans of Arthurian legend thanks to its association with the magical Forest of Brocéliande. The upper stretches of the Vilaine Valley to the south are more secretive, but full of tourist surprises, too.

The Forêt de Paimpont, or Brocéliande

The forest of Paimpont, or Brocéliande, as Arthurian aficionados call it, is one of those places where the imagination gets much the better of reality, or religion. To tackle the disorientating subject, we suggest you first read our special **Topic** devoted to Arthurian legend in Brittany on p.44. On the spot, the best way to get a feel for place and its legends is to go on a tour round the forest with an expert guide who knows the legends well – sign up at the Paimpont or Tréhorenteuc tourist offices (*see* practical box).

The famed forest covers a mere 7,000 hectares today, but once a far greater, dense woodland stretched across a vast swathe of central Brittany. Now, along with the traditional oak and beech, willow adds a touch of lightness, while many pines were planted from the 19th century. Forest fires in 1990 caused some damage, from which the woods have slowly recovered. However, much of the higher land of this so-called forest is in fact covered with heathery moors. Most of the Forêt de Paimpont is in private hands, but there is a network of walks you can follow around it.

Getting to and around the Forêt de Paimpont and Vilaine Valley

Public transport to the Forêt de Paimpont isn't good. To find out about **buses** from Rennes, contact TIV, **t** 02 99 31 34 31. There's an infrequent **train** service from Rennes to Montfort-sur-Meu. Down the Vilaine, Guipry-Messac has regular train links with Rennes, while Redon is just 3 hours from Paris on the TGV line to Quimper via Rennes, and reachable by train from Nantes.

To hire a **boat** on the Vilaine, try Crown Blue Lines, Port de Plaisance, Messac, **t** 02 99 34 60 11; Bretagne Plaisance, 12 Quai Jean Bart, Redon, **t** 02 99 72 15 80, *www.bretagne-plaisance.fr*; or Cris'Boat Croisières, 75 Rue de Vannes, Redon, **t** 02 99 71 08 05, *www.crisboat.com*. To **canoe**, ask at Messac tourist office. For general boating info contact the Comité des Canaux Brétons, **t** 02 97 25 38 24, *www.canaux-bretons.net*.

To try and stop you losing your historical bearings altogether in imaginary Brocéliande, here are a few solid stepping stones to guide you across the deep and treacherous marshes of legend. As in so many parts of Brittany, signs of neolithic civilization are scattered around, including dolmens, menhirs and gallery chambers. How the area might have been touched by British immigration in the Dark Ages, and how it became so intimately linked with Arthurian legend, remains very blurred.

Moving on swiftly, a significant if shadowy historical figure closely connected with the area is Judicaël, a local king, chief of a central Breton region known as Domnonia during the 7th century, credited with founding the priory of Paimpont around 640, and made into a saint in these parts. Religious authorities then held sway over the forest for a good many centuries, the abbey of Paimpont becoming a foundation of some standing. The bishop of Alet (St-Malo) had to intervene, though, when Eon, a hermit in these woods, went mad and claimed that he was the Christ of the Last Judgement. Rarely for the Ille-et-Vilaine, the place names here still show the influence of the Celtic language, and Breton continued to be spoken in the area up until the 12th century.

Iron production was the important industry as far back as Roman times, thriving down the centuries, as you can see at the 18th-century village of Les Forges in its quaint lakeside spot. These forges were highly productive in their day, supplying the major Breton arsenals of Rennes, Nantes, Lorient and Brest with arms. But the imagination began competing hard with industry in these parts during the 19th century, interest in Arthurian legend bringing the forest international renown.

Paimpont

One of the best places to get your bearings is Paimpont itself, a purple-stoned place with a typically atmospheric mirror of a lake, one of several in the forest. Historic Paimpont is modest, really a one-street village, entered by an archway at one end, finished at the other by a large abbey next to the lake. Between the two you'll find fairly simple places to eat, and, of course, the odd esoteric shop, proposing crystals, tarot-readings and the like . The tourist office beside the abbey offers more down-to-earth information on the forest, walking paths, and cultural events.

The **abbey's** roots go back to Judicaël's time, but the **church** dates mostly from the 13th to 15th centuries. Inside, below the big Gothic windows, the Baroque woodwork is ornate. Compare this refinement with Notre Dame de Paimpont, a blushing painted 15th-century Virgin holding her vacuously grinning Christ-child under a baldaquin. The rose window in the transept is one of the oldest in Brittany, dating from the beginning of the 13th century. The sacristy has preserved many of its treasures. The most amazing reliquary takes the shape of a silver arm, holding a book encrusted with precious stones. The arm, with a little window incorporated in it, is meant to contain a finger of St Judicaël.

A Tour of the Forest of Brocéliande

Our route takes you anti-clockwise round the forest. Heading northeast from Paimpont, branch off to look at the **Etang du Pas du Houx**, the largest of the forest's lakes, beautiful but private. A 20th-century castle named the Château de Brocéliande lies on its edge.

Some way northeast up the D71, look out for a turning for the **Tombeau de Merlin**. Viviane is supposed to have imprisoned Merlin here for ever, but in nine magic, invisible circles, so don't be surprised if you don't see much. You'll need to use your imagination, too, if you go down the lane from Merlin's tomb to the **Fontaine de Jouvence**, the Fountain of Youth, a basic watering hole but one whose waters were supposed, in legend, to possess rejuvenating powers.

Follow the northern edge of the forest towards Concoret and you come to the Château de Comper, home to the **Centre de l'Imaginaire Arthurien** devoted to Arthurian subjects. Inside, the annual exhibitions delve into different aspects of the legends, using waxworks scenes and textual explanations. The château stands right next to the **Lac de Comper**, one of the most atmospheric lakes in the forest. It's in its waters that Merlin is supposed to have built Viviane her magical home.

It's quite tricky finding your way to nearby **Folle Pensée** ('Mad Thought'). There may have been an asylum here, and patients may have been taken to the **Fontaine de Barenton** to drink from it in the hope that it might cure them, but the place was also associated with the power to unleash terrible storms. To get to the fountain, you pass through the red stone village of Barenton; it's a longish walk to and from the car park.

In the parish of **Néant-sur-Yvel** some way west, **Le Jardin aux Moines** is a neolithic rectangle of stones that appears to have avoided being touched by Arthurian legend. However, the Christian

Centre de l'Imaginaire Arthurien
www.centre-arthurien-broceliande.com, **t** *02 97 22 79 96; open April–June and Sept–Oct Thurs–Mon 10–5.30, July and Aug Thurs–Tues 10–7*

morality tale invented here has it that a group of orgy-loving monks were turned to stone by way of punishment.

Tréhorenteuc, a little village tucked in on the western side of the forest, really goes to town with the Arthurian theme. It boasts an extraordinary **church** (*small fee*) where Arthurian legend shares the limelight with Christian stories. A sparkling mosaic greets you, showing flaming red and haloed lions surrounding a white hart carrying a cross on its neck. Further panels illustrate scenes of Arthurian adventures, while the stained-glass windows represent both Joseph of Arimathea, the man who saved several of the crucified Christ's drops of blood in the Holy Grail, and St Onenne, sister of King Judicaël. She chose a life of chastity and retired to Tréhorenteuc, where she kept a flock of geese; apparently they warned her of the approach of soldiers with wicked intentions and fought off her assailants.

A purple hiking path leads up to the deeply atmospheric **Val Sans Retour**, reached via L'Arbre d'Or, a striking gilded tree. This is the vale where the bitter Morgane le Faye, sister of King Arthur, supposedly imprisoned unfaithful knights, turning them into her puppets. If they tried to escape, terrifying visions would stop them in their tracks. These knights were eventually liberated from their prison of pleasure by fellow knight Lancelot, who, despite having an adulterous relationship with Arthur's Queen Guinevere, won out because he remained faithful to his love.

Just southwest of the forest, the moat-surrounded **Château de Trécesson** makes quite a sight in its beautiful purple stone, even if you can't visit the property. However, you can walk up the hillside above it. Dramatic views open out over the countryside, but at the top of the crest you reach the boundaries of the enormous military camp of Coëtquidan. The **Ecole de St-Cyr-Coëtquidan** is France's equivalent to the British Sandhurst or US Westpoint. You can visit the interesting **military museum** within the camp. Among other subjects it covers, it movingly commemorates 17,000 graduate officers killed in battle.

Back north towards Paimpont, **Les Forges de Paimpont** were entirely purpose-built for iron production, but now they make a gorgeous, tranquil picture.

Quite some way northeast of the forest, the Arthurian theme is pursued at **Montfort-sur-Meu**, still in purple stone country. A single tower is virtually all that remains of a once massive medieval fort here. Its **Ecomusée** also has interesting displays on local costumes and on simple rural childhood toys of the past, cleverly fashioned out of basic country materials. The Forêt de Montfort south of the town is rather beautiful. If you're interested in traditional Breton games, consider contacting **La Jaupître** at Monterfil to organize a special outing.

Military museum
www.st-cyr.terre. defense.gouv.fr, **t** *02 97 70 77 50; open Tues–Fri 10–12 and 2.30–5 or 6, closed Thurs pm, Sat and Sun 10–12 and 2–6; you will need to show your passport at the entrance*

Ecomusée de Montfort-sur-Meu
www.ecomusee-montfort.com; open Oct–Mar 8.30–12 and 2–6, April–Sept Mon–Fri 8.30–12 and 2–6, Sat 10–12 and 2–6, Sun 2–6

La Jaupître
t *02 99 07 47 02*

The Purple Vilaine Valley: Rennes to Redon

Pretty in purple, **Pont-Réan** on the Vilaine has appealing restaurants by the 18th-century bridge which attract crowds from Rennes at weekends. The river scene is prettier still at the **Moulin de Boël** a few kilometres away. South of Pont-Réan, the road climbs steeply out of the Rennes Basin to Guichen. Below the town of **Bourg-des-Comptes** (on the river's east bank), look out for the streets leading to the tiny, unspoilt old **Port de la Courbe**, weeping willows on its banks, prunus on the old village square with its old village bar, the 18th-century château of Gai-Lieu standing nearby.

Cross the river at Pléchâtel-Plage and in the distance you get dramatic views of the massive spire of **St-Malo-en-Phily** rising above a scarred, quarried cliff. The village itself is unspoilt and exudes charm, located above its separate little port of Bruère. Back in the Middle Ages, the monks of Alet, precursor of St-Malo, went to collect relics of saint Malo from southwest France, where he had been buried, to return them to his Breton seaside home. As the relics were carried along the Vilaine, the local lord was cured of an illness; it seemed obvious to him that the saint's bones had done the trick, so in gratitude, he gave the monks a piece of land here.

The massive main church, which looks absurdly, even spectacularly, oversized for such a little community, isn't medieval. Regnault's early 20th-century extravaganza is in mixed neo-Byzantine, -Romanesque and -Gothic styles. Black and white patterned stones give impact to the façade's arches and the rose window. Walk out a few hundred metres from the village and you come to a **chapel** in much more typical, modest, Breton style.

The riverside at the combined ports of **Guipry** and **Messac** looks surprisingly industrial after the rural idyll above; but this is the main centre for hiring tourist boats for this stretch of the Vilaine. At **Lohéac**, northwest of Guipry, it's cars that are lined up row upon row in the **Manoir de l'Automobile**, but you can't drive any of these vintage numbers away. This vast collection was amassed by automobile press baron Michel Hommell.

The Neolithic Monuments of St-Just

Continue south via Pipriac to reach one of the most atmospheric prehistoric sites in Brittany, the neolithic monuments outside St-Just, visited by few tourists. The constructions stretch across several kilometres of open heathland. Head for the new **Maison Nature et Mégalithes** at St-Just, which offers a good introduction both to the range of neolithic sites and the natural environment.

Wandering along the exceptional ridge west of the village, you encounter groups of monuments erected at different periods,

Manoir de l'Automobile
www.manoir-automobile.fr, t *02 99 34 02 32; open July–Aug daily 10–7, rest of year Tues–Sun 10–1 and 2–7*

⭐ St-Just

Maison Nature et Mégalithes
www.landes-de-cojoux.com, t *02 99 72 69 25; info and departure point for tours, including guided moonlit tours*

dating from between 5000 BC and 3500 BC. The **Landes de Cojoux alignments** include small lines of unusual quartz standing stones. There are also schist megaliths, their dark tones contrasting with the quartz. Between some of these menhirs, holes have been discovered that may have been made to hold up further structures. A Bronze Age coffin was found in the top line of megaliths, dating to around 1500 BC.

A further set of megaliths lies close together at **Croix St-Pierre**. The tumulus here is marked by a rectangle of stones, with quartz used on the southern side, and schist on the northern one. It's reckoned to date from approximately 3000 BC. Some rather unorthodox archaeologists have been at work in this area – a colony of rabbits digging their warrens in this tumulus brought a polished axehead to the surface!

Next comes a half-restored **dolmen**, dated to around 5000 BC and used as a collective burial site. Experts particularly admire the floor, described by the guide as 'the Versailles flooring of its period'. By contrast, the **Dambiau tomb** was constructed around 4000 BC for an important individual – perhaps a sign of how hierarchies were evolving in neolithic communities in that period. **Le Tribunal** (the Law Court) is the name given to the monument that follows because its semicircle of stones reminded researchers of a court. A nearby standing stone may have served as a calendar marking special days. However uncertain the precise purposes of these neolithic structures, they make a strong impact even today.

The Vilaine via Langon

Back by the Vilaine, the country lanes to Redon are beautiful. At the **Sites de La Corbinière et de l'Ermitage**, the river runs through little gorges, where you can take a pretty towpath walk. At **Port-de-Roche** the river is crossed by a metallic bridge constructed for the Paris Universal Exhibition of 1867, and moved here in 1868.

Frescoes make an enjoyable little theme to pursue at the attractive village of **Langon**. The viciously pointed and slate-covered tower of the **Eglise St-Pierre** stands out as you arrive. Inside, a 12th-century mural of Christ blesses all comers. But the more extraordinary frescoes lie hidden in the tiny **Chapelle Ste-Agathe**. This building's fine, colourful masonry, consisting of little cubes of purple stone divided up by layers of orange tiles, dates back in part to Gallo-Roman times. Most rarely, the diminutive apse is covered with fish swimming around a figure of Venus, the Roman goddess of love. Her features have been effaced, but it's still possible to distinguish her elegant hair by the guide's meagre torchlight. It's thought that the frescoes were painted some time around AD 200, to decorate the baths of a substantial private villa – they certainly seem quite incongruous in a chapel!

Chapelle Ste-Agathe
Contact the mairie, t 02 99 08 76 55, to arrange a visit

07 Ille-et-Vilaine | The Forêt de Paimpont and Vilaine Valley: The Purple Vilaine Valley

Above the village stand further megaliths, the **Demoiselles**. The comical if rather nasty old Christian legend here claimed that a bunch of young girls, instead of going to church, went to dance on the heath. By way of punishment, they were literally petrified by God. Medieval chronicles and bishops' archives do mention pagan cults taking place on neolithic sites, but it's hard to judge how much truly went on, and how much was Church propaganda or paranoia. Such cruel Christian morality tales are associated with a good many neolithic monuments around Brittany.

Tour Du Guesclin
guided tours July–Aug
Tues–Sun 3–7

East of Langon, **Grand-Fougeray** has retained a solid keep, known as the **Tour Du Guesclin**, part of what was once a substantial 13th-century fort. Set beside a lake, the tower now makes a picturesque setting for summer exhibitions.

On the way from Langon to Brain-sur-Vilaine, a panel indicates a small stretch of Gallo-Roman road preserved under trees by the river. Apparently, a bitter sign here used to read: 'The Romans had this way built by their slaves, the Gauls.' **Brain-sur-Vilaine** is both a little port and a pretty old village; the locals keep their punts along the river. Around the village, spot some of the traditional local architecture, incorporating *palis*, thin slabs of stone used in place of wooden fencing – well, we are in Brittany. The river banks then give way to wide marshlands and flood plains. Seek out the ramshackle, atmospheric hamlet of **Gannedel** here.

Redon

The old town of Redon is trapped in the fork where the Vilaine and the Oust Rivers converge, surrounded by waterways and boundaries. It stands in the southwestern corner of the Ille-et-Vilaine. The Loire Atlantique *département* lies to the south, the Morbihan *département* to the west. The Canal de Nantes à Brest passes through the centre of town, as does a major railway line. The surrounding countryside is regularly flooded by winter waters.

Redon is known in Brittany above all for its **Romanesque church of St-Sauveur**, part of the abbey to which the town owes its existence. Redon's abbey is closely linked with the creation of Brittany's brief kingdom. In the Bretons' territorial expansion eastwards during the 9th century, the monk Conwoïon, close to the powerful Nomenoë, Breton administrator for the Frankish Carolingians, set up a religious community at Redon. He then appears to have encouraged Nomenoë to fight for Breton emancipation from the Carolingian kingdom. In fact, some 10 kilometres north of Redon, at La Bataille east of Bains-sur-Oust, a cross commemorates the Battle of Ballon in which Nomenoë effectively achieved Breton independence; Conwoïon's persuasive role is acknowledged there in the nationalistically pro-Breton text.

Through the Middle Ages, the abbey of Redon was one of the most influential religious institutions in Brittany. It benefited from a privileged position, not just with dukes of Brittany, but even with the Vatican, and its leaders saw to the foundation of several other abbeys in southern Brittany. It was also a place of pilgrimage on the journey to Santiago de Compostela, and held many relics.

The many-levelled Romanesque tower still has pride of place in the town centre. Inside, the transept, covered by an octagonal cupola, is a remarkable achievement of the 12th century, with the outlines of worn frescoes to pick out. A taller Gothic choir was added to the church in the 13th century, held up by flying buttresses, but its light was partly obscured by the enormous, ornate retable added in the 17th century.

Redon town has scattered points of interest, which you might follow using the panels of the Circuit Patrimonial. The **Grande Rue**, the main shopping street, boasts an interesting mix of façades, some of them in timberframe, some in stone, including elements in light tufa, a sign of strong links with the Loire.

The street leads down to where the Canal de Nantes à Brest crosses town. The Vilaine flows by just to the east. Along it, the name of **Quai St-Jacques** is a reminder of the fact that pilgrims for Compostela left from here by ship. Redon was for centuries a thriving inland port, acting as a stocking place for imports waiting to be carried up to Rennes. The Compagnie des Indes, the official French trading company with the Indies, had offices here. **Quai Duguay-Trouin**, the extension of Quai St-Jacques along the Vilaine, is overlooked by grand if now slightly wonky former merchants' houses. Redon's broad **marina** lies to the west.

Down **Quai Jean Bart**, the Musée de la Batellerie de l'Ouest explains the importance that Redon's inland waterways once had in Breton trading. A former Redon riverman may sometimes be on hand to talk about his experiences of this life, which continued until quite recent times..

Musée de la Batellerie de l'Ouest
t 02 99 72 30 95;
open mid-June–mid-Sept daily 10–12 and 3–6; rest of year Mon, Wed, Sat and Sun 2–6; closed mid-Dec–mid-Mar

(i) **Paimpont >>**
5 Esplanade de Brocéliande, 35380 Paimpont, t 02 99 07 84 23, www.paimpont.fr

Market Days in the Forêt de Paimpont and Vilaine Valley

Montfort-sur-Meu: Friday
Plélan-le-Grand: Sunday
Guipry: Thursday
Grand-Fougeray: Saturday
Pipriac: Tuesday
Redon: Monday
Guerche de Bretagne: Tuesday (since 1121)

Where to Stay and Eat in the Forêt de Paimpont and Vilaine Valley

Paimpont and Around ✉ 35380

**Relais de Brocéliande, 5 Rue des Forges, t 02 99 07 84 94, www. relais-de-broceliande.fr (€€–€). A typical, traditional country address situated opposite the arch into the old village, with good restaurant.

⭐ **La Corne de Cerf B&B** >

ⓘ **La Maison du Tourisme du Pays de Redon**
Place de la République, 35600 Redon, t 02 99 71 06 04, www.tourisme-pays-redon.com; for information on both Redon and the Upper Vilaine Valley

ⓘ **Pays d'Accueil de Brocéliande**
t 02 99 06 86 07, www.broceliande-tourisme.info; for general information on the Forêt de Paimpont

ⓘ **Langon**
7 Grande Rue, t 02 99 08 76 55, www.ville-langon.fr

ⓘ **Messac**
Square de la Liberté, 35480 Messac, t 02 99 34 61 60, syndicat.initiative.guipry. messac@wanadoo.fr

ⓘ **Montfort-sur-Meu**
4 Place du Tribunal, 35160 Montfort-sur-Meu, t 02 99 09 88 16, www.paysdemontfort.com

ⓘ **Tréhorenteuc**
Place Abbé Gillard, 56430 Tréhorenteuc, t 02 97 93 05 12, www.valsansretour.com

La Corne de Cerf B&B, at Le Cannée, a short way east of Paimpont, **t** 02 99 07 84 19 (€). A truly beautiful place, the rooms gorgeously done up by the Morvans, the artistic couple who own the place.

Les Forges de Paimpont, **t** 02 99 06 81 07 (€€). Provides good regional fare in this pretty spot. *Closed Sun eve and Mon.*

Aux Berges de l'Aff, Le Pont de la Lande, Beignon, **t** 02 97 75 74 25 (€). A crêperie in a forest setting by the Aff River, serving organic pancakes.

Pont-Réan ✉ 35580

Le Grand Hôtel, **t 02 99 42 21 72, *www.le-grand-hotel-bretagne.com* (€). Next to the bridge, with pretty, modern rooms and a riverside restaurant.

Guignen 35580

Ferme-auberge France, off the D42 about 3km west of Guignen (on the D177 between Guichen and Lohéac), **t** 02 99 92 05 56, *ferme auberge.france@wanadoo.fr* (€€). A welcoming historic manor where you can sample local produce (€€). *Advance booking required. Closed Wed out of season.*

Grand-Fougeray ✉ 35390

***des Palis, 15 Place de l'Eglise, **t** 02 99 08 30 80, *www.restaurant-les-palis.fr* (€€). Stylishly restored hotel in 17th-century village house, with sleek, contemporary rooms at a very reasonable price, a fine restaurant (€€–€) offering regional delights, plus an 'English pub' for those in need of reassurance.

La Tour Duguesclin, Rue du Château, **t** 02 99 08 31 30, *www.latourdu guesclin.com* (€€€–€€). Set in a park and affording a view onto the historic keep, and serving imaginative dishes. *Closed Sun eve and Mon.*

Brain-sur-Vilaine

La Grand' Maison B&B, Grande Rue, **t** 02 99 70 25 81, *www.la-grand-maison.com* (€). Excellent rooms in a fine 17th-century village house. *Table d'hôte* (€).

La Chapelle-de-Brain/Gannedel

L'Hôt Berge B&B, **t** 02 99 70 21 97, *www.gannedel.fr* (€). The unusual rooms here beside the marshes recently won a regional prize for ecological tourism. *Table d'hôte* (€).

Redon ✉ 35600

Chandouineau, 1 Rue Thiers, **t 02 99 71 02 04 (€€). A pleasant town house near the railway station, with refurbished, soundproofed modern rooms. The chef cooks a variety of interesting local dishes (€€), using Redon chestnuts and eels in season, in the warm dining room. *Closed Sat, Sun eve and 1wk Aug.*

La Bogue, 3 Rue des Etats, **t** 02 99 71 12 95 (€€). A quaint setting near the huge town hall in which to enjoy meat and fish dishes. *Closed Sun eve and Thurs.*

L'Île aux Grillades, 9 Rue de l'Enfer, **t** 02 99 72 20 40 (€€). Wood-fire grills and a 3-course *formule*. *Closed Sun, Mon.*

L'Akène, 10 Rue du Jeu de Paume, **t** 02 99 71 25 15 (€). Really good port-side crêperie with a garden terrace. (€10)

Le Moulin de Via, Route de Gacilly (D873), **t** 02 99 71 05 16 (€€). Refined cuisine from home-produced ingredients, in a lake-side location outside town. *Closed Mon, Tues and Sun eve.*

Bains-sur-Oust 35600

Ferme-Auberge Guérin, La Morinais, **t** 02 99 72 12 17, *www.fermelamorinais.com* (€€). Savour excellent home-reared food (duck and pig) in a lovely rural setting 4km north of Redon.

Côtes d'Armor

Pink rocks, orange boulders, mauve moorlands and emerald seas follow in quick succession as you travel along the Côtes d'Armor's shores, the most colourful in Brittany. Starting in the east, the gracious resorts of the Côte d'Emeraude give way to dramatic, unspoilt heathland running down to the sea. Then come the gorgeous greys of the Bay of St-Brieuc. Brittany's tallest cliffs rise around here, but tumble down into an intriguing, disorientating chaos by the time you reach the enchanting shores around Paimpol and L'Île de Bréhat. The outrageous pink boulders of the Côte de Granit Rose around Perros-Guirec make this the most fabulous stretch of French coastline.

Inland, up the main river estuaries, you soon hit upon fine historic towns such as Dinan, Tréguier, Lamballe or Guingamp.

Head deeper into the interior, and you'll find Brittany at its most authentic. In the heart of the province, the Lac de Guerlédan may only be a 20th-century creation, but it now blends in beautifully with the surrounds, its indented, wooded shores making it look surprisingly reminiscent of the Breton coast.

08

Don't miss

⭐ Kissing dromedaries
Dinan **p.173**

⭐ A dramatic coastal castle
Fort La Latte **p.186**

⭐ A beautiful bay
St-Brieuc **p.190**

⭐ Perfect peace
Lac de Guerlédan **p.201**

⭐ Absurd pink and orange boulders
Côte de Granit Rose
p.229

See map overleaf

Côtes d'Armor

10 km
5 miles

N

les Sept Iles
Côte de Granit Rose

Trégastel-Plage • Ploumanac'h
Ile Grande
Ploumanac'h
Perros-Guirec
Trébeurden • Pleumeur-Bodou
Trébeurden
Plougasnou
Baie de Lannion
Locquémeau
Trédrez
Locquirec
Le Yaudet
Lanmeur
St-Michel-en-Grève
St-Efflam
Plestin-les-Grèves
Ploumilliau
Château de Rosanbo
Château de Tonquédec
Plouaret
Les Sept Saints
Trégrom
Morlaix
Plounérin
Locmaria
Ménez Bré
Plougonven
Belle-Isle-en-Terre
Louargat
Loc Envel
Scrignac
Callac
Bulat-Pestivien
Huelgoat
St-Nicodème
Locarn
FINISTÈRE
Carhaix-Plouguer
Maël-Carhaix
Trémargat
Kergrist-Moëlou
Rostrenen
Abbaye de Bon Repos
Les Forges-des-Salles
MORBIHAN
Cléguérec
Stival
Pontivy

Port-Blanc
Trévou-Tréguignec
Plougrescant
Sillon de Talbert
Pleubian
Kermouster
Loguivy
Ile de Bréhat
Pointe de l'Arcouest
Tréguier
Ploubazlanec
Lézardrieux
Paimpol
Abbaye de Beauport
La Roche-Derrien
La Roche-Jagu
Pointe de Minard
TRÉGORROIS
Rûnan
Pontrieux
Lanleff
Pléhédel
Bréhec
Pointe de Plouha
Brélidy
Quemper-Guézennec
Kermaria
Plouha
Tréveneuc
Bégard
Lanvollon
St-Quay-Portrieux
Etables-sur-Mer
Guingamp
Trégomeur
Binic
Grâces
Châtelaudren
Pordic
Les Rosaires
Plouagat
Avaugour
Bourbriac
St-Péver
St-Fiacre
St-Brieuc
Château de Beaumanoir
Kerpert
Senven-Léhart
Quintin
St-Gilles-Pligeaux
St-Nicolas-du-Pélem
Corlay
Ploeuc-sur-Lié
Uzel
Gouarec
St-Gilles-Vieux-Marché
Le Quillio
Caurel
Lac de Guerlédan
Mur-de-Bretagne
St-Aignan
Forêt de Quénécan
Loudéac
Rohan

FRANCE

Don't miss

⭐ Dinan **p.173**
⭐ Fort La Latte **p.186**
⭐ St-Brieuc **p.190**
⭐ Lac de Guerlédan **p.201**
⭐ Côte de Granit Rose **p.229**

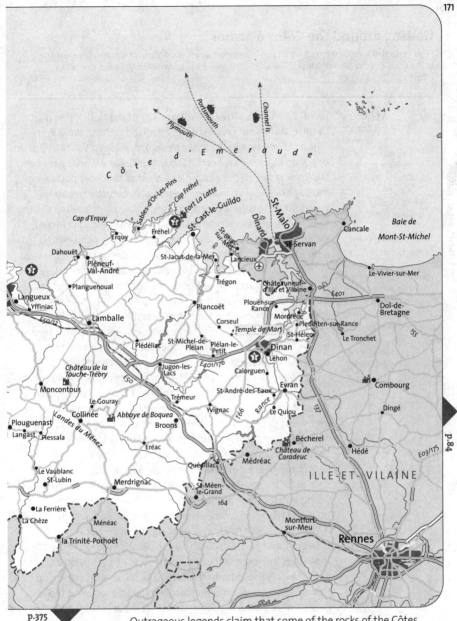

Côte d'Emeraude

Plymouth
Portsmouth
Channel Is

Baie de
Mont-St-Michel

Cancale
Le-Vivier-sur-Mer
Dol-de-Bretagne
Le Tronchet
Combourg
Dingé
Hédé

St-Malo
Dinard
St-Servan
St-Briac-sur-Mer
Lancieux
St-Jacut-de-la-Mer
Châteauneuf-d'Ille et Vilaine
Plouër-sur-Rance
Mordreuc
Pleudihen-sur-Rance
St-Hélen
Trégon
Plancoët
Corseul
Temple de Mars
St-Michel-de-Plélan
Plélan-le-Petit
Dinan
Léhon
Calorguen
Evran
St-André-des-Eaux
Le Quiou
Bécherel
Château de Caradeuc
Médréac

Cap d'Erquy
Sables-d'Or-Les-Pins
Cap Fréhel
Fort La Latte
St-Cast-le-Guildo
Fréhel
Erquy
Dahouët
Plérin-Val-André
Planguenoual
Langueux
Yffiniac
Lamballe
Plédéliac
Jugon-les-Lacs
Trémeur
Yvignac
Le Gouray
Moncontour
Château de la Touche-Trébry
Collinée
Abbaye de Boquea
Broons
Eréac
Plouguenast
Langast
Plessala
Landes du Ménez
Le Vaublanc
St-Lubin
La Ferrière
La Chèze
Ménéac
la Trinité-Porhoët
Merdrignac
Quédillac
St-Méen-le-Grand
Montfort-sur-Meu
Rennes

ILLE-ET-VILAINE

E50/12
E50
E401/176
E401
E03/175

p.84

P-375

Outrageous legends claim that some of the rocks of the Côtes d'Armor were turned red by the blood of persecuted saints. Many stretches of the shoreline here are truly startling. But as the name of the *département* indicates, you encounter a great variety of coasts travelling through these parts, rather than one homogeneous look. In the east, smart resorts cluster like mussels around the deep, calm bays. The scene turns wilder around Cap Fréhel, where heather and gorse cling on to the almost totally

Getting around the Côtes d'Armor

For up-to-date, precise information on public transport across the *département*, consult the website of the Côtes d'Armor Conseil Général, *www.cg22.fr*; there's a link to *www.tibus.fr*, which covers bus information in particular.

ⓘ **Côtes d'Armor**
Comité Départemental du Tourisme des Côtes d'Armor, Maison du Tourisme, 7 Rue Saint-Benoît, B.P.4620, 22046 St-Brieuc Cedex 2, t 02 96 62 72 00, www. cotesdarmor.com; the département's special booking service is available at www.cotes darmor-reservation. com, covering hotels, B&Bs, gîtes, ramblers' accommodation, youth hostels and even special short breaks or longer holidays

unbuilt-on slopes, although Brittany's most dramatic castle, Fort La Latte, stands out proudly on its headland, defying the waves.

Turn the corner and the vast, splendid, cliff-edged Bay of St-Brieuc opens up before you. Cheerful Erquy doubles as a working port and laid-back resort on the eastern end. Most of the other ports around the bay have long abandoned their traditional activities and transformed to offer a gentle tourism, taking on genteel airs, with their well-maintained promenades. Nature has the upper hand, though, by the time you reach the rugged cliffs around Plouha, among the tallest in Brittany. The Bay of St-Brieuc ends in the west with the extraordinary jumbled rockscapes around the historic port of Paimpol and L'Ile de Bréhat, the latter surely the prettiest island off the Breton coast, if sometimes overrun by tourist hordes. The city of St-Brieuc, capital of the Côtes d'Armor, sits at the bottom of the bay named after it. Sprawling across several deep valleys, it's not an obvious tourist destination, but it boasts excellent restaurants, and some intriguing port areas.

The Côtes d'Armor has some stunning historic towns a short way inland from the coast. The finest, and most touristy, are Dinan in the east and Tréguier in the west – typically for Brittany, these two gems lie well protected up their river estuaries. There's also a string of enchanting smaller historic towns encircling St-Brieuc; Lamballe, Moncontour and Quintin are all worth a visit, as is Guingamp, the last extremely Breton in feel.

Head for the southwestern corner of the Côtes d'Armor below Guingamp for some of the most unspoilt parts of the whole province. While the country churches often look amazingly pickled in the past, Breton folk music, dancing and other traditions still thrive in these parts – in fact, you can distance yourself from the modern world more easily here than in just about any other corner of Brittany. However, with the Côtes d'Armor countryside being heavily agricultural, including carrying the title for being the biggest pork-producing *département* in France, ground pollution has been an issue in recent times. That said, the ridges of hills reaching into the centre of the province give this area a peculiar wild beauty and the boulder-strewn countryside is rich in legends.

The Blavet River rises here, and provides the water for the gorgeous Lac de Guerlédan, right in the heart of Brittany. Created to provide central Brittany with hydroelectricity, now sweet little resorts have sprung up around the lake's shores, while a gorgeous handful of historic sights lie within close proximity.

Back beside the sea, the final, western stretches of Côtes d'Armor shorelines are the most extraordinary of the lot. The madly indented section from the Ile de Bréhat to Trégastel is without any doubt the craziest in all of France. Known as the Côte de Granit Rose, the rocks not only take on the most intense colours, but also the funniest forms and postures. One is even known as The Upturned Foot, while The Skull indicates there are others that touch the imagination in more sinister manner. Perros-Guirec, the main resort of this famous coast, is a joy, but the smaller stops share the magic. Along the final stretch of coast before the Finistère, Trébeurden is backed by the busy, buzzing high-tech town of Lannion just inland. But grandiose nature has the upper hand in the series of great headlands and the impressive bay of the Lieue de Grève with which the Côtes d'Armor ends in the west.

Dinan and Around

★ Dinan

A memorable, steep winding street bordered by timberframe houses links the two halves of Dinan, the port down by the Rance, and the upper fortified town. The medieval ramparts which still virtually encircle the place are the glory of Dinan, of staggering proportions and extent. Within these massive walls and towers, the main sights to visit include the Eglise St-Sauveur, and the château, the latter containing the town museum. But the main pleasure of Dinan is simply wandering through its picturesque streets and squares. Don't miss the charming banks of the Rance below, including the house of artist Yvonne Jean-Haffen, now a museum set in a garden seemingly made for Miss Marple.

A History of Dinan

The Bayeux Tapestry depicts William the Conqueror attacking a simple hilltop castle called Dinan in 1065. The stronghold was clearly a thorn in the formidable Norman's side. Important religious establishments were founded here before the close of the 11th century, Benedictine monks from the great abbey of St-Florent on the Loire were called upon to start one institution. They set up mills, organized fishing, and collected dues from boats passing along the Rance. The church dedicated to St Malo was in existence by 1060. The church of St-Sauveur went up in the 12th century.

Early in that century, the lordship of Dinan was split in two. King Henry II Plantagenet attacked the town in 1169, in part to tame Roland de Dinan, unruly lord of southern Dinan. Subdued, Roland then settled down to an important administrative post, taking charge of fiscal, judicial and military matters in Brittany, and also serving as tutor to King Henry's young son Geoffroy. Without heirs of his own, Roland adopted his nephew Alain de Vitré, who became

Getting to and around Dinan

To get to and from St-Malo and Dinard by **bus**, see the specialist *département* website. Dinan is on a **train line** that links it with Dol-de-Bretagne in the east and St-Brieuc in the west.

equally significant in Breton affairs, as would the latter's son-in-law, Juhel de Mayenne. As well as holding such important posts in the duchy, the lords of Dinan maintained important land holdings in England and Wales. You can read more about medieval Dinan and its English connections in *Dinan au temps des seigneurs*, written and researched by Peter Meazay, a Welshman who fell for Dinan in recent times.

Dinan's two lordships were briefly reunited by inheritance and marriage under Alain d'Avaugour in the 13th century. However, in a seeming act of folly, he sold them to the duke of Brittany. It was Duke Jean I who ordered the commencement of the construction of Dinan's striking ramparts, though most of these date from later than that, important additions being made in the 15th century.

The Breton War of Succession, which began in 1341, turned Dinan into a major theatre of war between France and England. Jeanne de Penthièvre, rightful heir to the duchy, was a direct descendant of Josselin de Dinan, of the d'Avaugour family. She was backed by the French monarchy, and her Breton cousins included most of the big feudal lords of northern Brittany. The English were on the opposing side and in 1342 sacked Dinan, stealing treasures from St-Sauveur. The town's walls were much strengthened after this first attack. In 1357, the English again laid siege to the town, now defended by the brilliant leader du Guesclin. A truce was then agreed, but a disputed ransome led to a joust that would be remembered in French history (*see* opposite).

The English-backed de Monfort side would eventually win the Breton War of Succession, however, and Duke Jean IV of Brittany invested in a wide castle-building programme, which included the construction of a new Château de Dinan. Its colossal keep went up in the 1380s.

During the vicious 16th-century French Wars of Religion, the ultra-Catholic leader in Brittany, the Duc de Mercoeur, briefly made Dinan one of his strongholds, although the townsmen rallied to the side of his Protestant opponent, Henri de Navarre, the future King Henri IV. With the triumph of Catholicism in 17th-century France, Dinan saw the building of substantial new religious institutions. The ramparts were strengthened further in the 18th century, war between France and Britain encouraging paranoia.

Dinan remained one of the most important towns in Brittany right through to the Revolution, the textile trade making many fortunes, as in many towns across northern Brittany, although few

One of the Most Famous Jousts in French History

In the period of truce in the mid-14th century, the great Breton and French leader Bertrand du Guesclin learnt that his brother Olivier had been captured by the English enemy, under the command of Thomas of Canterbury. The latter demanded an unusually high ransom for Olivier's release. Although not himself one to play precisely by the chivalric book, du Guesclin objected to Canterbury's action, both in taking a prisoner in time of truce and then in asking for an excessive transfer fee. He challenged his opponent to a duel, with God as arbiter. Du Guesclin comprehensively beat Canterbury, who was sent back, dishonoured, to the English army, while the Frenchman's feat would be feted in the country's chronicles and history books.

can boast such an exceptional legacy of stone and timberframe homes. The Dinannais cloth was exported very successfully between the 15th and 18th centuries, though evidence for its making goes back to at least the mid 13th century. The remarkable 15th-century town belfry, built by and for merchants, was a symbol of their power. Before the Revolution, the textile trade with the French Caribbean colonies and the Iberian peninsula proved particularly fruitful.

At the Revolution, the religious orders that had taken over such a large share of Dinan were disbanded and some religious buildings damaged. But the 19th century would see major developments beyond the old walled town, notably the building on the viaduct over the Rance, and the opening of the railway station.

During the Second World War, though, on 2 August 1944, a terrible rain of 2,000 shells fell on the town as American troops liberated Dinan from the Nazis. It's hard to spot many obvious marks on the restored historic centre, but Dinan has grown substantially beyond its ramparts since the war.

A Tour of Dinan

Old Dinan may be enclosed within three kilometres of the most imposing ramparts, but it isn't dauntingly large. Start a tour at the impressive joint squares of **Place du Champ Clos** and **Place du Guesclin**, lined with elegant 18th-century houses and many hotels, restaurants and bars, although the car parks dominate the scene, rather than the café terraces. Place du Guesclin is where the famous medieval joust took place (see box, above), signalled by a triumphant equestrian statue of the victor, the dumpy but indomitable du Guesclin; it was made at the start of the 20th century by Emmanuel Frémiet, best known for the striking statue of St Michael that crowns the Mont St-Michel.

Château-Musée de Dinan
open June–Sept daily 10–6.30, Oct–Dec and Feb–May daily 2–5.30

Head south for the **Château-Musée de Dinan**. It really looks more like one of the sturdiest sections of the town's ramparts than an independent castle. The separate Tour de Coëtquen and the massive Porte du Guichet gateway are generously considered part of the château these days.

Go down to the deep, dark, lowest chamber of the main museum first to follow the chronological order of the exhibits. The keep was made to be lived in, as you can see in the vaulted kitchen with its massive fireplace fit to roast whole animals. A small display of prehistoric finds starts off the collections. From Roman times, look out for the beautiful carved plaque showing a marine god fighting a seahorse. The ground floor includes the former chapel, and next to it, the Salle au Duc, with another major fireplace and a collection of engravings, maps, furniture and sculpture haphazardly recalling Dinan's past. Further levels present the local textile-making traditions and paintings of Dinan. Nineteenth-century works by George Clarkson Stanfield and Isidore Dagnan stand out, offering dramatic depictions of the town.

In the Tour de Coëtquen, the top floors are used for annual exhibitions, often of modern artists' works. Down the stairs hides the atmospheric, if dank and dimly lit **Salle des Gisants**. Don't miss the seven remarkably forceful medieval tomb effigies on display here, from that of Roland de Dinan, said to be the oldest armed effigy in western Europe, to big-headed Geoffroi le Voyer, chamberlain to Duke Jean III of Brittany, and his shrivelled, painfully thin second wife.

You can get out of the ramparts under the massive **Porte du Guichet**. A walk down the **Promenade des Petits Fossés** leads you past two further formidable medieval towers, the **Tour du Connétable** and the **Tour de Beaufort**. Below you'll find the pleasant **Jardin des Petits Diables** (Little Devils' Garden).

Rue de Léhon leads back into the centre of town and from here you can turn into remarkable **Rue de l'Horloge**. The Maison de la Harpe occupies the 16th-century **Hôtel de Kératry**, one of many exceptional old town houses in Dinan, although this one was in fact rescued from a village near St-Brieuc and transported here. Comical little carved men mince around the first-floor windows. The exhibition inside focuses on the history of the Celtic harp. A medieval tomb effigy was discovered during restoration work on one house opposite and is now displayed outside it, although it looks strangely ignored, lying headless on the pavement. The towering presence in this street is the **Tour de l'Horloge**, the 15th-century belfry, a major symbol of merchant pride. It's open for hoi polloi to climb now in summer.

Kissing dromedaries aren't a common feature of French churches, but they are one of the decorative delights that survive from the Romanesque period at the **Eglise St-Sauveur** on lovely tree-lined **Place St-Sauveur**. The story goes that a 12th-century chivalric hero from Dinan, Riallon le Roux, vowed that he would build a church in town if he got back alive from crusading. He returned, and appears to have communicated his strong memories of the Middle East to

Maison de la Harpe
www.harpe-celtique.com, t 02 96 87 36 69; open June–Sept Tues–Sat 3–9; harp festival 2nd week of July; workshops for children in summer

Tour de l'Horloge
open Easter–Sept 10–6.30

the masons. A few other wonderful elements of the Romanesque decoration have survived. Barbary apes count among the other visible signs of the influence of the crusades. The winged bull and lion on the outside are commoner Christian creatures, symbols of the evangelists Luke and Mark. Around the restored carving of Christ, hysterically gesturing figures dance about the central arch, while further down, a few of the larger statues in stone appear to have been gradually melting away down the centuries.

The bulk of the church was rebuilt in Gothic style in the 15th and 16th centuries. Inside, the single side-aisle offers a wonderful Gothic-pointed perspective down its length. The old wooden pews in the nave make delightful waves leading to the elaborate baldequin of the choir. The heart of Bertrand du Guesclin lies in a chest in the north transept. He's also romantically depicted in a 19th-century painting by Antoine Rivoulon, offered to the town by French king Louis-Philippe. As well as the dromedaries hidden behind the doors, look out too for the 11th-century baptismal font, with four beheaded figures holding its sides and a couple of stone fish carved inside it.

Behind the church, the former cemetery has been turned into the pretty **Jardin Anglais**, from where you can go out walking along stretches of the ramparts enjoying fabulous views down on the Rance far below.

Heading to the very centre of historic Dinan, **Rue Apport** boasts exceptional timberframe arcades. Many boutiques around here sell Breton specialities, while the **Musée de la Veilleuse Théière Arthé** is a tearoom that doubles as a museum dedicated to that most revered of household objects, the teapot. On **Place des Merciers** the restaurant Chez La Mère Pourcel boasts the most famous of the grand timberframe façades, but this quarter contains all manner of delightfully quirky old houses. **Place des Cordeliers**, an adjoining beautiful square, has an exceptional timberframe house standing out from the crowd on its wooden columns. You can get a good view from here on to the Gothic end of the grand **Eglise St-Malo**, rebuilt in the 19th century in Flamboyant style. Among its finest features are its stained-glass windows.

From the back of the church of St-Malo, **Rue Comte de la Garaye** takes you out to some of the most impressive portions of Dinan's ramparts. Turn right at the end of the street and you can walk along the **Promenade des Grands Fossés** below the Tour Beaumanoir and the Porte St-Malo. Up on the **Tour du Gouverneur** you get a wonderful view of old Dinan, its roofs and towers. Return to the centre of town via **Rue de l'Ecole**, lined with grand 18th-century houses. Some were owned by Compagnie des Indes sea captains who retired here, bringing many luxuries to adorn the interiors of their sober-faced homes.

Down to the Rance

Rue du Petit Four and **Rue de Jerzual** make for a fabulous winding walk down to the Rance, packed with fine houses all the way. Half-way along, these streets are divided by the mighty **Porte de Jerzual**; in the passageway passing through this vast tower, you feel the massive weight of history hovering over your shoulders. Too steep to be a main tourist trap, the reward for negotiating the dangerous gradient is rather fine craft shops along the way, some selling jewellery and sculptures, one specializing in leather articles, another in decorative old linen. Look out for occasional exhibitions in one of the very finest houses along the way, the **Maison du Gouverneur**. There is also the odd créperie, while once you reach the riverside, you're spoilt for choices of places to eat and drink.

Maison de la Rance
www.port-dinan-lavallay.com, t 02 96 87 00 40; open July and Aug daily 10–7, April–June and Sept–Nov Tues–Sun 2–6, rest of year Sun 2–6

The pretty Rance was once one of the major trade routes in Brittany. Textiles, wood, leather and cereals would be shipped up to St-Malo and abroad. Fish, salt and wine, and later tea and other luxury goods from foreign parts, would be hefted up the hill. Cross the bridge for the **Maison de la Rance**, which explains the history, ecology and workings of this tidal river with some verve. Guided visits are organized from here.

Maison d'Artiste de la Grande Vigne
t 02 96 87 90 80; open mid-May–Sept daily 2–6.30

Along the quays back on the other side of the river, the sweet little **Maison d'Artiste de la Grande Vigne** looks cute enough to serve as the set for an English country murder story. This house in its terraced gardens in fact served as home and studio to the prolific painter Yvonne Jean-Haffen from 1937 until the early 1990s. A student of that great recorder of daily Breton life, Mathurin Méheut (see p.196), Jean-Haffen was introduced to Brittany by him. The artists apparently became lovers in Méheut's later years, though she was married. Méheut's life is celebrated alongside hers here, even if most of the works on display are by Jean-Haffen.

Musée du Rail
www.museedurail-dinan.com, t 02 96 39 81 33; open daily April–mid-Sept 2–5

The **Musée du Rail** at Dinan's railway station can satisfy rail enthusiasts with its large collection of model railways and material on rail travel around Brittany.

South along the Rance to Léhon

Musée 39–45
www.militaire-musee.com, t 02 96 39 65 89; open 10–12 and 1.30–6.30 April–Oct daily, Nov–March Sat, Sun, public and school hols

On the southern outskirts of Dinan towards Léhon, a collector fascinated by the Second World War has created the **Musée 39–45**. As well as displaying war vehicles, it looks in detail at the daily life of the soldiers, both Allied and German.

Tucked just out of sight of Dinan, **Léhon** is an enchanting historic riverside village . Breton rebel leader Nomenoë gave land here to monks to build an abbey in the 9th century. These wily religious men are said to have stolen relics of St Magloire and then forged a manuscript on his life to add to the credentials of their new institution, which rapidly gained a reputation as a centre of learning. But the monks would soon be on the run; even though a fort had been built up on the hillside above, nothing could stop the Viking raids. The monks escaped east with their relics, their successors to return to rebuild the abbey in the 11th century.

In the 12th, the lords of Dinan erected a new château on the hill and it seemed that Léhon was set to thrive again. However, King Henry II Plantagenet swept through and had his troops sack the castle. A major new **Château de Léhon** was then erected, which knew its finest hours in the 13th and 14th centuries. Long in ruins, the remaining towers and ramparts have been secured, leaving visitors free to wander round them at certain times. Very picturesque they look, too, but compared with Dinan's vast defences just up the valley, they resemble mere toy models in size.

Château de Léhon
Mairie de Léhon,
t 02 96 87 40 40; open
April–Oct daily 10–7,
Nov–March weekends
10–7; free

The magnificent **Abbaye St-Magloire** has stood the test of time better. The main doorway into the church may be Romanesque, but the rest of the vast vessel is plainly 13th-century Gothic. Medieval tomb effigies are lined up along the walls of the nave. Several depict lords of the mighty chivalric Beaumanoir family. Another represents the niece of the warrior Bertrand du Guesclin, surrounded by coats of arms showing her noble credentials. On guided tours, you can visit the splendidly restored 13th- to 14th-century refectory, with its finely wrought Gothic openings. A palm tree adds an exotic touch amid the patterned hydrangeas in the calming ruined cloister.

Abbaye
St-Magloire
church and cloister
open year-round; the
rest open July and Aug
10–12 and 2–6

North of Dinan

A great Gallo-Roman city, capital of the Roman-subjugated Celtic Coriosolitae tribe, arose at **Corseul** *c.*10 kilometres northwest of Dinan from around the year 10 BC. It grew to cover some 100 hectares and more, and possibly counted up to 10,000 inhabitants. It thrived for four centuries, gradually being abandoned from around AD 360. The remains of one of the most important monuments from these times, a **Temple to Mars**, stands some three kilometres from the main settlement. The height of this badly damaged octagonal building is impressive.

In Corseul itself, the displays of Gallo-Roman finds are slightly disappointing unless you're an expert on the subject, although the town hall garden stands out on arrival, decorated with the stubs of Gallo-Roman columns found in digs, indicating the commercial area that once stood here. The **Musée de Corseul** is housed within the Mairie. The Gallo-Roman town was laid out on a grid plan, with the usual civic provisions such as forum and baths. A few little rooms on the top floor display finds from the local excavations, including dice, decorated pottery, statuettes, a phallic amulet and buttons, one amusingly showing the head of a wild boar.

Musée de Corseul
t 02 96 27 90 17 to
visit by appointment

08 **Côtes d'Armor | Dinan and Around**

On the east side of the Rance, the village of **St-Hélen** conceals more carved medieval tomb effigies in its church. This place lay at the centre of the fiefdom of the Coëtquens, an important feudal family in the area. The ruins of the Château de Coëtquen are nearby.

Musée de la Pomme et du Cidre
t 02 96 83 20 78; open daily July–Aug 10–7; April, May, June and Sept 2–7

At tiny **Lyvet** beside the Rance, local fishermen still sometimes use their *carrelets*, square nets left suspended above the bank until they're submerged to catch fish. Nearby, at **Mordreuc**, the views of the river are particularly gorgeous as it widens out. Go to **Pleudihen-sur-Rance** and the lively, well-laid-out **Musée de la Pomme et du Cidre** to learn about traditional Breton cider-making.

Market Days in and around Dinan

Dinan: Thursday

Dinan Activities and Festivals

ⓘ **Dinan-Pays de Rance**
9 Rue du Château, B.P.65 261, 22105 Dinan Cedex, t 02 96 87 69 76, www.dinan-tourisme.com

To enjoy the Rance by **boat**, you can opt for a longer cruise up to Dinard with Corsaire (*www.compagnie corsaire.com*, **t** 08 25 13 81 00), or a shorter journey to Léhon on Le Jaman IV (*www.vedettejamaniv.com*, **t** 02 96 39 28 41). You can also hire a boat from Danfleurenn Nautic, **t** 06 07 45 89 97. For **canoes**, contact the Club de Canoë Kayak de la Rance, **t** 02 96 39 01 50, *cckrance@yahoo.fr*. Les Cycles Gauthier, **t** 02 96 85 07 60, rent out **bikes**; you can cycle all the way to Dinard avoiding roads.

⭐ **Le Challonge** >>

The **Théatre des Jacobins** in the old town offers good dance, musical and theatrical performances year round (**t** 02 96 87 03 11; programme on tourist office website). **Rencart sous les Remparts** consists of free Wednesday street events in July and August, afternoons for children, evenings (from about 9pm) for adults. Many Dinannais get decked out in medieval dress to celebrate the **Fête des Remparts** (even years only, 3rd weekend in July, *www.fete-remparts-dinan.com*, **t** 02 96 87 94 94).

Where to Stay in and around Dinan

⭐ **d'Avaugour** >

Dinan ✉ 22100
***d'Avaugour, 1 Place du Champ Clos, **t** 02 96 39 07 49, *www.avaugour*

hotel.com (€€€€–€€€). Cosy, tastefully decorated rooms in a completely renovated 18th-century building on the largest of Dinan's squares, but with a delightful garden looking onto the ramparts. *Closed Nov–Feb.*

***Dugueslin**, 66 Rue de Brest, *www.residhotelduguesclin.com*, **t** 02 96 85 54 80 (€€). Contemporary-designed rooms and apartments in an elegantly converted barracks, with heated pool. There's also a restaurant.

***Jerzual**, 26 Quai Talards, **t** 02 96 87 02 02, *www.bestwestern-jerzual-dinan.com* (€€€–€€). This large but quite stylish new hotel, with big rooms and a pool, stands beside the Rance. The restaurant (€€€–€) has a nice riverside location.

****Le Challonge**, 29 Place du Guesclin, **t** 02 96 87 16 30, *www.lechallonge.fr.st* (€€). Well-appointed, up-to-date, decent-sized and good-value rooms in a flower-fronted hotel overlooking the main central square.

****Arvor**, 5 Rue Pavie, **t** 02 96 39 21 22, *www.hotelarvordinan.com* (€€€–€€). Comfy modern rooms on the site of a former Jacobin monastery, with private parking. *Closed most Jan.*

****Hôtel de la Porte St-Malo**, 35 Rue St-Malo, **t** 02 96 39 19 76, *www.hotelportemalo.com* (€). Extremely pleasant rooms opposite the ramparts, and private parking.

L'Hostellerie du Vieux St-Sauveur, 21 Place St-Sauveur, **t** 02 96 85 30 20 (€). A basic option on this delightful old square, with very cheap rooms above the sometimes noisy bar.

Le Logis du Jerzual B&B >

Le Logis du Jerzual B&B, 25 Rue du Petit Four, **t** 02 96 85 46 54, *www.logis-du-jerzual.com* (€€). Fine rooms in a very appealing historic house on the winding old street to the port.

La Villa Côté Cour B&B, 10 Lord Kitchener, *www.villa-cote-cour-dinan.com*, **t** 02 96 39 30 07 (€€€–€€). Outside the historic centre, in a less exciting quarter close to the station, but offering a haven of peace and elegantly furnished rooms with hydrotherapy bathrooms.

Plouër-sur-Rance ✉ 22490

Manoir de Rigourdaine >

Manoir de Rigourdaine, Route de Langrolay, **t 02 96 86 89 96, *www.hotel-rigourdaine.fr* (€€). This lovely converted smart farm around its courtyard lies in a tranquil spot with a pretty terrace, looking on to the Rance some 10km north of Dinan, on the west side of the river. *Closed early Nov–Feb.*

St-Michel-de-Plélan ✉ 22980

La Corbinais B&B, **t** 02 96 27 64 81, *www.corbinais.com* (€). Quite charmingly decorated, cute rooms under the eaves in a typical Breton long house near Corseul, with an adjoining 9-hole golf course. *Table d'hôte* available.

Eating Out in and around Dinan

Les 3 Lunes, 22 Rue de la Lainerie, **t** 02 96 85 10 32 (€€€–€€). A very stylish dining address looking across to Place des Cordeliers, serving inventive cuisine. Also has a delicatessen and tearoom.

Auberge du Pélican >

Auberge du Pélican, 3 Rue Haute Voie, **t** 02 96 39 47 05 (€€). For refined traditional cuisine in a fine half-timbered building. *Closed Mon, and Thurs eve.*

La Fleur de Sel, 7 Rue Ste-Claire, **t** 02 96 85 15 14 (€€€). A nice variety of fresh menus available here, including a *menu du marché*, and a vegetarian one. *Closed Sun, Mon and Wed eve in low season.*

La Courtine, off Rue de la Croix (no.6), **t** 02 96 39 74 41 (€). Grills and fish are a speciality at this well-regarded address.

Le Cantorbery, 6 Rue Ste-Claire, **t** 02 96 39 02 52 (€€). A popular place with Brits, and rightly so, offering delicacies such as jugged rabbit with ginger and spices, and speciality potted fish in atmospheric dining rooms. *Closed Sun in winter.*

Le Léonie, 19 Rue Rolland, **t** 02 96 85 47 47 (€). Tiny fish restaurant much appreciated by the locals. *Closed Sun, Mon and Thurs eve.*

Chez La Mère Pourcel, 3 Place des Merciers, **t** 02 96 39 03 80 (€€€). In one of the finest historic settings in town, with a lovely terrace. The food is fairly run-of-the-mill traditional. *Closed Sun and Mon in low season.*

L'Atelier Gourmand, 4 Rue du Quai, **t** 02 96 85 14 18 (€€–€). With its fine terrace by the Rance, one of the most tempting of Dinan's riverside restaurants, serving Breton dishes. *Out of season closed Sun eve and Mon.*

Crêperie Ahna, 7 Rue de la Poissonnerie, **t** 02 96 39 09 13 (€). One of the best crêperies in town, given a contemporary design, also serving grilled meat. *Closed Sun in low season.*

Crêperie du Roy, 40 Rue de la Lainerie, **t** 02 96 39 29 72 (€). A comical stone monster greets you above the door to this traditional little address serving tasty crêpes and good cider.

Crêperie des Artisans, 6 Rue du Petit Fort, **t** 02 96 39 44 10 (€). In a great location on the way to the port, with charming terrace.

Lanvallay ✉ 22100

Le Bistrot du Viaduc, 22 Rue du Lion d'Or, **t** 02 96 85 95 00 (€€). A restaurant not far from Dinan, past the viaduct, offering a fine view of the Rance Valley as well as good food. *Closed Sat lunch, Sun eve and Mon.*

La Vieille Braise, 23 rue Rennes, *www.lavieillebraise.com*, **t** 02 96 39 40 50 (€€). Refined traditional cuisine enlivened by familial atmosphere. *Closed Sun and Tues eve and Wed.*

The Côte d'Emeraude to Cap d'Erquy

A handful of dramatic spits reach out into the Channel along this stretch of coast between Dinard and the Bay of St-Brieuc. The first three have been colonized by the villas of the resorts of Lancieux, St-Jacut-de-la-Mer and St-Cast-le-Guildo, making the most of the sandy beaches and coves. The two western spits, Cap Fréhel and Cap d'Erquy, have a much wilder, emptier feel, covered with moors running down dramatic cliffs. The coastal rocks already start to turn pink here, while the moors change to a bright heathery mauve in season. The spectacular promontory fort of La Latte steals the tourist limelight in the area. The curious resort of Sables-d'Or-les-Pins boasts the most brilliant beach.

Lancieux to St-Cast-le-Guildo

Lovely villas punctuate the shore around **Lancieux**, the resort on the left bank of the Frémur (for St-Briac-sur-Mer on the other bank, see p.205). In summer time, shoals of fish-sized boats are left stranded on the extensive sands when the tide goes out. A new **Club Nautique** opened recently on Plage de St-Cieux, the main beach with its lifeguards, and offers all manner of watersports possibilities, from sea kayaking to sandyachting. Another recent creation is **Golf Gaea**, a nine-hole course in a beautiful coastal location, with a simple restaurant.

Club Nautique de Lancieux
t 02 96 86 31 50

Golf Gaea
t 06 26 37 72 32,
www.gaea.fr

It's an Irish saint who's credited with founding a community at **St-Jacut-de-la-Mer** in the Dark Ages, hence the name. The abbey grew into one of the most important in Brittany, and ran one of Dinan's large religious establishments, but virtually nothing remains today. Originally, fishermen here lived off mackerel-fishing in particular. But there has also always been an abundance of shellfish which the local women used to collect from the vast expanses of sand. Nowadays, you'll often find large numbers of local enthusiasts going out to fill their buckets at low tide. A small local community does stay on through the winter, once the tourist hordes have left. Some apparently still practise their *Jégui* together, not some kind of dance, but the local form of Gallo, the dialect of eastern Brittany whose roots go back to Gallo-Roman times.

The very alluring scattering of pine-clad rocks just out to sea from Lancieux and St-Jacut, the **Ebihen islands** (the name derives from the Breton, An Inizi Bihan – the Little Isles), are reachable on foot at most low tides, but you must check with the local tourist offices about timing any such walk.

The **Arguenon River**, which flows down from the Méné hills in central Brittany, once served as the medieval frontier between the lordships of Dinan and Penthièvre. You can walk freely around the impressive ruined walls of the medieval **Château du Guildo**, set

Getting around the Côte d'Emeraude

just above the estuary. Built for the lords of Dinan, it guards the eastern entrance to the Arguenon. The pretty quayside of the village of **Le Guildo** lies nearby.

Following the Arguenon inland, you come to the pleasant old town of **Plancoët**, serious, solid granite houses built up and down its slopes and along its curving main shopping street. One or two extravagant fountains add a jolly note, and help indicate that this place is known across Brittany for its bottled water. Near town, you can enjoy a free glass of the local mineral water; the Perrier group has been in charge of bottling at this source since 1961.

St-Cast-le-Guildo lies on a wider, less insular peninsula than St-Jacut. The two communities used to fight over their fishing territories; now they compete with their holiday beaches – St-Cast boasts seven. The first beach on the eastern side, the **Plage des Quatre-Vaux**, is a rural delight before the more built-up quarters. The big **beach of Pen-Guen** lies south of the main part of town, overlooked by the beautifully located 18-hole **Golf de Pen-Guen**. Wealthy holidaymakers began building spacious villas on the southern tip of the old town, Pointe de la Garde, from the second half of the 19th century. The *sentier touristique* encourages you to walk through these quarters, with their fine trees and views over to St-Jacut and the Ebihen islands. **La Garde**, the main beach, stretches some two kilometres below the town. The old fishermen's quarters, **L'Isle**, lie on the tip of the peninsula; a local association organizes fishing trips (spring–Oct) on a traditional vessel, or you can take a magnificent **boat excursion** to Cap Fréhel. You can sign up at the tourist office for these, or for guided walking tours of the oyster and mussel fields reachable when the tides are very low. The resort's **Centre Nautique** hires out watersports materials and organizes courses. The big event for 2009 has been the building of a brand-new **marina**, with 750 berths in deep water.

Boat excursion
summer only; see
www.compagnie
corsaire.com

Centre Nautique
t 02 96 41 86 42,
www.cnautique-
saintcast.com

A track leads to the very tip of the peninsula and sensational views. The way down the western side of the St-Cast peninsula along the Bay of La Fresnaye is more broken up by cliffs than the eastern side. Although there are lovely sandy coves to discover this way, at low tide, the bay turns into a vast mudflat where mussels and oysters are professionally cultivated.

Bloody Saint's Rocks

Ruddy streaks of colour stain some of Lancieux's rocks. One legend has it that a saint from the Dark Ages, Siog (in Breton) or Cieux (French for skies), was born here and cleared the land to make it fertile. Having gone off to convert the pagans inland, he returned battered and bruised, on the verge of death. The blood that poured from his wounds here is supposed to have turned the local rocks red.

08

Côtes d'Armor | The Côte d'Emeraude to Cap d'Erquy

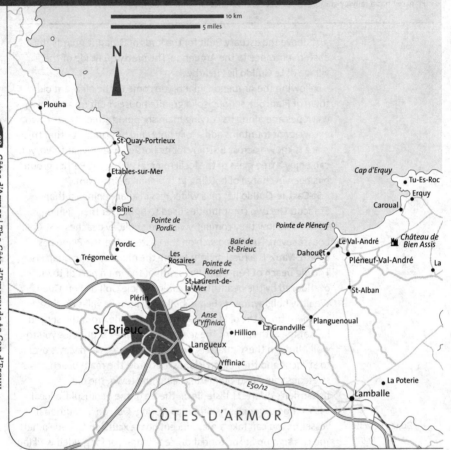

10 km
5 miles

N

Plouha

St-Quay-Portrieux

Etables-sur-Mer

Cap d'Erquy

Tu-Es-Roc

Erquy

Binic

Caroual

Pointe de Pordic

Pointe de Pléneuf

Le Val-André

Château de Bien Assis

Pordic

Baie de St-Brieuc

Dahouët

Pléneuf-Val-André

La

Trégomeur

Les Rosaires

Pointe de Roselier

St-Laurent-de-la-Mer

Plérin

St-Alban

Anse d'Yffiniac

Planguenoual

St-Brieuc

Hillion

La Grandville

Langueux

Yffiniac

E50/12

La Poterie

Lamballe

CÔTES-D'ARMOR

St-Cast's name evokes the memory of an important 18th-century battle between the British and the French. In 1758, during the Seven Years War, British commander General Bligh led an invasion landing at St-Lunaire to the east. His fleet withdrew to wait at St-Cast. Bligh's attack failed and he and his many thousands of soldiers headed rapidly for St-Cast to regain their vessels. However, the army of the Duc d'Aiguillon, royal governor of Brittany, was lying in waiting for them. In a chaotic battle, the French eventually triumphed, as the chivalric symbolism on top of the St-Cast column reflects, the greyhound vanquishing the English lion.

Matignon may be familiar to you as the name of the French prime minister's residence in Paris, but it is also the name of a pleasant Breton village inland from St-Cast-le-Guildo – in fact, Jacques Goyon-Matignon, of the local lordly family, once owned the Parisian house, hence its name. Another Goyon-Matignon,

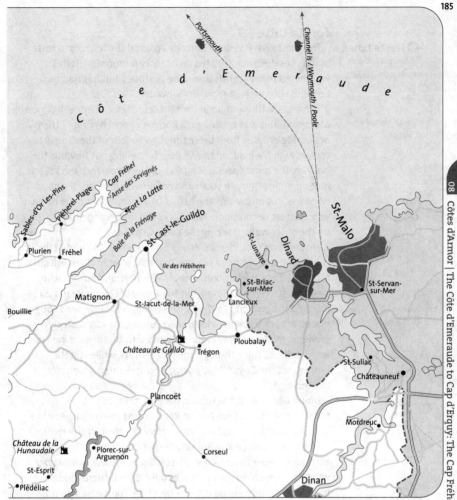

François, Comte de Thorigny, married the heiress of the Grimaldi family, becoming Prince of Monaco. A Matignon lord also ordered the building of the stupendous Fort La Latte much closer to home.

The Cap Fréhel Peninsula

What a change, after all the family resorts from St-Malo to St-Cast-le-Guildo, to come to the tremendous unspoilt wild heaths of this peninsula. Keen walkers should try the dramatic coastal path round the Bay of La Fresnaye. By car or by bike, enjoy the delightful traditional hamlets such as **La Motte** or **St-Géran**, with their ruddy-stoned houses and their apple trees. Follow the tracks to the deadends of St-Géran or **Château Serein**, and a steep walk down the slopes leads you to glorious, secretive stretches of shoreline.

Fort La Latte

❷ Fort La Latte
*www.castlelalatte.
com, t 02 96 41 57 11;
open daily July and Aug
10–7, April–June and
Sept 10–12.30 and
2.30–6.30; rest of year
Sat, Sun and hols 4–6*

The most sensational of Brittany's coastal castles, Fort La Latte stands out defiantly, isolated on its rocky promontory. It has weathered many storms down the centuries, but has had to contend with neglect more than invaders.

The first castle went up in the 14th century for Etienne III Goyon-Matignon, and was known as La Roche-Goyon. The first of the two drawbridges dates from these times, as do four of the rampart towers with their distinctive shapes, funnelling out towards the bottom. The most spectacular piece of the whole fort, the keep, is also original. Although sober and defensive, with virtually no windows, but arrow slits the height of a man, it does have its own very discreet decoration – symbols of the four evangelists placed on the outer walls, marking the cardinal points.

Brittany was rocked by its War of Succession in the mid-14th century. Then the king of France, Charles V, tried to claim Brittany for himself. His Breton-born army leader, Bertrand du Guesclin, took this stronghold in 1379, but the Treaty of Guérande in 1381 restored the property to the Goyon-Matignons. However, though placed in such a splendid lookout's position, the fort scarcely served in military terms in the 15th and 16th centuries. It was even left to fall into ruins through the 17th century, while still the property of the Goyon-Matignons, who appointed governors to oversee it.

Simon Garengeau, the man in good part responsible for fortifying St-Malo in the Ancien Régime, was given charge of the conversion of Fort La Latte's ruins before the close of the 17th century, with France and Britain at war. Although the Goyon-Matignons were to remain in possession of the place until 1720, when the French military finally bought it from them, these transformations were paid for by the state. The castle's guards continued to be recruited locally, but the governors stopped living at the fort, preferring to take more comfortable lodgings nearby. However, one famous guest did stay at Fort La Latte in 1715 – none other than the pretender to the English throne, James Stuart. He was forced to take refuge here on a stormy evening and wrote of the place being one of the grimmest, most godforsaken spots in which a man could spend a night. He complained that there were no comforts inside and not even wood with which to cook.

After all the effort spent adapting Fort La Latte, the 18th-century military action took place along other stretches of the Breton coast. Even during the Battle of St-Cast so close by, the fort played no role. During the Revolutionary period, a comical addition was made to the place – the French naval command had ordered that cannonball ovens be built along the north Breton coast, to respond to any passing enemy vessels, the aim being to set the ships on fire. Unfortunately it took two and a half hours to 'cook' a cannonball to the required heat, hardly swift enough to surprise the foe, who would anyway be warned by smoke from the oven. You can, though, still see the cannonball oven built at Fort La Latte.

By 1886, the military presence had been reduced to one castle-keeper. The estate was eventually put up for sale, and Frédéric Joüon des Longrais, passionate about the place since his childhood, bought the fort in 1931. With the assistance of the Monuments Historiques de France, he set about restoring the dilapidated buildings. Armies of tourists now come to visit this spectacular site each year.

The place may be rather empty within, but it makes for a magical tour. One of the most exhilarating parts of the visit is climbing onto the roof of the keep, which is covered with slabs of stone by way of tiles – they're unlikely to be blown away even in the strongest gales to hit this dramatically exposed point. Of course, the castle has all the drama needed to inspire Romantic artists and historical films. Kirk Douglas and Tony Curtis came here in 1957 to play at Dark Ages fighters in *Vikings*. The fort was also used as a set in the 1980s filming of Balzac's bloody Breton novel, *Les Chouans* (*see* box, p.138).

To Cap Fréhel

Energetic walkers go by fast from Fort La Latte, across the heathery coastal moors above the cliffs of the Anse des Sévignés with its fairy grotto of La Teignouse, to Cap Fréhel. The path offers a spectacular but at times precarious way to appreciate the varied colours of the cliffs and islets, made of schist and pinkish sandstone, with porphyry thrown in. The peninsula's roads are marred by traffic in summer, but virtually no houses have been allowed to sprout on the heather and gorse moorlands.

Phare de Fréhel
open April–Nov daily 10.30–12 and 2.30–5; small fee

The **Phare de Fréhel** stands out all the more given its isolated position on the moors. You can climb up it, taking you to almost 100 metres above the sea and to even grander views along wide stretches of the north Breton coast. During school holidays, the **Syndicat des Caps** organizes walks with guides who explain the flora and fauna. Guillemots, petrels and the odd gannet count among the rare species that nest on the island off shore. The largest colony of crested cormorants in France has settled at Cap Fréhel. To appreciate the soaring cliffs from a different angle, take a **boat trip** round Cap Fréhel from St-Malo, Dinard or St-Cast.

Syndicat des Caps
www.syndicat-des-caps.bzh.bh, t 02 96 41 50 83

Boat trip
www.compagnie corsaire.com, t 08 25 13 81 00

A glorious, open **corniche road** from the cape heads towards the resort of Sables-d'Or-les-Pins. Again, there are virtually no houses here, just moors and cliffs and the odd stretch of sandy beach reached via steep paths. For walkers, the views are staggering and unimpeded, as even the yellow-flowering gorse and the purple heather grow very low to the ground, avoiding the worst of the winds. **Pléhérel-Plage** is a friendly family resort, with a wonderfully situated village church overlooking the sea. As to its beaches, they benefit from tremendous views back to Cap Fréhel, and the rocky islands beyond its tip.

The great asset of the curious little resort of **Sables-d'Or-les-Pins** is its huge, stunning beach. The name of the place, invented by a pair of ambitious property developers in the 1920s, highlights the main attractions, both the glorious golden sands, and the pines planted on the dunes behind. Launay and Brouard called upon their architects to create a grand seaside town here from scratch. A first batch of large, Norman-style part-timberclad mansions went up, plus an unfortunately out-of-place arcaded Art Deco block close to the beach. It looked like the place and the social scene would take off, but the great crash, together with mismanagement, brought a swift halt to the development in the early 1930s. The resort has never been finished, leaving a strangely vacuous atmosphere to the place for some of the year, although the place does come alive in season, and money has recently been poured into the contemporary **Casino de Fréhel**, built in prime position just above the beach. There's also a well-located **golf course**.

The vast expanse of **beach** is superb, intact, magical, the protected bay here beautified by an island to the west and an island to the east, the western one, beyond the semi-natural marina, topped by a chapel to St Michael. At low tide, you can walk to this islet. White yachts often congregate around the eastern island. On the distant, eastern tip of the bay, the winds whip up dust from the stone quarry still in operation. Walk to the western end of the beach, and the Cap Fréhel headland with its moors and lighthouse comes beautifully into view. Continue round the protected **Flèche Dunaire** to explore the generous, sandy **Islet estuary**, a paradise for walkers, and for dogs to run across. Behind, the peaceful **Marais des Salines** is the domain of birds and ornithologists. Back on the heights, the village of **Plurien** has a quiet charm, and an intriguingly elongated old church in the centre.

Golf course
www.frehel-golf sablesdor.fr;
t 02 96 41 42 57

Market Days on the Côte d'Emeraude

Lancieux: Tuesday in season
St-Jacut-de-la-Mer: Friday
Plancoët: Saturday
St-Cast-le-Guildo: Friday; also Monday during summer
Matignon: Wednesday
Fréhel: Tuesday

Sables-d'Or-les-Pins: Sunday in July and Aug
Plurien: Friday

Where to Stay and Eat on the Côte d'Emeraude

Lancieux ✉ **22770**
***Les Bains**, 20 Rue du Poncel,
t 02 96 86 31 33, *www.dinan-hotel-*

ⓘ **Lancieux >>**
Square Jean Conan,
t 02 96 86 25 37, www.
lancieux-tourisme.fr

Pays Touristique de Dinan

*www.paystouristique
dinan.com; offers
general information on
the Côtes d'Armor's Côte
d'Emeraude resorts, as
well as on the area
around Dinan*

St-Jacut-de-la-Mer >
*Rue du Châtelet,
t 02 96 27 71 91;
out of season, contact
Plancoët tourist office*

St-Cast-le-Guildo >>
*Place Charles de
Gaulle, t 02 96 41 81 52,
www.saintcastle
guildo.com*

Plancoët >
*Rue des Venelles, t 02
96 84 00 57, www.
valdarguenon.fr*

★ L'Ecrin >

★ Manoir du Vaumadeuc >

★ Château du Val d'Arguenon B&B >

bretagne.com (€€€–€€). Comfortable modern rooms and a private garden, plus a tearoom to satisfy the British clientele.

St-Jacut-de-la-Mer ✉ 22750

*Le Vieux Moulin, 22 Rue du Moulin, **t** 02 96 27 71 02 (€). A delightful, simple hotel in an old mill in a superb location in the centre of the peninsula, with great views. Rooms may be old-fashioned, and not all have their own WC or shower, but they have charm. Hearty traditional French restaurant (€€).

Plancoët ✉ 22130

****L'Ecrin, 20 Les Quais, **t** 02 96 84 10 24, *www.crouzil.com* (€€€–€€). This hotel has smart, spacious, well-furnished modern rooms, but is best known for its reputed restaurant **Chez Crouzil** (€€€€–€€), where the chef adds exotic touches to his Breton dishes. *Closed most Jan.*

La Pastourelle B&B, L'Etang Quihouas, St-Lormel, a few km north of Plancoët along the west bank of the Arguenon river, **t** 02 96 84 03 77, *www.la-pastourelle.gitedarmor.com* (€). An old country house with good small, cosy rooms. Simple, copious *table d'hôte* (€).

Pleven ✉ 22130

****Manoir du Vaumadeuc, t 02 96 84 46 17, *www.vaumadeuc.com* (€€€€–€€). Very fine 15th-century manor and splendid rooms that look the part with their fireplaces and sober décor. Smart French-style gardens. *Closed Nov–Easter.*

Mme Blanchard B&B, La Rompardais, **t** 02 96 84 43 08 (€). Big classic, good-value rooms in a traditional Breton house.

Notre-Dame-du-Guildo ✉ 22380

Château du Val d'Arguenon B&B, t 02 96 41 07 03, *www.chateauduval.com* (€€€–€€). Beautiful property on the site of an earlier manor that was apparently destroyed by the British in the Battle of St-Cast. There are sumptuous B&B rooms, or stylish treehouses in the lovely grounds which go down to the beach. Tennis court too. *Closed early Nov–Easter.*

Le Gilles de Bretagne, Blvd Arguenon, **t** 02 96 41 07 08 (€€). Very pleasant restaurant by Le Guildo's port, with a great view onto the castle opposite.

St-Cast-le-Guildo ✉ 22380

***Les Arcades, 15 Rue du Duc d'Aiguillon, **t** 02 96 41 80 50, *www.hotels-saint-cast.com* (€€–€). Comfortable rooms, some with sea views, in the heart of the pedestrian zone, plus a brasserie.

Port Jacquet, 32 Rue du Port, **t 02 96 41 97 18, *www.port-jacquet.com* (€). An excellent hotel with a restaurant, situated right on the seafront. Prices vary depending on the view.

L'Espérance, 6 Rue Jacques Cartier, **t** 02 96 41 81 13, *www.hotel-de-lesperance. com* (€). A nice, tiny hotel with a handful of well cared-for rooms.

Ker Flore, **t** 02 96 81 03 79 (€€–€). Restaurant by the village church serving excellent fresh *cuisine du marché* in a 1920s-style decor. *Closed Mon, Tues eve, Wed eve and Sun eve.*

Crêperie Le Bretan'or, 8 Place Anatole Le Braz, **t** 02 96 41 92 45 (€). A holidaymakers' favourite. *Closed Wed out of season.*

Le Biniou, Plage de Pen Guen, **t** 02 96 41 94 53 (€€). Interesting seafood dishes served in dining rooms and on terraces with panoramic views over this beach. *Closed Mon.*

Bouchonneau Marie-France, Allée Roseraies, by port, **t** 02 96 41 18 80 (€). Sample mussels and oysters direct from the growers on the portside terrace. *Closed eves.*

Plévenon ✉ 22240

Le Trécelin, **t 02 96 41 46 82, *www.hoteltrecelin.com* (€). In the sweet village after which it's named, an appealing traditional hotel, some rooms renovated, with a restaurant for the clientele only. Pool.

Ushuaïa B&B and Crêperie, **t** 02 96 41 41 61 (€). In great location close to Fort La Latte, for crêpes and decent B&B rooms.

Le Relais de Fréhel B&B, Route du Cap Fréhel, **t** 02 96 41 43 02, *www. relaiscapfrehel.fr* (€). A little B&B within a family home, with its own wild garden. Warm welcome, family cooking and a wine shop.

ⓘ Fréhel
Place de Chambly,
t 02 96 41 53 81, www.
pays-de-frehel.com

★ La Voile d'Or >

ⓘ Matignon >>
Place du Général de
Gaulle, t 02 96 41 12 53,
www.tourisme.pays-de-
matignon.net

Le Victorine, Place de Chambly, t 02 96 41 55 55 (€€). On village square with terrace, prides itself on its fresh seafood. *Closed Sun eve and Mon in low season.*

La Ribote, Route du Cap, t 02 96 41 43 76 (€). Lovely spot at which to try good-value Breton specialities.

Sables-d'Or-les-Pins ✉ 22240

***La Voile d'Or**, Allée des Acacias, t 02 96 41 42 49, www.la-voile-dor.fr (€€€€–€€). The smartest hotel in the resort, set back by the sandy Islet estuary, across which the rooms have restful views, despite the road below. Its reputed restaurant, **La Lagune**, offers exciting seafood and regional cuisine in its stylish dining room (€€€€–€€; *closed Mon, Tues lunch, Wed lunch*). *Closed end Nov–mid-Feb.*

Manoir St-Michel, Le Carquois, Route du Cap Fréhel (north along the coast from Sables-d'Or), t 02 96 41 48 87, www.fournel.de (€€€–€). A real find, with a noble Breton exterior, excellent, spacious rooms complete with antique furniture, and wonderful

views onto the sea from the garden, which boasts its own lake. *Closed early Nov–March.*

Le Diane, Allée des Acacias, t 02 96 41 42 07, www.hoteldiane.fr (€€). On the boulevard leading to the beach, a typical Norman-style hotel with some period charm and a popular restaurant (€€€–€€). *Closed early Nov–mid-March.*

Les Pins, Allée des Acacias, t 02 96 41 42 20 (€€). Opposite Le Diane, another appealing, well-kept option.

Plurien ✉ 22240

***Manoir de la Salle**, Rue du Lac, t 02 96 72 38 29, www.manoirdela salle.com (€€€–€€). A smart 16th-century country farm set around a courtyard, hidden in its sweet garden on the edge of this pleasant village. The bedrooms are in relatively simple modern style.

Matignon ✉ 22550

Crêperie de Saint-Germain, village square, t 02 96 41 08 33 (€). Traditional crêpes made using top-quality local produce.

The Eastern Bay of St-Brieuc

★ St-Brieuc

The views across the immense Bay of St-Brieuc are staggering. They almost match those across the Bay of Mont St-Michel, but whereas the coast around that bay is flat as a pancake, cliffs line the shore almost all the way round the Bay of St-Brieuc. This bay is highly reputed for its *coquilles St-Jacques*, or scallops, but quotas are strictly limited. Anyway, most of the centuries-old fishing ports around the bay have been turning more and more into resorts since the Belle Epoque, with varying degrees of success. Villas predominate rather than apartment blocks, and many of the resorts' long, curving beaches are backed by well-laid promenades. Get away from the main settlements and your reward is exhilarating coastal walks and wilder beaches and coves.

The Peninsula and Port of Erquy

Archaeologists say that Celts and Gallo-Romans once guarded the coastline from the vantage point of the **Cap d'Erquy**. Heather and bracken dominate the scene today, with just a scattering of pines, leaving fabulous open views all round. The area had at one stage become ravaged by tourist hordes traipsing all across the heathland to enjoy the grandiose panoramas, but you're now

Getting around the Bay of St-Brieuc

herded along precise tracks. Well-marked paths lead around the peninsula. Beaches of varied character lie around the sides of this block of land. The **beach of Portuais** has impressive rocks as a backdrop. Closer to the western tip of the cape, the fine **Plage du Lourtuais** is favoured by nudists.

The **port** is the highlight of the sprawling seaside town of **Erquy** on the eastern end of the bay. Working boats and pleasure craft mingle quite happily in the beautifully clear waters. The quays provide an enchanting spot from which to watch the bustle. Tucked in below the colourful cliff face behind, appealing bars, restaurants and crêperies provided with generous terraces occupy virtually all the houses, plus there's the odd maritime shop, including a Comptoir Marin, and Itoha, a specialist clothes maker. At the rather dull modern shoebox of a building beside the water, the **Maison de la Mer** offers all sorts of seasonal watersports possibilities, such as yachting, kayaking, diving or sandyachting. In addition, they can give you details on getting out on the old sailing vessel, *La Sainte-Jeanne*.

The very northern tip of Erquy remains lively because of scallops and stone quarrying. Erquy is the most important port in France for scallop-catching, accounting for 50 per cent of the French quota, but this activity is severely restricted now to stop further depletion of stocks. The deep pink stone from Erquy has long been in demand, and apparently went into the building of Paris's Arc de Triomphe.

Big chunks of pink Erquy rock protect the **main beach** curving round from the port. There's an easy, flat promenade for walkers in front of the many car parks and the curve of buildings facing the sea, with only the rare hotel or restaurant set amid the villas. The ridge of houses climbing the bay's slopes may not be the most inspiring, but this is a very popular family resort. A strange, tall, truncated chapel marks the skyline above town.

There is an **older Erquy** just behind the promenade, houses built of purple-tinged stone clustering around the old **Eglise St-Pierre et St-Paul**, with its well-lit towers. Below the diminutive, shop-lined square beside the church, the tourist office has an exhibition space used for art shows in high season, close to the slickly simple contemporary covered market. Around the main shopping street, you'll find excellent fish shops as well as souvenir shops.

Turn the corner of the tall **Pointe de la Heussaye** on the western end of Erquy's bay and you come to the spacious **Plage de Caroual**, reputed for its fine, fudge-coloured sands. There's a simple café just behind, as well as a somewhat messy array of holiday homes.

Château de Bien Assis
www.chateau-bienassis.com, t 02 96 72 22 03; open mid-June–mid-Sept for guided tours, Mon–Sat 10.30–12.30 and 2–6.30, Sun and public hols 2–6.30; look out for special evening tours in high season

Inland, the **Château de Bien Assis** lurks behind an impressively solid wall. The sign *Douves!* warns you not to drive right into the well-concealed moat. Little remains of the 15th-century castle that was ordered by the Quélénec family, except for a mighty tower at the back. Look carefully at the façade and you'll see a dividing line running down the middle of the building – the château turns out to be something of a semi-detached house. One half was commissioned by Gilles Visdelou in the 1620s; the second half was added in the late 18th century by François-Hyacinthe Visdelou. Before the Revolution, the château became the property of the Comte de La Ville-Théart, the founder of a series of Breton stud farms. As the Terror raged in 1792, the count handily found himself in Britain buying thoroughbreds. Denounced as an émigré, he had his château ransacked. The place served briefly as a prison and then became the property of a Napoleonic general. The Kerjégus bought and restored it in the 1880s. The architecture inside and out contains many subtle references to the sea, as you'll learn during the guided tour.

Pléneuf-Val-André to St-Brieuc

Keen walkers should continue along the superb coastal path from Erquy to the resort of Le Val-André. The way leads you past the splendid **beaches of Ville-Berneuf** and the **Grève des Vallées**.

The **Ile Verdelet**, the Bay of St-Brieuc's answer to the Mont St-Michel's rock, draws the onlooker's eye magnetically across the waters. This dramatic, triangular island is a bird reserve, home to great cormorants, crested cormorants and all manner of gulls. At low tide, a causeway of pebbles and sand is revealed, making it possible to walk out to the island, but normally access is forbidden, to leave the birds in peace.

With the highly picturesque Ile Verdelet adding to the obvious attraction of its long sandy beach, **Le Val-André** was chosen as the site for a brand new Breton resort in the 1880s. The gabled villas built in crazy stone patterns still dominate right round the long curve of the seafront, with only a few modern developments muscling in. The long, pedestrian-only **promenade** is much appreciated. Although at high tide the waves come right up to slap the seawall, when the waters recede, the sands here are excellent for children; sand-yachts also come out to make the most of the wide expanse of beach. On the eastern end of the resort you'll find the **sailing school** next to the small **port**. Above the central section of the promenade, the **Rotonde complex**, with its cinemas, casino and restaurant and bar with sea views, attracts plenty of visitors. The main street parallel to the promenade is also lively in season with its shops and restaurants. Up the steep hillside, the older community of **Pléneuf** stretches out from the church.

The port of **Dahouët** hides away behind the Pointe de la Guette west of Le Val André. It has much older and deeper roots; apparently wily Viking raiders exploited its cunning location. It is certainly cleverly concealed down the narrowest of rock-lined estuaries, out of harm from lashing waves – a fact modern developers have exploited, too, creating a rather shiny new **marina**, hundreds of yachts crammed together here.

The ports around the Bay of St-Brieuc were historically renowned for their great long-distance, perilous fishing expeditions to the waters off North America and Iceland. Dahouët claims to have been one of the first French ports from which boats left for the gruelling cod-fishing journeys off Newfoundland, as early as the start of the 16th century. Overlooked by a protective Virgin Mary, colourful fishing boats still draw up by the quayside houses part of the year, bringing in scallops. You can go out on trips in the *Pauline*, a reconstruction of a local boat from the 1900s.

It makes for an enjoyable game, going in search of the discreet series of coves you can discover down to the bottom of the Bay of St-Brieuc. A breach in a cement wall leads on to the beach of **Le Port Morvan**, often particularly warm and cosy thanks to the high sides of the cliffs protecting it. The tarmac track ends before you get to the **Grèves du Vauglin**, a splendid little sandy spot enclosed by rocky points. Follow the winding village road through attractive **La Cotentin** to the cliffs. After the next creek at Jospinet, head down to **L'Hermot d'en Bas** and the **Chapelle St-Maurice**. Beyond a Nazi blockhouse, the little chapel on its hillock stamps its character on this stretch. At the beach of **St-Maurice**, a curious low cliff of orange earth forms the back wall to the beach. Beyond, the Gouessant River snakes its way through the mudflats to the sea at low tide; panels warn of this treacherous channel, disguised when the tide comes up. Above the **Plage de Béliard** you can get an excellent view of the incoming tide arriving to cover the lines of wooden posts on which mussels grow out in the bay. Head just inland to the village of **Morieux** to appreciate the intriguing medieval frescoes discovered in the **church**.

At the splendid expanse of the **Plage de la Grandville**, more signs alert you to the speed of the incoming tides. This is one of the most spectacular beaches along the north coast of Brittany. As to the **Dunes de Bon Abri**, the dunes here are gorgeous, hidden out of sight from St-Brieuc by the Pointe de Guette. Mussel-farming tractors work by these dunes, dogs race joyfully across the great tracts of sands at low tide, and the odd trotter-horse racers come out in their comical chariots to practise their skills. As you walk across the beach, mussels crunch underfoot.

West of the Pointe de Guette, the **Anse d'Yffiniac**, the deep, sharp, southerly point of the Bay of St-Brieuc, turns into a vast mudflat when the tide goes out, so this is not a place to come swimming. Sadly, pollution has become an issue at the back of the bay in recent times. However, many of the residents of **Hillion** keep a little boat by the shore. Suburban quarters have grown up around the village in recent years, but the coastal path remains unspoilt. You might visit the **Maison de la Baie de St-Brieuc** on Rue de l'Etoile first, before embarking on a magical walk. The visitor centre explains the bay's exceptional environment, subject to the fifth largest tidal range in the world. There's a project to build a more substantial centre. In nearby Langueux, **La Briqueterie** is another modern-style museum that focuses on traditional human activities around the bay, particularly brick-making, although there are also events put on here, for example on pottery.

Maison de la Baie de St-Brieuc
t 02 96 32 27 98, open all year

La Briqueterie
t 02 96 63 36 66; open July and Aug Mon–Fri 10–6.30, Sat–Sun 1.30–6.30

(★) **L'Escurial** >>

(i) **Erquy** >
3 Rue du 19 Mars 1962, t 02 96 72 30 12, www.erquy-tourisme.com

(i) **Pléneuf-Val-André** >>
Rue Winston Churchill, Le Val André, t 02 96 72 20 55, www.val-andre.org

(i) **Yffiniac**
t 02 96 72 00 37, www.yffiniac.com

Market Days on the Bay of St-Brieuc

Erquy: Saturday
Pléneuf: Tuesday
Le Val-André: Friday in summer

Where to Stay and Eat on the Bay of St-Brieuc

Erquy ✉ 22430
**Beauséjour, 21 Rue de la Corniche, t 02 96 72 30 39, *www.beausejour-erquy.com* (€€–€). On the resort's western slope, above a beach, a hotel in a typical gabled villa looking over the bay, many of its cheerful rooms with views. The restaurant has good views too (€€€–€€; *closed Mon*). *Closed mid-Nov–mid-March.*

**de la Plage, 21 Blvd de la Mer, t 02 96 72 30 09, *www.hotelplage-erquy. com* (€€–€). A modern option by the beach benefiting from big light windows both in the bedrooms and the restaurant.

**Le Relais, 60 Rue du Port, t 02 96 72 32 60 (€). Rooms with lovely views on the eastern end of town, and a popular seafood restaurant that remains lively year-round.

La Cassolette, 6 Rue de la Saline, t 02 96 72 13 08 (€). A great-value choice offering *cassolettes* such as crayfish with orange, plus other seafood dishes, on its covered terrace. *Closed Wed–Thurs in low season.*

L'Escurial, Blvd de la Mer, t 02 96 72 31 56 (€€). With a dining room perched above the central beach to benefit from the sea views, this restaurant offers carefully prepared, imaginative dishes.

St-Aubin ✉ 22430
Le Relais St-Aubin, Route de la Bouillie, t 02 96 72 13 22, *www.relais-saint-aubin.fr* (€€€–€€). In a 17th-century former priory with a lovely garden, 3km inland from Erquy. Seafood is a speciality in the restaurant (€€), and meats are grilled in a monumental fireplace. *Closed Mon, also Tues in low season.*

Pléneuf-Val-André ✉ 22370
**Grand Hôtel du Val André, 80 Rue Amiral Charner, t 02 96 72 20 56, *www.grand-hotel-val-andre.fr* (€€). The only hotel on the seafront, its grand façade separated from the promenade by a pine-shaded lawn. Many of the comfortable bedrooms have sea views, and the large windows of the big, smart restaurant (€€€–€€; *closed Mon, Tues lunch and Sun dinner*) also benefit from the location. *Closed most Jan.*

***Georges, 131 Rue Clemenceau, t 02 96 72 23 70, *www.partouche.com* (€€). This modern hotel a short way back from the promenade amid the shops has been given a good, trendy makeover. *Closed mid-Nov–Jan.*

de la Mer, 63 Rue Amiral Charner, t 02 96 72 20 44, *www.hotel-de-la-mer.com* (€€–€). Well-kept rooms, just a few with sea views, 50m from beach, plus traditional seafood restaurant. The **Motel Nuit et Jour offering studios (€) set further back in the resort is part of the same set-up. **Au Biniou**, 121 Rue Clemenceau, t 02 96 72 24 35 (€€). Sea-faring setting for succulent seafood, including delicious fish stews. *Closed Tues eve and Wed.*

Planguenoual ✉ 22400

***Château et Domaine du Val**, t 02 96 32 75 40, *www.chateau-du-val.com* (€€€–€€). Luxurious hotel in a medieval castle and its outbuildings, but offering all the modern comforts. You pay more to stay in the château itself. The grounds, situated less than 1km from the sea, are listed. There's a covered sports complex with indoor tennis court, two squash courts and a heated pool. The restaurant uses home-grown veg from the *potager*. **Manoir de la Hazaie B&B**, t 02 96 32 73 71, *www.manoir-hazaie.com*

(€€€€€–€€€). Grand accommodation in a beautiful 16th-century house 2.5km southeast. The bedrooms are extremely spacious, with antiques and often four-poster beds and/or monumental old fireplaces. The bathrooms are a dream.

Hillion ✉ 22120

Château de Bonabry B&B, t 02 96 32 21 06, *www.bonabry.fr.st* (€€€). Luxury rooms in a stern-faced little 14th-century castle close to the Bon Abri dunes. The bedrooms are sumptuously decorated and boast their own private salons. Intriguing grounds to explore. *Closed Oct–Easter.*

Langueux ✉ 22360

Crêperie des Grèves, Rue des Grèves, t 02 96 72 56 96 (€). A reasonably priced place using excellent local produce in its range of crêpes.

(i) **Hillion >>**
t 02 96 32 21 53 or
t 02 96 32 21 04
out of season

(★) **Château de Bonabry B&B >>**

(★) **Château et Domaine du Val >**

(i) **Langueux >>**
t 02 96 62 25 50,
www.langueux.fr

Historic Towns around St-Brieuc

A trio of fine little historic towns, Lamballe, Moncontour and Quintin, lies within easy reach of the southern tip of the Bay of St-Brieuc, but these delightful places also make good bases for exploring inland, rural Côtes d'Armor.

Lamballe

Once capital of the quarrelsome Breton county of Penthièvre, which stretched south from the Côte d'Emeraude and the Bay of St-Brieuc, Lamballe is now known as capital of the Breton horse, as well as being one of the most overlooked of Brittany's characterful market towns, set in its hollow in the Gouessant Valley.

Lamballe acquired particular political significance when Duke Alain III of Brittany gave the lordship of Penthièvre as an *apanage* to his brother Eudes in 1034, but from that time to the 15th century, the counts of Penthièvre frequently proved a thorn in the side of the Breton dukes. Lamballe inevitably became embroiled in the vicious Breton War of Succession of the mid-14th century; after all, the French-backed contender for control of the Breton duchy, Charles de Blois, was none other than the husband of Jeanne de Penthièvre. In 1420, well after the war had finished, the victorious Duke Jean V of Brittany had Lamballe's town ramparts torn down.

King Charles IX elevated the county of Penthièvre to a duchy in the 16th century. The Duc de Mercoeur, the feared ultra-Catholic

Getting to and around the Penthièvre Towns around St-Brieuc

Lamballe is on the TGV rapid **train** line from Paris (under 3hrs away) to Brest. There are regular trains to St-Brieuc (15mins away) and Rennes (*c.* 1hr away), and rail links with Dinan.

leader in Brittany during the French Wars of Religion at the end of that century, also took the title of Duke of Penthièvre. One of his greatest enemies, the Calvinist La Noüe, nicknamed Bras-de-Fer ('Iron Arm') because of an artificial limb he wore, came to attack Lamballe in 1591. He was seriously wounded in the siege, much to the chagrin of King Henri IV, for whose cause he had been fighting. 'He was worth a whole army on his own', the king is supposed to have said. After the Wars of Religion had been settled, Henri IV donated the Penthièvre to his illegitimate son, César de Vendôme. Under the rule of King Louis XIII, his half-brother César plotted against Richelieu; the cardinal had Lamballe's castle destroyed in 1626 by way of retaliation – only the chapel was left standing.

The titles bestowed on the rulers of the Penthièvre became ever more extravagant through time, however. By the Revolution, they styled themselves princes. The last one proved to be particularly dissolute; his debauchery put an end to him three months after his arranged marriage to a young princess from Piedmont. The widowed princess, later known as Mme de Lamballe, went on to serve Marie Antoinette as a lady-in-waiting for some 20 years, until she lost her head in the Revolutionary Terror of 1792 – it was infamously paraded through the Paris streets on a pike.

Although Mme de Lamballe was so savagely butchered in the Revolution, the **town hall** preserves a splendid painting of her in full courtly regalia, portrayed by Jean-Laurent Mosnier; it offers a stunning vision of the last flowering of the Ancien Régime aristocracy, and hints at the outrageous extravagance the courtly ladies indulged in.

In contrast, a more substantial artistic legacy left to Lamballe concentrates the mind on the lives of everyday Brittany and Bretons in the first half of the 20th century, as recorded by the Lamballe-born artist Mathurin Méheut (1882–1958). The **Musée Mathurin Méheut** preserves an extraordinary and enlightening collection of simple paintings and drawings, and reveals how the artist painted obsessively, daily. The works are displayed in one of the grandest old town houses, the timberframe **Maison du Bourreau** ('Hangman's House'), which also contains the tourist office and a little museum on local history, the **Musée d'Art Populaire du Pays de Lamballe**. The Maison du Bourreau is tucked away in a corner off the main historic square, the picturesque sloping rectangle of the **Place du Marché**. The tower of the substantial **church of St John** peers over one end.

Musée Mathurin Méheut
musee.meheut@wanadoo.fr; open June–Sept Mon–Sat 10–12 and 2.30–6; April–May and Oct–Dec Wed, Fri and Sat 2.30–5

Musée d'Art Populaire du Pays de Lamballe
t 02 96 34 77 63; open Tues–Wed 10–12 and 2.30–5, Thurs–Sat 2.30–5

Lamballe Haras
www.haraspatrimoine.
com, t 02 96 50 06 98;
open June–mid-Sept
for tours at 10.30,
2.30 and 4; rest of year
Tues–Sun at 3; mid-
July–Aug horse-riding
show Thurs at 5pm

Rue Villedeneuf leads north to the vast **Place du Champ de Foire.** On one side lies the **Lamballe Haras** or stud farm, very much in the centre of town. It's in good part thanks to the French predilection for eating horse meat that the stocky breeds of Breton horses survived the 20th century. Developed for strength, these squat, square-built steeds are the rugby men of the horse world. You can go and see some of the thick-necked, massive-rumped creatures in Lamballe's magnificent 19th-century stables. Founded in 1825, by the start of the 20th century the Lamballe stud was the biggest in France, with accommodation for 400 stallions. Now it houses up to 70 at any time. The bulk of these are either *chevaux de trait bretons*, Breton cart or draft horses, or Breton *postiers*, which are a mix between the traditional Breton trait and Hackney and Norfolk horses. They star in a number of events staged by the stud farm.

Across to the Arguenon Valley

La Ferme d'Antan
at St-Esprit
www.ferme.dantan22.
free.fr, t 02 96 34 80 77;
open April–May
Tues–Sun 2–6,
June–Aug Tues–Sat
10–6

East from Lamballe, it's a short way from Plédéliac to **La Ferme d'Antan at St-Esprit**, a re-creation of a Breton farm as it would have been at the start of the 20th century. Animals occupy the farm buildings, and the smell of horses comes right into the single room where the family would have lived.

Château de la
Hunaudaye
www.la-hunaudaye.
com, t 02 96 34 82 10;
open mid-June–
mid-Sept 10.30–6.30

Nearby, the ruins of the **Château de la Hunaudaye** rise from marshy lands not far from the Arguenon. This impressive pentagon of a medieval castle is marked by a huge tower at each corner. The château was owned for much of its history by the Tournemine family, related to the Plantagenets. Largely built in 1360, damaged in the Wars of Religion, it was the Chouannerie anti-revolutionary war of the 1790s that put paid to it. However, it's enjoyed a contemporary revival, being given a makeover to make it better suited to visitors and exhibitions. A medieval play, staged in summer within the ruins, brings life and comedy to this stern ruin.

Moncontour

Moncontour looks more like a picture-postcard village from southwest France than a typically Breton one, set on a rocky hilltop, surrounded by medieval fortifications. Long a stronghold of the lords of Penthièvre, sited above two small valleys, it guarded the road between Lamballe and Pontivy in central Brittany.

In the Breton War of Succession, when Moncontour was frequently besieged, the place gained the right to mint money. During the last independent years of the Breton duchy in the late 15th century, French troops seized the place, Duc François II himself trying, unsuccessfully, to liberate it. The administration of the French king, Charles VIII, allowed Moncontour to rebuild its much put-upon ramparts. In the late 16th century, the Huguenots and

**Maison de la
Chouannerie et
de la Révolution**
*t 02 96 73 49 57; open
Sept–June Tues–Sat
10–12.30 and 2–7 (not
Thurs pm), July–Aug
daily 10–12.30 and
2–6; closed 2 wks
Mar and Sep*

the ultra-Catholics battled over the site. Despite all these stormy periods, the little museum above the tourist office, the **Maison de la Chouannerie et de la Révolution**, concentrates on the civil war here through the Revolutionary period.

Montcontour's major legacy is the fine houses of the wealthy Ancien Régime linen merchants, particularly around the village church. The **Eglise St-Mathurin** has a startling 18th-century Baroque façade that looks quite out of proportion for such a small place. The unusual belfry added in the 20th century also draws attention to itself. The rest of the bulky church dates from the early 16th century. The bright old stained-glass windows are the highlight within, inspired by Flemish Renaissance models. A silver reliquary bust of St Mathurin stands out among the statues; he was reputed to help cure the mentally ill. The important **Pardon de St-Mathurin** takes place at Whitsun, but the community here stages all manner of cultural events and little festivals through the year, notably a Fête Médiévale, so check out what's on.

Southeast from Moncontour

The Abbaye de Boquen hides in its forest southeast of Moncontour. To get there you might go past the **Château de la Touche-Trébry**, a noble, moated castle with shapely roofs, dating mainly from the 16th century, a few of its rooms open in summer.

**Château de la
Touche-Trébry**
*mid-July–Aug
Tues–Sun 10–12
and 2–6*

Or meander towards the abbey via the heights of **Bel-Air**, one of the highest points in Brittany. Bel-Air lies in the **Méné range of hills**, also known as the **Landes de Menez**. These heights traditionally separated the Breton counties of Penthièvre and Le Porhouët. Streams to the north head for the Channel, those to the south for the Atlantic. You really feel you've arrived in the deserted centre of Brittany around here. Signs point to the **Site de Croquelin** (west of Le Gouray), a small scattering of boulders lost on a high ridge typical of the area.

The **Abbaye de Boquen** (east of Le Gouray) counts among the most peaceful religious sites in Brittany. Originally built in the 12th century, it had fallen into ruins by the 20th, but was restored thanks to a passionate local priest, Mathurin Presse, alias Dom Alexis, who roped in much help to bring the place back to life from 1936 on. His main aim was to see religious life restored to Boquen. It is now home to a group of nuns. The sisters sell gifts in the shop at the entrance to the abbey grounds. The touching story of Dom Alexis's almost superhuman efforts to revive the abbey is told in a room you can visit before heading down the track to the well-hidden church, while in the mill house on the way you'll find explanations on the work of the present-day Sisters of Bethlehem. Enter the **church**, and such is the tranquillity inside this vast, impressive, calming edifice that you could hear a pin drop.

South from Moncontour

South from Moncontour, you head deep into the Côtes d'Armor, the countryside strewn with chapels for you to unearth. Perhaps stop at the wonky village **church of Langast** – some of the Romanesque arches within look as though they're about to tumble over. Brilliantly stylized, frog-eyed figures, possibly painted as far back as the 10th century, stare out from the older arches. Beautiful stained glass fills the apse.

Continue down through the gorgeous village of **Le Vaublanc**, once entirely devoted to industry, purpose-built for iron production from the 1670s. The little **church of St-Lubin** to the south conceals charming features under its Romanesque helmet of a slate steeple. Old stained-glass windows present a striking depiction of Christ being crucified, while angels and dragons run along the carved stringbeams. Look out also for the painted statue of St Lubin with blue hands in one of the retables.

The **church of La Ferrière** also displays a fine collection of stained-glass windows and Breton statuary , close to the village of **La Chèze**, the latter located attractively by the Lié River. It offers up the ruins of a medieval castle to walk around, and a cluttered **Musée Régional des Métiers**, the objects divided up according to the old trades. **Loudéac**, the main town of central inland Côtes d'Armor, is best known for its Easter horse races, its Lent passion play and its useful flies – made for fishing in the local waters.

Musée Régional des Métiers
t 02 96 26 13 16; open July and Aug daily 10–12 and 2–6; May, June and Sept daily 2–6; March and Oct Sun–Fri 2–6

Quintin

As at Moncontour, the hill at Quintin appeared an excellent site for the lords of Penthièvre to fortify in medieval times – from here, they could guard an important inland route from St-Malo to Carhaix. However, the fortifications here were frequently subjected to attacks and one castle after another had to be built on the spot. The bits and pieces to have survived dominate one side of town.

A discreet gateway off Quintin's main market square leads into the quiet, lawn-covered courtyard of the **Château de Quintin**. Quirkily, the wings of what is now the main section were originally built as stabling; the remains of the unfinished 17th-century château lie derelict to one side, above the Gouët Lake. Although the ensemble looks scrappy, the property has the rare distinction of having kept most of its archives, and the Bagneux family that own the place love to tell its story, their enthusiasm compensating for any amateurish displays inside. Touring the chambers, you'll learn of the waves of castle building and devastation here from the Middle Ages on, how the place became a Protestant stronghold in the Wars of Religion, and how the Bagneuxs acquired the château.

Château de Quintin
www.chateaude quintin.fr, t 02 96 74 94 79; open daily June–Sept 2–6; school hols 2–5; Easter–October Sun 2–5; candlelit activities at Christmas

The houses on the splendid **old squares and streets** in the centre of Quintin date back in good part to the 17th and 18th centuries, when the local merchants made their fortunes manufacturing linen for export. **Place 1830** has all the timberframe charm you could wish for in a Breton provincial market town.

From one corner of the square, **Rue Notre-Dame**, with its finely carved doorways and a Breton fountain to one side, leads down to the grand 19th-century neo-Gothic **Basilique Notre-Dame**. The church has long held an ancient piece of cloth claimed to be a fragment of the Virgin's girdle from when she gave birth to Jesus; inevitably, this led to pilgrimages here by women desperate at not being able to conceive. A copy of the cloth displayed inside was even stolen in recent times – the power of very dubious relics still appears to be alive and well for some.

Back at Place 1830, the **Grand'Rue**, the principal shopping street, leads to the elegant cobbled **Place du Martray**, where, in medieval times, English prisoners were apparently brought after the Battle of La Roche-Derrien. The commander had promised that their lives would be spared. But the blood-curdling story goes that as they were led through town, Quintin's furious butchers savagely slaughtered them.

Leaving Place 1830 by sloping **Rue Emile Nau**, at the crossroads in the dip you come to the **Maison du Tisserand** where you can see traditional looms at work.

Maison du Tisserand
open June–Sept Tues–Sun 2–6; Fête des Tisserands 1st w/e in Aug

ⓘ **Jugon-les-Lacs**
Place Martray, t 02 96 31 70 75, www. jugon-les-lacs.com

★ **Manoir de Villeneuve B&B >>**

ⓘ **Loudéac**
1 Rue St-Joseph, t 02 96 28 25 17 out of season, www. centrebretagne.com

ⓘ **Lamballe >**
Place du Champ de Foire, t 02 96 31 05 38, www.otlamballe.com

Market Days in the Penthièvre Towns

Lamballe: Thursday
Jugon-les-Lacs: Friday
Moncontour: Monday
Loudéac: Saturday
Quintin: Tuesday

Where to Stay and Eat in the Penthièvre Towns

Lamballe ✉ 22400

La Tour des Arch'ants, 2 Rue du Docteur Lavergne, **t 02 96 31 01 37, *latourlarubelle@orange.fr* (€€). This centuries-old half-timbered town house, with garden, contains cosy old rooms and a restaurant (€€).

Le Lion d'Or, 3 Rue du Lion d'Or, **t 02 96 31 20 36, *www.leliondor-lamballe. com* (€). On a quiet street, with redone rooms under the eaves, plus garden.

Le Teno-Yannick B&B, 14 Rue Notre-Dame, **t** 02 96 31 00 41 (€). The birthplace of the artist Mathurin Méheut, with very good-value, spacious rooms.

Crêperie Ty Coz, 35 Place Champ de Foire, **t** 02 96 31 03 58 (€). A popular local restaurant.

Manoir de Villeneuve B&B, St-Aaron, **t** 02 96 50 86 32, *www.chambresau manoir.com* (€€€–€€). Enchanting traditional country manor offering three good rooms and a large garden a few km north of Lamballe.

La Poterie ✉ 22400

Manoir des Portes, **t 02 96 31 13 62, *www.manoirdesportes.com* (€€€–€€). Comfortable, colourful rooms set around the courtyard of a 16th-century manor, plus delicious cuisine in a dining room with great fireplace.

Plorec-sur-Arguenon ✉ 22130

***Château Le Windsor, Le Bois Billy, on the bank of the Arguenon opposite the medieval ruins of the Château de

ⓘ **La Chèze**
t 02 96 26 70 99,
www.centre
bretagne.com

ⓘ **Quintin** >>
6 Place 1830, t 02 96
74 01 51, www.pays-de-
quintin.com

(★) **Le Clos du**
Prince B&B >>

ⓘ **Moncontour** >
4 Place de la Carrière,
t 02 96 73 49 57, www.
pays-moncontour.com

la Hunaudaye, **t** 02 96 83 04 83, *www. chateau-le-windsor.fr* (€€€€€–€€). A clean, straight-lined 18th-century château with grand rooms. Splendid pool and extensive grounds. This hotel was being sold at time of going to print; renovations are on the cards.

Moncontour ✉ 22510

A La Garde Ducale B&B, 10 Place Penthièvre, **t** 02 96 73 52 18, *www.gitesd'armor.com/ala-garde-ducale, alagardeducale@orange.fr* (€). On the central square, with nice wood-panelled rooms and slightly twee furnishings. *Table d'hôte* (€) available.

Chaudron Magique, Place de la Carrière, **t** 02 96 73 40 34, *www.le-chaudron-magique.com* (€€). Waiters serve you in medieval costume in the evenings. If you order the medieval

menu, you dress up too! *Closed Sun eve and Mon*

Crêperie Au Coin du Feu, Place Penthièvre, **t** 02 96 73 49 10 (€). Good atmosphere. *Closed Mon.*

Quintin ✉ 22800

Le Clos du Prince B&B, 10 Rue Croix-Jarrots, **t** 02 96 74 93 03, *www.leclosduprince.com* (€€). An unforgettable, excellent-value B&B with a cavernous fireplace in the reception, a granite staircase leading to 18th-century panelled rooms, and hydrangea borders and ancient trees in the garden. Rooms are decorated with style and touches of humour.

Hôtel du Commerce, 2 Rue Rochenen, **t 02 96 74 94 67 (€). Peaceful, well-renovated rooms in a historic house. Good restaurant (€€€–€; *closed Mon, Fri lunch, Sun eve*).

Southwestern Côtes d'Armor

Were you to try to locate the geographical heart of Brittany, the Lac de Guerlédan might very well fit the bill. This lake was created when a major dam went up here in the early 20th century to generate electricity, radically altering this part of the Blavet Valley. Although born of such practical purposes, the Lac de Guerlédan has grown into a much-appreciated tourist spot. Even if set right in the heart of Brittany, its long, serpenting shores in some ways resemble the Breton coastline, with their deeply attractive, indented, wooded banks. Resorts have sprung up around the lake, there's a lovely hiking trail around it, and the historic sights close by are of exceptional beauty. To the west, along and above the Canal de Nantes à Brest, you can enjoy the gentler pleasures of inland Brittany and deeply rural southwestern Côtes d'Armor.

To the Lac de Guerlédan

(✪) **Lac de Guerlédan**

Mur-de-Bretagne stands on the slopes above the eastern end of the Lac de Guerlédan, and makes a pretty picture of a central Breton town with its mix of white-washed and stone houses. Its main cultural attraction is the 18th-century paintings covering the ceiling of the **Chapelle Ste-Suzanne** in the upper part of town. The edifice's classical tower makes for an unusually refined entrance to a Breton church. This tower is framed by an alley of splendid oaks that inspired the great French 19th-century landscape artist Corot. The chapel's own paintings, from the 18th century, are in typically

Getting around the Southwestern Côtes d'Armor

You'll need to rely on the *département* bus service (see *www.tibus.fr*) to get round by public transport.

Base Départementale de Plein Air de Guerlédan
www.base-plein-air-guerledan.com,
t 02 96 77 12 22

Jardins de Botrain
m 06 12 03 28 44;
open Easter–Oct
weekends

La Maison des Toiles
www.routedulin.com,
t 02 96 56 38 26; open
June–Sept daily 10.30–1
and 2–6.30, Oct and
April–May Tues–Sun
2.30–6, Nov–Dec
Sun 2.30–6

Musée du Pays et de l'Electricité
www.pays-pontivy.
com/culture/guerledan.
php; open daily
10–12.30 and 2.30–6.30
exc Sun am

Hydroelectric dam
t 02 97 27 51 39; tours
by appointment

Boat trip
To hire your own
boat or take a bateau
à pédales, t 02 96 28
52 64; for canoes,
t 06 30 95 48 04

Les Forges-des-Salles
www.lesforgesdes
salles.com, t 02 96 24
95 67; open July and
Aug daily 2–6.30; Sat,
Sun and bank hols
out of season 2–6.30

naïve Breton style, and depict the traumatic story of St Susan, falsely accused of adultery.

A road just west out of town leads to the **Base Départementale de Plein Air de Guerlédan** beside central Brittany's greatest lake. This place provides both for long-stay holidays, and for those who wish simply to enjoy one of the water or other sporting activities for half a day.

Go east from Mur towards St-Guen and look out for signs to the **Jardins de Botrain**, showing many different horticultural styles on its two hectares. Quite some way further east towards Loudéac, at **St-Thélo** on the Oust, La Maison des Toiles tells of how flax and linen-making deeply marked these parts in the Ancien Régime.

Back close to the Lac de Guerlédan, the adorable, flower-smothered village of **St-Aignan** a short way southwest of Mur has a lovely medieval **church** that holds a few artistic treasures, including a remarkable Tree of Jesse carved in wood, crammed with jostling regal figures; this extravaganza may have been made for the Abbaye de Bon Repos (*see* opposite). The deeply traditional village is also the surprising location for the **Musée du Pays et de l'Electricité**, a delightful museum of electricity (in fact explained by the proximity of Guerlédan's dam) that also includes a substantial old electric train set. The **hydroelectric dam** was a massive engineering project for the 1920s. Following Guerlédan's southern shore, at the **Anse de Sordan**, you'll find a quite charming small resort with a little artificial beach in its wood-surrounded inlet, as well as some boats and a bar.

The main resort lies on the Lac de Guerlédan's north side. You reach it by going down via **Caurel**, with its little row of attractive bars and restaurants, to **Beau Rivage**, with its lively summer beach. You can try your hand at all sorts of watersports here, or take a **boat trip** round the lake. In the southwestern corner of Guerlédan, an exceptionally beautiful road shaded by pines leads to Les **Forges-des-Salles**. It's hard to imagine an industrial site more beautiful than this purpose-built Ancien Régime iron-making village, tucked into its own little valley, set by its own little lake. Today, Les Forges-des-Salles looks simply like a gorgeous château with delightful outbuildings, but this was once a hard-working foundry. Iron production is an oft forgotten part of Brittany's industrial past, but small-scale production had been going on in these parts from the Middle Ages until the early 17th century. Then the powerful duke of Rohan decided to start up larger-scale works; slabs of cast iron were made here and transported via Brittany's central canal to the coastal naval yards. Although the place is tranquil nowadays, the noise must have been shattering when the works were in full operation.

Abbaye de Bon Repos
www.bon-repos.com,
t 02 96 24 82 20;
open daily 2–6

The lovingly restored ruins of the **Abbaye de Bon Repos** lie a bit north at Saint-Gelven. They too are extremely picturesque, and set by water, the Blavet meandering past. On a wander round the ruins, which are gradually being restored, you learn about Bon Repos's history and architecture, and the life of its abbots and monks. An abbey first went up in the 12th century – the charming story goes that Lord Alain III de Rohan fell asleep in this enchanting spot after a hunting expedition, and dreamt of the Virgin Mary, who inspired him to commission the religious foundation. Cistercian monks came to build the place, and for centuries the abbey exerted its influence over much of central Brittany. But the abbey was wrecked in the 16th-century Wars of Religion. In the late 17th century, major restoration work began, plus the building of a new, palatial wing. But the establishment deteriorated once again, and the last monks were thrown out at the Revolution. The abbey serves as the dramatic backdrop for a half-dozen major *son-et-lumière* evenings in August. The charming former outbuildings in mottled stone rival the sober abbey for attention. Fully renovated, they contain an information centre, craft shops and a restaurant with rooms.

To the north, the **Gorges du Daoulas** form a narrow, atmospheric stretch of valley, with boulders strewn all around, including in the stream. A fiendishly steep walk takes you up onto the open moors of the **Landes de Liscuis** with their unspoilt, almost prehistoric-looking landscapes and neolithic gallery chambers. For an easier route by which to reach them, go via Laniscat.

West and Northwest of Guerlédan

The main N164 road through central Brittany leads west from Guerlédan to the market town of **Rostrenen**, known in Brittany for its traditional Breton singing and dancing, best witnessed in the **Festival Ficelle**, a lively celebration held at the end of August and named after the special dance of the area – be bold and learn its steps. More peacefully, anglers should appreciate the rivers and lakes around here, but the sleepy Breton boulder-strewn landscapes are a pleasure any visitor can enjoy.

Parc Atelier Sculpture
www.cormand.com,
t 02 96 29 06 86; open
March–end Nov

At **Trohoar**, beside the Canal de Nantes à Brest a couple of kilometres from town, the prize-winning, exceptionally versatile sculptor Philippe Cormand has set up his **Parc Atelier Sculpture** to show off his skills in a whole variety of materials. You can often see him carving his pieces, here associated with Brittany's flora, fauna and legends. The setting above the canal proves intriguing, too.

The **Grande Tranchée de Glomel** west along the canal is a massive man-made curiosity running for several kilometres which

Centre Nautique
et d'Animation
de Glomel
www.cnpakb.org,
t 02 96 29 65 07

Maison du Cheval
t 02 96 29 42 90;
open July–Aug
Mon 2–6, Tues–Sat
10.30–12.30 and 2–6

Musée Rural de
l'Education
www.musee-ecole-
bothoa.blogspot.com;
open July–mid-Sept
and Easter hols
Tues–Sun 2–6

recalls the grizzly history of how the waterway was dug out in the 19th century, using prison labour. The canal-side **Centre Nautique et d'Animation de Glomel** makes the most of its location close to a series of locks to offer bicycles, rowing boats and rafting.

To the north, there's another line of little discoveries to enjoy. The small market town of **Corlay** is known for horse breeding and has a little **Maison du Cheval** on the history of local horses, in the remains of the castle. Corlay is known for its horse races, held a handful of times a year at the comically named Petit Paris track.

At **Bothoa**, just north of **St-Nicolas-du-Pélem**, the **Musée Rural de l'Education** sweetly recreates a 1930s country school.

West around **Trémargat**, you come into extraordinary rock-strewn countryside. Go walking in the atmospheric **Gorges de Toul Goulic**; you'll need to leave your car to descend into this boulder-filled section of the Blavet Valley, where mythical Breton creatures are said to guard hidden treasure. The place served as a hideout to real people in history, notably the anti-Revolutionary Chouan leader, Cadoudal, fleeing Republican troops.

Christ has lost his arms at the top of the exceptional **calvary of Kergrist-Moëlou**. He stands dying in isolation on his column, while the story of his life unfolds around the octagonal structure below. The calvary dates from the 16th century, the church from the 15th. Its outer gables feature many figures from the medieval bestiary, while here and there carved angels bear heavy coats of arms. Inside, your attention will be drawn to the painted ceiling, executed by a local artist recording the members of the Vatican One Council in 1871. The nave also contains the extraordinary sight of a large fireplace, apparently provided for baptisms on cold days.

Maison du
Patrimoine
t 02 96 36 66.11;
open mid-June–
mid-Sept am and pm,
rest of year just pm

At **Locarn**, the **Maison du Patrimoine** plays a double role, acting as a museum explaining the local culture, and as a place offering nature outings. Anyone can go exploring the **Menez and Menhir Guellec**, and walking on the moors. You can pay homage to a gorse-defended, hulking menhir overlooking a vast unspoilt section of inland Brittany. Archaeologists believe neolithic inhabitants dug for gold here, going by the presence of neolithic stone basins near the menhir. North of the Menez Guellec explore the mysterious **Gorges du Corong**, where you can admire further extraordinary rock formations. (For Carhaix nearby in the Finistère, see p.310.)

(i) **Mur-de-Bretagne/Guerlédan >>**
1 Place de l'Eglise,
t 02 96 28 51 41,
www.guerledan.fr

Market Days in the Southwestern Côtes d'Armor

Mur-de-Bretagne: Fri during summer
Rostrenen: Tuesday

Where to Stay and Eat in the Southwestern Côtes d'Armor

Mur-de-Bretagne ✉ 22530
★★★**Auberge Grand'Maison**, 1 Rue Léon le Cerf, **t** 02 96 28 51 10, *www.auberge-*

(i) **Pays Touristique de Guerlédan-Argoat**
www.centre bretagne.free.fr

(i) **Rostrenen >>**
6 Rue Abbé Gibert, t 02 96 29 02 72, www. tourismekreizbreizh.com

(★) **Merlin les Pieds dans l'Eau >**

grand-maison.com (€€€–€). Charming bedrooms and splendid food (€€), such as profiteroles filled with foie gras with a truffle sauce.
M. Le Boudec B&B, Le Pont Guer, t 02 96 28 54 52 (€). A pretty, flower-decked cottage by the Canal de Nantes à Brest.

Caurel ✉ 22530
**Beau Rivage, t 02 96 28 52 15, *www.le-beau-rivage.net* (€). Modern hotel in popular lakeside location by a beach. The restaurant (*closed Sun eve, and Mon off season*) has the benefit of a waterside terrace.
L'Auberge de Guerlédan, t 02 96 26 35 16 (€). A lovely traditional restaurant up in the old village of Caurel.

St-Aignan ✉ 56480
Merlin les Pieds dans l'Eau, Anse de Sordan, t 02 97 27 52 36, *www. restaurant-merlin.fr* (€). This gorgeous waterside restaurant on the southern side of the Lac de Guerlédan serves

tasty tapas-style options. *Closed Nov–mid-March.*

Abbaye de Bon Repos/ St-Gelven ✉ 22570
Les Jardins de l'Abbaye, Bon Repos, t 02 96 24 95 77, *abbaye.jardin.free.fr* (€). An atmospheric restaurant in the dark-stoned buildings by the abbey, plus a handful of basic rooms (€).

Gouarec ✉ 22570
Crêperie Au Bon Vieux Temps, Le Bout du Pont, t 02 96 24 82 95 (€). A good, pretty crêperie.

Rostrenen
L'Eventail des Saveurs, 3 Place du Bourg Coz, t 02 96 29 10 71 (€€€–€). Excellent Breton cooking in a nice setting.

Glomel ✉ 22110
Canal Chouette B&B, Kergérard, t 02 96 29 81 44, *www.canalchouette.fr* (€). Simple, sweet rooms by the canal and Tranchée de Glomel. *Table d'hôte* (€).

The Western Bay of St-Brieuc

Founded by the Welshman Brieuc, one of the seven saints credited with creating the first Celtic bishoprics of Brittany, the town of St-Brieuc has only kept the odd trace of its history, notably its forbidding medieval cathedral. Heading north from its Port du Légué, you can set off up and down the rollercoaster cliffs of the Côte du Goëlo. This coast forms the western side of the Bay of St-Brieuc, stretching from the Côtes d'Armor's capital to the port of Paimpol, and finishing with the colourful rocks of L'Ile de Bréhat.

St-Brieuc

St-Brieuc, administrative capital of the Côtes d'Armor, sprawls across several deep valleys, roads straddling these on tall bridges. It's a busy, workaday kind of town and port, although the place has strong literary connections. Louis Guilloux, one of the most respected Breton authors of the 20th century, was from St-Brieuc and set his most famous work, *Le Sang noir*, here. The absurdist Alfred Jarry (he of the zany *Ubu roi*), the defeatist Tristan Corbière, and the unsettlingly idealistic Villiers de L'Isle-Adam, all significant 19th-century French literary figures, were either born or went to school in St-Brieuc. The recent arrival of university faculties has brought in more bright young people today.

Getting to and around St-Brieuc and the Goëlo Coast

St-Brieuc has a small **airport**, *www.st-brieuc.aeroport.fr*, **t** 02 96 94 95 00; Skybus flies here from Newquay, *www.skybus.co.uk*, UK **t** 01736 334 234. Paris is 3hrs away by fast TGV train. The main **bus** station is located by the **train** station. Tí Bus, *www.tibus.fr*, **t** 08 10 22 22 22, operates buses to many nearby towns.

The **Cathédrale St-Etienne** is one of those stern Breton cathedrals that seem to have been built almost as much for defence as for worship. In fact, look at the towers on the entrance façade and you can spot arrow slits and machicolations. On a more peaceable note, Guillaume Pinchon, a 13th-century bishop of St-Brieuc, was celebrated in these parts for becoming the first Breton to be canonized by the papacy. In 1346, during the Breton War of Succession, English troops ruined the cathedral Guillaume would have known. During the Revolution, it was turned into an arms depot and stables, almost all its furnishings demolished. One altarpiece, the curvaceous Baroque masterpiece of Yves Corlay, was supposedly saved by being hidden under a great pile of straw.

Off the cathedral square, past the 19th-century **covered market**, the sloping **Rue Fardel** counts among the prettiest and most colourful streets in town. Just adjoining the other side of the cathedral square, you'll find an uncompromisingly modern shopping square, **Place du Chai**, with café terraces squashed in. **Place de la Résistance** close by includes the main cultural centre, **La Passerelle**, with a theatre, gallery and cinema.

Musée d'Art et Histoire de St-Brieuc
t 02 96 62 55 70; open Tues–Sat 10–12 and 1.30–6, Sun and hols 2–6; Oct–April closed Tues

The **Musée d'Art et Histoire de St-Brieuc** lies a short walk to the south on Rue Lycéens-Martyrs. The museum focuses on local art and history, as well as the traditional trades of the Côtes d'Armor. **Rue St-Guillaume**, east of Place de la Résistance, is the main shopping drag. The tourist office has published a special guide in English, Go Shopping, to steer you round to some of the best boutiques and restaurants in town.

Keep your eyes peeled for signs to St-Brieuc's port on the banks of the Gouët estuary; get onto the north side of the port unless you want to end up among the kaolin and fertilizer warehouses. The **Port du Légué** lies in a typically deep and narrow St-Brieuc valley, the legs of a great bridge crossing over it, the remains of a tall medieval tower, the **Tour de Cesson**, overseeing proceedings. On the north side of the river, the **marina** is followed by the fishing harbour. Tucked so discreetly away, the port turns out to be one of the biggest in Brittany, with an atmosphere all of its own.

Musée-Atelier du Jouet en Bois
www.junobravo.com, t 02 96 60 83 50; open May–Sept Tues–Sat 10–12 and 3–6

The latest tourist addition at the port is the **Musée-Atelier du Jouet en Bois**, a sweet museum with a workshop, dedicated to wooden toys and games, set in a surprising location, a converted former RAF boat from the 1950s called *Juno Bravo*. It makes for a cheering transformation to see wooden horses and other innocent toys in a former military ship.

Up the Gallo Part of the Goëlo Coast

Leaving St-Brieuc's urban sprawl behind you, the social pecking order appears to be reflected on the cliff of **St-Laurent-de-la-Mer**, the resort just around the corner from the Port du Légué. Here you'll find a line of swanky modern villas atop the steep cliff, while down below lies a characterful array of shacks.

Follow the coast northwards to the **Pointe du Roselier** for some of the most sensational views across the Bay of St-Brieuc. A 1980s granite monument recalls those from the area who have died at sea. You can go walking along the cliffs, passing a cannonball oven and a coastguard's cottage. Heading steeply down from the point, you come to the little grey pebble beach of **Martin-Plage**, but beware, tides and currents can be dangerous here.

Les Rosaires, by contrast, is welcoming and relaxing, a chic resort that feels surprisingly cosmopolitan. The seafront looks very neat. A wide pedestrian promenade parallels much of the two-kilometre beach. Wealthy Briochins go on their dog-jog along it on weekend mornings. The place has a mix of villas, some pre-war, in mottled stone, some more contemporary and experimental.

The next tiny resort to the north, **Tournemine**, is a much more private little place than Les Rosaires, difficult to get to and with a pebbly beach. Then you reach the **Pointe de Pordic**, offering further fabulous views across the bay.

Inland to Trégomeur and Châtelaudren

Inland from the Pointe de Pordic, the **Zoo de Trégomeur** lies down a steep valley north of the village of Trégomeur. It has recently been totally modernized, with dozens of new shelters built for the animals, including tigers, gibbons and playful lemurs, the last the passion of the devoted founder of this zoo, Monsieur Arnoux. The whole place has been imaginatively landscaped, and there's a smart new information centre and café.

Head west for **Châtelaudren**, historic capital of the Goëlo area. In the centre, it has a few attractive streets of 18th-century stone houses, while the old printworks that stands out by the Leff River now houses the **Musée du Petit Echo de la Mode**, explaining the history of this once hugely influential French fashion magazine that lasted from the 1880s to the 1980s, its practicality outdone by the glossiness that counts more in our times.

Otherwise, the town may look slightly dull, but one of its churches conceals a very colourful attraction. The **Chapelle Notre-Dame-du-Tertre** – not to be confused with the church in Châtelaudren's main square, lying up the slope on the other side of the river – has an extraordinary series of late-medieval painted cycles. Almost one hundred biblical scenes adorn the choir ceiling.

Zoo de Trégomeur
www.zoo-tregomeur. com, t 02 96 79 01 07; open Easter weekend and April–Sept daily 10–7; Oct–Mar Mon–Fri 1–5, weekends, public hols and school hols 10.30–5.30

Musée du Petit Echo de la Mode
t 02 96 74 20 74, www.petit-echo-de-la-mode.fr; open June–Sept 3–7

Chapelle Notre-Dame-du-Tertre
open Mon–Sat 10–12 and 4–7

The paintings were executed between 1450 and 1480, by a team of craftsmen. The wealth of detail makes the ensemble look overwhelming at first sight, but a guide is normally to hand to explain the order of the scenes, in French at least. Beginning with the Creation, God is portrayed as a rather noble oriental king going about his duties. A striped serpent with a woman's head tempts Adam and Eve, then the familiar tales of Cain and Abel, Noah (the animals sadly left out of the ark!), Abraham and Isaac, Joseph and Moses unfold. Twelve prophets take up the next row, prefiguring the arrival of the son of God on earth. And so the action moves on to the New Testament. Jesus' life is told as though it were some courtly tale, Pilate like a medieval lord, a jester sometimes in tow.

The stories of St Marguerite and St Fiacre portrayed in a side chapel may be less familiar to you. The persecution of 3rd-century Marguerite for sticking firmly to her Christian principles is harrowing. Fiacre is described as a 7th-century Irishman, born of royal parents, who became a monk and sailed to France, where he performed saintly deeds but was also harassed by a trouble-making woman, La Becnaude. The artist has used Fiacre's noble background as an excuse to depict a colourful medieval joust and a medieval war scene. Yet more scenes focus on Mary Magdalene.

Resorts Back on the Goëlo Coast

Back on the coast, the port of **Binic** boasted one of the most important long-distance cod-fishing fleets in 19th-century Brittany. A few old houses and streets recall those major fishing days, but Binic has long converted to tourism – part of its very central port has been transformed into a marina, and bar and restaurant terraces cluster around here. There's also a sandy beach either end of the port.

Binic Museum
t 02 96 73 37 95;
open July–Aug daily,
April–Sept Wed–Mon
2.30–6

Binic Museum is, appropriately enough, set in a disused fish-canning factory, although it doesn't make for the most inspiring of settings. *Coiffes* are comically displayed in what look like disused butchers' showcases, perhaps a fitting image for the disappearance of traditional Breton costume. There are plans afoot to redo the museum.

Steep roads lead down to the pair of dramatic beaches at **Etables-sur-Mer**, the next resort, reputed for its seaside villas. To get to the Plage des Godelins at the foot of steep cliffs, though, you pass a neo-Gothic horror of a mansion. A bit north, the **Plage du Moulin**, set between further cliffs, has lovely fine sand.

The old port of **St-Quay-Portrieux** has also converted into a beach and marina resort. The transformation in fact began back in the mid-19th century. Two wealthy women from the nearby town of Guingamp were told by their doctor to go and take the sea air. They stayed with nuns of the Sacrés-Cœurs de Jésus et Marie, and from

Man in Stone Boat Beaten by Gorse

Arriving exhausted from Ireland in a stone boat during the Dark Ages, as the legend would have it, the extraordinary Quay didn't get the warmest of receptions when he landed, beaten with gorse by the local women. Knocked out, he slumped to the ground, but where he fell, a spring rose up and revived him. Unfazed, he went on to found a religious community in the area.

these unlikely sounding beginnings the fashion for seaside stays here was launched. The nunnery is no longer an option, and modern developments have sprung up, with a somewhat suburban look.

The port area lies to the south, its first **marina** now superseded by a large 1990s development, surrounded by crude walls made from piled up blocks of rock. This was built to make sure that the harbour was provided with deep water at all times rather than being at the mercy of the tides.

Heading north, you come to the **Plage de la Comtesse**. The **Ile de la Comtesse**, joined to the mainland at low tide, was bought by the town in the 1970s, so you can enjoy walking out onto it when the sea withdraws. The coastal path leads up to the third and prettiest part of St-Quay-Portrieux. A white-balustraded path provided with brightly coloured benches looks down on a series of delightful beaches. The **Plage du Châtelet** and **Plage du Casino** are the two main stretches. Two pretty seawater pools, as well as the casino, add to the attractions on this side of town.

Market Days in St-Brieuc and up the Goëlo Coast

(i) Pays Touristique de Saint-Brieuc
www.baiedesaint brieuc.com

St-Brieuc: Wednesday, Saturday and Sunday
Plérin: Sunday
Pordic: Friday
Châtelaudren: Monday
Binic: Thursday
Etables-sur-Mer: Tuesday
St-Quay-Portrieux: Monday and Friday

Where to Stay and Eat in St-Brieuc and up the Goëlo Coast

(i) St-Brieuc >
7 Rue St-Gouéno,
t 08 25 00 22 22, www.
baiedesaintbrieuc.com

St-Brieuc ✉ 22000

***de Clisson, 36 Rue de Gouët, t 02 96 62 19 29, *www.hoteldeclisson.com* (€€–€). The smartest address in town, with warmly decorated modern rooms and a garden.

**Le Duguesclin, 2 Place Duguesclin, t 02 96 33 11 58, *www.hotel-duguesclin. fr* (€). A hotel with a decent restaurant specializing in smoked fish.

**Le Ker Izel, 20 Rue de Gouët, t 02 96 33 46 29, *hotel-kerizel.com* (€). Comfortable, refurbished rooms in a cosy old house in the historic part of the town. Pool in garden.

Aux Pesked, 59 Rue du Légué, t 02 96 33 34 65 (€€€). Delicious, refined cooking in a restaurant on the way down to the port, looking across a typical St-Brieuc valley. *Closed Sat lunch, Sun eve, Mon.*

La Croix Blanche, 61 Rue de Genève, t 02 96 33 16 97 (€€€€). For highly original haute cuisine. *Closed Mon.*

L'Amadéus, 22 Rue de Gouët, t 02 96 33 92 44 (€€). A smart restaurant offering quirky dishes mixing seafood with Breton meat specialities. *Closed Sat, Sun, Mon lunch.*

Crêperie Le Ribeault, 8–10 Rue Fardel, t 02 96 33 44 79 (€). Good crêpes and more in heart of old quarter.

(i) **Binic >>**
*Ave Général de
Gaulle, t 02 96 73 60 12,
www.ville-binic.fr*

(★) **La Maison du
Phare B&B >**

(i) **Etables-
sur-Mer**
*9 Rue République,
t 02 96 70 65 41, www.
etables-sur-mer.com*

(★) **Manoir de
Keryos B&B >**

(i) **St-Quay-
Portrieux >>**
*17 bis Rue Jeanne
d'Arc, t 02 96 70 40 64,
www.stquay
portrieux.com*

(★) **Ker Moor >>**

(★) **Char à
Bancs B&B >**

(i) **Châtelaudren**
*2 Rue des
Sapeurs Pompiers,
t 02 96 74 12 02, www.
cdc-chatelaudren-
plouagat.com*

Plérin/Port du Légué ✉ 22190
La Maison du Phare B&B, 93 Rue de la Tour, t 02 96 33 34 65, *www.maison phare.com* (€€–€). Lovely rooms, with balconies, in a former shipowner's house at the Port du Légué.

La Vieille Tour, 75 Rue de la Tour, t 02 96 33 10 30 (€€€–€€). Highly sophisticated cuisine served in a stylish contemporary dining room that hosts changing exhibitions of local artists' work.

Pordic ✉ 22590
Manoir de Keryos B&B, t 02 96 79 17 32, *www.keryos.gitedarmor.com* (€€–€). This lovely villa set in spacious grounds close to the sea has four delightful rooms, some with sea views, and a wonderful artistic feel.

Plélo ✉ 22170
Char à Bancs B&B, La Ville des Guerfault, t 02 96 74 13 63/02 96 79 51 25, *www.aucharabanc.com* (€€). Elaborately decorated, large, luxurious B&B rooms by village of Plélo, 3km north of Châtelaudren. The food, served in a converted watermill, is traditionally Breton. The whole Lamour family plays an enthusiastic part here; sometimes Monsieur does guided tours of the old farm on the hill, now a museum illustrating old Breton ways.

Binic ✉ 22520
**Le Neptune, Place de l'Eglise, t 02 96 73 61 02 (€). A modest hotel in this unpretentious resort, with sea views.

A la Table de Margot, 7 Place de L'Eglise, t 02 96 73 35 56 (€€). Fine Breton seafood dishes served in Binic's oldest building. *Closed Mon.*

Nord Sud, Quai de Courcy, t 02 96 73 30 77 (€€). One of the best options on the port, serving seafood specialities.

Crêperie An Arvor, Quai de Courcy, t 02 96 73 37 98. Really good port-side crêperie.

St-Quay-Portrieux ✉ 22410
***Ker Moor, 13 Rue du Président Le Sénécal, t 02 96 70 52 22, *www. ker-moor.com* (€€€€–€€€). A startling extravaganza, an oriental-looking hotel with onion-shaped domes set in a pretty garden above the bay. Many rooms with sea views and balconies. *Closed mid-Dec–mid-March.*

**Le Gerbot d'Avoine, 2 Boulevard du Littoral, t 02 96 70 40 09, *www.gerbotdavoine.com* (€€–€). A traditional French hotel, some of its 20 bedrooms boasting sea views, plus a restaurant (€€€–€€), a bar, a billiards room and a reading room. *Closed mid-Nov–mid-Dec and early Jan–early Feb.*

The Northern Goëlo Coast to Paimpol

You arrive at the Breton-speaking part of the Côtes d'Armor coast here and the look and feel are immediately more typically Breton. Some of the highest cliffs in Brittany plunge into the sea, littered with scatterings of rocks. Curious religious sights stand inland.

The Coast around Plouha

The cliffs grow taller heading north from St-Quay-Portrieux, this stretch of coast left almost untouched by modern housing. Roads shaded by tall trees run steeply down narrow valleys to flat stretches of sand or makeshift, tiny harbours. The dramatic clifftop coastal path seems a world apart from the beaches below. If you follow this path on foot you could still be tempted down a precipitous descent from time to time. Seek out **Port Goret** with its lovely beach, east of Plouha. Just a bit north, the spectacular

Getting to and around the Northern Goëlo Coast

Paimpol is on a slow train line linking it to Guingamp, where you can pick up the fast TGV service.

location of the **Plage des Palus** has attracted a pleasant little group of simple restaurants behind the long curve of its pebble bank.

Up on the clifftop path, the views from the **Pointe de Plouha** are stunning. Rocky cliffs melt into the distance and St-Quay-Portrieux is reduced to model size. These cliffs are said to be the highest in Brittany, rising more than 100 metres above sea level.

Up until Paimpol, the same pattern of steep cliffs and sandy coves repeats itself. The makeshift port of **Gwin Zégal** is exceptional, however. Protected by the Ilot de Gwin Zégal, little boats are simply tied up to a handful of rows of tall thin wooden posts planted in the water. This antiquated but utterly picturesque port has been listed as a European Maritime Heritage Site. **Port Moguer** to the north is a tiny harbour better sheltered than Gwin Zégal, with a pink granite wall to help protect it from the elements.

Nearby, **Plage Bonaparte** is a beach known for its vanishing tricks. Twice daily, at high tide, its glorious expanse of sands simply disappears. On the cliff tops above the Plage Bonaparte stands a major **Second World War memorial**. Stone plaques donated by Allied troops salute the efforts of the Resistance here.

Skeletons dancing with the rich and powerful tellingly illustrate the vulnerability of life for all, regardless of worldly status, at the **chapel of Kermaria-in-Isquit** west of Plouha village. This *danse macabre*, a popular theme in art and writing all over Europe in the Middle Ages, counts among the most striking of church paintings in Brittany. The frieze of the dance runs along both sides of the nave, above lovely pointed Gothic arches. The paintings are thought to date from between 1488 and 1500; the figures, apart from the skeletons of course, are dressed in period costume, and in descending social rank.

West of Kermaria the **Temple de Lanleff** was long thought to have been a Gallo-Roman sanctuary, but dates from the medieval Romanesque period. Much of the church has fallen into ruin, but parts are still in a reasonable state of repair, while the capitals have retained their engrossing motifs.

A Pro-British Bonaparte

Despite the Plage Bonaparte's provocative-seeming appellation, the nickname derives from the Second World War codename given to it, when the place was used by the French Resistance to help evacuate Allied soldiers hiding behind enemy lines. In the course of the war, 135 Allied aviators and agents who had been shot down across France and subsequently rescued by Resistance members were secretly brought to this location, where, on dangerous night operations, they were transferred onto Royal Navy gunboats that came in close to the shore to pick them up. Eight successful rescue missions were carried out here between January and August 1944.

The Coast from Bréhec to the Abbaye de Beauport

Back on the coast, heading towards Paimpol, at **Bréhec**, with its wide, long, unspoilt beach below the cliffs, the boats are pulled in on to the sand behind the jetty. A couple of further spectacular clifftop points, the **Pointe Berjule** and the **Pointe de Minard**, look out onto the Bay of St-Brieuc. At the **Pointe de Bilfot**, marked by its purple granite, Paimpol and its bay come into view. From the point you can go down to the steep-sided **Port Lazo** below St-Riom.

After failed attempts to create a monastery on the island of Riom out in the Bay of Paimpol in the 12th century, Count Alain de Penthièvre et de Goëlo paid for a new foundation on the coast early in the 13th century, giving charge of this **Abbaye de Beauport** to monks from a Norman abbey near Mont St-Michel. The abbey quickly assumed an important role in north Breton religious affairs. It was placed under direct authority of the papacy and its abbot was allowed to don a mitre, a symbol of his high status. Most of the buildings went up during the Gothic period. Under the Ancien Régime, the abbey fell into decline; it was sold off at the Revolution. Although the place stands mainly in ruins now, the Gothic chapterhouse with its splendid period vaulting, the *salle au duc* and the *salle aux hôtes* have survived best, and you can see the vestiges of various other rooms. Concerts and cultural events take place within these walls on Thursday evenings in summer.

Beyond the beaches around the Anse de Beauport, or Anse de Poulafret, you can walk to the end of the curious spit named the **Pointe de Guilben**, where black basalt rock mingles with the pink granite. The mild climate here encourages relatively exotic flora, and also attracts birds in large numbers.

Abbaye de Beauport
www.abbaye-beauport.com, t 02 96 55 18 58; open mid-June–mid-Sept daily 10–7; Oct–May daily 10–12 and 2–5; night visits July–Aug Sat and Sun 10pm–1am

Paimpol and its Peninsula

Paimpol drowning under a tidal wave of sea-widows' tears – that's the popular French image of this renowned Breton port, which became something of a symbol of the sufferings involved in the cruel centuries-long trade of long-distance cod-fishing. Expectations are somewhat disappointed at first sight. Rather than facing boldly out to sea, Paimpol hides like a coward down an inlet, which drains to a black marsh when the tide goes out. And the quays of Paimpol are no longer lined with granite shipowners' mansions; instead, a modern quayside has been built, with all the character of a modern shopping arcade, which is basically what it is. To add insult to injury, the French national merchant navy school so long based in Paimpol closed down only to be replaced by a catering college. Tough cod-fishing has given way to cod cuisine here. Not everyone is complaining.

Yet an atmosphere lingers in the air. Behind the quayside you can find old squares and winding, cobbled streets, especially around **Place du Martray** and **Place de l'Eglise** – by the shattered old church, of which only the steeple remains, a monument pays its respect to Théodore Botrel, an early 20th-century Breton crooner who became popular across France and had a big hit with a song called *La Paimpolaise*, about fishermen from the port far away at sea wistfully remembering their beautiful women back home... here depicted in stone. On a bright note, Paimpol hosts the fine **Festival du Chant Marin**, celebrating Breton sea shanties with great verve.

Two very small museums give you an image of Paimpol frozen in the past. The **Musée du Costume**, which is located in a typical little fisherman's cottage, has a collection of traditional furniture on the ground floor and on the first floor a display of local costumes. The **Musée de la Mer** pays its respects to Paimpol's maritime past. Appropriately enough, its collections are housed in a former cod-drying building.

Fishermen from these parts went cod-fishing on the lucrative banks off Newfoundland as early as the 16th century. They would sail away at the end of February for gruelling stints in the terrible waters of the Atlantic. Before they went, a religious *pardon* was held, the boats decked out for the occasion. In the 19th century, sailors switched their attention from Newfoundland to Iceland. Each boat had a crew of around 20 men and boys; the catch was collected in larger vessels that could return frequently to France in a season, but the fishermen themselves stayed a pretty hellish half-year out at sea. The Icelandic fishing came to an end in 1935. One study has estimated that about 2,000 men died on the Paimpol expeditions in one 80-year period alone.

Many Paimpolais still feel strongly attached to their fishing past, despite changing times. The attachment to Breton culture generally is particularly evident here. There's a Breton-speaking Diwan school in town and plenty of Breton activities. Contact the tourist office about participating in special Breton dancing lessons.

To get out to sea, either for a fishing trip, to sail, or for a kayak adventure, contact the **Centre Nautique Paimpol Loguivy de la Mer**. From May to September you can also take a pretty trip on

Festival du Chant Marin *every second year, early Aug, next in 2009 and 2011*

Musée du Costume *open July–Aug daily 10.30–12.30 and 2.30–6*

Musée de la Mer *open daily mid-June–Aug 10.30–12.30 and 2.30–6.30, April–mid-June and Sept 2–6; at other times call t 02 96 22 02 19 for an appointment*

Centre Nautique Paimpol Loguivy de la Mer *www.pole-nautique-paimpol.com, t 02 96 20 94 58*

08 Côtes d'Armor | The Northern Goëlo Coast to Paimpo: Paimpol and its Peninsula

Reduced to Tears by Cod's Emotional Wallop

The extravagant romantic writer and naval officer Pierre Loti saw his tear-jerker of a novel, *Pêcheurs d'Islande*, published in 1886. It's a tale of tragic romance, set in Paimpol and the Icelandic seas, which rapidly became a bestseller across France. Loti himself never went on a cod-fishing expedition, but he did have his naval background to draw on; in his past he had crossed the oceans. And he came to stay in Paimpol, befriending many fishermen from these parts. Realizing that life on the Breton fishing boats was extremely harsh, he also tried to emphasize the simple camaraderie on board, and the heroism of the fishermen. *Mon Frère Yves*, Loti's other highly successful Breton fishing novel, tackled the painful reality that many Breton fishermen were driven to drink by their desperate lives at sea.

La Vapeur du Trieux
www.vapeurdutrieux.com, t 08 92 39 14 27

Le Vapeur du Trieux, a **steam train** that transports you along the lovely Trieux Valley between Paimpol and Pontrieux.

North along the coast enjoy the little ports around the northern Bay of Paimpol. Climb the **Tour Kerroc'h**, a 19th-century tower, to take in wide views of the peninsula. The village of **Ploubazlanec** that follows contains an extremely moving reminder of just how many local men lost their lives in the cod-fishing expeditions between 1853 and 1935; black plaques along the **cemetery wall** are inscribed with the names of the sailors who disappeared at sea. Fishing still goes on from the little port of **Porz Even**, before you arrive at the heavily touristy **Pointe de l'Arcouest** and its little terminal for boat trips to the splendid island of Bréhat. Because of Bréhat's massive popularity, the roads tend to get very clogged up around here in season.

As a walker, you're privileged to be able to follow the coast westwards from the Pointe de l'Arcouest, along the top of the Paimpol peninsula, without traffic. You arrive at the diminutive port of **Loguivy**, another great spot for practising watersports (see Centre Nautique above), or you can embark on beautiful, peaceful walks down the Trieux estuary from here.

Market Days on the Northern Goëlo Coast

Plouha: Wednesday
Paimpol: Tuesday

ⓘ Plouha
5 Avenue Laënnec, t 02 96 20 24 73, www.plouha.com

Where to Stay and Eat on the Northern Goëlo Coast

Pléhédel ✉ 22290

Château Golf du Boisgelin, t 02 96 22 37 67, www.chateauduboisgelin.com (€€€–€). A delightful little château converted to offer lovely smart B&B rooms at varied prices, with a pool at the heart of things, and a golf course. There's a brasserie, too.

ⓘ Paimpol ›
Impasse Herland, t 02 96 20 83 16, www.paimpol-goelo.com

⭐ K'Loys ›

Paimpol ✉ 22500

★★★K'Loys, 21 Quai Morand, t 02 96 20 40 01, www.k-loys.com (€€€€–€€). Eleven very lovely, spacious, traditional rooms in one of the remaining old ship owners' homes looking onto the harbour.

★★de la Marne, 30 Rue de la Marne, t 02 96 20 82 16 (€). Simple Breton architecture, tastefully done rooms

and delicately spiced food in the excellent restaurant (€€). Closed Mon.

★★L'Origano, 7 bis Rue du Quai, t 02 96 22 05 49 (€). Quirky shaped, rather spartan rooms in a characterful old house just behind Quai Morand.

★Berthelot, 1 Rue du Port, t 02 96 20 88 66 (€€€). A simple option offering great value.

La Vieille Tour, 13 Rue de l'Eglise, t 02 96 20 83 18 (€€). For inventive Breton fare, served in a warm dining room in an inn dating back to the 16th century. Closed Sun eve and Tues.

Le Restaurant du Port, 17 Quai Morand, t 02 96 20 82 76, www.paimpol-restaurant-du-port.com (€€). With a first-floor dining room looking out over the port, offering good seafood platters.

L'Islandais, 19 Quai Morand, t 02 96 20 93 80 (€€). Serves a well-appreciated menu to a consistently packed salle.

La Cotriade, Quai Armand Dayot, t 02 96 20 81 08 (€€). Named after the traditional Breton fish soup, a good seafood restaurant looking onto the port.

Crêperie L'Agapanthe, 12 Quai Duguay Trouin, t 02 96 20 42 09 (€). A cosy place that's worth seeking out for its Paimpolaise with artichoke.

Crêperie Morel, 11 Place du Martray, **t** 02 96 20 86 34 (€). A good, authentic Breton crêperie.

Porz-Even, Ploubazlanec and Pointe de l'Arcouest ✉ 22620

Pension Boucher, 44 Rue Pierre Loti, Porz-Even, **t 02 96 55 84 16 (€). A pleasant, traditional home with old-fashioned rooms, but in a charming port-side location and serving good food (€€).

Hôtel Le Barbu, Pointe de l'Arcouest, **t** 02 96 55 86 98, *www.lebarbu.com*. In a fabulous location beside the ferry jetty to Bréhat, this hotel is undergoing a complete makeover in 2009 to reopen in grand style in 2010.

Loguivy ✉ 22620

Au Grand Large, Le Port, **t 02 96 20 90 18, *www.hotelrestaurantaugrand large.com* (€€). Another superbly located port-side choice, some of its simple rooms benefiting from great sea views. Enjoy very good traditional French cuisine in the restaurant.

Ile de Bréhat

The Bréhat archipelago is rather like a beautiful object that has shattered into a thousand pieces; just the odd larger fragment remains. The rocks strewn here, there and everywhere in the seas around it are of a rare beauty, even by Brittany's standards, with their many gradations of pinks and oranges.

Bréhat, the main island, consists of two large pieces of rock joined together by a small bridge. The south island proves very different from the north, much more lush and densely populated. The north island is barren and wild, exposed to the wind. Bréhat's ecosystem is in danger as a result of tourism, so treat it with respect.

History

There are no obvious signs of the neolithic or Gallo-Roman settlements said to have existed on Bréhat. Nor can you see anything to prove that St Budoc came here in the 5th century. He is, though, supposed to have founded one of the oldest Breton monasteries, on the island of Lavrec just east of the main island, around AD 470. This monastery is thought to have exercised its influence over a good portion of Brittany in the early period of Dark Ages immigration from Britain.

Bréhat was fortified in the medieval period. A château was built facing the island of Lavrec. The original church in the main village dates back to the 12th century. As to St-Riom, it was constructed in the northeastern corner of the island to serve as a small lepers' colony, provided with its own tiny chapel. In the 15th century, Duke Jean V of Brittany called on the English for help against the French; they landed on Bréhat, but ransacked the place. At the end of the 16th century, the ultra-Catholic leader, the Duc de Mercœur, had the battered castle repaired. However, in 1591, English General Norris came to Bréhat in support of Protestant King Henri IV of France. Norris had several of the Ligueurs hanged from the sails of

Getting to and around the Ile de Bréhat

Ferries to Bréhat are run by Les Vedettes de Bréhat (*www.vedettesdebrehat.com*, **t** 02 96 55 79 50) from the Pointe de l'Arcouest north of Paimpol; book well in advance during high season. (No cars are allowed on the ferries, so leave time to find a parking.) Be aware, leaving Bréhat, that given changes in the tide, you may need to leave via a different jetty from the one you arrived at. You can go for magnificent walks or cycle rides round Bréhat; it's roughly 12km all the way round; or take a boat tour to see it all from the water.

the windmill of Crec'h Tarek; Mercœur then sent Spanish allies to wreak his revenge on the island. Finally, King Henri IV ordered the destruction of Bréhat's castle.

Under King Louis XIV's warring reign, Vauban apparently came to see about fortifying the island; a meagre causeway seems to have been the only result. A tidal mill was added in the 17th century, located by the Bay of La Corderie, between the island's two halves, the wide inlet there serving as the new port for the local fishermen for many centuries. Port-Clos, built in 1770, gave the island a safer harbour. Many of the island's menfolk were drafted into the navy in the Ancien Régime. Others became corsairs, notably the captains Corouge and Lambert.

In the 19th century, two lighthouses went up to improve safety in these rocky parts. The southwestern tip of Bréhat was fortified with a Second Empire citadel, and the chapel of St-Michel was rebuilt on top of the highest point of the island, serving a double purpose, as a seamark for sailors as well as a place of worship.

Artists began to come from afar, attracted by the otherworldly beauty of the place. Bréhat gradually turned chic and chichi after the Second World War. It used to be local fishermen who would retire here, buying a small plot of land to cultivate, but the gorgeous hideaway became increasingly fashionable for a wealthy intellectual set. It was in this period that exotic flowers were brought in in large number on to the southern island – until then, potatoes are said to have been the islanders' main love.

A Tour of Bréhat

You land in well-protected **Port-Clos**, where you can hire bikes. The pine-wooded, cliff-sided point to the west is the site of the 19th-century citadel. Extraordinary views open out from the **Bois de la Citadelle** on that side. The point to the east leads to the **Grève du Guerzido**, the best-known beach on Bréhat, backed by gardens where exotic plants and fig trees, eucalyptus and palms prosper.

Le Bourg, up the eastern side of the south island, is the unimaginatively named main village, but it is an attractive place, centred around a cheerful circular square shaded by plane trees. Cast an eye inside the church, in small part dating back to the 12th century, but mostly a mid-17th-century edifice. Just up from Le Bourg lie the vague ruins of the castle.

On the western side of the south island, a track leads past the ruins of the windmill on its hill. Then head up to the **Chapelle St-Michel**, the highest point on Bréhat, clearly visible from afar with its deliberately colourful and most un-Breton orange roof tiles. Up by the basic whitewashed chapel you get sensational views across the archipelago. From the mound, you can look down on to the very pretty 17th-century **tidal mill** restored to working order and occasionally open to the public. In olden days, at high tide, boats could come right up to a handy window in the building and deliver the grain to be milled. Another great viewing point on Bréhat is from the **Croix de Maudez**, a cross erected on the most westerly tip of the island in 1788.

Crossing the tiny Pont ar Prat, you come onto the wilder **northern half of the island**. This part of Bréhat contains far fewer houses. Moors rather than carefully tended gardens dominate here. If you head up the western side to the whitewashed naval watchtower and lighthouse of Le Rosédo, you can pass the 19th-century granite **chapel of Keranroux** with its little spire and whitewashed interior.

Next, head for the northernmost tip of the island and the **Phare du Paon**. Here, several legends revolve around the deeply pink rocks and the chasm below, in which the waves roar. The hackneyed story concerns young women wanting to know if they might get married; they were supposed to throw a stone into the abyss, and if it plopped straight into the water, then they would supposedly be married in the year, but if the pebble hit the sides, then they would have to wait as many years as it bounced against the rocks.

A much more gruesome story tells of an evil pair of children whose father, Mériadec, was a wealthy lord of Goëlo. Greedy to grab hold of his riches, they plotted to kill him. But Mériadec got wind of their plans and fled to Bréhat. His diabolical children tracked him down to the northern end of the island and murdered him here. As they were about to dispose of his body, Justice took its revenge, and they were transformed into the cruelly lacerated rocks you now see, stained with their father's blood.

Market Days on the Ile de Bréhat

Ile de Bréhat: Daily in July and August

Where to Stay and Eat on the Ile de Bréhat

ⓘ **Ile de Bréhat >**
t 02 96 20 04 15,
www.brehat-infos.fr

Ile de Bréhat ✉ 22870
**Bellevue, Port-Clos, t 02 96 20 00 05, www.hotel-bellevue-brehat.fr

(€€€€). A pretty portside hotel, with simple but very expensive rooms, some with sea views. The restaurant terraces are invaded by visitors with each boat that arrives.

**La Vieille Auberge, Le Bourg, t 02 96 20 00 24. (€€€). A small hotel in the main village. Again with expensive rooms and a touristy restaurant with nice terrace. *Closed Nov–Easter.*

La Brazérade, main street, t 02 96 20 06 30 (€€). A simple option for *moules frites. Closed Nov–Mar.*

Inland Trégor to Guingamp

The historic Breton region of **Trégor** stretched along the coast from the Trieux estuary, in what is now the Côtes d'Armor, to the Morlaix River, in what is now northeastern Finistère. It also extended far inland; it was basically the territory overseen by the bishops of the city of Tréguier. One of the four distinct dialects of the Breton language developed in the Trégor. Although the notion of the Trégor has somewhat dwindled in modern times, its various parts have retained typically Breton looks and remained close to their Breton traditions.

In this section we start with Pontrieux, an inland port located, not too surprisingly, by the Trieux River, and which served as an outer harbour for the town of Guingamp. Around Guingamp, you can seek out some deeply rural Breton retreats.

Pontrieux and Around

At **Pontrieux**, a quaint little historic river town, the squares and streets almost mirror each other either side of the Trieux. The two halves have clearly lived as separate communities in past times. Each had its own *coiffeur* and café, as well as its own church. Although the Trieux was used for river trading down the centuries, now it's just little pleasure boats that go up and down, including those for tourists run by Barques des Lavoirs – contact the tourist office to sign up. The riverbanks are lined with boathouses and former washhouses that the townspeople now smother with flowers. They've also placed models of washerwomen in traditional costume along the way, although these figures aren't exactly convincing. Mid-August sees a big celebration along the river, the **Fête des Lavandières**, or festival of the washerwomen.

Pontrieux's merchants grew wealthy from their riverside mills (used both to make flour and paper) and from the linen trade, as houses such as the towering timberframe **Maison d'Eiffel** (now home to the tourist office) demonstrate. A fair number of craftspeople have set up shop today. On the northern side of town lies the **marina**. From the railway station nearby, you can take the delightful tourist steam train, **La Vapeur du Trieux**, along a dramatic stretch high above the Trieux to Paimpol.

The impressive castle you may spot on the west bank of the Trieux is the **Château de la Roche-Jagu**, a severe defensive block built in the 15th century. The ornate chimney stacks do add a decorative touch. An annual exhibition on a Côtes d'Armor theme is held in the otherwise rather empty chambers within, with their vast fireplaces and beams. The carefully restored gardens are the main focus of many visitors' attention.

La Vapeur du Trieux
www.vapeurdutrieux,
t 08 92 39 14 27;
open May–Sept

Château de la Roche-Jagu
open daily July and Aug 10–1 and 2–7, April–June and Sept–Oct 10–12 and 2–6; exhibition mid-June–11 Nov

Getting to and around Inland Trégor

Guingamp, the main centre of travel in the area, is conveniently served by the TGV fast train from Paris to Brest. The local train line between Guingamp and Paimpol also has some useful stops.

In the Middle Ages, the dukes of Brittany had a castle, Châteaulin-sur-Trieux, in the vicinity. This may have disappeared, but the dukes also used to attend the local **church at Runan** (just west of Pontrieux), as did the lords of La Roche-Jagu, hence the unexpectedly rich decorations on this fairly basic Breton edifice. The south porch is packed with finely sculpted figures. Above, a stone panel represents a couple of major scenes from the New Testament. A dozen coats of arms, elaborately carved in stone, are also encrusted into the south side, symbols of the place's very wealthy patrons. The extravagant decoration continues inside.

Guingamp

Guingamp, a traditional Breton market town, may be quite widely known for its strong defence of Breton traditions, but it's also become a househould name in France in recent years thanks to its successful football team, which punches far above its weight. On a more modest note, the little **Musée de la Boule Bretonne** at the tourist office covers regional boules down the ages.

In high summer, **Les Jeud'his de Guingamp** consist of a programme of free street events, including music and dance, for children and adults alike. **Le Bugale Breizh**, early in July, brings around a thousand children from across Brittany to perform traditional dances here. **La Fête de la St-Loup**, a week-long celebration of Breton dancing, starts the Sunday following 15 August. *La Dérobée de Guingamp* is known as one of the liveliest Breton dances, although it turns out that it may have been imported back here by Napoleonic soldiers fighting in Italy.

The main church is dedicated to the Black Virgin known as **Notre-Dame de Bon Secours**, much venerated in these parts. Her *pardon* counts as a major event for local Catholics, taking place on the first Saturday in July. But in this instance the pilgrims don't parade their protector by day, but wait until nightfall to start their torchlit procession. At any time of year in Guingamp, however, you'll find believers coming to light candles to the Black Virgin sheltering in one of the church's porches. The whole sturdy edifice mixes several periods of architecture, partly because the right-hand side of the Gothic church fell down in 1535. That section was rebuilt using swanky new Renaissance forms.

Inside, the church is darkly spectacular, the main ceiling held up by Gothic vaulting. The contrast between the aisle on the left, resting on Gothic arches, and that on the right, supported by Renaissance ones, could hardly be more marked, providing a good lesson in the differences between the two styles. The design of the gallery above the Renaissance arches is wilder, turning Baroque with its extravagant curves. The heavier, earlier Romanesque period makes its weighty presence felt in the crossing, where the solid arches almost entirely separate off this part of the church from the rest of the edifice. Beyond the crossing, the choir looks lightly Gothic by comparison.

Down from the church, the lovely triangular square known as **Place du Centre** is the focal point of the town. Bordered by grand houses, some stone, some timberframe, its charm is added to by the **Fontaine de la Plomée**, uncharacteristic of Brittany in its finesse. This Renaissance fountain is decorated with spectacular winged griffins, women and putti. Two of the three vases of the fountain are made from lead – *plomb* in French – hence the name *Plomée*. At the foot of the old town, the **banks of the Trieux** have been redone to allow walkers and cyclists to enjoy the riverside.

Back during the Breton War of Succession, Jeanne de Penthièvre's husband, Charles de Blois (or de Chastillon) defended her interests supported by the king of France. A deeply religious man, de Blois also made donations to many foundations in northern Brittany, for instance in Guingamp. But he would lose the war, dying at the Battle of Auray in 1364. His remains lie in a reliquary box in the **church at Grâces**, a village just west of Guingamp. After his death, a cult grew up around him, and the religious warrior was in fact eventually declared a saint.

Grâces' grand Gothic church only dates from the late 15th century, but it was funded by the last Breton duchess, Anne, also countess of Penthièvre – hence the presence of the Breton ducal insignia on the building. The whole edifice is in fact rich in all manner of details; a pair of baboonish-looking rampant lions hold up a coat of arms on one of the gabled sides of the church, and a Breton bagpipe player is carved over the door to the belltower. Still funnier animals are represented inside, haring along the stringbeams in hunting scenes and comically illustrated cautionary tales.

South of Guingamp

To hunt down a near-forgotten corner of Breton villages and chapels, head for the area around St-Péver. Some of the sights along this route have a desolate beauty; some are badly neglected. To visit some of the run-down, almost windowless chapels here, you need to get the keys from local houses (details are posted on the chapel doors). At the basic, severe-looking **Chapelle Notre-Dame d'Avaugour** (a little north of St-Péver), the architecture is strikingly ascetic. The Breton statues prove the main wealth within. The most touching sculpture depicts a crudely carved crucified Christ resting on God's knees in a touching family scene.

The virtually windowless **Notre-Dame de Restudo** just south of St-Péver seems still more detached from the modern world. Some very worn frescoes have just about survived, painted on the Gothic arch dividing up the nave. Beyond this arch, look at the side chapel, its wall covered with horseshoes – the place is dedicated to St Eloi, patron saint of farriers. In the **chapel of St-Fiacre** nearby, boxes containing the bones of the dead were still displayed in the ossuary until not that long ago. While in these parts, explore the beautiful **Forêt d'Avaugour**, with its well-laid-out hiking paths.

Follow the steep country road south to **Senven-Léhart** and you come to a **chapel** with one of the most easterly of the typical Breton calvaries. This was the 16th-century work of the studios of Roland Doré. The neat drapery folds of the figures resemble the furrows of seashells.

Just to the south, the rock-strewn village of **St-Connan** looks particularly pretty. A tiny road then leads you down to **St-Gilles-Pligeaux**, a village with a photogenic ensemble of church and chapel. The two fountains below them are particularly lovely. Venture west to the vestiges of the **abbey of Coat-Mallouen at Kerpert** to view these attractive if somewhat unstable ruins.

Back west of St-Péver, **Bourbriac** has a vaingloriously large church on its big barren square. The crypt goes back to the 11th century or even earlier, and the church contains a Merovingian tomb, claimed by some to be that of the Breton saint Briac, once said to be able to cure epilepsy.

Some way west, Pestivien and Bulat-Pestivien boast an exceptionally interesting religious legacy. The **Chapelle St-Blaise** and its **calvary at Pestivien** are set in a green-grassed enclosure. They were made from lovely light grey stone, now covered with grey lichen . On the calvary, peculiarly intense, elongated figures look down on the dead Christ. The chapel also contains interesting carvings. Apparently, two memorable *pardons* were traditionally held here, the *pardon au beurre* (the butter pilgrimage) on Trinity Sunday, when butter used to be offered to St Blaise, and the *pardon du coq*, the first Sunday of February, when the tradition was for a slaughtered cockerel to be thrown down from the tower onto the congregation – presumably not a practice of which today's EU health and safety regulators would approve.

The **Eglise Notre-Dame de Bulat** in **Bulat-Pestivien** is a much more substantial affair. It towers above its village, out of all proportion with it. Bulat-Pestivien became a particularly revered spot in Brittany because Yves, the saintly 13th-century Breton lawyer who defended the region's poor (*see* box, p.225), came to pray to Notre-Dame de Bulat on numerous occasions. The church dates mainly from the 14th and 15th centuries. Its soaring tower has a typical curving Gothic accolade arch on its front, but 16th-century French Renaissance details have been carved around it, while Renaissance-style windows put in an appearance as well. A smart stone couple in Renaissance attire even greet you on either side of the main doorway. By contrast, to the right of the main entrance, a series of lively skeletons acts as a chilling reminder of the frailty of human life. One of these figures of the Grim Reaper, *l'Ankou* in Breton, is shown impassionedly preaching, brandishing bones.

Enter the church via the porch with its severe statues of the apostles. The conspicuous lord's loggia inside was built so that the local nobles could sit comfortably apart from the rest of the congregation. Curious sculptures to look out for include Charles de Blois, portrayed in mock-chivalric style, and a Breton in clogs holding up the lectern.

Maison de l'Epagneul Breton
t 02 96 45 57 89; open mid-July–Aug daily exc Sun pm 10–12.30 and 3–6

The area around Bulat-Pestivien and Callac to the west is known for breeding the Breton spaniel, a much-appreciated hunting dog in France. At **Callac**, the cute little **Maison de l'Epagneul Breton** may satisfy dog-lovers' curiosity about this wonderfully alert breed. Hunters of mysterious neolithic sites should head a bit east to **Maël-Pestivien**, its atmospheric rocks including **La Chaire des Druides**, the stone marked by what looks like the imprint of a human body, inevitably a catalyst for wild speculation.

West of Guingamp around the Menez-Bré

The N12 dual carriageway rushes west through the countryside from Guingamp to Morlaix, passing below the **Ménez-Bré**, a long-sacred hill, sometimes known as the Good Giant to Bretons from this area. From up on its heights, you can enjoy fine views of the western Côtes d'Armor stretching in all directions.

Armoripark
www.armoripark.com, t 02 96 45 36 36; open July–Aug 11–7, April–June and Sept 11–6

Bringing you back down to the modern day with a joyous bump, **Armoripark**, north of the Ménez Bré at Bégard, is a thriving Breton theme park offering both indoor and outdoor activities and attractions, from pools and waterslides, to farm animals, bouncy castles and group games.

West along the N12 stands **Belle-Isle-en-Terre**, a picturesque village along the Léguer River, if slightly disturbed by the dual carriageway passing close by. The story most often told here is of Maï Manac'h, born in 1869, the daughter of a local miller. She would climb the social ladder in spectacular fashion. First, she

Saint Hervé's Strange Gifts

The Ménez-Bré is associated with the blind 6th-century Breton saint, Hervé, who went around guided by a wolf. His blindness was considered a gift from God, to stop him from being deceived by appearances. Hervé is said to have had powers of healing and exorcism; he is also credited with discovering the spring on the side of the hill.

married a market porter who took her to live in London. After he died, she became the lover of Prince Antoine d'Orléans, grandson of King Louis Philippe of France, before marrying British industrialist Robert Mond, nicknamed the King of Nickel and knighted by King George V. Lady Mond, as she became known, remained generous to her home village, eventually even donating her château. Having served as a school, it has now been transformed to hold the **Centre Régional d'Initiation à la Rivière**, encouraging visitors to learn about river flora and fauna, and organizing outings in the summer.

Belle-Isle has kept touch with many Breton traditions. There's a clog-maker on Place de l'Eglise, and a specialist Breton biscuit maker. The place was strongly associated with traditional **Breton wrestling**, and contests bring particular life to the village the third Sunday in July. A museum may be created one day on the subject.

One thing to have disappeared from the area is the paper-making tradition. However, at **La Vallée des Papeteries**, the vestiges of the paper mills have been nicely restored. It makes a pretty walk out from the village along the Léguer to visit this free sight.

Lord and Lady Mond's mausoleum, with its massive plain pink granite tomb, lies by the pretty **chapel of Locmaria** on a hillside a couple of kilometres north of Belle-Isle-en-Terre. The chapel is best known for its elaborately carved rood screen. The 12 flat-faced, bearded apostles lined up on one side of it were all seemingly made to the same model.

Southwest from Belle-Isle-en-Terre the charming slope-side **church of Loc Envel** is set in a forest-bordered village and boasts another elaborate rood screen. Many decorative features stand out inside, such as the 18th-century clock, or the figure of a praying, kneeling lord. Look out too for the host of angels above your head.

Centre Régional d'Initiation à la Rivière
t 02 96 43 08 39,
www.eau-et-rivieres.asso.fr

ⓘ **Pays Touristique Terres d'Armor**
www.terres-darmor.com

ⓘ **Pontrieux**
Maison Eiffel, t 02 96 95 14 03, or t 02 96 95 60 31 out of season,
www.pontrieux.com

ⓘ **Bourbriac**
12 Place du Centre,
t 02 96 43 46 03, or t 02 96 43 40 21 out of season

ⓘ **Callac**
Place du Centre, t 02 96 45 59 34, or t 02 96 45 50 19 out of season,
www.callac-argoat.fr

ⓘ **Belle-Isle-en-Terre** >>
Place de la Mairie,
t 02 96 43 01 71,
www.ot-belle-isle-en-terre.com

ⓘ **Guingamp** >
Place du Champ au Roy, t 02 96 43 73 89,
www.ot-guingamp.org

★ **La Demeure B&B** >

Market Days in Inland Trégor

Pontrieux: Monday
Guingamp: Friday and Saturday
Bourbriac: Tuesday
Callac: Wednesday
Louargat: Thursday
Belle-Isle-en-Terre: Wednesday

Where to Stay and Eat in Inland Trégor

Guingamp ✉ 22200

La Demeure B&B, 5 Rue du Général de Gaulle, t 02 96 44 28 53 (€€€–€€). Spacious, lovely, well-furnished rooms in an atmospheric 18th-century, central town house. Closed Jan.

La Boissière, 90 Rue de l'Yser, t 02 96 21 06 35 (€€). Characterful restaurant in a grand house with picturesque grounds, serving grills and fruits de mer. Closed Sat lunch, Sun eve and Mon.

Crêperie St-Yves, Rue St-Yves, t 02 96 44 31 18 (€). Tiny, popular crêperie.

Belle-Isle-en-Terre ✉ 22810

**Le Relais de l'Argoat, 9 Rue du Guic, t 02 96 43 00 34 (€). Classic French provincial hotel with reliable restaurant. (€€)

Crêperie Ti Ar Ch'rampouz, 13 Place de l'Eglise, t 02 96 43 00 01 (€). Opposite the church, serving excellent crêpes.

Tréguier and the Presqu'île Sauvage

Back with the coast, the Presqu'île Sauvage may look an unkempt peninsula compared with the famed Côte de Granit Rose that follows, but it is a curiously fascinating place. As to the little city of Tréguier, historic capital of the Trégor, it's renowned for its cathedral, its cloister, and its religious son, 13th-century St Yves, but it isn't all spiritual stuff – the place makes a cheerful tourist stop.

The Presqu'île Sauvage

Lézardrieux makes the most of its position overlooking the beautiful Trieux estuary. It has a successful fleet of oyster boats and an outrageously sized marina for such a small place. If you're in search of coastal walks without the hordes of the Côte de Granit Rose, the Presqu'île Sauvage fits the bill. Consider a guided kayak trip into the rocky seas around here from the **Club Nautique de Trieux**. Curious spits of land stick out into the sea north of here. On **Pen Lan**, looking across to Bréhat past seaweed-covered rocks, the **Centre d'Etude et de Valorisation des Algues** offers detailed presentations on algae and their varied uses in a suitable setting. The CEVA also organizes seaweed-hunting tours on the Sillon de Talbert. You may also spot the Breton whisky shop, Celtic Whisky.

The **Sillon de Talbert** needs to be seen to be believed. It's a natural phenomenon, but how this low, narrow strip of sand and pebbles reaching far into the sea hasn't been washed away by the tides seems a miracle. You can learn more about it at the **Maison du Sillon**, where you can also find out about guided walks. The **Phare des Héaux** stands out in the distance, at 45 metres the highest lighthouse in the sea off the French coast. Two warnings, though, about walking along the Sillon de Talbert by yourselves – it is extremely dangerous to try to wander out beyond the end of the cordon at low tide, as you may well get caught out by the incoming sea; and when the terns are nesting, visitors are forbidden.

At **Pleubian**, take a look at the richly carved if weather-worn round granite **outdoor pulpit**, a variation on the theme of the stone calvaries so numerous further west in the Finistère, dating back to the 15th century.

Club Nautique de Trieux
t 02 96 20 92 80

Centre d'Etude et de Valorisation des Algues
Maison de l'Algue, www.ceva.fr, t 02 96 22 89 16; open for tours Easter hols Thurs–Fri 2.30, second half June and first half Sept Mon–Fri 2.30, first half July and last week Aug Mon–Fri 10.30 and 2.30, mid-July–mid-Aug Mon–Fri 10.30, 2.30 and 4

Tréguier

My son, live in a way that will make you a saint.
Azou de Quinquis to her son Yves Helory de Kermartin. (He did become a saint – talk about living up to parental expectations.)

Getting to and around the Presqu'île Sauvage and Tréguier

Lannion and Paimpol have the nearest train stations. For bus services, see *www.tibus.fr.*

The soaring steeple of its remarkable cathedral certainly makes clear who was boss in Tréguier in centuries past. Tréguier still has its serious, sober side, but nowadays this little city makes for a relaxing stop before the follies of the Côte de Granit Rose, and its river has been turned into something of a marina.

History

Tréguier lays claim to being one of the original seats of Christian power in Brittany. Tugdual, a monk from Wales, became the first bishop of Tréguier in 540. The town then grew into one of the most important spiritual centres in Brittany.

The Gothic cathedral of Tréguier was begun in 1339. From 1347, the tomb of St Yves was installed there and for a small sum pilgrims were allowed to touch his skull. Pilgrims also came in large numbers during the second half of the Middle Ages on the Tro Breizh, the religious tour of the seven Breton cathedrals. Trade prospered during this time, as did printing, as this ground-breaking industry took off here from the late 15th century.

After suffering in the nightmare of the French Wars of Religion, when Tréguier briefly supported the Protestant side and as a result was severely damaged by Catholic attacks, the city centre up on the hillside became largely dominated by Catholic religious establishments. But, with the French Revolution and the demise of the Church, Tréguier lost much of its importance. However, the fertile vegetable fields of this stretch of the north Breton coast brought back some prosperity in the 19th century, until tourism helped to revive Tréguier's fortunes. Pilgrims have never stopped coming though, including many lawyers, perhaps seeking inspiration, or forgiveness.

Tréguier Cathedral
Open June–Sept daily 9–7, Oct–May daily 9–12 and 2–6

Tréguier Cathedral

The cathedral is definitely the heart and soul of Tréguier. It's also wonderfully eccentric, the most appealing, and possibly the most

St Yves – How a Lawyer Can Become a Saint

In 1253, Yves Helory de Kermartin was born into a local noble family. He headed to Paris to train to become a talented Church lawyer, but then took on a position as an ecclesiastical judge in Brittany, serving at Rennes and Tréguier. He became exceptionally respected by the common people for his fairness and his concern for the poor. Yves eventually changed career to serve as a priest, and with incredible energy went around Brittany preaching God's word. It's said that he sometimes delivered four or five sermons a day. He also turned part of his family home at Kermartin into a hospital for the poor and the sick and was considered to have performed many miracles during his lifetime. Dying on 19 May 1303, he was buried in Tréguier cathedral. A cult grew up around his memory and relics and he became the only Breton parish priest to be canonized in the Middle Ages.

interesting, of all Brittany's major churches. Rather than entering the cathedral via the main west door, known as the **Porche des Ladres**, or Lepers' Door (apparently lepers weren't allowed in during services but could listen from here), you'll probably be forced to enter by the south porch, the **Porche des Cloches**, sticking out from under the soaring steeple; its delicate tracery held up by just one slender column shows how seductive Gothic architecture can be.

Much of the interior decoration, however, was destroyed in a single day of Revolutionary fury. The feared Bataillon d'Etampes swept through on 4 May 1794, destroying tombs, furnishings and stained glass. Off the nave, inside the **Chapelle au Duc**, you'll find the tomb of Duke Jean V of Brittany. He had his chapel added in the mid-15th century – imprisoned by Marguerite de Clisson, he made a vow to build it if he regained his freedom. He donated his weight in silver, a reasonably healthy 95 kilos, to the cathedral. Disappointingly, the reworked 1945 ducal tomb is relatively plain.

The much venerated tomb of St Yves is a copy of the medieval one that Duke Jean V also ordered. It's in the neo-Gothic chivalric style. A further monument recalls the last bishop of Tréguier, who fled to England at the Revolution. Lawyers from around the western world attend the annual **Pardon de St Yves** – one of the stained-glass windows was even donated by the US bar. Recent *ex votos* show how many Bretons still put their trust in St Yves.

Towering arches spring up from the **cathedral crossing**. Up high, you can make out paintings of angels; they carry flowing banners made to contain quotes from the Bible. The **south transept** is lit by a tall window divided up by sensational Flamboyant Gothic tracery, but the bright glass is rather overwhelming. Reaching the **choir**, you come to a much more harmonious piece of Gothic architecture, built in the late 14th and early 15th centuries. The stalls, from the early 16th century, have delightfully carved misericords displaying the usual Gothic bestiary.

In the **north transept** much of the Romanesque architecture has survived. A huge wooden Christ with an even bigger wooden head looks down from on high. From here, you can go out into the

Cloister
Adm

peaceful 15th-century **cloister**. Behind the lacy Gothic stone tracery, the walkways serve as something of a museum for a collection of fine **medieval tomb effigies** collected from churches and abbeys around the Côtes d'Armor that were destroyed in the Revolution; several come from the abbeys of Bonrepos, Bégard and Beaulieu.

In the **treasury** you can pay your respects to the skull of St Yves. This prized relic was hidden under one of the cathedral's flagstones during the Revolution. Among other curiosities is a revolving *chasublier*, an original piece of furniture made to hold all the bishop's finery in an easily accessible manner – a godsend for your dandy ecclesiastic.

From the cloisters, notice the three different cathedral towers in a dramatic row. The outrageously tall spire over the south porch (63 metres high) is cut with simple patterns like a child's toy.

Tréguier Beyond the Cathedral

On one side of the cathedral, the grand bishop's palace has been converted into town hall and library, while a statue of a grieving Breton woman signals the war memorial, set below the staggering trio of the cathedral towers. The other side of the cathedral, the fine mix of houses in both granite and timberframe look utterly dwarfed by the great religious vessel. A melodramatic statue stands out defiantly in one corner, representing Ernest Renan. Although born in this Church-dominated little city, he wasn't a follower of the faith, far from it, becoming one of the greatest French 19th-century minds to attack the foundations of Christianity with his brilliant intellectual rigour. Visitors to town tend to take a mellow attitude to Tréguier, either drinking in the dramatic scene from a café table, or perusing the shops.

Streets lined with splendid historic houses stretch up and down the slope from the cathedral square. Head up to the **Chapelle des Paulines** and you'll often find art exhibitions inside. The finest streets slope down towards the Trieux. Passing behind the cathedral to reach them, you come to enchanting **Place Coat**, in a lively, touristy shopping quarter, with the **Musée Renan** just beyond occupying one of the very finest timberframe houses in town. The museum pays homage to the anti-religious hero.

Gently sloping, curving **Rue Renan** is lined with major merchants' houses all the way down, some with appealing shops on the ground floor. The architectural display ends with two dramatic matching towers, signalling the main way out to the **riverside port**. Cafés and restaurants look across the wide parking spaces (used by boats as well as cars) to the Jaudy, and the completely unspoilt river bank opposite. Follow the river south a short way, and before the arch of the bridge, you come to Tréguier's **marina**.

At **La Roche-Derrien**, a village just a short way inland upriver, and sometimes described as a mini-Tréguier because of its fine historic buildings, notably around its square, the **Club de Kayak de la Roche-Derrien** can provide canoes for exploring the Jaudy estuary.

Musée Renan
t 02 96 92 45 63; open April–June and Sept Wed–Sun 10–12 and 2–6, July–Aug daily 10–12 and 2–6, Oct–Mar by appointment

Club de Kayak de la Roche-Derrien
www.kayak-roche-derrien.fr, t 02 96 91 51 48

Market Days on the Presqu'île Sauvage and Tréguier

Lézardrieux: Friday
Pleubian: Saturday
Tréguier: Wednesday

Where to Stay and Eat on the Presqu'île Sauvage and Tréguier

Quemper-Guézennec ✉ 22260
Ferme Auberge de Kerpun, Le Marlec, a few km east of Pontrieux, **t** 02 96 95

ⓘ **Pays Touristiqe de Trégor et Goëlo**
www.tregorgoelo.com

ⓘ **Presqu'île de Lézardrieux >**
Kévantour, 22740 Pleudaniel, **t** *02 96 22 16 45, www. cc-lezardrieux.com*

★ **Château de Brélidy >**

★ **Château de Kermezen B&B >**

★ **Manoir de Kergrec'h B&B >>**

ⓘ **Tréguier >**
67 Rue Ernest Renan, **t** *02 96 92 22 33, www. ot-cotedesajoncs.com*

66 47, *www.kerpuns.com* (€). Pleasant, simple B&B rooms in a granite farmhouse surrounded by flowers and known locally for its hearty country cooking (€).

Lézardrieux ✉ 22740

Le Littoral, 8 Rue St-Christophe, **t 02 96 20 10 59, *lelittoral-lezardrieux@ wanadoo.fr* (€). A pleasant family-run village hotel close to the Trieux estuary.

L'Auberge du Trieux, 1 Impasse du Four Neuf, **t** 02 96 20 10 70 (€). A lovely restaurant in an old house, serving refined Breton cuisine.

Brélidy ✉ 22140

***Château de Brélidy, **t** 02 96 95 69 38, *www.chateau-brelidy.com* (€€€). A small, much-restored 16th-century castle with luxurious bedrooms. Two rivers flow through the grounds, where you can go fishing in season. You'll also find fun extras, like a Jacuzzi under an arbour in the garden and a billiards room.

Pommerit-Jaudy ✉ 22450

Château de Kermezen B&B, **t** 02 96 91 35 75, *www.chateaux-france.com/ kermezen* (€€€€). A splendid little Breton castle down an oak avenue just south of La Roche-Derrien, offering the most luxurious type of B&B experience in rooms with old-fashioned charm. The Kermel family has roots here going back some 500 years. A couple of the rooms have useful galleries where children can sleep.

Tréguier ✉ 22220

***Aigue Marine, 5 Rue Marcellin Berthelot, Port de Plaisance, **t** 02 96 92 97 00, *www.aiguemarine-hotel.com* (€€). A large modern hotel by the marina, with comfortable traditional rooms, a heated pool, a Jacuzzi, a gym, a sauna and good food in the restaurant (€€€–€€; *closed Sat lunch, Sun eve and Mon*). *Closed early Jan–late Feb.*

***Kastell Dinec'h, Route de Lannion, Minihy-Tréguier, west of Tréguier, **t** 02 96 92 49 39, *kastell@club-internet.fr* (€€). A converted Breton manor in the

countryside, with romantic little rooms, an excellent, stylish restaurant (residents only; dinner only) offering wonderful seafood specialities, and delightful gardens with a pool. *Closed Nov–mid-March.*

Manoir de Troguindy, Minihy-Tréguier, **t** 02 96 92 20 89, *www.breton-manoir. com* (€€). There has been a fortified château in this prime position in a bend of the river Guindy since the 12th century. Recently rebuilt, it now offers lavishly decorated rooms with direct access to charming gardens and a park with its own lake, chestnut avenue and grotto chapel.

Hôtel de l'Estuaire, 5 Place Général de Gaulle, **t 02 96 92 30 21 (€). A clean, modern hotel.

Le St-Bernard, 3 Rue Marcellin Berthelot, **t** 02 96 92 20 77 (€). Good-value menus down by the marina.

Crêperie La Dentellière, 4 Rue de St-Yves, **t** 02 96 92 33 54 (€). In a pretty building, a popular place for crêpes or regular *formules*.

Moulinet Jean-Pierre, 2 Rue Renan, **t** 02 96 92 30 27 (€). A fishmonger's just behind the cathedral with a takeway service and a first-floor dining room for seafood sit-down.

Plougrescant ✉ 22820

Manoir de Kergrec'h B&B, 15 Hent Kergrec'h, **t** 02 96 92 59 13, *www. manoirdekergrech* (€€€). Gorgeous luxury rooms in a solid 17th-century manor by the coast.

Mme Janviers B&B, 15 Hent Castel Ment, **t** 02 96 92 52 67 (€). A friendly stop with simple, pleasant rooms.

Auberge de Pen-Ar-Feunteun, Route de Penvénan, **t** 02 96 92 51 02 (€). A simple rustic restaurant. On the second Wed of every month it serves *tête de veau* and *langue de boeuf*.

Porz Hir ✉ 22820

Hôtel Restaurant Pors Hir, 1 La Plage, Hent Pors Hir, just north of Plougrescant, **t** 02 96 92 52 14 (€). Looking out over a delightful tiny port, with extremely basic bedrooms. It's run by a former fisherman, so it comes as no surprise that the seafood is excellent (€€).

The Côte de Granit Rose

✪ Côte de
Granit Rose

Here you arrive at one of the most famous stretches of coast in France and some of the most gorgeous and preposterous granite formations on the planet. It's not just that the boulders are pink and orange along the 20 or so kilometres of the Côte de Granit Rose; it's also that they've been carved by the elements into some of the most bizarre shapes. Seek out such comical natural sculptures as the Upturned Foot, the Bottle or Napoleon's Hat. The resorts are as delightful as the rockscapes. From the well-to-do main port of Perros-Guirec, boats leave for the ornithological reserve of Les Sept Iles, where puffins, gannets and seals can be seen in spring and early summer.

From the Plougrescant Peninsula to Perros-Guirec

The wonderful craziness begins north of Tréguier, on the Plougrescant peninsula. Past the little **oyster port of La Roche Jaune** on the west bank of the Jaudy estuary, from the fabulous coast road, islands beckon temptingly, not just the **Ile Loaven**, where the splendidly named Ste Eliboubane was venerated in the Dark Ages, but also the **Iles d'Er** further out. With very low tides, these islands become accessible by foot.

At the top of the Plougrescant peninsula, you come to the tiny boulder-surrounded port of **Porz Hir**. Here you already come across houses set among vast boulders. The **Pointe du Château**, better known as **Castel Meur**, claims one of the most famous houses in the country, trapped among its rocks. It looks as though two huge boulders have been dropped at either end of it, imprisoning it in their stony embrace. To divert attention from this celebrity home (there are quite a number more such houses along this coastline), the Conservatoire du Littoral, the national body set up to protect the French coastline, has created a **Maison d'Accueil** to inform visitors about the striking natural environment. Continuing west, the sea can come raging into the great split between two rocks at the **Pointe du Gouffre**. The magical rockscapes continue around **Pors Scarff**, sonorous pebble slopes running down from the boulders to the sea. The **Plage de Ralevy** follows.

Don't miss the curious chapel at **Plougrescant** village just back from the coast. One end of it looks as crooked as a building from a fairytale, topped by a leaning, barbed little lead tower that resembles a medieval torture instrument. Monstrous gargoyles drool down from this sinister steeple. The chapel dates back to the Romanesque period. Local people will show you round the interior for a paltry sum, though the commentary may be delivered as unemotionally as the Massacre of the Innocents is depicted on the ceiling – the chapel's glory is the striking series of Biblical paintings

Getting to and around the Côte du Granit Rose

Lannion a short way south of Perros-Guirec has a TGV train station and airport (*www.aeroport-lannion.fr*) with regular flights to and from Paris. For buses, consult *www.tibus.fr*.

daubed on the wooden planks of the vault. In the main panels, Old Testament stories are told against a red and flowery background, while Adam and Eve are memorably shown being expelled from Eden, clad in a wonderful pattern of leaves. Selected New Testament scenes are represented below them. There are other elements of decorative wealth inside the chapel, including tombs for a vainglorioius 16th-century bishop of Tréguier, Guillaume du Halgouët, and for the local saint, Gonéry, son of Ste Eliboubane. Gonéry's supposed skull is also on display, as brown as a berry.

Heading west along the coast, at the **Anse de Gouermel**, you come to a bay with wider views. Around **Buguélès**, houses mingle in greater number with the boulders, making for a truly fantastic sight. The small islands visible just out to sea make up the **Penvénan archipelago**. From Buguélès, it's amusing to try and reach Port-Blanc by car or by foot by the shortcut across the **Anse de Pellinec**, only passable at low tide when the causeway is revealed. Fertile fields surround the bay, producing crops of artichokes and cauliflowers.

Port-Blanc is absolutely stunning, though not very white, despite the name. However, some white seamarks do stand out like sugarloaves on the pink rocks. The rockscapes here are more tranquil than those to the east, and the waters temptingly blue. The **Plage de Rohanic** is particularly splendid.

You can follow the coast westwards on foot, but a glorious high road leads from Port-Blanc to **Trévou-Tréguignec**. Two spectacular rock-protected beaches lie down from the village, **Les Dunes** and **Royau**. Big rectangular blocks of quarried pink granite, patterned with the cuts of the drills, act as sea walls. Out to sea, you can make out the barren Ile Tomé and the Sept-Iles. The coast around tiny **Port Royau** is so strewn with rocks that it seems like quite an act of folly to have placed a port here at all. **Port l'Epine** just west has further beautiful rocky creeks and pebbly beaches.

Perros-Guirec

One of the most dramatic resorts in Brittany, Perros-Guirec has grown up around a stunning peninsula. Grand villas and hotels climb the steep slopes above a magical array of beaches framed by pines. The more ordinary, busy town shopping centre stands on the hilltop, but most of the attention focuses on the coast.

Perros-Guirec's **port and marina** lie on the flat, eastern side of town, the number of posh yachts far outdoing the number of

Maurice Denis and the Colour Pink

Maurice Denis was one of the greatest French painters at the turn of the 19th to 20th centuries to have been seduced by Brittany. Influenced by Gauguin and Sérusier, with the latter he founded the Ecole des Nabis, seeking inspiration in Ancient, Oriental and esoteric sources, which lent a dreamy tone to many of his works. He came to Perros-Guirec over many years, painting dazzling seaside scenes here, and even bought a villa in the resort called Silencio. The extraordinary tints of the rocks on this coast seem to have had a profound effect on his imagination. In fact, he became a bit obsessed by the colour pink, the trademark colour in so many of his works.

traditional boats. There are a couple of beaches this side of the resort, the **Plage des Arcades** and **Plage du Château**.

In such a glamorous seaside spot, it comes as a slight surprise to find a museum by the port commemorating a painful time in Breton history. The **Musée de Cire** focuses on the anti-Revolutionary Chouannerie, with waxwork scenes re-creating the bloody events that took place in the area. Respects are also paid to Ernest Renan (*see* p.227) and to Maurice Denis.

Musée de Cire
t 02 96 91 23 45; open April–Oct and school hols daily; June–Aug 9.30–6.30; April, May and Sept 10–12.15 and 2–6

The dramatic rocky headland of the **Pointe du Château** separates the two sides of Perros-Guirec. Two large **beaches**, **Trestrignel** and **Trestraou**, lie to the west. Framed by great rocks, and backed by beautifully wooded slopes, they appeal immediately to the aesthetic. With their fine sands and very gentle inclines, they make excellent stretches for toddlers to play on. Trestraou has the luxury thalassotherapy centre, the **Thermes Marins de Perros-Guirec**, as well as a casino and nightclubs. From a jetty to one side of the beach, boats leave for trips around the Les Sept Iles, one of the richest reserves in France for rare marine birds.

Thermes Marins de Perros-Guirec
t 02 96 23 28 97

At the **Eglise St-Jacques** in the old part of upper Perros, masons put some of these colourful local rocks into building the church. The dome is such a deep pink, it looks like an Englishman suffering from a bad case of sunburn. Inside, the nave is clearly divided between earlier and later medieval halves.

A Boat Trip Around Les Sept Iles

Even in the height of summer, one of the islands making up Les Sept Iles appears to be covered in snow: the gannet colony turns the north side of the Ile Rouzic completely white with the sheer number of nesting birds. The gannets, with their distinctive black-tipped wings, yellow heads and piercing blue eyes, stay from spring until roughly late September. They don't fly to the mainland, keeping well away from people; the Ile Rouzic is the only place in France where they come to reproduce.

Boat trip around Les Sept Iles
try Armor Découverte, Trestraou, t 02 96 91 10 00, www.armor-decouverte.fr, or Vieux-Gréement, Sant C'hirey, t 06 85 92 60 61, www.santguirec.com

The mascot of Perros-Guirec, though, is the puffin; from spring to around mid to late July you can spot a colony of these 'sea parrots' on Les Sept Iles. They almost died out because of men hunting them up to the early 20th century. It was due to this danger that the Ligue pour la Protection des Oiseaux (LPO) fought to have Les

Sept Iles declared an ornithological reserve, which it has been since 1912. Spring is the best time to come if you're a keen ornithologist. Then you can also spot cormorants, razorbills, guillemots, manx shearwaters, fulmars and kittiwakes, among others. The other major attraction around this archipelago is the grey seals. The babies in fact come into the world white; they grow darker in colour with age.

On calm days, the tour includes an hour-long stop on **L'Ile aux Moines**, the name of this steep barren rock recalling the fact that monks tried valiantly to colonize the place at one time. Otherwise, the boat trip lasts around 90 minutes.

To Ploumanac'h via the Pink Coast or the Pink Quarries

You could go by foot from Perros-Guirec to Ploumanac'h along the beautiful **coastal path**, which becomes increasingly cluttered with a chaos of pink rocks. Views of Les Sept Iles accompany you all the way on clear days. Sculptors have long enjoyed working the rare local rock, and a mixed bag of monumental works are displayed in the **Parc de Sculptures Christian Gad** on the road from Perros-Guirec to Ploumanac'h. The place has looked slightly unkempt for some time, but there are plans to smarten it up.

It feels a bit unsettling looking on the dramatic **quarries** still in operation in the hillsides behind, around **La Clarté**. Here you can see enormous pieces of pink granite piled up in the quarry craters, like huge building blocks destined for some vast, camp building project. Mammoth lorries thunder out from here. On a gentler theme, several artisans have set up shop in the village. Here, take a look at the extraordinary pink **Eglise Notre-Dame de Clarté**, looking down to the sea from its height. The story goes that the church was constructed thanks to a vow made by the Seigneur du Barac'h, a nobleman from these parts who once found himself stuck in fog in the treacherous seas around Les Sept Iles. He prayed to the Virgin for assistance and the pea-souper suddenly lifted. The depictions of the stations of the cross within were designed by Maurice Denis.

Pink Geology

The pink granite here was formed across the same period as the rest of Brittany's granite, some 300,000 million years ago, when great veins of magma bubbled up beneath enormous mountains that then covered the region, reaching higher than the Alps. The magma cooled and turned to granite, while the mountains were slowly eroded by the elements. Eventually, after an inconceivably long period, the granite was exposed on the surface. Apparently, a geological vein on the Côte de Granit Rose remained open and active for some 10 million years, giving more diverse types of magma the time to reach this level. The science all sounds as unbelievable as the Breton legends.

Ploumanac'h

To see the funniest, craziest rocks in Brittany, head on to Ploumanac'h. First have a look at the **Plage St-Guirec**, one of the most dramatic beaches in France, tucked away on the western side of the Ploumanac'h peninsula. The little oratory perched on its beachside rock is dedicated to St Guirec, said to have landed here in the 6th century. The wooden statue of the man has a mutilated nose – traditionally, young women anxious to get married would come to stick a hairpin into his proboscis, due to which action it has now completely worn off. Outside the walls of **St-Guirec's chapel**'s enclosure, which is set a bit back from the beach, the religious man's so-called 'bed' turns out to be a stone basin; water taken from it used to be claimed to have miraculous properties.

A dream of a castle stands out on the **Ilot de Costarès** a little way out to sea. Built in the 1890s for a Polish engineer, Bruno Abdank, it has seen several famous visitors and further owners. Abdank's most celebrated guest was the author Henryk Sienkiewicz, said to have completed his best-known work, *Quo Vadis*, at the castle.

The **coastal walk** around the **Parc Municipal** guides you past Ploumanac'h's absurd pink geological formations. They turn a particularly fiery colour in the setting sun. Because of the damage that was being caused to this extraordinary coastal strip by the hundreds of thousands of tourists who used to traipse all too freely over the rocks, you're now sensibly restricted to marked paths. They take you from the Plage de St-Guirec round the **Pointe de Squewel**. The names given to some of the rocks here give you a good indication of just how fanciful they look, for example *Le Rocher des Amoureux* (The Lovers' Rock), *La Tête de Mort* (The Skull), *La Bouteille* (The Bottle) and the easily recognizable *Pied Renversé* (The Upturned Foot).

Behind the lighthouse (in pink granite too, of course, rebuilt after it was destroyed in the Second World War), you come to the **Maison du Littoral**, which tells the geological story of these parts. Explanations are also given on the various local flora and fauna. Some of the postcards on display show that the very poor used to make shelters under the rocks and live there in makeshift caves. Today, the pink granite is used as much for art as for shelter.

To appreciate further absurdly shaped rocks in the shade, go walking in the deep **Vallée des Traouïero**, the path heading inland from Ploumanac'h to Trégastel village (as opposed to the resort of Trégastel-Plage). Small exhibitions are held in the tidal mill along the way.

Trégastel-Plage

Trégastel-Plage boasts the most absurd pink rocks of the lot. Head up to its sensational **aquarium**, some of its chambers set

Aquarium de Trégastel
www.aquarium-tregastel.com; open Jan–Mar and Oct–Dec school hols only, Tues–Sun 2–5; April–June and Sept Sat–Mon 2–6 and Tues–Fri 10–6; July–Aug 10–7

08 | Côtes d'Armor | The Côte de Granit Rose

under a very judiciously arranged pile of the most enormous pink slabs. This extraordinary architectural phenomenon turns out to be purely natural, even if the white statue of God the Father plonked on top looks preposterously out of keeping. The tanks have been updated recently, the whole place enlarged and modernized, and made more welcoming and educational.

The sea deserts the resort at low tide. Then you can go on a fabulous voyage of discovery on foot among all the rocky piles and isles. The walk onto the Ile Renote takes you past some particularly spectacular rock formations, including the Skull, the Pile of Crêpes, the Die and the Great Chasm.

Actually, at any time of year you can also go swimming at Trégastel-Plage, at the **Forum** (at time of writing, being restored after storm damage; should reopen soon), an indoor sports complex built overlooking the spectacular **beach of Coz-Porz**. Its modern design caused a scandal, but it has been relatively sensitively landscaped, keeping low to the ground beside the beach – it's the modern blocks above that don't fit in with the natural setting, but their cafés do offer good front-row seat onto all the rocky drama. From inside the Forum, you can enjoy excellent views out onto the rockscapes and swim in warm waters even in mid-winter. The facilities are luxurious and up to the minute, with jet sprays and jacuzzis around the pool. West of here seek out further wacky rocks towards the Grève Blanche, such as the *Tirebouchon* (the Corkscrew).

(★) **Les Feux des Iles** >>

(i) **Côte du Granit Rose**
www.cotede
granitrose.fr

(★) **Le Manoir du Sphinx** >>

(i) **Perros-Guirec** >
21 Place de l'Hôtel de
Ville, **t** 02 96 23 21 15,
www.perros-guirec.com

(★) **L'Agapa** >

Market Days on the Côte du Granit Rose

Perros-Guirec: Friday
Trégastel-Plage: Monday

Where to Stay and Eat on the Côte du Granit Rose

Perros-Guirec ✉ 22700
****L'Agapa, 12 Rue des Bons Enfants, **t** 02 96 49 01 10, www.lagapa.com (€€€€€–€€€€). This sumptuous hotel set among pine trees has breathtaking sea views from its luxurious rooms, many decorated in very elegant, contemporary style. Large modern annex houses spa and sophisticated dining room of the restaurant Le Belouga (€€€€–€€). Pool, gym and lovely garden.

***Les Feux des Iles, 53 Blvd Clemenceau, **t** 02 96 23 22 94, www.feux-des-iles.com (€€€). Wonderful views over to the Sept Iles from many of the characterful rooms, divided between a traditional resort home in stone and a recent addition with more spacious modern rooms. There's a pretty garden, a tennis court and a traditional restaurant (€€€€–€€; dinner only).

***Le Manoir du Sphinx, 67 Chemin de la Messe, **t** 02 96 23 25 42, lemanoirdusphinx@wanadoo.fr (€€€). A stylish Belle Epoque villa in its own gardens lording it over the Plage de Trestrignel, with enchanting sea views from many of the comfy rooms. The good restaurant (€€€–€€; closed Mon lunch and Fri lunch) has a panoramic conservatory and offers such delights as spit-roasted turbot.

***Le Grand Hôtel, www.grand-hotel-trestraou.com (€€€€–€€). A 1930s hotel with plenty of atmosphere

(i) **Trévou-Tréguignec**
at Trestel, t 02 96 23 71 92, www.trevou-treguignec.fr

(i) **Trégastel-Plage >>**
Place Ste-Anne, t 02 96 15 38 38, www.ville-tregastel.fr

(★) **Castel Beau Site >**

overlooking the beach, and next door to the thalassotherapy centre, with which it has close links. Over half of the rooms have great sea views. Panoramic restaurant, too.

Le Levant, 91 Rue Ernest Renan, **t 02 96 23 20 15, *www.le-levant.fr* (€). A modern block in a fantastic location, the nice, practical, bright, good-value rooms with their big windows and little terraces looking over the marina and to sea. There's a good restaurant (€€€–€; *closed Fri, Sat lunch and Sun eve*) on the first floor benefiting from the same views.

Le Suroît, 81 Rue Ernest Renan, **t 02 96 23 23 83, *www.lesuroitperros.com* (€€€–€). Neighbour and rival of the above, its rooms recently renovated.

Morgane, Plage de Trestraou, **t 02 96 23 22 80, *www.hotel-morgane.com* (€€€–€). A hotel in an old-style house, with plain modern rooms and a covered, heated pool.

Au Bon Accueil, 11 Rue de Landerval, **t 02 96 23 25 77, *www.au-bon-accueil.com* (€). Comfortable, modern rooms, some with views of the port.

La Suite, Plage de Trestraou, **t** 02 96 49 09 34. Refined new restaurant at the end of the beach, offering excellent French fare in various formulae.

Digor Kalon, 89 Rue du Maréchal Joffre, **t** 02 96 49 03 63 (€). A tranquil haven of a café-restaurant, offering seasonal delights on a good-value tapas-style menu.

Les Vieux Gréements, 19 Rue Anatole le Braz, **t** 02 96 91 14 99 (€). A good crêperie with nautical decor.

Ploumanac'h ✉ 22700

***Castel Beau Site, Plage St-Guirec, **t** 02 96 91 40 87, *www.castelbeau site.com* (€€€–€). This 1930s building that once served as barracks has been converted into a fine modern hotel that has undergone a major make-over. The rooms have wonderful sea

views, shared by the restaurant (€€€; *dinner only exc July–Aug; closed Sun*). *Closed Jan.*

Le Phare, 39 Rue Saint-Guirec, **t 02 96 91 41 19, *www.hotel-le-phare.fr* (€). Modern rooms overlooking the beach.

du Parc, 174 Place St-Guirec, **t 02 96 91 40 80, *www.hotelduparc.com* (€€€). Hotel in a simple stone house opposite one of the main car parks, but close to the beach and the amazing rock formations. The seafood restaurant (€€€) is permanently packed out with tourists.

Trégastel ✉ 22730

***Belle Vue, 20 Rue des Calculots, **t** 02 96 23 88 18, *www.hotelbellevue tregastel.com* (€€€–€€). Some of the rooms in this refurbished 1930s building have sea views, others give onto the garden. The restaurant (€€€–€€; *open dinner only, May–Sept*) has a terrace looking to the sea. *Closed mid-Nov–mid-March.*

Beau Séjour, Plage du Coz Pors, **t 02 96 23 88 02, *www.beausejoursarl.com*. (€€€–€€). With a variety of different-sized rooms, many with sea views. The restaurant (€€€; *dinner only*) serves modern dishes and has a terrace looking out on to the rocks. *Closed mid-Nov–mid-Dec and mid-Jan–mid-Feb.*

Hotel de la Mer, Plage du Coz Pors, **t 02 96 15 60 00 (€€–€). Another appealing option beside the rocks, with decent rooms.

Crêperie L'Iroise, 29 Rue Charles Le Goffic, **t** 02 96 15 93 23, *www. creperieliroise.fr* (€). Good crêperie.

Crêperie Ty Maï, 21 Place Ste-Anne, **t** 02 96 23 41 95 (€). A decent basic option. *Closed Wed.*

Auberge Vieille Eglise, Trégastel-Bourg, **t** 02 96 23 88 31 (€€–€). Near the delightful church in the old village to the south, a traditional-style Breton inn with terrace, serving tasty dishes. *Closed Sun eve, Mon and Tues eve.*

Ile Grande to Plestin-les-Grèves

After Trégastel, some of the pinkness goes out of the rocks and the crowds thin out somewhat, too. This piece of coast is still sensational. Travel inland up the Léguer beyond the historic and high-tech town of Lannion to enjoy the calm sights along this very

Getting to and around Ile Grande and Plestin-les-Grèves

Lannion has an **airport** with regular flights to and from Paris and a **railway station** with good connections.

pretty, unspoilt valley. The coast southwest of Lannion turns wilder, lined by spectacular cliffs. This final coastal stretch of the Côtes d'Armor leads you to the Lieue de Grève, a stunning wood-fringed bay that has served as the setting for many a legend.

Ile Grande

The Ile Grande is now permanently joined to the mainland by a bridge. The granite here has bluish-grey tinges, and the land is covered with dense gorse and bracken. Past the large neolithic gallery chamber near the top of the island, you can scramble up to the rocks marking the highest point. Among the islets to the east, the wooded one puts in its claim to being the Avalon of Arthurian legend, where King Arthur went to die... or at least to rest until he should be brought back to life to fight once more (see p.44).

The Ile Grande is best known now for its reputed ornithological centre and bird hospital, run by the Ligue Pour la Protection des Oiseaux (LPO), the official French agency for the protection of birds. The **Station LPO de l'Ile Grande** opened in 1984, in good part to deal with the effects on birds of oil slicks caused by tankers running aground on the Breton rocks. It covers the birds of Les Sept Iles, too.

Station LPO de l'Ile Grande
www.lpo.fr/reseau/ile-grande, t 02 96 91 91 40; open July–Aug Mon–Fri 10–1 and 2.30–7, Sat–Sun 2.30–7; June and school hols daily 2–6; outside school hols Sat and Sun 2–6; birdwatching tours in summer

Pleumeur-Bodou and Around

Built in the shape of the most enormous golf ball, the **Radôme** is the most striking element of **Cosmopolis**, a concentrated group of tourist sights at **Pleumeur-Bodou**. The Radôme may look like an outrageous new golfing complex, but the massive structure was actually part of a pioneering satellite centre built many decades ago – the first satellite broadcast between America and Europe was effected from here. The national telecommunications company, France Télécom, now Orange, has opened a hi-tech museum here, the **Cité des Télécoms**, which tells the story of the development of French telecommunications over the past century and a half in an appealing interactive fashion. Special futuristic sound-and-light shows are put on inside the Radôme itself.

Cité des Télécoms
www.cite-telecoms.com, t 02 96 46 63 80; open July and Aug daily 10–7; May and June daily 10–6; April and Sept Mon–Fri 10–6, Sat and Sun 2–6; school hols Mon–Fri 10–6, Sun 2–6

The **Planétarium du Trégor** close by, and also part of Cosmopolis, runs a regular programme of shows on the sky and the stars. Although the **Gaulish village of Meem**, a third element in this collection of tourist sights, is fake, with reconstructions of Celtic huts, this is popular with families with young children, and run by a humanitarian organization raising money for community schools in the bush in Togo, Africa, hence the reconstruction of African huts alongside Gaulish ones.

The one remarkable, genuinely old monument around Pleumeur-Bodou is the **Menhir de St-Uzec**. However, this neolithic standing stone was typically vandalized by overzealous Christians in the 17th century, who carved primitive Christian symbols on it. On the slope above the menhir, you can enjoy a hilarious view of the crudely Christianized prehistoric monument with the Radôme appearing in the background like a huge, miraculous moon.

To Trébeurden

Back with the coast, amid the wide landscapes of the **beach of Groas Trez**, lie the **marshlands of Quellen**, where ornithologists can make the most of three observatories. You can also spot the odd Camargue white horse brought in to graze the land here.

Trébeurden brings you back into major beach holiday country after the little nature break to the north. The commanding presence of the **Ile Millau** close to the shore marks the sea views from Trébeurden and gives shelter to some of the resort's beaches. When the tides are particularly low you can actually walk out to this island and discover its contrasting sides, the windswept west as well as the more protected east, rich in flora.

At the northern end of Trébeurden, a couple of upmarket hotels stand high above the first beach. Then you come to the **Plage de Pors-Termen** with a modern **marina** that caused a local stir. It is made from big, chaotic piles of granite. The money to finance this project came from those responsible for the environmental disaster of the oil tanker *Amoco Cadiz*, which badly affected the area. Sailing is a passion here, and it's a good place to learn, to go by the number of little boats that often head out like colourful shoals. There's also a diving school. **Le Castel** is the name of the entirely natural fort of rock that towers to one side of the port. Take the hiking path round it and you're taken away from the busy bars, restaurants and car parks that hog the territory behind.

To the south stretches Trébeurden's principal beach, the kilometre-long **Plage de Tresmeur**, set in its own well-protected bay, backed by lots of modern apartments, with villas further up. The spectacular **Pointe de Bihit** at the southern end takes you out of the sprawling resort. Follow the path to the end and you can walk onto a wonderfully wild, overgrown, low round headland. From here you get glorious views of the last coastal stretch of the Côtes d'Armor, and on good days you can see as far as Roscoff and the island of Batz in the Finistère. Under the tip of the Pointe de Bihit, **Porz Mabo** has a gorgeous long stretch of beach looking out onto the large bay of Lannion.

There are some more intimate beaches along the bay towards the Léguer estuary. You might go in search of the **Crique de Mez-an-Aod**, with its wonderful sandy shore, particularly appreciated by nudists who favour the northern end, or settle for the delightful **Plage de Goalagon**. At the headland of **Beg Léguer** you get enchanting views down onto the Léguer estuary. The town of Lannion lies inland on its banks.

Lannion and Around

A remarkably bustling town, Lannion grew prosperous thanks to its protected port tucked away up the Léguer River. The banks are busy with traffic, and the waters have been canalized, so it's not the prettiest scene, although the challenging canoeists' course to one side means that international professionals as well as locals come to test their skills here.

Up the eastern slope, you come to the smart historic parts of town. Thanks to its wealthy merchants, Lannion has a fine legacy of grand houses, particularly around the main square, the highly picturesque **Place du Général Leclerc**. Some of the buildings are tall timberframe numbers, others were built in chunky granite, while the most striking were clothed in tight-fitting slate. An impressive, if clichéd picture of a 19th-century French town hall marks one corner of the square. Below it you'll find the typical 19th-century covered market, still in active use. The main market square, **Place du Marchallac'h**, is a short walk up the hill from Place du Général Leclerc, and is similarly surrounded by old town houses. Many of the former merchants' homes have been turned into chic boutiques. They cater to the well-off workers in the high-tech industries that have settled in and around Lannion.

The main cultural attractions lie outside the centre – two beautiful churches set in a couple of old outlying villages now caught in Lannion's sprawling suburbs. You could in fact climb the 143 steps from the town centre to the **church of Brélévenez** on its hilltop, apparently fortified by a branch of the crusading-rich Knights Templar. The church dates in part from the 12th century, with fine Romanesque details. Very narrow stairs lead down to the crypt. For the **chapel and fountains of Loguivy-lès-Lannion**, cross to the west bank of the Léguer. Here, you enter a much quieter atmosphere. The double-fountained chapel in 15th-century Breton Flamboyant Gothic style is delightful.

Down the Léguer Valley

Head south out of Lannion down the D11 and the Léguer Valley to step into the deeply rural, inland Côtes d'Armor that so contrasts with the crowded coastal strip. A string of surprising chapels and châteaux line the way.

The **Chapelle de Kerfons**, discreetly hidden away on its chestnut-covered slope above the Léguer just southeast of Ploubezre, is one of those rural Breton chapels full of appealing elements. The most striking aspect inside is a late-15th-century rood screen, still in place, dividing the nave from the choir, decorated with swooping angels and cheeky monkeys as well as the apostles. The choir end is full of surprises. Some of the original 15th-century stained glass remains in place. Below, a rococo altar drips with little caryatid figures, pomegranates and pears. The pulpit too is extravagant. The tombs of the Marquise de Goulaine, who once owned the lands round and about, and her daughter, are to be found here. (Goulaine is a famous château in Muscadet country – see p.498.)

The **Château de Tonquédec** a short way south presents a spectacular, sturdy image of a medieval castle, its walls strengthened by enormous towers. These have lost their roofs and the walls have had to be much restored. A first château went up in the 13th century but was destroyed. The second, constructed for Guy de Coetmen, viscount of Tonquédec, was brought down by order of Duke Jean IV of Brittany in 1395. So the fort you see dates mainly from the 15th century; it was built for Roland IV de Coetmen, who went off to die on crusade. In the early 17th century, supporters of Marie de' Médicis, rebellious mother of the young King Louis XIII, took the castle. Once they had been defeated, Tonquédec was in good part demolished again.

The **Château de Kergrist** a little further south is sometimes open too. In contrast with the Château de Tonquédec, this castle hides timidly behind its wall, only a handful of pepperpot towers sticking out. The architecture is rather grand, the original 16th-century house much added to in the 18th and 19th centuries, though visits focus on the gardens and tearoom.

South again, branch off for the sleepy hamlet of **Les Sept Saints**. Its early 18th-century **chapel** contains a crypt made from a prehistoric dolmen. Images of seven early Christian saints, walled up alive for their beliefs, were found here; they have been reproduced as typical Breton statues above the altar.

The Coast to the Legendary Lieue de Grève

La Côte de Bruyère, or 'Heather Coast', is the tourist name given to the stretch of shore west of Lannion, and it gives an indication that nature still has the upper hand; the stunning series of dramatic, high promontories along here has proved unsuitable for holiday developments.

The village of **Le Yaudet**, set high above the southern end of the Léguer estuary, occupies a privileged position on its high promontory looking out over the sea. This great location was much appreciated by earlier civilizations. A panel in the village tries to point out where you can supposedly make out curious traces of mysterious prehistoric goings-on.

The charming **church** dates almost entirely from the 19th century, although it's in neo-Gothic style. It contains some admirably tacky Catholic kitsch, including a large figure of the Virgin with her baby Jesus, lying tucked up in a bed covered with lace. Eccentric literature in the chapel used to claim Celtic roots for this strange image of the recumbent Mary; actually it looks Spanish in its extravagance.

Le Yaudet would be delightful enough without trying to claim the additional distinction of being the site of Astérix's and Obélix's village. However, such a steep and awkward location goes against the cartoon evidence – close observation of Uderzo's drawings over the years suggests that the village of the indestructible Gauls was set down close to a beach, not on a promontory, we're sure serious historians will agree.

You can walk down and around Le Yaudet's steep promontory. The path isn't particularly easy, but you're rewarded with fine views for the effort. The port, really not much more than a jetty, is located on the eastern side. Most of the boats are left at anchor in the river.

The extremely steep street west from Le Yaudet takes you down to **Port Roux**, very prettily tucked behind a small sandy cove. Unless you're walking, you then have to leave the coast for a short distance to get to Locquémeau. Either way, head for the **Pointe du Dourven**. An atmospheric, shaded path of boulders and trees leads to a modern house, the **Domaine du Dourven** (*see* the page on *www.oddc22.com* for more details) where **contemporary art exhibitions** are often held. The setting alone, high above the sea, is tremendous, whatever your views of the presentations.

Locquémeau still has an active fishing port and a couple of pleasant sandy beaches, Notigou and Kiriou. At the western end, you reach the **Pointe de Séhar**. This extraordinary barren, flat peninsula is made up almost entirely of pebbles and boulders. The place has a messy charm, with a little port, a fish market, shops and cafés all breathing life into it. The houses are a hotchpotch, their gardens mostly made up of jumbled piles of stones.

The coastal path heads due south, along the **cliffs of Trédrez**, among the most impressively unspoilt in Brittany. If you're in your car, you can only rejoin the coastal path again around five kilometres to the south, so walk this sensational stretch if you can. Also visit the **village of Trédrez**. The place feels lost in the Breton countryside and in time. This was where Brittany's great saintly lawyer, Yves (*see* box, p.225), served as priest for a time in the 13th century. The pretty church you now see dates from the late 15th century to early 16th century, built in the distinctive so-called Beaumanoir Gothic gabled style.

The spit of land beyond Trédrez is the glorious **Beg ar Forn**. Cars have to be left well away from the coastal path high above the sea. Once on the coastguards' track, you can watch the waves sweeping in to crash against the cliffs stretching up to the Pointe de Séhar. Westwards, you can see across to the Locquirec peninsula in the Finistère. Turn the southern corner of the headland and the splendid protected bay of the Lieue de Grève comes into view.

Around the Lieue de Grève

Extremely steep country roads lead down to **St-Michel-en-Grève**, beautifully located on the eastern end of the Lieue de Grève. The church stands right above the beach, while the cemetery reaches out into the sensational bay. There are apparently traces of masonry from a couple of Roman baths in the cemetery wall. Rich Gallo-Romans appear to have appreciated this corner of Armorica, given the number of finds from the period that have been discovered along this stretch of coast. Today, St-Michel-en-Grève offers a lovely place to sit and contemplate the tides. The seawaters withdraw some two kilometres at their lowest ebb, the views stretching between four and five kilometres to the other side of the bay and the village of St-Efflam.

As a traveller or pilgrim arriving at the Lieue de Grève by foot or on horseback centuries ago, you had to time your crossing of the sands carefully. Horror stories have lingered of those caught out by the rising tide and its currents. For centuries, the **Croix de Mi-Lieue**, a cross planted in the middle of the bay, served as a marker indicating to voyagers when they could start out over the sands – if, when you arrived at the bay, the cross's base was clear of the water, it was fine to continue. As one expression had it, the journey would be safe as long as *la croix nous voit* ('the cross can see us').

Nowadays, you can follow the coast road along the back of the Lieue de Grève. A large rock here, the **Grand Rocher**, protrudes from the hills roughly in the middle of the curve. A dragon once lived within this great rock, local legend has it, a creature King Arthur himself came to fight (*see* box, p.242). After the Grand Rocher, a longish line of villas signals the start of the village of **St-Efflam**, a resort that has known more fashionable days. Look out into the bay from here, and you can clearly make out the dragon form of the Rocher Rouge with its spiky spine and tail.

On the façade of the modest whitewashed **chapel** tucked into the western side of the bay, statues in granite represent the Irishman St Efflam and his virginal wife, St Enora, figures from the 4th or 5th century. Efflam is said to have left Ireland just after they had got married to go abroad and proselytize; Enora apparently

Legends around the Lieue de Grève

St Efflam became heroically linked with legend, even Arthurian legend, in these parts. Different versions tell how the Irishman helped Arthur to slay the evil dragon terrorizing the area. One rather begrudging account gives only a small part of the action to Efflam. Arthur and the evil monster had been engaged in violent combat. The exhausted British king was running out of energy. Efflam came to the rescue, discovering a source of water to refresh Arthur. The noble warrior was able to take up the fight again and triumph, killing the dragon.

Other versions give Efflam more of the glory. For much of the Middle Ages, priors from the Mont St-Michel were given lands and rights around the Lieue de Grève. Some local priests were apparently incensed at this gift to the powerful Norman abbey, and waged a long campaign against the Norman presence. Local historians say that it was to rival the story of St Michael slaying the dragon that the local legend of St Efflam taking on his own beast grew in importance. The great 17th-century collector of Breton saints' lives, Albert Le Grand, recorded a version of the tale where Efflam ordered the dragon to drown itself in the sea, the mesmerized monster obeying his saintly word. A popular song embellished the tale, claiming that Efflam enchanted the beast by making it play to itself, morning, noon and night, music that would keep it forever captivated by its own tunes.

It's also said that the dragon guarded a great treasure in the Grand Rocher. This rock was supposed to open up just twice a year, in the time the bells rang for midnight signalling Christmas and Pentecost. As the bells fell silent, the rock closed up again. None of the men foolhardy enough to have ventured inside the rock in that all too brief interlude ever escaped to say what lay inside.

demonstrated saintly chastity in his absence. The elaborately domed fountain down from the chapel used to be said to have a power often associated with Breton springs – of telling girls when they were going to get married.

It's sobering to remember how the Lieue de Grève was affected by the Second World War. The Nazis mined the beach, destroyed many of the villas along the coast and built a great number of defensive blockhouses along the hills; these monstrosities are now quite well hidden by vegetation. The Germans were anxious that the bay might provide a favourable spot for an enemy landing. In the event, this did become the only place along the north Breton coast where an Allied landing took place in 1944. Today, a recurring problem that plagues the back of the bay in hot weather is the proliferation of green algae; although said not to be dangerous to humans, they can mar the beaches, and leave a stench at times.

Inland behind the Lieue de Grève, the village of **Ploumilliau** has strong links with the dark Breton legends of the Grim Reaper, l'Ankou in Breton (*see* box, opposite). It's renowned for its wooden statue of the much-feared fellow. This typically Breton figure is to be found in the Flamboyant Gothic church.

Château de Rosanbo
www.rosanbo.net,
t 02 96 35 18 77; open
July and Aug daily
11–6.30, April–June
and Sept daily 2–5,
Oct Sun 2–5

South of Ploumillau, the **Château de Rosanbo** sits aloof and alone above the calm Bo valley. A great driveway leads to the enormous round dovecot in front of the walled property; this outbuilding acts as a powerful reminder of the grandeur of the owners of the château under the Ancien Régime. Visiting the place, you learn of the very important network of aristocratic connections the family built up down the centuries, and how it became the seat of a

Anatole le Braz and Legends of *l'Ankou*, the Grim Reaper

Anatole Le Braz was one of the major figures in the late 19th century to write down Breton legends previously only passed down by word of mouth. His father had come to teach at Ploumilliau in the 1860s, and the young Anatole's imagination was fired by tales he heard. His classic book, *La Légende de la Mort*, collected together Breton legends associated with death, and in particular with l'Ankou, the Grim Reaper, who pays his chilling visit on those about to die.

One of the stories in *La Légende de la Mort* is set in Ploumilliau itself. One Christmas Eve, the blacksmith Fanch ar Floc'h was still busy at work. He preferred to carry on working rather than attend midnight mass. He told his wife and children to go without him. His wife asked him to show some Christian respect, and at least to stop working by the time the Host was lifted in the church for the congregation's adoration. But Fanch forgot. Before the service was over, there was a knock at his workshop door. A tall man in a wide-brimmed hat stood in the doorway. 'I have the most urgent of services to ask of you,' the man declared. He showed Fanch his scythe, whose blade was turned outwards. 'It just needs a nail put in it,' the stranger explained. Fanch obliged, repairing the scythe. 'I will not pay you for your trouble', the tall stranger said by way of thanks, 'but I will only give you a warning. Go to bed right now, and when your wife returns, tell her to fetch the priest. The work you have just done for me is the last you will do in your life.' Fanch's wife returned home with the children to find her husband in agony. As the cock crowed at dawn, Fanch passed away. Of course such christianized stories reveal the way the Church manipulated folk tales to put psychological and moral pressure on the Breton people, and to instill fear in their hearts.

marquis. Despite the Marquis de Rosanbo at the end of the Ancien Régime going to the guillotine, the present owners can trace the family line back some 1,000 years, and once again carry the title. The buildings date mainly from the 17th and 18th centuries, but the interiors you see are dominated by the 19th-century neo-Gothic style. In 1910, the landscape designer Achille Duchêne was called upon to redesign the gardens, and you can enjoy their shaded alleys and long romantic arbours.

An autumn organ festival of Baroque music is held at **Lanvellec**, the village closest to the château, to show off the restored mid-17th-century instrument in the church. It was made by Robert Dallam and is a copy of the one in King's College, Cambridge.

Back close to the Lieue de Grève, **Plestin-les-Grèves** serves as the market town for the bay. Due north of it, the coast road follows the fairly built-up peninsula of Plestin round to the Côtes d'Armor's border with the Finistère. The site of the vestiges of the Gallo-Roman **Thermes du Hogolo** shows how the wealthy knew how to locate their baths far back in time. The **Douron estuary** divides the two counties, its sandy sides lined by turreted properties. The hamlet stretching along the estuary has a sweet chapel; tempting *crêperies* encourage you to stop to drink in the picturesque scene.

Thermes du Hogolo
free access

Market Days between Trégastel and Plestin-les-Grèves

Ile Grande: Thursday

Trébeurden: Tuesday
Lannion: Thursday
St-Michel-en-Grève: Monday
Ploumilliau: Saturday
Plestin-les-Grèves: Sunday

(i) **Trébeurden** ›
Place de Crech-Héry,
t 02 96 23 51 64,
www.trebeurden.fr

(★) **Ti al Lannec** ›

(★) **Manoir de
Kerguéréon
B&B** ››

(★) **Manoir de
Lan Kérellec** ›

(i) **Pleumeur-
Bodou**
11 rue des Chardons,
t 02 96 23 91 47,
*www.pleumeur-
bodou.com*

(★) **L'Ancien
Presbytère B&B** ››

(i) **Plestin-les-
Grèves/Lieue
de Grève**
Place de la Mairie,
t 02 96 35 61 93,
*www.officetourisme-
delalieuedegreve.com*

(i) **Lannion** ›
2 Quai d'Aiguillon,
t 02 96 46 41 00,
www.ot-lannion.fr

Where to Stay and Eat between Trégastel and Plestin-les-Grèves

Trébeurden ✉ 22560

****Ti al Lannec, 14 Allée de Mezo Guen, **t** 02 96 15 01 01, *www.tiallannec. com* (€€€€€–€€€€). A hotel lording it over the sea, with characterful rooms, luxury sea-water spa treatments, and terraces set among gardens. It has a great restaurant (€€), a choice of bars and salons. *Closed mid-Nov–Feb.*

***Manoir de Lan Kérellec, **t** 02 96 15 00 00, *www.lankerellec.com* (€€€€€–€€€€). A 19th-century manor on the heights, with luxurious rooms with sea views, and super bathrooms with maritime touches. The splendid luxury restaurant (€€€€; *closed lunches Mon-Thurs*) resembles the interior of a ship and serves delicate Breton dishes. The grounds include a tennis court and a plush terrace. *Closed mid-Nov–early March.*

Ker An Nod, 2 Rue de Pors Termen, **t 02 96 23 50 21, *www.kerannod.com* (€). A hotel in a perfect location to enjoy the sunsets, with a restaurant making the most of the views thanks to its wide bay windows. The rooms are small but neatly presented, many with sea views.

Ile Millau Gîtes, reserve via the Trébeurden tourist office (**t** 02 96 23 51 64, *www.trebeurden.fr*) (€€). The rugged little crofters' cottages on this tiny isle have been turned into cosy hide-outs. Only accessible at low tide.

Servel ✉ 22300

Manoir de Crec'h Goulifern, Route de Beg Léguer, **t** 02 96 47 26 17 (€€–€). Cosy rooms in a typical Breton home southeast of Pleumeur-Bodou, about 3km from the beach, with menhirs as well as tennis courts to hand.

Lannion ✉ 22300

Le Serpolet, 1 Rue Félix Le Dantec, **t** 02 96 46 50 23 (€€). Good food served in a quirky dining room with a fireplace. *Closed Sat lunch, Sun eve and Mon.*

Le Tire-Bouchon, 8 Rue de Keriavily, **t** 02 96 37 10 43 (€€–€). Pleasing Breton fare at this address in the historic centre.

Rospez ✉ 22300

La Ville Blanche, Route Lannion–Tréguier, **t** 02 96 37 04 28 (€€€€–€€). Delicious, fine French cuisine, enhanced by produce from the herb garden, just east of Lannion. *Closed Sun eve and Mon, and Wed exc July–Aug.*

Ploubezre ✉ 22300

Manoir de Kerguéréon B&B, **t** 02 96 38 80 59, *www.chateaux-france.com* (€€). Two rustically luxurious rooms up the spiral staircase in this atmospheric Breton manor.

Tonquédec ✉ 22140

Le Queffiou B&B, **t** 02 96 35 84 50, *lequeffiou.free.fr* (€€). Spacious, individually styled rooms and bathrooms in a slate-roofed house with a large garden.

Douau Ha Mor, 4 Rue du Général de Gaulle, Cavan (east of Tonquédec), **t** 02 96 35 89 99 (€€). A rustic restaurant serving good food in an ivy-covered old house.

Trégrom ✉ 22420

L'Ancien Presbytère B&B, Plouaret, **t** 02 96 47 94 15, *tregrom.monsite@ wanadoo.fr* (€). Enchanting B&B opposite the church, with charming rooms. Walled garden and pool in the orchard. *Table d'hôte* available (€€). *Closed Oct–Feb.*

Le Yaudet ✉ 22300

Ar Vro, **t 02 96 46 48 80 (€). In the village, a hotel with old-style rooms, but an excellent regional restaurant.

Trédrez ✉ 22300

Auberge St-Erwan, 6 Rue des Fontaines, **t** 02 96 35 72 51 (€€–€). A wonderfully rustic inn serving crêpes and grilled meats.

St-Michel-en-Grève ✉ 22300

Hôtel de la Plage, 1 Place de l'Eglise, **t 02 96 35 74 43, *www.hoteldela plage.be* (€). Good-value rooms, many with wonderful views across the bay. The restaurant does summer BBQs.

Au Bon Accueil, Landebouch, Ploumilliau, **t 02 96 35 74 11, *www. aubonaccueil-ploumillau.fr* (€). Simple country-style rooms and excellent seafood.

Finistère

The most Breton of Brittany's départements, the Finistère (or Penn ar Bed – 'End of the Earth' – in Breton) spans the sensational western tip of the region. The countless kilometres of sandy and rocky coasts along three of its four sides are guarded by some of the tallest lighthouses in Europe. Grittily picturesque ports and boulder-surrounded resorts from Roscoff to St-Guénolé face the waves full on in these dramatic parts. Others, like Brest and Douarnenez, or Quimper and Concarneau, hide at the back of bays, or far up river estuaries. Out to sea lie the feared, legend-filled islands of Ushant and Sein, although Batz and Les Glénans offer calmer havens. Along the Finistère's gentler southern shores, Gauguin was famously inspired by Pont-Aven.

Head inland to avoid the tourist maelstrom. Here, enchanting Breton openwork steeples mark the countryside with their delicate silhouettes, set above the Elorn and Aulne valleys, or against the atmospheric hills of the Monts d'Arrée and Montagnes Noires. The majority of the elaborate Breton calvaries are to be found here, while the Breton language clings on tenaciously in parts.

09

Don't miss

⭐ **Wind-battered islands**
Ouessant, Batz, Sein and Les Glénans p.278

⭐ **An enchanting corsairs' den**
Morlaix and its Bay p.254

⭐ **A legend-steeped bay and magical cliffs**
Douarnenez and Crozon p.320

⭐ **Wonderful spires, ceramics and museums**
Quimper p.328

⭐ **Shocking art**
Pont-Aven p.366

See map overleaf

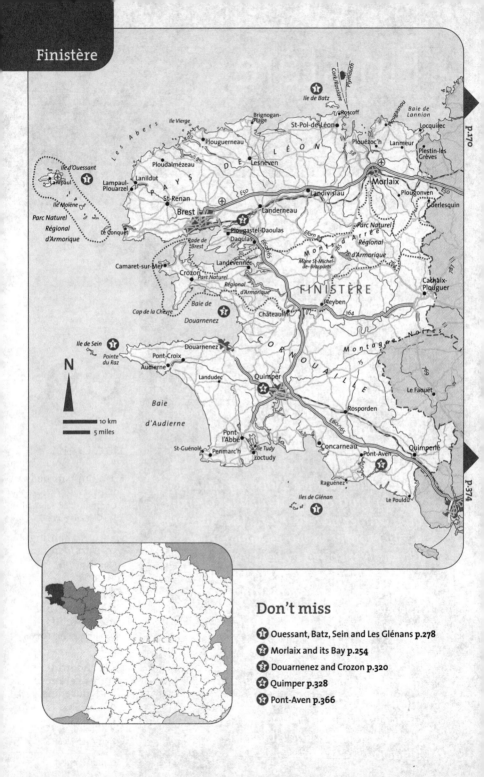

Don't miss

- Ouessant, Batz, Sein and Les Glénans **p.278**
- Morlaix and its Bay **p.254**
- Douarnenez and Crozon **p.320**
- Quimper **p.328**
- Pont-Aven **p.366**

ⓘ Comité Départmental du Tourisme du Finistère
4 Rue du 19 Mars 1962, 29018 Quimper Cedex, t 02 98 76 20 70, www.finisteretourisme. com. The first port of call for tourist information of all kinds on the whole of Finistère; also offers holiday packages and short-break ideas on www.finistere-resa.com; to plan trips on public transport around the Finistère, see www.via0029.fr

Huge lighthouses, including the tallest one in Europe, warn stray vessels away from the exceptionally rocky coast of northern Finistère, traditionally known as the Léon. While waves of people migrated here from the British Isles in the Dark Ages, the area's mariners through the Middle Ages and Ancien Régime were often involved in terrible battles with the English. Now, happily, Roscoff, surely the most picturesque ferry port in France, greets visitors from the north with open arms.

Two splendid historic towns deserve your attention just south of Roscoff: St-Pol-de-Léon with its soaring spires proudly showing off its religious legacy, and mercantile Morlaix hiding its riches down an estuary guarded by the formidable Château du Taureau. In recent times, the enchanting resorts of Locquirec and Carentec have grown up in the sandier spots close by. The Léon coast west from Roscoff is known as the Côte des Légendes, its confusion of rocks inspiring fantasy and fables, although small resorts have found footholds here too. Algae-coated reefs dominate, turning the corner to the deep river estuaries of the *abers*.

Heading down the Finistère's west coast, the wild archipelago of Ouessant (or Ushant), feared by shipping, but beloved of tourists, comes into view at the French entrance to the Channel. Naval Brest, by contrast, lies in an almost cowardly location, protected from the enemy and the rough Atlantic by a splendidly calm bay known as the Rade de Brest. That didn't stop the Second World War bombardments, but the modern city that reemerged is much more enticing than you might imagine. Inland, cloth-making brought prosperity to the Elorn Valley for centuries, so the communities put up showy churches and remarkable stone calvaries – the last, like elaborate outdoor pulpits, tell Christ's story in caricatural scenes.

The hills of the rugged Monts d'Arrée and of the more wooded Montagnes Noires separate the Léon from Cornouaille, or southern Finistère. The exposed slopes of the Monts d'Arrée have a fine sprinkling of unspoilt villages, plus centres devoted to the flora and fauna, including one on wolves, creatures that once roamed freely here.

The Monts d'Arrée form part of the swathe of central Finistère protected as the Parc Naturel Régional d'Armorique. This exceptionally beautiful park stretches westwards to take in the Crozon Peninsula and Ouessant. The Presqu'île de Crozon offers the most dramatic scenery of all in the Finistère. Staggering cliffs defy the Atlantic along its western shore. In contrast, the Aulne meanders its way gently to the Presqu'île from central Finistère, backed by the Montagnes Noires – quiet hills rather than great peaks. Journey up the Aulne, and it feels like a journey back in Breton time.

09 Finistère

Southern Finistère has vibrant Quimper as its capital. This very Breton city by the Odet, known for its soaring cathedral spires, its ceramics and its Breton celebrations, is also administrative capital of the Finistère. Close to the perfectly preserved village of Locronan, the Cornouaille coast begins in the northwest with the soothing Bay of Douarnenez, although the disturbing legend of the drowned city of Ys haunts these parts. The Pointe du Raz beyond is considered France's Land's End, looking out to the mysterious island of Sein, seemingly always in danger of being swamped by the sea.

South from the Pointe du Raz, you can sweep down the ocean-exposed curve of the Baie d'Audierne, which ends with one of the longest beaches in Europe, although the thundering waves aren't conducive to swimming. The southwestern tip of Cornouaille is guarded by notoriously savage rocks which feature large in one of Chaucer's *Canterbury Tales*, yet a whole string of fishing ports have tucked themselves into the coast here and are still thriving on their *langoustine* trade.

At Loctudy, the southern Finistère coast becomes much more gentle, the soft, sandy beaches greatly appreciated by families. The gorgeous, wooded river estuaries – here known as *avens* rather than *abers* – famously attracted artists before the yachtsmen arrived. Even the major fishing port of Concarneau, prettified by its fortified island turned enchanting tourist trap, boasts a huge marina. As to Pont-Aven, it's the victim of its international renown, but head inland into the cider-making countryside, for example around quaint Quimperlé, and you can find more tranquil spots.

The Trégor Finistérien: Locquirec to Morlaix

Locquirec has all the ingredients of a chic Breton coastal resort to tempt you into savouring it a while: bars and restaurants packed close together on **Place du Port**, all looking out onto the beautifully clear waters of the well-protected harbour and bay; a picturesque **church** just behind, proposing longer-term protection to those with faith, plus some amusing elements to entertain the casual passer-by, most noticeably the statue of a saint perched up by the steeple, like a boy playing a dangerous prank; a couple of galleries for those who've sold out to Mammon, or at least the art and antiques dealers; a couple of hotels right by the action; and **beaches** facing both east and west. At the port, lined by magnolias mimicking sun umbrellas, the shy little beach is washed twice daily

Getting to and around the Trégor Finistérien

The nearest **railway** station is at Morlaix, with TGV connections; then get local buses.

right behind the ears by the tides. Even the waterside tourist office here sells tasteful art and books, as well as dispensing advice. The rougher, tougher beach west round Locquirec's dramatic headland is a particular joy for surfers, overseen by the odd grand villa on the slopes above.

You can only get round Locquirec's headland on foot, and the best way to appreciate the series of dramatic, **unspoilt points** plunging into the sea west of the resort all the way to Plougasnou is to go hiking along the **Sentier Côtier**, although the beautiful **corniche road** is provided with some car parks which allow drivers to stop and appreciate the stunning views too. There is just the odd rather pebbly beach along the way, that of **Poul-Rodou** boasting the delightful surprise of a café-cum-bookshop, Caplan et Co.

Otherwise, the steep slopes plunge from on high into the sea, their sides densely covered with broom, bracken and heather. The best known headland along here, **Beg ar Fri**, also has brambles along the final stretch to its tip, blackberries the reward for reaching it in late summer. The views stretch right across the Baie de Lannion in the east, while as you continue westwards, the Roscoff peninsula and the Ile de Batz appear dramatically on the horizon.

Just inland, the village of **Christ** – not the only one in the Finistère to carry this rather vain-sounding name – has been completely renovating its chapel. A bit futher inland, on the edge of **Lanmeur**, the **chapel of Notre-Dame de Kernitron** reveals its Romanesque roots with its stocky frame and a typical doorway decorated with the symbols of the Evangelists surrounding Christ. What is possibly a much older piece of Christian architecture lies below the mainly reconstructed central **village church**. Here, disturbing, fat serpentine forms in stone writhe around the pillars of the crypt. Evil feels to hand. The saintly 6th-century nobleman Mélor is said to have been buried here after being hounded to death by his evil uncle Rivod.

Back by the coast, the pretty old village of **St-Jean-du-Doigt** lies in a flat dip in the cliffs, behind a pebbly beach. In fact, the very elegant **church** tower seems to be sticking its long neck out above the houses in a desperate bid to get a glimpse of the sea. It certainly draws attention to itself. Up close, it's very charming too, its stone enclosure, reached through an elaborately carved gate, containing a plethora of tombs and crosses, but also the surprise of a grand Renaissance fountain. The curious name of the place, St John of the Finger, derives from the fact – or could it be the fiction? – that a crusading lord of the Middle Ages returned from afar with

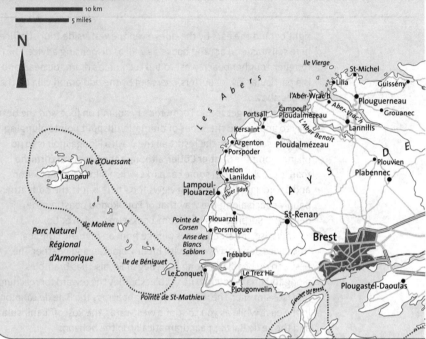

what he thought was a rather famous digit, said to have belonged to none other than John the Baptist himself. The miraculous healing properties attributed to this dubious *doigt* long drew droves of sick pilgrims to the *pardon*, held here on 23 and 24 June.

North of the village of **Plougasnou**, you return to a coast of crazy, chaotic, captivating rock formations. You also return to more built-up slopes, many lovely villas sprouting up in these rather magical parts. At the slightly unkempt little resort of **Primel-Trégastel**, it's quite a demanding walk just clambering over the small but dramatic headland of the **Pointe de Primel** with its bobbly granite rock formations. A customs cottage was added at the top in Napoleonic times, but as early as the Bronze and Iron Ages, men had already enhanced the natural fortifications here, turning the headland into an *éperon barré* (a barricaded spur). You can go diving, canoeing or even sand-yachting at Primel.

The next little resort, **Le Diben**, is enchanting, the entrance to its port surrounded by clumps and bouquets of boulders. This is the best place from which to embark on a sea **voyage to the Château du Taureau**, a staggering island fort in the Bay of Morlaix (*see* p.252). Otherwise there are plenty of pleasure boats here, and a

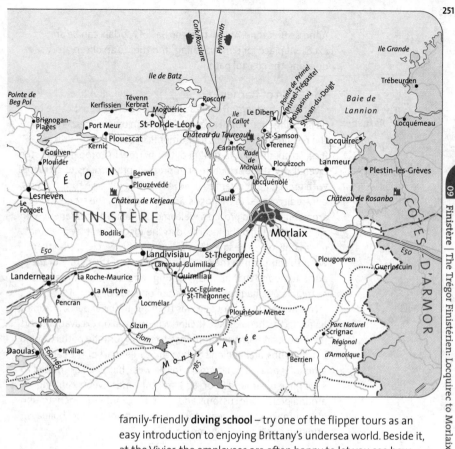

family-friendly **diving school** – try one of the flipper tours as an easy introduction to enjoying Brittany's undersea world. Beside it, at the Vivier, the employees are often happy to let you see how shellfish, lobsters and the like are handled before delivery onto the restaurant plate.

Turning the coastal corner, the large beach of **St-Samson** is overlooked by a pretty chapel. Well-protected **Terenez** has superb views on to Barnenez's spit of land and the spectacular Château du Taureau. Tucked away from the rough seas, the tranquil little **Bay of Terenez** looks mirror-like on calm days. On its western side, between two lovely traditional old hamlets, the lower one of the two with oyster farms on the water's edge and an appealing crêperie-cum-oyster bar, stands one of the largest neolithic burial mounds ever unearthed (*see* below).

Continuing down the **Rade de Morlaix**, views of the oyster parks and the Château du Taureau add to the natural beauty. The prettiest route takes you through Plouézoc'h and past the lovely little port of **Le Dourduff**. This spot, next to the excellent natural harbour in front of Morlaix, is where one of the most famous ships of medieval Brittany, *La Cordelière*, was built, by order of Duchess

Anne de Bretagne. At low tide, the Bay of Morlaix can be an excellent place for bird-watching, and there's an observatory set up along the coastal path.

The Cairn of Barnenez

The Cairn of Barnenez
check relevant website page on www.monuments-nationaux.fr for opening times across year; guided visits summer daily at 10.15 and 11.15, and between 2.15 and 5.45

Neolithic builders often had an aesthetic eye when it came to positioning their burial sites, and the cairn of Barnenez is one of the best located neolithic monuments in the whole of Brittany. It's also possibly the largest neolithic barrow in Europe, a vast, step-layered, dry-stone structure of impressive proportions, constructed with great care. It's hard to believe that this massive tumulus was only rediscovered in the 1950s, and by accident. The stones amassed here had proved a welcome find to an entrepreneur with a contract to build the local road in the 1950s. The story goes that it was only when he failed to pay some of his workers, who then went to complain to the local authorities, that the nature of the ancient mound that he was wrecking came to light. By that point a sizeable bite had been taken out of one side of the cairn.

This highly significant site was then left to the experts, including respected archaeologist P. R. Giot, who worked on excavations and restoration at Barnenez from 1955 to 1968. From the pottery found in the tombs, archaeologists date the earlier part of the cairn to around 4500 BC. The later part, to the west, has been estimated to have gone up around 4000 BC. In recent times, events centring around prehistoric customs and ways, for example demonstrations of tool-making, have been staged here in various school holidays, bringing neolithic society more to life.

The Château du Taureau

The Château du Taureau
book via Morlaix Chamber of Commerce, t 02 98 62 29 73, www.chateaudu taureau.com; depending on tides and programmes, you can take the boat either from Carentec (15 mins trip), or from the port of Le Diben (45 min trip)

The Rade, or Bay, of Morlaix is strewn with viciously beautiful rocky islands, some unsettlingly resembling sinking ships, as though by way of warning. It's hard to find a clear channel through to the town of Morlaix, hidden down its river estuary. But in 1522, English troops seeking revenge for the devastating attacks on the English coast led by local man Jean Coatanlem snuck through to wreak devastation.

The Morlaisien were left terribly shaken by this traumatic event, and decided extra protection was needed in addition to the bay's natural defences. A strategic island was chosen to become the town's fortified outpost. It was called L'Ile au Taureau, or Bull Island, although no one quite remembers how it got this name, whether it was for the shape of the original rock, or maybe through a deformation of a Breton word for a hillock.

In time, the island's defences became more elaborate. A major round keep was added early in the 17th century, as you can still see, but virtually all the rest dates from after the 1680s, when Vauban came to inspect Brittany's coastal defences for Louis XIV. He drew up amazing plans for a horse-shoe-shaped fort making use of the entire island. His protégé Garangeau would somewhat modify the forms, but the result was a superbly conceived island defence with excellent amenities for men, provisions, arms and, of course, gunpowder.

However, the formidable place would never serve in battle, as warring moved on. Instead, the crown turned it into an out-of-the-way prison – in the first instance, for degenerate young aristocratic men, their distraught families paying for them to be locked up out of harm's way for a time; then, at the Revolution, for recalcitrant types, especially priests, before they were sent to the galleys or the gallows; and after that for political prisoners.

The military authorities tired of looking after the isolated fort at the end of the 19th century. A posh Parisian family, the Vilmorins, turned it into an eccentric holiday bolt hole to escape the beau monde in the 1930s, then it served as a magical sailing school for several decades, before being abandoned in the 1980s, as it was proving too difficult to maintain. The town of Morlaix recently took up the challenge, aided by the state, to restore the place. For the most magical trip to this magnificent site, definitely take the longer boat journey from Le Diben. You're only allowed one hour to visit the exceptional fort, either following an interesting guided tour, or exploring the chambers yourself – explanatory panels fill you in on relevant themes. The views from the terraces up top are grandiose and memorable.

ⓘ Pays Touristique de Morlaix
www.tourisme. morlaix.fr; general tourist info on the coast from Locquirece to Carantec, as well as inland around Morlaix

ⓘ Locquirec ›
Place du Port, t 02 98 67 40 83, www. locquirec.com

⭐ Le Grand Hôtel des Bains ›

Market Days in the Trégor Finistérien

Locquirec: Wednesday

Where to Stay and Eat in the Trégor Finistérien

Locquirec ✉ 29241

***Le Grand Hôtel des Bains, 15 bis Rue de l'Eglise, t 02 98 67 41 02, www.grand-hotel-des-bains.com (€€€€). A joy of a hotel in front of the church, with exclusive grounds going right down to the sea. Some bedrooms have splendid terraces. Half board obligatory in high season. Heated indoor pool, plus spa treatments. The stylish restaurant (€€€–€€) offers dinner only.

L'Hôtel du Port, 5 Place du Port, t 02 98 67 42 10 (€). In prime location, by port and beach. Old-fashioned rooms in need of renovation, but they've got fabulous views at bargain price. The restaurant terrace (€€–€); (closed Tues and Wed, exc July and Aug) gives you a ringside seat on the summer bustle. The food is classic Breton seaside fare. There are many other simple restaurants with terraces around the port. Closed mid Nov–Feb.

Caplan & Co, Poul Rodou beach, 29620 Guimaêc, t 02 98 67 58 98 (€). Atmospheric literary café in lovely location just above a wild beach west of Locquirec, serving light salads as well as literature. Closed Sun–Fri in winter.

St-Samson ✉ 29630

**Roc'h Velen, t 02 98 72 30 58, *www.hotelrochvelen.fr* (€). A good-value option, a little hotel in a good location just 200m from the sea.

Plouézoc'h/Le Dourduff ✉ 29252

Café du Port, on Le Dourduff's port (€). A nice place with a terrace close to the water where you can enjoy local oysters and mussels.

Inland to Morlaix and Around

Morlaix

Morlaix and its Bay

Morlaix bridges the medieval counties of the Trégor and the Léon. Tucked out of sight from the sea down its deep river estuary, the town became one of the great havens for Breton corsairs, as well as a major trading port. Its extraordinary theatricality comes from the massive arches of the 19th-century viaduct that dominate the centre.

History

English alliances and enmities profoundly marked the history of Morlaix. In the Breton War of Succession, the town supported the French claimant Charles de Blois. But the English-backed de Montforts won the battle for the duchy and most unpopularly stationed English troops here, leading to a revolt. The Morlaix corsair Jean Coatanlem crossed the Channel to create havoc among the Bristol fleet at the end of the 15th century and even plundered the city once. A few decades later, the English under King Henry VIII took their revenge; English sailors mounted a surprise attack on Morlaix in 1522, finding a time when the town was poorly defended, and wrought widespread destruction, even if the local tale to try and gloss over the horror says that many of the English attackers were punished for their greed, slaughtered as they became slowed down by all the booty they were carrying. It was after this calamitous incident that the town decided to build the outer defence of the Château du Taureau on an island to the north (*see* above).

In the terrible 16th-century French Wars of Religion, Morlaix became one of the last strongholds of the ultra-Catholic Ligueurs under the fanatical Breton leader Mercoeur. King Henri IV's Marshal d'Aumont, supported by English troops, laid siege to the Ligueurs, who had eventually to give in, Spanish support for them having failed to materialize. The castle of Morlaix was then destroyed.

From the 14th to the 17th centuries Morlaix's merchants thrived in particular on exporting Breton cloth. Trade with the Iberian peninsula was particularly lucrative, and it may be that Morlaix's

Getting to Morlaix

Fast TGV **trains** between Paris and Brest stop regularly at Morlaix. There are useful **bus** services between Morlaix and the ferry port of Roscoff nearby.

distinctive *maisons à lanterne* derived certain features from the typical Spanish house built around a patio.

In the mid-18th century, Charles Cornic of Morlaix became one of the great scourges of the British at sea. Less reprehensibly perhaps, Tristan Corbière, the son of a local 19th-century ship's captain, developed into a notorious avant-garde poet of the 19th century. With his black but humorous ways and verse, the Morlaix fishermen of his day nicknamed him *l'Ankou*, the Breton Grim Reaper.

The year 1863 saw the building of the impressive viaduct. It survived attempts by RAF bombers to cut off the German route to the west during the Second World War. Central Morlaix looks so bourgeois today that it's hard to associate it with some of the most violent farmers' demonstrations in Brittany of the past decades. Most memorably, in 1961, Alexis Gourvennec, fiery leader of the Breton farmers, led the occupation of the town's administrative buildings.

A Tour of Morlaix

Viaduct
open July–Aug daily; free

Start a visit to Morlaix in the shadow of the great **viaduct**. Under it you'll find car parks and the tourist office. In high summer, climb up from the valley and you can go on an exhilirating walk through the monumental arches. From on high, enjoy the drama of the architecture and the views down on to the centre of town and the port.

Coming down off the viaduct, **Rue Ange de Guernisac** passes behind the grand Flamboyant Gothic **church of St-Melaine**. The slate-covered and timberframe sides of the houses give the street great appeal. Picturesque alleyways known as *venelles* lead up the slopes from here. Continuing along Rue Ange de Guernisac you come to Place des Viarmes, and a little beyond, to **Place des Jacobins**.

Here, a major former medieval monastery dominates the scene. These 13th- and 14th-century religious buildings were long home to a Dominican community. The place welcomed both Anne de Bretagne and Mary Queen of Scots – the latter passed through Morlaix as a girl in 1548, on her way to join the French court on the Loire. Of greater consequence for Breton culture, the monk Albert Le Grand studied here in the early 17th century. His book on the life of the Breton saints, *La Vie des saints en Bretagne*, became a bestseller across the province for centuries, a crucial book for the

Musée de Morlaix
*www.musee.ville.
morlaix.fr, t 02 98 88 68
88; open July and Aug
daily 10–12.30 and
2–6.30; April, May and
Sept Mon and Wed–Sat,
plus Sun pm, 10–12 and
2–6; June, and
Oct–March Mon
and Wed–Sat 2–5*

**Maison de
Pondalez**
*run by the Musée
de Morlaix; open
same times*

**Maison de la
Duchesse Anne**
*open April–Sept
Mon–Sat; call t 02 98
88 23 26 for times*

A Fer et à Flots
*www.aferaflots.org,
t 02 98 62 07 52;
outings mainly
summer weekends*

Breton psyche. Much abused from the Revolution on, the monastic buildings were at one stage even turned into stables. Some time ago parts of it were transformed into the **Musée de Morlaix**, which puts on changing exhibitions through the year, while elements of the Gothic architecture are a permanent highlight.

Wandering along the main shopping drag, the **Grand'Rue**, look upwards to see how the old houses lean right in towards one another. No.9, the **Maison de Pondalez**, is a grand 16th-century *maison à lanterne* that has been renovated to a high standard. The exteriors of these extraordinary houses may look typically French, the most wonderful examples of late-Gothic fancy, with their elaborate, highly entertaining wood carvings. Inside, though, things look more unusual. These homes centre around a cavernous central space which stretches way up to the roof. This is really like a covered patio, only provided with a monumental fireplace and staircase, and is the main feature of the *maisons à lanterne* – the inner courtyard was traditionally covered by an opaque roof from which a lantern was hung to give added light to the silo-sized room, hence the name. The Maison de Pondalez displays many historic riches from Morlaix, including goldsmiths' elaborate works.

Head over to the nearby sizeable **Place Allende** and you can visit another remarkable *maison à lanterne*, the **Maison de la Duchesse Anne**. This famous house may be in need of love and attention, but look closely at the carvings and you'll be engrossed. You can make out numerous figures on the façade, including saints and archetypal Gothic figures, such as the jester, the wild man, or the mad mother. The interior details are impressive too. The courtyard staircase opens out in very bold fashion. A guide once described it to me as being *en décolleté* – it takes a French person to describe a staircase as having a pretty cleavage.

A little south through town, there are many intriguing artistic curiosities to admire at the **Eglise St-Mathieu**, including the exterior carvings in stone, and an amazingly ornate statue of the Virgin within, who opens up to reveal a host of figures she's been protecting for centuries under her skirts. Make the steep climb nearby to the meagre castle ruins on **Square du Château** for a splendid view over the historic town crammed into its valley.

Wandering back in the direction of the viaduct, maybe stop at a café to sample Coreff, the locally brewed bitter. North, at the **river port** and quays, the splendid 18th-century **Manufacture de Tabac**, designed by royal architect Jacques François Blondel, oversees the many yachts moored here, giving a grand look to the area. Cigars were manufactured in the building up to the end of the 20th century. Now, the place contains an art gallery, among other things. For an enjoyable round trip by water and rail from Morlaix to L'Ile de Batz and back, contact **A Fer et à Flots**.

Les Jardins de Suscinio
open most school hols; t 02 98 72 05 85 *for times*

Les Jardins de Suscinio, a botanical garden set round a 17th-century château in the Suscinio area on the Ploujean hillside a few kilometres from the centre, presents plants that follow the trail of the famous corsair Cornic. Children may be more excited by the new **Espace Aquatique**, a state-or-the-art indoor pool complex that has recently opened just south of town.

East of Morlaix

East of Morlaix, you enter a much quieter, slower world than the bustling coastal strip. At the sleepy little town of **Plouigneau**, they've recently created the Ecomusée de la Métairie which recalls old country ways in these parts with extensive displays of objects, well laid out in the buildings set around the courtyard of a farm located practically at the centre of the *bourg*. In the area, farming has been thriving up to recent times, and although many farmers are now abandoning the profession, you can still see lots of dairy herds round these parts.

Ecomusée de la Métairie
www.ecomusee.ploui gneau.fr, t 02 98 79 85 80; *open April–Oct daily exc Sat 10–12 and 2–6*

North of Plouigneau, the village of **Plouégat-Guérand** feels set in a filmic time-warp, the broad, plain, main street spreading out below the fine **church**. The latter, set in its enclosure, has two lovely hunting dogs guarding its main entrance, while the south porch is packed with charming religious decorations, the words of the angels above the Annunciation scene mysteriously painted backwards.

Heading a little south of Plouigneau to **Plougonven**, the Monts d'Arrée hills form a painterly backdrop of ridges. The **church** is relatively unknown, although it has a major 16th-century **calvary** on which scenes from Christ's Passion are dramatically sculpted. The church itself is from earlier in the century, topped by a typical steeple.

Directly east, gorgeous **Guerlesquin**'s historic centre basically consists of one extremely elongated, sloping square divided up by various important buildings along the way. Beyond a pompous bust of a now-forgotten 19th-century Breton bard and the big mistake of a modern rainbow fountain, the 17th-century **Présidial** (*often open*) surely ranks among the prettiest prisons ever built, with its cute corner towers. Then comes the imposing arcaded 19th-century **covered market**, followed by the enchanting **church**, its Breton rose window in the choir best viewed from **Place du Champ de Bataille**, once the local training ground to prepare against English invasion, now a delightful flower garden with Breton fountain and a statue of a music player.

Southwest of Plougonven, following the pretty course of the Queffleuth River, you arrive at **Le Relec** (*see* p.300).

Market Days in and around Morlaix

Morlaix: Saturday
Plougonven: Tuesday
Guerlesquin: Monday

Where to Stay and Eat in and around Morlaix

(i) **Morlaix >**
Place des Otages,
t 02 98 62 14 94,
www.morlaix
tourisme.fr

(★) **Manoir de Roch Ar Brini B&B >>**

(★) **La Grange de Coatélan B&B >>**

(★) **Manoir de Coat Amour B&B >**

(i) **Guerlesquin >>**
t 02 98 72 84 20
(summer) or 02 98 72 81
79, www.guerlesquin.fr

Morlaix ✉ 29600

Hôtel de l'Europe, 1 Rue d'Aiguillon, t 02 98 62 11 99, *www.hotel-europe-com.fr* (€€€–€€). The most stylish option in the centre, with quite smart, sober bedrooms. The **Brasserie de l'Europe next door has a modern split-level design and a teak-tinted basement bar; the cuisine here is modern and good.

**Le Port, 3 Quai de Léon, t 02 98 88 07 54 (€€–€). A comfortable modern choice up the quays, although the road outside can be a bit noisy.

Manoir de Coat Amour B&B, Rue de Paris, t 02 98 88 57 02, *www.gites-morlaix.com* (€€). Fine 19th-century house on the heights with elegant rooms. Run by Brits. *Table d'hôte* (€€€).

La Marée Bleue, 3 Rampe St-Melaine, t 02 98 63 24 21 (€€€–€€). A warm, cosy, tranquil restaurant offering well-prepared seafood in refined surroundings. *Closed Sun eve and Mon.*

La Reine Anne, 45 Rue de la Mer, t 02 98 88 08 29 (€€). Really good traditional Breton fare in a central restaurant with terrace. *Closed Sun eve, Mon, and Wed eve.*

Les Bains Douches, 45 Allée du Poan Ben, t 02 98 63 83 83 (€€). Eccentrically located in the former public baths,

providing French bistro fare. *Closed Sun, Mon and Sat eves.*

Crêperie L'Hermine, 35 Rue Ange de Guernisac, t 02 98 88 10 91 (€). A rustic, very pretty place for traditional crêpes, plus algae fillings.

Crêperie du Kiosque, 11 Place des Otages, t 02 98 88 41 40 (€). A quite sophisticated, central place preparing crêpes the old-fashioned way.

Le Tempo, Quai de Tréguier, t 02 98 63 29 11 (€). With a terrace looking onto the river port, good spot for a salad or simple food. *Closed Sat and Sun.*

Ploujean ✉ 29600

Manoir de Roch Ar Brini B&B, t 02 98 72 01 44, *www.brittanyguesthouse.com* (€€). Exceptional B&B rooms in a grand stone villa 3km from the town, built in the 1840s for Edouard Corbière, father of famed local poet Tristan Corbière.

Plougonven ✉ 29640

La Grange de Coatélan B&B, t 02 98 72 60 16 (€€). A lovingly converted 16th-century farm in a peaceful setting, with attractive B&B rooms in the outbuildings. *Table d'hôte* (€€).

Plouégat-Moysan ✉ 29650

Le Puits de Jeanne, Voie Romaine Le Ponthou-Plouegat, t 02 98 79 20 15. Lovely country inn serving traditional Breton dishes. (€€). Ring in advance to check if serving; outside of Aug, mainly open weekends only.

Guerlesquin ✉ 29650

**Les Monts d'Arrée, 14 Rue du Docteur Quéré, t 02 98 72 80 44 (€). A provincial village hotel, but it has some charm. Rooms are simple, the menus (€€–€) quite imaginative.

Crêperie du Martray, t 02 98 72 83 21 (€). Nice option for tasty crêpes.

The Haut-Léon via Roscoff

Coming to Brittany from Ireland or southwest England, you may well land in the Haut-Léon, at the gorgeously rocky and lively Roscoff, protected by the unspoilt island of Batz. The great religious figure of the area, St Pol Aurélien (St Paul Aurelian), got here early, coming from Wales to spread the gospel to these parts in the 6th century, and is still very much remembered in the towering-spired

Getting to and around the Haut-Léon

Ferries from Plymouth, Cork and Rosslare arrive at Roscoff – *see* Planning Your Trip chapter for ferry companies. Roscoff and St-Pol-de-Léon have railway stations and frequent **trains** to Morlaix, where you can join the fast TGV network. **Buses** run regularly between Roscoff, St-Pol-de-Léon and Morlaix.

little city of St-Pol-de-Léon. The name Léon, by the way, is thought to derive from Caerleon in south Wales.

The Carantec Peninsula

A short distance northwest of Morlaix, the village of **Locquénolé** is full of charm, with a little *enclos paroissial* to go with its Romanesque church. Its natural harbour looks across to the small port of Le Dourduff on the other side.

Carantec was 'discovered' by posh tourists at the start of the 20th century and has remained one of the most exclusive resorts on the Finistère's north coast. It has many glamourous sides to it, with a splendid array of **beaches**, notably the central **Kelenn**, backed by tempting restaurant with terraces. Exclusive villas line the lanes along the headland of **Penn-al-Lann**, around which you can venture down to wilder beaches. The views over the rock-strewn seas are enchanting. This side of the resort, there's also a 9-hole **golf course**, just separated from the sea by a beach. As to the **Centre Nautique**, it offers a host of activities through the year, including sea kayaking. One particular delight at Carantec is simply walking north at low tide over to the **Ile Callot** to appreciate its sandy creeks and little chapel.

The resort has a small **Musée Maritime**. Across the road, an exhibition space focuses on the work of Ernest Sibiril, a local shipbuilder who, during the Occupation, risked his life operating a number of dreadfully difficult passages for French volunteers and Allied pilots.

Carantec golf course
*t 02 98 67 09 14,
www.golfde
carantec.com*

Carantec Centre Nautique
*t 02 98 67 01 12,
www.carantec-
nautisme.com*

Musée Maritime
*open daily mid-
June–mid-Sept, plus
Easter hols 10.30–12
and 2.30–6*

St-Pol-de-Léon

Behind the Léon coastline, wide, flat vegetable fields dominate the scene, prettified by surprisingly comely artichokes, cabbages and cauliflowers in season. Amid the fertile plains, the staggering spires of St-Pol-de-Léon can be seen from afar, clearly signalling what an important religious centre this once was. The religious roots go back to the Dark Ages, at least, and the great Welsh evangelist, St Pol (*see* box, p.260).

During the Middle Ages the town became one of the major stops on the Tro Breizh, the great Breton pilgrimage route. Only with the Revolution did St-Pol-de-Léon lose its important religious status as the centre of a diocese. The last bishop, Jean-François de la Marche,

St Pol, a Founding Father of Celtic Christian Brittany

St Pol is considered to have been one of the seven founding saints of Celtic Christian Brittany in the Dark Ages. The story goes that he was born in Wales in the late 5th century, became the pupil of the great St Ildut and then went to serve King Marc'h at his Cornish court in Tintagel. But he headed off to convert non-believers abroad to Celtic Christianity.

It's said he set sail for Armorica around 512, landing first on the Island of Ouessant (Ushant). There he met with strong resistance from the inhabitants. He quickly left, going off to found a monastery on the island of Batz above Roscoff, where he triumphed over the local dragon. On the invitation of the local lord Withur, he then crossed to the mainland to help the people there – the place having just been devastated by raiders. Pol gave the community the impetus to rebuild their settlement and Kastell-Paol soon flourished. It became the seat of Pol's bishopric, the diocese seemingly founded at the end of the 520s.

also happened to be the last count of Léon. St-Pol's harbour of Pempoul was extremely active down the centuries too... until it silted up and the port had to be moved north.

The two main churches in St-Pol-de-Léon contrast markedly in style, although both were inspired by Norman buildings. The Gothic **cathedral** was strongly influenced by the cathedral of Coutances on the Cherbourg Peninsula. It went up painfully slowly, building work on the nave and aisles lasting through the 13th and 14th centuries, the side chapels and choir completed in the course of the 15th and 16th centuries. The stone employed within came from Caen in Normandy, in contrast to the Breton granite used on the outside. The long nave with its pointed Gothic arches and decoration has a sober simplicity. Saint Pol's tomb lies in front of the main altar, while you can seek out his supposed skull in a reliquary in one of the aisles, plus a miraculous bell that legend says a fish carried away from King Marc'h's court in Cornwall when Pol left there. The great organ was the work of Robert Dallam, who also made the one in King's College, Cambridge.

D'une légèreté inquiétante ('of a worrying lightness') wrote Breton art historian Victor-Henry Debidour of the sensational steeple of the **Chapelle Notre-Dame du Kreisker**. This rocketing feat definitely tries to steal the show from the cathedral. From a distance, its defiant arrow, more than 75 metres in height, does eclipse the bishops' church. It was apparently commissioned out of pride by Léonard merchants, not the Church. For some time the town council used to meet here. Not surprisingly, Notre-Dame du Kreisker looks rather top-heavy from close up. Some of it was built in the 14th century, but the flamboyance of 15th-century Gothic triumphs. The tower was added between 1439 and 1472, following the model of that at St-Pierre de Caen. It's held in place by the massive pillars of the crossing. You can climb nearly 170 steps up to the viewing gallery.

Several of the streets around these dominating religious buildings contain some splendid houses, many from the 16th and

Maison Prébendale
t 02 98 69 01 69,
www.laprebendale.fr;
open July–Aug
Tues–Sun 3–7;
Sept–June Wed and
Fri–Sun 2–6; free

17th centuries. One canon's house, the **Maison Prébendale**, with its remarkable showy stairtower, has been turned into an exhibition space, featuring contemporary artists. Except on market days, the calm little city of St-Pol-de-Léon can seem to lack soul, or at least the bustling spiritual and commercial activity it must have once enjoyed. The life of the area is today concentrated in Roscoff.

Roscoff

trou de flibustiers, vieux nid de corsaires (buccaneers' hideout, corsairs' den)

Tristan Corbière, 19th-century local poet

Don't be put off by Corbière's description – Roscoff makes a deeply attractive tourist stop nowadays. The modern ferry port lies east of the old harbour town. Central Roscoff is a delight, although it's somewhat chaotic at the best of times and gets extremely busy during the summer months. It makes rather too much play of its pirating past to be healthy, you might think, but it's now well geared to meeting the needs of the very many English-speaking visitors. The place also pays homage to its cross-Channel onion sellers, the so-called Breton 'Johnnies'.

History

The silver sailing ships crossing blue waters depicted on the arms of Roscoff recall the times before ferries became the main shipping interest of this port. The shipowners, corsairs and smugglers of Roscoff were engaged in a centuries-long struggle with the English. In the course of medieval conflicts, one lord of Arundel came and destroyed much of the town in the 14th century. In the early 15th century, the Amiral de Penhouët set out from here to fight the English navy. Through the Ancien Régime, Roscoff corsairs sailed off to join in the battle for control of the seas that raged between France and England. England wasn't the only party Roscoff regularly feuded with – its merchants often entered into conflict with the bishops of St-Pol-de-Léon, who tried to impose their authority over the port.

On a more positive diplomatic note, Roscoff is where Mary Queen of Scots landed in 1548, coming over as a child bride to the French court. Many of Roscoff's merchants prospered on honest trade down the centuries, dealing with the Hanseatic League, Flanders and the Iberian peninsula in particular. Tragi-comically, in 1746 Bonnie Prince Charlie, Young Pretender to the English throne, landed here, having escaped from England disguised as 'Betty Burke', supposedly Flora Macdonald's maid.

The serious onion-selling to Britain began relatively early in the 19th century, and local men continued to head across the Channel to sell door-to-door from their bikes until well after the Second World War. Since the setting up of the European Union, the Breton vegetable producers have become much more highly organized. They first created a cooperative to market their produce, and after that it was in large part due to them that Brittany Ferries was established in 1972, quickly becoming a successful shipping enterprise. The deep-water port to the east of old Roscoff came into existence in 1973, leaving the historic port to the fishing fleet and to yachts.

A Tour of Roscoff

The merry steeple of **Notre-Dame de Kroaz Batz** looks as if it's built up out of stone bells. The graceful openwork forms of the many levels of Renaissance lanterns cheerfully mark the Roscoff skyline. The rest of the church's architecture, completed in 1548, is in Flamboyant Gothic style. Roscoff shipowners contributed considerable amounts to the construction, which probably explains why carvings of sailing vessels were permitted in the stone. These were executed as *ex votos*, to thank God for sparing a ship. Around the church, the grand granite houses of the 16th and 17th centuries, often with stylish dormer windows, reflect the prosperity of some of Roscoff's merchants.

One of the joys of visiting Roscoff is promenading up and down the quays of the **old port**, so often full of life, thanks to the fishing fleet, the boats setting out for the island of Batz, and the holiday yachts. The protective sea walls stick out at odd angles into the port, like strange tentacles. Fishing is still thriving here, with large numbers of vessels making the most of Roscoff's proximity to rich grounds – crab is a particular speciality. You can visit the **Criée**, where the catch is sorted and sold, a guide talking you through the elaborate processes. Ask at the tourist office about signing on for this special tour, and the possibility of going out on a fishing trip. A walk east along the harbour takes you to the **Pointe de Bloscon**, with its tiny **Chapelle Ste-Barbe**, whitewashed to double as a seamark for boats.

Thalado
www.thalado.fr,
t 02 98 69 77 05; open
Mon–Sat 9–12 and 2–7

Maison des Johnnies
t 02 98 61 25 48; open mid-June–mid-Sept daily exc Sat 10–12 and 3–6; if closed ask at tourist office

Head west along the seafront to reach **Thalado**, where you can learn a lot about Brittany's 800 different types of algae. As well as the slide show and tour, the place organizes special algae nature walks, and even puts on algae gastronomic events – seaweed is featuring more and more in Breton cuisine.

As to the **Maison des Johnnies**, on Rue Brizeux at the entrance to the town centre, it's dedicated to a sweet story of entente cordiale. It tells how the local onion sellers crossed the Channel from Roscoff, getting on their *vélos* to make a living purveying their vegetables on British doorsteps – and helping to maintain that favourite English image of the bereted Frenchman cyling around in his stripy top, garlands of onions around his neck. Since this is a happpy tale of Breton–British cooperation, you'll find plenty of elements in English, and many amusing details.

Algoplus
www.algoplus-
roscoff.fr, **t** 02 98 61 14
14; open shop hours

As you approach the ferry terminal, you come to **Algoplus**, a manufacturer of algae products offering a guided tour, during which you learn about how algae are harvested and transformed, plus tastings.

**Jardin Exotique
de Roscoff**
www.jardinexotique
roscoff.com, **t** 02 98 61
29 19; open July and
Aug daily 10–7;
April–June and
Sept–Oct daily
10.30–12.30 and
2–6; Nov and
March daily 2–5

Roscoff, like the island of Batz, has its own exotic garden making the most of the temperate climate. The **Jardin Exotique de Roscoff** is located east of town, near the ferry terminal, and looks out over the spectacular Bay of Morlaix. Even palm trees, cacti and plants from the southern hemisphere prosper here. The major development in these parts will be the building of a major new marina below the Jardin Exotique in the coming years – completion expected around 2011.

Ile de Batz

As Breton islands go, Batz has remained mainly agricultural and relatively unspoilt by tourism. The whole island is less than four kilometres long and around a kilometre and a half wide, so you can walk around the coastal path in three to four hours. While early Christian teaching may have thrived for some time on the island, frequent Viking attacks seem to have put paid to the monastery. Fishing and farming were the main activities for the islanders for countless centuries, along with the production of seaweed fertilizer – you'll notice that the stuff is scarcely lacking in these rocky waters. The lighthouse marking the western end of the island went up in the middle of the 19th century, in a period when Batz's port became relatively busy. Electricity came reasonably early to the island, in 1938, but the inhabitants had to wait as late as 1970 to receive fresh piped water.

A Tour of the Island

The main **village** stretches round the large **Baie de Kernoc'h**. Plots of vegetables still keep their place among the houses. There are some lovely gardens here, with such exotic plants as cacti, agapanthus and echium growing in profusion, as well as a fair number of trees such as tamarisks and palms. The 19th-century church contains a statue of St Pol (*see* boxes, p.260 and p.264), as well as a piece of cloth once claimed to have been Pol's stole, and said to have come in handy in helping him drag the island's dangerous dragon to its death.

Getting to the Ile de Batz

Three **ferry** companies run boats to Batz: **Armein**, t 02 98 61 77 75, *www.armein.fr*; **Armor Excursions**, t 02 98 61 79 66, *www.vedettes.armor.ile.de.batz.fr*; and **CFTM**, t 02 98 61 78 87, *www.vedettes-ile-de-batz.com*. A spectacular crescent of a footbridge leads across to the embarcation point; the sea crossing only takes *c.*15mins.

Jardin Delaselle
t 02 98 61 75 65; open July–Aug daily 1–6.30; April–June and Sept–Nov daily exc Tues 2–6

It's a pretty walk to the southeastern tip of the island and the **Jardin Delaselle**. After he had fallen in love with the spot and decided to convert it into a garden in the late 1890s, Georges Delaselle had an artificial string of dunes dug to protect it. In the process, many mysterious old tombs were discovered. Then Delaselle imported all manner of exotic species from the colonies, and palms in particular – more than 40 species of that tree are nurtured here. It seems extraordinary that in such a windy, salty environment so many exotic plants survive, but this part of the Breton coast remains fairly mild year round. The ruins of the **Chapelle Ste-Anne**, also in the east, are the remains of a Romanesque building from around the 10th century. They may stand on the site of Pol's original monastery.

Batz's best-known **beaches**, the Grève Blanche and the Porz Mellok, lie not far off, on the northeastern side of the island. Their sand is sometimes likened to flour, it's so white and fine. Further north, things get rockier and much wilder. Ships were sometimes torn to pieces on the sharp reefs just out to sea, the wreckage often landing here. The **western side** of Batz is dominated by the **lighthouse** (*contact tourist office for opening times*), not actually on the shore, but inland. You can climb it to get a stunning view of the whole island and the Léon coast. The **Trou de Serpent** recalls where Dark Ages hero Pol supposedly finished off the dragon of Batz (*see box, below*).

Along the Artichoke Coast

West of Roscoff, the **beach of Le Dossen** is a favourite among sand-yachters. At low tides, a causeway makes it possible to go for a magical walk out to the private **island of Sieck** just to the north.

Pol the Dragon-Slayer

When Pol arrived on the island of Batz from Ouessant, he was quickly adopted by the populace. If the claims are to be believed, he immediately set about miraculously curing three blind people, two mutes and one paralytic. The legend goes that the local lord also asked Pol if he could help fight off the dragon on Batz, which had been indiscriminately devouring livestock and people. Donning his religious ceremonial clothes and accompanied by an armed warrior, Pol went off to see what he could do. The dragon was perhaps mesmerized by the glorious religious finery, submitting straight away to Pol's will; the holy man then tied his stole like a lead around the dragon's neck, took it to the rocky shore and ordered it to jump into the foaming waters. The dragon obediently followed Christian orders and plunged to its death. Pol then set about establishing his monastery on the island.

Across the Quillec River, embark on a curious trip along the **artichoke coast** between Sibiril to Plouescat. Vegetables grow among strange rocks, almost right up to the sea. Further bizarre rock formations lie out to sea. At times, the proprietors of the Château de Kérouzeré will show you round their picturesque medieval fort close to the sea just above Sibiril. The tiny port of **Moguériec** is beautifully located on the western side of the Quillec estuary.

Château de Kérouzeré
open certain days mid-May–Oct; check on t 02 98 29 96 05

Continue along the coast to the enticing beach of **Tévenn Kerbrat**, as well as **Kerfissien**, with a series of creeks along the way. More beaches have found a spot among the rocks along the coast between Poulfoen and the Bay of Kernic. Those to the west at **Pors Meur and Pors Guen** prove particularly attractive. Pors Guen is home to the area's main **Centre Nautique**, offering all manner of watersports possibilities. The area around the **Baie de Kernic** is a favourite with sandyachters and volleyball players. All these beaches lie a short distance from the little resort of **Plouescat**, with its 16th-century covered market.

Centre Nautique de Plouescat
www.plouescat-nautisme.net; t 02 98 69 63 25

West of Plouescat, sensational wild sandy dunes stretch to the Grève de Goulven, strewn with huge dollops of granite. A section of them was donated to the Conservatoire du Littoral, official guardian of the French coasts, which has opened a **Maison des Dunes at Keremma**, explaining the formation and action of the dunes. Already back in the 16th century, great quantities of sand were on the march, pushed westwards by the prevailing winds. In the period that followed, many of the old coastal field-divides were eradicated; when an almighty storm struck in 1666, the sands where pushed inland without obstacle, accelerating the natural phenomenon of dune formation along this stretch of Léon coast. The Maison organizes nature walks, and has a boutique and cafeteria. Lining the road behind the cordon of dunes, the glorious thick, towering pines help stabilize the earth.

Maison des Dunes at Keremma
www.maisondesdunes.org, t 02 98 61 69 69; *open July–Aug daily exc Sat 10.30–6; Sept–June Sun programme of events*

Château de Kerjean and St-Vougay

The **Château de Kerjean**, the grandest pre-Revolutionary castle of the Léon, set on a fine estate, lies south of Plouescat, just below St-Vougay. Superb alleys of towering beeches surround it. A bulging dovecot gives you some notion of the former importance of the Kerjean lords' estates. A gibbet still stands in one corner close to the château.

This substantial home was built for Louis Barbier in the second half of the 16th century. Although this was the period of the French Renaissance, bringing new refinement to French architecture, as can be seen here, Kerjean was also clearly built with an eye to defence. The French Wars of Religion would, after all, be raging through the period of its construction. The château suffered

Château de Kerjean
www.chateau-de-kerjean.com, t 02 98 69 93 69; *open July and Aug daily 10–7; April–June and Sept–Oct daily exc Tues 2–6; Nov–Dec Wed and Sun 2–5*

considerably in the ensuing centuries. Early in the 18th century, a fire destroyed part of it, while during the Revolution the place was pillaged and the widowed owner, Mme de Coëtanscourt, sent to Brest to get the chop.

The place still looks impressive, built around a spacious courtyard, two wings coming off the main lord's quarters. Unfortunately, this central section was partially destroyed by fire, hence the skeletal look up top, with just the frames of aristocratic windows reaching out above the walls. The château contains a permanent collection of Léonard furniture from down the centuries, although the items don't have the grandeur you might expect for a castle – many were in fact rescued from local farms. You can wander round the massive, cold, stone rooms looking at the snug box beds that remained popular across Brittany for so long, or at the chests in which Bretons stored linen and provisions. Wardrobes became fashionable around the mid-17th century, and a tradition arose for well-to-do families to give prettily carved ones to newlyweds. Apparently the ordinary people of the parish were allowed to attend services in the ornate **chapel** before the Revolution, but the lord's family had its private oratory. The beams here are carved with angels, dragons and figures of the Evangelists.

The château puts on interesting temporary **exhibitions** in one of the renovated wings, covering a wide range of themes relating to the château and its period, and it hosts an extensive **cultural programme**, going from concerts to theatrical evenings.

Parc Animalier La Ferme d'Eden
www.ferme-eden.fr,
t 02 98 29 55 80

A few kilometres away, the **Parc Animalier La Ferme d'Eden** makes for a jolly excursion for families with young children, as here you can walk around among a large array of friendly farmyard animals. At the little restaurant, you can sample Breton fare and Breton teas.

Market Days in the Haut-Léon

Carantec: Thursday
St-Pol-de-Léon: Tuesday
Roscoff: Wednesday
Plouescat: Saturday

ⓘ Carantec >
4 Rue Pasteur,
t 02 98 67 00 43,
www.carantec-tourisme.com

★ Hôtel de Carantec >

Where to Stay and Eat in the Haut-Léon

Carantec ✉ 29660

★★★Hôtel de Carantec, Rue du Kelenn, t 02 98 67 00 47, *www.hotel decarantec.com* (€€€€). Enchanting hotel next to the beach at Kelenn, with 12 excellent rooms, five with terraces. The views are stunning. The fabulous restaurant (€€€€) offers daring dishes, such as red mullet cake with Léon raspberries. There's a garden, too.

Manoir de Kervezec B&B, Kervezec, c.1.5km from Carantec, **t** 02 98 67 00 26, *www.manoirdekervezec.com* (€€–€). Relatively simple, sober rooms in a grand 19th-century villa. The grounds, home to llamas as well as horses, look over the Bay of Roscoff.

Le Cabestan, at the port, **t** 02 98 67 01 87 (€€€). In a romantic spot by the port, offering brasserie-style classic French dishes. *Closed Tues, and Mon out of season.*

Pays Touristique du Léon
www.payduleon.com. Information on the area from Roscoff south

St-Pol-de-Léon ›
Place de l'Evêché, t 02 98 69 05 69, www.saintpoldeleon.fr

⭐ **L'Ecume des Jours** ››

⭐ **Les Alizés** ››

ⓘ **Roscoff** ›
46 Rue Gambetta, t 02 98 61 12 13, www.roscoff-tourisme.com

⭐ **Le Brittany** ›

⭐ **Le Temps de Vivre** ›

ⓘ **Ile de Batz** ››
25 Rue de la Plage, t 02 98 61 75 70, www.iledebatz.com

⭐ **Ty Va Zadou** ››

⭐ **Hôtel du Centre – Chez Janie** ›

La Chaise du Curé, 3 Place de la République, t 02 98 78 33 27 (€€). A restaurant in the centre, offering a selection of traditional Breton food in a family atmosphere.

Plouzévédé ✉ 29440
Hôtel des Voyageurs, 1 Rue de St-Sol, t 02 98 69 96 84, voyageurs.berven @wanadoo.fr (€). A charming old Breton house with small but nicely done rooms at excellent price. The traditional Breton restaurant is also recommended (€€).

St-Pol-de-Léon ✉ 29250
**France, 29 Rue des Minimes, t 02 98 29 14 14, www.hoteldefrancebretagne. com (€€–€). Set in a historic building, with well-priced, comfortable, often spacious bedrooms giving on to the courtyard or the pretty shaded garden.

La Pomme d'Api, 49 Rue Verderel, t 02 98 69 04 36 (€€€€–€€€). A restaurant in an old Breton house, with refined décor and excellent regional food, such as melting artichoke hearts.

Dans la Grand' Rue, Rue du Général Leclerc, t 02 98 19 16 24 (€€–€). Really good fresh French fare served in this new restaurant in the heart of town.

Roscoff ✉ 29680
***Le Brittany, 22 Boulevard Ste-Barbe, t 02 98 69 70 78, www.hotel-brittany.com (€€€€–€€€). A wonderfully located stone manor on the old port water's edge, with very comfortable rooms, many with sea views, some in a modern annexe. The cuisine (€€€€€) is extravagant and adventurous, such as John Dory served in a blue cheese sauce. Heated, covered pool.

***Le Temps de Vivre, 19 Place Lacaze Duthiers, t 02 98 19 33 19, www. letempsdevivre.net (€€€€€–€€€€). An excellent address in an old corsair's house, many of the sleek contemporary rooms with sea views. In the restaurant (€€€€€), you'll find luxurious, inventive dishes on the menus, for example spider crab galette with fresh vegetables and foie gras.

**Hôtel du Centre – Chez Janie, 5 Rue Gambetta, t 02 98 61 24 25,

www.chezjanie.com (€€). In another fine old stone house in a great location right by the old port, its rooms redone in most appealing contemporary style.

**Les Tamaris, 49 Rue Edouard Corbière, t 02 98 61 22 99, www.hotel-aux-tamaris.com (€€–€). Really good 2-star, a welcoming address well located by the sea, some of the bright rooms looking out to Batz.

**Talabardon, 27 Place Lacaze-Duthiers, t 02 98 61 24 95, www. talabardon.com (€€€€–€€€). Comfortable, set in an imposing 19th-century stone building, some of the refurbished rooms looking onto the sea, others onto the church square. The restaurant (€€€€–€€€) has panoramic views.

**La Résidence, 14 Rue des Johnnies, t 02 98 69 74 85 (€€–€). With recently refurbished rooms, a jolly, good-value address. Closed Dec–Jan.

L'Ecume des Jours, Quai d'Auxerre, t 02 98 61 22 83 (€€€). Utterly delightful restaurant serving fine food in a 16th-century house looking out to sea. Terrace too. Closed Sept–June, Wed lunch, and Wed eve out of season.

Les Alizés, Quai d'Auxerre, t 02 98 69 75 90 (€€€€–€€). Top-notch cuisine, including perfectly cooked fish, plus a magnificent view to sea from its stylish modern dining room.

Le Surcouf, 14 Rue de l'Amiral Réveilière, t 02 98 69 71 89 (€€–€). Worth visiting for its good-value seafood menus. Closed Tues, and Wed Oct–June.

Crêperie de la Poste, 12 Rue Gambetta, t 02 98 69 72 81 (€). With appealing rustic décor.

Crêperie Ti Saozon, 30 Rue Gambetta, t 02 98 69 70 89 (€). Very small, but very popular, as it offers interesting fillings such as artichoke hearts with cream of seaweed. Closed lunch.

Ile de Batz ✉ 29253
Roch Armor, t 02 98 61 78 28 (€). A cheerful, old-style, basic option with bargain-priced rooms with views on to the sea.

Ty Va Zadou, (right just before the village church), t 02 98 61 76 91 (€). The most delightful place to stay on the island, with lovely views from the fresh first-floor bedrooms.

Le Bigorneau Langoureux, t 02 98 61 74 50 (€). Adorable bistro by the port, with outdoor terrace, but an interior packed with atmosphere too.

Crêperie La Cassonade, t 02 98 61 75 25 (€). A lovely spot for a crêpe, again by the port.

Plouescat ✉ 29430

Le Bistrot des Halles, Place des Halles, **t** 02 98 69 88 66 (€€–€). A pretty

restaurant with courtyard terrace, serving good regional dishes.

St-Vougay ✉ 29225

Crêperie du Château, Kerfao, **t** 02 98 69 93 09 (€). Good crêpes in a restored farmhouse near the Château de Kerjean.

Porz Meur ✉ 29430

Roc'h-ar-Mor, t 02 98 69 63 01 (€€). A very basic but well-located hotel, its restaurant offering simple, decent seafood and a glorious spot to catch the sunset.

The Pays des Abers and Pays d'Iroise

Brittany's most northwesterly corner is known for its strong Breton roots and legends, and for its seaweed, which thrives on the particularly rocky strip of coast here. Towering lighthouses try to warn off stray ships from the reefs on which the algae thrive, but they haven't always been successful: the sinking of the oil tanker the *Amoco Cadiz* here was one of the greatest ecological disasters in Europe in the 20th century. The *abers*, the atmospheric river estuaries along this stretch, make deep little cuts into the land.

The Mer d'Iroise is the name for the stretch of sea where the Channel and the Atlantic merge off the Breton coast. Along this invigorating stretch, the Pointe du Corsen boasts of being the closest point in mainland France to North America; the viewing table helpfully records that New York lies a mere 5,080 kilometres away. Most visitors simply settle for a short trip from the port of Le Conquet to the virtually treeless archipelago of Molène, which includes Ouessant, the savagely beautiful island of Ushant – the waters around here, with their crazy rocks and choppy seas, have time and again proved fatal for ships, but holiday-makers don't seem to be put off. Directly south of Le Conquet, the Pointe de St-Mathieu counts among the most famous of the major westerly peninsulas in Brittany. It marks the northern entrance to the huge, calm bay concealing the superbly located port of Brest.

The Pays Pagan

Before you hit the more exposed coasts, seek out a couple of sheltered corners east of the Abers themselves. **Goulven** is a little village hidden away behind a vast bay, but there's nothing modest about its **church**'s massive Flamboyant Gothic steeple. This contrasts comically with the building's second, ridiculously small steeple, over the crossing. The major one, erected over the entrance porch, is a towering achievement from 1593, if completely out of proportion to the building below it.

Getting around the Pays des Abers

Bus services loop around these areas from Brest.

At the western end of the **Baie de Goulven**, vast stretches of firm sand are left stranded at low tide, allowing the sand-yachters to come out to play, flitting around at breakneck speed. The beach of **Plounéour-Trez** is particularly renowned for the sport.

Continuing westwards, the shore becomes increasingly otherworldly, with a fantastical array of massive rocks that seem to have landed from outer space. The resort of **Brignogan-Plages** curves round a horseshoe-shaped bay full of unruly boulders. Further formations come out at low tide as the seawater retreats. A few too many rather uninspiring buildings have gone up at Brignogan itself.

To the north and west of Brignogan, the splendid **beaches of Les Chardons Bleus** and **Ménéham** are particularly worth seeking out. Between these two, take a look at the massive **Menhir Men Marz** (or Miracle Stone), abandoned by the roadside. It looks like some monumental nose that has slipped off the face of a colossal statue.

Nearby, the **Chapelle Pol** is almost swamped by enormous boulders. From here, marked coastal paths take you past **Pontusval** and its **lighthouse**, surrounded by a ring of fierce-looking rocks.

The exceptional old hamlet of **Ménéham** above Kerlouan was set up amid the dunes and boulders as a coast guards' and customs officers' settlement in the 18th century, these officials later joined by fishermen and algae farmers. Gradually abandoned, the whole place was bought up by a property developer after the war, but the locals who remained had the place listed to stop modern developments. The Conservatoire du Littoral stepped in, and now Ménéham has been restored and at the time of writing, the whole place was set to relive. The **Maison du Site** (*to open school hols*) will welcome visitors with its short films on Ménéham, together with temporary exhibitions. The **guards' house** set between the rocks has been turned over to a permanent exhibition on coastal forts. The remarkable **Maison Salou** with its characteristic lean-to will now be a museum recalling the hamlet's history. Even the inn, L'Auberge de Ménéham, has been re-thatched and restored. West of here, yet more boulders stack up along the coast round to **Guissény**.

Lesneven and Le Folgoët

Musée du Léon
open May–Sept Mon 2–7, Tue–Sun 10–12 and 2–7; Oct–April Mon 2–7, Tue–Fri 10–12 and 2–7

Inland, Lesneven isn't a touristy town, but it is proud of its history as administrative capital of the Léon and houses a fairly interesting historical museum, the **Musée du Léon**, in a former Ursuline convent. The main magnet for visitors, though, is the imposing **Basilique du Folgoët**, which looks out of place on the southwestern

An Extraordinary Horticultural Happening Gives Birth to a Church

The simpleton Salaun lived in these parts in the middle of the 14th century, while the Breton War of Succession was bringing misery to Brittany. He's said only ever to have learnt to speak a few words, but he became obsessed by the Virgin and the singing of her praises. He went around proclaiming her name all the time, all over the place – while he ate his bread, while he bathed in the fountain, even when he climbed trees, a favourite pastime of his. The villagers merely looked on him as a madman. But after his death a curious lily arose near where he was buried, and the sweet-smelling plant supposedly grew to spell out the name of the Virgin. This was taken to be a miracle of considerable significance, and news of the extraordinary horticultural happening travelled across Brittany faster than a bramble spreads its roots. Local churchmen decided to try to track down the source of the mysterious plant, and discovered that it had grown from the dead Salaun's mouth, which they took as a sign of God's joy in the madman's naïve piety.

outskirts of town, lording it over a modest village. This Flamboyant Gothic monster of a pilgrimage church was constructed roughly from the 1420s to the 1460s in honour of the Virgin Mary... and the piety of a local village idiot – Folgoët means Madman of the Wood in Breton (*see* box, above).

The two west towers contrast markedly with each other, just one given a typically soaring Léon spire. The plentiful details around the outside of the church are absorbing, especially the statues. One of the most important art historical facts at Le Folgoët is that it was here, for one of the first times in the province, that Breton stone sculptors started to use the peculiarly dark granite of Kersanton for their works, which stand out curiously against the lighter granite used for the buildings.

Look around the ornate doorways to appreciate the wealth of sculptural decoration. Over the main entrance you can make out scenes from Christ's Nativity, including the lively arrival of the Three Kings. The Virgin is shown naked-breasted, a surprisingly unprudish representation for the Catholic Church. In the Pietà scene of the calvary, Christ had his head chopped off just like so many French nobles. Look out for the image of the Breton St Yves, typically shown standing between the rich man and the poor man, or for the depiction of a medieval warrior holding a sceptre and a book. The last may be meant to portray Breton Duke Jean V – a Latin inscription on the west porch recognizes him as the founder of Le Folgoët. The most moving figure of all is that of the *Mater dolorosa*, the mother of Christ shown in her grief, her thick tears carved in stone.

The interior has been heavily restored – the place served as a barracks and for pigsties at the Revolution. Some decorative features stand out, notably the rood screen. Most such Breton screens were carved out of wood; this one is made from stone, but it looks remarkably light and elegant, a model of Flamboyant Gothic style. The choir, virtually cut off from the rest of the church, is graced by the elegant tracery of a rose window.

On the green outside the basilica, some picturesque old buildings stand to one side. One of them, a former hostel for pilgrims, contains the little **Musée de la Basilique et de la Piété Populaire**, focusing on Breton popular religious faith, fervour and legend. The *pardon* at Le Folgoët remains one of the best-attended in Brittany. It takes place on the first Sunday in September.

Musée de la Basilique et de la Piété Populaire
open mid-June–mid-Sept Mon–Sat 10–12.30 and 2.30–6.30, Sun 2.30–6.30

Plouguerneau and its Curious Coast

Plouguerneau, a bastion of Breton culture, is also a popular destination for tourists, although the main attractions in these parts are the sensational dunes, lighthouses and rocks on the nearby coast, the last providing huge quantities of algae. This crop was of great importance to the coastal farmers here, as is recalled at the unusual museum in the village, the **Ecomusée de Plouguerneau et du Pays Pagan**.

Ecomusée de Plouguerneau et du Pays Pagan
www.club-internet.fr/perso.bezhin, t 02 98 37 13 35; open mid-June–Sept daily 2–6, May and June weekends 2–6 and Easter school hols 2–6; rest of year Sun 2–6

Moving to the varied coasts around Plouguerneau, a little way northeast, admire the splendid **dunes of Zorn and Vougot**. Directly north of Plouguerneau, the scruffily enchanting little port of **Le Corréjou** lies on the end of the peninsula of Penn Enez. Its beautifully coloured waters have attracted artists as well as boat lovers. A wag of a **stone sculptor** has created amusing to silly works around the port, curious human figures in stone popping up here and there. As to the **Maison de Gardes** on its little hillock observing the fabulous shoreline here, it has been turned from look-out-post to cute seasonal art exhibition room. Wandering around here, you can spot disused algae ovens, although an annual festival brings the activity fleetingly back to life.

The old village of **Tremenac'h** just west of Le Corréjou was largely engulfed by dunes in the early 18th century. Abandoned, it lay forgotten under the sands for a long time. As the land settled, new buildings started to go up on top of its remnants. However, in the 1960s, a bulldozer was shifting earth to start on the foundations of another modern house when it hit on the old church and cemetery. The parish bought the site and cleared it, opening **Iliz-Koz**, which centres around the cemetery and church of Tremenac'h, although a small museum has recently been added to explain the whole story (*see* box, below). A dense patchwork of medieval

Iliz-Koz
open 15 June–15 Sept Tues–Sun 2.30–6.30; rest of year Sun and bank hols 2.30–5

Don't Mess with the Devil's Cat

The legend claims that the church of Tremenac'h was buried under the sands by way of punishment of a band of unruly youths from the parish. Led astray by that great evil, boredom, one day they captured the devil's cat and brought it to the blind parish priest to be baptized. When the innocent priest threw water over the diabolical puss, it gave out a blood-curdling cry and even the blind man felt the ball of fire that then shot out in front of him. The boys' act brought down the wrath of God. At midnight, a wind whipped the sand dunes into a frenzy and they swirled over the village, burying it. It has to be said, the punishment sounds a bit harsh for such a prank, but then Breton Christian fables often carry a heavy-handed moral lesson.

tombs, around 100 in number, was revealed by the digs, both outside the church ruin and within it. The most exciting feature of the place was that many of the tombstones were engraved – the swords and the gloves were symbols of high social standing, but other details such as caravels and scissors no doubt represent families who practised specific trades.

The small **Chapelle St-Michel** sits on the spit of land north of Tremenac'h. The even smaller oratory next to it was built in honour of **Michel Le Nobletz**, who marked the area with his preaching in the early 17th century. At that time, northwestern Léon could still be a wild place where superstitions thrived. The fervent religious figure settled here for a time, attempting to reinforce Catholic belief among the poorly educated masses, although he didn't always get the best reception. He used specially made, cartoon-like missionary paintings to get across the Christian message simply. Often executed on sheepskins, sometimes on wood, they became known as *taolennou* in Breton. The tradition of painting these continued right into the 20th century, although the main period in which they were made lasted between 1613 and 1639. A cross out on one of the rocks beyond the religious edifices was erected in memory of those who died when the British liner *The Kurdistan* sank off the coast here in the early 20th century.

West of St-Michel lies the well-protected little bay of **La Grève Blanche**, with its fine sands. Turn the corner, though, and the waters look more disturbing, with big lumps of rock standing out to sea. However, the tallest lighthouse in Europe, the towering **Phare de l'Ile Vierge**, marks its authority over the scene. Built at the very end of the 19th century, it reaches 80 metres above sea level, and has one step for every day of the year. It dwarfs the previous lighthouse, which looks childlike by its side, at a mere 33 metres in height.

Phare de l'Ile Vierge
open April–Sept, tours with Vedettes de l'Aber, www.vedettesdesabers. com, t 02 98 04 74 94

Round a further bay you come to **Lilia**. Take in the magical rockscapes around its port, where you can often see seaweed being unloaded. Sticking high out of the sea to the west, the **Phare de l'Ile Vrac'h** looks like a modest house that has suddenly sprouted up like a straight beanstalk into the sky, its steep little sloping roof perched far above the ground. This lighthouse on its small island contains a small exhibition on that almost vanished breed, lighthouse keepers, and also puts on temporary exhibitions.

Phare de l'Ile Vrac'h
open June–Sept; only reachable at low tides

Around Aber Wrac'h and the Aber Benoît

The Ile Vrac'h lies out to one side of the mouth of **L'Aber Wrac'h**. Various other islands remain stranded in the estuary as the tide goes out. The legendary settlement of Tolente supposedly lies somewhere out in the waters, a drowned city. The best way to appreciate the natural setting of L'Aber Wrac'h, the Fairy's Estuary, is to go to **Paluden** and the south side of the bridge to take a boat trip or a canoe out on to its waters. A corniche road takes you to the little **port of L'Aber Wrac'h**, a lively spot thanks to its cafés. At neighbouring **Landéda**, the disused **semphore building** now holds temporary exhibitions in season; visiting them, you can benefit from great views. Out on its island, **Fort Cézon** was ordered by the great military architect Vauban in the late 17th century. The coast road leads along the **Baie des Anges** past the ruins of a religious foundation to the dunes of the peninsula of **Ste-Marguerite**.

The **Aber Benoît** estuary comes out into the Channel just south of L'Aber Wrac'h. This estuary is wilder than Aber Wrac'h's, and best appreciated on foot. Various bird observatories have been posted along the way. One route leads to the little port of **St-Pabu**, where a Maison des Abers is planned to open in the coming years, explaining the coastal features here.

Westwards, wide stretches of splendid dunes lie to the north of **Lampaul-Ploudalmézeau**. Following the beach of **Tréompan**, from the point above the dunes, you look out to **Carne**, this island with its prehistoric tumulus reachable at low tide.

Piles of rocks litter the dunes and sea on the way to the port of **Portsall**. This village had the misfortune of being all too closely linked with the environmental disaster of the *Amoco Cadiz*. The port recovered some time ago from the effects of the oil pollution. However, it has kept the vessel's massive anchor as a kind of memorial. The little resort of **Kersaint** is tucked into the bottom of Portsall's bay.

Along the Coast to L'Aber Ildut

The low coastal strip down to L'Aber Ildut looks more exposed, and more than a touch melancholic, with wild grasses and heather growing on the rocky ground that slopes gently down to the water. The terribly exposed stretch around **St-Samson** is, though, greatly appreciated not just by surfers, but also by kite-surfers.

Out to sea lie the vicious rocks of Argenton, the enormous **Phare du Four** lighthouse warning ships off them. Further out still, the island of Ouessant (Ushant) comes into view in the distance on clear days. The port of **Argenton**, enclosed in its little bay, looks reasonably picturesque. But go out on to the **Presqu'île de St-Laurent** to get the most sensational views of the Phare du Four on windy days, when the waves fly at the lighthouse.

The little harbours of **Porspoder** and **Melon** that follow are somewhat dominated by rocks. The tiny port of Melon is particularly atmospheric, and protected from the worst of the waves by the island that lies in front of it.

After Melon you come to the estuary of **L'Aber Ildut**, the southernmost and smallest of the three *abers*, its entrance marked by the Rocher du Crapaud, 'Toad Rock'. Tucked into the estuary you'll find the fine new marina of **Lanildut**. The place also boasts the distinction of being the largest seaweed-gathering port in France. You can go and see all the algae action down on the quays between mid-May and mid-October. The village itself, with flower-covered houses, has charm, especially as the granite in this area has attractive pinkish tinges. You can best appreciate the southern bank of L'Aber Ildut by taking the hikers' path from Port Reun.

St-Renan to Le Conquet

Set a bit back from the coast, **St-Renan** is the now quiet historic capital of the Pays d'Iroise. The story goes that it was founded by an Irish religious man, Ronan, who crossed the seas to settle here in the late 5th century, but he moved on further south in the Finistère (*see* pp.325–26). The town was much more important in the Léon in medieval times, but in 1681, the court and administration of the area were moved to Brest and the previously prosperous merchants' town declined. Some splendid old houses around the sloping hillside **Place du Marché** give you an indication of the past wealth of some of the local traders. The **Musée d'Histoire Locale** off the square holds a classic collection of Léon furniture and *coiffes* and recalls the history of the town, including its once thriving pewter industry. Today, the place is best visited for its Saturday morning market, when it regains some of the vibrant life it knew in centuries past.

Musée d'Histoire Locale
open July and Aug Tues–Sat 10–12 and 2–6, Sept–June Sat 10.30–12

For a very lively time, families head for the enormoulsy popular adventure park, **La Récré des Trois Curés** at nearby **Milizac**. The cheeky name could be translated as 'Break Time for the Three Priests'. The place includes roller-coasters, giant slides, bumper cars, a lake for boating, but also large indoor games areas.

La Récré des Trois Curés
www.larecredes 3cures.fr, t 02 98 07 95 59; open year-round on Wed, Sat and Sun pm

Back on the Atlantic, the first stretch of coast south of L'Aber Ildut is relatively built up. The port of **Porscave** and **Grève de Gouérou**, the latter with its algae ovens, are followed by the popular **beach of Lampaul-Plouarzel** and the pretty port of **Porspaul**.

The last, set in a remarkably rounded bay, has the distinct advantage of being protected by the headland of the Beg ar Vir. Dunes shifting with the winds have frequently been a bit of a problem in these parts, though, even swallowing up a ruined church. Selling sand to Brest in fact became a local industry for some time.

The area around the Pointe de Corsen stands out for its lighthouses. The **Phare de Trézien** looks as though it's gone awol and strayed inland into the countryside. It's possible to climb the 200 steps to the top on a tour. For a demanding walk along the coast, go in search of the wild creeks of **Ruscumunoc**. To reach the **Pointe de Corsen** by road, turn towards the ruined house at the

Phare de Trézien
open July–Aug 2.30–6 contact Plouarzel tourist information on t 02 98 89 69 46 for tour details

funky radar base. Maritime traffic along this dangerous coast is regulated from here. Out on the headland you can view the cliffs and creeks along the coast.

A dramatic stretch of coastal path links the Corsen headland to the protected bay of **Porsmoguer**. Further south, the **Anse des Blancs Sablons** boasts an extremely well-known beach, wild and wonderful, with around a kilometre and a half of sand curving round the bay. There's a nudist section. You can make out the island of Molène from here, but views of the whole archipelago reveal themselves more spectacularly at the **Pointe de Kermorvan**.

Most visitors come to **Le Conquet** to take the ferry out to Ouessant, so the place often gets clogged with tourist cars. The steep-sided harbour is quite charming, though, and panels scattered around the place recall its history. The fishermen specialize in catching shellfish now, but in earlier centuries wine and salt from southwest France was shipped via here. However, in 1558 the old houses of Le Conquet were destroyed by an invading English force, apparently avenging a defeat off the nearby Pointe de St-Mathieu at the hands of the Breton admiral Jean de Penhoët.

Notre-Dame de Bon Secours looks down on the port. Michel Le Nobletz, that stirring 17th-century missionary (*see* p.271), is buried inside. Copies of some of the *taolennou*, the simple Catholic cartoons he used to help spread the Christian message across the province, are displayed within. Le Conquet does have its own little beach, but a few kilometres to the south the **Plage de Porz Liogan** is a very appealing alternative.

From the Pointe de St-Mathieu to Brest

The **Pointe de St-Mathieu**, one of several contenders for Brittany's Land's End, looks a frightful architectural mess at first sight, with its abbey ruins, its radio transmitters, its inconsequential village and its towering lighthouse. The place can appear a touch sinister too at times, looking like a suitable setting for a horror movie, although it's certainly a compelling spot.

This **abbey church of St-Mathieu**, an enormous Benedictine construction from the Middle Ages, was abandoned at the Revolution, then much of its stone pillaged by builders. The ruins reveal an austere architecture, with little decoration except for some rudimentary designs on some of the capitals left standing. Although this location is said to have been the site of a religious establishment as early as the 6th century, the place wasn't dedicated to a local saint from across the Breton seas, but to a biblical one – it's said that local sailors journeyed all the way to Ethiopia to collect St Matthew's skull and bring it back here.

Phare de St-Mathieu
open French school hols, and daily through July and Aug; adm

The **Phare de St-Mathieu** serves as an information centre for this headland; there's a little museum attached, focusing on the abbey,

09

Finistère | The Pays des Abers and Pays d'Iroise

and you can also climb the lighthouse during holiday periods for exhilarating views.

To the northwest, you see the scattered islands and rocks of the Molène archipelago. The closest island, the **Ile de Beniguet** (a transformation of Benedict), derived its name from the fact that the Benedictines of St-Mathieu also owned it. To the west, on clear days, the red and white stripes of the solid **Pierres Noires lighthouse** may be visible far out into the ocean, indicating another of those daring 19th-century feats of engineering built to make the Breton seas safer.

Turning the coastal corner, the rocky cliff path east from the Pointe de St-Mathieu leads to the daunting **Fort de Bertheaume** on its island, only just attached to the mainland by what looks like a flimsy bridge as you approach. This fort guarding the northern approach to Brest was designed by Vauban in the late 17th century. It belonged to the French military until just a few years ago. **Arbreizh Aventure** offers adrenaline-rush trips around the fort, by high wire Tyrolean or *via ferrata* ladders. The company also has a tree-top assault course nearby. Spectacular events are staged at the Fort de Bertheaume in summer.

Plougonvelin and **Le Trez Hir** became popular among wealthy Brest families early in the 20th century, as some of the grand villas testify. Now the people of Brest flock here at weekends as soon as there's the slightest sign of good weather. It's a long walk home along the coastal path from Le Trez Hir to Brest, but the path is by far the best way to appreciate the spectacular **Goulet de Brest**, the Narrows or Bottleneck of Brest. This is the very tight waterway through which all vessels have to pass to make it into the glorious natural bay of the Rade de Brest. This strategic channel has been heavily fortified for centuries. You can see oil tankers, container ships, naval vessels and yachts of all descriptions passing in and out of the Goulet, the views particularly wonderful from the **Pointe du Minou** with its small lighthouse.

Fort de Bertheaume
open July and Aug daily 10–7, April–June and Sept Tue–Sun 2–6.30

Arbreizh Aventure
www.arbreizh.com, t 06 64 24 06 41

Market Days in the Pays des Abers and Pays d'Iroise

ⓘ **Pays Touristique des Abers-Côte des Légendes**
www.aberslegendes-vacances.fr

Goulven: Sunday in July and August
Brignogan-Plages: Friday in July and August
Lesneven: Monday
Plouguerneau: Thursday
Lilia: Tuesday 5–7pm in summer holidays
Ploudalmézeau: Friday

St-Renan: Saturday
Lampaul-Plouarzel: Thursday
Le Conquet: Tuesday

Where to Stay and Eat in the Pays des Abers and Pays d'Iroise

Plouider ✉ 29260
***La Butte**, 10 Rue de la Mer, t 02 98 25 40 54, *www.labutte.fr* (€€). Spacious, comfortable refurbished

(i) Brignogan-Plages >
t 02 98 83 41 08,
www.ot-brignogan-plage.fr

(i) Ploudalmézeau >>
t 02 98 48 12 88,
www.ot-ploudalmezeau.com

(i) Guissény >
t 02 98 25 67 99,
www.guisseny-tourisme.fr

(i) Plouguerneau >
Place de l'Europe,
t 02 98 04 70 93,
www.abers-tourisme.com

(i) Le Conquet >>
Parc de Beauséjour,
t 02 98 89 11 31,
www.leconquet.fr

(i) Lesneven/Le Folgoët
t 02 98 83 01 47,
www.lesneven-tourisme.com

(i) Pays Touristique d'Iroise
www.vacances eniroise.com

(★) La Baie des Anges >

(★) Hostellerie de la Pointe St-Mathieu >>

rooms in this modern hotel with views onto the Bay of Goulven. The restaurant (€€€–€€) is much appreciated for its Breton produce.

Brignogan-Plages ✉ 29890

**Castel Régis, Plage du Garo, t 02 98 83 40 22, *castel-regis@wanadoo.fr* (€€€–€€). In its own grounds on a wonderful promontory by the sea, this hotel was undergoing a makeover at time of going to print, so check on developments. Heated seawater pool, tennis court and sauna.

La Corniche, Rue de la Corniche, Baie de Pontusval, t 02 98 85 81 99. Good regional and fish dishes to accompany the sea views.

Guissény ✉ 29249

**Auberge de Keralloret, t 02 98 25 60 37, *www.keralloret.com* (€€). Pleasant rooms in a restored farmhouse, plus copious, good-value, home-made Breton dishes (€€) served in the evenings only.

Plouguerneau Coast ✉ 29880

**Castel Ac'h, Lilia, t 02 98 04 70 11 (€). Wonderfully located by Lilia's rocks, and many of the rooms have sea views, but let's hope that they'll soon refurbish the outdated rooms. The restaurant is rightly popular though for its excellent fresh seafood.

Trouz ar Mor, Le Corréjou, t 02 98 04 71 61 (€€). Appealing restaurant perched high enough to enjoy the views across the port from both dining room and terrace.

Lannilis/Paluden

L'Auberge du Pont, t 02 98 04 16 69. At this hamlet halfway down the Aber Wrac'h, this good, nicely decorated waterside restaurant also has a terrace, and puts on musical evenings.

L'Aber Wrac'h ✉ 29870

***La Baie des Anges and La Villa des Anges, Route des Anges, t 02 98 04 90 04, *www.baie-des-anges.com* (€€€). A fine hotel divided between two locations close to the lovely river estuary.

St-Pabu ✉ 29830

Crêperie de l'Aber Benoît, Pors ar Viln, t 02 98 89 86 26 (€). A delightful Breton crêpe joint.

Ploudalmézeau ✉ 29830

Crêperie du Château d'Eau, Route de Brest, t 02 98 48 15 88 (€). A memorable place in which to eat, more than 50m up in a Breton watertower (take the lift, or, to work up an appetite, the 278 stairs). The food is basic, the views fantastic.

Portsall ✉ 29830

La Demeure Océane, 20 Rue de Bar al Lan, t 02 98 48 77 42 (€€). A charming B&B with characterful rooms in a substantial old house set in its own garden. *Table d'hôte* (€) is available on reservation.

Trébabu ✉ 29217

Le Grand Keruzou, t 02 98 89 11 92 (€). The very picture of a tough yet loveable old Breton manor, offering B&B in charming if relatively sober rooms decorated with a mix of antiques and modern furnishings. *Table d'hôte* is available by reservation only.

Le Conquet ✉ 29217

La Vinotière, 1 Rue du Lieutenant Jourden, t 02 98 89 17 79, *www.lavinotiere.fr* (€€€–€€). A lovingly renovated old house a stone's throw from the old port, offering lovely contemporary rooms with bare stone walls, plus a *salon de thé*.

**Hôtel Au Bout du Monde, Place de Llandeilo, t 02 98 89 07 22, *www.auboutdumondehotel.fr* (€€–€). Another stylish new option with relaxing wood interiors to the rooms, a few with balcony.

Crêperie des Boucaniers, 3 Rue Poncelin, t 02 98 89 06 25 (€). Tasty crêpes served in a characterful old house.

Pointe de St-Mathieu ✉ 29217

***Hostellerie de la Pointe St-Mathieu, t 02 98 89 00 19, *www.pointe-st-mathieu.com* (€€€–€€). A fine hotel on this highly touristic headland, the rooms a mix of modern

St-Renan
Place du Vieux Marché, **t** *02 98 84 23 78,* www.tourisme-saint-renan.com

and traditional, some with a balcony. The restaurant has two styles of dining room (€€€–€€) too, traditional and contemporary, in a charming Breton stone house.

Le Trez Hir ✉ 29217
La Maison Lyre, 5 Allée Verte, Locmaria–Plouzané, **t** 02 98 48 53 50 (€). An interesting B&B full of books and travel mementoes, towards Trégana.

The Islands of Molène and Ouessant

Qui voit Molène voit sa peine. Qui voit Ouessant voit son sang.

⭐ **Ouessant, Batz, Sein and Les Glénans**

This alarming rhyme warns those sailing by the archipelago that they'll know grief if they set eyes on Molène, and shed blood if they see Ouessant. It's not a rhyme taken up by the tourist brochures. Innumerable ships have been wrecked on the devilish rocks strewn all around these islands. However, the tourist boats know their way very well. While the main islands you can visit off the north Breton coast nestle close in to the shore, protected enough to allow semi-tropical gardens and palms to thrive, these exposed islands some way off western Brittany are flayed by the winds. Virtually no trees grow on them. But they're exhilarating places. Ouessant, known in English as Ushant, is the largest and most westerly fragment of the Molène Archipelago. It's a fascinating island to visit and has two interesting museums. You can also stop off at the much tinier Molène Island. The archipelago is a UNESCO Réserve de la Biosphère, meaning that its unique marine environment is specially protected.

Molène

This island is both vertically and follically challenged – some claim its name comes from the Breton *moal enez,* 'bald island', and it has been nicknamed L'Ile Chauve in French. Molène is also minuscule. A local joke goes that a cow on Molène can simultaneously stand in one field, graze in a second, and deliver a cowpat in a third.

If you want to get away from the world, Molène is a great place to come. But you will find Brits for company... in a cemetery by the church, which had to be made specially for those who drowned in the tragic sinking of *The Drummond Castle* in 1886. The **Musée du Drummond Castle** behind the village hall recalls this harrowing accident of a vessel returning from Cape Town to London, many of the passengers attending the captain's final celebratory ball as the ship struck the Pierres Vertes rocks. The islanders spent several days recovering bodies washed on to the shore and gave them as dignified a burial as possible. Queen Victoria thanked them for their pains. On a rather brighter note, the newer **Maison de**

Musée du Drummond Castle
t *02 98 07 38 41; open daily July–Sept 2.30–6, Oct–June 3–5*

Getting to Molène and Ouessant

The **Compagnie Penn ar Bed** (*www.pennarbed.com*, **t** 02 98 80 80 80) runs **ferry** services to both Molène and Ouessant every day of the year from Brest and Le Conquet. There's also a service from Camaret in high season. Book places well in advance in holiday season. You can **fly** to Ouessant with **Finist'Air** from Brest Bretagne **airport** (*www.finistair.fr*, **t** 02 98 84 64 87). The easiest way to travel around Ouessant is by **taxi** or **minibus**. Hiring a **bike** is also extremely popular, although **walking** is the only way to appreciate the coast to the full.

---

l'Environnement Insulaire helps visitors focus on the island's flora and fauna.

Ouessant, or Ushant

Ouessant's little ecomuseum crams a lot of information on the island's history and life on Ushant into two small houses. The island was only isolated from the mainland after the end of the last Ice Age, some 10,000 or so years ago; just small signs of neolithic and Iron Age inhabitants have been found. In the Dark Ages, the extremely influential Welsh evangelizer Pol first set foot on dry land across the Channel here. He seemingly founded a monastery on the island in the 6th century. Lampaul and Pors Paul on Ouessant are both named in memory of this man, considered the great Celtic apostle of northern Finistère (*see* box, p.260).

From the 13th century to 1589, the island became the property of the bishops of Léon. They sold it to the powerful René de Rieux de Souréac, governor of Brest, who added fortifications. Later, in 1764, Ouessant was bought by the Crown. Numerous naval battles between French and English ships were fought off Ouessant until the end of the 18th century.

The population remained extremely poor down the centuries. Local fishing was difficult, given the lack of natural harbours, the extremes of the weather and the dangers of the rocky reefs all around. Ouessant men would join long-haul fishing expeditions, or the navy, with Brest so close by. Their men so often far away or, all too often, dead young, the women and widows of Ouessant had to tend the land, which was divided up into tiny walled allotments that they hoed, planted and harvested. They took turns too in collecting seaweed, used as fertilizer. Today, the food-growing allotments of Ouessant have been abandoned. The other traditional mainstay of the community, sheep, remain, although the tiny Ouessant chocolate-brown variety peculiar to the island is very rare. Such was the singular position the women of Ouessant held that they even took on the right to propose to men rather than having to wait to be asked.

A terrible number of shipwrecks has occurred down the centuries around Ouessant. Towering lighthouses, their names legendary to the French, were built all around the island to try to improve warnings to ships. The massive lighthouse of Le Stiff, its name with unintentionally comical and macabre undertones in English, has its origins in the early 18th century. The others went up in the 19th century, daring engineering feats. Since the major oil tanker disasters off this coast in the 1960s and 1970s, more measures have been put in place to survey shipping traffic.

Only about 700 people live on the island year round now, but numbers swell to some 3,000 in summer, and in 2008, Ouessant staged its first international music festival, quite a feat for such a forbidding place, but one that draws people irresistibly to it.

Touring Ouessant

You land on the **eastern side of the island**, in the protected **Baie du Stiff**. The enormous **Phare du Stiff** marks the highest point on the island. If you head south you come to the hamlet of **Penn Alarn**. Some ruins possibly indicate where the governor's castle once stood; now migrating birds favour the spot. A steep path leads down to the little port of **Porz Arlan**. In the sea to the south, the **Kéréon lighthouse** stands out on a rock towards Molène. There's a little sandy **beach** on the **Pointe de Penn Alarn**, much more tranquil than the beaches on the western side of the island, though the water is chillier.

The advantage of the **south coast** of Ouessant is that it's much less well known and quieter than the northern one, if less spectacular. However, particularly stirring views open up at the **Penn ar Roc'h** headland. As you reach the **Pointe de Roc'h Hir**, the **Jument lighthouse** comes dramatically into view out to sea. The **Pointe de Porz Doun** marks the most southerly point on the island. The coastal path then turns to head into the Bay of Lampaul, and you come to the main beaches on Ouessant, the **Plage de Prat** and **Plage de Corz**.

The bustling village of **Lampaul** opens out on to a surprisingly friendly bay. The hotels, restaurants and bike hire shops are clustered close together by the church. In the atmospheric graveyard, you can see how few different family names crop up on a little isolated island such as this.

Ouessant's two museums stand in the **northwest corner of the island**, the busiest part of Ushant after Lampaul, with lots of low stone walls. The little pointed shelters you pass were built for sheep, not pixies. Conditions were cramped in traditional Ouessant cottages though; experience something of their claustrophobia in two that have been turned into the **Maison du Niou Uhella or Ecomusée d'Ouessant**, the first *Ecomusée* to be created in France, celebrating local life.

One cottage presents the history of Ouessant, as well as details on the everyday life of the women on the island and the men out

Maison du Niou Uhella or Ecomusée d'Ouessant
www.parc-naturel-armorique.fr, t 02 98 48 86 37; open June–Sept and school hols Tues–Sun 10.30–6.30 (mid-July–Aug also 9pm–11pm), Oct–May Tues–Sun 2–6

to sea. The more charming cottage retains traditional Ouessant furniture, compactly functional and full of hidden surprises. While there may be nothing radically different from your average mainland Breton peasant's home of the past centuries, the place has the distinct feel of a ship's cabin, of a family boat moored on the island. Virtually everything shuts tight, as though to guard against the wind that might force its way in at any moment. The cottage basically consists of one room, the separations formed by the pieces of furniture, much of which might have been made from wood gathered from shipwrecks. The blue and white paint makes the interior look surprisingly bright and gay. The layout inside the cottage follows a formal pattern, with two distinct sides. To the right lies the *penn lous*, the 'end of the ashes', with fireplace and cooking corner. The *penn brao* is the other, 'beautiful end' of the house, for display.

The island used to be covered with windmills, and you can pass a rare one to have been maintained on the way from the Ecomusée to the Créac'h lighthouse on the northwestern tip of Ouessant. You also pass the **Centre d'Etude du Milieu de l'Ile d'Ouessant**, which organizes nature walks round the island in summer.

The **Centre d'Interprétation des Phares et Balises** is an unusual lighthouse museum set right beneath the massive, black-and-white-striped **Créac'h lighthouse**. Flashing green and red harbour lights greet you as you enter the substantial museum, dedicated to some of the world's most powerful light beams. The place may blind you a little with its science of lighthouses, beacons, buoys and other sea markers; take comfort in the aesthetic wonder of many of the objects, displayed in what were the huge electricity-generating rooms once required for the lighthouse above.

Head on to the enormous bristling mounds of rocks of the **Pointe de Pern**, the island's most westerly point. Another great lighthouse, the **Phare de Nividic**, stands just out to sea from here.

It's along the **northern coast of the island** that you'll find the most spectacular rock formations of Ouessant. The **Ile de Keller** makes a particularly sensational feature, just detached from the island. On stormy days, Brittany doesn't get more dramatic than this, although seals feel most at home in these parts.

Centre d'Etude du Milieu de l'Ile d'Ouessant
www.parc-naturel-armorique.fr,
t 02 98 48 82 65

Centre d'Interprétation des Phares et Balises
www.parc-naturel-armorique.fr, **t** *02 98 48 80 70; open same hrs as Ecomusée*

Market Days on Ouessant

Ouessant: Tuesday, Thursday and Friday

Where to Stay and Eat on Molène and Ouessant

Ile de Molène ✉ 29259
For details of B&B accommodation on the island, contact the *mairie*: t 02 98 07 39 05, *www.molene.com*.

09 Finistère | The Islands of Molène and Ouessant: Ouessant, or Ushant

(i) Ouessant >>
*Place de l'Eglise,
Lampaul, t 02 98 48 85
83, www.ot-ouessant.fr*

**(★) Ti Jan Ar
C'hafé >>**

Kastell an Daol, quayside, **t 02 98 07 39 11 (€). A neat, welcoming option, some rooms looking over the harbour. The restaurant is the obvious place to eat on Molène (there isn't a wide choice), lobster stew the speciality, and the bar is the social hub of the island. Ask here about boat trips to the rarely discovered, otherworldly little islands of the archipelago, Banneg and Balaneg to the north, and Trielen, Quéménès and Beniguet to the south.

Ile de Quéménès

Ile de Quéménès B&B, m 06 63 02 15 08, *www.iledequemenes.fr* (€€€). To escape the rest of humanity and spend a weekend on an extraordinary island, contact the only inhabitants of Quéménès, a young couple who've settled into leading a self-sufficient life here since 2007 and offer B&B breaks .

Ile d'Ouessant ✉ 29242

**Ti Jan Ar C'hafé, t 02 98 48 82 64 (€€). Charming colourful rooms in this exclusive new little hotel between port and Lampaul, the latter under half a mile away.

**Roch Ar Mor, t 02 98 48 80 19, *www.rockarmor.com* (€€). Probably the most attractive of the hotels in Lampaul, many rooms with sea views and balconies. Restaurant (€€€–€€).

Crêperie du Stang, Route du Stiff leading out of Lampaul, **t** 02 98 48 80 94 (€). A good alternative to the hotel restaurants, with excellent filled crêpes.

Brest

Brest overlooks one of the most beautiful great bays in France, the Rade de Brest. For centuries France's main naval harbour, the town has a fascinating history. The roots of its massive castle overseeing the bay go all the way back to Roman times, but Brest really grew mightily in importance when Richelieu and then Colbert decided to turn it into one of the main centres for the French fleet, and French shipbuilding, exploiting its amazingly well-protected natural harbour. Between 1660 and 1790, over 180 major vessels, 70 frigates and 100 additional boats were built here, often cruelly exploiting prisoners' labour – their lives were cheap back in the Ancien Régime. Taken over by the Nazis in the Second World War, Brest became one of the Germans' main naval bases, and was consequently smashed to smithereens by Allied bombing.

So Brest's architecture is mainly modern, set on an American-looking grid-plan of streets sloping down to its string of ports. The naval harbour now counts as the second most important such base in France, after Toulon on the Med, and despite recent cuts, there are still many thousands of sailors stationed here. Brest is roughly divided in two by the Penfeld River, the naval town stretching to the west, civilian and student Brest to the east. Many tourists are only tempted to venture into the eastern outskirts of town to visit Océanopolis, the best aquarium in Brittany. Venture further west and the hulking ports, ramparts and castle, plus the broad, airy streets and the museums may take you by surprise.

Getting to and around Brest

Brest Bretagne **airport** (**t** 02 98 32 86 00, *www.brest.aeroport.fr*) lies 11km northeast of the centre. Ryan Air operates flights between London-Luton and Brest certain days of the week. Flybe flies to Brest from Birmingham, Exeter, Manchester and Southampton. Aer Arann also has some flights to the city. A navette shuttle bus runs between the airport and town centre several times a day. Brest is linked to Paris by fast TGV **trains**, and there's a rail network to many other major north Breton towns. For **buses** around greater Brest, consult *www.bibus.fr*. To research trips further afield, see *www.viaoo29.fr*. The main bus station is next to the railway station.

Océanopolis and the Vallon du Stang Alar

Océanopolis
www.oceanopolis. com, **t** *02 98 34 40 40; open July–Aug daily 9–7, early May–June and first half Sept daily 9–6, rest of year daily exc Mon 10–5*

Océanopolis is an outstanding and entertainingly educational aquarium, gently encouraging a little more understanding of marine life and clarifying Brittany's sometimes murky waters. You can follow several main themes including scientists' knowledge of the world's oceans and their latest research into them; navigation and security at sea; and the sea life of the Breton coasts. You can also embark on a kind of world tour of the planet's underwater life via the Tropical Pavilion, the Temperate Pavilion (here the Brittany coast is recreated inside a mock-up marine base), and the Polar Pavilion.

Opposite Océanopolis, entering the waterside suburb of **Le Relecq-Kerhuon**, the sandy **Plage du Moulin Blanc** attracts bathers on warm days, but the new, swanky **Spadium** (a mix of spa and indoor pool complex), recently opened on the other side of the road, means they can enjoy the surroundings year-round from inside, in what is the largest indoor pool in Brittany. Plus you can get a pampering in the spa below.

Conservatoire Botanique National de Brest
www.cbnbrest.fr, **t** *02 98 41 88 95; main gardens free, open daily 9–6; greenhouses open July–15 Sept Sun–Thurs 2–5.30*

To get away from the hordes on the coast, head for the peaceful **Conservatoire Botanique National de Brest** in the **Vallon du Stang Alar**, a gorgeous public garden, set apart from the town in its long, deep valley, and free to visit. A stream runs through it, supplying a whole chain of small lakes and ponds full of water lilies. Great clumps of elephant-eared gunnera and bamboos, clusters of palms and even of cacti and agaves make for an exotic atmosphere.

Port de Commerce and Ferry Port

West from Océanopolis, you can drive through the huge docks of the **commercial port**, some of its vast berths built for supertankers, to reach the **ferry port**, which has become a trendy spot, with its clusters of bars and restaurants, several major buildings around here plastered with gigantic murals. In July and August, the **Jeudis du Port** add a vibrant note of excitment with their free programme of Thursday evening concerts.

Yachts flit across the Rade in far greater numbers than naval vessels these days, and you can choose between a number of

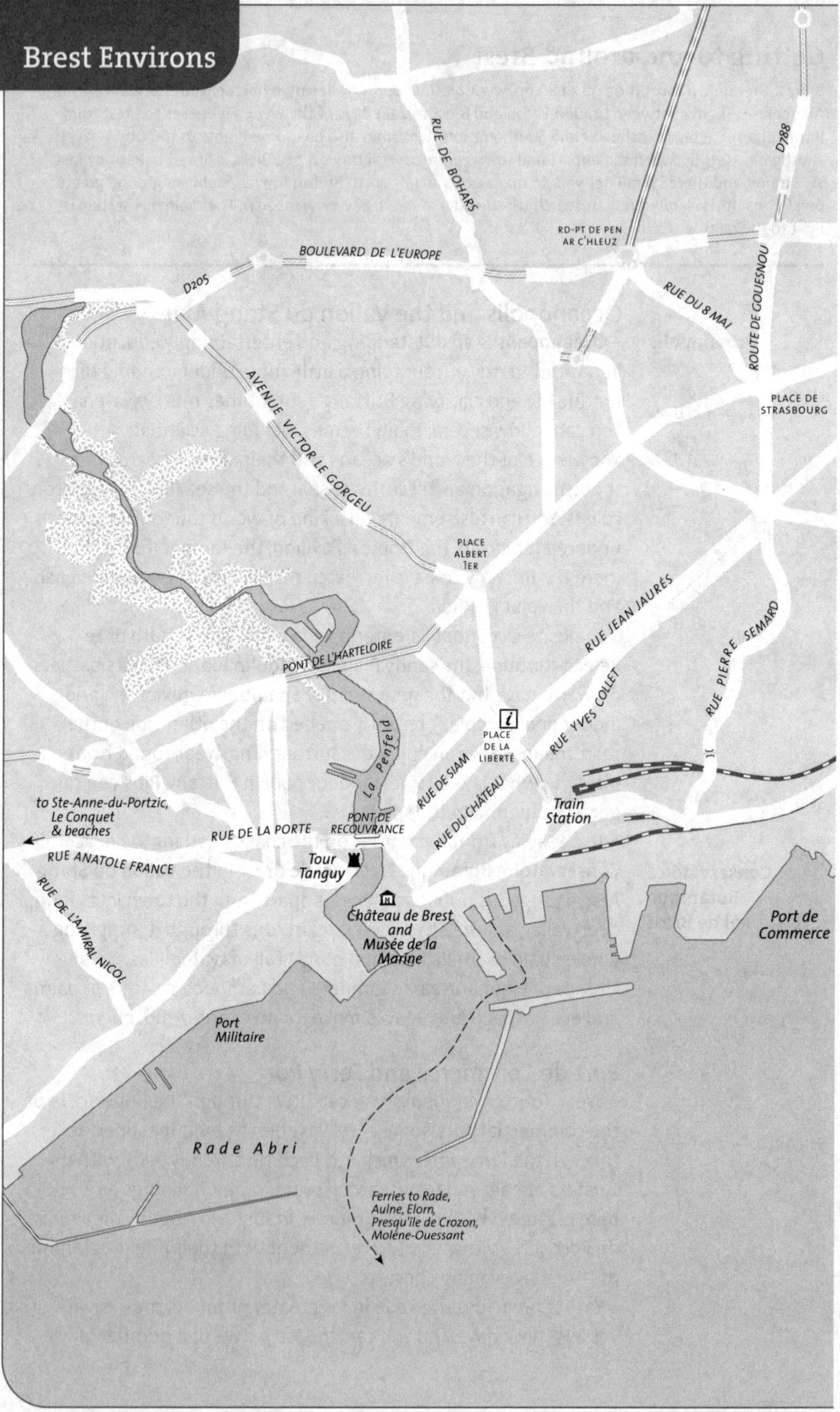

RUE DE BOHARS

RUE DE L'EUROPE

D788

BOULEVARD DE L'EUROPE

RD-PT DE PEN AR C'HLEUZ

D205

RUE DU 8 MAI

ROUTE DE GOUESNOU

PLACE DE STRASBOURG

AVENUE VICTOR LE GORGEU

PLACE ALBERT 1ER

RUE JEAN JAURÈS

PONT DE L'HARTELOIRE

RUE YVES COLLET

RUE PIERRE SEMARD

La Penfeld

PLACE DE LA LIBERTÉ

RUE DE SIAM

RUE DU CHÂTEAU

Train Station

to Ste-Anne-du-Portzic, Le Conquet & beaches

RUE DE LA PORTE

PONT DE RECOUVRANCE

RUE ANATOLE FRANCE

Tour Tanguy

RUE DE L'AMIRAL NICOL

Château de Brest and Musée de la Marine

Port de Commerce

Port Militaire

Rade Abri

Ferries to Rade, Aulne, Elorn, Presqu'île de Crozon, Molène-Ouessant

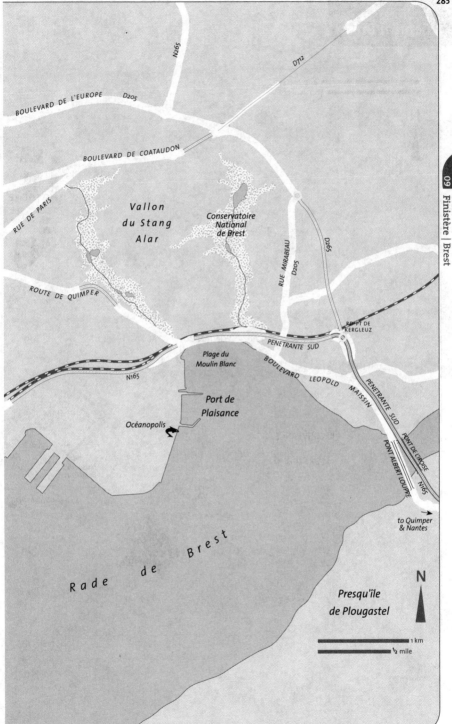

400 metres
400 yards

N

PLACE
ALBERT
1ER

AVENUE MARECHAL FOCH

RUE DE PORTZMOGUER

RUE DE LA MOTTE PICQUET

RUE DU GUESCLIN

R. TOURVILLE

RUE LANNOURON

HARTELOIRE

PONT DE L'HARTELOIRE

RUE PIERRE PUGET

RUE DE FOSSE SAVOIRE

AVENUE GEORGES CLEMENCEAU

University

BOULEVARD JEAN MOULIN

RUE GENERAL GALLIENI

RUE DE CARPONT

RUE DU 2EME R.I.C.

RUE FAUTRAS

RUE DE LYON

RUE DUQUESNE

RUE D'ALGESIRAS

RUE LIEUT VAISSEAU PARIS

RUE SAINT - EXUPERY

RUE DE MAISSIN

RUE DE PONTANIOU

PONTANIOU

R. MICHELET

PLACE
ST-LOUIS

PASTEUR

RUE DE CARPONT

RUE V. ROSSEL

La Penfeld

RUE LOUIS

ST-LOUIS

RUE DE SIAM

BOULEVARD CDT. MOUCHOTTE

RUE D'AIGUILLON

RUE JEAN MACÉ

CENTRE
SIAM

RUE EMILE ZOLA

PLACE
WILSON

RUE TRAVERSE

RUE DU CHATEAU

RECOUVRANCE

RUE DE LA PORTE

PLACE DE
LA PORTE

PONT DE RECOUVRANCE

RUE DU REMPART

RUE AMIRAL LINOISE

RUE VOLTAIRE

RUE ANATOLE FRANCE

RUE VAUBAN

Tour
Tanguy

Musée des
Beaux-Arts

BOULEVARD DES FRANCAIS / LIBRES

RUE BROSSOLETTE

US Memorial

RUE DE L'EGLISE

PLACE GÉN.
DE GAULLE

RUE DE DENVER

COURS DAJOT

RUE F. ROOSEVELT

QUAI DE LA DOUANE

Château de Brest
and
Musée de la
Marine

QUAI DU CDT MALBERT

Arsenal

To Porte
Grande Rivière

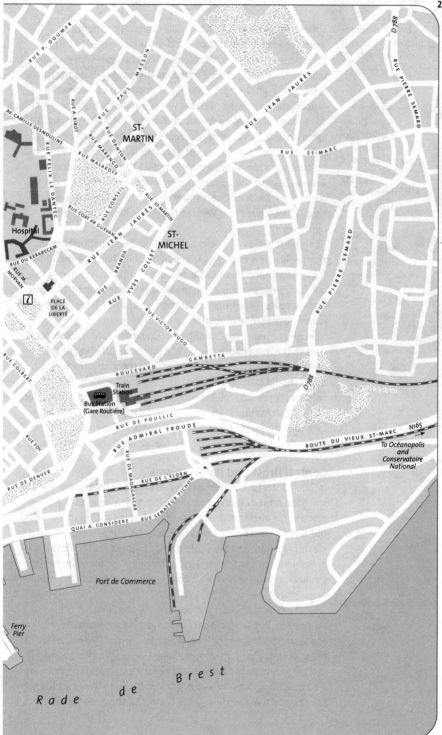

La Recouvrance
www.larecouvrance.
com, t 02 98 33 95 40

Notre-Dame
de Rumengol
www.antest.net,
t 02 98 20 06 58

Société
Maritime Azénor
t 02 98 41 46 23,
www.azenor.com

Compagnie
Penn ar Bed
t 02 98 80 80 80,
www.pennarbed.com

options for getting out on the waters alongside them. *La Recouvrance* is the best known old-fashioned vessel to carry passengers. It's a much-vaunted replica of an early 19th-century schooner, named after one of the most high-profile quarters in Brest, although the boat was originally built to sail along the African and Caribbean coasts. It works out pretty expensive for a day trip aboard it. *Notre-Dame de Rumengol* is the real thing, a listed historic monument of an old sailing vessel, but sailings are rare, and once again pricey. For easy, regular trips out into the Rade de Brest in modern-style vessels, contact the **Société Maritime Azénor**. Or with the **Compagnie Penn ar Bed** you can take a ferry out to the islands of Ouessant, Molène or Sein from here. More simply, hire a bike from **Vélozen** to take on Brest's ports and upper town.

Behind this area, the no-man's land has been gradually giving way to slick new buildings, in the main office blocks, although a funky new **concert hall**, **La Carène**, draws attention to itself, done out in distressed orange, the trendy architecture calling to mind rusting boats. This venue lies at the foot of a remarkable length of towering old stone **ramparts**.

Every four years, Brest, along with Douarnenez to the south, plays host to the most phenomenal international gathering of special vessels, including tall ships, from around the globe. The next such event should take place in 2012. The city and the Rade de Brest go wild for these huge celebrations. In 2008, the impressive new **Port du Château marina** at the foot of Brest castle was put into action for the first time, to receive a good number of the vessels, the brand-new facilities opening to general use at the start of 2009.

Central Brest and its Museums

The architecture of the **Château de Brest** has been greatly altered since the famed chronicler Jean Froissart, writing in the 14th century, claimed that it was one of the largest castles in the world, but this fort is still very impressive and daunting, guarding the western entrance to the Penfeld River. As Brest shot to naval prominence in the Ancien Régime, the irrepressible military genius Vauban got his hands on the plans, and redesigned the place, giving it its angular looks.

Musée National
de la Marine
www.musee-
marine.fr, t 02 98 22 12
39; open Wed–Mon
April–Sept 10–6.30,
Oct–mid-Dec, Feb and
March 10–12 and 2–6;
closed Jan

Most of the château is still occupied by the French naval authorities, but the front section houses Brest's maritime museum, the **Musée National de la Marine** mainly devoted to the strikingly gruesome shipbuilding traditions here, though certain major events in the history of the castle and the town are also told along the way, as you go from tower to tower and along the ramparts. Astonishingly, the bottom of the walls formed part of an impressive defensive *castrum* built here as far back as the 3rd century.

A splendid tree-lined **promenade, Cours Dajot,** follows the top of the ramparts, from which you can enjoy amazing views over the Rade de Brest. The **monument** which sticks out so prominently on its terrace is a **Franco-American war memorial** in pink granite, paying tribute to combined American and French naval achievements 'in the World War' – the reference is to the First World War; they didn't realize that Brest was going to be annihilated in a second. The US was given a tiny territory of 424 square metres here.

The area around the ramparts featured in steamy goings-on in Jean Genet's notorious and quite brilliant novel describing an imagined murky underworld in the city. *Querelle de Brest* paints a disturbing picture of drunken sailors, corrupt cops and homosexuality, creating a very heady cocktail for those times; the disturbing piece was turned into a shocking but celebrated film by the German director Rainer Werner Fassbinder.

Musée des Beaux-Arts de Brest
*t 02 98 00 87 96;
open daily exc Sun am
and Mon 10–12 and 2–6*

In the grid of broad streets leading up the slope from the castle, the **Musée des Beaux-Arts de Brest** stands on Rue de Traverse. Some of the fabulously detailed old school paintings of the town on display at this museum of fine arts give you further fine views of how Brest looked in its heyday. But this museum is best known for its Symbolist collection, notably works by the Pont-Aven School. The lush greens and yellows of Paul Sérusier's *Les Blés verts au Pouldu*, painted in 1890, make it one of his most appealing works. Emile Bernard's depiction of the pink rocks of St-Briac show off the typical *cloisonné* effects of the school. The painting adopted as the symbol of the museum, though, is Georges Lacombe's view of the cliffs at Camaret-sur-Mer, the rocks taking on vaguely human shapes against a bilious yellow sea. Striking as this work may be, it is rather harder to stomach than the canvases of the Pont-Aven artists. You'll also find quite an engrossing collection of paintings here showing Breton religious processions.

Rue de Siam is Brest's most famous street, now a broad shopping avenue. However, the name commemorates the visit to the town in 1686 of one of the earliest exotic Asiatic diplomatic missions, when ambassadors sent by the king of Siam (Thailand) arrived here on their way to visit King Louis XIV. They carried with them the most precious of letters, engraved on gold. The way leads up to the major **Place de la Liberté** with the town hall. Here you really feel as if you've arrived in 1950s urban America, although some interesting new university buildings have been going up close by. Behind the Hôtel de Ville, **Rue Jean Jaurès**, with its big stores and shopping malls, leads up to the **Quartier St-Martin**, where you might go in search of a few traces of pre-war Brest.

Cross the Penfeld River by the massive **Pont de Recouvrance** back near the bottom of Rue de Siam and you'll be struck by the sight of the medieval **Tour Tanguy** standing above the lines of naval vessels moored below. The tower has been turned into a little museum on Brest's mainly vanished history. Further west, the shore down from the centre of town is dominated by the military quarters and military boats, which you won't be allowed to go and see unless you can show a French passport. Out towards Le Conquet, the **Mémorial des Finistériens** tells the harrowing story of Brest in the Second World War, in the setting of the Fort Monbavey, built under Louis XIV.

Mémorial des Finistériens
t 02 98 05 39 46; open Jan–Dec Mon–Fri 9–12 and 2–6

Market Days in Brest

There's a Sunday-morning market around the Rue de Lyon, and other markets daily.

Where to Stay in Brest

ⓘ **Brest >**
Place de la Liberté, B.P. 91 012, 29210 Brest Cedex 1, t 02 98 44 13 75, www.brest-metropole-tourisme.fr

Brest ✉ **29200**
***Océania-Centre, 82 Rue de Siam, t 02 98 80 66 66, *www.oceania hotels.com* (€€€€–€€€). One of the best choices in the centre, this big, well-run hotel which has been given a complete make-over has stylish rooms. The cuisine at its restaurant, **Le Nautilus** (€€; *closed Sat lunch and Sun lunch, and most Aug*), is highly recommended. The same group owns **Le Continental** and **L'Amirauté**, further good three-star in the centre, and has a good branch at the airport too – see website.

**La Rade, 6 Rue de Siam, t 02 98 44 47 76, *www.hotel-de-la-rade.com* (€€–€). At the heart of the city, with recently renovated rooms, some with sea views.

**Cîtotel de la Gare, 4 Blvd Gambetta, t 02 98 44 47 01, *www.hotelgare.com* (€€). A good choice, some rooms with great sea views, and close to the rail station.

Eating Out in Brest

⭐ **Le M >**
Le M, 22 Rue du Commandant Drogou, t 02 98 47 90 00 (€€€€). Extremely refined cuisine, with the added bonus of being set in a lovely house with its own quiet grounds, north of Place Albert 1er. *Closed 1wk end Aug, Sun eve and Mon.*

La Fleur de Sel, 15 bis Rue de Lyon, t 02 98 44 38 65 (€€€–€€). High quality central restaurant with cool contemporary dining room.

La Maison de l'Océan, 2 Quai de la Douane, Port de Commerce, t 02 98 80 44 84 (€€€–€€). A great, buzzing restaurant serving excellent fresh fish and seafood by the water, with some outdoor tables for warm days. *Closed Sun and 2wks Sept.*

L'Armen, 21 Rue de Lyon, t 02 98 46 34 (€€–€). A lovely restaurant serving very good French food in a former *patisserie* with exuberant decor. *Closed Sun and Mon.*

Ma Petite Folie, Port de Plaisance du Moulin Blanc, t 02 98 42 44 42 (€€). A most delightful restaurant by Océanopolis, set in a former lobster fishing boat and offering excellent seafood. *Closed Sun and 2wks Sept.*

Blé Noir, Vallon du Stang Alar, t 02 98 41 84 66 (€). The best-located crêperie in the city, at the northern end of the Stang Alar gardens.

Café de la Cale, 53 Rue de la Corniche, 29480 Le Relecq-Kerhuon, t 02 98 28 13 19 (€). Out east, a simple, amusing café with a couple of terraces offering fabulous views over the Rade de Brest. Go for a drink, or weekday lunchtimes, a simple traditional home-made meal.

Elorn Calvaries and Enclos Paroissiaux

Brittany's most distinctive and well-known art, the religious art of the *enclos paroissiaux*, or parish church enclosures, flowered particularly finely in the stretch of land between Brest and Morlaix in the 16th and 17th centuries. A distinct sense of rivalry became evident between the parishes around the Elorn Valley. Their churchyards were embellished with ornate entrance arches, ossuaries and, most distinctively, stone calvaries (*see* box, below). Inside, many very colourful altarpieces, or retables, were commissioned in crude Baroque style.

Why did these communities build some of the most sumptuous and showy of Breton churches? The main reason was their huge commercial success in selling cloth to England, Flanders, Spain, and even South America. This was shipped out from the river ports, such as Morlaix and Landerneau. There's a well-trodden Breton art history pilgrimage you can make to a series of *enclos paroissiaux* along the Elorn. The way goes from Plougastel-Daoulas, south of Brest, to St-Thégonnec, close to Morlaix (or vice versa).

Plougastel-Daoulas and its Strawberry Peninsula

The peninsula of **Plougastel-Daoulas** just south of Brest is by far the most attractive natural area along this religious route, though

The Traditional Breton Calvary Scenes

Breton calvary scenes generally concentrate on the best-known stories of the gospels. They often begin with the Annunciation of the virgin birth to Mary. The Visitation might follow, when Mary goes to see her cousin Elizabeth, expecting her own divinely inspired boy, John the Baptist. Sometimes Mary's marriage to Joseph is added in. Following the highly picturesque scenes of the Nativity, the Adoration of the Magi, and the Flight to Egypt (occasionally Jesus's circumcision is also shown), Jesus grows up fast.

The main focus is on the harrowing stages of Christ's crucifixion following his entry into Jerusalem. The Last Supper is always a central theme. His praying in the garden of Gethsemane often features too. Then follow his arrest, maybe his appearance, bound, before the high priest Annas, his encounter with the Roman Pilate, and his flagellation. The painful way of the cross is dwelt on in detail. Crowned with thorns, Christ is helped along with his burden. The veil of Saint Veronica, which she offered Christ on the way to his crucifixion and which retains the imprint of his face, makes for a striking additional scene, carved in low relief.

Christ's crucifixion always occupies the high point of the calvary. Generally the two thieves are also represented, much more contorted, troubling figures on neighbouring crosses. Sometimes, a local Breton saint creeps into the scene, maybe given a place just below the main cross. The Pietà, or grieving mother of Christ mourning her dead son slumped across her lap, conveys the most powerful emotion, along with the entombment scene, with Christ's body laid out in front of a group of mourners, the tears of the onlookers sometimes actually thickly carved on the faces. Christ may descend into limbo before the great image of hope that ends the story – the resurrected Christ stepping out of his tomb.

Getting to and around the Elorn Valley

Local **trains** between Brest and Morlaix stop at Landerneau, La Roche-Maurice, Landivisiau, Guimiliau and St-Thégonnec. A few fast TGV trains from Paris to Brest stop at Landivisiau and Landerneau.

the town of Plougastel-Daoulas, relatively close to Brest, was badly damaged by Second World War bombs. Its church had largely to be rebuilt, hence the funky neo-Gothic steeple aping the old Breton style, but made of concrete.

The famous **calvary** is the main attraction. Covered with some 180 sculpted figures, it too was damaged by bombing, but was restored in good part thanks to the dynamic support of John D. Skilton, a US officer with a strong interest in art history. Among the most substantial in Brittany, the calvary went up between 1602 and 1604, after the parish had suffered terribly from the plague in 1598. Some say that this may in fact be a plague calvary, indicated by the bubo-like protrusions on the crosses.

It is certainly one of the most engrossing calvaries in Brittany. While the structure is of light stone, the carvings are in dark Kersanton granite, extracted from nearby quarries. Kersanton stone would become the favoured medium of many sculptors across Brittany from the mid-15th to the mid-17th centuries. This stone was particularly appreciated by the sculptors as it was relatively easy to carve and also resisted the elements better than others. The calvary's human figures may look rather stilted, but they sport elaborate, refined costumes. The donkeys and horses that feature in the stories are a delight. A staircase up to the top of calvary platform meant it could be used as an outdoor pulpit.

Musée de la Fraise et du Patrimoine
www.musee-fraise.net, **t** *02 98 40 21 18*; *open June–Sept Tues–Fri 10–12.30 and 2–6 and weekends 2–6, Easter hols Tues–Fri 10–12.30 and 2–5.30 and Sun 2–5.30, Feb–May and Oct–Dec Wed–Fri and Sun 2–5.30*

The small, modern **Musée de la Fraise et du Patrimoine** concentrates not just on the long-reputed strawberries of Plougastel-Daoulas, but also on local costumes and traditions, as well as highlighting the little chapels strewn across the **peninsula**, their fountains ascribed various healing powers. Most tourists bypass the Plougastel-Daoulas area because it doesn't have any beaches or resorts, but its maze of badly signposted country lanes are a joy in which to get lost. Its peninsula has often been compared to a hand reaching into the waters of the Rade de Brest; have a look at a regional map and you'll see why.

Dirinon and Daoulas

In the wrist of the glove of the peninsula's hand, Dirinon and Daoulas are two fascinating religious gems. **Dirinon**, set on its height, boasts lovely views. Its charming church is topped by one of those Breton steeples that looks absurdly top-heavy for the size of the place. Above a Gothic accolade arch, spot a statue representing Ste Nonne, a figure of vital importance in Welsh history as well as

Patron Saint of Wales Born to Ste Nonne in Brittany?

The 6th-century Melarie, nicknamed Nonnita (the little nun), or Nonne, when she took the veil, was the daughter of Brecan, a Welsh chieftain, and of Dinam, an Irish princess. A Breton version of her story has it that one day, as Nonne was crossing a Welsh forest, she encountered a wicked prince who had his way with her and made her pregnant. The shamed Nonne sailed off to Brittany to give birth to her son, Divy (Dewi in Welsh, David in English). She came to Dirinon (the place now named in part after her). The rock by which she gave birth to her baby supposedly softened to form a cradle for the newborn infant. A fountain also sprang up, enabling Nonne to baptize her son. She remained here for the rest of her life as a recluse. Divy, the Breton story continues, went back to Wales, where he became a great defender of the Christian faith and a celebrated Celtic evangelizer. Canonized in 1120, he would be made patron saint of Wales. Welsh versions of the life of Ste Nonna differ somewhat. Rhygyfarch, writing in the 11th century, wrote that Nonna was a nun in Dyfed. Seduced by a prince called Sant, as a consequence she gave birth to Dewi or David. She went off to settle at Altarnon in Cornwall for a time, only after that travelling to Brittany, where she would end her days.

being much venerated in Brittany, and said to have died here in the 6th century (*see* box, above).

The church interior is highly decorated. Ceiling paintings along the nave, dating from the Ancien Régime, depict male saints to one side, female saints to the other. Ste Nonne has pride of place in the procession. Her tomb effigy lies in a chapel in the cemetery.

Slopeside **Daoulas** is packed with religious edifices. This very reverend village also grew rich through commerce – *daoulas* even became the name given to a reputed, particularly fine Breton cloth produced around these parts. Merchants came from far and wide, up through to Rade de Brest to the Daoulas River estuary, to buy the prized linen.

The place's longer-lasting fame rests in its **abbey**. Its substantial main **church** still retains some of its lovely Romanesque lines, although it has been much altered through time. The west front and the nave look typical of the grand religious architecture of the late 12th century, and the rounded ends of the apse also clearly date from the Romanesque period.

In 1985 most of the other abbey buildings were bought by the *département* of the Finistère, and a major Breton cultural centre was created within them. Since then, important annual ethnic exhibitions have been held here. Enter the former abbey buildings to see the **exhibitions**; organized with the help of internationally reputed archaeologists and ethnographers, they've won wide acclaim. Recent ones have focused on the Vikings and the Berbers of North Africa.

Abbaye de Daoulas exhibitions
www.abbaye-daoulas.com, **t** *02 98 25 84 39*; *open mid-May–early Jan 10.30–6.30*

The small **Romanesque cloister** you can also see is unique in Brittany, the only one to have survived from its period, although it was much restored during the 19th century. Quite delicate columns hold up the arches, their capitals decorated with foliage and geometrical patterns. A sweet medicinal **herb garden** copying a medieval design has been laid out above the cloister.

Wander down into the village for the 16th-century **oratory of Notre-Dame des Fontaines** and its Breton fountain. Several statues adorn the interior of the oratory with its openwork façade. The **fountain**, with three basins perhaps recalling the Trinity, is watched over by a statue of the Virgin and St Catherine of Siena offering her heart to the Lord. The waters were supposed to cure illnesses of the eye and sterility.

Just east, near Irvillac, go in search of the strangest of Breton calvaries, by the chapel of **Notre-Dame-de-Lorette**. This experimental piece was made in 1644, seemingly copying the curved forms more commonly adopted by goldsmiths. Also of interest at the chapel is a touching carving of Christ's Entombment.

Just southwest of Daoulas, it's quite easy to get lost amidst the tiny lanes on the peninsula of **Logonna-Daoulas**, the traditional houses here employing the area's distinctive yellow stone. Views open up on to the Rade de Brest. **Moulin-Mer**, just south of the pretty village of Logonna-Daoulas itself, is a particularly enchanting spot with its tidal mill, and there's a lively **watersports centre** down here, allowing all manner of possibilities for getting out on the Rade de Brest.

The unappealingly named but prettily located **Hôpital-Camfrout** lies nearby, at the bottom of another river estuary, and just within the Parc Régional Naturel d'Armorique. A little detour from Hôpital-Camfrout takes you to the picturesque **Ile Tibidy**. Although this hasn't been an island for a good long time now, it looks across the waters to the site of Landévennec on the Crozon peninsula, where the most famous Breton abbey of the Dark Ages was constructed (*see* p.312).

The Elorn from Landerneau to Landvisiau

Moving to the Elorn Valley, historic **Landerneau** has preserved a few lovely houses, most obviously some of those built on the spectacular **Pont de Rohan**. It was the nobleman Jean de Rohan who had this amazing bridge built in 1510, sturdily enough to carry the weight of the beautiful chaos of houses to be constructed upon it. They are still lived in – a rarity in Europe. Some further grand blocks line the **Quai de Léon** on the north bank and the **Quai de Cornouaille** to the south. All this indicates what a prosperous river port Landerneau was in past centuries, and well protected upriver from the Rade de Brest. During the Revolution, Landerneau was briefly made capital of the newly formed *département* of Finistère, but lost out to Quimper. In the 20th century, Edouard Leclerc, nicknamed the Grocer of Landerneau, created one of the largest supermarket chains in France, becoming a household name around the country. Yachts moor along the Elorn's quays. On the south side of the river, you might pay your respects to Thomas of Canterbury, to whom the Renaissance-style **Eglise St-Thomas** is dedicated. In July, the town hosts a major Celtic cultural gathering, **Le Festival Kann al Loar** (*www.kann-al-loar.com*)

On its height a little way to the south, the **church of Pencran** is set in a pretty *enclos paroissial*, mostly built in the 16th century. A simple calvary with various branches shows a little figure, arms raised, above Christ, a symbol of his departing soul. The church steeple rises in Renaissance fashion, but the main doorway is Gothic in style. Wonderfully elaborate carvings decorate the outside of it. In the archivolts, you can make out scenes from the Old Testament, from the temptation of Adam and Eve to Noah gathering grapes and then falling into his drunken sleep. A wealth of beam carvings give interest to the interior, the heads of strange men peering down from between foliage motifs.

Welsh visitors might like to make a special detour west of Landerneau to **St-Divy**, dedicated to the Breton version of Dewi, or David. His life story was painted on the **church** ceiling in the 17th century, and one of the statues in the church represents him. The 1552 calvary outside bears the arms of the Rohan family.

Continue east, inland up the wooded Elorn Valley from Landerneau, for pretty **La Roche-Maurice**. The **ruins of a medieval fort** stand out on a bald spur here. Clamber up to them to get fine views down on to the valley. The 16th-century **church of St-Yves** below is best known for its decorated rood screen. The barrel vault is also heavily painted. Much more elegant 16th-century stained glass lights up the choir end, showing scenes from Christ's Passion and his resurrection. The Rohans financed both church and windows. Outside in the parish enclosure, the ossuary of 1639 was built in Renaissance style. Look out, above an outer font, for *l'Ankou*, the Breton Grim Reaper, shown here as a mockery of a Cupid with his arrow of love; here you know that the arrow is deadly. The revered St Yves puts in a more reassuring appearance on the exterior of the ossuary. As ever, he is settling a dispute between a rich man and a pauper.

The *enclos paroissial* of **La Martyre** (south of La Roche-Maurice) reserves a memorable welcome for you along a lovely old village street. This little place gained enough riches to pay for such a magnificent **church** through its popular annual textile fair, to which English, Irish and Flemish traders would come. The church feels almost walled in here. You enter the enclosure under an elaborate arch. The delightful crooked Flamboyant Gothic church porch beyond is one of the oldest of its type in Brittany. The best piece of sculpture on it represents the Nativity, although unfortunately Mary's baby Jesus has disappeared from the scene. Under the porch, the statues of the apostles were added in the 16th century.

A Renaissance ossuary stands next to the porch. The remarkably sinister caryatid figure on this little building certainly shows foreign influences; this naked-breasted, emaciated woman has a stiff skirt wrapped around her legs like the bandages of an Egyptian mummy. However, the elaborate warning carved on the building, reminding us that death awaits us all, is inscribed in Breton.

The stained glass in the main window is sumptuous in its representation of Christ's crucifixion. The influence of elegant northern European style shines through. The wooden arch carrying a cruder Crucifixion scene, the carved stringbeams in the north chapel (in particular the ploughing scene and that of a funeral procession), and the carved panels set around the apse count among the sculptural riches inside the church.

Ploudiry, La Martyre's immediate neighbour to the east, has another distinctive *enclos*, with a very striking **ossuary**, featuring a *danse macabre*. The church's south porch also contains particularly fascinating decorations. (For the *enclos paroissial* of Sizun a short distance southeast, *see* the Monts d'Arrée section, p.299).

A short way west of Landivisiau, the village of **St-Servais** puts its parish enclosure to unusual use, as part of the **Musée Yan'Dargent**. This 19th-century artist, born in the village, produced melodramatic Breton paintings. Religious works of his are displayed around the parish church, a visit to which is included as part of the museum tour.

Musée Yan'Dargent
t 02 98 68 15 21; open July–Sept daily exc Thurs 2–6

Enclos Paroissiaux East of the Elorn

The *enclos paroissiaux* east of the Elorn Valley between Landivisiau and St-Thégonnec don't stand in such picturesque locations as those around the Elorn, but the elaborate Breton church art of the Ancien Régime reaches its pinnacle in the church closes here, paid for by particularly wealthy linen merchants in that period.

Landivisiau to St-Thégonnec

Landivisiau lacks the charm of many other Finistère towns, but it has opened the **Espace Culturel Lucien Prigent** in its own little park, which puts on engaging temporary painting and sculptural exhibitions.

Lampaul-Guimiliau, with its houses built of thin layers of stone, has charm aplenty. The little **Maison du Patrimoine** contains a collection of Breton costumes and furniture. However, it's the

Maison du Patrimoine
open July and Aug daily 10–1 and 2.30–6.30, Sept–June Mon–Fri 2.30–6.30; free

enclos paroissial that's the focus of attention. Inside, the **church** boasts an extraordinarily rich series of six 17th-century **retables**. The most famous one depicts stages in the life of St John the Baptist below some tender 16th-century stained-glass figures. Looking down the nave, you'll be struck by the organ perched on stilts and the remarkable *poutre de gloire*, the main crossbeam, with a colourful crucifixion scene rising from it. As to the baldaquin-covered baptismal font, it looks rustically entertaining, almost vulgarly bright. Among many other artistic features to focus on, the Entombment scene is unusually fine, not a Breton work, but carved from Loire limestone by Antoine Chavagnac in the 17th century. The separate **ossuary** too contains a retable, covered with saints associated with the plague. The plague of commercialization has struck here, though, this ossuary now serving as a shop, selling some particularly ugly statues.

Two naïve riders greet you at the arch leading into **Guimiliau**'s *enclos paroissial*, perhaps the most charming of the major ones of the Léon, with some of the most intriguing, lively and confusing **calvary** scenes. The figures are so blotched with lichen it looks as though they've been struck by a rampant disease. From the Annunciation scene, the Virgin depicted with the symbolic lily of purity, to the monster swallowing sinners destined for hell, the detail and expressions of the carvings are engrossing and more filled with life than on any other Breton calvary. In the depiction of the Last Supper, for example, several of the apostles peer round from behind Christ's shoulder to see what's on the table – and there awaits the roast. In fact most of the apostles appear more interested in the thought of a good feast than in religious matters. A statue of St Pol de Léon stands on a kind of altar under the main classical arch, and a stairway leads to the top of the platform.

Elaborate carving continues as a theme within the **church**, dating back to the Flamboyant Gothic period, but with later additions standing out. The richly wrought organ, an early example of the art, dating from 1677, sticks out on stilts again. The baptismal baldaquin, from the same period, rests on twisting Baroque pillars. The unusual building with its rounded little roofs tacked on to the church is the 17th-century **sacristy**. The **ossuary** here has also been turned into a shop selling wooden statues, among other things. Its retable is dedicated to Ste Anne.

St-Thégonnec boasts the most grandiose of the Léon's *enclos paroissiaux*, rivalled in Brittany only by the one at Pleyben (*see* p.308). Set in the centre of the village, the *enclos* isn't particularly well situated, although its cluster of architectural elements is quite imposing. You enter via a chunky gateway, constructed in 1587 by the builders of the Château de Kerjean (*see* p.265). This gateway reads like a lesson in Renaissance motifs, with its niches, shells, orbs and ornate scrolls, all topped by lanterns. A depiction of the Annunciation has been added into the corners.

Well known for its **calvary**, St-Thégonnec's was one of the last major ones made, dating from 1610. The saint, Thégonnec, is presented with an ox and a deer below him, one of several Breton saints closely associated with oxen, ploughing and the fertility of the soil. The holy man is said to have sailed across the sea to Ireland to become bishop of Armagh later in life. This calvary is relatively simple compared with that at Guimiliau, with just one layer of scenes below the crosses. The story of Christ is limited pretty well to the time from his arrest to his resurrection. The costumes show the fashions of the time the calvary was made, the rounded hats standing out in particular. In certain scenes of the way of the cross, the guards show off bulging codpieces, while their barbaric cruelty is reflected in their monstrously grinning faces.

On to the **church** itself. The end belltower of 1563 is the only remnant of an earlier, Gothic-style church. The other much more imposing tower went up in the first part of the 17th century, competing with the great Renaissance tower that had recently been erected at Pleyben. The elaborate riot of carving inside was badly damaged by a terrible fire in the late 1990s, but a good deal has now been well restored.

⭐ **Le Domaine de Moulin-Mer B&B >>**

ⓘ **Landerneau >>**
Pont de Rohan, t 02 98 85 13 09, www.tourisme. landerneau.daoulas.fr

ⓘ **Pays Touristique des Rives d'Armorique**
t 02 98 21 37 67, www.rives-armorique.fr

ⓘ **Landivisiau**
14 Avenue Foch, t 02 98 68 33 33, www.ot-paysdelandivisiau.com

Market Days in the Elorn Valley

Plougastel-Daoulas: second and last Thursdays in the month; there's also a small Saturday market

Daoulas: Sunday

Landerneau: Tuesday, Friday and Saturday

Landivisiau: Wednesday

Where to Stay and Eat in the Elorn Valley

Plougastel-Daoulas ✉ 29470

Le Chevalier de Lauberlac'h, 5 Rue Mathurin Thomas, **t** 02 98 40 54 56 (€€€–€€). Charming wood-panelled restaurant serving quite refined cuisine.

Daoulas and Logonna-Daoulas ✉ 29460

Ar Baradoz Bihan B&B, 12 Rue de l'Eglise, Daoulas, **t** 02 98 85 04 87 (€). A couple of lovely rooms in a 17th-

century house owned by a former English teacher.

Le Domaine de Moulin-Mer B&B, 34 Route de Moulin-Mer, **t** 02 98 07 24 45 (€€€–€€). Very elegant rooms in this lovely property.

Landerneau ✉ 29800

Le Brunch Breizh, Quai de Léon (€). Restaurant by the water serving original crêpes topped with Breton specialities.

La Roche-Maurice ✉ 29800

Auberge du Vieux Château, 4 Grand-Place, **t** 02 98 20 40 52 (€€–€). A good-value country inn. Advance booking is essential. *Closed lunch.*

Lampaul-Guimiliau ✉ 29400

**Hostellerie des Enclos, t 02 98 68 77 08 (€). A traditional French provincial hotel by the church, not that exciting, but well run.

Ty-Dreux, near Loc-Eguiner-St-Thégonnec ✉ 29410

Ty-Dreux, t 02 98 78 08 21 (€). Delightful rural B&B rooms in a former weaver's village.

St-Thégonnec ✉ 29410
***Auberge St-Thégonnec**, 6 Place de
la Mairie, t 02 98 79 61 18,
www.aubergesaintthegonnec.com
(€€€–€€). Not exciting from the
outside, but with comfortable rooms

and a plush restaurant (€€€–€€) with
good-quality cooking.
Ar Prespital Coz, 18 Rue Lividic, t 02 98
79 45 62, *ar.prespital.koz@orange.fr* (€).
Six spacious B&B rooms in a former
priest's house. *Table d'hôte* (€)
possible.

Into the Monts d'Arrée

Other Bretons were long suspicious of the people of the isolated Monts d'Arrée, an eerie ridge of hills visible from far across northern and central Finistère. In centuries past, this area was considered a kind of no-man's-land between the counties of the Léon to the north and Cornouaille to the south. You may read tales of religious festivals that turned into pagan rituals. You may hear of Monts d'Arrée priests in times past performing exorcisms. Even the locals claimed that the gates to hell lay hidden within the forbidding peat bog of Yeun Elez. But nowadays these hills, and especially their southern slopes, seem particularly appealing and peaceful, with some of the prettiest chapels in Brittany decorating the open, traditional villages. The area is being well preserved as part of the Parc Naturel Régional d'Armorique.

Along the Northern Side of the Monts d'Arrée

Head up the western slopes of the Monts d'Arée for **Sizun**, a pretty crossroads town further up the Elorn Valley. Here we continue with the theme of the *enclos paroissiaux* of the previous touring section, only this enclosure has no proper calvary. But the **church**'s soaring steeple visible from great distances, together with the very substantial entrance gateway to the close, make up for that. The splendid **ossuary** dates from the 1580s, like the gateway. It offers the cheering sight of the apostles neatly put away in their Renaissance niches. The curious caryatids and atlantes carved between the windows below further reflect the Renaissance influence that inspired the sculptors here. The church itself dates almost entirely from the 16th and 17th centuries, except for the steeple tower and porch, added for show in the 18th century. The interior is very noticeably more sober than the rich churches to the north.

Maison de la Rivière
www.maison-de-la-riviere.fr, t 02 98 68 86 33; open July–Aug daily 10–7, out of season Mon–Fri 10–12 and 2–5.30

The **Maison de la Rivière** in the Vergraon mill just northwest of Sizun reveals all sorts of details above the life of the waters of the Monts d'Arrée. A handful of kilometres southeast lies the **Drennec**

reservoir, formed when a dam was built here across the Elorn River in 1982.

Between Sizun and Commana, the Ecomusée des Monts d'Arrée at the Moulins de Kerouat, or watermills of Kerouat, are now home to a charming museum on the traditions of the rural community in these parts, spread around the buildings in a very verdant little setting.

Today a quiet village on its hilltop, **Commana** has a fairly elaborate *enclos paroissial*, indicating that in past times commerce here might have been brisker. The impressive spire went up in 1592. Inside the **church**, the most ornate piece of decoration is the 17th-century retable devoted to Ste Anne. Two large statues, one of the Virgin, one of her revered mother, are shown seated in a riot of Breton–Baroque decoration.

East past Plounéour-Ménez, the grounds of the **abbey of Notre-Dame du Relec** at the foot of the Monts d'Arrée are a pleasure to visit throughout the year, what with their towering trees, monumental Breton fountain and remnants of a moat. The solid Romanesque **church** is the only building still fully standing from the Cistercian monastery that developed here over six centuries. At the **exhibition building** you can learn more about the place and related themes, while in the shop you can sign on for a guided tour and find out about the series of cultural events staged here across the year, including concerts.

Nearby, at **Le Cloître-St-Thégonnec**, the new **Musée du Loup** is prettily set in the village, but recalls a feared animal that used to roam wild in the Monts d'Arrée countryside – the wolf. The last wolves were eradicated from these parts at the end of the 19th century; in fact, this village was the last place in these hills where a hunter was paid for bringing in a dead wolf, back in 1884. Wolves haven't been seen as man's best friend down the centuries, but this modern museum tries to give them a better press, if a little late in the day, as well as focusing on lupine fears exploited in legends and literature. You can actually see living wolves not far off in the Parc d'Armorique, in captivity at the Domaine de Menez-Meur (*see* p.305).

The **Menez Kador**, or Tuchen Gador, and **Roc Trévézel** dominate the backgrounds to these northern Monts d'Arrée villages, these heights sharing the honours for the highest peak in Brittany, at 384 metres, or some way over 1,000ft. The Roc Trévézel stands out for its jagged dinosaur's back of a shape. Head up to these summits, and just a short walk along the rugged crest of the Monts d'Arrée might tempt you into trying a longer hike along the 40-kilometre **Chemin des Crêtes**, which takes you through heather and myrtle tracks, past sharp slices of slate rock sticking viciously out of the ground, while from up high, magnificent views open out to the

Sidebar

Ecomusée des Monts d'Arrée at the Moulins de Kerouat
ecomusee.mont darree@wanadoo.fr, t 02 98 68 87 76; open July and Aug daily 11–7; June Mon–Fri 10–6, Sat and Sun 2–6; mid-March–May and Sept–Oct Mon–Fri 10–6, Sun 2–6

Abbaye de Notre-Dame du Relec exhibition building
www.abbayedurelec. com, t 02 98 78 05 97; open May–Sept daily 10–7, rest of year Wed–Sun 2–6

Musée du Loup
www.museeduloup.fr, t 02 98 79 73 45; open July–Aug daily 2–6, plus Sun only March–June and Sept–mid-Dec

north on to the steeples and patchwork of fields of the Léon. To the south, the Montagne St-Michel-de-Brasparts looks at one and the same time satisfyingly rotund and strangely barren, with just a small chapel placed at the top – see below.

The **St-Michel Reservoir** and **disued Brennilis nuclear power station** are conspicuously visible below. Shut down in 1985, the latter's dismantlement is the subject of an ongoing dispute between the owner company and the environmental movement. This hasn't curbed the enthusiasm of the family who run the curious, cluttered **Auberge Expo du Youdig** near Brennilis. They cheerfully advertise their place as being 'a dream at the gates of hell' – the reference being to an entrance to the underworld said to exist in these parts long before the nuclear power station was built. If you visit this eccentric farm, you can eat at the traditional inn, where Breton song and dance are sometimes on the menu, head out on guided walks, or be treated to strange legends while looking round the twee model of a rag-and-bonemen's village. The itinerant rag merchants of the Monts d'Arrée, *pilhaoueriens* in Breton, became known as great storytellers, though they were often despised. They sold the used cloth they collected to be converted to paper in some of the Breton watermills

In the village of **Brennilis**, the enviromentally aware *Association Bretagne Vivante* runs the new **Maison de la Réserve du Venec et des Castors**, a small museum covering the reintroduction of beavers to the area in particular. The association organizes themed nature walks. Another good organization that organizes a whole programme of special guided walks around the Monts d'Arrée, with Breton teas or music often thrown in, is **ADDES**.

Auberge Expo du Youdig
www.youdig.fr,
t 02 98 99 62 36;
open year-round

Association Bretagne Vivante
www.bretagne-vivante.asso.fr,
t 02 98 79 71 98

Maison de la Réserve du Venec et des Castors
open July–Aug

ADDES
www.arree-randos,
t 02 98 99 66 58

On the Southern Side of the Monts d'Arrée

Huelgoat and its Giant Boulders

Giant boulders clutter the Argent Valley at Huelgoat in fabulous fashion (*see* box, p.304). Head to the town's pretty **lake** marked by the extremely picturesque **Moulin du Chaos** by the bridge. From the mill, then follow the *Sentier Pittoresque* into the extraordinary, deeply dappled valley. Even for adults, it feels like you've been turned into an elf as you descend amid the boulders, picking your way round the contorted tracks. The place is magical, the trunks of the trees covered in as shaggy moss as the rocks. You may be tempted into squeezing into the **Grotte du Diable** ('Devil's Grotto') with the aid of little rungs hammered into the rock. Another secretive, often slippery little path takes you down to the **Ménage**

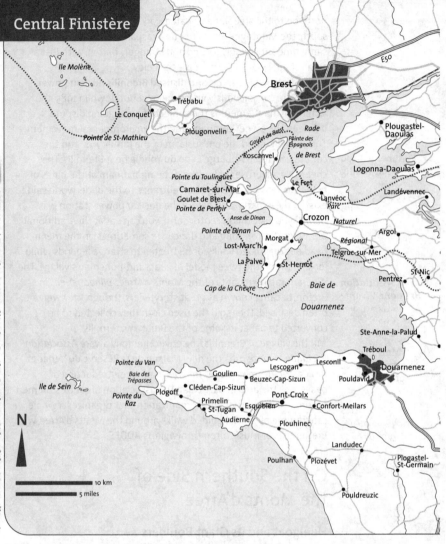

Brest

Ile Molène

Le Conquet

Trébabu

Plougonvelin

Pointe de St-Mathieu

Rade

Pointe des
Espagnols

de Brest

Roscanvel

Plougastel-
Daoulas

Logonna-Daoulas

Pointe du Toulinguet

Camaret-sur-Mar

Goulet de Brest

Pointe de Penhir

Le Fret

Lanvéoc

Landévennec

Parc

Anse de Dinan

Crozon

Naturel

Pointe de Dinan

Morgat

Régional

Argol

Lost-Marc'h

La Palve

St-Hernot

Telgruc-sur-Mer

St-Nic

Pentrez

Cap de la Chèvre

Baie de

Douarnenez

Ste-Anne-la-Palud

Tréboul

Pointe du Van

Baie des
Trépasses

Goulien

Lescogan

Lesconil

Douarnenez

Ile de Sein

Plogoff

Cléden-Cap-Sizun

Beuzec-Cap-Sizun

Pouldavid

Pointe du
Raz

Primelin

Pont-Croix

St-Tugan

Esquibien

Audierne

Confort-Meilars

Plouhinec

Landudec

Plogastel-
St-Germain

Poulhan

Plozévet

Pouldreuzic

N

10 km

5 miles

de la Vierge, where it takes some imagination to make out the Virgin's bed, the cradle for Christ and a cauldron supposedly carved out in the rocks. In a more open location, the **Roche Tremblante** is an enormous boulder that even a child can get to move, if leaning on it in the right spot. There's also an outdoor theatre and a crêperie down in this wacky valley.

Celtic men from the Iron Age appear to have gathered around Huelgoat. You might fancy a walk further out to the **Camp d'Artus**, one of the few vestiges of the pre-Roman Armorican tribes that you can see in Brittany. Later, legend claimed that this was one of King Arthur's camps.

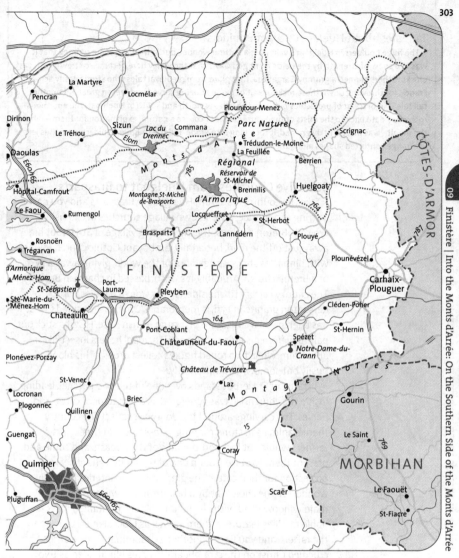

We shouldn't forget the appealing little **town** of Huelgoat itself, mirrored in the calm lake that was only created in the 18th century to help exploit a silver-bearing lead mine down below in the valley – Argent means silver in French. There are some bars with terraces beside the lake, and you'll find a number of galleries and pottery shops on the streets above, while the traditional main square overseen by the church also has bars and crêperies to tempt you in.

From the former station at nearby **Locmaria-Berrien**, **A l'Ouest** offers outings on a simple Breton horse-drawn cart, a popular trip for children.

A l'Ouest
t 02 98 99 73 28

Tall Tales about Huelgoat's Giant Boulders

The huge boulders in Huelgoat's valley are a natural wonder, but in the past, some claimed that it was in a show of strength by the Celtic giant god Gawr that the valley here became so strewn with vast blocks. Others blamed a grumpy Gargantua, that giant from medieval tales who strode easily across France, for throwing down these rocks in a fit of pique at being served bad Breton gruel. Yet another tall tale told of a war of projectiles between the villages north and south of Huelgoat. The enormous rocks may date back to the mists of time, but there is of course a natural explanation for them – where the granite was more thickly grained, it took longer to erode and the tougher boulders were thus left in strange contorted shapes along the river bank.

Secretive Churches from Huelgoat to Brasparts

Take the country road from Huelgoat to Brasparts and you pass a string of adorable, little-known village churches in exquisite, typically Breton settings. The enchanting village of **St-Herbot** hides away just off the road, but a tall Flamboyant Gothic church tower with pinnacles sticks its head out of the wood, giving away a gem of a Breton **church**. Arguably, it's unsurpassed in charm in Brittany. The chunky calvary to one side, carved from a big block of Kersanton granite in 1571, is memorable. On it, the crucified Christ has been given a caricature of a large Jewish nose. His ribs stick out painfully from his emaciated body. An angel hovers insect-like above him, while two robed figures collect drops of his blood, busily but somewhat indifferently.

A statue of St Herbot stands over one of the two porches leading inside the church. He was venerated as a protector of cattle and horses. The carvings around the doorways reflect the country theme, animals in stone running across them. In times past, local farmers would cut locks off the tails of their beasts and come and present them to St Herbot on one of the church altars, seeking protection for their cattle. The granite-floored interior is utterly wonderful. The choir is lit by a beautiful rose window and by a main window filled with splendid 16th-century stained glass – noble families feature in them as well as biblical ones. Look up to the rafters, and you'll spot another extraordinary figure of the crucified Christ on the stringbeam, his eyes blindfolded as two angels collect his blood. Come back down to earth at the deliciously quaint café beside the church, open in season.

Loqueffret, in its lovely open slopeside location, benefits from great views of the Monts d'Arrée to the north and the Montagnes Noires to the south. Its Gothic **church** and its calvary are coloured with bright lichens, orange on the church roof, green on the calvary. Two remarkably acrobatic angels hold up one of the latter's branches. Go round the outside of the church to appreciate the exterior stone carvings; one figure sticks out like a merry sailor peering out to sea, even if lost so far inland.

Carved deer frolic all over the place in the *enclos paroissial* of **Lannédern**. One is stuck on the simple calvary, being ridden by the cowled St Edern himself. The story goes that this religious man offered refuge in his hermitage in the woods to a terrified deer that was being pursued by hunters. The church and village of Lannédern lie on one of the brightest, prettiest and most open slopes of the southern Monts d'Arrée, with the Montagne St-Michel-de-Brasparts in the distance. The whole *enclos paroissial* is photogenic in the extreme. The ossuary includes the figure of a comically puffy-cheeked angel between a skull and cross bones. *L'Ankou*, the Breton Grim Reaper, puts in an appearance too.

The **church close** occupies the prime position in the traditional hilltop village of **Brasparts**. It's a moving place, with one of the most powerful Breton Pietà carvings on its calvary, the three women around the dead Christ stiff with the shock of grief, their faces almost oriental in look. St Michael pokes his very long, sharp sword into the devil's mouth below. On the ossuary, *l'Ankou* appears twice, in one image holding an arrow, in the other his scythe, looking like a very laid-back Grim Reaper having completed his chores. Beyond the close, the cemetery tumbles down the hillside, while in the distance, you can spot the remarkable form of the Montagne St-Michel-de-Brasparts.

The Montagne St-Michel-de-Brasparts and St-Rivoal

Ferme des Artisans
t 02 98 81 46 69;
open July–mid-Sept
daily 10–7.30, April–June
and rest of Sept
weekdays 2–6.30,
weekends 10.30–7;
rest of year
weekends 10.30–7

Heading north up to the rugged, rounded hilltop of the Montagne St-Michel-de-Brasparts, stop at the **Ferme des Artisans**. All manner of crafts, and artisans from across western France, are represented in the exhibition spaces here, some of the work of a high quality.

The circular hill of the **Montagne St-Michel-de-Brasparts** is said to have been venerated by the pre-Roman inhabitants of Armorica, its roundness symbolizing the sun god Belenos. The 17th-century **chapel** on top of it is battered by the winds, but the views from this treeless summit are sensational.

Maison Cornec
t 02 98 68 87 76;
open July–Aug daily
11–7, June daily 2–6;
first half Sept daily
exc Sat 2–6

Set in unspoilt Breton countryside, the little **Maison Cornec** at St-Rivoal is a traditional village farm that has been subtly restored by the Parc Régional Naturel d'Armorique and turned into a little museum on rural life in centuries past. The farmhouse dates from 1702; the name of the first occupant, Y. Cornec, is inscribed over the door. For an enjoyable taste of rural produce from these parts, try the **Bro ar Are grocer** in the village, specializing in local delights, organically made.

Domaine de Menez Meur
domaine.menez.meur
@pnr-armorique.fr, t 02
98 68 81 71; open
May–Sept daily 10–6;
March–April and
Oct–Nov Wed and Sun
1–5.30; Dec–Feb, school
hols daily exc Sat 1–5

The **Domaine de Menez Meur**, the Monts d'Arrée's animal park, lies a little west of St-Rivoal. From the car park, a beautiful old Breton track, with beeches planted on the moss-covered earth walls to either side, leads to the farmyard with its explanatory panels on Breton horses – the Domaine incorporates the **Maison du Cheval** explaining the history of these sturdy breeds. On certain days you can take a ride around the park on a Breton horse-drawn cart. In the neatly separated fields on the property, go in search of tiny Ouessant sheep, wild boar and wolves, all among the animals most strongly associated with Brittany. Endangered types of Breton cattle and several species of deer are also kept here.

ⓘ **Parc Naturel Régional d'Armorique**
t 02 98 81 90 08, www.parc-naturel-armorique.fr

ⓘ **Pays Touristique du Centre Finistère**
t 02 98 26 60 25, www.tourisme-centrefinistere.com

ⓘ **Brasparts >>**
Place des Monts d'Arrée, t 02 98 81 47 06, www.yeun-elez.com

ⓘ **Huelgoat >**
Moulin du Chaos, t 02 98 99 72 32, www.tourisme huelgoat.fr

Market Days in the Monts d'Arrée

Sizun: 1st Friday of the month

Huelgoat: 1st and 3rd Thursdays of the month

St-Rivoal: 1st day of the month in April, July, Aug and Sept

Where to Stay and Eat in the Monts d'Arrée

Plounéour-Menez/ Le Relecq ✉ 29410

Restaurant du Relecq, t 02 98 78 06 88 (€€). Opposite Le Relec abbey, a nice quiet country spot at which to dine, tables set outside on good days. *Closed Sat.*

Scrignac ✉ 29640

Lesénéchal, t 02 98 78 23 13 (€€). Fine restaurant serving elaborate Breton cuisine.

Trédudon-le-Moine, northwest of Berrien ✉ 29690

Ferme-auberge de Porz Kloz, t 02 98 99 61 65, www.monsite.wanadoo.fr/porzkloz (€€–€). A converted farmhouse set in picturesque moorlands in the Monts d'Arrée, with pretty, comfortable studio rooms.

Huelgoat ✉ 29690

Hôtel du Lac, 12 Rue de Brest, **t 02 98 99 71 14 (€). A reasonable budget option that looks out prettily over the lake of Huelgoat.

Crêperie des Myrtilles, 26 Place Aristide Briand, **t** 02 98 99 72 66 (€). A crêperie in a beautiful house in the centre of town, with Breton furniture.

L'Autre Rive, t 02 98 99 72 58 (€). Out in the forest of Huelgoat, this enchanting café-cum-bookshop does delightful lunch dishes.

Poullaouën ✉ 29246

Les Tilleuls de Goasvennou B&B, t 02 98 93 57 63, www.chambres lestilleuls.free.fr. Four nicely presented rooms in a traditional Breton long house, where you'll be pampered by the young farmer's wife.

Auberge de la Tour d'Auvergne, 5 Ave de la Tour d'Auvergne, **t** 02 98 93 52 64 (€€). For good, fresh Breton country cooking.

Brennilis ✉ 29690

Auberge du Youdig, t 02 98 99 62 36, www.youdig.fr (€). Offers B&B accommodation and typical Breton meals, as well as its eccentric museum (see p.301).

La Feuillée ✉ 29690

Auberge de la Crêpe, t 02 98 99 68 68 (€). A typical Breton stop for a bite to eat, in the pretty village itself.

Brasparts ✉ 29190

Les Roulottes des Korrigans, t 02 98 81 41 62, www.roulottes-korrigans.com. Smartly done up wagons set in countryside near the village, available for B&B nights or longer.

Domaine de Rugornou Vras, t 02 98 81 46 27, www.vacances-arree.com (€). A very good-value B&B option in a traditional building. *Table d'hôte.*

Garz ar Bik, t 02 98 81 47 14 (€). Similiar to the above, also with *table d'hôte.*

Up the Aulne Valley

Ignoring the Aulne estuary covered in the section on the Crozon peninsula (*see* p.311), this route takes you back up along the winding banks of the Aulne, past rustic chapels, from Châteaulin to Carhaix-Plouguer. This beautiful stretch of river became the final westerly link to the sea for the Canal de Nantes à Brest, built in the early 19th century, with locks making it navigable for barges transporting materials between the two great Breton ports, thus helping avoid more dangerous trips by sea, on which convoys could be attacked in time of war. Abandoned for some time, the locks and towpaths have recently been restored; many of the lock-keepers' cottages have been turned into little *centres d'interprétation*. Our Aulne Valley trip offers a beautiful, mellow bucolic route into central Finistère. The hill range of the Montagnes Noires or 'Black Mountains' rises along the river's south bank, from the Ménez-Hom looming over the Baie de Douarnenez to the heights to the east where the three Breton *départements* of the Finistère, the Côtes d'Armor and the Morbihan meet.

The Aulne from Châteaulin to Pleyben

The lovely country **chapel of St-Sébastien-en-St-Ségal** sits quietly above a meander in the Aulne northwest of Châteaulin. It was built in the mid-16th century, apparently to help in the Christian fight to ward off the plague. On the monumental gateway, St Sebastian, a saint closely associated, in his bearing of suffering, with the dreaded epidemic, is being shot at from close range by archers. Near the gateway, the calvary, in darker Kersanton stone, lies just outside the enclosure wall. The chapel's interior looks rather empty, but the choir end is abuzz with carved activity. Typically Breton–Baroque, incredibly sickly-sweet, it dates from around 1700. Look out for the Nativity scene, in which one of the shepherds has brought along his Breton bagpipes. A separate set of panels tells the hilarious story of the Virgin Mary's miraculous flying house doing its tour of Europe, carried by angels.

Heading east, the road continues to a beautiful meander in the Aulne at **Port-Launay**, the crescent of old houses reflecting the river's path. This was clearly a good spot for trading in times past, while a 50-metre high train viaduct crosses the valley, adding to the drama.

Round the corner, you arrive at the appealingly picturesque but untouristy small town of **Châteaulin**, with its substantial quayside houses on either side of the river. A row of bridges connects the two banks. In season, you can see locals fishing on the boulders out in the water; angling is a major activity along the Aulne. A **passe à**

Getting around the Aulne Valley

Carhaix-Plouguer has a **railway** station and is roughly 2hrs from Rennes by train, or 4hrs 30mins from Paris. Châteaulin also has a railway station on the north–south Brest to Quimper line. A local **bus** service links Châteaulin with Carhaix-Plouguer. Further bus routes link Carhaix-Plouguer with Morlaix to the north, and Pleyben with Quimper to the south.

poissons was installed by the river so that you can go and view the fish going up and down it.

Do venture up the left bank of the river at Châteaulin to the **Chapelle Notre-Dame**, a lovely Breton chapel set in a picturesque corner by the meagre ruins of Châteaulin's château. In fact the chapel was built to serve the lords of this fortress. The very primitive calvary, dating from the late 15th century, carries a carving of the Last Judgement on one side.

Although not as attractive as Châteaulin, **Pleyben** draws more tourists, as it boasts possibly the grandest of all the Breton *enclos paroissiaux*, church and enclosure dominating the centre of town. The **calvary** is the most famous feature of the place. It looks like a massive triumphal arch. Because its base is much taller than that of most of the other Breton calvaries, it makes the sculpted scenes that much harder to look at in detail. However, on the two levels below the crosses, episodes in Christ's life unfold in fascinating detail. Some of the figures were carved in the mid-16th century, more in the mid-17th – look at how much Christ changes in character.

The **ossuary**, one of the oldest in Brittany, dating from the mid-16th century, now houses a tiny museum. The **sacristy**, with its typical period roundedness, was added for further show in 1719. The **church** itself is dedicated to St Germain l'Auxerrois – not a local saint but a national one. Two competing towers rise from the edifice. The choir is lit by a refined 16th-century stained-glass window once more illustrating Christ's Passion, the stylized trees shaped like vases.

Pleyben's other claim to fame is its Breton butter biscuits, the *galettes de Pleyben*. On the broad squares around the church, you'll find several outlets selling them, as well as competing crêperies.

Châteauneuf-du-Faou to Carhaix

Châteauneuf-du-Faou, a little town to the east, looks down on another meander of the Aulne and across to the Montagnes Noires to the south. The painter Paul Sérusier, so closely associated with the Pont-Aven School (*see* box, p.367), came and settled here for much of his life. In 1919 he decorated the little chapel that contains the baptismal font in the town church.

There are several points of interest at the riverside. There's a **Base Fluviale** at **Penn ar Pont**, to help you get out on the water, and where you can even hire a barge for a weekend – contact **Aulne Loisirs Plaisance, t** 02 98 73 28 65. As to the **Maison Eclusière**, it holds an exhibition on the fauna of the area. It's quite some walk along the towpath eastwards to the **Chapelle du Moustoir**, but the way is rather beautiful. This chapel has been saved from ruin by a passionate local group that has gone a bit crazy with the flower planting – the place can look as gaudily colourful on the outside as Breton retables so often look on the inside of Breton chapels. However, here, the restored interior proves pleasantly simple.

Château de Trévarez
www.trevarez.com,
t 02 98 26 82 79; open
July and Aug daily
11–6.30; April–June and
Sept daily 1–6; Oct–late
Nov and March Wed,
Sat and Sun 2–5.30

South of the Aulne and out of town, the **Château de Trévarez** stands out on the wooded slopes of the Forest of Laz. Although known as the *château rose*, the building actually looks more ruddy orange than pink. It is quite rare to see brick at all in western Brittany, and the structure sticks out a bit like a sore thumb in these traditionally Breton parts, but the place has undeniable grandeur. In fact it was built in mock Loire Renaissance style from the late 19th century, for the ambitious Marquis de Kerjégu, president at that period of the Conseil Général du Finistère and a member of the French parliament. It fell into disrepair after the Second World War, but the Conseil Général du Finistère bought it in 1968 and it has now been fully restored.

All manner of **exhibitions** take place here across the year, not in the castle itself, but in the well-adapted stables. Much of the interest of the place lies in the large **grounds** and their special plants; the Domaine de Trévarez is well known for its seasonal collections, of camellias, azaleas, rhododendrons, hydrangeas and fuchsias in particular. Look out too for **seasonal festivals** here.

Country roads lead up through the dense Forêt de Laz to some of the highest heights of the **Montagnes Noires**. These aren't mountains at all, but a line of wooded hills following the course of the Aulne. They don't get much above 300 metres above sea level, but do offer fine views over inland Brittany from their quiet crests. Neolithic men built burial mounds along them. You can see the very meagre remains of one at **Kastell Ruffel at Coat Plin-Coat**, marked by a big golf ball of a radar station; what's more moving is the fabulous view over central Finistère at your feet.

These parts on the border with the Morbihan still feel deeply rural. Superstitious priests sent up here in centuries past claimed that the devil encouraged the locals to participate in all manner of satanic rituals. L'Ankou, the Breton Grim Reaper who sharpened his scythe on human bones, was also said to enjoy hanging out here. The next height east of Kastell Ruffel is marked by a statue, **Notre-Dame-des-Montagnes-Noires**, set up by an extraordinarily eccentric aristocrat who settled here. Vefa de Saint-Pierre had no time for the local superstitions, but was crazy about her hunting. An exquisite recent French biography about her, *Une Amazone* *bretonne*, by Claire Arlaux, tells her life, from the time, as a young girl, when 'she handled guns the way other girls handled knitting needles'. The **Roc de Toullaeron** a hike further east is one of the very highest points of the Montagnes Noires, at 326 metres. Gourin just across in the Morbihan, styles itself capital of these 'mountains' (*see* p.391).

Back down close to the Aulne, **Spézet** is a traditional village deeply proud of its Breton culture; it organizes a festival of the Breton language every Whitsun, and is home to a dedicated Breton publisher, Keltia, which has an excellent bookshop, the **Coop Breizh**, on the edge of town, selling books in both French and Breton, covering all manner of regional topics, from Breton songs to Breton surfing, via history and culture.

The **chapel of Notre-Dame du Crann**, slightly hidden by trees off a road to the south, is renowned for its 16th-century Renaissance stained-glass windows. They are of exceptional finesse and sophistication for Brittany, let alone a deeply rural spot like this, and were apparently paid for by parishioners. The windows tell the stories of Christ, the Virgin, and the man who became the patron saint of blacksmiths and goldsmiths, Eloi – there was clearly some money around in these parts. The stories of St Brigid's connections with Brittany are recounted beneath a striking naive statue of the great Irish saint, whom, legend had it, could get a full bucket of milk from her cows three times a day, clearly a miracle of great proportions for such country areas.

To the east, the Canal de Nantes à Brest branches off from the Aulne, flowing close to **St-Hernin**, a village centred around an exceptionally pretty church enclosure. The scene is full of engrossing details. On the calvary, the two thieves crucified alongside Christ are shown in the most contorted poses. A Pietà, Mary grieveing over her dead son, has been placed on the ossuary. Hernin, one of the saintly wave of immigrants from Dark Ages Britain, is depicted over one of the church's porches. A hilarious series of carvings is lined up above the main entrance, including a giant saint stamping on a monster, and the hand of God holding the globe like a football. The neighbouring village of **Cléden-Poher** closer to the Aulne also has a remarkable calvary, framed by two memorably caricatural Roman soldiers on their horses.

The market town of these parts, **Carhaix-Plouguer** has known more important days. It may have been a Gallo-Roman town of some significance, going by the renown of Vorgium; it became the legendary capital of the evil Breton chieftain Comorre in the Dark Ages; it was intimately linked with the legend of Tristan and the second Yseut, she of the white hands; and in reality, it became the capital of the central Breton county of Poher. It still has a few pretty old streets, notably Rue Brizeux. The **Maison du Sénéchal**, with its

Pays Touristique du Centre Finistère
www.tourisme-centrefinistere.com, for information across the area

ⓘ Châteauneuf-du-Faou >>
Place Ar Segal, t 02 98 81 83 90, www.chateauneuf-du-faou.com

ⓘ Carhaix-Plouguer >>
Rue Brizeux, t 02 98 93 04 42, www.poher.com

★ Manoir de Kerledan >>

ⓘ Pleyben >
Place Charles de Gaulle, t 02 98 26 71 05, www.ville-de-pleyben.com

ⓘ Châteaulin
Quai Cosmao, t 02 98 86 02 11, www.tourisme-porzay.com

Market Days in the Aulne Valley

Châteaulin: Thursday
Pleyben: Saturday and 2nd Tuesday of the month
Châteauneuf-du-Faou: 1st, 3rd and 5th Wednesdays of the month
Spézet: last Friday of the month
Carhaix-Plouguer: Saturday

Where to Stay and Eat in the Aulne Valley

Pont-Coblant, south of Pleyben ✉ 29190
Le Poisson Blanc, t 02 98 73 34 76 (€€–€). Nicely located restaurant by the Aulne.

Pleyben ✉ 29190
La Blanche Hermine, 1 Place du Général de Gaulle, t 02 98 26 61 29 (€€). Traditional Breton food. *Closed Wed exc July and Aug, Mon and Tues eves in winter.*
Crêperie de l'Enclos, 51 Place Charles de Gaulle, t 02 98 26 38 68 (€). A popular crêpes stop.

Châteauneuf-du-Faou ✉ 29520
**Le Relais de Cornouaille, 9 Rue Paul Sérusier, t 02 98 81 75 36, *www.le relaisdecornouaille.com* (€). Old-style French provincial hotel with modest rooms. The restaurant (€€–€) serves good country fare.
Crêperie Le Petit Rozell, 6 Rue de la Mairie, t 02 98 73 25 49 (€). A good rustic crêperie.

Carhaix-Plouguer ✉ 29270
**Noz Vad, 12 Blvd de la République, t 02 98 99 12 12, *www.nozvad.com* (€€–€). Pleasingly modernized.
Manoir de Kerledan, t 02 98 99 44 63, *www.kerledan.com*. Gorgeous tasteful rooms in this manor renovated by Brits in the countryside outside town.
La Rotonde, Place des Droits de l'Homme, t 02 98 93 30 41 (€). Traditional Breton meat dishes served in an old town house.
Crêperie Ty Gwechall, 25 Rue Victor Massé, t 02 98 93 17 00 (€). Plenty of Breton charm.

Port-de-Carhaix ✉ 29270
Auberge du Poher, t 02 98 99 51 18. Country inn serving fine dishes.

carved timbers, contains the tourist office and the little local history museum.

Carhaix isn't wholly pickled in the past. Every year it hosts a major **rock festival**, by the misleadingly quaint title of **Les Vieilles Charrues**, the Old Ploughs. In school holidays, the indoor pools of **Plijadour** please the kids. Year round, you can visit the **Coreff Breton beer maker** opposite the station. Head out a couple of kilometres to the **Vallée de l'Hyère** where you can enjoy a little golf course, a treetop assault course or the equestrian centre all benefiting from the beautiful forest setting.

The Crozon Peninsula

Nowhere in Brittany does the coast look more unrelentingly sensational than along the alarmingly beautiful cliffs of the Presqu'île de Crozon, specially protected as part of the Parc Naturel Régional d'Armorique. In the east, at the mouth of the Aulne River, the ruins of the abbey of Landévennec are the major cultural

Getting around the Crozon Peninsula

Châteaulin has the nearest **train** station, with **buses** from there taking you onto the peninsula. You can also get buses from Brest and Quimper.

attraction, while at the other end of the peninsula, Camaret and Morgat are the main resorts. Two interesting new tourist routes have been laid out recently around the Presqu'île, encouraging you to follow a couple of major themes. The **Route des Fortifications** takes you round via a whole series of defences, dating from prehistoric times to the Ancien Régime, dotted around the coast, and emphasizing that the Crozon peninsula, with its amazing natural fortifications, has long been a major strategic spot – France's naval officers are still trained along its northern shore. The **Cheminements du Roi Marc'h** focus on sites associated with Celtic legends in these parts – this loop starts on the flanks of the Ménez-Hom hill that dominates the views at the back of the Presqu'île.

The Northern Crozon Peninsula via Landévennec

Le Faou, northern gateway to the Crozon peninsula, is a sweet old village set back in a typical Breton estuary. The slate-covered sides of the fine 16th-century houses in the centre show that the merchants here once enjoyed great prosperity thanks to river trading. At one period, timber used to be brought down from the forests to the east to be shipped over to Brest for the building of the massive wooden naval vessels of the Ancien Régime.

An exceptionally pretty corniche road leads you from Le Faou to the **Pont de Térénez** spanning the Aulne. From the bridge you can admire the most gorgeous wooded river valley.

Abbaye de Landévennec

Abbaye de Landévennec
www.parc-naturel-armorique.fr, **t** *02 98 27 35 90; open July–mid-Sept daily 10–7; April–June, second half Sept, and French school hols 15–30 Sept Sun–Fri 2–6*

Quite impressively, in 1985 the abbey of Landévennec celebrated its 1,500th anniversary. A Gallo–Roman religious edifice may even have preceded the Dark Ages Breton one so feted in 1985. However, the mysterious Celtic Christian foundation is the most intriguing of the chain of religious establishments to have succeeded one another at Landévennec. The very hazy memories of it centre around stories of Guénolé, one of the great Breton saints of the Dark Ages (*see* box).

The abbey ruins are a bit of a mess, and a bit of a let-down if you don't know the deep historical significance of this Breton spiritual centre. Archaeological digs have been going on here for many

Whiter than White – St Guénolé

'Bold White' might be a translation for the name Guénolé, giving you a hint about the guy's purity. The stories of his life derive from hagiographies devoted to him, notably the work by a Landévennec monk named Clément, writing around AD 860 – that is, some three centuries after Guénolé is reckoned to have lived. Guénolé's father, Fracan, was apparently a man of some standing, cousin of the Breton chieftain Catovius, but his mother, the purely named Gwenn-Alba ('White White'), had higher ambitions for her son. Guénolé was sent as a boy to St Budoc's monastic school on the island of Lavret near Bréhat (*see* p.215) to prepare for his future. Having learnt to work miracles, as one clearly did in Celtic religious school, Guénolé headed off to perform them in western Brittany. He first stopped on the Ile Tibidy. Then, driven on by a vision, he crossed the sea to Landévennec (without getting his feet wet, of course), followed by 11 disciples. They set about building a Christian monastery that would grow rapidly in influence. A cult developed around St Guénolé after his death. He was supposed to be able to assist with problems of fertility and to help babies grow strong and walk. This was in addition to his powers for curing neuralgia and warts. His cult spread far, to several places in southern England even. Guénolé and Landévennec are also intimately associated with the powerful Breton legends of Gradlon, King of Cornouaille, and of the fabulously opulent and immoral town of Ys, said to be lost somewhere under the waters of the Bay of Douarnenez (*see* box, p.324).

years, and the funky modern museum next to the ruins displays some of the finds.

Almost nothing concrete is known about Guénolé's Celtic Christian monastery. However, some evidence exists of Landévennec in the 9th century. While Roman Catholicism was spreading its influence ever more widely across France, this was quite possibly the last place where Celtic Christianity kept a foothold on the European continent. With St-Sauveur in Redon, this abbey had become the main centre for spiritual and literary endeavour in Brittany. Some weird and wonderful illuminated manuscripts were prepared at Landévennec in this period. The most famous depict the Evangelists, but with strange animal heads. These manuscript treasures are now in the hands of the New York Public Library, but copies of them are visible around the museum. Vikings brought this period of influence to a swift end. Landévennec fell prey to the pillaging Norsemen in 913. The monks fled. England's Anglo-Saxon King Athelstan apparently helped the abbey start to get back on its feet.

The Romanesque reconstruction of Landévennec lasted through the 11th and 12th centuries, in a period of relative prosperity. But during the 14th century, few parts of Brittany would be spared the effects of warring, and Landévennec was once again largely ruined. Following dark times, Jehan du Vieux Chastel ordered the abbey's rebuilding early in the 16th century. He also commissioned a statue of St Guénolé that you can see here. However, time and again through the Ancien Régime the abbey would experience a cycle of revival and collapse.

By the 19th century, the place lay in ruins. However, towards the end of the century, one Comte de Chalus fell for the place and devoted his energies to restoring it, albeit to his tastes. He it was who had the palm trees planted around the ruins, giving them their vaguely exotic air. He apparently enjoyed wandering around the property dressed up as a monk. Taking Landévennec rather more seriously, a group of Benedictine monks bought the place from the count's heirs in 1950, built the separate modern abbey, and encouraged restoration and research work on the ruins.

The **ruins** you can walk around are basically those of the early medieval church, some of the columns that remain decorated with typical period motifs. The nave of seven bays had cruciform pillars to hold up the ceiling. The wide transept was followed by a choir with an ambulatory and three rounded ends. Two chapels stood next to the south transept. One is still known as King Gradlon's Tomb, but it only dates from the 12th century, while the remains of frescoes are from the 16th and 17th centuries. The other chapel was where the tomb of St Guénolé was housed for a time, its walls one of the oldest vestiges of Landévennec, dating from Carolingian times. The south transept of the Romanesque ruins leads out to where the abbey cloisters stood.

The **museum** displays finds going back beyond the Breton Dark Ages and well beyond the confines of the abbey. Statuettes and an amphora are signs of Gallo–Roman settlements around the Rade de Brest. Models and plans give an impression of what successive monasteries at Landévennec looked like. To bring more life to the place, in recent years it has hosted concerts, evening walks and classes, for example in manuscript-making. Each summer, they also create a new temporary garden.

You can attend services at the **new abbey**, built of sturdy granite. There's a monastic shop as well, which helps fund the monastery. The small village of **Landévennec** is charming, so well protected from the worst of the Atlantic weather that Mediterranean plants thrive here.

The North Shore of the Crozon Peninsula

You can walk a stretch of coastal path westwards from Landévennec, but after that a large portion of the north shore of the Crozon peninsula is reserved for the French navy – the Anse de Poulmic is where France's naval officers are trained. A little way inland, by Les Quatre Chemins, signs lead you to the **Musée du Cidre**, basically a glorified farm shop with a makeshift cider museum tacked on. Of more substance is the Musée des Vieux Métiers at **Argol**. Here, on selected afternoons, you can see a variety of craftspeople demonstrating different old trades, such as weaving, basket-weaving or forging.

Back on the peninsula's northern shore, west of military Lanvéoc, the little old ports of **Le Fret** and **Rostellec** look quite innocent with

Musée des Vieux Métiers
www.argol.fr,
t 02 98 27 79 30; open April–Sept Tues, Thurs and Sun 2–5.30

their old fishermen's cottages, but they lie at the foot of the submarine base of L'Ile Longue. From Le Fret, the **Société Maritime Azénor** runs little ferry services to Brest, offering a fabulous trip across the Rade de Brest.

West of here, the coast road leads up to the large **peninsula of Roscanvel**. The top of this peninsula forms the south bank of the Goulet de Brest, the narrow straits controlling the entrance to the great Bay of Brest. The **Pointe des Espagnols**, the most northerly outpost, stands guard right over this strategic point. It was occupied by Spanish soldiers at the end of the 16th century, during the French Wars of Religion, hence the name.

Société Maritime Azénor
www.azenor.com,
t 02 98 41 46 23

To Camaret-sur-Mer

You finally emerge from the naval terrain dominating the north side of the Presqu'île de Crozon around the **Plage de Trez Rouz**, or Red Beach. The rocks do have rather orange tinges, but the strand apparently got its name for more gory reasons, to recall the blood of English and Dutch sailors whose bodies were washed ashore here after the epic naval battle fought in the **Anse de Camaret** in 1694.

The extraordinary natural feature of **Camaret-sur-Mer**, its pebbly jetty, curves out into the well-protected Bay of Camaret. Along this flat spit, known as a *sillon*, the wooden skeletons of several large abandoned fishing boats add a melancholic but picturesque note to the scene – Camaret used to be a major fishing port until quite recently. Modern yachts have replaced these redundant fishing vessels.

The light-coloured stone of the **Chapelle Notre-Dame de Rocamadour** on the *sillon* wonderfully mimics marble, with its swirling traces of colour. The edifice is said to have lost the top of its steeple to an English cannonball in the violent 1694 battle. Inside, *ex voto* models of boats hang from the nave crossbeam.

The **Tour Vauban** is named after Louis XIV's famed military architect Sébastien de Vauban. Practically all the fortifications he planned out for France's borders have been listed as part of a UNESCO World Heritage Site in his honour, including this one. The fort is one of his more curious works, an eccentric-looking piece of architecture with its deeply pigmented orangey-red walls. Camaret's bay clearly presented enormous advantages for the French navy, though, offering an obvious safe haven, and an outer harbour for Brest, hence Vauban's interest in the place. He came to see to its fortification in 1689. The sea used to provide a moat for further defence. Vauban's military and engineering genius and achievements are recalled in the modest museum inside the tower.

Tour Vauban
open daily July and Aug 10–6; Sept, Oct and April–June daily 3–6; Nov–March Sat and Sun 3–6

North of the *sillon*, the **beach of Corréjou**, part pebbly, part sandy, stretches along to the unspoilt **Pointe du Gouin**, which you can walk round. Camaret offers a variety of delightful possibilities for getting out to sea to admire the Crozon peninsula from the water. **Pesketour** proposes either sea tours or fishing off the coast in a former trawler, for small numbers. With **Autour de l'Eau**, small groups can go out around the peninsula on a large catamaran. The **Société Maritime Azénor** operates the classic crossing to and from Brest. As to the **Compagnie Penn ar Bed**, this ferry company runs boats from Camaret to the islands of Ouessant, Molène and Sein, April to September only.

The Western Headlands of the Crozon Peninsula

The many headlands along the western coast of the Crozon peninsula vie with each other in drama. Beyond Camaret's suburbs, you come to the **Pointe du Toulinguet**. After the protected Anse de Camaret, suddenly you're exposed to the vastness of the Atlantic ocean. On the north side, you can look down onto some particularly weirdly shaped rock formations, one pierced by a natural arch, others topped by pinnacles.

Past the disconsolate neolithic **Alignements de Lagatjar**, some messy former Nazi fortifications provide spaces for a bird and seashell museum, the **Musée Ornithologique et des Coquillages**, and for a museum devoted to the Second World War Battle of the Atlantic, the **Musée Mémorial International de la Bataille de l'Atlantique**. French, US, British and European flags fly over this museum in such a fitting location. An anchor memorial outside pays homage to the 45,000 Allied merchant navy sailors who lost their lives between 1939 and 1945 in the vital actions to keep supply convoys going between Britain and North America in the Second World War. The success of all the Allied operations against the Nazis depended to a great degree on keeping this transatlantic link open. Some 30,000 German submariners would also die in this atrocious Atlantic conflict – their average age was just 20.

The Pointe du Toulinguet is breathtaking enough, but the **Pointe de Penhir** eclipses it. The most sensational natural element to this headland is the **Tas de Pois**, a series of massive lumps of rocks ricocheting out to sea. A huge cross of Lorraine marks out the headland. This huge cement memorial commemorates the efforts of Breton fighters in the Second World War. The adventurous among you might contact **Face Ouest**, a young team that organizes exhilarating rock-climbing and sea-canyoning in this tremendous site; clearly these activities aren't for the faint-hearted.

The coastal path leading from the Pointe de Penhir right down to the Cap de la Chèvre takes you along a gloriously rugged coast.

Pesketour
pesketourarmement
@wanadoo.fr,
m 06 07 70 76 49

Autour de l'Eau
www.autourdeleau.
com, m 06 63 62 95 10

Société Maritime Azénor
www.azenor.com,
t 02 98 41 46 23

Compagnie Penn ar Bed
t 02 98 80 80 80,
www.pennarbed.com

Musée Mémorial International de la Bataille de l'Atlantique
call t 02 98 27 92 58
for opening times

Face Ouest
www.faceouest.fr,
t 02 98 27 44 76

First comes the great **Plage de Veyrach**, followed by further smaller sandy creeks below the next few headlands. Follow the coastal path round to Kerloc'h and the **Anse de Dinan**. This bay changes dramatically with the tides. At low tide, a tremendous, enormous sandy beach is uncovered across the bay. The sea has carved grottoes into the geologically colourful cliffs. Close to here, **Marc'h Ambilli** offers outings in a horse-drawn cart led by a typical Breton cart horse.

Marc'h Ambilli
m 06 23 30 30 67

Looking into the distance to the west, you can see why the **Pointe de Dinan** is also known as the Château de Dinan – although there's no man-made castle, the rocks have formed what looks like a massive fort, complete with a drawbridge of an arch of rock in front of it.

The territory stretching down from the Pointe de Dinan to the Cap de la Chèvre is especially wild, with the odd old Breton hamlet popping up along the way. A series of untamed beaches succeed one another. The **Plage de Lost Marc'h** is certainly lost, situated far down a sandy track surrounded by heath. Swimming is supposed to be forbidden here, but that doesn't stop surfers from coming out, and naturism is permitted. The headland above the beach was the site of an Iron Age fort, and you can still clearly make out the trenches built to defend the promontory. To the south, the **beach of La Palue** is more substantial, but has the same dangers as well as a sense of drama.

Inland from La Palue, you come to the sleepy old village of **St-Hernot**, with its **Musée des Minéraux**. It's rare to go into a museum and discover that you can be more illuminated by turning off the lights than leaving them on – one highlight of this geological museum is the room full of fluorescent rocks. The place also runs interesting guided walks in July and August on which you can learn not only about the local geology, but also the traditional architecture, and the flora and fauna, all while appreciating the exceptional natural setting.

Musée des Minéraux
www.maison-des-mineraux.org, t 02 98 27 19 73; open summer season daily 10–7, rest of year Mon–Fri 10–12 and 2–5, plus Sun pm

The views suddenly open up on to the enormous, more tranquil Baie de Douarnenez once you reach **Cap de la Chèvre**, the most southerly Crozon headland. On clear days, the Ménez-Hom hill rises like a mountain at the back of the huge bay. Back on the 'Goat's Cape' (*see* box, p.318), the naval watchtower rather spoils the immediate natural surroundings. Looking out to the Atlantic, an alarming war memorial to naval air pilots shows the tail of an aeroplane sticking out of a hole in the ground. For a fascinating self-guided tour of this headland, hire the special headset from the Musée des Minéraux, with recordings in French.

Dahut and the Keys to the City of Ys

The splendid, debauched, legendary city of Ys is supposed by tradition to lie drowned somewhere out in the Bay of Douarnenez. A place close to the Cap de la Chèvre, Poul-Dahut ('Dahut's Hole'), recalls the evil daughter of King Gradlon of Cornouaille, whose unbridled desires and callous murdering led both to the creation and the destruction of this fabulous, godless city. In the story, Dahut, having seduced and killed countless lovers on Ys, falls for a fiery-bearded stranger who refuses to tell her his name. Such is her all-consuming passion for him that she accepts his challenge to prove her love for him by stealing the keys to Ys's protective sea gates from her sleeping father. It's only once she's delivered the keys to the stranger that she realizes where her evil has finally led her. As the storm gathers force to wipe out Ys, she follows the stranger to the top of her castle. But by the time she arrives he has disappeared, leaving only the trace of a goat's hoof, the sign of the devil. Ys's fate is sealed. Read the fuller story on p.324.

The Southern Presqu'île de Crozon and its Resorts

The southern side of the Presqu'île de Crozon brings you back to gentle, restful Breton seaside territory, with gorgeous views across the Bay of Douarnenez. The look resembles an Emile Bernard painting here and there (*see* p.367), the big *cloisonnée* blocks of colours of the fields descending to a calm sea.

Tucked away from the pounding ocean, **Morgat** boasts a still better-protected beach resort than Camaret, with a long stretch of sand reaching round its fabulous bay. Morgat has been popular with holidaymakers since the end of the 19th century, as you can see from some of the old villas. A big marina was later added, built behind the embracing arm of a jetty.

There are **grottoes** you can visit on both sides of town. Some can only be reached by boat... or by kayak – contact the **Point Passion Plage** to find out about the sea-faring possibilities. The most spectacular cave, the **Grotte de l'Autel**, is often described as a 'cathedral of the sea' with its natural 'altarpiece' and the rich decoration of its naturally coloured rocks.

Point Passion Plage
www.cncm.fr,
t 02 98 16 00 00

The town of **Crozon** just above Morgat serves as a good shopping centre, with daily morning market, but isn't inspiring. The one cultural thing you might stop to see is the retable in the **church**. It so teems with carved figures that it's known as the 'retable of the 10,000 martyrs'. The packed panels retell the story of soldiers in Emperor Hadrian's Roman army, persecuted for converting to Christianity. Breton art doesn't get much more cartoon-like than this.

East of Morgat, the fields slope down to the deep blue waters at the **Plage de Postolonnec**, where families build low stone walls on the pebbly beach to stake out their territory. Steep roads lead down to the sensational **Plage de l'Aber**. Continuing east, **Trez-Bellec Plage** is home to the **Telgruc Centre Nautique** offering watersports facilities. The spot is beautiful too, but the caravan parks are rather noticeable.

Telgruc Centre Nautique
www.cntelgruc.free.fr,
t 02 98 27 33 43

(i) **Pays du
Ménez-Hom
Atlantique**
*www.menez-
hom.com*

(i) **Camaret-
sur-Mer >>**
Quai Kléber,
t 02 98 27 93 60,
*www.camaretsurmer-
tourisme.fr*

(i) **Le Faou >**
t 02 98 81 06 85,
*www.cc-aulne-
maritime.fr*

(i) **Landévennec**
t 02 98 27 78 46
(summer) or
02 98 27 72 65

(i) **Telgruc-
sur-Mer**
t 02 98 27 78 06,
*officetourisme.
telgruc@wanadoo.fr*

(★) **Hostellerie
de la Mer >**

(i) **Crozon-
Morgat >>**
*Boulevard de
Pralognan-la-Vanoise,*
t 02 98 27 07 92,
www.crozon.com

Market Days on the Crozon Peninsula

Le Faou: last Saturday of the month; June–Sept Fri farmers' market
Camaret-sur-Mer: 3rd Tuesday of the month, plus every day in high season
Crozon: 2nd and 4th Wednesdays of the month
Telgruc-sur-Mer: Tuesday and Friday

Where to Stay and Eat on the Crozon Peninsula

Le Faou ✉ 29580

***De Beauvoir La Vieille Renommée**, 11 Place de la Mairie, t 02 98 81 90 31 (€€). Some of the spacious rooms in this traditional hotel have been refurbished recently. The place has a well-reputed restaurant (€€€€–€€€).

Crêperie La Frégate, 50 Rue du Général de Gaulle, t 02 98 81 09 09 (€). A fine crêperie in a typical lovely village house. *Closed Tues and Wed.*

Rosnoën ✉ 29580

Ferme Apicole de Térénez, Route de Crozon, t 02 98 81 06 90 (€). B&B accommodation in a beautiful place that both produces honey and has a little *écomusée* on the subject. *Table d'hôte* is available on reservation.

Ferme-auberge du Seillou, Le Seillou, t 02 98 81 92 21 (€). A pretty stone farm with a few bright B&B rooms. Advance reservations are essential.

L'Ermitage, along the road to the Térénez bridge, t 02 98 81 93 61 (€€). Fish and grills *du jour* served on a covered terrace facing on to the Aulne, with lovely views.

Vivier du Térénez, shortly before L'Ermitage, t 02 98 81 93 61 (€). A kind of lakeside *poissonnerie* where you can sample the daily catch marinated, smoked or filleted, on a little terrace by the water.

Le Fret ✉ 29160

***Hostellerie de la Mer**, Quai du Fret, t 02 98 27 61 90, *hostellerie.de.la.mer @wanadoo.fr* (€€€–€). A lively, well-kept hotel on the shore looking across

to Brest, with a good restaurant (€€€€–€€€) attached, local produce the speciality. *Closed Jan.*

Camaret-sur-Mer ✉ 29570

***Thalassa**, Quai du Styvel, t 02 98 27 86 44, *www.hotel-thalassa.com* (€€€–€€). A modern hotel that gives directly on to the *sillon*. It has comfortable rooms, some with balconies overlooking the sea, plus a heated seawater pool, a sauna, a gym and a jacuzzi. *Closed Dec–Easter.*

***de France**, 19 Quai Toudouze, t 02 98 27 93 06, *hotel-france-camaret@ wanadoo.fr* (€€–€). A hotel on the waterfront, with good rooms, its restaurant (€€€–€€) with a view serving fine Breton food. *Closed Nov–Easter.*

***Le Styvel**, Quai du Styvel, t 02 98 27 92 74, *hotelstyvel@wanadoo.fr*. (€). A small, traditional-style family hotel with a good restaurant (€€) and a number of rooms with sea views.

***Vauban**, 4 Quai du Styvel, t 02 98 27 91 36 (€). A basic cheap option with some charm, including good views, plus a garden. *Closed Jan–Feb.*

Crêperie Rocamadour, 11 Quai Kléber, t 02 98 27 93 17 (€). An enticing crêpe house looking out on to the port.

Morgat ✉ 29160

***Grand Hôtel de la Mer**, 17 Rue d'Ys, t 02 98 27 02 09, *thierry.regnier@vvf-vacances.fr* (€€€–€€). A big hotel dating back to the Belle Epoque. Located between the beach of Morgat and a wooded park, it was refurbished in the 1990s and has a wide array of facilities, including a tennis court. *Closed Oct–March.*

***Hôtel Julia**, 43 Rue de Tréflez, t 02 98 27 05 89 (€€€–€€). A bright, white hotel with some quite pretty rooms and a garden. *Closed Oct–March.*

Hôtel de la Baie, on the port, t 02 98 27 07 51 (€). A simple but charming choice.

La Flambée, 22 Quai Kador, t 02 98 27 12 24 (€). A crêperie with a first-floor dining room that looks out over the delightful bay.

Crozon ✉ 29160

La Presqu'île, Place de l'Eglise, t 02 98 27 29 29, *mutin.gourmand1@*

wanadoo.fr (€€–€). A new hotel that's been given plenty of Breton style, plus it includes the already well-established, reputed restaurant **Le Mutin Gourmand** (€€€€–€€; *closed Mon lunch, plus Sun eve and Tues lunch in low season*) presenting fine regional cuisine in a modern decor.

Crêperie du Menez Gorre, 86 Rue de Poulpatré, **t** 02 98 27 19 66 (€). A good choice in a pleasant 19th-century stone house on the eastern edge of town.

Crêperie Le Korrigan, Plage de Postolonnec, **t** 02 98 27 14 37 (€). On the beach a few km southeast of town, with a fabulous view of the bay. *Open April–Sept daily exc Mon; rest of year weekends and school hols.*

Tal ar Groas ✉ 29160

Crêperie Maëligwenn, Tal ar Groaz, **t** 02 98 26 18 02 (€). Its first-floor dining room offers fabulous views to go with the good crêpes.

The Eastern Bay of Douarnenez

⊕ Douarnenez and Crozon

The imposing hill of the Ménez-Hom dominates the extraordinarily beautiful, rural coastal strip on the eastern side of the Bay of Douarnenez. The two main tourist attractions beyond the long stretches of beach are the splendid old towns of Locronan and Douarnenez. This area is absolutely steeped in Breton legends.

Around the Ménez-Hom

From the top of the **Ménez-Hom** hill you get the grandest views across the Finistère and the Bay of Douarnenez on good days. At 330 metres, this summit is the highest of the chain of the Montagnes Noires, which stretch away eastwards, while a patchwork of fields descends west to the sea. Nowadays, the hilltop may look slightly undignified in its balding state, with what look like the scrappy remnants of a green-rinse grass toupee clinging to its bare, rounded pate. The brave among you might like running off it on a paragliding trip – contact **Vol Libre du Menez-Hom**.

Vol Libre du Menez-Hom
www.vol-libre-menez-hom.com, **m** 06 80 32 47 34

The Ménez-Hom clearly held great significance in past societies. Some say that a sun god was worshipped on its summit in prehistoric times. Legend claims that an ancient tumulus hidden on the north side of the mount is the tomb of King Marc'h. Today, this major legendary figure (*see* box, opposite) has inspired a new tourist route, the **Cheminements du Roi Marc'h**, that starts here, and loops right round the Presqu'île de Crozon to end in Locronan, telling tales of this unfortunate Celtic king along the way, while focusing your attention on scores of interesting religious, historical and natural sights along the way. Panels tell you more, and there's a booklet to accompany the tour. Tasty goat's cheese is also produced around these parts.

North of the Ménez-Hom, head along delightful country tracks towards Trégarvan to seek out the isolated old rural Breton school

Getting around the Eastern Bay of Douarnenez

The **bus** service from Quimper to Camaret-sur-Mer passes through Plogonnec, Locronan, Plonévez-Porzay, Plomodiern and St-Nic. Another bus route links Quimper with Douarnenez.

Musée de l'Ecole Rurale
www.musee-ecole.fr,
t 02 98 26 04 72; open daily July and Aug 10.30–7, June 1.30–7, Sept 2–6

that has been turned into the interesting **Musée de l'Ecole Rurale**, capturing the nostalgia of more innocent school days, but also recalling the way that some Breton children were made to feel ashamed of speaking their mother tongue in times past – however, it should be said that many rural teachers were understanding of their pupils' difficulties in learning French when only Breton was spoken at home. Continue along the gorgeous road to **Trégarvan** and its **church**, set on a lovely slope above the Aulne River. A curious carving of the Pietà stands in the cemetery through which you have to walk to get to the lovely Gothic edifice, in which an old clock ticks like a slow heartbeat.

Coming down off the southern side of the Ménez-Hom, you arrive at the village of **Ste-Marie-du-Ménez-Hom**. Its **chapel** looks surprisingly rich for such a small and remote hillside village. In fact, Ste-Marie-du-Ménez-Hom lay at a crossroads where an important regional fair used to be held four times a year. Over the period, a tax was put on all purchases made at these fairs, raising money to construct the chapel. Most of the building dates from the late 16th century, but you enter the *enclos paroissial* under a pompous 18th-century gateway given a Baroque top comically resembling a

Chasing an Undignified King with Horse's Ears

King Marc'h – meaning King Horse in Breton – is a complex figure to have come down to us from Celtic mythology. Diverging stories make him a chieftain on both sides of the Channel, in both British Cornwall and Breton Cornouaille. It seems the character of the different cross-Channel legends may have some links to a real 6th-century leader, but that's really of little concern in the wild tales told of Marc'h.

Endlessly unlucky, he became caught up in several intertwining tales, and in the end would even be forbidden from being buried in a cemetery because of his bad conduct. The most famous story in which he plays an unfortunate part is that of Tristan and Yseut. He's the third figure in this famed love triangle. Marc'h becomes the champion of his orphaned nephew Tristan, whom he wishes to make his successor. Tristan is even sent off to accompany Marc'h's chosen bride Yseut from across the seas, but she and Tristan fall fatefully in love after accidentally drinking a love potion meant for her and Marc'h. Somewhat understandably, Marc'h is left in turmoil, but in the end he shows some sympathy for the unpredictable nature of love – finding the lovers sleeping next to each other, separated only by Tristan's sword, the king replaces his nephew's weapon with his own to show them he knows.

In the Finistère, Marc'h is also embarrassingly linked with the evil Dahut from the great legend of the Ville d'Ys. Out hunting in these parts one day, he shoots an arrow at a beautiful white hind he's tracked down. To his horror, the arrow, instead of killing the doe, boomerangs back to kill his beloved steed. The doe, it turns out, is the wicked Dahut in disguise. To humiliate Marc'h still further, she imposes immovable horse's ears on his head. He tries all manner of ways to hide his shame, but, once again, the tale makes him into the object of ridicule... and this time a cruel one, as every barber who cuts his hair has then to be killed, to try and keep the secret from anyone. (For more on Ys, read boxes, pp.318 and 324.)

Napoleonic hat. Statues of the Virgin and St Hervé adorn the gateway. The calvary, dating back to 1544, has been restored. Inside the church, the most exuberant of richly carved retables runs across the whole length of the choir end.

The Coast from Pentrez-Plage to Ste-Anne-la-Palud

A league of spectacular, broad beach runs down from the village of **Pentrez-Plage**. As at Trez-Bellec to the north, just the camp sites detract from the utter tranquil beauty of the place. In recent years, there's sometimes been a proliferation of algae in the waters at the back of the bay, making swimming offputting.

The scattering of chapels close to the coast have some lovely wood carvings: the **Chapelle St-Jean** with its decorative stringbeams, and the **church of St-Nicaise** with the grotesque figures in its porch (as well as some restored 16th-century stained glass). Most ornate of the lot is the **Chapelle St-Côme et St-Damien**, with its monsters seemingly trying to swallow the crossbeams, and miserable figures holding their hands to their stomachs on the rafters. The **Pointe de Talagrip** is one of the best spots from which to appreciate the full sweep of the bay. Further chapels lie along the way south to Ste-Anne-la-Palud.

After the colourful Celtic adaptation of St Anne's Biblical story (see box), the 19th-century church of **Ste-Anne-la-Palud** looks disappointingly drab in its present form, lost by the dunes. Inside stands a 16th-century painted granite statue of the 'Breton princess'. She has been greatly venerated over the centuries, and the *pardon* of Ste-Anne-la-Palud, on the last Sunday in August, remains one of the most popular in Brittany. The rest of the year, Ste-Anne-la-Palud is admired for its fine long sands and the turquoise waters caught within the claws of its bay. Fields slope gently down to the strand. The currents are dangerous on the southern end of the beach, but you can enjoy the walk to the **Pointe de Tréfeunteuc**. Further highly picturesque beaches curve round the **Anse d'Ar Veche**n to Douarnenez.

St Anne, Mother of Mary and Princess of Cornouaille?

Among the most wildly implausible of Breton legends is the one that claims that Anne, mother of the Virgin Mary, was originally a princess of Cornouaille. The story goes that she was flown away from this corner of Brittany by angels who wanted to rescue her from her first husband, who had been mistreating her. She was supposedly taken to Judaea, where she remarried and went on to give birth to the mother of Christ. She returned to Brittany to live out her old age, the local tale has it. Jesus, that kind boy, is supposed to have paid a visit to his distant grandmother, creating the spring of Ste-Anne-la-Palud for her. The absurd association of St Anne with the place may stem from storytellers playing on the Breton word for a moor or marsh, *ana*.

Douarnenez

Douarnenez is a port both practical and poetic, deeply immersed in Breton fishing and Breton legend – the ruins of the glorious but evil city of Ys are supposed to lie under the waves nearby. Douarnenez actually sits in an enchanting location at the back of the peaceful bay named after it, but when its canneries opened, it became, for a time, a centre of Breton class warfare.

Fish has been the backbone of the place up till now. In ancient times, it produced quantities of garum, a salty fish-gut paste considered a delicacy in the Roman world. After a seemingly busy period, Dark Ages Douarnenez is a bit of a mystery, just the tragic tale of the Ville d'Ys coming down to us. As to the island in front of Douarnenez, it carries the name of Tristan, reflecting how further legends would take root here.

Through the Middle Ages, the port became part of the estates of the dukes of Brittany, although its fortunes waxed and waned. The morals of the people of the area do appear to have worried the Church from time to time; in the 17th century, the formidable evangelizer Michel Le Nobletz (*see* p.271) settled in town for a while, no doubt intent on bringing some of the inhabitants back to the straight and narrow.

The first fish-canning factory opened in 1851. Workers flocked to Douarnenez and were housed in conditions almost as cramped as the fish they were tinning. The place grew into a bastion of working-class militancy after the First World War. In 1921, its citizens elected the first ever French Communist mayor. Three years later they voted for a woman to join the town council, but she was barred from office by French law. From 1924 to 1925 the Douarnenez workers took on their employers in one of the first epic union battles in the country. During the Second World War, Douarnenez became an important recruitment centre for the French Résistance.

In the last few decades, things have quietened down, many fishermen doing quite well, until the recent downturn. There's no longer a colourful coastal fishing scene to attract visitors. In contrast, the boat museum is a major pull, as are the huge gatherings of old sail boats held in the bay every few years. On those special occasions, the Bay of Douarnenez takes on an even more picturesque look, with the tall ships and the tanned brown sails of the past flitting across the waters. Publishing is one of the new small-scale industries to have developed in town. Two excellent, beautifully produced magazines devoted to Breton culture, *Chasse-Marée* and *Armen*, are put together here and are well worth reading if you speak French.

The Legend of the Ville d'Ys

The precise location of the legendary Ville d'Ys is, understandably, disputed, but down the centuries, inhabitants of Douarnenez have claimed to have spotted vestiges of the city 'where the poorest were richer than kings' under the waters near the fishing harbour. King Gradlon of Cornouaille, the story goes, had Ys built to satisfy the unbridled desires of his wild daughter Dahut, also sometimes referred to as Ahès. Dahut's mother died at sea while giving birth to her; her grieving father was anxious to indulge her every whim. In Quimper, she grew into an exceptionally beautiful young woman few could resist... except Corentin, Bishop of Quimper, who warned Gradlon of Dahut's immodest clothing, her frivolous conversation, her mocking attitude towards the clergy, and her refusal to go to church. Corentin tried to show Gradlon that his blind paternal love might lead to disaster.

Dahut, meanwhile, was becoming frustrated by Quimper, considering it to be in the grip of joyless religious orders. She asked her father whether he hadn't become the prisoner of the Church, for Christianity, she said, was stifling her. She felt an overwhelming desire to live next to the ocean on which she had been born. Seeing her pining so, Gradlon asked her how he might make her feel better; she told him that building a magnificent new city by the sea for her was the answer...and a place without churches. Gradlon replied to Dahut that her hopes were impossible, but in secret he called his architects together and ordered the building of a city so splendid, he said, that even the ocean would be surprised. When it was complete, the delighted Dahut went to reign in the churchless city of Ys. The place became increasingly debauched and wicked, however, and Dahut and its inhabitants would be punished by a wrathful God.

After Dahut falls for the devil (*see* box, p.318), all hell breaks loose. In the terrible foaming finale to the tale, King Gradlon manages to escape from the city being ripped apart by giant waves on his stallion Morvark, nimble enough to run over the waves. But the doting king tries to save his daughter too. The weight of her evil drags the horse down and it looks as though they'll all be drowned. The monk Guénolé arrives on the scene at the last minute to save Gradlon from the engulfing waves. He reassures the king that God will pardon him for his blindness because of the churches he had founded, including Landévennec (*see* p.312). But he tells Gradlon that he must push Dahut from the horse. His diabolical daughter is swallowed up by the waves and torn apart by the rocks. The Christian and parental morals are pretty clear.

Douarnenez's Different Ports

On the eastern side of town, colourful houses look down on to the **Vieux Port** and the **Port de Rosmeur**, Douarnenez's working port. This counts among the dozen largest fishing ports in France, but most of the catch arrives from afar at night. Enormous refrigerated lorries come to carry away some of the haul. Large quantities of fish are still canned in the Rosmeur quarter; you can't visit the **canneries**, but they do have **shops**. The **Vedettes de Rosmeur** have been running tours of the bay going in high summer from this side of town. Just west of Rosmeur, central Douarnenez offers the surprise of its own little beach, the **Plage des Dames**.

Turn the corner for the estuary harbour of **Port-Rhu**. Along the east bank, below the church, stetches the substantial **Musée du Bateau**. At this boat museum, you go round looking at real, not model, vessels. A wide variety of old fishing and transport boats is displayed inside a large converted canning factory. Some come from Brittany, others from Britain and Ireland, but among the most striking are the flamboyantly shaped Portuguese marsh boat with its amusing paintings, and the Vietnamese paddy field boat, which

Vedettes de Rosmeur
t 02 98 92 83 83

Musée du Bateau
www.port-musee.org, t 02 98 92 65 20; open mid-June–mid-Sept daily 10–7; Easter–mid-June and mid-Sept–Oct Tues–Sun 10–12.30 and 2–6

really resembles a very large basket. The old Douarnenez fishing industry is also recalled. Several larger vessels are moored outside, and you can climb on board to take a good look round them. A few maritime craft shops have set up along the quay.

Just out beyond the estuary stands the picturesque **Ile Tristan**. On the rare occasions when especially low tides allow it, the tourist office organizes a guided tour of the island, crossing on foot. Otherwise, there are lovely, easier walks to be enjoyed along the main coastal paths from Douarnenez.

Tréboul, on the other bank from Port-Rhu, is where you'll find the **marina**. Some façades as brightly coloured as those at Rosmeur look down on it. Tréboul is also home to the the **Centre Nautique de Douarnenez**, which offers courses in sailing, windsurfing and even kite-surfing. On the slopes above the intimate **St-Jean beach**, you can go up via the secretive winding lanes to the little chapel by the Hôtel Ty Mad. A bust of the 20th-century Quimper poet and artist Max Jacob stands behind it. He stayed at the hotel with his talented young English artist friend, Christopher Wood, in 1930. The latter was inspired by his Breton visit, but would soon tragically kill himself. One of the best views to be had of the Bay of Douarnenez is from the splendidly located cemetery on the nearby slope, surely one of the most uplifting spots in which to be buried. To end on a relaxing note, try the **Centre de Thalasso de Douarnenez** beside Tréboul's **Plage des Sables Blancs** for a fine seawater pampering. The heated indoor seawater pool here also benefits from a fabulous bay view.

Centre Nautique de Douarnenez
www.centre-nautique-douarnenez.fr,
t 02 98 74 13 79

Centre de Thalasso de Douarnenez
www.thalasso.com,
t 02 98 74 48 62

Locronan

Just one look at Locronan's central square tells you how wealthy the sail and cloth merchants of Locronan were in centuries past. The gorgeous, substantial granite houses surrounding the enchanting **Place de l'Eglise** date mostly from the 18th century, with their dormer windows sticking their heads so charmingly out of their silvery-grey slate roofs.

Tourism dictates life in Locronan today. Virtually all the houses have been turned into restaurants, crêperies or boutiques. The tourist invasion is the price Locronan pays for being one of the most picturesque of all Breton villages. Many films have been shot here. Director Roman Polanski came here to make his version of Thomas Hardy's *Tess of the d'Urbervilles*. Nastassja Kinski, playing the role of tragic Tess, was even sent to brood over the tomb of Ronan in the church. Ronan, a saint who came to Armorica from Ireland in the Dark Ages, ironically moved down to Cornouaille from Léon to try to find a little peace and quiet here for contemplation (*see* box overleaf).

Ronan Refutes the Evil Kéban

Miracle-working Ronan (also known as Renan) was so pestered by requests for help after he had settled in the northern Finistère that he began to fear for his sanity and decided to move south in order to get away from all these demands. He settled in the deep forest of Névet behind the Bay of Douarnenez. He lived there as a hermit, in harmony with the natural world, taming the wilder animal passions of the creatures of the woods.

However, a deranged woman from the area accused him of a heinous crime. One day, Kéban went to the court of King Gradlon in Quimper screaming for justice against Ronan. She claimed that he had come to her cottage, transformed himself into a wolf, and then carried away her little daughter to devour her in the forest. The chieftain decided to have Ronan face a primitive kind of trial. He had him bound to a tree and set his two mastiffs on him. The bloodthirsty dogs came bounding up to tear him apart. But as Ronan made the sign of the cross, they stopped in their tracks.

Convinced of Ronan's innocence by this feat, Gradlon apologized to the hermit and asked him what he wished for by way of reparation. Ronan asked that Kéban be forgiven. The saintly man also went on to reveal that Kéban had hidden her daughter in a chest in her cottage. A crowd ran there and found that the poor little girl had suffocated inside the chest. But the story was to have a happy ending: miracle-working Ronan resuscitated the girl.

The focal point of the town, and of its history and its ceremonies, the slightly unstable-looking old **church of St-Ronan**, just about offers an escape from the commercialism beyond. When the great French Romantic, Chateaubriand, visited the building in the 18th century, he memorably described it as 'a masterpiece of humidity, with its large silvery patches of lichen decorating the walls like the clouds of eternity'. The building is a graceful piece of granite architecture dating from the 15th century. It was funded by Breton dukes, who came here on pilgrimage to pray to Ronan for fertility. Lovely Flamboyant Gothic tracery rails run above the main entrance gable, along the top of the church tower and down the sides.

A cavernous entrance porch leads into the church under the stocky main tower, a statue of Ronan looking over those who come to worship. But generally these days you have to enter the church via the side chapel, commissioned by Duchess Anne of Brittany early in the 16th century – she too came to pray for fertility here. The arresting 15th-century tomb effigy of Ronan lies inside the chapel, while an elaborate carved pulpit in the main church illustrates scenes from his legendary life. The main church window does however focus on the biblical story of Christ!

Locronan has attracted quite a number of artisans, what with its great tourist potential; you'll find a glass-blower, a book antiquarian and a shop specializing in Breton beers, as well as boulangeries selling the very buttery Breton speciality of *kouign amann*, and boutiques touting touristy trinkets.

On the lower end of the main square, the Compagnie des Indes (the French equivalent of the East Indies Company) kept offices at Locronan. Nearby, you can head down the steep **Rue Moal**, lined with delightful old houses and offering beautiful views on to the countryside. The way leads to **Notre-Dame de Bonne Nouvelle**. A fine Breton fountain and washplace lie by this chapel.

From the upper end of the main square, **Rue St-Maurice** leads steeply up the hillside. Once you're past the cottages, spectacular views open up across the countryside to the sea. Up here, there are a few more galleries in splendid locations.

The Locronan *pardons* count among the most celebrated in Brittany, and are known as Troménies, from the Breton *tro minihy*, the 'tour of the sanctuary'. Pilgrims accompany the religious statues and banners up and around Locronan's hill, possibly following a sacred path that has existed here since the days of the Celtic druids.

Country Churches North of Quimper

Pretty **Plogonnec** southeast of Locronan has a **church** with marvellous stained-glass windows. These depict memorable scenes, not just of the Crucifixion, but also of the Apocalypse, with some frightfully active purple and green demons. In the Resurrection window, Breton saints surround Christ, a couple riding stags, another shoeing a horse, yet another sailing along in his galleon.

The pain of crucifixion has bent the legs of the two thieves crucified with Christ into almost acrobatically impossible poses on the very worn calvary of **Guengat**, southwest of Plogonnec. Enter the **church** through the Gothic porch and a much more gruesome and painful crucifixion awaits you, portrayed in the exceptional 16th-century stained glass in the choir. Look out too for an amazing gilded processional cross dating from 1584, the figures on it quite naïvely portrayed. Much cruder Breton art still is packed into the stringbeams, where, among the cider-barrel and milk-churning scenes, you can also make out a number of carved animals.

A couple of rare Breton **triangular-based calvaries** can be seen by the very peaceful rural chapel at **St-Venec** and at the delightful village of **Quilinen**, both west of Briec. Whereas most of the Breton calvaries balance horizontal scenes with the verticality of the crosses, on these all the figures and forms emphasize ascension. North above Briec, the delightful **Notre-Dame-des-Trois-Fontaines** has just been restored.

Market Days in the Eastern Bay of Douarnenez

Douarnenez: Monday, Wednesday and Friday
Locronan: Thurs evening markets in summer, 7–midnight

 Auberge des Glazicks >>

Where to Stay and Eat in the Eastern Bay of Douarnenez

Plomodiern ✉ 29550

Auberge des Glazicks, 7 Rue de la Plage, t 02 98 81 52 32 (€€€€). One of the most exciting (and expensive) of

⭐ Hôtel de la Plage >

⭐ Ty Mad >>

ⓘ Plonévez-Porzay >
*t 02 98 92 53 57,
www.tourisme-
porzay.com*

⭐ Manoir du Moëllien >

ⓘ Locronan >
*Place de la Mairie,
t 02 98 91 70 14,
www.locronan.org*

ⓘ Pays du Ménez-Hom Atlantique
*Maison du Tourisme,
B.P. 45, 29160 Crozon,
t 02 98 26 17 18,
www.menez-hom.com,
for information across
the area*

ⓘ Douarnenez >
*2 Rue du Docteur
Mével, t 02 98 92 13 35,
www.douarnenez-
tourisme.com*

recent restaurants to open in the Finistère, run by a young chef with great flair. *Closed Mon and Tues.*

Ste-Anne-la-Palud ✉ 29550

****Hôtel de la Plage**, t 02 98 92 50 12, *www.plage.com* (€€€€€–€€€€). The only hotel giving onto the beach of Ste-Anne-la-Palud, with posh rooms, some with sea views. The restaurant (€€€€; most often dinner only, exc Thurs and weekends) has glorious views to accompany extremely refined seafood dishes. The grounds have pool and court. *Closed Nov–mid-March.*

Plonévez-Porzay ✉ 29550

Manoir du Moëllien, t 02 98 92 50 40, *manmoel@aol.com* (€€€–€€). The rooms are set in the outbuildings of this characterful 17th-century manor and are rather special, as is the restaurant (€€€–€€; dinner only for residents). *Closed mid-Nov–mid-March.*

Kervel Izellla, Plage de Kervel, t 02 98 92 51 81. Good-quality crêperie at the beach.

Locronan ✉ 29180

Le Prieuré, 11 Rue du Prieuré, t 02 98 91 70 890 (€€–€). By the western car parks on the edge of this beautiful village. There's a large dining room (€€€–€) with a front conservatory section to receive the hordes. *Closed mid-Nov–mid-March.*

You'll find a handful of very pretty, very touristy crêperies to tempt you in the centre of the village.

Douarnenez and Tréboul ✉ 29100

***Le Clos de Valombreuse**, 7 Rue Estienne d'Orves, t 02 98 92 63 64, *www.closvalombreuse* (€€€–€€). The rooms have just been renovated in this imposing early 20th-century residence set in a private garden with pool, 20m from the beach. Restaurant (€€€–€).

***Thalasstonic**, above Plage des Sables Blancs in Tréboul, t 02 98 74 45 45, *www.hotel-douarnenez.com*, (€€€–€€). Plain, smartish rooms, some spacious, in this hotel close to a beach and with sea-water treatment centre attached. The restaurant (€€€€–€€) offers traditional cuisine, or special dietary options.

****Ty Mad**, above Plage St-Jean in Tréboul, t 02 98 74 00 53, *www.hoteltymad.com* (€€€–€). A delightful hotel, in Tréboul's quiet lanes. The rooms have been charmingly redone. Restaurant (€€) open for dinners, serving seasonal dishes. *Closed Nov–March.*

****Auberge de Kervéoc'h**, 42 Route de Kervéoc'h, t 02 98 92 07 58, *www.auberge-kerveoch.com* (€€–€). A converted country farmhouse outside town, with peaceful guest rooms.

****Hôtel de France**, 4 Rue Jean Jaurès, t 02 98 92 00 02, *www.lafrance-dz.com*. (€€–€). A good traditional option in the town centre, its comfortable rooms recently refurbished. Its restaurant, **L'Insolite** (€€€€–€€), serves fine cuisine.

****Le Kériolet**, 29 Rue Croas Talud, t 02 98 92 16 89, *www.hotel-keriolet.com* (€). A decent simple option, some rooms with a view of the bay, and a restaurant serving jolly good fresh Breton dishes (€€€–€).

Chez Fanch, 49 Rue Anatole France, t 02 98 92 31 77 (€€€–€€). Great for seafood. *Closed Fri eve.*

Au Goûter Breton, 36 Rue Jean Jaurès, t 02 98 92 02 74 (€). Excellent crêperie with a relaxing atmosphere, and a garden terrace out the back. *Closed Sun.*

Quilinen ✉ 29150

L'Auberge de Quilinen, t 02 98 94 50 02 (€€). Small inn 100m up from the enchanting village church, serving fine Breton fare. *Closed Mon, and most Aug.*

Quimper

✪ Quimper

In Quimper castle lived Gradlon, King of Cornouaille, in great mourning, in great sadness.

La Légende de la ville d'Ys

Getting to Quimper

Quimper is easily reached from Paris by TGV fast **train**. You can also **fly** from Paris to Quimper-Cornouaille airport (*www.quimper.aeroport.fr*, **t** 02 98 94 30 30) at Pluguffan west of town.

The capital of the historic Breton county of Cornouaille, Quimper has lost its castle, but its great legendary figure, King Gradlon, still rides sadly through the city, up between the splendid twin spires of the cathedral. Those joyous soaring spires tower over Quimper's old town, which is not in the least melancholic, but a lively, cheerful place. A row of merry bridges spans the Odet River flowing through the centre of town. Kemper (the Breton for Quimper) actually means confluence, the Steir River joining the Odet here.

In artistic and cultural terms, Quimper is best known abroad for its pottery, with its characteristic naïve decoration of Breton figures, but it's also home to two excellent museums and the major Festival de Cournouaille celebrating Breton culture.

Some Quimper History and Some Quimper Legend

Known as Aquilonia under the Romans, Gallo-Roman Quimper developed a port by the Odet, and, quite significantly for the future, a pottery-making tradition. During the Dark Ages, legend claims that Quimper became the seat of power of King Gradlon of Cornouaille. The story goes that he appointed Corentin, a holy hermit whom he encountered while out hunting one day, as Bishop of Quimper (*see* box, p.331). The city is still dedicated to Corentin, regarded as one of the major saintly figures in the founding of Celtic Christian Brittany after the fall of the Roman Empire.

In the early Middle Ages, pottery-making flourished in the quarter south of the Odet named in honour of the Virgin, Locmaria, overseen by its solid Romanesque church. The 13th century saw the start, on the Odet's north bank, of the building of Quimper's mighty cathedral, the raising of ramparts and the establishment of a Franciscan monastery. The bishops ruled within the city walls, the dukes of Brittany outside them. Quimper cathedral counted among the seven cathedrals to be visited on the medieval pilgrimage around Brittany, the *Tro Breizh*. In the Breton War of Succession, Charles de Blois's soldiers stormed Quimper and pillaged it.

You can still feel the prosperity of some of the Quimper merchants of the 15th and 16th centuries walking along such streets as Rue Kéréon leading to the cathedral. The major Breton family of the Rohans left their mark on the town too, constructing the 16th-century portion of the bishops' palace. In the Wars of Religion that scarred the second half of that century, Quimper was split between Catholics and Protestants. After several bloody

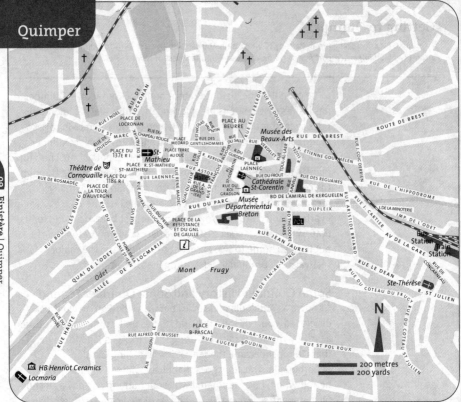

switches in power, eventually the Catholics had to give in to the troops of Henri de Navarre (the future peace-seeking King Henri IV), who bombarded the city from the Frugy hillside rising on the Odet's south bank.

At the Revolution, Quimper was briefly dechristianized, the cathedral badly damaged, and the city pompously renamed Montagne-sur-Odet, which rather exaggerates the size of the Frugy. With the creation of the French *départements*, Quimper fought it out with Landerneau to become the administrative capital of the newly formed Finistère, and won.

Among the Quimper specialities to thrive in the 19th century were its potteries and its *crêpes dentelles* (feather-light Breton biscuits), both still going strong. The pottery has gained an international reputation, known above all for its hand-painted Breton rural figures, which put in their first appearance in the mid-19th century with the 'Petit Breton', a caricatural Breton wearing traditional baggy pants, bright breeches and a waistcoast, and sporting a black Breton hat. This quaint, if rather patronizing vision of a Breton quickly caught on.

While some of the city ramparts were torn down in the 19th century, Quimper cathedral was embellished with its magnificent twin spires, the work of Joseph Bigot, who designed other significant buildings in town. The equestrian statue of Gradlon on top of the cathedral also dates from that time, while inside, the building received a make-over to make the most extravagant of today's television designers green with envy. As to the Odet, it was tamed, and the bourgeois living on the south bank ordered the many little bridges across the canalized river.

From the 1920s, a number of Breton artists formed the association of 'Seven Brothers' (the name playing on the long tradition of the seven founding saints of Dark Age Brittany) to revive Breton crafts at the same time as taking into account new, more experimental trends. The city's potteries encouraged these and a host of other Breton artists. Perhaps the most interesting cultural figure to emerge from Quimper in the 20th century was Max Jacob, who enjoyed frequenting the Café de l'Epée, *the* place to be seen along the Odet. After brilliant studies, he went up to Paris to live a Bohemian existence, but you can see some of his works of art at the Quimper fine arts museum.

Quimper is known in French postwar politics as the place where de Gaulle gave his last major speech as president, in February 1969. He thanked those Bretons who had helped in the Resistance, and spoke of encouraging regionalism, even employing a few Breton

King Gradlon and Bishop Corentin

The stories of Gradlon, legendary King of Cornouaille, probably combine memories of a number of local Breton leaders with pure fantasy to make for a moving, rip-roaring morality tale. The painful Gradlon stories retold in Charles Guyot's *La Légende de la Ville d'Ys* indicate the influence on the Breton imagination of battles with Scandinavians and of a powerful Church leading a crusade against pagan beliefs, sexual license and rampant materialism.

At the beginning of Guyot's version, Gradlon lies wailing in his castle in Quimper, his cries like the agonized howling of a wolf or the love-sick barking of a rutting stag. He is grieving for Malgven, the formidable Queen of the North with whom he fell in love as he was besieging her castle in Scandinavia. She had asked Gradlon to kill her odious husband and the two had then sailed off together. Lost at sea, they enjoyed a long period of passion on the salty waves. One stormy night Malgven gave birth to their daughter Dahut on the ship, but died immediately afterwards.

Back in Quimper, the grieving Gradlon wanted to spoil his daughter Dahut, who grew increasingly capricious, debauched and godless, asking him to build her a city by the sea without any churches – the legendary Ys. One day, out hunting in the forest, the king encountered a hermit, Corentin, who soothed his troubled soul and conjured up a miraculous meal for him out of fish and sacred water – only half a fish was eaten, to avoid destroying one of God's creatures, for Corentin's fish could rejuvenate itself endlessly. Gradlon was so impressed he made Corentin Bishop of Quimper, and under him, to Dahut's chagrin, the nature of Quimper changed to a city ruled over by the clergy. *See* boxes , pp.318 and 324 for the rest of the story.

phrases. Quimper has certainly gone on to wear its Bretonness with pride, as you can well see in its streets, museums and the great Festival de Cornouaille.

Cathédrale St-Corentin and Surrounding Squares

Admire the cathedral's soaring west front from the large cobbled square in front of it, **Place St-Corentin**. Some of the boutiques here try to distract your attention from the towering religious edifice, one particularly extravagant timberframe tourist shop completely covered with Quimper ceramics on the outside, making quite an impression.

The **Cathédrale St-Corentin** is mainly medieval, but it is a surprise that those wonderful twin spires were only added in the 19th century, as they look the epitome of uplifting Gothic style. Strain your eyes to make out the tragic figure of King Gradlon riding along between the towers, his horse's head bowed. Far down below, a grand Gothic arch decorated with rows of angels leads into the building. The lion above this entrance carries the Breton banner that was the symbol of the de Montfortist side who won the Breton War of Succession in the 14th century.

Looking down the interior, you can't help noticing that this is a cathedral with a kink in it. The nave is 15th century, while the choir is in great part 13th century. Some 15th-century stained glass high up in both nave and choir survived the Revolution, the figures representing religious leaders and lords with their guardian saints. A few late-medieval bishops' tombs also made it through the destruction, along with the 17th-century pulpit, its scenes representing the life of St Corentin.

Most of the decoration, however, is from the 19th or early 20th centuries. You'll see how the cathedral spires feature as much inside the building as outside, depicted several times in Romantic paintings and stained-glass windows, all helping to reestablish Quimper's solid Catholic credentials after the revolutionary battering. Breton saints get their fair share of the action too. The Santik Du, or Black Saint, who fought the plague in medieval times, is much revered here, along with St Corentin. The most amusing of many Breton-inspired themes shows a Catholic figure receiving the gift of the Breton language... by an angel putting its finger on his tongue. If only languages, not to mention faith, could be so easily acquired.

A couple of major, stylish cafés with broad terraces where Quimpérois and tourists gather to chat stand across the spacious **Place Laënnec** from the cathedral. The statue of the seated Dr Laënnec recalls the local medical man who gave the world the stethoscope, whose cold feel we've all experienced on our chest in the doctor's surgery. There's also a carousel here to please the kids, set in front of the fine arts museum. If you're after a Breton kilt, pop round the back of the cathedral for the specialist shop on saucy-sounding **Rue du Frout**.

Musée des Beaux-Arts

Musée des Beaux-Arts de Quimper
www.musee-beauxarts.quimper.fr,
t 02 98 95 45 20; open July and Aug daily 10–7; April–June and Sept–Oct daily exc Tues 10–12 and 2–6; Oct–March Mon and Wed–Sat 10–12 and 2–6, Sun 2–6

This museum was built in 1864 in order to present the substantial collections that had been donated to the town by Jean-Marie de Silguy. The architecture was designed by Joseph Bigot once again. Behind the 19th-century façade lie very modern, well-lit museum rooms. Representative works of European art going from the 14th century to the present are on show, but de Silguy was particularly interested in Flemish painting from the late 16th century to the early 18th century and French art from the 18th and 19th centuries.

The curators of the new museum early set about acquiring additional works inspired by Brittany, and have done so ever since. Several of the ground-floor rooms concentrate on Breton-inspired art and Breton artists. One of the most impressive works is by Boudin, *Le Port de Quimper*, painted in 1857. The Pont-Aven School (*see* box, p.367) is represented by striking pieces by Paul Sérusier, Charles Filiger and Emile Bernard. One of the most famous depictions of a Breton religious procession is the highly realistic canvas by Alfred Guillou showing beautifully coiffed women arriving by boat for the *pardon* of Ste-Anne-de-Fouesnant. Charles Cottet painted darker pictures that convey how tough Breton life could be before the First World War. Breton legend isn't forgotten, Evariste Luminais depicting the end of the city of Ys.

One room is devoted to the Quimpérois Max Jacob, a fascinating figure, a gay Jew who converted to Catholicism, but died being deported to Germany. His own Breton paintings tend to the caricatural, but there are some fine portraits of him, including one by Picasso, with whom he briefly shared a place when he first went up to Paris. The museum puts on excellent temporary exhibitions, often involving major artists from Brittany, or who were drawn to the region.

Musée Départemental Breton and the Odet

Musée Départemental Breton
musee-breton@cg29.fr, t 02 98 95 21 60; open June–Sept daily 9–6; Oct–May Tues–Sat 9–12 and 2–5, Sun 2–5

The Musée Départemental Breton is the Finistère's ethnographic musuem, housed in the grand former bishops' palace glued to other side of the cathedral from the Musée des Beaux-Arts. Among wonderful exhibits on display, one of the best, a stunning but simply designed gold chain, turns out to be one of the very oldest – a Celtic piece dating back many centuries before Christ. Archaeological fragments recall Gallo-Roman Finistère, but with nothing much to show from the Dark Ages, the displays move swiftly on to early medieval carved capitals and tomb effigies. The collection of later, painted statues of saints stands out.

The steps up the enormous spiral staircase lead past further extravagant religious items and the odd sword, recalling terrible warring times. Upstairs, fine collections of Breton costumes, furniture and pottery take up the spaces – the costume collection is particularly colourful. From the beginning of the 19th century to the period between the two World Wars, the embroidery used to decorate Cornouaille festive garments became increasingly elaborate. You can also see here how certain contemporary designers have adapted traditional Breton styles to modern fashions.

Beside this museum stands an impressive section of the town's **medieval ramparts** overlooking the river, with a **public garden** below. From here, you can see the lovely line of **footbridges crossing the Odet**. The other side is a modern cinema complex, and the grandiose 19th-century theatre. Keep on the north side of the Odet heading west and you come to the famous **Café de l'Epée**, with its Breton decorations.

Old Shopping Quarters

The most remarkable street in Quimper, with some of the finest old houses in town, some timberframe, some slate covered, is the wonderful **Rue Kéréon** – Kéréon is the Breton word for cobblers, but now the street is lined with all manner of interesting shops. Further delightful shopping streets head northwards up the slope. From either **Rue Elie Fréron** or **Rue des Boucheries**, get onto **Rue du Sallé** for **Place au Beurre**, where you'll find a fabulous concentration of tempting crêperies with terraces. Around here, you can discover shops specializing in Celtic music and some interesting art galleries. A little further up the slope, opposite the bulky Chapelle des Jésuites, the **Jardin de la Retraite** offers a calm little oasis of greenery looking down on the city centre.

To the south of Rue Kéréon, the wacky architecture of the modern covered market, or **Halles**, rebuilt after a fire in 1979, draws shoppers in large numbers with its excellent selection of food stalls, plus there are many other shops on the square around it. A little way further west you come to the **Place Terre-au-Duc**, another shopping square surrounded by fine timberframe facades, while on adjoining little **Place Médard**, modern fountains stand beside the Steir River. This was where the western limit lay of the old medieval town. A watchtower remains. Beyond, the spire of the 19th-century **church of St-Mathieu** stands out. You can reach it via lively **Rue du Chapeau Rouge**, with more shops and bars, and places selling fresh crêpes that sometimes perfume the air.

Across broad Rue de Franklin, a whole cutting-edge new quarter has arisen recently, the brand-new Médiathèque having taken over a smart old barracks building, while **Le Quartier**, Quimper's big contemporary art centre nearby, supports present-day artists by putting on temporary art shows. The neighbouring **Théâtre de Cornouaille** is a big bruiser of a contemporary theatre. Walk down from here to the **Quai de l'Odet**, lined by more traditional grand old Breton blocks.

Le Quartier
www.le-quartier.net,
t 02 98 55 55 77; open
Tues–Sat 10–12 and
1–6, Sun 2–6

Quimper's Outer Quarters

The **pottery quarter** lies in the shadow of the big Romanesque church of **Locmaria**, west along the opposite bank of the Odet, past the wooded Mont Frugy and the big car parks at its feet. Visit the workshops of **HB Henriot Faïenceries de Quimper** to see how the traditional Quimper pottery is still made and decorated. This is one of the few major French potteries still painting designs entirely by hand, without using transfers. Each piece is unique and signed by the artist who executed it. The tours are extremely popular and the shop sells a large selection of Quimper pottery and seconds. You can also sign up to try your hand at decorating your own piece.

HB Henriot
Faïenceries
de Quimper
www.hb-henriot.com,
t 02 98 90 09 36, open
Mon–Thur 9–11.15 and
1.30–4.15, Fri 9–11.15 and
1.30–3; call t 08 00 62
65 10 for times of tours

From the quay close to the pottery quarter, or from further down river, depending on the tides, you can embark on a cruise down the Odet with **Les Vedettes de l'Odet** in high season. Or hire a **kayak** to explore the beautiful river. Continue along the south bank to visit the **Jardins de Lanniron**, the rather fine terraced gardens that lead down from the former bishops' palace to the Odet, whose banks you can continue exploring using the towpath. As a reward for children going round town, consider **Aquarive**, also out along the banks of the Odet, boasting one of the best indoor pool complexes in the region, with a major wave machine to mimic the sea.

Les Vedettes
de l'Odet
www.vedettes-
odet.com,
t 02 98 57 00 58

Kayak
www.kayak
quimper.neuf.fr

Aquarive
t 02 98 52 00 15

In the less exciting commercial outskirts of town, **Armor Lux** and the **Crêpe Dentelles biscuit makers** have popular if architecturally uninspiring stores at which to stock up on their specialities. There are some prettier cider-producing farms to visit close to town – the tourist office can supply a list.

Market Days in Quimper

Markets are held in various parts of town on Wednesday, Friday, Saturday and Sunday.

Festivals in Quimper

The **Festival de Cornouaille** is a major annual Breton festival, one of the best in Brittany, held every year the third or fourth week in July.

Where to Stay in Quimper

Quimper ✉ **29000**
★★★Manoir Hôtel des Indes, 1 Allée de Prad ar C'hras, **t** 02 98 55 48 40, *www.manoir-hoteldesindes.com*

**ⓘ Pays
Touristique de
Quimper**
*www.paystouristique-
quimper.fr, for
information on the
wider area around
Quimper*

(€€€€€–€€€). For the charming, exclusive hotel of Quimper, head c.2km out of the centre towards Douarnenez. Pool, too.

***Gradlon, 30 Rue de Brest, **t** 02 98 95 04 39, *www.hotel-gradlon.com* (€€€€–€€). A hop and a skip east of the old centre, with prettily decorated rooms and a courtyard.

***Kregenn, 13 Rue des Réguaires, **t** 02 98 95 08 70, *www.hotel-kregenn.fr* (€€€€–€€). Again a tiny bit east of the historic centre, a well-refurbished modern hotel.

Le Dupleix, 34 Blvd Dupleix, **t 02 98 90 53 35, *www.hotel-dupleix.com* (€€€–€€). A modern building with the advantage of some spacious rooms looking out over the Odet River and onto the cathedral spires.

Logis du Stang B&B, 41 Allée de Stang-Youen, 10mins southeast of old Quimper, **t** 02 98 52 00 55, *www.logis-du-stang.com* (€€). The most charming B&B in Quimper lies a fair way southeast of the centre.

Mme Le Garrec B&B, 1A Rue St-Nicolas, **t** 02 98 95 61 63 (€). A nice, good-value central option.

Eating Out in Quimper

La Fleur de Sel, 1 Quai Neuf, **t** 02 98 55 04 71 (€€€–€€). Light fish dishes served at this good riverside restaurant opposite Locmaria. *Closed Sat lunch and Sun.*

L'Ambroisie, 49 Rue Elie Fréron, **t** 02 98 95 00 02 (€€€€–€€). A restaurant with a friendly 1950s feel serving inventive Breton cuisine. *Closed Mon.*

Café de l'Epée, 14 Rue du Parc, **t** 02 98 95 28 97 (€€€–€€). A stylishly decorated brasserie well known as an elegant meeting place, with good seafood on the menu.

Crêperie La Krampouzerie, 9 Rue du Sallé/Place au Beurre, **t** 02 98 95 13 08 (€). Among the cluster of tempting crêperies around Place au Beurre, this one does excellent, original crêpes. *Closed Sun and Mon.* (Also recommended in this lovely area are the atmospheric **Crêperie du Sallé**, **t** 02 98 95 95 80, with large terrace opposite, or **Le Jardin d'Eté**, **t** 02 98 95 33 00, with fresh, wider menus [€€–€] and little courtyard.)

Au Vieux Quimper, 20 Rue Verdelet, **t** 02 98 95 31 34 (€). A good option where you can watch the *crêpières* at work and enjoy the Breton décor. *Closed Sun and Mon.*

The Cap Sizun and the Ile de Sein

Moving to the coast of Cornouaille west of Douarnenez, a stunning, precipitous coastal path leads west from that well-protected port to two of the most famous headlands in France, the Pointe du Van and the Pointe du Raz. The French feel they can find their Land's End at the latter. Audierne, the major town of the Cap Sizun, offers the archetypal Breton fishing scene. From here, boats leave for the tiny island of Sein, seemingly always on the verge of being submerged by the sea. Celtic druids, it's said, thought they could depart from here for the afterlife; it is very atmospheric.

The Coast from Douarnenez to the Pointe du Van

You have to walk along the coastal path to appreciate the beauty of the Baie de Douarnenez from its southern side. Starting from Tréboul west of Douarnenez, the brackeny trail takes you past the dramatic **headlands of Leydé and the Jument**. The Baie de Douarnenez below is often spotted with sails. Inland, **Lesconil**

Getting around the Cap Sizun

Buses from Douarnenez and Quimper serve this area.

has a quite impressive neolithic gallery chamber. Also just inland from the coastal path, the **Moulin de Keriolet** still has its metallic wheel in place; a little exhibition inside focuses on local watermills.

The **Pointe du Millier** is a well-known viewing point along this coast, its lighthouse still in operation. Below, to the west, you can find one of the rare sandy beaches along this unspoilt stretch. Remnants of a neolithic settlement lie scattered around **Lescogan** inland. Heading on past **Lillouren**, you can see a large block of stone by a mill, claimed by legend to have been the stone boat in which St Conogan arrived, another Dark Ages religious immigrant from across the Channel.

Back at the coast, past another beach, the Plage de Pors Péron, and the Pointe de Trénaouret, you come to the exhilarating **Pointe de Beuzec** or **Castel Coz** ('Old Castle'), with its traces of an Iron Age fort and its scary coastal track, for which you need to be sure of foot. The **Fête des Bruyères**, or Heather Festival, celebrating Breton music, dance and ceremony, takes place at nearby **Beuzec-Cap-Sizun** on the second Sunday of August. The way continues dramatically until you reach the area of the **Cap Sizun bird reserve**.

Past the reserve, the shore looks much more savage and unforgiving, although a small number of yachts can draw into the tiny harbour below the **Pointe de Penharn** with its monumental rock formations. Spectacular views open out from the **Pointe de Brézellec**, while a little further on, the **Pointe de Castel Meur**, site of another Iron Age defence, looks particularly scary.

Cap Sizun bird reserve
reserve-cap-sizun@bretagne-vivante.asso.fr, t 02 98 70 13 53; open daily 15 April–June 10–12 and 2–6, July and Aug 10–6

To the Breton Land's End

On the end of the Cap Sizun, two exceptionally dramatic rocky peninsulas stick out into the ocean like the pincers of a great sea creature trying vainly to catch the Ile de Sein beyond their grasp.

The **Pointe du Van** ('van' means headland or point in Breton, so the French name rather labours the... point) doesn't reach quite as far out to sea, which makes it slightly less iconic than its rival, the Pointe du Raz. Tourist cars are herded into car parks sensitively surrounded by low stone walls. Walking across the heath to the edge of this treeless headland, among the scrub you can make out the remains of much older stone walls, a sign, amazingly, that this land was once cultivated, divided into small protected plots. The **chapel of St-They** stands out dramatically to one side. The spirit of this saint supposedly used to get the bells to ring to warn ships away from this lethal coast. That didn't stop many being wrecked. You get spectacular views of further headlands from here,

Legends of Death

Legends of death have piled up at La Baie des Trépassés like so many bits of wreckage after a ship goes down. The eerie name possibly derives from a misinterpretation of the Breton *aon*, meaning 'river', for the Breton *anaon*, meaning the dead. One intriguing tale recounts how deceased Celtic druids were transported from here to be laid to rest on the island of Sein – this bay was seemingly considered, at one time, a point of departure for the afterlife. In more recent times, it was said that on All Saints' Day, the Catholic day of the dead, you could hear the sound of the souls of wailing sailors lost at sea gathering here.

including the more famous and much more touristy Pointe du Raz nearby.

The road between these two leads you down and across the **Baie des Trépassés**, the Bay of the Dead. With its hotel, large car park and broad beach, plus its grottoes to go and see at low tide, the bay doesn't feel as frightening today as the legends make it sound (*see* above). Ignore the touristy stuff, though, and looking out from the beach to the rock-strewn seas beyond, the captivating views do take on an otherworldly quality.

La Pointe du Raz
*www.pointe
duraz.com*

Arriving at **La Pointe du Raz**, a Grand Site de France and one of the most famous headlands in France, it can feel at times as if you're caught in the weekend queues for a big city hypermarket. And you have to pay to park here. In the 1990s, much was done to try to protect this overpopular, tourist-worn French Land's End. A hotel was demolished and the tourist boutiques moved to new, more discreet buildings. At the **Maison du Site** visitor centre, you can find out about the history of the promontory and its area, while a video tells the story of the city of Ys (*see* box, p.324); there are also guided tours you can pay to go on, some specially geared to children.

Maison du Site
*open July–Aug
daily 9.30–7.30,
April–June and Sept
daily 10.30–6; free*

As you walk to the end of the wild promontory, the landscape still looks lunar in parts, the rocks polished so smooth by visitors' feet. One unfortunate monument that hasn't been removed is a white statue of the Virgin, the vulgar Catholic **Notre-Dame des Naufragés** (Our Lady of the Shipwrecked), inaugurated at the *pardon* in 1904. A fair number of visitors clamber out quite far on to the tortuous rocks that tail off so spectacularly into the ocean.

One particularly rough chasm on this headland, where the sea boils down below, is known as the **Gouffre de Plogoff**. The name is a reminder of the pathological evil of Dahut, daughter of King Gradlon, in the legend of Ys. Each night, the story goes, she chose a new partner. After they had made love, she had her latest paramour (or should that be pas-amour?) suffocated with a silk mask and the body discarded in this tormented cauldron.

On good days at the Pointe du Raz, you can see north to the Pointe de St-Mathieu in the Léon and south to the Pointe de Penmarc'h at the end of the vast Bay of Audierne. Straight out to the west, the **Phare de la Vieille** and the **Phare de la Plate** count among the best-known lighthouses in France. You may be able to make out the island of Sein, too, floating like a mirage in the distance.

The Southern Cap Sizun to Audierne

To appreciate the southern coast of the Cap Sizun to the full, you need to walk the coastal path once again. The road to Audierne runs parallel to the coast just inland and takes you past villages with pretty churches and chapels – in fact, in July and August, a dozen of them across the Cap Sizun serve as so many contemporary art galleries for **L'Art à la Pointe**.

L'Art à la Pointe
*get details from local
tourist offices*

The road passes through the village of **Plogoff**, with Cléden-Cap-Sizun just to the north. The churches here have ships sculpted in stone on the walls. Plogoff is the village renowned for its successful protests in the 1970s against the outrageously insensitive French government plan to build a nuclear power station nearby. *Des Pierres contre des fusils* (*Stones Versus Guns*) was the name of a well-known film made of the almost epic environmental battle.

After cute coastal **Primelin** tucked at the bottom of a well-protected little bay, the **Anse du Loch**, branch off to visit the delightful Flamboyant Gothic **Chapelle St-Tugen**. This substantial 16th-century chapel stands in a traditional Breton parish enclosure, the entrance to it making a memorable picture, the accolade arch of the gateway echoed in the porch entrance. This porch holds statues of the apostles and of St Tugen. Tugen was one of the best-known healing saints from the Breton Dark Ages. A story goes that he tried in vain to put a stop to his sister's unbridled pleasure-seeking. In frustration, Tugen cried out that it would be easier to stop a rabid dog from biting than getting a wanton girl to give up her evil ways; God supposedly consoled the man by giving him the power to cure rabies. At the St-Tugen *pardons*, it's said that keys were sold that believers were meant to throw at a mad dog if it approached them. The eccentric interior is richly decorated with all manner of quirky Breton craftsmanship.

Southwest of St-Tugen, seek out tracks to the beautiful beach in the **Anse du Cabestan**, one of the few stretches of sand along the south coast of the Cap Sizun before Audierne. The coastal path becomes rocky again from the old fortifications of the Penn an Enez on the eastern end of the Anse du Cabestan to the Pointe de Lervily. Round the corner, you come in view of **Ste-Evette**, the merry seaside resort attached to Audierne, with lovely beaches below the coastal road. This is also where **boats** leave for **L'Ile de Sein**.

Audierne, safely anchored up the Goyen estuary, still feels like a busy fishing port. Its west bank is lined with former shipowners' houses. The port has its fair share of seafood restaurants as well as supplying restaurants all around France with shellfish. The small **Halles**, or covered market, by the tourist office is open mornings, selling fish, crêpes and other local produce. A local association runs the little **Musée Maritime du Cap Sizun** close by, recalling the fishing traditions of the area. Once a month, a Scottish guide, Fiona McLeod, organizes a guided tour round the Cap Sizun, recounting Celtic legends. Sticking with old Audierne, you can get enjoyably lost in the charming maze of steep streets above the quays. Squeezed in among them, Audierne's **church** has a ship carved in stone over its entrance, appropriately enough.

Musée Maritime du Cap Sizun
check opening times and tour dates at tourist office

Aquashow at the back of the estuary heads the list of tourist attractions in town. As well as aquaria, with one large one devoted to sharks, the place also keeps owls, which feature in flying shows. If the weather isn't good for bathing, **Aquacap** at **Esquibien**, just west of town towards Raz, offers warm waters year-round, plus giant slides and the like.

Aquashow
www.aquarium.fr, t 02 98 70 03 03; open April–Sept daily 10–7

Aquacap
www.recrea.fr/aquacap, t 02 98 70 07 74

Cross the Goyen for **Plouhinec**, where you can go to watch the local **fishing boats** come in on summer afternoons, and even enjoy the **Criée**, or fish auction. For less touristy beaches, head down to the **Plage de Kersigny** and **Plage de Mesperleuc** below Plouhinec.

Île de Sein

Qui voit Sein voit sa fin. (If you see Sein you see your end.)

It seems a miracle that this island hasn't been swallowed up by the ocean. The highest point on this southwestern outpost of Brittany doesn't even manage to reach 10 metres above sea level. Treacherous reefs spread out from Sein, hence the grisly rhyme above, warning sailors against straying this way. A pair of imposing lighthouses mark the island's tips, while 10 kilometres west of Sein, the **lighthouse of Ar Men** ('The Rock') is one of the most famous symbols of Brittany to French people.

Beyond the single village with its ugly church and little museum in particular commemorating the heroic action of the islanders in the Second World War, there's very little to visit on Sein. The place is about as barren as Brittany gets, almost ceaselessly windswept, and you can wander round to most parts of the island in half a day. But it has a compelling atmosphere; and there are a number of restaurants and bars in which to take refuge.

Mythology and History of the Île de Sein

Neolithic men clearly came to Sein millennia before any Senes (*see* box, right), one or two monuments remaining from that period. No trace has been found, however, of a religious

Getting to the Ile de Sein

The **Compagnie Maritime Penn Ar Bed** (*www.pennarbed.fr*, **t** 02 98 80 80 80) runs services to Sein from both Audierne and Brest through the year. The **Vedette Biniou** (*www.vedettebiniou.freeserve.fr*, **t** 02 98 70 13 78) offers an alternative service in July and Aug.

establishment from the Dark Ages. Down the centuries, even the island's name seemed uncertain, its spelling changing time and again, but the fear that it instilled in sailors remained unaltered. The small number of Sénans, as inhabitants of Sein are known, also gained a filthy reputation as wreckers. The Christian story goes that the wayward islanders had, basically, to be reconverted during the 17th century.

Sein has often been under threat from the seas. In 1756, after a tidal wave crashed over the island, the royal governor of Brittany, the Duc d'Aiguillon, offered the Sénans money to move to the mainland. They refused, but did accept the building of a jetty. The 19th century saw the building of great lighthouses around the island, but useful as these may be, they don't help on those rare occasions when Sein is engulfed by raging tides. The most dramatic incident occurred in 1868, when the islanders took refuge in the highest attics; such was the feeling of desperation that Sein's priest is supposed to have offered everyone the last rites. A similar rush to take cover under or on the village roofs has occurred on a couple of other occasions since. As compensation for their troubles, the inhabitants of Sein are apparently exempt from paying most taxes.

Tour of the Ile de Sein

You feel you can take in the whole of Sein in one easy glance as you arrive by sea. The **port-cum-village** occupies the centre of the

Sein, the Senes and Saints

Sein, despite being so small, has featured large in Breton mythology. Strange stories survive of nine virgin Celtic priestesses who lived totally isolated on the island, guardians of a Celtic oracle, endowed with awesome supernatural powers. These Senes were supposed to be able to whip up storms, change into terrifying beasts, cure terrible diseases, and tell the future. They would only use their powers for sailors who made it to the island to consult them.

The Senes play a part in versions of the legend of the city of Ys. The debauched and godless Dahut, daughter of King Gradlon, comes to ask them for help, distraught at the building of a church in her beloved irreligious town on the ocean. To counteract this encroachment of Christianity, together they chant Dahut's wishes, including the building of a new castle. *Korrigans*, Breton pagan fairies, are sent out to accomplish its construction in just one night.

Despite their superhuman powers, the Senes foresee the arrival of a god from the Orient who will bring about their end. They lament that 'the Senes will die one by one, and with the death of the last one, the old gods of Armorica will die'. The history of Sein indicates that old pagan ways weren't so easily eradicated here and Christianity not so simply espoused. In the Dark Ages, two powerful Breton saints are said to have tried to plant the Christian faith firmly on its soil, St Guénolé and St Corentin.

When Sein Made Up One Quarter of France

The Senans knew their most honourable hour at the outbreak of the Second World War in France. While the rest of the country capitulated so meekly to the Nazis in 1940, the men of Sein made the most of their isolated position to take up General Charles de Gaulle's call to join him across the Channel and go and fight for a free France. A large number of the adult population of able and fit men, approximately 150 in number, took to their boats on hearing de Gaulle's message and immediately headed for England. 'So the island of Sein makes up a quarter of France, does it?', de Gaulle is claimed to have remarked wryly as he inspected the first batch of French arrivals in Britain. Several thousand further Frenchmen got away to Britain from Sein in the ensuing weeks. Some 30 Sénans died in the Second World War.

island. The village itself does have its secretive side, with its very narrow, crooked streets – they're supposed to be just wide enough to roll a barrel along. The favoured mode of transport in fact appears to be the wheelbarrow – there are no cars. Up by the church, the two **menhirs** face each other like slightly irascible if close friends; they're comically known as the ***Pregourien***, 'the Chatters'. The **church**, in neo-Romanesque style, dates from the late 19th century but is dedicated to the Celtic Christian Guénolé. Inside, it contains interesting postwar stained glass. On the northern end of the village, the **Kador** ('Seat') rock is traditionally associated with those powerful pagan priestesses of Sein, the Senes.

Narrow isthmuses either side of the village lead to scrub-covered tips. Heading southeast, you can walk along the wide sweep of sand and stones protected by the arm of the port's jetty. The isthmus here can be a tricky place to negotiate with its great number of rockpools. The southern tip of the island is now totally uninhabited, but the labyrinth of stone walls swallowed up by scrub makes you feel like you're walking over a ruined settlement. The easier, concrete path takes visitors west to the lighthouse, the **Phare St-Corentin**, the one substantial building on the island. Before you arrive, a very inconsequential chapel dedicated to St Corentin tries its best to hide in the undergrowth in these unforgiving parts.

Pont-Croix and Around

Back on the mainland and up the picturesque Goyen River from Audierne, cobbled little streets as treacherously steep as alpine slopes lead up from the waterside to the historic town of Pont-Croix on its height. You'd do best to don mountain boots to make it up the **Grande** or the **Petite Rue Chère**, lined by minute old cottages. The site of Pont-Croix is fit for a castle. And in fact a fort did used to stand here, marking the frontier between the Cap Sizun and the Pays Bigouden to the south. This was the seat of power of a lordly Cornouaille family during medieval times. The port back down at the foot of the town would once have been bustling with activity. In fact Pont-Croix was the proud capital of the Cap Sizun, before the Goyen began to silt up.

The story of Pont-Croix's medieval wealth is written in the stones and finery of the **Eglise Notre-Dame de Roscudon**, a Breton church that was influenced by English architecture. The edifice dates back in fair part to the 13th century. A whole string of other religious buildings followed this style, forming what became known as the Pont-Croix school of architecture. The two main outer features of the church are a towering spire and a sensational Flamboyant Gothic porch, added on to an otherwise reasonably sober building. Inside the church, tightly ranked semicircular arches in the Romanesque style hold up the dark nave. Only in the choir do lighter Gothic pointed arches take over. The west façade and the sacristy both date from the 18th century.

The streets of the upper town have plenty of charm. Stop in at the Musée du Marquisat to see the Breton furniture and objects displayed in this fine old town house.

To the east of Pont-Croix, at **Confort-Meilars**, the outdoor calvary looks grandiose, but the niches for the apostles stand empty. The most exciting curiosity of this finely decorated church is its chime wheel, with 12 bells, each playing a different note. It is said to have been a gift from Alain de Rosmadec and Jeanne de Chastel to thank the Virgin for getting their mute child to speak.

Musée du Marquisat
www.pont-croix.info, t 02 98 70 40 38; open July–Aug daily exc Sat am 10.30–12.30 and 3.30–6.30, second half June and first half Sept daily 3.30–6.30

ⓘ **Association Ouest Cornouaille Promotion**
www.ouest-cornouaille.com, for information across the area

ⓘ **Audierne >>**
8 Rue Victor Hugo, t 02 98 70 12 20, www.audierne-tourisme.com

ⓘ **Beuzec-Cap-Sizun**
64 Rue des Bruyères, t 02 98 70 55 51, www.beuzec-cap-sizun.fr

Market Days in Cap Sizun and the Ile de Sein

Plogoff: Friday
Cléden-Cap-Sizun: 4th Thursday of the month
Audierne: Saturday
Pont-Croix: 1st, 3rd and 5th Thursdays of the month

Where to Stay and Eat in Cap Sizun and the Ile de Sein

Plogoff ✉ 29770

**La Baie des Trépassés, t 02 98 70 61 34, *hoteldelabaie@aol.com* (€€–€). A large modern hotel overrun during the day by the Pointe du Raz hordes, but otherwise in a great position for you to make the most of the spot.
Kermoor, Plage du Loch, **t 02 98 70 62 06, *www.hotel.kermoor.com* (€€).

A good hotel, and the owner-chef can cook up a storm in the restaurant (€€€–€).
Crêperie du Loch, Plage du Loch, **t 02 98 70 36 26** (€). A good crêperie close to the above.

Cléden-Cap-Sizun ✉ 29770

L'Etrave, Route de la Pointe du Van, **t 02 98 70 66 87** (€€€–€€). Unfussy restaurant with sea views, known above all for its excellent if expensive lobster dishes. *Closed Oct–March.*

Audierne ✉ 29770

***Le Goyen, Place Jean Simon, **t 02 98 70 08 88**, *www.le-goyen.com* (€€€€–€€). A smart waterside hotel ideal for lapping up the atmosphere, many of the rooms with views over the port. The restaurant (€€€€–€€) with its conservatory front serves fine seafood. *Closed Dec–March.*
Au Roi Gradlon, 3 Ave Brusq, **t 02 98 70 04 51, *www.auroigradlon.com* (€€–€). Hotel right next to the beach, with sea views from many rooms (lots

ⓘ Pont-Croix >>
Rue Laënnec,
t 02 98 70 40 38,
www.pont-croix.info

★ Crêperie
l'Epoké >>

ⓘ Plouhinec
Place Jean Moulin,
t 02 98 70 74 55,
www.plouhinec-
tourisme.com

with balconies) and a restaurant (€€€€–€) specializing in seafood.

**Hôtel de la Plage, 21 Blvd Brusq, t 02 98 70 01 07, *www.hotel-finistere.com* (€€–€). A sunny seafront hotel just a hop and a skip from the beach, with lots of cheerful rooms with sea views. Bright restaurant (€€€€–€€) open for residents only. *Closed Oct–April.*

L'Iroise, 8 Quai Camille Pelletan, t 02 98 70 15 80 (€€€€–€). Refined cuisine at this smart restaurant overlooking the port.

Côté Jardin, 1 Rue du 14 Juillet, t 02 98 75 04 45 (€€€–€). For fresh cookery by the covered market.

Pont-Croix

Crêperie l'Epoké, 1 Rue des Partisans, t 02 98 70 58 39 (€). Enchanting old-stone home by the main church, serving delicious crêpes, with summer terrace.

Ile de Sein ✉ 29990

**Ar Men, Route du Phare, t 02 98 70 90 77, *www.hotel-armen.net* (€€–€). Charming hotel, the last before America, giving onto the beach. Several of the island's restaurants offer the speciality of lobster stew.

The Pays Bigouden

The Pays Bigouden occupies one of the wildest corners of the whole Breton peninsula. Pont-l'Abbé is its capital, where a uniquely tall *coiffe* was traditionally worn. This towering headdress of the women of the area, worn by some until quite recently, is surely one of the most architectural manifestations of fashion in the world. It makes such a powerful image that it has become one of the main symbols of Brittany to outsiders.

On the western side of the Pays Bigouden, an immense, gently curving but challengingly wild beach runs down the Baie d'Audierne. The chapel of Tronoën, boasting the most famous calvary in Brittany, looks over at the barren scene. A whole string of fishing ports lines the southern shore of the Pays Bigouden, despite the sinister rocks of the area. Their forces combined, they make up one of the biggest fishing fleets in all France. Between these ports, the invigorating beaches are particularly appreciated by windsurfers.

The Bay of Audierne

The predominant feature of the Bay of Audierne is the great sweep of its sands disappearing into the distance. Sea spray often obscures the view of the entire curve, while the Atlantic waves thunder in incessantly. On the northern end of the bay there is a rough, rocky stretch of coastline before you arrive at the immense, long beach. The Pays Bigouden officially starts at **Pors-Poulhan**, where René Quillivic's statue of a Bigoudène girl used to blush orange with lichen at her prominent role marking the frontier with the Cap Sizun – her face has been scrubbed clean recently. The cute

Getting around the Pays Bigouden

Bus services radiate out from Pont-l'Abbé, making it possible, if slow, to get to the ports and resorts. There's a good bus service between Pont-l'Abbé and Quimper.

little harbour here, tucked away from the roaring Atlantic, makes a good halt for a drink.

The exposed coast road sticks close to the rocks as you head south past the **Menhir des Droits de l'Homme**, at the **beach of Canté**. The top of this neolithic standing stone snapped off in a storm in 2008, but the 19th-century memorial curiously engraved on it remains, recalling that it was just out to sea from here that the ship *Les Droits de l'Homme*, part of a large French fleet sent out on an abortive expedition to support insurrection in Ireland against the British, was hounded, holed and sunk by English frigates in 1797.

A diminutive manmade harbour at **Penhors** tries to protect the local boats from the elements. Many passers-by stop to drink in the bay views from the simple cafés behind it, although the building of a new sea-rescue centre here has caused a recent controversy. Some visitors are tempted into the highly commercial **Musée de l'Amiral**, with its huge collection of shells, stuffed sea birds and sharks, and marine fossils stretching behind its extensive shop. The **Chapelle de Penhors** adds a serious, but picturesque, religious note in the background, set by the old village, looking out over the bay. Like many other chapels in the area, its appealing architecture follows the Pont-Croix style.

Musée de l'Amiral
*www.museedelamiral
.com,* **t** *02 98 51 52 52*

Inland from Penhors, **Pouldreuzic** is known above all as the setting for Pierre Jakez Hélias's famous book (*see* box, below). The

The Bitch of the World and the Horse of Pride

As I'm too poor to buy any other kind of horse, at least the horse of pride will always have a place in my stable.

The subtitle to *Le Cheval d'Orgueil*, a deeply evocative autobiographical book by Pierre Jakez Hélias, reads *Mémoires d'un Breton du Pays Bigouden*. Originally written in Breton, then translated into French by the author, it has become the most read book on Brittany and even been turned into a French film. It tells the story of a Bigouden community centred around Pouldreuzic and how its people lived in the first half of the 20th century.

Most of the locals' lives were dominated by the 'bitch of the world' – poverty. In an area and a time where a horse remained the sign of a wealthy man, the poor were still tied to their overlords, their employers and the clergy, in an almost feudal, medieval manner. After a hard day working for the master, they would sometimes gather by moonlight to clear by hand a piece of meagre earth to cultivate for themselves. Children slept in *lits-clos* on bedding stuffed with seaweed. The cottage floors were of beaten earth: 'Each head of a family had his own recipe for preparing his floor, just as each wife had hers for preparing her stew,' Hélias explains. Despite the harshness of life for most in the parish, the rituals, the pleasures and the comedy of everyday events, conversations and ceremonies fill the pages. The Bigoudens' comments on life can be coarse and subtle at the same time. Pettiness, rivalry and superstition go hand in hand with heartfelt love and intelligence.

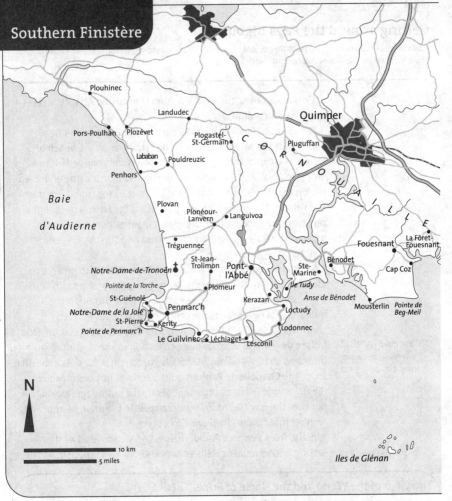

Maison Hélias is a small museum dedicated to the subject, set in the house where the author was born. Pouldreuzic is also a place of important Breton culinary traditions. The popular Breton crêpe-making machines by Krampouz are manufactured and sold here. The village is also home to the family firm that makes Brittany's very popular pork Pâté Hénaff, which has a cult following in France and features in many epic Breton yachting adventures, international and familial; it has even opened a museum for its devoted followers, the **Maison du Pâté Hénaff** – or simply sample and buy the stuff at the shop. Good cider is also produced in these parts, the **Cidrerie Kerné** at Mesmeur claiming to be the oldest craft cider-maker in the Finistère. There's also the beer-making **Brasserie de Pouldreuzic**, located in a beautiful farm where Breton cultural events, including *fest-noz* evening dances, are sometimes staged.

Maison du Pâté Hénaff
www.henaff.fr,
t 02 98 51 53 76;
open June–Sept

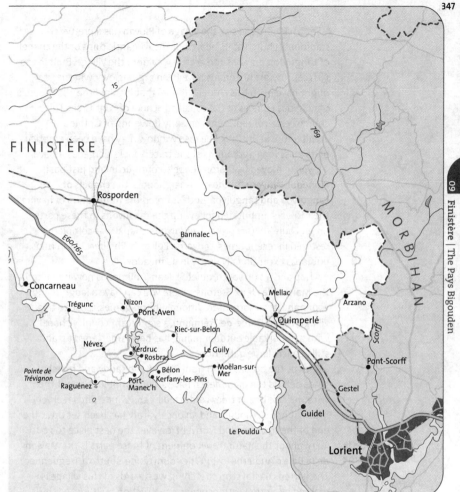

One of the Longest Beaches in Brittany

South of Penhors, one of the longest beaches in Brittany curves gently round the Bay of Audierne down to St-Guénolé. This is also one of the wildest strands in the province, backed by a curious bank of ancient pebbles. The odd Nazi blockhouse has toppled down to deface the sands. Going back in time, it was along this coast that the wrecks from the Pointe de Penmarc'h tended to be blown ashore. The poor would comb the beaches to recuperate remnants. They long had a reputation as wreckers, deliberately trying to get ships to go astray on their shore. Behind the beach, many of the old houses were built without any openings on the Atlantic side, to give no opportunities to the ocean's draughts to enter.

Set back from the sea, the village of **Plovan** has a pretty, traditional church at its heart, but the romantic ruins of the **chapel of Languidou** draw visitors a little way from the village. Built in the 13th century, art historians have been arguing over whether it might have been this church's model that inspired the whole series of religious edifices of the so-called School of Pont-Croix. This church certainly represents an early flowering of Gothic architecture in Brittany. The rose window may have been emptied of its glass long ago, but its stone tracery looks gorgeous as lace.

If you're moved by Breton chapels, continue inland just past **Ploneour-Lanvern** for the near-neighbours, the **chapels of Languivoa and Languivoa**. Both suffered the humiliation of having their towers amputated following the tax revolts in these parts under Louis XIV (*see* p.354). Languivoa's chapel was completely restored in recent times. Lanvern's Eglise St-Philibert lies in ruins, but looks exceptionally pretty in its meadow.

A hop and a skip south, quiet **St-Jean-Trolimon** is now home to the **Maison des Jeux Bretons**, where you can have a laugh trying your hand at all sorts of traditional Breton games. Close to this village, **Notre-Dame-de-Tréminou**, a significant country chapel with a remarkable outdoor pulpit, has been smartened up and still attracts large gatherings for its *pardon*.

Back by the ocean, south from Plovan, the sandy and marshy lands behind the great beach have an unkempt look about them, with the rare line of trees contorted by the winds. Birds feel very much at home, though, and an observatory has been set up at the end of the track beyond Trunvel. However, the best place to go to learn about the natural environment of these parts is the **Maison de la Baie d'Audierne** lost in the countryside south of **Tréguennec**. The barren coastal strip stretching westwards of this village is marked by a grimly atmospheric construction built for the Nazis. This didn't form part of their Atlantic defences, but was a factory the Germans set up to have the beach pebbles sorted 24 hours a day using virtual slave labour; they were then transported for construction work in Brest, Lorient and elsewhere.

Of the many rural chapels lost in the small valleys and plots just inland, seek out the doll-sized **Chapelle de St-Vio** for its sheer comical charm, while the pretty **Chapelle de Beuzec** stands in a hamlet that boasts the unforgettably named Camping de la Crêpe.

Maison de la Baie d'Audierne
t 02 98 87 65 07; open summer Mon–Fri 2–6; spring and autumn Wed 2–6; free, exc for guided visits

Tronoën, the Little 'Cathedral of the Dunes', and its Calvary

Its Breton steeple standing out of the melancholy countryside like a lichen-rusted trident, the **church of Tronoën** possesses the most famous **calvary** in Brittany, and one of the oldest, dating from around 1450. The two levels of sculpted friezes around it tell many stories from Christ's life and Passion. The exposed stone figures may have been eaten away by the salty winds, but Tronoën's sculptures count among the most expressive of any on the Breton calvaries.

Perhaps the best-known panel shows the Virgin after Jesus's birth, Mary earthily depicted naked-breasted in bed. Other striking scenes stand out: Jesus blindfolded as he's beaten; Pilate, in what slightly resembles a pirate's hat, washing his hands; Christ carrying his cross; the Virgin, almost as rigid as an Egyptian mummy in her grief, being supported by the women surrounding her. Three crosses rise like bent masts from the top of the calvary. At the foot of the central one, the Pietà scene has a particular tragic tenderness, as two figures reach up to draw back the Virgin's veil.

Archaeological digs have revealed Gallo–Roman vestiges and a large number of Dark Ages tombs in the area, indicating that this has long been a holy site. Nowadays, though, it comes as a surprise to see that a good portion of the land around Tronoën, once considered unsuitable for cultivation, is being exploited by commercial flower producers – tulips and other colourful blooms set the fields ablaze at the end of each picking season.

On the southern end of the Baie d'Audierne, the slashed piles of rocks of the dramatic spit of the **Pointe de la Torche** are often lashed by crashing waves, but these assailants are reduced to cascading foam by the encounter. It makes for an exhilarating walk to the tip of the point. A discreet dolmen and German concrete bunkers mark the crowning points of the headland. One of the Nazi posts has been turned into an information centre. The first world windsurfing championships were held here in 1983 and several others have taken place here since. The spot is also much-favoured by surfers, although the sea is dangerous for swimming.

The beautiful **beach of Pors Carn** curves round to the gritty port of St-Guénolé, a modest beach-side café making the most of the view up the Baie d'Audierne, and serving *kouigns*, like Scotch pancakes. Behind the café, the old-fashioned **Musée Préhistorique Finistérien** presents menhirs, dolmens, steles and a gallery chamber outside, while within, the gathered archaeological evidence can teach you something about the prehistoric societies that have inhabited the Finistère down the millennia .

Musée Préhistorique Finistérien
open 10–12 and 2–6 Wed–Mon June–Sept, Wed–Sun Oct–May

The Fishing Ports of the Southern Pays Bigouden

Set defiantly amid menacing rocks and reefs, the big ports of St-Guénolé, Le Guilvinec/Léchiagat, Lesconil and Loctudy are what are termed *ports de pêche artisanale*, or craft fishing ports, to distinguish their activity from *pêche industrielle*. Together they form the largest centre for this type of fishing in the whole of France, specializing in delicious langoustines. The harbour streets of these towns that live so largely by seafood sometimes smell pungent, the screech of greedy gulls often filling the air. The people of the area have been living off the ocean for a long time, and fishing remains close to the heart of these communities. Virtually all the Criées, the fish-auctioning halls, can be visited on guided tours. From the lovely beaches of the area, many framed by rocks, you can see the local vessels heading into port at teatime. You'll find shops selling seafood specialities and Breton clothes in all these ports.

The Penmarc'h Peninsula

Eterne God, that thurgh thy purveiaunce
Ledest the world by certein governaunce,
In ydel, as men seyn, ye nothyng make.
But, Lord, thise grisly feendly rokkes blake,
That semen rather a foul confusioun
Of werk than any fair creacioun
Of swich a parfit wys God and a stable,
Why han ye wroght this werk unresonable?
The noble lady Dorigen bemoaning the danger of the Pointe de Penmarc'h's rocks in Chaucer's 'Franklin's Tale' from *The Canterbury Tales*

As Lady Dorigen laments in Chaucer's great work, the rocks of the Penmarc'h Peninsula can seem very forbidding, but they also beautify this extraordinary stretch of the Breton coastline. **St-Guénolé** appears quite sinister on first acquaintance, surrounded by serrated, evil-looking rocks, but it proves a compelling place. Although a vicious storm in winter 2008 managed to breach the harbour wall, the **port** is at the technological forefront of the fishing industry with computerized auctioning of the catch. It's possible to go walking on the savage **rocks** north of the port, but beware – the Rocher du Préfet is named after the head of a French *département* who was swept out to sea from here with his family by a freak wave

South from St-Guénolé, a memorable rockscape opens out in front of you. The rocks resemble a shower of meteorites scattered over the waters. On top of many stand small beacons like coloured candles, warning boats away. The church of **Notre-Dame de la Joie** was seemingly built among the reefs, and a stone boat is even carved on one gable. The name of the building, Our Lady of Joy, may seem ironic given the treacherous setting, but this is the church where sailors came to pray in thanks to the Virgin Mary for sparing their lives on dangerous journeys. It also served as the house in which materials salvaged from wrecks were stored. A famous old Breton song, the 'Gwerz Penmarc'h', tells a chilling story, though, cursing the people of the Pointe de Penmarc'h for lighting fires in their church in order to mislead sailors and wreck their ships. Not surprisingly, with so many local people depending on the risky work of fishing for their livelihood, the church gathered a deeply devoted following, its *pardon* of 15 August becoming one of the most important events in the Pays Bigouden.

Turn the corner and you come to the gorgeous **port of St-Pierre**, although the algae-strewn rocks around it can give off quite a whiff. Dwarfing the diminutive place stands the Phare d'Eckmühl, completed at the very end of the 19th century. It looks regal, wearing its crown of a lantern, and generously spreads its light over 60 kilometres out to sea. It also serves as a landmark for many kilometres around. Visitors can climb almost to the top of its 65 metres for sensational views over the ocean and the Pays Bigouden.

Phare d'Eckmühl
www.penmarch.fr,
t 02 98 58 60 19; open
April–Sept daily
10.30–6.30

Two much smaller towers stick out in front of the Phare d'Eckmühl. One belongs to the older 19th-century lighthouse, made to seem quite poxy by the larger erection, but it still serves a purpose – these days, it holds the small but interesting Centre de Découverte Maritime, which puts on fascinating exhibitions on sea-related themes on the ground floor, and good art exhibitions on the first. As to the 15th-century **chapel of St-Pierre**, its tower doubled as a lighthouse long before the other two upstarts. In summer, it plays host to very local painting exhibitions.

Centre de
Découverte
Maritime
open July–Aug daily
2–6, April–June and
Sept daily exc Tues 2–6

The **Société Centrale des Naufragés** (the 'Central Company for the Shipwrecked') at the port, run by the Association Papa Poydenot, named after an old life-saving boat from 1900 lovingly preserved here, also merits a visit. Stories of maritime disasters and rescues around Penmarc'h are told around the walls. All these sights should help you work up a thirst to visit the appealing crêperies and bars clustered round the skirts of the Phare d'Eckmühl, Ty Mone even with a *boule* ground looking across to the port.

Association
Papa Poydenot
www.papapoydenot.
com, t 02 98 58 67 36;
open April–Sept
daily; free

Starting along the southern side of the Pays Bigouden, you soon come to the jolly port of **Kerity**, but with the reefs of the Ecots rocks just out to sea serving as a vicious defence. The place's present appearance belies its much grander past. This area was cosmopolitan in its heyday in the 16th century; Kerity was then the largest port in the Pays Bigouden, serving the whole Penmarc'h area, and one of the most important in Brittany. Ships coming up from Bordeaux laden with wine would frequently stop here on the way to England and Flanders. Now tourists come to enjoy the lively

**Centre Nautique
de Penmarc'h**
t 02 98 58 64 87

line of bars and restaurants behind the quay. The **Centre Nautique
de Penmarc'h** is based to the east, where you'll find long, sandy
stretches of beach.

Inland, **Penmarc'h's church of St-Nonna** stands out by its grand
dimensions, rising high above the town's little houses. In contrast
with the generally minute chapels of the area, St-Nonna is on an
impressive scale. It was built early in the 16th century, when
Penmarc'h was thriving. The church was dedicated to Nonna, a
saintly man from the Dark Ages, and not to be confused with Ste
Nonna, mother of St David (*see* box, p.293). The bulky west tower
was never completed, but you can see several ships in stone
sculpted on the elaborate side gables – a sign of wealthy shipping
merchants' donations. Inside, the spaces supported by towering,
wide Gothic arches seem cavernous in comparison with all the tiny
chapels of the Pays Bigouden.

To see some exceptional contemporary stained-glass windows
in a Breton chapel, head for the **Chapelle de la Madeleine**, just
northwest of central Penmarc'h, clad in palest grey stone. Inside,
the flaming semi-abstract religious figures by the artist Jean
Bazaine flow with energy and emotion.

From Le Guilvinec to Loctudy

Haliotika
*www.leguilvinec.com,
t 02 98 58 28 38; open
15 March–15 Oct and
school hols Mon–Fri
2.30–7, Sat and
Sun 3–6.30*

Le Guilvinec and **Léchiagat** face each other across their inlet, but
have joined forces to form one very lively, workmanlike port. Le
Guilvinec's harbour seems the busiest place to be after 4pm on
weekdays in the Pays Bigouden, when the fishing boats return,
laden with langoustines in particular. Learn more about the fishing
trade in these parts at Haliotika, which covers the contemporary
realities of the maritime fishing profession through imaginative
presentations, and also allows you to visit the fish-sorting and
auctioning hall. The maze of lanes in both Le Guilvinec and
Léchiagat have all the atmosphere you'd expect of such Breton
ports, and it comes as no surprise that there are numerous bars
either side of the water. Les Brisants, at the end of the Léchiagat
quays, takes marine decoration to amusing heights. Back with Le
Guilvinec, temporary art exhibitions are put on at the converted
Abri du Pêcheur, the first of a dozen such houses in Brittany,
ordered by the benefactor Jacques de Thézac early in the 20th
century to help lessen the sufferings of sailors in dire straits. These
places offered education and practical training, plus eucalyptus tea
to try and stop the scourge of alcoholism that blighted these
communities. At the back of the estuary, you can still see the
skeletons of old wooden boats, left gradually to disintegrate.

A series of long, lovely, quite wild **beaches**, separated by rocky
outcrops and backed by tallish sand dunes, runs to Lesconil, that of
Kersauz especially beautiful. **Lesconil** is a popular little fishing port

that doubles as a charming small resort. Its old fishermen's houses are kept immaculately whitewashed. The bars behind the port are often lively with locals and tourists, while several maritime boutiques have opened around the harbour.

Turning the corner after Lesconil, the coast to Loctudy is more protected from the open seas, and partly because of this, has become more and more built up with Breton holiday homes in recent decades. The sands are particularly white along here, contrasting all the more with the black algae that come to die on the strands.

Loctudy, one of several places around these parts named after an influential Dark Ages saint, Tudy, is both bustling fishing port and lively holiday resort. It lies in a lovely, well-protected location just beyond the mouth of the Pont-l'Abbé River. Its popular **beaches** look east. The odd grand 19th-century villa stands out among the modern seaside homes, recalling the fact that rich families from the area took early to the new fashion of sea-side holidays.

The **ports** are tucked in on the north side, with glorious views looking across to the peninsula of L'Ile-Tudy and the wooded interior beyond. With its large fishing fleet, Loctudy has the biggest market for live langoustines in France. In high summer, **cruise boats** from here can take you up the Odet or out to the Glénan islands. The large **marina** lies in a bit of an isolated position further west of town.

In the centre, the **church of St-Tudy** is surrounded by a sandy graveyard into which the tombstones seem to be sinking. A pre-Christian stele stands out behind the church, like a finely grooved menhir; the Christian Church had to put its own mark on it in the shape of a cross. Although the church was given a classical facade in the 18th century, inside, it's Romanesque. It conceals a rare sight for a Christian place of worship – a carving of a male erection, but then the Church authorities were maybe a little less hung up about these matters in the early medieval period. The erection turns out to be a little affair to be spotted at the base of a column in the choir. Otherwise, some of the column capitals are carved with intriguing Celtic-style patterns that you can see reproduced on the traditional embroidered Bigouden men's jackets.

Manoir de Kérazan
www.institut-de-france.fr, t 02 98 87 50 10; open mid-June–mid-Sept daily exc Mon 10.30–7, Easter–mid-June and 2nd half Sept daily exc Mon 2–6

North of Loctudy, the **Manoir de Kérazan** is a fine Breton house dating from the 16th and 18th centuries, the eccentric shapes of its slate-covered roofs giving it immediate appeal. The manor's last private owner, Joseph Astor, left it to the Institut de France on condition that it be turned in part into a museum, in part into a school of embroidery for young Bigoudènes. The last pupils left during the 1960s, but the museum survives. The place is filled with paintings by well-known names of the Breton art scene, including Maurice Denis, Charles Cottet and Auguste Goy, plus period furniture and rare ceramics. There are also temporary exhibitions, and the farmyard has animals you can go and see.

Ecomusée du Pays Bigouden
open Mon–Sat Easter–31 May 10–12 and 2–5, June–Sept 10–12.30 and 2–6.30

Also situated between Loctudy and Pont-l'Abbé, the **Ecomusée du Pays Bigouden** at the Ferme de Kervazégan contains a pretty collection of Bigouden rural furniture, and occasionally hosts craft events in high summer.

Pont-l'Abbé

Pont-l'Abbé is a friendly little town that stretches out from the river now named after it. It originally grew up around the place where an abbot of Loctudy decided to build a bridge, hence the name. Subsequently the barons of the bridge became powerful lords in the region and from the 12th century had a château on the river. Pont-l'Abbé long benefited from its inland port, as the houses along the quays indicate, but this area no longer plays centre stage. Instead, tourist attention focuses on the very large number of Breton gift shops in the shopping streets and squares up the slope.

Musée Bigouden
www.letriskell.com, t 02 98 66 09 03; open June–Sept daily 10–12.30 and 2–6, Easter–May daily 2–6

The **castle**, Pont-l'Abbé's major building, nowadays houses the town hall, the tourist office and the **Musée Bigouden**, the last holding a rather lifeless collection of items in its big granite chambers. Livelier exhibitions by contemporary painters are put on in the basement in summer. On one side, the castle overlooks 'a big sad lake', as the writer Maupassant accurately described it. This was much cleaned up in the 1980s, and a quite un-Breton-looking modern cultural centre, the **Triskell**, went up on another side to host all manner of events.

Otherwise, Pont-l'Abbé has a strongly Breton feel. In fact, for Maupassant this was one of the most Breton towns of Breton-speaking Brittany. Either side of the river, there's an interesting church to visit. On the far bank stands the lovingly preserved shell of the **Eglise de Lambour**, one of several decapitated churches in the Pays Bigouden. In 1675, popular wrath at punishing new royal taxes brought in by Louis XIV's chief minister Colbert was particularly strong in many parishes around Pont-l'Abbé. In a premature revolution, the loal protesters became known as the Bonnets Rouges, for their red bonnets. They drew up a Peasants' Code calling for major political change, but were violently put down by the troops of the royal governor of Brittany, the Duc de Chaulnes. Not only were many Bigoudens hanged or sent to the galleys, but half a dozen parishes also had their church tower decapitated, including this one.

On the opposite bank, **Notre-Dame-des-Carmes** stands out above the quays, with its eccentric slate-covered roofs. This 15th-century church was built as part of a Carmelite monastery. Its most admirable features are its two rose windows with their fine Gothic tracery. Notre-Dame-des-Carmes, like the Triskell, organizes a series of annual **summer concerts** that attracts internationally respected musicians.

Notre-Dame-des-Carmes lies close to the shopping heart of town. Fine granite buildings stand out along the main drag leading up from one side of the castle. Shoppers seeking Breton specialities are spoilt for choice. The massive, rather vacuous main square, **Place de la République**, has some enticing shops around it, too, while the **Halles**, or covered market, built in sturdy granite on one end, also contains tempting food shops. The smaller, tree-shaded **Place Gambetta** has more charm and a friendlier feel, plus more bars with terraces.

Pont-l'Abbé is at its liveliest for the **Fête des Brodeuses**, the major folk festival of the Pays Bigouden, held each year on the second Sunday in July, when local associations parade in traditional Breton costume. Even at the start of the 21st century you could still see the odd old Bigoudène wandering around town in her towering *coiffe* (*see* box), although most have sadly now passed away.

The best thing of all at Pont-l'Abbé is taking the magical walk south alongs the **river**. Before heading down the quays, maybe take a look at Le Minor, a shop specializing in Breton embroidered items; on certain days, you can see a traditional Breton embroiderer at work here. Following the **towpath** offers a beautiful, peaceful walk, the inky-dark clumps of pines reflected in the waters as though in

---

The Tallest *Coiffe* in Brittany

A popular story had it that the towering Bigoudène *coiffe* grew to its extraordinary height as a sign of protest at the churches decapitated in the region with the revolt of the Bonnets Rouges. This is a purely invented tall tale, if highly attractive. In fact, the local *coiffe* only gradually edged skywards from the middle of the 19th century, to reach its dizzying height of more than 30cm around 1935.

Generally speaking the origine of the *coiffe* as a headdress can be traced back to the medieval hats worn by the nobility. In time, the fashion for an elegant headpiece moved down through the social classes. A desire for show and rivalry between neighbouring Breton *pays* seems to have played a major part in creating the huge Bigoudène *coiffe*. So too did the machine manufacturing of lace, making such extravagance easier. The *coiffe* consists of a tube of patterned lace, closed at the top, and fixed with a curved comb and a piece of velvet onto the wearer's hair, which has to be gathered up over a little bonnet. Another piece of lace closes the back of the *coiffe*. Finally, two broad lace ribbons are tied together under the left ear and allowed to trail down over the costume.

After the war, many women opted for shorter hair, and fashions from Paris caught on rapidly. The tradition of the *coiffe* became not merely a chore, but also unfashionable, viewed as backward by a good number of Bretons. But for those women brought up in the tradition of wearing a *coiffe* every day, it proved hard to abandon the custom. More than that, many women in the Bigouden countryside who had always worn it would have felt uncomfortable, perhaps even a little ashamed, to be seen by others, as the expression put it, *en cheveux* ('in their hair'). The Bigoudène *coiffe* was the only Breton headdress to have been worn daily by a group of Breton women right through to the turn of the 21st century.

a Japanese print. Most extraordinarily, after around half an hour, you come to a **menhir** that lies half-submerged in the river water; it looks like a scene from an Arthurian fantasy. Just as satisfying to children may be a visit to Pont-l'Abbé's new indoor pool complex, **Aquasud**, up on the way out of town towards Quimper.

Aquasud
*www.cc-pays-
bigouden-sud.fr,*
t 02 98 66 00 00

To L'Ile-Tudy and Ste-Marine

On the way east from Pont-l'Abbé to L'Ile-Tudy, you pass a small botanical garden, the **Parc Botanique de Cornouaille**, with its seasonal collections of camellias, magnolias, azaleas, rhododendrons, maples and roses, plus a large collection of unusual rocks.

Adorable **L'Ile-Tudy** isn't quite an island; it's a long, thin spit of land connected to the mainland by a sandy causeway. The wide estuary of the Pont-l'Abbé River with its wooded islands stretches away on one side, the Bay of Bénodet on the other. Tudy, a saint of the Dark Ages, is said to have founded his hermitage in this tranquil setting before moving to Loctudy 'on the continent' across the water. For a long time only fishermen and their wives lived here, their houses huddled together in the narrow, picturesque lanes. There's a cute church in the midst of them, while cafés reserve some of the best seats looking across the gorgeous waters to Loctudy. The other side, a great stretch of **beach** heads round to Ste-Marine.

The crescent of shaded Breton houses around the tiny port of **Ste-Marine** have almost all been converted into restaurants and cafés in order to make the most of this extremely beautiful location on the Odet estuary. Ste-Marine's diminutive 16th-century chapel has so far resisted being turned into an eatery, although its stringbeams are carved with fish. The estuary walk south is divine.

At the southern end of Ste-Marine, you come to the **Pointe de Combrit**, with its spectacularly flat horizons. Out to sea, the slabs of rock are the Iles des Glénan. Just set back from the point, hiding in very cowardly fashion in a dip, lurks a coastal **fortification** dating back to the mid-19th-century reign of Emperor Napoleon III. So well hidden from sight, it's in immaculate condition and serves as a local art gallery.

It's only in recent decades that it's been possible to cross the Odet by road, thanks to the great span of the modern **Pont de Cornouaille** to Bénodet; walk across it to take in some of the most glorious estuary views in Brittany.

Market Days in the Pays Bigouden

Plozévet: 1st Monday of the month
St-Guénolé: Friday

Guilvinec: Tuesday, and Sunday in July and Aug
Léchiagat: Saturday
Lesconil: Wednesday
Loctudy: Tuesday

(i) **Association Ouest Cornouaille Promotion**
www.ouest-cornouaille.com, for information across the area

(★) **Ker Ansquer** >

(i) **Plozévet**
Place de l'Eglise, t 02 98 91 45 15, www.hautpays bigouden.com

(★) **Château de Guilguiffin** >

(★) **Les Rochers** >>

(★) **Domaine de Lesvaniel** >

(i) **Pouldreuzic**
Salle Per-Jakes Hélias, t 02 98 54 49 90, wwwpouldreuzic.org

(i) **Le Guilvinec** >>
62 Rue de la Marine, t 02 98 58 29 29, www.leguilvinec.com

(i) **Penmarc'h**
Place du Maréchal Davout, B.P. 47, St-Pierre, 29760 Penmarc'h, t 02 98 58 81 44, www.penmarch.fr

Pont-l'Abbé: Thursday (all day), Place de la République
Ile-Tudy: Monday in July and Aug

Where to Stay and Eat in the Pays Bigouden

Lababan ✉ 29710
***Ker Ansquer**, t 02 98 54 41 83, *www.keransquer.fr* (€€). Very comfortable rooms in a small neo-Breton manor with artistic touches, set a few km northwest of Pouldreuzic. Smart restaurant (€€) open dinners only. *Closed Oct–May.*

Landudec ✉ 29710
Château de Guilguiffin, Route de Quimper, t 02 98 91 52 11, *www.guilguiffin.com* (€€€€–€€€). Enchanting 18th-century Breton castle in countryside southeast of Landudec, converted into holiday apartments but with a few luxurious B&B rooms. Beautiful grounds. *Closed most Jan.*

**Domaine de Lesvaniel, t 02 98 91 55 05, *www.domainedelesvaniel.com* (€€–€). A beautifully landscaped combination of stables and hotel in the middle of the countryside, with rooms decorated according to different themes. There's a library and a salon where they serve crêpes and other traditional food.

Penhors ✉ 29710
**Breiz Armor, t 02 98 51 52 53, *www.breiz-armor.fr* (€€€–€€). Appealing modern complex in great location by the wild coast. All 23 rooms have sea views. The restaurant (€€€€–€) benefits from them too.

Plonéour-Lanvern ✉ 29720
Manoir de Kerhuel, at Kerhuel, t 02 98 82 60 57, *perso.wanadoo.fr/manoir-kerhuel* (€€). A grand little hotel set in a splendid-looking Breton manor in its own grounds, with a pool and tennis court. Restaurant. *Closed Dec–March exc Christmas–New Year.*

St-Guénolé ✉ 29760
***L'Ocean**, 31 Rue Lucien Le Lay, t 02 98 58 71 71 (€€). A recently renovated little hotel, some rooms with sea views, plus smart covered pool. *Closed Nov–Easter.*

***Le Sterenn**, Rue de la Joie, t 02 98 58 60 36, *www.le-sterenn.com* (€€–€). Right on the coast, many rooms looking over rocks and reefs. The restaurant (€€€€–€), open dinner only, has great views too, and does excellent seafood and fish. *Closed Nov–March.*

**de la Mer, t 02 98 58 62 22, *www.hotelstgue.com* (€€–€). In a traditional Breton house with rustic Breton furniture, some of the simple rooms with good views on to the rocks, but the place is best known for its first-floor restaurant (€€€€–€€), serving intersting Breton fare along with the sea views.

**Les Ondines, Rue Pasteur, t 02 98 58 74 95, *www.lesondines.com* (€€–€). An appealing hotel tucked away a short distance from the rocks, with nice nautically themed rooms, and a sweet restaurant (€€€–€) serving appealing menus. *Closed Dec–March.*

Les Rochers, Rue des Embruns, t 02 98 58 75 30. Great new restaurant in converted canning factory, the first floor turned contemporary dining room, making the most of fabulous rocky views. Excellent fresh seafood on the small menu, plus great puds.

Kerity ✉ 29760
Le Doris, t 02 98 58 60 92 (€). Great institution of a lively seafood restaurant on the first floor above a local bar, views onto the sea and rocks through windows and portholes

Le Guilvinec-Léchiagat ✉ 29730
**Le Poisson d'Avril, 19 Rue de Men-Meur, t 02 98 58 23 83, *www.lepoissondavril.fr* (€€€–€). Set right by the sea at the western end of the port, a little hotel with rooms with great sea views, and a restaurant with patio that makes the most of the spot.

Plomeur ✉ 29120
Chaumière de Keraluic, t 02 98 82 10 22, *www.keraluic.fr* (€). High-quality B&B rooms in a renovated thatched cottage close to St-Jean-Trolimon. *Table d'hôte* available.

Fouen et Plouz, at Kerflouz, t 02 98 82 01 60, *bernardlebreton@aliceadsl.fr*.

Sweet country accommodation for a short break, run by Monsieur Le Breton, an accomplished Breton musician.

Le Jardin de la Tulipe Consistently good, and good-value cuisine served at this smart restaurant in the village.

Le Champ des Sirènes, 2 Route de la Torche, t 02 98 82 09 31. A cheerful country stop on the way to La Torche, offering both crêpes and Breton fare, plus Breton music nights.

Crêperie Men-Lann-Du, Route de Penmarc'h, t 02 98 82 01 06 (€). A popular place serving good crêpes in a simple old Breton farmhouse that has kept its traditional beaten-earth floor.

Loctudy and Lodonnec ✉ 29750

**La Porte des Glénan, 19 Rue du Port, t 02 98 87 40 21, *www.laportedes glenan.fr* (€€–€). A sweet hotel for its price, close to the port and its bars. With small neat rooms, and a bar serving seafood. Sauna and jacuzzi too.

Le Relais de Lodonnec, 3 Rue des Tulipes, Plage de Lodonnec, 2km south of Loctudy, t 02 98 87 55 34 (€€). A restaurant in an old granite fisherman's cottage, serving flavoursome seafood dishes. *Closed Mon in July and Aug; Tues eve and Wed in low season.*

Crêperie de Lodonnec, Plage de Lodonnec, t 02 98 87 98 29 (€). In great location with terrace overlooking the beach.

Pont-l'Abbé ✉ 29120

**de Bretagne, 24 Place de la République, t 02 98 87 17 22, *www.hoteldebretagne29.com* (€€–€). An old-style house on the big market square, with garden behind. Small,

decent rooms. Good restaurant (€€€€–€) looking onto the garden.

**La Tour d'Auvergne, 22 Place Gambetta, t 02 98 87 00 47, *www.tourdauvergne.fr* (€). On the smaller central square, another decent option, with bistrot below.

Crêperie Courot, Rue du Lycée, t 02 98 87 02 61, (€). For excellent crêpes.

Ile-Tudy ✉ 29980

**Euromer, 6 Ave du Téven, t 02 98 51 97 00, *www.euromer.fr* (€€€–€). A large, often lively modern hotel in the newer, northerly part of Ile-Tudy. The place is built around a large pool, although the beach is only c.150m away. Rooms are quite comfortable. *Closed Oct–Easter.*

Ste-Marine ✉ 29120

***Villa Tri Men, 16 Rue du Phare, t 02 98 51 94 94, *www.trimen.fr* (€€€€€–€€€). Beautifully located large villa recently converted into a gracious hotel. The spacious rooms have lovely views onto the Odet estuary through the pine-shaded garden. Smart restaurant with small but appealing menu.

**Sainte-Marine, 19 Rue du Bac, t 02 98 56 34 79, *www.hotelsaintemarine. com* (€€). Enchanting place at the port, with delightfully decorated rooms, and an enticing restaurant (€€€€–€) with a gorgeous terrace looking over the water.

Café du Port, 2 Quai Jacques de Thézac, t 02 98 56 44 36 (€). Stylish bistrot by the port beach, looking to Bénodet.

Café de la Cale (€). A wonderfully located café right on a waterside tip one end of the port, serving light dishes.

Crêperie La Misaine, t 02 98 51 90 45 (€). A very cheerful place to eat, also by the port.

(i) Ile-Tudy >>
1 Rue des Roitelets,
t 02 98 56 30 14,
www.ile-tudy.com

(i) Loctudy >
Place de la Mairie,
t 02 98 87 53 78,
www.loctudy.fr

(i) Ste-Marine and Combrit >>
Pont de Cornouaille,
29120 Ste-Marine,
t 02 98 56 48 41,
www.ville-de-combrit.fr

(★) Villa Tri Men >>

(★) Sainte-Marine >>

(i) Pont-l'Abbé >
Place Gambetta,
t 02 98 82 37 99,
www.pontlabbe-lesconil.com

The Pays Fouesnantais

After the wild shores and gritty fishing ports of the Pays Bigouden, the Pays Fouesnantais east from Bénodet to Concarneau proves much gentler, but more touristy. Bénodet has long been lorded as one of the most genteel of Breton resorts, its marina

Getting to and around the Pays Fouesnantais

Bus services are the only option for public transport.

popular with sailors from north of the Channel – Winston Churchill even came to paint here. Following the long swathes of beaches either side of the Pointe de Mousterlin, one sweet resort succeeds the next, making the most of the protected beaches around the Baie de la Forêt, with further huge marinas at Port-la-Forêt and Concarneau. While the first of these two is wholly modern, the second lies beside a delightful historic, ramparted town. Inland, the cheery countryside of the Pays Fouesnantais produces some of the finest Breton cherries and some of the best Breton cider.

Bénodet

Bénodet is Ste-Marine's much bigger brother, across on the eastern bank of the Odet, and an exceptionally handsome resort it is too. The beautiful siblings are joined by the **Pont de Cornouaille**, with its sensational estuary views. Bénodet's gorgeous **marina** lies below the bridge, well protected from the sea. Many regattas start out from this lovely harbour.

Before the Bénodet quays were built, it's said that when the tide was very high, the waves would wash up into the port-side **church**, further down the estuary. It's dedicated to Thomas à Becket, with a typical delicate Breton steeple making it stand out. In front of the church, a line of trendy quayside cafés rival each other with poseurs.

Les Vedettes de l'Odet
www.vedettes-odet.com,
t 02 98 57 00 58

Tourist cruising boats leave from the quay here. They offer a delightful dilemma to tourists, as to whether to take the trip up the Odet to Quimper, or out to the magical, tiny archipelago of Les Glénan. Both trips are wonderful. Contact **Les Vedettes de l'Odet**. The **Odet cruise** takes you along the twisting, wood-lined river with its rocky banks and creeks. From time to time, pastures and lawns open out, leading to smart châteaux and manors. Up in Bénodet town centre, the **Musée du Bord de Mer** recounts the story of how Bénodet became a premier seaside resort and yachting destination.

Musée du Bord de Mer
open June–Sept

Relais Thalasso Bénodet
www.thalasso-benodet.com,
t 02 98 66 27 00

Back at the estuary, the glorious **balustraded coastal path** takes you south past small beaches, under a remarkably glamorous Art Deco boat of a building and the lighthouse, round to the south side of Bénodet. Here you come to the curve of the resort's **main beach**, backed by a concrete promenade, changing rooms, hotels and the casino. There's also the possibility of enjoying relaxing sea-water treatments at the new **Relais Thalasso Bénodet**.

Out to sea, you can make out what look like giant stepping stones on the horizon. These are the islands of the tiny Glénan archipelago. Go round the wooded tip of the **Pointe de Bénodet** and they come even more clearly into view. East round the point, you arrive at Bénodet's adjoining village of **Le Letty**, looking across a seawater lagoon known rather grandly as **La Mer Blanche**, or 'White Sea', which some enjoy wading across to reach the thin strip of beach that goes all the way to Mousterlin. At low tide, aficionados gather shells. It comes as no surprise to find an 18-hole golf course close to Bénodet, the **Golf de l'Odet**, inland at Clohars-Fouesnant.

Golf de l'Odet
www.formule-golf.com/odet,
t *02 98 54 87 88*

Glénan Islands

Bénodet is just one of the resorts from which you can take a boat out to Les Glénan, an exquisite archipelago some 20 km from the shore, well known for its glorious waters, its sailing and diving schools, and for the numerous old wrecks scattered around it. You can only land on the **Ile St-Nicolas**, with its couple of bars. If you're not diving, just walk around the magical island, or forget the world on its lovely beaches.

La Chambre has been called the prettiest lagoon in Brittany, its glorious see-through emerald waters encircled by the close-knit archipelago. The plant Narcisse des Glénan, said to be unique in the world, was supposedly brought here by the ancient Phoenicians. It only flowers late spring.

The Pays Fouesnantais

Two long, flat stretches of beach curve away from the **Pointe de Mousterlin**, one of the best places from which to view the Glénan Islands. Mousterlin itself doesn't have a real centre but has grown into a rambling maze of lanes dotted with holiday homes. The point ends with a jetty and little rocks. To the west, the beach on its narrow spit reaches almost all the way back to Bénodet. The beach east from the Pointe de Mousterlin stretches round to Beg-Meil, backed by a curious marshland that attracts birds and ornithologists.

Beg-Meil has long-established credentials as a smart resort. The writer Marcel Proust and the actress Sarah Bernhardt counted among its more illustrious early visitors. The **beaches** on the western side of Beg-Meil offer expansive views out to sea, while the little ones on the eastern side hide away in shaded creeks giving on to the gentler **Baie de la Fôret**.

Don't miss **Cap Coz**, an enchanting little resort set along an astonishing sandy spit stretching across the back of the bay. The road behind the safe, glorious beach is shaded by beautiful pines. The marshy inlet further makes is highly picturesque too.

Coming to the small twin towns of Fouesnant and La Forêt-Fouesnant, you arrive in a land of cherry trees and apple orchards. **Fouesnant**, with its cheerful old centre, is synonymous with good cider in Brittany. It also has a quite impressive modern **indoor pool**, should the weather let you down, and a Romanesque **church** of some repute. Built in the late 11th and early 12th centuries and since restored, it looks surprisingly light inside, given its period. Outside, the calvary and the sacristy with its little roof in the shape of an upturned hull were both added in the 17th century.

La Forêt-Fouesnant climbs delightfully up the slope from a densely wooded valley. It's more low-key than Fouesnant, but with hotels and restaurants aplenty. Outside the Flamboyant Gothic **chapel** half way up the hillside, the simple calvary is surrounded by an outdoor preaching pulpit, its four corners marked by Gothic pinnacles. Inside, the nave is surprisingly decorated with chandeliers.

From La Forêt-Fouesnant, you may spot a forest of masts across the waters, giving away the location of the modern, purpose-built **marina of Port-La-Forêt**, created in the 1970s. This harbour is on an impressive scale, with a massive array of yachts at berth and for sale. The artificial village behind it, with the odd bar and restaurant and sailing-related shops is certainly functional, but can scarcely be said to have any charm. Anyway the place is swamped by parking facilities... for yachts as well as cars, of course. Walk south round the corner from the port and you quickly find yourself back at a typically gorgeous Breton **beach** scene with **Kerleven**. There's a tempting 18-hole golf course, the **Golf de Cornouaille**, nearby at the Manoir du Mesmeur.

Golf de Cornouaille
www.golfde cornouaille.com,
t 02 98 56 97 09

Concarneau

Concarneau is a fishing port with many enticing facets. It has long attracted artists as well as tourists. Its beach resort looks west across the Baie de la Forêt. However, turn the corner beyond the Marinarium sea-research centre, and the Ville Close comes into view. This ramparted island in the Moros estuary is the main tourist magnet, with a major marina just in front. The large fishing harbour hides away behind the bustling tourist quarter, although it counts among the very largest fishing ports in France, ranked third in the country.

French fishermen have of course been facing difficulties in recent years, but this isn't the first fishing crisis the place has experienced – the sardine banks which had given Concarneau's fishermen a stable catch for a long time suddenly moved on from their familiar waters in 1905, causing terrible hardship. However, a number of artists who had been coming regularly to Concarneau from outside Brittany to paint showed their solidarity with the community, and assisted many fishermen's families through dire times.

The Ville Close

The Ville Close, the defensive historic heart of Concarneau, was fortified as early as the 14th century. Its island offering such a good obvious natural defence, it also became an obvious point to attack. English troops took it for the de Montfortist side during the Breton War of Succession, but du Guesclin's men eventually wrested it from them. The sturdy ramparts that you can now walk round were largely remodelled for Duke Pierre II of Brittany in the mid 15th century, much added to in the mid-16th century, then altered by Vauban in the late 17th century. Vauban notably chopped off the tops of the towers along the ramparts, to make artillery platforms.

You arrive on the island close to the comical clock tower, an irresistibly twee 20th-century addition. Through the triangular fortifications, you enter the somewhat claustrophobic old town – the Ville Close measures a mere 100 metres by 350 metres, so conditions have always been a bit cramped. Today, this definitely feels like a tourist trap, even if it is all very quaint. The main street is absolutely crammed with touristy shops and places to eat. The focal point is **Place St-Guénolé** with its monumental fountain, featuring a turtle, an otter and a crocodile among other animals. Go for a stroll up on the **ramparts** (*small fee*), where you can catch your breath.

Musée de la Pêche
open daily July and Aug 9.30–8, Sept–June 10–12 and 2–6

Near the entrance to the Ville Close, the **Musée de la Pêche** spreads its net wide in retracing the history of fishing, not just in these parts. The place gives you an introduction to the international history of fishing and fishing techniques down the centuries. Much closer to home, fish canning developed into an extremely important trade in Concarneau, which explains why a rare, rusty-topped mid-19th-century tin is reverentially included among so many other more impressive exhibits. Numerous large models of fishing boats, and even whole boats, are on display in and around the buildings that once made up the arsenal of the Ville Close, and you can even climb on board the *Hémérica*, a 34-metre trawler moored outside the ramparts. Back inside, aquaria present the variety of marine life to be found off the Breton coast.

Concarneau Beyond the Ville Close

You can breathe more easily in Concarneau beyond the Ville Close. **Place Jean Jaurès**, the large square opposite its entrance, has a spacious feel to it, and has been nicely redone recently. It's lined with lively bar and restaurant terraces. The solid granite **Halles**, or covered market, in one corner has also undergone a makeover, and makes a great sight with its daily food stalls. Painters and art dealers are still attracted to Concarneau, so take a look at the galleries dotted around here.

Although there's no longer the possibility of visiting the fish-auctioning hall from the harbour behind, ask at the tourist office if you're interested in going on a fishing excursion on the former sardine boat, *Le Santa Maria*. Or contact **A L'Assaut des Remparts**, run by Simon Alain, an ex-fisherman well used to dealing with English-speaking visitors. He organizes all manner of boat tours around the area; he can also take you on board fishing vessels moored in the harbour, and to visit a couple of the canneries still going strong.

A L'Assaut des Remparts
www.alassautdesrem parts.fr, **t** 02 98 50 55 18

Wandering south along the quays next to the large modern **marina**, statues have been placed beside the water, adding artistic interest to the stroll. Turn the corner and you come to the **Marinarium** on the southern point of Concarneau. This place may be a bit old fashioned, but it's a serious marine research centre, part of that august French academic institution, the Collège de France, and it puts on really good exhibitions that can teach you a fascinating thing or two about life in the ocean. Heading onto the western side of Concarneau, past a little coastal chapel and further outdoor sculptures, a good walk brings you to the lovely white-sanded **beach of Les Sables Blancs**.

Marinarium
open daily Easter–Sept 10–12 and 2–6.30

Concarneau's best-known traditional festival, the **Fête des Filets Bleus**, named after the blue nets employed in sardine fishing, gathers together Breton musicians and dancers in large numbers in August. The **Salon Livre et Mer**, at Easter, is dedicated to books about the sea.

Château de Keriolet
open June–mid-Sept daily 10.30–1 and 2–6

Above town, the **Château de Keriolet** at **Beuzec-Conq** makes for an eccentric visit, with its neo-Gothic architecture and its links with Russian prince Felix Youssoupov, the castle's one-time owner, more notoriously known as Rasputin's assassin.

Market Days in the Pays Fouesnantais

Bénodet: Monday
Fouesnant: Friday
La Forêt-Fouesnant: Sunday
Concarneau: Monday and Friday

ⓘ Bénodet >>
29 Ave de la Plage,
t *02 98 57 00 14,*
www.benodet.fr

Where to Stay and Eat in the Pays Fouesnantais

Bénodet ✉ 29950
***Kastel, t 02 98 57 05 01,
www.hotel-kastel.com (€€€–€€).
Engaging hotel just behind the

La Forêt-Fouesnant >>
*2 Rue du Vieux Port,
t 02 98 51 42 07,
www.foret-fouesnant-
tourisme.com*

Manoir du Stang >>

Concarneau >>
*Quai d'Aiguillon,
t 02 98 97 01 44,
www.tourismecon
carneau.fr*

Les Sables Blancs >>

Ker Moor >>

Fouesnant-Les Glénan >
*Espace Kernévéleck,
t 02 98 51 18 88,
www.tourisme-
fouesnant.fr*

seafront, many rooms with balconies. Pleasant restaurant too (€€€–€€).

***Grand Hotel Abbatiale, 4 Ave de l'Odet, **t** 02 98 66 21 66, *www.hotel abbatiale.com* (€€). An imposing block of a hotel just behind the port restaurants, many of its sober rooms with beautiful estuary views. Has its own restaurant (€€€–€€).

Les Bains de Mer, 11 Rue de Kerguélen, **t 02 98 57 03 41, *www.lesbainsdemer.com* (€€–€). A modern, friendly hotel in the centre, with pool. Choice of simple or more elaborate food (€€€€–€). *Closed Dec–Feb.*

Restaurant du Centre, 56 Avenue de la Plage, **t** 02 98 57 00 38 (€€–€). A classic French restaurant with authentic seafood platters, plus pizzas in summer. *Closed Oct–March, and Tues Sept–July.*

Crêperie La Boulange, 11 Rue de l'Eglise, **t** 02 98 57 17 71 (€). The best-known crêperie in town.

Pointe de Mousterlin ✉ 29170

***La Pointe de Mousterlin, **t** 02 98 56 04 12, *www.mousterlinhotel.com* (€€€–€€). A hotel just behind Mousterlin's beaches, rooms divided between the old part and the modern wing, some with balconies looking to sea. Little luxuries include a pool, jacuzzi, a sauna and tennis courts. *Closed Feb and March.*

Beg-Meil ✉ 29170

Thalamot, 4 Le Chemin Creux, **t 02 98 94 97 38, *www.hotel-thalamot.com* (€€–€). A charming old-style hotel near the southern end of the resort, with traditional restaurant (€€€€–€€).

Fouesnant ✉ 29170

Auberge du Bon Cidre, 37 Rue de Cornouaille, **t 02 98 56 00 16, *www.aubergeduboncidre.com* (€). A well-run and cheap family option.

L'Orée du Bois, 4 Rue de Kergoadic, **t 02 98 56 00 06, *www.hotel-oree-du-bois.fr.st* (€). A decent, low-priced little family hotel.

Le Cap Coz ✉ 29170

Hôtel de la Pointe, 153 Ave de la Pointe, **t 02 98 56 01 63, *www.hotel-capcoz.com* (€€). Wonderfully situated,

just a bit above the beach, overlooking a delightful bay. Many rooms have sea views, as does the appealing restaurant.

La Forêt-Fouesnant ✉ 29940

***Manoir du Stang, **t** 02 98 56 96 38, *www.manoirdustang.com* (€€€€–€€). A splendid Breton stone manor dating from the 15th and 18th centuries, hidden in its own wooded valley, with a tennis court. The rooms are wonderfully atmospheric. *Closed mid-Sept–mid-May.*

Concarneau ✉ 29900

Les Sables Blancs, 45 Rue des Sables Blancs, **t** 02 98 50 10 12, *www.hotel-les-sables-blancs.com* (€€€€–€€€). Splendidly renovated, stylish beach-side hotel, its glorious rooms with sea views and balconies. Contemporary restaurant (€€€€–€€) with sea views, of course.

***de L'Océan, 2 Rue des Sables Blancs, **t** 02 98 50 53 50, *www.hotel-ocean.com* (€€€–€€). Large, more prosaic modern hotel just set back from the beach, some rooms looking to sea, others over the heated pool. Restaurant.

Ker Moor, 37 Rue des Sables Blancs, **t 02 98 97 02 96, *www.hotel-kermoor.com* (€€€). An enchanting little beach-side hotel in an old Breton house with a beautiful interior. The caringly decorated rooms offer a high degree of comfort as well as sea views, plus there's a stylish terrace.

Les Halles, Place de l'Hôtel de Ville, **t 02 98 97 11 41, *www.hoteldes halles.com* (€€–€). Beside the main square looking across to the Ville Close, quite charming hotel rooms with marine décor.

La Coquille, 1 Rue du Moros, **t** 02 98 97 08 52 (€€€€–€€). An excellent seafood restaurant with a very pleasant terrace overlooking the port, and a dining room decorated with Breton paintings. At lunchtimes, there's the option of the cheaper **Le Bistrot** (€€). *Closed Sun eve and Mon.*

Le Buccin, 1 Rue Duguay Trouin, **t** 02 98 50 54 22 (€€€–€€). Fancy place serving good seafood. *Closed low season Sun and Thurs eves, Mon lunch in season.*

Chez Armande, 15 bis Ave du Dr Nicolas, **t** 02 98 97 00 76 (€€€–€). A pleasant, generous restaurant with wood panelling, opposite the marina.

Le Penfret, 40 Route de Vauban, **t** 02 98 50 70 55 (€€). Restaurant mainly serving crêpes in a very fine old granite building in the heart of the Ville Close, plus terrace. *Closed Oct–Jan.*

Les Remparts, 3 1 Rue Théophile Louarn, **t** 02 98 50 65 66 (€). A more tranquil spot in the Ville Close, with flowerly facade, a good choice of crêpes, and a terrace. *Closed Nov–April.*

The Avens

Between Concarneau and Pont-Aven there's a slightly wilder stretch of coast leading down to the Pointe de Trévignon, then you can explore the series of well-hidden narrow estuaries known as *avens*. The village of Pont-Aven is anything but secretive, famous for inspiring Gauguin; in this beautiful spot every second house has been turned into an art gallery. The other gorgeous villages and ports in this area are hugely popular in summer.

The Coast from Concarneau to Pont-Aven

From the rocky **Pointe de la Jument**, long, exposed beaches and dunes extend south, this coastal stretch only to be appreciated on foot. The **Pointe de Trévignon** seems a rough and uninviting spot at which to have established a little port, but it remains an active harbour, a concrete sea wall offering protection. As to the crenellated fort on the point, it has a Scottish air.

East of Trévignon, you come to the coast of the *avens*. Gorgeous sandy creeks replace the great stretches of beaches to the west. Adorable hamlets lie in the countryside behind. First, the coast road follows the beaches to **Raguenèz and its island**. Walking out to the latter is a popular activity here at low tide.

Next, the **Anse de Rospico** looks like the perfect pirate's sandy cove. The **Jardins de Rospico** beside it offer the possibility of a relaxed tour around a variety of different gardens, from British and Mediterranean to Japanese, the last with a curious pagoda looking to sea.

Jardins de Rospico
www.rospico.net,
t 02 98 06 71 29; open mid-March–mid-June daily exc Sat 2–6, mid-June–mid-Sept daily exc Sat 11–7, mid-Sept–mid-Nov daily exc Sat 2–6

Inland, the hamlet of **Kerascoët** comes under siege from photographers in summer because of its splendid little granite and thatched cottages. Some of the buildings are made with walls of standing blocks of granite. These *pierres debout*, or *mein zao* in Breton, were used both in the local architecture and as field divides in times past, and you may come across other remnants of them in the area around Névez and Trégunc.

Back along the coast, the little resort of **Port-Manec'h** serves as a good introduction to the typical harbours of the *avens*, located at the western end of the mouths of the Aven and Bélon rivers. The wooded slopes give the harbour a warm feel. The way north leads

Getting around the Avens

Quimperlé and Rosporden both have **train** stations on the fast TGV line running from Paris to Quimper. Otherwise, use the Finistère bus services to get around the area.

to the gorgeous little estuary port of **Kerdruc**, with equally cute **Rosbras** immediately opposite. The waterside scenes here are typical of the twin harbours you'll find along these tidal rivers around Pont-Aven.

Pont-Aven

 Pont-Aven

Pont-Aven is a divine Breton village where Paul Gauguin is God. A bit of an absent God, mind – you're likely to see only a very few genuine works of his here, as most of the canvases he painted in the area have been whisked away across the globe, snapped up by mega-wealthy institutions and individuals. In fact, you're liable to spot more Gauguin works featuring on the tins of buttery biscuits for which Pont-Aven is also famous than in the museum. In recent times, a granular bust of the big-nosed, big-hitting artist has been placed on the central square, even if it looks a bit crude. Frustrating as all this may be, there is plenty of real enchantment to be found in and around Pont-Aven, if you can cope with the hordes of pilgrims come to worship at this site of the Nativity of a *New Art* (*see* box, opposite) at the end of the 19th century.

Musée des Beaux-Arts de Pont-Aven
*www.pontaven.fr,
t 02 98 06 14 43; open
July and Aug daily 10–7,
Feb–June and Sept–Dec
daily 10–12.30 and 2–6*

A hundred years after Gauguin and Emile Bernard brought a radically new look to French art, the **Musée des Beaux-Arts de Pont-Aven** opened its doors just off the main street. It has grown astonishingly quickly, developing its own collection from nothing. As well as that, a short video rapidly presents the outlines of the story of the Pont-Aven School, and old photos help give you some idea of the village's atmosphere in the late 19th century. Look at the snaps of Gauguin, and you can see him change rapidly from a fresh-faced young man to a hardened character. Paul Sérusier stands out because of his wacky haircuts.

The works of art on display include some interesting engravings and excellent zincographs by Gauguin, and such intriguing peripheral pieces as a painted studio door and the sign from the Pension Gloanec, where many of the artists stayed. There are wonderful paintings by the well-known Bernard, Denis and Sérusier, but also fascinating pieces by the likes of lesser-known figures such as Filiger, Jourdain, de Haan, Moufra and Moret. It all adds up to an amazing display of the avant-garde art of the 1880s and 1890s. On top of that, the museum puts on some great temporary exhibitions.

The Pont-Aven School of Art, 1886 to 1896

European art took a great leap forward in the little Breton village of Pont-Aven during the 1880s, although in many ways it was a deliberate leap backwards too. Gone was the academic painters' obsession with perspective. Gone was the imperative that a painting should jolly well look like nature. And away went the obsession with accurate detail.

It is true that during the 1870s the Impressionist movement had already got rid of many rules of traditional academic painting. But the artists who gathered together at Pont-Aven around Paul Gauguin and Emile Bernard from 1886 on moved away from the feathery-looking touches of Impressionism, too, and from the tenderness and movement that Impressionist techniques were so adept at conveying.

Gauguin, Bernard and their followers painted big bold blocks of colour on to their canvases. Horizons were flattened out and forms greatly simplified. When the pictures of the so-called Pont-Aven painters were depicting such scenes as Breton festivals that would have been full of movement in real life, they generally turned the occasions into frozen images on the canvas. People were transformed into statues. Haystacks and trees became boulders in the landscape. These painters often exploited shockingly bright colours that exaggerated or provocatively contradicted the much more muted tones seen in the natural world. The seeds of abstract art lay in these works.

Paul Gauguin and Emile Bernard, the artists jointly at the forefront this new movement, settled in Pont-Aven for large periods in the second half of the 1880s. During the preceding decades, Pont-Aven had already become well known to artists hailing from far and wide. For example, a colony of American painters had fallen for the place before Gauguin and Bernard. But these and others were more interested in rendering traditional views of Brittany than in devising a new aesthetic.

Emile Bernard should rightfully be regarded as the instigator of the new style in western European art, before Gauguin. He pioneered *Cloisonnisme* in painting, copying the thickly partitioned *cloisonné* effects of enamel work. Even if Bernard only adopted this technique for a short while, the results of his *cloisonniste* period match Gauguin's works in intensity and power. The style of the Pont-Aven School was also officially described as Synthetism.

The Pont-Aven painters lived extremely close together, sharing their ideas and enthusiasms. Many stayed at the Pension Gloanec, run by Marie-Jeanne Gloanec. Gloanec is portrayed as a kind of mother figure for the movement, spoiling her artistic children with her warmth and good food.

The majority of the Pont-Aven School artists were French but not Breton. Several came from abroad. Paul Sérusier and Maurice Denis are two other crucial figures in the Pont-Aven School. Gauguin's tips to the young Sérusier make for some of the most memorable quotes, showing the aims of the new artistic movement. *Ne copiez pas trop la nature, mais rêvez devant elle* ('Don't copy nature too much, but dream in front of it'). Charles Filiger, Armand Seguin and Emile Jourdan count among other important Pont-Aven artists.

A Tour of Pont-Aven

Art galleries and souvenir shops occupy practically every house on the main street through the village, knowing that art-loving tourists are drawn here like bees to honey. The paintings on sale vary widely in quality; many are derivative of the original Pont-Aven School, others take contrasts in colours to gaudy extremes, while others still show genuine talent of their own. Along with the galleries, you can't avoid the biscuit shops, where the tins decorated with tempting copies of works by the famous Pont-Aven artists inevitably come at extra cost.

There is, though, a free, interesting **trail of panels** you can follow around the village, with reproductions of famous works placed in the spots where they were executed. The way leads you down, past the former mills on the rock-strewn stretch of the river, to the gorgeous **harbour**, often full of yachts and pleasure boats, although this was once a busy working port. Walking down either bank makes for an idyllic Breton stroll. The **Vedettes Aven Bélon** allow you to embark on a delightful river cruise downstream from here in summer.

Vedettes Aven Bélon *www.vedettes-aven-belon.com,* *t 02 98 71 14 59*

You may notice that Pont-Aven is a place that has attracted its fair share of poets as well as painters. By the port, the acclaimed Breton bard, Auguste Brizeux, is recalled in a memorial. Back up in the village, on the central square, you may spot a plaque in English on the Ajoncs d'Or hotel recalling the passage of expansive writer Ernest Dowson in the late 19th century. Dowson, you read, was the 'author of *Cynara* and other beautiful poems'; he may be largely forgotten now, but *Cynara* contained a rather famous phrase to be exploited in film – 'gone with the wind'.

The Breton poet most associated with this artistic village is Xavier Grall, a fiery postwar writer portrayed as a wild-eyed figure in a bust of him set among the little river crossings north of the main bridge. Follow the **Promenade Xavier Grall** this way and it takes you up past many little wash-houses and former mills, some in a better state of repair than others. It used to be said that there were as many watermills as houses in Pont-Aven. The waterside path north leads via the wonderful big natural stepping stones of the **Chaos de l'Aven**, a fabulous spot to take children. Further on, you can wander along the **Promenade du Bois d'Amour**. Picturesque spots in this 'Wood of Love' inspired many an artist from the Pont-Aven School, but this route now has something of a neglected air.

The village **church** may be a neo-Gothic building rather than a more typical old Breton edifice, but its steeple makes its mark, and inside it contains a few contrasting works by Emile Bernard. A famed Breton crooner of the early part of the 20th century, Théodore Botrel, is buried at Pont-Aven. Botrel helped to get the local **folklore festival of Les Fleurs d'Ajonc** (Gorse Flowers) off the ground.

To Gauguin's Yellow and Green Christs

You can go in search of one or two of the local representations of Christ that inspired some of Gauguin's most famous works at the churches around Pont-Aven. There's no more obvious example of how the Pont-Aven School was directly influenced by Breton country art than Gauguin's *Le Christ Jaune*, the jaundiced, crucified body a close copy of the naïve but bold 17th-century statue of Jesus that you can still see hanging in the **Chapelle de Trémalo** above the village. A beautiful tree-lined lane leads to this chapel with its roofs trailing down to the ground in typical Breton Gothic style. Inside, also enjoy the carvings on the stringbeams that look like illustrations for a children's book. A Goldilocks lookalike is terrorized by a wolf of a monster; a green-spotted dog holds on to its bone, a man on to his fish.

Nizon's church is located in a peaceful village northwest of Pont-Aven. Its 16th-century calvary looks shockingly new because of the way it has been restored – the figures now appear as though they're made of tightly moulded, granular sand. The crucified Christ here inspired a *Green Christ* by Gauguin. Inside, the collection of wooden statues is interesting, too. However, the most extraordinary of all the figures around this church lies outside at the fountain – the most primitive of stone Virgins in Brittany.

River Estuaries from Pont-Aven to Le Pouldu

A series of *avens* indent the coast between Pont-Aven and Le Pouldu. Down the east side of the main Aven from Pont-Aven, seek out **Rosbras**, sharing the enchanting wooded estuary port with Kerdruc opposite. A short but winding way east, the village of **Bélon** is synonymous with fine oysters, to be tasted in the bars and restaurants of the area. Bélon's crescent of houses looks over to a miniature château. The walk south takes you down to the **Pointe de Penquernéo**, where Bélon and Aven Rivers meet.

It's a really awkward but rewarding drive round from the west to the east side of the Bélon River. The walking track takes you past countless oyster beds. On the east bank, **Port-Bélon** has a little chapel overlooking the creek. The **Vedettes Aven-Bélon** organize boat tours around the Bélon and Aven estuaries. Close by, **Brigneau** is another delightful pocket-sized port east along the coast from Kerfany.

Vedettes Aven-Bélon www.vedettes-aven-belon.com, t 02 98 71 14 59

Further on, **Merrien** and **Doëlan** are two further absolutely adorable *aven* ports. The former is tiny, the latter slightly more substantial, with little lighthouses marking the estuary. The **Compagnie des Iles** runs a boat from here to the island of Groix, lying so temptingly out to sea, in summer.

Compagnie des Iles www.compagnie desiles.com, t 08 25 13 41 00

Steep-sided **Le Pouldu** may have lost some of its old charm to sprawling modern buildings, but despite all the construction, the slopes lead down to a pretty port and glorious beaches. Le Pouldu drew its fair share of artists in the 19th century, including Gauguin. The mural paintings you can view at **La Maison de Marie Henry** are, though, a colourful, amusing fake of the decorations the many artists who stayed at Marie Henry's boarding house created there.

La Maison de Marie Henry open for guided tours July and Aug daily 10.30–7; April–Sept Wed–Sun 3–6

Follow the coastal path west, and you can plunge down from on high to some glorious rocks, where local fishermen find nooks in which to lodge. Then there follow fabulous beaches, including the **Plage de Kérou**, the island of Groix beckoning from afar. The coastal path follows the cliff edge undisturbed by traffic.

On the eastern side of Le Pouldu, the beautiful **Laïta River** ends softly, with deeply sandy banks lining its estuary. Explore the quaint little riverside port area here. **Laïta Croisières** operates short boat crossings over to Guidel on the Morbihan side, but also offers

Laïta Croisières m 06 64 27 62 15

cruises up the glorious black waters of the Laïta to Quimperlé. The GR34 hiking trail also follows the river's course.

Site Abbatiale de St-Maurice
t 02 98 71 65 51

On the way to Quimperlé, you pass the **Site Abbatiale de St-Maurice**. The vestiges of this medieval abbey have been renovated, and on a visit to this peaceful spot you can learn about the Cistercian order. The monks may have left long ago, but bats have hung on, and the special observatory allows visitors to view them at certain times. Guided nature walks are on offer sometimes too. The nearby **Forêt de Carnoët** also makes for a deeply atmospheric walk, what with its megaliths its legends, and the ruins of the castle of Comorre, described as the Breton Blue Beard.

Quimperlé and Around

This delightful waterside town grew up where the Isole and Ellé Rivers meet to form the Laïta. A Gallo-Roman settlement may have arisen here, on the border between the territories of the Osismi and the Veneti tribes. The town also has shadowy Dark Ages links with Guntiern, Prince of Cambria (Wales). The story goes that during the 6th century he fled here, having killed his nephew, and became a hermit. Viking raiders raced upstream in the 10th century, ravaging the settlement that had grown up around this hermitage.

Quimperlé appears to have blossomed in medieval times, to go by the architectural legacy. The town developed around the abbey of Ste-Croix, founded in 1029. This monastery brought the place prosperity, encouraging trade. The settlement spread up the hillside, where another church was begun in the 13th century. Quimperlé became embroiled in the Breton War of Succession, serving as a stronghold for the de Montfort side, backed by the English. The Breton leader of the French troops, du Guesclin, took the place in 1371.

The **Eglise Ste-Croix** makes a very bold statement, built on the round model of the famed church of the Holy Sepulchre in Jerusalem. Although it dates back to the late 11th century, the edifice was heavily restored during the 19th century. Even if much of the decoration isn't original, this remains an extraordinary church. On entering the building, glance back at the refined sculptures behind you; many of the figures look as though they're peering down on to a procession passing below them. You can then walk all the way round the ambulatory, while a bridge leads up to the main area of worship. Underneath, the church's treasures are well displayed beneath the central platform, and include tomb effigies.

Close to Ste-Croix, the pretty **pedestrian quarter** has several enticing food shops, including in the small, patterned brick **Halles**, or covered market. The streets around here boast some remarkable old houses. The finest timberframe one, the 16th-century **Maison des Archers**, is concealed down a side street, but is decorated with carvings that very much draw your attention. The interior makes a fine setting for temporary art exhibitions, as does that of the

Présidial nearby – this former law court built in solid granite lies in a more prominent position along the main shopping street, which is also marked by the picturesque ruins of a chapel. Up the western slope, there's a whole additional quarter to go and see around the Gothic church of **Notre-Dame de l'Assomption et St-Michel.** The flowery **Laïta River banks** leading south out of town are a delight. You can take the trip downstream by canoe; contact the **Canoë Kayak Club de Quimperlé.** Northwest of Quimperlé, the serious **Manoir de Kernault** outside Mellac was lovingly restored during the 1990s for the *département* of the Finistère. As well as learning about the ways in which such a typical manor with its farm evolved down the centuries, you can also appreciate different aspects of Breton culture highlighted in the interesting regular exhibitions held inside.

Canoë Kayak Club de Quimperlé
t 02 98 39 24 17,
www.ckcq.free.fr

Manoir de Kernault
open high season daily 10.30–12.30 and 2–7; rest of year school hols, public hols and Sun 2–6

Market Days for the Avens

ⓘ **Pays des Portes de Cornouaille**
www.cornouaille.com, for information across the area

Trégunc: Wednesday, plus Sunday in July and Aug
Névez: Saturday
Pont-Aven: Tuesday
Riec-sur-Bélon: Wednesday and Saturday
Moëlan-sur-Mer: Tuesday
Quimperlé: Friday

ⓘ **Pont-Aven** ›
5 Place de l'Hôtel de Ville, t 02 98 06 04 70, www.pontaven.com

Where to Stay and Eat in the Avens

★ **Moulin de Rosmadec** ››

ⓘ **Trégunc** ›
16 Rue de Pont-Aven, t 02 98 50 22 05, www.tregunc.fr

★ **Les Grandes Roches** ›

Trégunc ✉ 29910
***Les Grandes Roches**, Rue des Grandes Roches, t 02 98 97 62 97, *www.hotel-lesgrandesroches.com* (€€€–€€). Here a charming old Breton farm has been turned into an enchanting hotel with peaceful grounds. Some of the cosy, delightful rooms have fireplaces. The smart restaurant (€€€€) is a delight too. Pool.

Raguenèz ✉ 29920
Ar Men Du, Rue des Iles, Raguenèz-Plage, t 02 98 06 84 22 (€€€–€€). This small hotel in the style of a typical smart modern Breton home is set in a magnificent, exclusive location beside the sea. The stylish restaurant (€€€€–€€€) shares the same advantages; it's a joyous place to eat. *Closed Nov–March.*

★ **Ar Men Du** ›

ⓘ **Névez/Port Manec'h**
18 Place de l'Eglise, t 02 98 06 87 90, www.nevez.com

Kerdruc ✉ 29920
Pen Ker Dagorn, 9 Chemin des Vieux Fours, t 02 98 06 85 01 (€). A delightful B&B 200m from the port of Kerdruc, set in an exuberant garden, offering homely rooms.

Le Bistrot de l'Ecailler, t 02 98 06 78 60 (€€€€–€€). Wonderful stylish place serving excellent seafood in a lovely spot by the port. *Closed Oct–Easter.*

Auberge de l'Aven, t 02 98 06 78 51 (€€). A gorgeous portside inn reputed both for its cuisine and its lovely terrace. Studio accommodation is also available.

Pont-Aven ✉ 29930
Moulin de Rosmadec, Venelle de Rosmadec, t 02 98 06 00 22, *www.moulinderosmadec.com* (€€). A magical converted 15th-century mill in the centre of the village, surrounded by water, set somewhat apart from the tourist hordes, and beautifully shaded by riverside trees. It has a small number of sober, smart but sweet rooms, but is better known for its excellent restaurant (€€€€–€€€).

***La Chaumière Roz Aven**, 11 Quai Théodore Botrel, t 02 98 06 13 06, *www.hotelpontaven.online.fr* (€€–€). Four of the rooms are in the unmissably beautiful thatched house on the quay, but the others in the annexe also have river views.

Les Ajoncs d'Or, 1 Place de l'Hôtel de Ville, t 02 98 06 02 06, *www.ajoncsdor-pontaven.com*. At the very heart of the village, a popular traditional hotel with very touristy restaurant.

Hôtel Les Mimosas, 22 Square Botrel, t 02 98 06 00 30, *www.hotels-pont-aven.com* (€). More peacefully located choice at the southern end of the quays, with traditional rooms all

ⓘ Le Pouldu/ Clohars-Carnoët >>
*Place de l'Océan,
t 02 98 39 93 42,
www.cloharscarnoet
tourisme.com.*

ⓘ Quimperlé >>
*45 Place St-Michel,
t 02 98 96 04 32,
www.quimperle-
tourisme.com*

**ⓘ Riec-sur-
Bélon >**
*2 Rue des
Gentilhommes,
t 02 98 06 97 65, ot-
riec.sur.belon@
wanadoo.fr*

**★ Domaine de
Kerstinec >**

**ⓘ Moëlan-
sur-Mer >**
*20 Place de l'Eglise,
t 02 98 39 67 28,
www.moelan-
sur-mer.fr*

**★ Manoir de
Kertalg >**

looking onto the river. The restaurant, specializing in seafood, has a terrace with great views, plus there's a lively bar appreciated by the locals.

Le Bistrot sur le Pont, 11 Place Gauguin, t 02 98 06 16 16 (€€–€). Very stylish central new contemporary restaurant by the river, serving refined fare, run by the Moulin de Rosmadec crew.

Le Talisman, 4 Rue Paul Sérusier, t 02 98 06 02 58 (€). A good crêperie a walk east of the centre. *Closed June.*

Crêperie Au Vieux Chêne, 1 Place de l'Eglise, Nizon, t 02 89 09 11 10 (€). Appealing place in the centre of Nizon village, doubling as an art gallery sometimes.

St-André ✉ 29930

La Taupinière, Route de Concarneau, t 02 98 06 03 12 (€€€€). Highly reputed restaurant on the main road c.4km west of Pont-Aven, offering lovingly prepared Breton fare. Diners can watch the talented chef and his team at work. *Closed Mon and Tues, and mid-Sept–mid-Oct.*

Riec-sur-Bélon ✉ 29340

★★★Domaine de Kerstinec, Route de Moëlan (3km south of Riec), t 02 98 06 42 98, www.hotelbelon.online.fr (€€€–€€). Some of the smartest, largest rooms in the area, set in the converted buildings of a 19th-century farm dominating the surrounding countryside. Its restaurant, **Le Kerland**, overlooks the Bélon River.

Port-Bélon ✉ 29340

Chez Jacky, t 02 98 06 90 32 (€€€€–€€). Classic seafood restaurant in an oyster farmer's house on the Bélon estuary, with terrace. *Closed Sun eve and Mon, and Oct–Easter.*

Crêperie du Bélon, t 02 98 71 12 14 (€). Crêpe house with a view.

Moëlan-sur-Mer ✉ 29350

★★★★Manoir de Kertalg, t 02 98 39 77 77, www.manoirdekertalg.com (€€€€–€€€). An enchanting 15th-century manor within large private grounds, with very comfy rooms, woods and river-fishing on the Bélon. *Closed mid-Nov–mid-April.*

★★★Les Moulins du Duc, Route des Moulins, t 02 98 96 52 52, www.hotel-

moulins-du-duc.com (€€€€–€€). Lovely riverside setting to rooms in cottages by the Bélon. The restaurant (€€€€–€€€) takes up the old mill. Covered pool; lakes for fishing. *Closed Dec–Feb exc Christmas.*

La Petite Gargotte, t 02 98 39 77 01 (€). Very sweet little restaurant offering international cuisine.

Le Pouldu ✉ 29121

★★Le Panoramique, Route de la Plage de Kérou, t 02 98 39 93 49, www.hotel-panoramique.fr (€). Small modern hotel in a residential coastal quarter west of town, with basic, bargain rooms a walk up from the beaches. Basement crêperie open high summer. *Closed early Nov–Easter.*

Quimperlé ✉ 29300

★★★Le Vintage, 20 Rue Bremond d'Ars, t 02 98 35 09 10, www.hotelvintage. com (€€). In an imposing, converted 19th-century bank on the main street close to St-Croix church, with well decorated rooms.

La Maison d'Hippolyte, 2 Quai Surcouf, t 02 98 39 09 11 (€). Delightful B&B by the River Isole. Also hosts exhibitions of contemporary Breton painting and photography.

La Cigale Egarée, Zone Villeneuve, t 02 98 39 15 53 (€€€€–€€€). A striking new restaurant towards Lorient, creating a stir with its style and fine dining. Cookery lessons possible.

Le Bistro de la Tour, 2 Rue Dom Morice, t 02 98 39 29 58 (€€€€–€€). Fine central restaurant, offering classic dishes with experimental touches in a vibrant 1930s decor. *Closed Sat lunch, Sun eve and Mon.*

Crêperie des Archers, 6 Rue Dom Morice, t 02 98 39 09 54 (€). A favourite with the locals.

Crêperie Ty Gwechal, 4 Rue Mellac, t 02 98 96 30 63 (€). A restored 17th-century house in which to enjoy a wide selection of crêpes.

Arzano ✉ 29300

Château de Kerlarec, t 02 98 71 75 06, chateau-de-kerlarec@wanadoo.fr (€€€). Refined B&B accommodation in a grand 19th-century villa. *Table d'hôte* (€€€€–€€€) available. Tennis court and art gallery.

Morbihan

Morbihan *means 'little sea' in Breton. The sensational little sea after which this département is named is the Golfe du Morbihan, a magically protected, island-strewn stretch of water below the highly picturesque towns of Auray and Vannes. You can visit a trio of its islands, including Gavrinis, which conceals the finest neolithic tomb in Brittany. To the French, the name Morbihan also means megaliths, as this is where the many thousands of menhirs of Carnac stand in their long rows. A visit to lesser-known neolithic sights at Locmariaquer, Kerzehro or Arzon can be just as rewarding... and baffling.*

The Morbihan boasts blissfully varied seascapes, and two of the largest Breton islands, Groix and Belle-Ile, the latter out beyond Quiberon, the resort where luxurious sea-water treatments were introduced to Brittany.

Exceptionally beautiful valleys lead inland to enchanting châteaux, villages and chapels. There are eccentricities to uncover, too, such as the contemporary art at the Château de Kerguéhennec or the ground-breaking Cité de la Voile at Lorient, the Morbihan's naval port, now turning its military inheritance to uplifting new uses.

10

Don't miss

⭐ **Neolithic masterpieces**
Carnac, Kerzehro, Locmariaquer and Gavrinis p.415

⭐ **Bracing Atlantic islands**
Groix and Belle-Ile p.385

⭐ **A string of attractions**
The Blavet Valley p.392

⭐ **Historic villages**
La Roche-Bernard, Josselin and Rochefort-en-Terre p.446

⭐ **A magical gulf**
Golfe du Morbihan p.425

See map overleaf

Morbihan

FINISTÈRE

Montagnes Noires

Laz

Gourin

Le Saint

Abbaye de
Langonnet

Abbaye de Bon Repos
Les Forges-des-Salles

Mur-de-
Bretagne

Lac de
Guerlédan
Forêt de
Quénécan

St-
Aignan

Coray

Scaër

Le Faouët

St-Barbe

Lac du Bel-Air

Ploërdut

Cléguérec

Stival

Quimper

Rosporden

St-Flacre

Meslan

Berné

Lignol

Kernascléden

Guémené-
sur-Scorff

Quelven

Pontivy

CORNOUAILLE

E60/165

Bannalec

Plouay

Melrand

St-Nicodème

Quistinic

Blavet

St-Nicolas-
des-Eaux

St-Barthélemy

Baud

Concarneau

Pont-Aven

Quimperlé

Lanvaudan

Ferme Archéologique

Bubry

Site de
Castennec

St-Nicolas-
des-Eaux

St-Adrien

MORBIHAN

Scorff

Pont-Scorff

Inzinzac-
Lochrist

Camors

24

Raguénez

Port-
Manec'h

Kerngornet

Gestel

Guidel

Hennebont

Languidic

Pluvigner

Iles de Glénan

Guidel-Plage

Plœmeur

Lanester

Lorient

Brandérion

Landévant

Ste-Anne-
d'Auray

N

Larmor-
Plage

Kerroc'h
Lomener

Port-Louis

Plouhinec

Nestadio

Belz

Auray

Kernourz

Gâvres

Etel

St-Cado

Erdeven

Port-Blanc

Larmor-
Baden

Arzon

Port-Tudy

Groix

Ile de Groix

dolmens and tumulus
Plouharnel

Carnac

Port-Navalo

10 km

5 miles

St-Pierre-Quiberon

Presqu'île de
Quiberon

Quiberon

Baie de

Quiberon

Ile d'Houat

Pointe des
Poulains

Sauzon

Le Palais

Port Goulphar

Bangor

Locmaria

Belle-Ile

Ile
d'Hoëdic

FRANCE

CÔTES D'ARMOR

ILLE-ET-VILAINE

M O R B I H A N

LOIRE ATLANTIQUE

Loudéac
Le Vaublanc
Merdrignac
St-Méen-le-Grand
Montfort-sur-Meu
Rennes
164
La Chèze
Ménéac
Tombeau de Merlin
Iffendic
Mordelles
Chapelle Ste-Noyale
Rohan
la Trinité-Porhoët
Mauron
Comper
Noyal-Pontivy
Naizin
Lanouée
Guilliers
Néant-sur-Yve
Tréhorenteuc
Brocéliande Forêt de
Paimpont
Etang du Pas du Haux
Plélan-le-Grand
Val Sans Retour
Les Forges-de-Paimpont
Réguiny
Josselin
St-Servant
Ploërmel
24
Guer
Guignen
Locminé
Château de Kerguéhennec
Guéhenno
Lizio
Sérent
Monteneuf
Maure-de-Bretagne
St-Jean-Brévelay
Malestroit
St-Marcel
Plaudren
Pleucadeuc
St-Martin-sur-Oust
La Gacilly
Pipriac
Guipry
Messac
Elven
Landes de Cojoux
St-Just
Port-de-Roche
Glénac
Rochefort-en-Terre
Langon
St-Avé
Questembert
Redon
Allaire
St-Nicolas-les-Pins
Guéméné-Penfao
Vannes
166
775
775
Zooparc de Branféré
Théix
Le Guerno
Bégganne
Vilaine
Surzur
Muzillac
Izernac
St-Dolay
Tréhillac
Billiers
Arzal
La Roche-Bernard
St-Gildas-des-Bois
Blain
Damgan
Kervoyal
Trébiguier
Camoël
Missillac
Brest
Sarzeau
Pénestin
Pointe de Penvins
Pen Bé
Herbignac
St-Colombier
St-Gildas-de-Rhuys
Quimiac
St-Lyphard
Piriac-sur-Mer
La Turballe
Guérande
Savenay
Le Croisic
La Baule

Canal de Nantes à Brest

Don't miss

1. Carnac, Kerzehro, Locmariaquer and Gavrinis **p.415**

2. Groix and Belle-Ile **p.385**

3. The Blavet Valley **p.392**

4. La Roche-Bernard, Josselin and Rochefort-en-Terre **p.446**

5. Golfe du Morbihan **p.425**

ⓘ Comité
Départemental du
Tourisme (CDT) du
Morbihan
*Allée Nicolas Leblanc,
56010 Vannes, t 02 97
42 61 60 or t 08 25 13 56
56 (premium rate),
www.morbihan.com.
For up-to-date
information on public
transport across the
département, see
www.morbihan.fr with
full details on the TIM
network (within France,
t 08 10 10 10 56 –
premium rate) around
the Morbihan. The CDT
also offers packages
and online reservations
– consult www.
morbihanresa.com*

The Morbihan coastline is remarkably friendly and open, in the main, characterized by long, broad, sandy beaches strewn with fewer rocks than in the north or west and by genteel resorts where sailing and watersports are major passions. To add to these delights, Brittany's most famous neolithic sights often stand just a stone's throw from the shore.

There are unmissable military scars along the Morbihan's western shore, around Lorient, the *département's* major port, where we start this touring chapter. Much battered, this naval harbour has been transforming its grim legacy, most excitingly opening a cutting-edge centre devoted to sailing, boldly placed right in front of the indestructible Nazi U-Boot installations left from the war. Across Lorient's bay, the splendid beach-side Ancien Régime fortifications of Port-Louis now contain a fine museum of colonialism. In addition, every year, Lorient hosts the great annual gathering of Western European Celts, the August Festival Interceltique.

Head inland from Lorient up either of the Scorff or Blavet Valleys, and you'll be treated to a journey into traditional Brittany, the sights vying with one another in quaintness. Tempting you out to sea from Lorient, the island of Groix has remained wonderfully unspoilt and unpretentious.

Continuing east along the Morbihan coast, past the extraordinary indented estuary of the Etel, you come to the Quiberon Peninsula, only connected to the mainland by a dramatic, thin strip of sand. The lively port of Quiberon, renowned for its seawater treatment centre and its culinary specialities, serves the extremely popular but rather posh Belle-Ile, the largest island off the Breton coast. Here, Claude Monet and Sarah Bernhardt found inspiration; now the place has become chic enough to charge Parisian prices.

Exploring the fabulous landscapes and seascapes of the Golfe du Morbihan, it becomes confusing as to what is mainland, what island. The best way to enjoy this extraordinarily beautiful inland sea is take a boat trip around it. Two of the Morbihan's major historic towns hide at the back of the Golfe, but are well worth unearthing, Auray for its picture-postcard port, and Vannes, the *département's* capital, for its great mix of architectural and cultural attractions. Close to Auray, Ste-Anne d'Auray, as the largest pilgrimage site in Brittany, draws Catholics in droves; the place also recalls the huge number of Bretons who fell in the First World War. Back by the ocean, the Morbihan coast comes to a very pretty end around the Vilaine estuary.

One significant advantage of heading up into inland Morbihan is that the coastline gets terribly clogged up with traffic, especially around the gulf, Carnac and Quiberon, and not just in holiday season. Anyway, a journey up the Oust Valley or Canal de Nantes à Brest takes you to enchanting old towns and villages such as Rochefort-en-Terre, La Gacilly, Malestroit and Josselin.

Lorient and Around

The western Morbihan coast is dominated by the oddly compelling, if in parts grizzly-grey military and fishing port of Lorient. However, the place has been turning its attention more and more to culture and sport in recent times. Anyhow, you don't feel Lorient's presence on the most western stretch of the Morbihan coast between Guidel-Plage and Larmor-Plage.

From the Laïta to Lorient

The **Laïta** River heading down from the town of Quimperlé forms the beautiful border between the Finistère and the Morbihan near the coast. You can enjoy exploring its shaded wooded banks. In summer however, attention is focused at the well-protected Laïta estuary. On the Morbihan side, **Guidel-Plage** makes a joyous first stop, with its small **Port du Bas Pouldu** tucked up the estuary, facing Le Pouldu across the water. The coastal strip heading southeast is quite wild, a good stretch for windsurfers. Continuing down the coast to the typical little port of **Kerroc'h**, the island of Groix comes more closely into focus. Past the tip of the **Pointe du Talud**, the equally small port the other side is **Lomener**.

The **Centre Nautique de Kerguelen** is a highly reputed school for learning water sports and diving, set behind the sandy beaches on the western side of **Larmor-Plage**. In the centre of town, the unusual design of the well-scrubbed church stands out. The interior contains rich carvings, notably the painted apostles in the north porch. Apparently, in centuries past, the tradition was for naval vessels leaving Lorient to head off to war to fire cannon shots as they passed this church. The priest was supposed to respond in nationalist manner by ringing the bells and raising the French flag on the spire. At Larmor-Plage's northern end, smart yachts moor at the chic modern **marina of Kernével**.

Lorient

Some stalwart Lorientais may have campaigned to return the town's name from Lorient to L'Orient or 'The Orient', but there's no reviving the port's once-opulent Ancien Régime look. Built from

Getting to and around Lorient

Lorient airport is at Lann-Bihoué-en-Ploemeur, t 02 97 87 21 50, *www.lorient.aeroport.fr*. There are flights from Ireland to Lorient from Waterford, Kerry, Cork and Galloway with Aer Arann (*www.aerarann.com*). Lorient is easily reached by TGV fast trains in c.3hrs from Paris. You can reach the ports along the coast by bus from Lorient. For details contact CTRL at the Gare d'Echanges, Cours de Chazelles, 56100 Lorient, t 02 97 21 28 29, *www.ctrl.fr*.

scratch in the second half of the 17th century to serve as one of France's main colonial ports, the new town of L'Orient became the base of the Compagnie des Indes, France's equivalent to the British East India Company, and grew wealthy on lucrative trading. When the colonial sources dried up, it transformed into a major naval harbour, and after the First World War a large-scale fishing port was added.

Disastrously for Lorient, in the Second World War, the Nazis established one of their most important U-Boat submarine bases here, constructing the thickest of concrete pens specially for them at Keroman. Allied bombers desperately tried to hit these installations, but wiped out the civilian parts of town instead. By the end of the war, 80 per cent or more of Lorient's buildings had been left in ruins.

The town has suffered badly not just from recent cuts in the French military budget, but also cuts to fishing quotas, causing unemployment and despondency, but it's by no means all doom and gloom. Yes, this is a place marked by naval installations, industry and some dreary postwar quarters, but in other parts it has been sprucing itself up in surprising manner. Palms line some of the central streets, the navy has liberated some of the most attractive historic areas recently, and one port in the heart of town has turned into a swanky marina. On top of that, Lorient has won the prestigious Ville d'Art et d'Histoire label for its postwar legacy. The most exciting development has been the 2008 opening of the Cité de la Voile Eric Tabarly, a great new tourist magnet, devoted to sailing for aficionados and the general public alike, its uplifting contemporary architecture defiantly placed in front of those dreadful Nazi U-Boat pens left on the western edge of town. It shouldn't be forgotten either that Lorient plays host every year to the largest, merriest, yet also most serious international gathering of Celts in Brittany, the Festival Interceltique (*see* box, below).

Festival Interceltique

Lorient may have had its links with the past brutally cut off, but it has become the proud rallying point for Brittany's most important annual display of Celtic culture, the **Festival Interceltique**. Breton, Irish, Welsh, Scottish, Manx, Galician and Asturian people unite in the first week of August to celebrate their Celtic roots, both with music, dance and other cultural events, and with serious meetings on the defence of Celtic culture. Information is available from 2 Rue Paul Bert, t 02 97 21 24 29, *www.festival-interceltique.com*.

Keroman and the Cité de la Voile

On the western side of Lorient, at Keroman, where the Germans built their vast submarine base, things have been changing extremely rapidly in the last few years. Although it's too difficult and expensive to get rid of the U-Boat pens, the town authorities have decided to develop exciting new projects around them. The modern submarine base here may have been shut down by the French navy, but many of the skilled local workers have transferred to developing state-of-the-art yachts. A new business park has been going up in Keroman with companies at the technological forefront of boat design. For tourists, though, the major excitement is the sparkling new Cité de la Voile.

Cité de la Voile Eric Tabarly

Cité de la Voile
Eric Tabarly
www.citevoile-tabarly.com; open July
and Aug daily 10–8,
April–June and Sept
daily 10–6, Oct–Dec and
Feb–Mar Tues–Sun 10–6

As a coastal region inevitably obsessed by the sea, Brittany has produced many of the most famous record-breaking sailors in the world in the last century. The most celebrated of the lot to date is Eric Tabarly, who tragically died in 1998. One reason why Lorient's Cité de la Voile bears his name is to honour his memory. The creation of the place was in great part down to the determination of his widow and friends to find a safe home for his series of ground-breaking yachts, virtually all called *Pen Duick*, in which he broke many world sailing records (see box, below). The Lorient authorities joined forces to back the project in dramatic fashion.

A Breton Sailing Legend – Eric Tabarly

Eric Tabarly's passion for sailing developed when his father donated the disintegrating family yacht to him after it had been left to fall apart through the Second World War. In fact this was not a Breton-built boat, but a late-19th-century vessel designed by the great Scottish boat-builder William Fife. The craft had been rechristened with a Breton name, *Pen Duick*, meaning black-headed tit. Realizing the lamentable state of the boat, Tabarly practically rebuilt it.

Following this experience, in the ensuing decades, he would go on to conceive a whole series of ground-breaking yachts, all given the name Pen Duick, and won an amazing number of races in them. Although he trained to be a fighter pilot in the French airforce, and did serve in Indochina, the army realized that his skills lay elsewhere, and released him to pursue his passion for sailing.

In 1964, when the British felt that Sir Francis Chichester ruled the waves, Tabarly won the solo transatlantic race. An extraordinary string of major victories followed, including, most impressively, a stunning second solo transatlantic victory in 1976. What was particularly remarkable was that Tabarly himself came up with so many of the pioneering design elements. As to the *Pen Duick IV* he sailed in 1968, it has been described by some as the greatest yacht of the 20th century, because it was so innovative, a great trimarin with aluminium hull.

Tabarly became a hero to many French people for his successes, but many others simply loved him because of the quiet way he transmitted his passion for sailing. He is credited with making sailing into the great hobby it is for so many French people today. Settled happily on the Odet in the Finistère, he would tragically lose his life to the sea. Tabarly died in an accident in 1998, falling off one of his beloved boats and drowning. His death fuelled the legend. Numerous books have been written about the modest man; but the opening of the Cité de la Voile is an amazingly uplifting legacy and tribute to a great Breton figure.

Architecturally, the Cité de la Voile is spectacular, a great wave of a building overlooking the pretty Le Ter river estuary. The place was designed by architect Jacques Ferrier, and is covered with aluminium which changes colour according to the daylight. An aerial walkway leads from the main building to the Tour des Vents, a vertical stairtower that takes you down to see the *Pen Duicks* from close up.

In the main exhibition spaces, you might begin by watching a couple of intriguing films, one covering Tabarly's career, the other on the extraordinary Tara polar expedition run from a pioneering vessel which set out from Lorient in 2006 on its major scientific and environmental expedition, only returning in 2008.

On the first floor, the history of sailing down the centuries is evoked in an experimental sound and light show, then with interactive sections. But the most fun is to be had in the last sections, which are probably as educational for adults without a clue about sailing as for children. The presentations may be too simple for seasoned sailors, but the skilled yachtsmen among you might appreciate the recorded interviews with leading sailors on their passions and philosophies of sailing. Bruno Peyron and Francis Joyon have been the dominant names in the French yacht-racing world in recent times, the latter the Breton champion who shattered Ellen McArthur's solo round-the-world sailing record at the start of 2008.

Then take the pedestrian bridge out to the Tour des Vents and down to the pontoon. Here, as well as taking a close look at Tabarly's *Pen Duicks*, sometimes other state-of-the-art racing yachts may be on display. If you book well ahead, small groups can also go out on a boat with an instructor to be taught the rudiments of sailing techniques.

Just south of the Cité de la Voile, the new **BSM marina** is fast developing into a major port of call for the most glamorous cutting-edge racing yachts in the world, rivalling La Trinité-sur-Mer down the Morbihan coast. Wander down from the Cité de la Voile, and you should see an amazing array of super-yachts parked here, or receiving a make-over. Passenger services are starting to operate from this new harbour too.

Now the initials BSM are a way of subtly disguising the fact that the marina lies in front of the **Base de Sous-Marins**, the vast Nazi submarine installation, its haggard concrete structures forming quite a daunting backdrop, but one with a gritty quality that brings to mind so many action adventure films. You can visit the base, described as one of the largest fortresses of the 20th century, on special guided tours taking in the **Musée Sous-Marin** and the **Tour Davis**, the latter built during the war for submarine training.

Tour Davis
normally open July–Aug daily 1.30–6.30, rest of year Sun 2pm – check Lorient tourist website and see also www.tourdavis.com

A Tour of Lorient's Other Ports

Heading eastwards, you can take a glimpse into the separate lives of Lorient's other ports. To appreciate the extensive **Port de Pêche**, or fishing harbour, at its bustling best, you should go there at crack of dawn, in order to see the streaming quantities of fish being auctioned. The tourist office organizes early-bird tours.

If you prefer to avoid an early alarm call, start at the **Bassin à Flot** marina in the heart of town. On its north bank, along the **Quai des Indes**, go and view the vast murals at the Art Nouveau **Chambre de Commerce** for a pictorial glimpse of Lorient as a colonial port. Further along the quay stand some of the few remaining stocky granite houses that were constructed for rich merchants during the 18th century.

The area just beyond used to be the naval arsenal, and was strictly out of bounds, but in the last few years it has been liberated to the public as is now known as **L'Enclos du Port**. Here you can explore one of the few remaining original historic quarters of town, including the Hôtel Gabriel, where the Compagnie des Indes sold its produce, and its flour mills. Indeed, on guided tours you can see inside the mills and even climb the Tour de la Découverte observation tower. Simply walking up the hill here you get wide views over the port.

On the southern side of the Bassin à Flot, the **Quai de Rohan** shows off with its slick modern development of shops and bars, which look down on the beautiful boats moored right in the centre of town.

La Thalassa
www.la-thalassa.fr,
open February, Easter
and All Saints school
holidays Mon–Fri
9.30–12.30 and 2–6,
Sat and Sun 2–6; July
and Aug daily 10–7;
May–June and Sept
Tues–Fri 9.30–12.30 and
2–6, Sat–Mon 2–6

La Thalassa at the quayside is located on the veteran Fremer trawler. One of the *espaces découvertes* series of museums that have been opened around the Morbihan, this presents experiences at sea from four different perspectives, those of captain, seamen, fisherman and oceanographer, each devoted their own deck. It all makes for fascinating viewing, with good use of interactive displays.

Quai de Rohan leads out to **Boulevard de l'Estacade**, where you'll find the car park as well as the **Gare Maritime** for trips out to the island of Groix. Beyond this, the interesting wedge of a modern building, the **Club Nautique**, has a lively bar open to all. From the tip of the Estacade, you may see the rare container ship or tanker carefully parking at the Port de Commerce, while up the Scorff, one of several rivers flowing into the Rade de Lorient, the naval vessels come into view. You can drive along the **Port de Commerce** quays, though huge petrol and grain storage tanks predominate here.

Back in the town centre, you might take a look at the circular **Halles Merville**, a covered market, or the **Jardins Jules Ferry**, the central public gardens. The grid of streets that lie to the north are quite vibrant, while **Rue du Port** is the busiest shopping artery. Little palm trees grow along **Rue de Liège**, giving it an exotic touch. Head up to **Place Alsace-Lorraine**, one of the rare spots in Lorient where you can see stone among the building materials. It seems only appropriate that the town's central, modern church has a tower sticking into the sky like a stylized fish bone.

Port-Louis and Gâvres

Just a short hop across the Rade de Lorient by water, but a long drive round by road, Port-Louis has kept so much of the Ancien Régime atmosphere that Lorient mostly lost. The long, thin Gâvres peninsula makes for a curious visit, still largely given over to the military.

Port-Louis, its Citadel and Museums

The **village** of Port-Louis on its slope is sweet, but quite separate from the major, sharp-angled citadel standing right beside the sea. Impressive lengths of stone **ramparts** stretch along the shore between the two. Gateways through the wall lead to a glorious, well-protected **beach**, with laid-back café – from both, you can enjoy fabulous views out to Groix.

The citadel itself lies behind layer upon layer of further defences, recent war memorials set amidst them, marked out by the fluttering flags. Spaniards originally began the fortifications, called upon during the French Wars of Religion to support the ultra-Catholic cause here. Early in the 17th century, Cardinal Richelieu convinced Louis XIII of the great strategic potential of the Rade de Lorient – the citadel was named Port-Louis in that king's honour. Under Louis XIV, from 1664, the place became the base for the Compagnie des Indes Orientales. Its role as a major colonial port would be shortlived, however, as virgin marshland on the opposite bank of the Blavet was chosen to develop a larger port for the expanding colonial trade – L'Orient.

Musée de la Compagnie des Indes
musee.lorient.fr,
t 02 97 82 56 72, open Wed–Mon Feb–April and Sept–Dec 1.30–6, May–Aug 10–6.30

The citadel now conceals several museum collections within its thick stone walls. The **Musée de la Compagnie des Indes** is the main one. It brings to the fore not just the significant link between the Rade de Lorient and France's colonies, but also the wider story of the French colonial adventure of the Ancien Régime. It tells of the development of France's 17th- and 18th-century colonies and trading posts, and the bitter battle over them with the British and the Dutch. At times, the historical complexities can get daunting. Basically, after King Henri IV's administration allowed for the creation of an Indies trading company in 1604, a series of floundering companies succeeded one another through the reigns of the Louis.

The museum focuses in particular on the period from 1664 on, as Colbert, that mastermind of a minister to Louis XIV, established a French fleet to rival that of the Dutch and the English. In 1664, the Compagnie des Indes Orientales, or Compagnie Colbert, was created and given near exclusive French trading rights with Africa, the Americas and the East. When this vast enterprise collapsed, splinter companies were formed to exploit specific territories again. John Law, a madly ambitious Scot who had settled in France, saw to their reuniting in 1719 as the Compagnie Perpétuelle des Indes, then creating the first catastrophic stock market bubble in history. Later, the Compagnie des Indes's resources were drained by the Austrian War of Succession through the mid 1740s, followed by the crippling Seven Years' War from 1756 to 1763, before it lost its privileges and died with the Revolution. However, these French overseas companies exercised huge authority over their territories and trading posts, minting coinage, dispensing justice, drawing up treaties... it was about much more than simply trading.

All this globe-trotting history unfolds in a series of galleries ordered chronologically or geographically. Copies of maps and documents, and fine objects in glass cabinets, give visitors a visual notion of how colonial trade developed and what products were brought back to France. Highlights include a collection of porcelain of the Compagnie des Indes, the odd piece of period furniture, and printed calico imported from the East.

Much more could be explained about the slave trade from which the colonial companies, Lorient, Brittany and France benefited so greatly during the Ancien Régime. One hundred and fifty-six slave-trading expeditions were recorded departing from Lorient in the 18th century – a slightly smaller number than was recorded from St-Malo, although a tenth of the vast number that set sail from Nantes.

Musée National de la Marine
www.musee-marine.fr; same hours

The citadel also contains the Musée National de la Marine, which has displays of boats, arms and models, but is most interesting for its good presentations on sea rescue through the ages and on marine archaeology.

To Gâvres

Maison de l'Ile de Kerner
www.maison-kerner.fr; open Easter and All Saints hols Mon–Fri 9.30–12.30 and 2–6, Sat–Sun 2–6; July–Aug 10–7; May–June and Sept Tues–Fri 9.30–12.30 and 2–6, Sat–Mon 2–6

Continuing eastwards, the pretty coast road takes you along the north side of the **Petite Mer de Gâvres**, a broad but shallow inlet which draws large numbers of shell pickers. At **Riantec**, the little Maison de l'Ile de Kerner overlooking the Petite Mer is another espace découverte, this one showcasing the area's ecosystem. The displays are beautifully executed, with terracotta reproductions of native birds made by a local craftsman, the wave-based soundtrack adding to the atmosphere. Accompanied nature walks are offered from here in summer.

The sign to the military peninsula of Gâvres, *Vue Imprenable* ('Unbeatable View'), reads with unintentional irony. This absurdly thin finger of land is a mixture of ugliness and beauty, scarred by military use yet for all that one of the most atmospheric places along the generally splendid Morbihan coast. Be warned that this is a serving army shooting ground, though panels indicate that you can visit the unspoilt beaches on certain days. The views out to Groix are spectacular. You can follow signs through **Gâvres's** labyrinth of little streets to reach the **Tumulus du Goërem**, a neolithic burial site now indecorously squeezed between two town houses.

Market Days in and around Lorient

Guidel: Wednesday and Sunday
Larmor-Plage: Sunday
Lorient: Wednesday and Saturday
Port-Louis: Saturday

Where to Stay and Eat in and around Lorient

Ploemeur ✉ 56270

Le Vivier, 9 Rue de Beg er Vir, **t 02 97 82 99 60 (€€€–€€). Sweet hotel in fine location on a rocky point right by the sea, many rooms with views, some with balcony. Very good restaurant (€€€€–€€).

Larmor-Plage ✉ 56260

Les Mouettes, Anse de Kerguelen, **t 02 97 65 50 30, *www.lesmouettes. com* (€€). Comfortable, modern, cheerful rooms behind the dunes on the western edge of the town. The hotel has side-on views along the beaches and a restaurant serving fine seasonal cuisine, including on the large terrace looking to sea.

Lorient ✉ 56100

***Mercure, 31 Place Jules Ferry, **t** 02 97 21 35 73, *www.accorhotels.com* (€€€–€€). Offering a taste of typical post-war Lorient architecture, it's comfortable and close to the Bassin à Flot.

Victor Hugo, 36 Rue Lazare Carnot, **t 02 97 21 16 24, *www.hotelvictorhugo-lorient.com* (€€–€). Decent option near the marina.

L'Amphitryon, 127 Rue du Colonel Muller, Route de Quimperlé, **t** 02 97 83 34 04, (€€€€). An exclusive restaurant outside the centre, serving the most refined cuisine, especially fish, in contemporary setting. *Closed Sun and Mon.*

Henri & Joseph, 4 Rue Léo le Bourgo, **t** 02 97 84 72 12 (€€€€–€€€). Top fish-cooking dog in town. *Closed Sun and Mon.*

Le Jardin Gourmand, 46 Rue Jules Simon, **t** 02 97 64 172 4 (€€€). Creative cuisine, with garden dining possible in summer.

Le Pic, 2 Blvd Maréchal Franchet d'Esperey, **t** 02 97 21 18 29, *www. restaurant-lorient.com* (€€). With a relaxed atmosphere, serving fresh seafood, tables set out on the street in summer.

Tavarn Ar Roue Morvan, 17 Rue de la Poissonnière, **t** 02 97 21 61 57 (€). Celtic hot spot that puts on evenings of Breton food and music. *Closed Sun.*

Port-Louis ✉ 56290

Les Magnolias, 1 Place du Marché, **t 02 97 82 46 05, *www.hotel-magnolias.com* (€€). A well-kept hotel with good food, on a pleasant, shady square.

Avel Vor, 25 Rue de Locmalo, **t** 02 97 82 47 59 (€€€€–€€). Elaborate seafood dishes served in a dining room overlooking the Mer de Gâvres. *Closed Sun eve, Mon and Tues.*

Le Bistroy, 18 bis Route de Locmalo, **t** 02 97 82 48 41 (€€–€). Glorious bargain of a restaurant also beside the Mer de Gâvres, serving remarkable fresh dishes in a pretty stone home.

ⓘ **Guidel**
9 Rue St Maurice,
t *02 97 65 01 74,*
www.guidel.com

ⓘ **Ploemeur-Bourg >**
Place de l'Eglise, **t** *02 97 85 27 88; Easter–Sept and school hols*

★ **Le Vivier >**

ⓘ **Larmor-Plage >**
Ave du Général de Gaulle, **t** *02 97 33 70 02 (Easter–Sept and school hols), larmor-plage@ lorient-tourisme.fr*

ⓘ **Port-Louis >>**
1 Rue de la Citadelle, **t** *02 97 82 52 93, www.ville-portlouis.fr*

ⓘ **Lorient >**
Maison de la Mer, Quai de Rohan, **t** *02 97 21 07 84, www.lorient-tourisme.com; a good first port of call, as it offers tourist info right across the area covered here, known as Cap l'Orient*

★ **Avel Vor >>**

★ **Le Bistroy >>**

The Island of Groix

 Groix and
Belle-Ile

The short boat trip out to Groix takes you decades back in time from the modern town of Lorient. Here gulls and rabbits rule the roost, and in the summer season the island is scented with wild honeysuckle. A couple of days on Groix should enable you to discover many of its hidden corners.

Groix seems like a sanctuary of innocence after military Lorient and Gâvres. One of the most noticeable features of its hamlets are the wash-places... although islanders did use to nickname these 'the courts', implying that the washerwomen's gossip could be harsh. Ties with mainland Brittany and Breton culture have traditionally been strong here, but the geology of the island sets it quite apart. The diversity of its rocks makes it a geologist's dream, but Groix has had to protect itself against rock thieves. The island has a couple of exceptional beaches, the most extraordinary being the Plage des Grands Sables, its sands tinted red because of the local powdered garnet that blows over it.

History

You can learn a great deal on the island's history from a visit to the Ecomusée at the main harbour, Port-Tudy. A certain number of megaliths, both menhirs and dolmens, shows that neolithic people settled here. As to Port-Tudy, it carries the name of a Dark Ages Breton saint also closely associated with Loctudy and L'Ile-Tudy in the southern Finistère.

Sadly, no artefacts remain from the most famous archaeological find made on Groix – a Viking burial mound containing the remains of a man, a child, a dog and other animals, all burnt in a Viking boat. Arms, utensils and decorative objects were found in this cache, shipped off to the Musée des Antiquités Nationales outside Paris.

Groix was divided into two parts under different ownership in medieval times, the more prosperous east known as the Primiture, the slightly harsher west called the Piwisi. The two sections were brought under joint ownership by the powerful Breton family, the Rohans, in 1384. Maritime activities became increasingly important down the centuries. By the Ancien Régime, the great majority of the men of the island would go to sea, either fishing or joining the navy, leaving the women to tend the soil. The Dutch and the British, fighting for control of the seas and new colonies in the second half of the 17th century, troubled Groix on several occasions. But it was only in the mid-18th century that the French military built serious fortifications on the island to protect it from invasion.

Getting to Groix

Boats for Groix mainly leave from central Lorient. The **Compagnie Océane, t** 02 97 64 77 64, or 08 20 05 61 56 (premium rate), *www.compagnie-oceane.fr* runs its services year-round. The **Société Morbihannaise de Navigation, t** 08 20 05 60 00 (premium rate), *www.smn-navigation.fr*, operates its crossings April–Sept. Or for a more personalized service, try the **Bateau Taxi de L'Ile de Groix, t** 02 97 65 52 52, *www.bateautaxi-iledegroix.com*, which can go from the BSM marina or Port-Louis. Hire bikes on the quayside on arrival, but they aren't allowed on the coastal paths.

The islanders remain proud of their fishing traditions, even though the activity has dwindled drastically. Sardine-fishing formed the backbone of the catch until the mid-19th century, when more advanced boats made long-haul trips possible. Between 1870 and 1940, Port-Tudy was one of France's biggest tuna-fishing ports. The first fishermen's school in France was founded here in 1895, as the captains of Groix were held in particularly high esteem on the mainland. But between the wars, the island's fishing fleet collapsed, and during the Second World War the people of Groix experienced intense German occupation. One fort, Surville, served as a detention camp, while the Bourg briefly contained a camp for Jewish prisoners.

The Groisillons, the 2,500 or so people of Groix, still divide the island into the Primitures to the east and the Piwisis to the west. The east is much more populated, and the people on that side have traditionally been wealthier. After all, the eastern side of the island benefits from much better climatic conditions – even the vegetables ripen earlier, they say...

A Tour of Groix

The Breton novelist Henri Queffélec wrote of the tuna dundees at **Port-Tudy** 'touching each other like animals crammed together in a livestock truck'. The description gives you some idea of the claustrophobic crush of boats that would have greeted you in the 19th century. Now yachts and passenger ferries take up much more of the picturesque harbour.

Ecomusée de Groix
t 02 97 86 84 60,
ecomusee.groix.free.fr;
open July–Aug
Tues–Sun 9.30–12.30
and 3–7; April–June and
Sept–Nov Tues–Sun
10–12.30 and 2–5;
Dec–Mar Wed, Sat and
Sun 10–12.30 and 2–5;
Feb, Easter and All
Saints hols Wed–Sun
10–12.30 and 2–5

It is fitting enough that the **Ecomusée** should have taken over a former Groix canning factory. Footprint trails painted on the floor lead you past cabinets explaining the history of Groix. Large models show how the local fishing boats became more streamlined through time. The toughness of the fishing trade is well brought out, and the section on sailmaking is a reminder of the days when Port-Tudy would have been lined with sailmakers, ships' carpenters, chandlers and painters, all long gone. One of the worst storms in the island's history occurred in September 1930, when six boats were wrecked and many people died. Reference is made to this disaster here and in several other spots around Groix. The museum also pays homage to a reputed Breton poet born on Groix, Jean-Pierre Calloc'h.

Up the hill from the port, the main settlement of the island is known to the locals as **Le Bourg**, although it's sometimes called St-Tudy and maps mark it as 'Groix'. Le Bourg has a quiet charm. The weather vane on the church takes the form of a tuna, appropriately enough.

Port Lay lies a short distance northwest. Down from the flowery upper village, this pretty and well-protected little harbour is tucked into a narrow inlet. Port Lay was the site of the fishermen's school where so many Groix sailors were once trained. Inland and up from Port Lay, between Kermario and Clavezic, you can go in search of the **Grand Menhir**, a tall, eroded monolith now submerged in scrub. Not that long ago, though, it was still prominent enough to be used by sailors as a seamark.

West along the coast from Port Lay, the main reservoir for the island lies behind **Port Melin**, where a statue honours the poet Calloc'h, known in Breton as Bleimor, killed fighting for France in the First World War. Further on, you can walk almost to the rocky tip of the island, at **Pen Men**, though this is now a nature reserve. As well as a good number of birds and a profusion of honeysuckle in season, it's home to the *glaucophane bleu*, not a rare bird, but a rare type of rock, which makes it a protected geological area.

Starting down the southern coast, you go past the sites of the **Trou du Tonnerre** and the **Grotte aux Moutons**, on past a prehistoric camp and a stretch inland where several megaliths lie low in the undergrowth. The typical hamlet of **Kerlard** stands close by.

Continuing along the coast you come to **Port St-Nicolas**, the most makeshift harbour imaginable, where small boats are simply tied with ropes to two rocks. Groix has a reputation for excellent sea diving, and this is one much-favoured spot from which to explore underwater. Sights include the wreck of the U-Boat *U171*, lost with all hands in 1942. (For diving around Groix, ask at the tourist office.) The dolmen nearest the port is where legend has it that the Breton Grim Reaper, *l'Ankou*, sets out at night to collect those about to die on the island.

The **Trou de l'Enfer** is the major tourist attraction of Groix after the beaches, a great hole formed in one of the cliffs. From here, on clear days, you can see the length of the south side of the island, the lighthouses at opposite ends both coming into view.

To the west of Locmaria, at **Les Saisies**, natural black jetties of rock stretch into the sea; if you're lucky you can find a deserted if tiny patch of sand for yourself among the rocks. **Locmaria** can offer you a more generous beach. The village itself has a simple church, **Notre Dame de Placemance**, and a particularly well-kept wash place. The area from Locmaria to the southern tip of the island, the **Pointe des Chats** ('Cats' Point'), is the corner of land with the most interesting geology on Groix. The *millefeuille* effects of the rocks,

Where to Stay and Eat on Groix

Port-Tudy ✉ 56590

**Escale, t 02 97 86 80 04 (€€€–€). A loud, cheerful option on the quay, its rooms with lovely views on to the harbour.

**La Jetée, t 02 97 86 80 82, *erwan. tonnerre@wanadoo.fr* (€€–€). Nicely presented rooms on the quay, plus oyster bar.

**Ty Mad, t 02 97 86 80 19, *www. tymad.com* (€€–€). Just 100m from where the boat gets in, with views down on the port. Restaurant. Pool.

Groix (Le Bourg/ St-Tudy) ✉ 56590

La Marine, 7 Rue du Général de Gaulle, **t 02 97 86 80 05, *www. hoteldelamarine.com* (€€–€). A charming hotel with a front courtyard shaded by a mighty yew. The shell-decorated restaurant (€€) is a good place to try rod-caught sea bass, plentiful around Groix.

La Renaissance B&B, t 02 97 86 54 57, *www.larenaissance-groix.fr* (€€–€). Very pleasant pretty, simple rooms at a former bistrot; the woman who runs the place also owns a boutique.

Le Cinquante, 22 Place de l'Eglise, **t** 02 97 86 51 10 (€€€–€€). A little restaurant by the church that serves good if pricey food.

Chez Sandrine, 6 Rue Maurice Gouronc, **t** 02 97 86 89 72 (€). An appealing family-run crêperie on the market square, with a lovely stone floor and little fireplace. Serves both traditional and more adventurous crêpes.

Locqueltas ✉ 56590

La Criste Marine B&B, t 02 97 86 83 04, *www.groix-chambredhote.com* (€€). Monique Poupée's cottage facing the ocean has simple, nice rooms with fantastic sea views.

L'Ocre Marine, 22 Rue Tromor, Locmaria, **t** 02 97 86 53 98, *ocre-marine@wanadoo.fr*. This charming crêperie by the sea makes its own jams and caramels.

Mez Carnelet ✉ 56590

Sémaphore de la Croix B&B, t 02 97 86 86 43, *www.semaphoredelacroix.fr* (€€€€–€€€). Luxury roooms, all with sea views, in a former semaphore building in a magnificent coastal setting a couple of minutes' walk from the Sables Rouges beach. *Closed Nov–Feb.*

⭐ La Criste Marine B&B >>

ⓘ Ile de Groix >
t 02 97 86 53 08,
www.ile-de-groix.com,
or *www.lorient-tourisme.com*

⭐ Sémaphore de la Croix B&B >>

with their occasional veins of quartz, count among the wonders that draw geologists to the island.

The eastern coast is the place to go to find the island's most curious beaches. A light powdering of red dust streaks the shore at **Les Sables Rouges**, the result of eroding garnet. These beaches were not always so small – a holiday village and restaurant were built above the more spacious sands... before they shifted swiftly north. The main beach on the island, the **Plage des Grands Sables**, is constantly on the move. Year by year it nudges closer to Port-Tudy. A delightful stretch of coastal path leads west from the beach back to this harbour, passing by the typical old hamlet of **Le Méné**, a good place to appreciate the traditional architecture of Groix.

Up the Scorff and Blavet

Our next touring section takes you inland into northwestern Morbihan, along the two main rivers that spill into the Rade de Lorient, the Scorff and the Blavet. Travelling up the Scorff, the trip

Getting around the Scorff and Blavet

Hennebont has a **railway** station on the line from Paris to Quimper via Rennes, but virtually no TGVs stop there. Pontivy also has a station, on the line crossing central Brittany north to south, from St-Brieuc to Vannes. **Bus** services are limited – see Transports de Cap L'Orient, Gare d'Echange, Lorient, **t** 02 97 21 28 29, *www.ctrl.fr*. There is a line from Lorient to Gourin, and one heading up the Blavet Valley from Lorient to St-Brieuc, stopping at Hennebont, Languidic, Baud and Pontivy.

leads you as far as the hills of the Montagnes Noires. The Blavet River flows through an exceptionally gorgeous valley, its beauty only embellished by the enchanting tourist sights created in recent times along its banks between Hennebont and Pontivy, the stretch we concentrate on here.

Up the Scorff

The trip along the Scorff is of especial interest for its exceptional Breton chapels clustered around Le Faouët, with more varied attractions on offer around Pont-Scorff.

Around Pont-Scorff

Ignore the main road up from Lorient into northwestern Morbihan; instead, take more rural routes up the Scorff Valley, sticking quite close to the river. A Grande Randonnée hiking path keeps to the river along a particularly beautiful stretch here.

Pont-Scorff has a thriving artistic community that welcomes visitors, and offers a circuit tour of artisans' studios (ask at the tourist office) to see them at work on a range of materials, centring on the **Cour des Métiers d'Art**, 8 Rue de Prince Polignac.

L'Atelier d'Estienne on Rue Terrien puts on interesting contemporary art shows in summer, while the **zoo** to the south of town appeals to large numbers. The **Odyssaum** is another *espace découverte*, an eco-museum exploring the lifecycle of the River Scorff's wild salmon. The exhibition, which follows their surprising odyssey, is beautifully located in a renovated mill, the Moulin des Princes. The presentation is lively. Cycling enthusiasts might head north for the the **Musée du Vélo** at the Domaine de Manehouarn at **Plouay**.

Kernascléden

Go happily to hell by visiting the village of **Kernascléden** north of Plouay. Colourless on the outside, its **chapel** contains a splendid array of 15th-century frescoes. This is one of many Morbihan religious buildings constructed thanks to the wealth of the mighty Rohan family. It went up between 1420 and 1464, and the style is typical Breton Flamboyant Gothic.

You'll find hell in the southern transept; it looks like a diabolical funfair in full swing. It's all very grizzly, but the cartoon-like scenes

Cour des Métiers d'Art
t 02 97 32 55 74, courmetiersd'art@ orange.fr; open July and Aug Tues–Sat 10–12 and 2.30–6.30, Sun 2.30–6.30; Sept–June Wed 2–6, Thurs–Sat 10–12 and 2–6, Sun 3–6

L'Atelier d'Estienne
www.atelier.estienne. free.fr, t 02 97 32 42 13; open July–Aug Tues–Sun 2.30–6.30, second half June and first half Sept weekend pm only; free

Zoo de Pont-Scorff
t 02 97 32 60 86; open summer 9.30–7, winter 9.30–5

Odyssaum
t 02 97 32 42 00, www.odyssaum.fr; open July–Aug daily 10–7; May–June and Sept Tues–Fri 9.30–12.30 and 2–6, Sat–Mon 2–6; Feb, Easter and All Saints hols Mon–Fri 9.30–12.30 and 2–6, Sat–Sun 2–6

Musée du Vélo
t 02 97 33 15 15; open mid-June–mid-Sept Tues–Sun 2–6, plus weekend afternoons rest of June and Sept

10 Morbihan | Up the Scorff and Blavet: Up the Scorff

are hard to take seriously nowadays. Memorable depictions include the damned, impaled on sharp branches, being plucked by devils to be cooked in great cauldrons – it makes you think a bit what it must be like to be a battery-farmed chicken.

More elevating scenes have been painted on the choir. Immediately above the arches you can make out the events of Christ's Passion. The finer art fans out above, in between the ribs of the Gothic vaulting, the refined scenes here illustrating the life of the Virgin and the baby Jesus. Large painted figures of angels with peacock-like wings make music in the north transept. With their tambourines and viols, they are apparently singing an Agnus and a Sanctus, as musicologists have apparently worked out. This is sophisticated art for a Breton chapel, possibly done by an artist from outside the region.

Kernascléden has another, new sight to scare those of a sensitive disposition, the small **Maison de la Chauve-Souris**, dedicated to bats. You may learn to love the furry creatures by learning more about them here, as the place is run with passion. Children are encouraged to take an interest through special activities.

Maison de la Chauve-Souris
www.maisondela chauvesouris.com, t 02 97 28 26 31; open July–Aug Tues–Sun 10–12 and 1.30–6.30, April–June and Sept–Oct Wed–Sun 2–5.30

Le Faouët and Around

Before Le Faouët, stop at the **church of St-Fiacre**, a fine example of awkward yet appealing Breton architecture. The interiors were commissioned for the Boutteville family, who appear to have wanted to rival the work ordered by the Rohans at Kernascléden. Inside, you'll be attracted like a child to the colours of the *jubé*, or rood screen. Its carver, Olivier Le Loergan, composed a fantastic multicoloured piece of art, the wood seeming almost as light as lace. However, Christ's placid crucifixion and Mary's suffering call for reflection. The original stained glass, made in the mid-16th century, shows Christ watched over by guards in period armour. Fiacre, patron saint of gardeners, also features.

The great sloping roofs of the **covered market** dominate the large central square of **Le Faouët**, indicating that the town, now a drowsy place, once held important fairs. A former Ursuline convent off one corner of the square has been converted into the **fine arts museum**. The interiors don't have the charm of the country chapels nearby, but have been redone to show a quite charming little permanent collection of works by the artists who formed something of a colony here in the early 20th century, drawn by the picturesque scenes they found. It comes as no surprise that lots of the works represent the local chapels. Each year the museum also puts on a substantial temporary exhibition.

Musée du Faouët
t 02 97 23 15 27, www.museedu faouet.fr; open Easter and mid-June–Sept daily 10–12 and 2–6

The **chapel of Ste-Barbe** just north of Le Faouët was one of these artists' favourite spots, and from the hilltop above it, you can still look out onto an unspoilt section of inland Brittany. The place was used as a location for the film *Marion du Faouët*, which retold the story of a local 18th-century highwaywoman who imposed her own sense of justice on the area, robbing the rich to feed the poor.

The chapel was built from 1483, in Flamboyant Gothic style. The story goes that Jean de Toulbodou was out hunting when lightning struck the rocks above him, causing large blocks to tumble down around him. He escaped unscathed – miraculously he felt, and therefore vowing to erect a chapel on the very spot where his life had been so generously saved. Tall twin Gothic accoladed doorways make for a noble entrance. Among the statues, one represents Ste Barbe, patron saint of firemen. The most beautiful feature inside is the French Renaissance stained-glass windows from around 1520, showing not just scenes of Ste Barbe's life, but also the story of the lucky local lord.

East at **Priziac**, explore typical inland Breton countryside at the Parc Aquanature Le Stérou, where you can go walking, fishing or on a horse and carriage ride, as well as appreciating the large herd of deer reared here.

Parc Aquanature Le Stérou
t 02 97 34 63 84,
contact@parc-aquanature.com; open April–Oct daily 11–7

To Gourin and Guémené-sur-Scorff

North of Le Faouët, the rather forgotten town of **Gourin** claims the title of capital of the Montagnes Noires, a chain of central Breton hills rather than mountains (*see* p.309), on whose southern slopes it lies. The place also boasts of being the crêpe capital of Brittany. It hosts the **Fête de la Crêpe** on the third weekend in July, in the grounds of the **Château de Tronjoly** a short walk from the centre. The festival, which includes a crêpe-making competition and traditional Breton dancing and music, promotes the tradition of the hand-made crêpe, despite the fact that Gourin is also the largest industrial producer of crêpes in Brittany. Regular art exhibitions by contemporary (often local) artists are also held in the outbuildings of the château.

Some way east, **Guémené-sur-Scorff**'s culinary reputation rests on a speciality that's rather harder for most Anglo-Saxons to stomach...of *andouille*, salted pigs' intestines stuffed in concentric circles into a casing of cow's stomach. *Andouille* is considered a delicacy in Brittany, although in the French language, the term is used as an endearing insult to another person's intelligence. Along the town's pleasant, sloping main street, butchers fight it out as to who produces the best specialist sausage. The vestiges of the mighty Rohans' **castle** (free to visit) here have been receiving attention recently. Some of the ramparts have been restored, and the medieval bathroom known as the **Bains de la Reine** has been brought partially back to life – it's really like a sumptuous sauna, with carvings around the wall, including of the well-connected lady and her husband for whom these very modern features for the time were put in.

From Lorient up the Blavet

⭐ The Blavet
Valley

Now we concentrate on the utterly enchanting stretch of the Blavet River between Hennebont, just north of Lorient, and Pontivy, a market town deep in the centre of Brittany. Along this stretch, you can go in search of a clutch of sights that have been exceptionally well done up in the last few years.

Hennebont

Hennebont is the most northerly of four semi-detached towns strung along the Rade de Lorient. Southwest of it, Lanester, Lorient and Ploemeur stretch out in a fairly unbroken urban chain. Hennebont, though not the most obvious of tourist stops, boasts some fine features, including sections of its old ramparts that are still standing. Two impressive towers along these walls house the interesting local history museum, the **Musée des Tours Broërec'h**. A traditional Breton **church** towers over the town centre and draws you ineluctably inside with its gaping entrance. Thursday is Hennebont's market day, a big event in the western Morbihan. The Hennebont tourist office organizes day trips in summer from the **river port**, down the Blavet estuary, and out to and around the island of Groix. Or hire a canoe from the club here.

The **Haras National d'Hennebont** a short way outside the historic heart of town is a big pull for horse-lovers. It stands in formal grounds that once belonged to a Cistercian nunnery. The château-like main building has a ground floor partly occupied by stabling, where you can admire many traditional sturdy Breton horses, as well as a collection of rather lighter-looking carriages. The tour includes a visit to the farrier's, the saddlery and the massive feed room. The latter has been converted into another of the *espaces découvertes* in the Lorient area, presenting a sizeable exhibition on the history of the Breton horse and horse-breeding as an industry. Temporary art exhibitions are also hosted here.

Ironworks used to cover some two and a half kilometres along the Blavet river bank north of Hennebont, at **Inzinzac-Lochrist**. Several large industrial buildings have been left standing. At the **Ecomusée des Forges and Musée des Métallurgistes** you can learn, through remarkably well-displayed panels, plans and tools, how these ironworks developed. Hire bikes to go exploring more of the Blavet Valley from **Blavet Cyclo**, or there's a good canoe club here.

Another *espace découverte* has been set up in **Brandérion**, east of Hennebont. **La Tisserie** offers a small, meticulously presented tour of Brittany's weaving history, but it also puts the craft in its wider, global context. There are temporary exhibitions in the summer months and off-season classes on how to weave on an ancient loom.

Musée des Tours Broërec'h
t 02 97 36 29 18; open June–Sept daily 10.30–12.30 and 1.30–6.30

Haras National d'Hennebont
www.haras-hennebont.fr; open Feb, Easter and All Saints hols Mon–Fri 9.30–12.30 and 2–6, Sat and Sun 2–6; May, June and Sept Tues–Fri 9.30–12.30 and 2–6, Sat–Mon 2–6; July–Aug daily 10–7

Ecomusée des Forges and Musée des Métallurgistes
t 02 97 36 98 21, ecomusee.lochrist@wanadoo.fr; open June Sat 2–6; July–Aug Mon–Fri 10–6.30, Sat–Sun 2–6.30

Blavet Cyclo
t 02 97 36 98 48

La Tisserie
www.la-tisserie.fr, t 02 97 32 90 27; open Feb, Easter and All Saints hols Mon–Fri 9.30–12.30 and 2–6, Sat–Sun 2–6; July–Aug daily 10–7; May, June and Sept Sun 2–6

Up the Blavet to Pontivy

North up the Blavet stands the absurdly picturesque thatched hamlet of **Poul-Fetan**. However, Poul-Fetan isn't absolutely perfect – you have to pay to get into it, for starters, and it isn't always open. The place had been virtually abandoned when the local authorities decided to buy it in 1977, to turn it into a showpiece village for the benefit of tourists and the local community. The restoration work is too immaculate for some tastes. The dozen houses, mainly dating from the 16th century, are regularly re-thatched, with exquisite blue irises left to grow along their crests. Enthusiasts dressed in Breton period costume bring life to proceedings on many weekends of the year, providing displays of old-fashioned spinning, millet-making and butter-churning, among other activities.

To discover a rival to Poul-Fétan in beauty, but a genuine village which makes slightly less of a song and dance about things, head west for enchanting **Lanvaudan**, with a superb collection of cottages set around its traditional Breton church.

The curious-sounding main reason for visiting **Baud** is to study old Breton postcards at the **Cartopole or Conservatoire Régional de la Carte Postale**. Even curiouser, the collection is housed in the town's former public baths. However, the modern exhibition space here has been extremely well conceived. Looking through the enormous number of postcards helps to create a surprisingly rich and diverse picture of the development of Brittany and Breton culture over the past century or so. There are hundreds of postcards you can view on CD-ROM, allowing you to magnify images of old Breton festivals and weddings, or of the ports in the times when fishing boats still had sails.

Baud is also known for the peculiar **Vénus de Quinipily** statue, to be found just to the south, by the Evel, a tributary of the Blavet. This naked Breton colossus, reaching more than two metres in height, may date back to Gallo-Roman times. Gustave Flaubert, on his 19th-century tour of Brittany, wrote of the statue having a 'a sensuality both barbarous and refined'.

Head on to the western side of the river to visit **Melrand's Village de l'An Mil**, next to the well-hidden **ruins of Lann Gouh Verlan** (same hours), or old Melrand. At the beginning of the 20th century, it was thought that the low moss- and grass-covered humps which form the remaining vestiges of the village's walls dated back to the Gallo–Roman period. It's now known that these are in fact the remains of an early medieval settlement from around AD 1000.

Several copies of early medieval houses have been constructed nearby. They share an extremely heavy thatched look, the shaggy roofs almost reaching to the ground making them comically reminiscent of Dougall the Dog from *The Magic Roundabout*. You should find a fire warming the interior of one of the houses even in

---

Poul-Fetan
t 02 97 39 51 74, www.poul-fetan.com; open Nov–Jan 10–12 and 2–5, Oct and Feb–Mar 10–12 and 2–6, April–Sept 10–7

Cartopole or Conservatoire Régional de la Carte Postale
www.cartolis.org, open mid-June–mid-Sept 10–12.30 and 2–6 (July–Aug 'til 7), mid-Sept–All Saints and Easter–mid-June Wed, Thurs, Sat and Sun 2–5.30

Melrand's Village de l'An Mil
t 02 97 39 57 89; open Mon–Fri 11–5, Sat and Sun 11–6

summer, as fire not only provided warmth, but also light, cooking facilities and fumigation to keep the insects away. It was the norm for animals to share the living quarters with families.

East of Melrand, back by the Blavet, head on via the beautiful hilltop **Site de Castennec**, caught in a tight meander of the river. Just west, **St-Gildas's chapel**, at the foot of a large rock overlooking the valley, is where the important early Celtic Christian, St Gildas, founder of a major abbey named after him down the Morbihan coast (*see* box, p.442), is said to have died as a hermit in 570.

The **church of St-Nicodème** lies on the other side of the river, east of the hillside village of St-Nicolas-des-Eaux. Approaching it through the surrounding fields, all you can make out of it is the top of its ornate steeple, rising sharply out of the rolling countryside. The church turns out to be of impressive size for such a remote little community. It was built in Flamboyant Gothic style in 1537. Within, a large sculpted Resurrection greets you, only Christ appears to have disappeared from the scene. Further carved wooden figures attract your attention around the church, including angels and musicians along the string-pieces. An elaborate fountain stands outside. St-Nicodème marks the southern starting point of a circuit of historic churches in central Morbihan given over to contemporary art installations through the summer, **Art dans les Chapelles**.

Art dans les Chapelles
www.artchapelles. com, t 02 97 51 97 21; chapels open early July–mid-Sept daily exc Tues 2.30–7; free

An even more startlingly substantial church towers over the lovely granite village of **Quelven**, west of the Blavet. **Notre-Dame de Quelven** is a huge Gothic building that would appear more suitable in size for a large town. The edifice went up at the end of the 15th century. An amazing thin pencil of a Gothic tower was stuck on to the main one. Big dragon gargoyles, carved dogs and semi-human creatures cling to the outside of the building. The curvaceously roofed outdoor pulpit with its double staircase was added in 1738.

The statuary within this church is wonderful. At the back of the nave, a large-scale scene shows a Little Red Riding Hood of a Virgin looking on as an emaciated St George on his thin white horse clinically lances the dragon. In another extraordinary scene, a muzzled wolf accompanies a holy man – this is the traditional representation of the Breton St Hervé (*see* p.41). The most famous statue of the whole collection, though, is the cross-eyed Virgin of Quelven.

All of a sudden, at the start of the 19th century, **Pontivy** had a substantial, straight-lined Napoleonic town tacked on to the traditional winding-laned medieval one. Pontivy was in fact briefly rebaptized **Napoléonville** when Bonaparte's government decided to exploit it's central position in Brittany, and in particular its waterways, in order to build a new administrative town here. The

Ste Noyale Arrives on Tree Leaves

Noyale, otherwise known as Nolwenn, was carried across the Channel to Brittany on tree leaves, so the legend poetically has it. Of royal lineage, she had given away all her material possessions to the poor and decided to cross the waters in search of a hermitage. She arrived in Armorica in the 6th century, accompanied by her former wet-nurse. Captured by a tyrant of a chieftain, named Nizall, she refused to submit to his carnal desires; in retaliation he had her decapitated. Unperturbed, she headed off, her head in her hand. She found a rock on which to pray, and where she planted her baton an ash tree rose up. Noyale then shed three drops of blood that turned into a fountain before wandering into the wilderness to finally die.

grandiose 19th-century new town is interesting to visit, if a little pompous in character.

As to the streets of the **old town**, they meander in gentle fashion down towards the Blavet from the castle and the adjacent former religious quarter; this part of town includes the long, thin **Place Leperdit**, which is home to a nice mix of old houses. Rue du Fil, a narrow, curving old shopping street with some beamed houses, takes you down to **Place du Martray**, the old heart of town, although it was somewhat cruelly cut through by Rue Nile, a long, straight shopping street, one of the main arteries of the Napoleonic new town.

Château de Pontivy
www.casteland.com,
t 02 97 25 04 10; open
July and Aug daily
10.30–7, Sept–June
Wed–Sun 10–12
and 2–6

The **Château de Pontivy** has two of the fattest, squattest towers you're ever likely to see on a French castle. It was one of a string of defences belonging to the mighty Rohan family. In fact, from 1396, Pontivy served as the capital of the Rohans' viscounty. Several châteaux have succeeded each other here; the stocky outer forms that you see now were built between 1479 and 1485. In summer, temporary exhibitions are held inside.

The area **around Pontivy** is rich in modest chapels and churches, several used as settings for contemporary art installations in the summer programme of **Art dans les Chapelles** (see above for practical details), the circuit well indicated.

The **Chapelle Ste-Noyale**, northeast of Pontivy, is exceptional. It may lie close to a wide, dull plain scarcely embellished by vast grain silos; but the mass of wall paintings in this chapel, which tell the terrible legend of Ste Noyale (see box, above) – twice – transport you to different times. Looking up to the painted ceiling, beware of suffering a cricked neck trying to decipher the panoply of martyred female saints represented there. Luckily, in high season, a guide can provide some enlightenment as to who they all are, and their dreadful sufferings.

ⓘ **Pays du Roi Morvan**
www.paysroimorvan.
com, for general
information on the area

Market Days up the Scorff and Blavet
Le Faouët: 1st and 3rd Wednesdays of the month
Gourin: Monday

Guémené-sur-Scorff: Thursday
Hennebont: Thursday
Baud: Saturday
Pontivy: Monday

ⓘ **Le Faouët** >
*3 Rue des Cendres,
t 02 97 23 23 23,
officedetourisme.le
faouet@wanadoo.fr*

⭐ **Le Ty Mat B&B,
Penquesten** >>

⭐ **Les
Chaumières de
Lézorgu B&B** >>

ⓘ **Gourin**
*24 Rue de
la Libération,
t 02 97 23 66 33,
si.gourin@wanadoo.fr*

⭐ **Le Roseau
Rando Plume** >>

ⓘ **Guémené-
sur-Scorff** >
*1 Rue Haha, t 02 97 39
33 47, ot.guemene@
wanadoo.fr*

ⓘ **Pont-Scorff**
*Rue de L'Orient,
t 02 97 32 50 27,
www.pont-scorff.com*

ⓘ **Hennebont** >
*9 Place du Maréchal
Foch, t 02 97 36 24 52,
www.hennebont.fr*

⭐ **Château de
Locguénolé** >

ⓘ **Baud** >>
*Place Mathurin
Martin, t 02 97 51 02 29*

Where to Stay and Eat up the Scorff and Blavet

Le Faouët ✉ 56320

**La Croix d'Or, 9 Place Bellanger, t 06 88 46 70 50, *www.lacroixdor.com* (€€). Once frequented by artists, this little hotel overlooking the main square has been completely renovated.

Crêperie La Sarrasine, 1 Rue du Château, t 02 97 23 06 05, *creperie.la. sarrasine@wanadoo.fr* (€). A pretty, rustic setting for excellent-value crêpes. *Closed Mon in low season.*

Auberge de Kérizac, (towards Le Scaër), t 02 97 34 44 57, *auberge kerizac@wanadoo.fr* (€€). Excellent hearty food served in a gorgeous country setting, in a lovely converted barn. Rooms sometimes available.

Roudouallec ✉ 56110

Le Bienvenue, 84 Rue Nicolas Le Grand, t 02 97 34 50 01 (€€). In a village up in the Montagnes Noires, a restaurant serving fine local produce.

Guémené-sur-Scorff ✉ 56160

**Le Clos des Princes, 18 Rue J Pérès, t 02 97 51 20 08, *www.closdesprinces. com* (€). A modernized traditional hotel, with wide range of rooms and fine restaurant. *Closed Sat lunch, Sun eve and Mon.*

Crêperie des Rohan, 24 Rue Bisson, t 02 97 39 35 14 (€). A bright, clean place on the main street, popular with locals.

Hennebont ✉ 56700

****Château de Locguénolé, Route de Port-Louis, Kervignac, a few km south of Hennebont, t 02 97 76 76 76, *www.chateau-de-locguenole.com* (€€€€€–€€€). Luxurious property in large grounds sloping down to the Blavet. Rooms are divided between the château and adjacent manor. There's a highly reputed restaurant (€€€€; *closed Mon*) too. Tennis court and heated pool.

L'Orchis, 25bis Quai du Port-Louis, t 02 97 36 19 19 (€€). Good-value traditional regional food in a modern setting with river views. *Closed Sat lunch, Sun eve and Mon.*

Le Jardin des Sens, Place du Calvaire, 1 Ave Ambroise Croisat, t 02 97 36 21 44 (€). Simple, renovated rooms in the centre. The restaurant's [*closed Sun eve and Mon*] elaborate cooking is highly regarded.

Inzinzac-Lochrist ✉ 56650

Le Ty Mat B&B, Penquesten, t 02 97 36 89 26, *pro.wanadoo.fr/ty-mat* (€). A lovely little manor with large rooms on the edge of woods.

Languidic ✉ 56440

Les Chaumières de Lézorgu B&B, t 02 97 65 81 04, *www. leschaumieres-morbihan.com* (€€–€). Enchanting 17th-century thatched home by the Blavet, offering good rooms.

L'Escale du Blavet Rando Plume, Keryvallan, t 02 97 65 28 74, *www. escaledublavet.com*. Good rooms in a restored old farm, with pool. Meals available.

Lanvaudan ✉ 56240

Le Roseau Rando Plume, Place de l'Eglise, t 02 97 33 33 04, *www.le- roseau.com* (€). Hikers' stop offering B&B rooms in enchanting cottage in this beautiful village, with Breton specialities to eat.

Quistinic ✉ 56310

Tavarn Poul-Fetan, Poul-Fetan, t 02 97 39 79 73 (€). In a gorgeous setting in this extraordinary hamlet, lovely spot for Breton specialities. *Open April–Sept daily 11–7, then weekends and school hols exc Christmas–Feb.*

Crêperie Au Coin Tranquille, St Trugdual, t 02 97 39 70 76 (€). A typical Breton crêperie in a quiet spot. *Closed Mon–Fri outside school hols.*

Baud ✉ 56150

**Auberge du Cheval Blanc, 16 Rue de Pontivy, t 02 97 51 00 85, *www.hotelduchevalblanc56.fr* (€). An old-fashioned, central posting-inn hotel with a good restaurant.

Melrand ✉ 56310

La Tourelle, Place de l'Eglise, t 02 97 39 51 13 (€€). A very simple hotel with restaurant in a pleasant old village house.

⭐ Poterie de Lezerhy B&B >

⭐ Ty Bihui Rando Plume >

ⓘ Pays d'Accueil de la Vallée du Blavet

Zone Artisanale Kermestre, 56150 Baud, t 02 97 51 09 37, www. blavet.com, for general information on the Blavet Valley

ⓘ Pays touristique de Pontivy

31 Rue Jean Moulin, 56303 Pontivy, t 02 97 25 01 70, www.pays-pontivy.com

ⓘ Pontivy >

61 Rue du Général de Gaulle, t 02 97 25 04 10, tourisme@pontiv communaute.com

Bubry ✉ 56310

Poterie de Lezerhy B&B, **t** 02 97 27 74 59, *www.charme-traditions.com* (€). Rooms in a darling thatched cottage, run by a potter.

Le Jardin, at St-Yves-Bubry, **t** 02 97 51 77 63, *www.lejardin-bubry.com* (€). Nice rooms in a most elegant 17th-century stone house.

Bieuzy-les-Eaux ✉ 56310

Ty Bihui Rando Plume, Rue du Presbytère, **t** 02 97 28 81 60, *www. cap.blavet.free.fr* (€). Magnificent hikers' stop in former priest's house, offering B&B accommodation for a bargain.

Quelven ✉ 56310

Auberge de Quelven, **t 02 97 27 77 50 (€€). Very appealing address; it has comfy rooms with views over the church green in this quiet village.

Aux Anges, **t** 02 97 27 75 92 (€). A sweet café de pays opposite the church, which puts on a regular programme of mainly Celtic music.

Pontivy ✉ 56300

***Le Rohan, 90 Rue Nationale, **t** 02 97 25 02 01, *www.hotelpontivy.com* (€€€–€). A fine building in Napoleonic style, converted into a charming hotel with good prices for its rooms.

***de l'Europe, 12 Rue François Mitterrand, **t** 02 97 25 11 14,

www.hotellerieurope.com (€€€–€€). Ostentatious, old-fashioned 19th-century looks, with some large rooms with period feel. With restaurant.

Aux Berges du Blavet, 9 Place Ruynet du Tailly, **t** 02 97 25 51 11, *www. auxbergesdublavet.com* (€). Clean, neat rooms and classic cooking. €35

La Pommeraie, 17 Quai du Couvent, **t** 02 97 25 60 09 (€€€). A restaurant run by a young couple, offering unusual cuisine near the old town. *Closed Sun and Mon.*

Le Martray, Rue du Pont, **t** 02 97 25 68 64 (€€). Good-quality traditional cuisine in the centre. *Closed Tues and Wed.*

Ploërmel ✉ 56800

***Le Roi Arthur, Le Lac au Duc, **t** 02 97 73 64 64, *www.hotelroiarthur.com*. Smart, modern golfers' hotel, with fine indoor pool and well-being treatments; the 9-hole course is beside the Lac au Duc.

Château de St-Malo B&B, **t** 02 97 73 58 20, *www.chateau-saint-malo.com* (€€). Smart rooms in a manor in grounds 1km from the town centre leading to views of the Lac au Duc.

Le Thy 19, Rue de la Gare, **t 02 97 74 05 21, *www.le-thy.com* (€). Enjoyably decorated bedrooms, each embodying the style of an artist, from Klimt to Van Gogh. Also enjoy the bohemian 'cabaret' and café.

The Etel Estuary and Quiberon Peninsula

Dividing the Lorient military area to the west from the major neolithic sights and holiday resorts to the east, the Etel estuary is the least known of the Morbihan's series of enormous river mouths. It is extraordinarily beautiful in parts, often tranquil, with few modern additions.

Below the Etel estuary, a precariously narrow strip of land is all that connects the Quiberon Peninsula to the mainland. Only as far back as the 11th century, the land mass of Quiberon was an island, but intensive deforestation caused the movement of large quantities of sand, which formed the spit of land known as a *tombolo* joining the island to the mainland. Who knows how long it might be before the peninsula reverts to being an island once again...

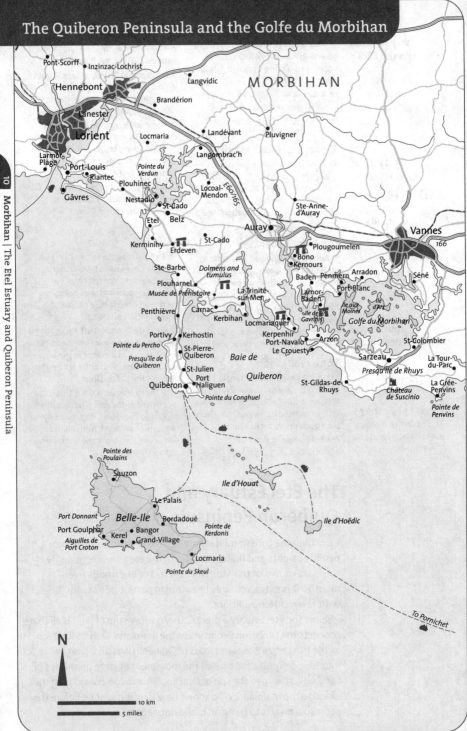

Getting around the Etel Estuary and the Quiberon Peninsula

Auray can be reached by **TGV** rapid train from Paris in just over 3hrs. In summer, the regional railway service from Auray down to Quiberon comes to life; this line serves Plouharnel, Les Sables Blancs, Penthièvre, L'Isthme, Kerhostin and St-Pierre-Quiberon (tickets from the tourist office: runs July–Aug daily, June and Sept weekends). There's also a good bus service along the Quiberon Peninsula – see Quiberon's tourist office website.

As it is, such is the weight of traffic trying to get up and down this spit in holiday time, it can feel as difficult as crossing a clogged-up bridge onto an overpopular island. Many of the cars are bound for the ferry to Belle-Ile, Brittany's biggest, chicest island. Quiberon, the resort, is renowned for being the place where thalassotherapy (sea-water treatments) was first begun in France. The two sides of the Quiberon Peninsula contrast markedly, one wild, the other tranquil. We don't forget the Battle of Quiberon Bay, the clash in which the English navy wiped out the French...

The Etel Estuary and Erdeven's Beaches

You could start out by going to take a look at the mouth of the Etel with its sand bar just out to sea, then head for the unspoilt Plouhinec side. A strikingly beautiful, **wild beach** runs westwards from the headland here, the sand deeply golden, with curious red lifeguards' ladders growing out of it. This beach still forms part of the long military shooting ground that goes as far as Gâvres to the west. Signs announcing *Servitude militaire* remind you of the fact, but this area is actually open to the public.

Heading up the western side of the Etel estuary, the skeletons of two large boats lie decaying opposite the workaday port of Etel town, symbols of the estuary's loss of its traditional trade. Seek out a narrow winding track to the secretive **Port du Vieux Passage**. Then turn off for **Nestadio**, the beautiful road taking you to a deadend with a little whitewashed chapel. Opposite Nestadio, the beautiful village of St-Cado looks very close across the water, but proves far to reach by car.

The north end of the Etel estuary has some charming **chapels**, notably those of **Kergoh**, **Locmaria** and **Legevin**. Descending the eastern side of the estuary, take a quick look at the village of **Langonbrac'h**, then cross the N165 for the Jardin du Château de Kerambar'h towards Landaul, with a whole range of gardens inspired by different periods.

Jardin du Château de Kerambar'h
open April–Nov 11–6

Back at the Etel water's edge, the **Pointe du Verdon** reaches deep into the centre of the ria, views opening out onto a confusion of further spits of land. On the way to the point, keep your eyes peeled for the Kegil Berhed or **Quenouille de Brigitte**, a neolithic

St Cado Has a Cat Killed for His Causeway

Cado is a Breton saint of the Dark Ages thought to have come across from Glamorgan in Wales to convert the local people. A familiar tale goes that once he had chosen the site where he was going to settle, he first had to chase the snakes from the land. He then began building his island monastery, but realized that he didn't have the funds he needed to make the causeway he wanted to attach the island to the mainland. Satan came and offered to construct it for him in exchange for the first life that crossed it. Clearly considering an animal's life much less valuable than a man's, Cado managed to get a black cat to go over first, thus sparing any human life.

In later times, St Cado became associated with miraculous cures for the deaf, and visitors would come to the saint's stone 'bed' in the church and put their bad ear to the hole in it – their ear was pronounced better when they could hear the waters lapping below the church.

menhir that, in the christianizing tale, turned into Ste Brigitte's spinning distaff. Follow the long branch of water to **Locoal-Mendon**, from where you can explore the beautiful scorpion's tail of land to the west.

Continue south for Belz and look for signs to the historic village of **St-Cado**. A scattering of tiny islands marks the estuary here. One, connected to the village by an old stone bridge, will draw you to it with its extraordinary huddle of houses. This is old St-Cado, and you're not allowed to take cars across. The main point of interest on this island is the old church, with its Romanesque elements.

The working port of **Etel** to the south has known better days, but the town has developed a small **marina** despite the annoying obstacle of the estuary's sand bar, which makes coming in and out awkward.

Erdeven, with its neolithic alignments of Kerzehro, is reserved for the section on mega megaliths (*see* p.414). But to the south of it, wide stretches of low dunes separate the old villages from the sea. The bulky, stern farms of the area did once live off the sandy lands, as the many old stone walls still separating former plots indicate.

The most westerly beach along this stretch, located close to the Barre d'Etel, is that of **Kerminihy**, a golden stretch favoured by nudists, while **La Roche Seiche beach** follows to the east, two lovely rocky islands a little way out to sea adding great charm to the seascapes.

Although the village of **Kerhillio** has come out in a rash of modern developments, the **beach** lies well away from the buildings, and its beautifully curving bay looks out on to two lighthouses. The sea can get wild along here, attracting windsurfers and even surfers.

The Quiberon Peninsula

The very narrow spit of land connecting the Quiberon Peninsula to the mainland starts just below Plouharnel. A curious little

Musée de la Chouannerie
www.musee-vendee-chouannerie.com, t 02 97 52 31 31; open April–Sept daily 10–12 and 2–6

museum, the inward-looking **Musée de la Chouannerie**, has taken over a Second World War Nazi bunker along here. This museum commemorates an anti-Revolutionary uprising in these parts (*see* **History**, p.31). Copies of portraits of the anti-Revolutionary leaders, models, weapons and short texts explain the importance of the Chouannerie in Brittany, particularly in this area.

Heading south down the **sandy spit**, turn left to reach the flat **beaches** by the bay, which are colonized here by campers. On this side, the sea withdraws a long way at low tide. The first couple of turnings on the right take you to what might be called specialist beaches, where the rough waters beyond the lovely sands attract surfers in large numbers, and the extensive dunes behind, littered with abandoned German fortifications, gay nudists in droves. Following the beaches south, at low tide the sand-yachts come out on the **Plage de Penthièvre** to make the most of its wider stretches of sand.

At the **Fort de Penthièvre**, an 18th-century coastal defence still owned by the French military, a big road-side panel reminds passers-by that some 60 Resistance fighters were executed here in the Second World War. They were also tortured before they died. An earlier massacre took place here during the Revolution, when troops of the feared Republican general, Hoche, regained the fort from the anti-Revolutionary Chouans who had occupied it, and wrought their revenge.

Past the cute village of **Kerhostin**, look out for the turning to Portivy and the **Côte Sauvage**. The name of **Portivy** conveys well the diminutive size of this port, protected from the worst of the waves by its northerly position on the peninsula, and by a small sea wall defending its boats. The village huddles cosily around the harbour, while the pretty **Chapelle Notre-Dame de Lotivy** is one of the few interesting religious buildings on the peninsula, although like all the churches on the Quiberon Peninsula, it was pillaged by British soldiers in the 18th-century colonial wars which scarred this stretch of coast. On Tuesday afternoons in April, May, June and Sept, you can embark on a **boat journey** along the Côte Sauvage (see Quiberon tourist website) from the port.

Once you turn the **Pointe du Percho**, the Côte Sauvage rocks start in earnest. Belle-Ile comes increasingly clearly into focus as you head down the coast road, which is lined by quite barren land, the grasses mown by the salt winds. You can spot the odd menhir along this wild side of the peninsula. Car parks near **Port du Rhu** and **Port Bara** give good opportunities to view dramatic stretches of the Côte Sauvage, but note that the waters here are only for experienced surfers. The most spectacular views are to be had from the **Beg er Goalennec headland**, nearing the town of Quiberon.

On the western point of town, **Beg er Lann**, the turreted mansion also known as the Château Turpeau, or even the Château de la Mer, stands out as a symbol of the era when very grand tourists used to swan in to the resort of **Quiberon** at the start of the 20th century to enjoy the sea air, the seawater, and the views on to Belle-Ile. Today, Quiberon may not be the most beautiful Breton seaside town, nor one of the most harmonious, but it is very popular, getting extremely crowded.

As well as the very popular ferries to Belle-Ile, you can embark on short afternoon **outings to sea from Port Maria**, either enjoying the natural beauty of the sea cliffs, or joining in a fishing expedition (see Quiberon tourist website). This port once knew the bustle of the largest sardine-fishing fleet in France; it's still a lively fishing harbour, the boats supplying the Criée.

The **Grande Plage**, the main arc of sand on the seafront, turns into one of the busiest family beaches in Brittany in summer, while past the Beg er Vil headland, you come to the **Pointe du Goulvars**, dominated by Quiberon's Centre de Thalassothérapie, with its adjoining hotels. The history of the ground-breaking seawater treatments here is intimately linked with the great Breton cyclist Louison Bobet, who pioneered them. Today, the pamperings available here are highly regarded, and the heated seawater pool benefits from wonderful sea views. More than 50,000 people a year come to Quiberon to follow one of the seawater treatments. However, far more simply use the resort as a staging post for Belle-Ile.

Beyond this area, the **Pointe du Conguel** is the curious southerly headland that throws itself into the water, a favourite place for walks, as this area has been protected by the Conservatoire du Littoral. The ovens along the way once served for burning algae to extract iodine. You can walk out to the **Ile de Toul Bihan** at very low tides. Out to sea stands the **Teignouse lighthouse**.

Quiberon boasts a number of **culinary attractions**. Those with a sweet tooth shouldn't miss the **Pâtisserie Riguidel** at 38 Rue Port Maria, while **La Maison d'Armorine** on 5 Blvd Chanard is well known to French visitors for its speciality, *niniches* (a kind of lollypop), but also produces all manner of Breton biscuits and sweets, with an Espace Visite in the Zone Artisanale Plein Ouest (at appropriately named 1 Rue des Confiseurs) where you can inspect how all their sugary delights are made. While in this quarter, consider visiting the fish-canning factory of La Belle-Iloise, where they continue to prepare their *poissons* the old-fashioned way, the workers wearing traditional blue-and-white-striped Breton shirts as they can sardines, pilchards, tuna and fish paste. Pursuing the culinary theme on this well-established Circuit des Saveurs,

Centre de Thalassothérapie
www.accorthalassa.com, t 02 97 50 20 00 or 02 97 50 48 88

Espace Visite
t 02 97 50 24 25; open Feb–Nov

La Belle-Iloise fish-canning factory
www.labelleiloise.fr, t 02 97 50 08 77; open Mon–Fri 10–11 and 3–4, Sat 10–3; free

La Maison Lucas specializes in high-quality smoked fish, and has both an outlet in the Zone Artisanale, and a restaurant, La Criée, on the quays. Lots of the tourist shops by the waterfront in the town centre sell the usual wide range of Breton specialities; you can also uncover all sorts of **art galleries** around these touristy parts.

The Eastern Side of the Quiberon Peninsula

The protected eastern side of the Quiberon Peninsula seems a great big windbreak apart from the wild western side. The beaches are much more protected and look peacefully across to the coast around Carnac and the Golfe du Morbihan. This is an excellent place for children to learn to sail or windsurf. There isn't a coastal road to follow except the short stretch to Port-Haliguen.

Port-Haliguen has been converted from a fishing port into the peninsula's main **marina**, boasting over 1,000 berths divided between two areas; the old harbour is squeezed between the two, and hosts a weekend art market in summer. Many sailing regattas set out from Port-Haliguen. But this is also a good place to learn to sail, with the help of the sailing club **A. S. N. Quiberon**. For a restful time, enjoy the **Plage du Porigo**.

A. S. N. Quiberon
www.basenautique.
asnq.free.fr, **t** *02 97 30*
56 54

Back during the French Revolution, Port-Haliguen was the site of a terrible battle after the landing here in 1795 of a royalist Catholic army of emigrés, come to take on the Revolutionary forces. The much-feared Republican leader General Hoche, having got wind of the invasion plans, was waiting for them when they arrived. A monument recalls the fateful event and the Republican leader. The persecuted Jewish army officer Alfred Dreyfus also landed here in 1899, returning from his period of imprisonment on Devil's Island off French Guyana. **La Maison du Patrimoine** can fill you in on more local history, and on local shipwrecks.

La Maison du Patrimoine
open mid-June–Sept
daily 2–6

Continuing north from Port-Haliguen, you come to the discreet resort of **St-Pierre-Quiberon**, where finds of Celtic pottery and Gallo–Roman coins show that this delightfully protected harbour has long been appreciated. It's a good spot to try sea-kayaking – contact **Sillages**. There are surf schools based here too, though the action takes place to the west. As to the **Centre Haliotis Plongée**, it organizes both diving and boat outings.

Sillages
www.kayak-
sillages.com,
t *06 81 26 75 08*

Centre Haliotis Plongée
www.haliotisplongee.
com, **m** *06 87 49 25 68*

North still, keen followers of the neolithic might seek out the **Mégalithes de Kerbourgnec**, an alignment with five rows of standing stones, plus a cromlech, but all slightly obscured by the surrounding private houses. To the east, mesmerizing stretches of sand are uncovered at low tide, reaching across the bay to the western side of the resort of Carnac. (*See* box, p.411 for details on the famous Anglo–French naval Battle of Quiberon Bay.)

ⓘ **Erdeven** >>
*7 Rue de l'Abbé Le
Barth, t 02 97 55 64 60,
www.ot-erdeven.fr*

ⓘ **Quiberon** >>
*14 Rue de Verdun,
t 08 25 13 56 00
(premium number),
www.quiberon.com*

ⓘ **Etel** >
*Place des Thoniers,
t 02 97 55 23 80,
www.etel-tourisme.com*

Market Days on the Etel Estuary and Quiberon Peninsula

Etel: Tuesday
Quiberon: Saturday

Where to Stay and Eat on the Etel Estuary and Quiberon Peninsula

Plouhinec ✉ 56680

**de Kerlon, Kerlon, t 02 97 36 77 03, *www.auberge-de-kerlon.com* (€€–€). A friendly, comfortable, simple hotel in a converted farm in the countryside. The owners rear their own fowl and lambs for their country restaurant.

Locoal-Mendon ✉ 56550

L'Arbre Voyageur B&B, Ty er Chir, t 02 97 55 32 71, *www.larbrevoyageur.com* (€€€–€€). Gay-run, with quite stylish rooms in modern-style Breton house. Covered pool. *Table d'hôte.*

Belz ✉ 56410

**Le Relais de Kergou, Route D'Auray (1km out of the village), t 02 97 55 35 61, *www.relais-kergou.com* (€€). A pleasant modern hotel, some rooms with balcony. Reasonable restaurant (€€). Pool.

Les Algues Marines, 8 Place Pen er Pont, t 02 99 55 33 30 (€€). A simple little restaurant where you can feast on fresh seafood.

Etel ✉ 56410

**Le Trianon, 14 Rue du Général Leclerc, t 02 97 55 32 41 (€). Comfortable rooms and a smart restaurant.

Ballanger B&B, L'Escale de la Ria, 9 and 27 Rue Amiral Schewerer, t 02 97 55 48 59, *dom.ballanger@cegetel.net* (€). A B&B in the home of former commander of the liner *France*.

Le Chat qui Pêche, 2 Cours des Quais, t 02 97 55 24 70. A lively, trendy little brasserie at the port which puts on bands.

Le Bistrot à Thon, Ruelle des Quais, t 02 97 55 32 50 (€€). A bar-cum-restaurant with a repertoire of 50 tuna recipes. *Closed lunch, and Sun and Mon out of season.*

Crêperie La Gourmandine, 8 Rue Général Leclerc, t 02 97 55 47 34 (€). A pretty little crêperie.

Erdeven ✉ 56410

**Auberge du Sous Bois, Route du Port-Louis, *www.auberge-erdeven.com*, t 02 97 55 66 10 (€€). Tranquil rooms in a neo-Breton house set in a large park.

St-Pierre-Quiberon ✉ 56510

***La Plage, 25 Quai d'Orange, t 02 97 30 92 10, *www.hotel-la-plage.com* (€€€–€€). Many rooms in this modern hotel have balconies looking onto the bay. *Closed Oct–Easter.*

**St-Pierre, Kéridenvel, 34 Route de Quiberon, t 02 97 50 26 90, *www.hotel-st-pierre.com* (€). Another well-kept hotel.

Hôtel des Deux Mers, 8 Ave Surcouf, t 02 97 52 33 75, *www.hotel-des-deux-mers.com* (€€). In great location right on the Penthièvre beach, with stylishly decorated rooms and fabulous sea views. *Closed mid-Nov–Easter.*

La Ferme Bretonne, 2 Rue du Manoir, t 02 97 30 95 23, *www.laferme bretonne.fr* (€). Crêpes in an old granite house with a walled flower garden. *Closed Mon and Tues out of season.*

Quiberon ✉ 56170

****Sofitel Thalassa, Pointe du Goulvars, t 02 97 50 20 00, *www.accorthalassa.com* (€€€€€–€€€€). A very large, rather uninspiring-looking hotel, but highly regarded for its modern seawater treatments. It lies right by the beach east of the town, and has pool, tennis court, sauna, gym and restaurant (€€€).

***Bellevue, Rue de Tiviec, t 02 97 50 16 28, *www.bellevuequiberon.com* (€€€– €€). A comfortable, modern hotel set back just behind the beach, with lovely pool in its garden. Restaurant. *Closed Oct–March.*

**La Petite Sirène, 15 Blvd René Cassin, t 02 97 50 17 34, *www.hotel-lapetitsirene.fr* (€€). A reasonably priced modern option next to the seawater treatment centre, with great sea views. *Closed mid-Nov–Easter.*

de l'Océan, 7 Quai de l'Océan, **t 02 97 50 07 58 (€€–€). A decently priced family-run option with pretty views on to the fishing harbour. *Closed Nov–Easter.*

La Criée, 11 Quai de l'Océan, **t** 02 97 30 53 09 (€€). One of the best seafood restaurants here, with reasonable prices, home-smoked fish a speciality.

La Chaumine, 36 Place du Manémeur, Manémeur village, **t** 02 97 50 17 67 (€€). Restaurant in a former fisherman's cottage, with good traditional marine cuisine. *Closed Sun eve and Mon, and mid-Nov–mid-March.*

⭐ **Crêperie du Manoir >**

Crêperie du Manoir, 2 Rue du Puits, **t** 02 97 50 13 86 (€). Classy crêpes served in a beautiful 18th-century house with a walled garden.

Port-Haliguen ✉ 56170

***Europa, Blvd de la Teignouse, **t** 02 97 50 25 00, *europa.hotel@wanadoo.fr* (€€€). A hotel with comfortable rooms, dominating a little bay. Inside, it has a covered pool, jacuzzi and a reputable restaurant.

Le Relax, 27 Blvd Castero, **t** 02 97 50 12 84 (€€). Good, simple dishes served in a dining room overlooking the sea. *Closed Mon and Tues out of season.*

Crêperie du Vieux Port, 44 Rue Surcouf, **t** 02 97 50 01 56 (€). Stylish stop.

The Islands of Belle-Ile, Houat and Hoëdic

The well-named Belle-Ile (Beautiful Isle) is the largest island off the Breton coast, and although the mainland remains within view, the Bellilois have traditionally somewhat distanced themselves from the Breton region and Breton culture, proud of their own independence and energy. Unlike the other Breton islands, Belle-Ile isn't so easy to acquaint yourself within a day. Around 20 kilometres long and almost 10 kilometres across in parts, it has a spectacular coastal path, reserved for walkers, and secretive coves. Take time to savour the place.

'Duck' and 'duckling' are the Breton names for these two joyous little islands south of Quiberon, but actually it's seagulls whose strident screams fill the air. In the major tourist season, these islands do suffer a daily summer invasion, but go outside July and August and you shouldn't unduly interrupt the islanders' life. Belle-Ile may be beautiful, but Houat and Hoëdic, reached by ferry from Quiberon, are more magical.

Belle-Ile

At 50, Sarah Bernhardt, that feisty superstar of a *tragedienne* from the late-19th and early-20th centuries, fell so much in love with this island that she bought a disused fort and built a house for her daughter on it. She apparently liked to be carried from boat to shore by sailors – mind you, she did have the excuse of an amputated leg from 1915, although that didn't stop her acting, or travelling. The Musée Sarah Bernhardt, in the villa-fort where the

Getting to and around Belle-Ile, Houat and Hoëdic

The usual way to get to these islands by **boat** is departing from Quiberon, taking about 40mins. The company running year-round services is **Compagnie Océane, t** 08 20 05 61 56 (premium rate), *www.compagnie-oceane.fr*. For other services at certain times of year, and from different ports, also consult: the **Société Morbihannaise de Navigation** at the Gare Maritime in Quiberon, **t** 08 20 05 60 00, *www.smn-navigation.fr*; **La Compagnie des Iles, t** 02 97 31 55 68 operating services from Quiberon to Sauzon mid-April–Sept; and **Navix, t** 08 25 13 21 00, *www.navix.fr*. For more exclusive bateau taxi services, contact **Atmos'Air Marine**, Le Palais, **t** 02 97 31 55 55. In summer, various ferries operate from Vannes, Sauzon, La Turballe and Pornichet.

Certain boats have a limited number of spaces for **cars**; they're expensive and you have to book ages in advance. Many visitors hire **bicycles** or **mopeds** to get around Belle-Ile. Cars Verts and Cars Bleus (opposite the *débarcadère*) run a **bus** tour service round the island.

actress once entertained King Edward VII at one of her famous soirées, has become Belle-Ile's newest attraction.

The Impressionist Claude Monet found inspiration here too, painting scenes of the savage southern shore. By contrast, in the 18th century, a small number of Acadians, French settlers in North America, came less happily, forcibly repatriated here after Britain had removed them from the New World in the colonial wars. Since the age of popular tourism, many Parisians have 'discovered' Belle-Ile. A glamorous crowd still loves the place, even if we haven't seen many of them follow the Bernhardt tradition with the sailors.

History

A couple of neolithic menhirs still stand on the island, nicknamed Jean and Jeanne, while the great 2nd-century Greek cartographer Ptolemy noted the place down, but as Vindilis. No self-respecting Breton island would be complete without a tale of saintly men arriving heroically in the Dark Ages to save it from ungodly wickedness; in this case it was a band of monks from Bangor, hence the name of one of the main villages.

In the course of time, the island would become known by the Latin Bella Insula, changing ownership several times, from the Vikings and the counts of Cornouaille to the duke of Brittany Geoffrey I, who took hold of it at the start of the 11th century. Control over the everyday running of the island, however, then lay in the hands of monks either attached to Quimperlé or Redon for five and more centuries. As naval conflicts broke out across western Europe, Belle-Ile became more strategically important, and more vulnerable; this caused Pope Nicholas V to proclaim in 1454 that all the pirates who were regularly ransacking the vulnerable island would be excommunicated. It's not entirely clear whether such a threat would make your average pirate tremble in his boots.

Fortifications at Le Palais, the island's capital, were constructed in the mid-16th century, but a couple of decades later, in 1572, English troops caused havoc on Belle-Ile for three weeks. In 1674, it was the turn of the Dutch to lay waste to the place, after which the French royal authorities called on the great military architect Sebastien de Vauban to put up some serious defences.

The incessant warring between France and Britain in the 18th century led to Britain again taking over the island in 1761, destroying many of its chapels. The Treaty of Paris in 1763 saw Belle-Ile returned to France in exchange for Minorca! Further pawns in the colonial conflicts, a group of 78 Acadian families from North America were packed off to live on Belle-Ile in 1763, after they had languished for some time in a number of British ports as forgotten prisoners. A few decades before the Revolution, the families of Belle-Ile, including the recent Acadian immigrants, became the proprietors of their island. Since the Second World War, strong ties have been revived between the Belle-Ile Acadians and their New World relatives; the Acadian flag, a French tricolore with a yellow star of Mary, even flies over Le Palais's citadel.

People harp on about Belle-Ile's artistically inspiring 19th-century past, but during that time the island fort served as a prison of note. The list of Belle-Ile's most famous 19th-century detainees reads like a summary of social upheaval against the status quo. The anti-Revolutionary Chouan, Georges Cadoudal, was held here, as was anti-slavery campaigner Toussaint Louverture. Napoleon III's administration decided to fortify the island on a grand scale in the mid 19th century, and many of the Second Empire forts survive in a good state of repair. Even the beaches on the protected, northeastern side of the island (the *dedans* or 'inside', as the locals call this coast facing the Breton mainland) were fortified. For the ordinary population of Belle-Ile, the 19th century was the time when fishing brought increased prosperity.

In the First World War, German prisoners of war were interned on the island, though roles were reversed in the Second World War, when Belle-Ile was heavily occupied by the Nazis. Unfortunately, it became one of the last German-occupied territories to be surrendered to the Allies, in May 1945. Since then, many foreigners have fallen for the charms of the place, many Bellilois heading off to the continent to seek their fortune.

A Tour of Belle-Ile

The island is divided into four parishes, Le Palais, Sauzon, Bangor and Locmaria. Our tour starts at Le Palais, where the boats arrive, then heads northwest to Sarah Bernhardt's beloved Pointe des Poulains beyond Sauzon, before following the Côte Sauvage southeast to the village of Locmaria, on the eastern end of Belle-Ile. Finally, comes the north coast stretching back up to Le Palais, which has some of the best beaches. A remarkable and intensely rewarding voyage of discovery is in store for those who follow the

coastal path right round the island, which can be done in four to six days. Motorcycles and mountain bikes are banned from the coastal path. Many **aquatic pursuits** are on offer around the island, from sailing, sea-kayaking and diving to boat trips – the Belle-Ile tourist website gives up-to-date listings.

Le Palais, capital of the island, is dominated by the star-shaped structures of the **citadel** designed by Sébastien de Vauban. As you approach the town by sea, you get a great view of it. A wealthy couple purchased the property during the 1960s and began its gradual restoration, now completed.

Citadelle du Palais
t 02 97 31 84 17; open daily July–Aug 9–7, April–June and Sept–Oct 9.30–6, Nov–Mar 9.30–12 and 2–5

Fortification upon fortification has in fact succeeded one another on the site of the citadel. Monks were given a castle here in the Middle Ages, then one Duc de Rohan saw to the building of another one. A larger fort then went up slowly before Vauban came towards the end of the 17th century and put his stamp on the place. Thanks to restoration work, the grander sections of the citadel have now been spruced up.

The museum inside covers the history of Belle-Ile from the time of the Ancien Régime in particular. The first room concentrates on the 16th to 18th centuries, the second on the 19th and 20th. There are lots of copies of engravings and portraits, and a rather confusing clutter of objects. The Battle of Quiberon Bay (*see* box, p.411) doesn't go unmentioned here, and homage is paid to some of the most successful 19th-century military men from the island. Most of the **quaysides** of Le Palais lie on the opposite side of the estuary from the citadel.

Sauzon has a good deep river harbour, which gave its inhabitants a natural advantage in fishing. Nowadays, a string of touristy restaurants and cafés occupy the colourful houses along its quays.

The dramatic rocks of the **Pointe des Poulains**, or Foals' Headland, mark the northwest corner of the island. The place might be rechristened Sarah Bernhardt Point, given the fuss made over her stays; introduced to Belle-Ile by her artist friend Clarin, she bought a small old military fort on this site and then a curious brick house known as the Manoir de Penhouët. However, in the Second World War the Nazis destroyed her house, as its red roof risked drawing the attention of the enemy.

Musée Sarah Bernhardt
t 02 97 31 61 29; open April–Sept daily 10.30–5.30

The **fort and Villa des Cinq Parties du Monde** have been brought back to life and turned into the **Musée Sarah Bernhardt**. The great actress may only have discovered this paradisiac corner of the planet at the age of 50, but she fell for it completely and came here every year for the next 30 years. It can't be said she entirely fled the Parisian *beau monde*, as she came with an army of artists, luvvies and personalities in tow. King Edward VII of England counted among her most honoured guests. She gave some thought to the difficulties of the local people, sponsoring a cooperative bakery, and becoming known as the Bonne Dame de Penhouët. To bring this huge personality back to life, the museum has called on Fanny Ardant to record the guided tour. Bernhardt's extraordinary Belle Epoque life is recalled, while some attention is also paid to the natural environment of this grandiose site.

The frightening **Grotte de l'Apothicairerie**, south past the island's ornithological reserve, although signalled on many tourist maps, can no longer be visited as it's considered too dangerous and there is no way anyone could hear your cries of distress if you fell from the slippery sides of this roaring cavern. The rock surfaces above are intriguing enough; their mother of pearl colours and rough texture make you feel like you're walking on a giant oyster shell. Continuing southwards along the main central road down the island, you pass the two menhirs **Jean** and **Jeanne** (to the south of the road), said to be star-crossed lovers turned to stone by displeased druids. The petrified pair are only supposed to be able to meet up again once a year, on New Year's Eve.

Port-Donnant, on the coast below Jean and Jeanne, draws the young of the island in droves to practise their greatest passion, bodyboarding. Port-Donnant isn't a port with houses and quays, but a beach of wide golden sands backed by a big dune, covered with wild roses in season – in Brittany, the word port or *pors* can simply mean a slightly sheltered place where fishermen might once have pulled their boats onto the beach.

Grand Phare
open summer daily
10.30–12 and 2–5.30

The **Grand Phare** is unmissable at 47 metres in height (213 granite steps and one iron ladder). On really clear days you can view vast stretches of the south Breton coast from it. When you visit Carnac you're told with disgust that many of the menhirs of the Petit Menec alignment were transported here to help create firm foundations for this colossus.

Port Coton with its **Aiguilles** (needles) of rock is the site most associated with Claude Monet's work on Belle-Ile. He depicted these dramatic parts subjected to raging, violent, churning storms. You can find beautifully illustrated books of Monet's works around the island, and other art volumes on the diversity of painters who have been inspired by Belle-Ile, including the Australian John Peter Russell. The latter brought many English-speaking artists in his wake.

A luxury hotel complex dominates the deep creek of **Port Goulphar** just southeast of the Aiguilles. The village of **Bangor** lies inland, but the focus is on the beautiful stretch of coast to the south of it. Various rocks lie just out to sea, and after passing **Port Kérel**, which boasts what is claimed to be the warmest beach on Belle-Ile, you can view the Ile de Bangor. Between the **Pointe du Grand Village** and the **Pointe de St-Marc** are little beaches (one for nudists) to stop and rest on, although they're hard to reach. The clifftop walk is sublime; don't miss the exquisitely shaded cove of the **Plage d'Herlin**, again only accessible on foot. The final stretch of coast along this side of the island takes you to its most southerly point, the **Pointe du Skeul**, also known as the Pointe de l'Echelle.

The track then turns up the east coast to Port Blanc and Port Maria. You now find yourself in the eastern parish of **Locmaria**. This village is home to a dazzlingly whitewashed little church that boasts a squat, curving slate steeple. Inside, you will see two *ex votos* of boats hanging from the roof, and a Madonna stretching her gaze up to the sky, said to be the work of a follower of the sentimental Spanish painter Murillo. Locmaria appears to be a quietly charming place, but other island dwellers long suspected the villagers of practising magic.

To the north of Locmaria, the **Pointe de Kerdonis** with its little lighthouse marks the most easterly point of the island; from here you get the best views on to the neighbouring islands of Houat and Hoëdic.

Heading up along the coast that looks to the mainland is the biggest beach on the island, **Les Grands Sables**, a splendid curve of sand, the major 19th-century fortifications built behind it forming a theatrical backdrop. Above lies the pretty hamlet of **Samzun**. A couple of other particularly lovely fortified beaches lie along the coast back up to Le Palais, **Port York** and the **Plage de Bordardoué**, separated from each other by the Pointe du Gros Rocher.

Houat

Houat, pronounced like an astonished Frenchman trying to say 'What?', is an amazing place. The boat trip from Quiberon takes you through cormorant waters and by a string of curious uninhabited rocks before arriving at the port – a grand word for the landing quay with its single building. The island is a langoustine-shaped rock measuring around five kilometres at its longest. If you wish to head straight for the beautiful beaches, they lie around the outstretched 'pincers' on the eastern end. But the island has two other special attractions: an enjoyable, modern museum telling of the heroic role of plankton in the world's creation; and its coastal path, especially round the western parts of the island.

First, to the village of **Port St-Gildas** (above the landing quay). It looks as brightly whitewashed as a Spanish *pueblo blanco*, only here the little houses are roofed with slate. Two squares lie side by side: the tiny church square, the serious administrative and spiritual capital of the island; and the business square – that's to say there's a *boulangerie*, a newsagent-cum-gift shop, and a bar.

Inside the church, with its picturesque stone tower, a large *ex voto* of a ship hangs from the new, honey-coloured wood ceiling while a statue of Joan of Arc shows a little of her armoured leg.

You can take the road out by the end of the church to the gorgeous **eastern beaches**. The gentle arc of sand that curves towards the mainland is one of the finest in the whole of Brittany, with lovely views, and a place from which you can restfully watch the boating activity around the landing stage. Heading across the rougher dunes, you come to the island's biggest beach, with views out to Hoëdic.

Eclosarium
t 02 97 52 38 38; open May–Sept 10–6

The walk from the village to the **Eclosarium** isn't particularly charming, but you do pass in front of a football pitch where the island's finest standing menhir has been comically left as a permanent spectator on the sidelines. The lovely museum tells the island's local history alongside that of plankton.

Going at a steady pace you can walk round the **coastal path** from the Eclosarium, via the western tip and back to the port, in three to four hours. It's never far from one side of the island to the other – around 500 metres – and if you get tired of the coastal path, you can take the central track. From the Eclosarium, head down towards the coast, an Avalon-like isle beckoning out to sea. Resist it, turn right on to the southern coastal path and you soon leave any sign of human civilization or habitation behind. You're just left with beautiful landscapes and seascapes, and gull-garrisoned points.

It takes roughly an hour to reach the glorious **western tips** of Houat with their ruddy-coloured rocks and gull islands. Go up to the fortified northwest point to appreciate the panorama. The northern coastal path leads you back to the village; although it can get overgrown, this indicates that you won't find crowds on the route.

The Battle of Quiberon Bay

Between 1756 and 1763, Britain and France were locked in the vicious Seven Years War over colonies and commerce. In 1759, a British naval fleet led by Admiral Hawke rushed to the west coast of Brittany, waiting there to take on the French fleet sheltering in the Rade de Brest. The British were caught napping, though, and the French admiral, Conflans, slipped out with his fleet onto the open seas round the south Breton coast.

However, Admiral Hawke's men-of-war were soon snapping at the heels of the French ships, racing past the Quiberon Peninsula and Belle-Ile, catching up with them. In one of the most devastating defeats in European naval history, the British managed to wipe out a great portion of the French fleet. It went down in British history as the celebrated Battle of Quiberon Bay, but in France the disaster became known as the Bataille des Cardinaux, because the reefs off Hoëdic are called the Petits Cardinaux and Grands Cardinaux. The colonial consequences were far reaching. France found its powers on the seas severely depleted. The British navy had established its superiority in this utterly crushing victory; in 1763, the Treaty of Paris ended the Seven Years War, and France was forced to cede major portions of its colonies to Britain.

Hoëdic

Hoëdic, shaped a bit like a whelk, lies south of the langoustine contours of Houat. It is smaller still, two and a half kilometres long, barely a kilometre at its widest, and surrounded by reefs. Sandy coves alternate with rocky points along its secretive coastline. Finds of extraordinarily old civilization have been found on this granite isle (*see* the Musée de la Préhistoire Miln-Le Rouzic in Carnac, p.416), and though most of the remains were taken away, you can still search out the island's menhir and dolmen.

The **Port d'Argol** at which you arrive was constructed in 1973, as the older Port de la Croix was only accessible at high tide. The new port lies by the Pointe du Vieux Château, and its coarse grass, scattered with thistles, suits the little frogs that proliferate on the island. French soldiers posted here in centuries past apparently used to complain about these critters jumping into their cooking pots and pockets. The village church is dedicated to St Goustan, a 10th-century pirate who turned preacher after a shipwreck.

ⓘ Iles du Ponant
*www.iles-du-ponant.com.
Information on Houat,
Hoëdic, Arz, Groix, Ile de
Moines and Belle Ile*

★ La Citadelle ›

**ⓘ Belle-Ile: Quai
Bonnelle**
*56360 Le Palais,
t 02 97 31 81 93,
www.belle-ile.com*

**★ Château de
Bordeneo B&B ›**

Market Days on Belle-Ile

Le Palais: every day in summer; otherwise Tuesday and Friday

Where to Stay and Eat on Belle-Ile

Le Palais ✉ 56360

★★★★La Citadelle, t 02 97 31 84 17, *www.citadellevauban.com*. The citadel's barracks have recently been converted into a large posh hotel making the most of the historic site, with excellent rooms. The restaurant, **La Table du Gouverneur** (€€€€–€€), serves fine food. *Closed mid-Oct–March.*

Château de Bordeneo B&B, **t** 02 97 31 80 77, *chateau-bordeneo.fr* (€€€€–€€€). Around 1km from the port, 300m from Port Fouquet creek, this grand 19th-century bourgeois house has five luxurious rooms. There's also a heated indoor pool, and fine grounds.

★★★Le Clos Fleuri, Route de Sauzon, **t** 02 97 31 45 45, *www.hotel-leclos fleuri.com* (€€€–€€). A peaceful hotel about 500m up from the port, offering free bike hire to guests.

Rooms are spacious and comfortable, some with little terraces.

★★Le Vauban, 1 Rue des Remparts, **t** 02 97 31 45 42, *www.hotelvauban.com* (€€). Looking down on to the port from the opposite side to the citadel, away from the quayside crowds, this hotel has very neat rooms with lovely views to sea. Excellent fresh seafood (€€€€€) is available for residents with advance booking. *Closed mid-Oct–mid-Feb.*

★★L'Atlantique, Quai de l'Acadie, **t** 02 97 31 80 11, *www.hotel-atlantique.com* (€€). Right by the port, with extremely comfortable rooms, some with sea views. It has a respectable waterside restaurant, and offers algae baths and a sauna.

Annick Paulic B&B, Port Halan, **t** 02 97 31 85 20 (€). Sweet rooms in a pretty, whitewashed hamlet on the southern outskirts of Le Palais.

L'Annexe, t 02 97 31 81 53. Trendy restaurant opposite the citadel, serving good seafood.

Le Verre à Pied, t 02 97 31 29 65. Fun place for simple dishes.

Sauzon ✉ 56360

★★★Le Cardinal, Port Bellec, **t** 02 97 31 61 60, *www.hotel-cardinal.fr* (€€€€). In a glorious location overlooking the coast, rooms with great sea views. Lots of activities possible, including with heated pool. Good restaurant. *Closed Oct–Easter.*

Hostellerie La Touline, Rue du Port Vihan, t 02 97 31 69 69, *www.hostellerielatouline.com* (€€€). One of the oldest houses on the island, this pink-fronted former fisherman's house has charming rooms a short distance from the lighthouse. The garden has a good view of the port.

★La Désirade ››

**Les Tamaris, 11 Allée des Peupliers, t 02 97 31 65 09 (€€–€). Quite comfortable rooms in a modern house.

Le Contre Quai, Rue St-Nicolas, t 02 97 31 60 60 (€). A hotel-restaurant with a simple rustic feel and serving well-regarded cuisine (€€).

L'Aubergerie B&B, Borgroix, t 02 97 31 64 61, *www.aubergerie-belleile.com* (€€). Sophisticated, homely rooms in a lovingly restored property 1.5km south of Sauzon, run by a charming host.

Le Roz Avel, Rue du Lieutenant Riou, t 02 97 31 61 48 (€€€). Very tasty dishes, including Belle-Ile lamb. Tables outside on warmer days.

Crêperie Les Embruns, t 02 97 31 64 78 (€). An extremely pink and popular crêpe house. *Closed Wed.*

Port Goulphar ✉ 56360

★★★★Le Castel Clara, t 02 97 31 84 21, *www.castel-clara.com* (€€€€€–€€€€). The size of this luxurious modern hotel on the rough, south side of the island comes as a bit of a surprise, and the prices will blow you away. It has a thalassotherapy and beauty centre, and excellent seafood cuisine. You can appreciate the rugged coast from the rooms and the restaurant, but you

ⓘ Houat ››
Information Point,
t 02 97 30 66 42
(summer) or Mairie,
t 02 97 30 68 04

★Le Castel Clara ›

ⓘ Hoëdic ››
Mairie,
t 02 97 52 48 88

can't swim in the sea here, so a heated seawater pool is provided, as are tennis courts, among many facilities.

**Le Grand Large, t 02 97 31 80 92, *www.hotelgrandlarge.com* (€€€–€€). A reasonably priced alternative in great location beside the coastal rock formations, rooms recently redone. *Closed Nov–Easter.*

Le Petit Cosquet ✉ 56360

***La Désirade, t 02 97 31 70 70, *www.hotel-la-desirade.com* (€€€€–€€€). A charming cluster of little houses around a swimming pool, located inland, near the little airport. Its excellent restaurant (€€€€–€€€) is just across the road. *Closed mid Nov–Easter.*

Bangor ✉ 56360

Crêperie Chez Renée, t 02 97 31 52 87 (€). The best-known crêperie on the island, set in a delightful, typical Bellilois house with a garden. *Closed Mon.*

Houat ✉ 56170

***La Sirène, Route du Port, t 02 97 30 66 73 (€€). A cheerful hotel on the outskirts of the village, with a bare-breasted mermaid signalling it on the outside. *Half board obligatory.*

*Les Iles, Le Bourg, t 02 97 30 68 02 (€€). A budget option set just back from the shore, with views across the sea to the Breton coast.

Hoëdic ✉ 56170

**Les Cardinaux, Le Bourg, t 02 97 52 37 27 (€€). A simple hotel.

Chez Jean-Paul, t 02 97 57 42 26 (€). A café-bookshop where you can eat among the books.

Mega Megalith Country via Carnac

The most famous concentration of neolithic monuments in the Western world is crammed into the short stretch of the Morbihan coast from Erdeven to Gavrinis, passing via the two most famous neolithic sites in Brittany, Carnac and Locmariaquer, also neighbouring resorts. The river port of La Trinité-sur-Mer between the two is a magnet for the best sailors in the world, with its staggering marina.

Getting around Megalith Country

Buses are the only form of public transport serving the area, but bicycles are a good alternative for getting around – for example, see *cyclo.erdeven.free.fr.*

Megaliths from Erdeven to Plouharnel

The little town of **Erdeven** (the name derives from the Breton for dunes), a quiet place with a few simple restaurants, is often passed through in a flash but some major megaliths lie scattered south out of town along the main road. It's possible not just to drive by the **alignments of Kerzehro**; you can even drive right *through* a section of them.

These alignments are impressive. You can count 10 rows at the thickest part. The ensemble still contains more than 1,000 standing stones, stretching over some two kilometres. Still more striking than the alignments themselves are the **géants de Kerzehro**, separate massive granite blocks lying apart. One of

An Introduction to the Neolithic Civilization Around Carnac

Such is the density of neolithic stone alignments and burial places in the region around Carnac that today's local authorities seem slightly at a loss as to what to do with them all. As to the academics who study the matter, they find it painfully difficult to pin down specific meanings to all these monuments. What is clear is that the area was of immense significance to the powerful neolithic people who became attached to these parts... whoever they may have been. The intriguing and mysterious vestiges scattered about stir the imagination, but remain quite puzzling for amateurs and experts alike.

The sheer chutzpah of the people determined enough and crazy enough to have erected the famed alignments of Carnac so many thousands of years ago certainly inspires reflection. Why did they do it, how, in what cause, through what beliefs, sufferings and hopes? All these are questions that have remained largely unanswered. Enjoy reading about some of the very potty theories that have been advanced on the alignments in our Topic on the matter, on p.40.

Despite so many puzzling mysteries, actually, more and more fragments of reliable information on neolithic times are being pieced together by archaeological surveys, making the study of this civilization increasingly lively. For a long period up to the 19th century, though,many considered these megaliths to date back to Celtic Iron Age times – that is, to the millennium before Christ. Modern research and dating techniques have shown that some of the monuments go back as far as 4500 BC and maybe beyond, almost a couple of thousand years before the great pyramids of Egypt went up. The research also indicates that neolithic civilization here evolved over many thousands of years, and lasted longer than our Christian civlization has been going – a sobering thought on the vanity of present-day religions.

Much of the neolithic study around Carnac has concentrated on the deaths of neolithic people and their burial rituals, because that's the clearest evidence which remains. Dolmens ('tables of stone', in Breton) are burial chambers built from huge blocks of granite; originally, they would all have been covered by a tumulus, a mound of stone and earth, although these have often been removed.

Despite the concentration on the morbid, you shouldn't forget that these neolithc people did have a life, and, it seems, a pretty complex one, with highly organized communities and beliefs. The extent of their achievements in this Carnac area, their buildings, their finely wrought tools, and the forms they engraved on stones show that theirs was certainly in many ways a sophisticated civilization.

Beyond visiting the monuments, go to the prehistory museum and La Maison des Mégalithes at Carnac to help you appreciate the subject. The main site at Locmariaquer also has an informative display, and Vannes presents a further museum of prehistory.

these has a side worn into a weird fantastical face, like a fossilized, monstrous whale-man. A ring of stones appears to encircle the giants.

Continue on past them, then follow the signs for the Mané-Bras, on the **Grand Arc megaliths walk** signposted around Erdeven. You can do this eight-kilometre track on foot or by mountain bike, though it's quite a distance to the **Mané-Bras dolmen**, unusual for having a chamber with four separate cells off the central corridor.

Two further prettily located dolmens stand southeast of the Kerzehro alignments, off the main road to Plouharnel. The **Dolmen de Crucuno**, dated to around 4000 BC, has been left bizarrely exposed in the middle of a hamlet. The **Dolmen de Mané-Groh** lies 500 metres further inland, past a stone cross carved with a primitive figure of Christ, and is photogenically set among small oaks and pines. Constructed some time between 4000 BC and 3500 BC, it's practically identical to that of Mané-Bras.

The quietly charming hamlet of **Ste-Barbe** is signalled by its typical Breton steeple on the other side of the main road towards Plouharnel. Among its small delights is another dolmen. The place has magical views down from its slope towards unkempt dunes, which stand in front of a stunning beach.

Plouharnel, in contrast, stands at a major tourist crossroads. It has its appealing sides, but is often clogged with traffic heading to or from Quiberon and Carnac. Further neolithic monuments, and pretty historic chapels are strewn around it. Distracting keen golfers from all the prehistoric excitement, there's a fine country course, the **Golf de St-Laurent**, a few kilometres north.

Carnac

Carnac, Kerzehro, Locmariaquer and Gavrinis

Carnac, Europe's neolithic capital, doesn't just boast one great prehistoric site; it contains a dense concentration of varied edifices, including tumuli, dolmens, and, most famously, four great alignments of standing stones, Le Ménec, Kermario, Kerlescan and Le Petit Ménec.

But Carnac doesn't only attract millions of visitors every year because of its neolithic riches. The place has a delightful old upper town with a remarkable church. And down below, it boasts a vibrant, chic beach resort. From the pine-scented woods among which so many of the dolmens hide to the mesmerizing, wide open sands of the Pô oyster bay to the west, the whole area is exceptionally beautiful. To reduce confusion, let's divide Carnac into three; first comes neolithic Carnac, then Carnac-Ville or Carnac-Bourg, the town, and finally, Carnac-Plage, the modern seaside resort.

Neolithic Carnac

The famed alignments stand just north of Carnac old town. It proves slightly tricky going to visit them. As to understanding them, and the neolithic civilization from which they emerged, best head first to the specialist museum in the old town.

Musée de la Préhistoire Miln-Le Rouzic

Discoveries about the prehistoric societies around Carnac are advancing so fast that this museum has trouble keeping up with them. But then many of the biggest questions still remain unanswered. The serious studying of neolithic Carnac began in the 19th century, slowly leading to the debunking of wild theories and extreme myths. Excavations by archaeologists go back to the 1820s, and this museum is named after two of the most important and passionate among them, Scotsman James Miln and his helper Zacharie Le Rouzic. Although the museum isn't old, it demands an old-fashioned slog round, reading panels covered with dense text. The displays, while containing a large number of interesting artefacts, are sometimes a little hard to decipher.

A brisk introduction rushes you through time and the vast-seeming Palaeolithic Era, divided into Lower, Middle and Upper periods, going from millions of years ago to the end of the last ice age some 12,000 years ago. As recently as 1977, remains of a community dating to around 450,000 BC were discovered in St-Colomban, just west of Carnac-Plage.

The period roughly from 12,000 to 3000 BC is referred to as the Mesolithic era, which witnessed great progress in the production of miniature tools, and therefore all manner of ground-breaking crafts. One of the first showcases displays the reconstruction of a Mesolithic grave from the island of Hoëdic beyond Quiberon. Buried among kitchen debris, one figure wore a long shell necklace and was decorated with antlers. The end of the Mesolithic age merged with the start of the Neolithic, said to go from some time in the 5th millennium BC to around the close of the 3rd. The most important change that neolithic culture brought was the shift from a hunter-gathering way of living to one where stable agriculture and cattle-rearing were mastered.

This museum is one of the most important repositories of neolithic artefacts in the world, found in and around burial sites of the area. Neolithic graves are well represented by a whole corridor lined with carved tombstones. A number of neolithic sites from the Morbihan were decorated with engraved stones, which may well reflect some of the civilization's major concerns, but they are hard to interpret. The recurrence of axes and horns might indicate the importance of felling and of cattle. Other symbols are thought to refer to leadership and female fertility.

For whom exactly the great tumuli of Carnac were built is still not known, but the panels talk of a powerful élite emerging in these parts, who probably introduced extremely important changes in technical skills and culture, such as the development of pottery and weaving. Neolithic daily life is evoked , although some of the fantastically polished axes are clearly rare, rather than everyday, pieces. One room is given over to an appealing, useful model of the Carnac alignments.

Further displays include curiosities such as a neolithic canoe and healing beads. Apparently such stones were still used in the Breton countryside in the 19th century. Additional sections dwell on the Celts (with some coins and even one or two ornaments on display), and on Gallo–Roman Brittany. The distinction is clearly made between prehistoric Celts of Armorica and Dark Age Bretons.

Prehistory can appear a rather dry subject if you're not taken by the passion, so the museum has been organizing an increasing number of events to offer a livelier approach – look out for what's on when you're visiting.

The Carnac Alignments and Maison des Mégalithes

Voilà donc ce fameux champ de Carnac qui a fait écrire plus de sottises qu'il n'a de cailloux (Here then is Carnac's famous field, which has inspired the writing of more idiocies than there are stones.)

Gustave Flaubert, *Voyage en Bretagne*

The Carnac Alignments and Maison des Mégalithes
carnac.monuments-nationaux.fr;
Oct–March you can wander freely around the alignments;
April–Sept you can only go in among them on guided tours, known as visites-conférences, most of which are in French, although in high season there's a programme of such visits in English – book in advance at the Maison des Mégalithes, Le Ménec, t 02 97 52 29 81; open daily July–Aug 9–8, May–June 9–7, Sept–April 10–5

The **Maison des Mégalithes** beside the Le Ménec alignments is the tourist centre dedicated specifically to Carnac's staggering rows of standing stones. Inside, there's a reasonably helpful model, a small permanent exhibition on the neolithic, plus a video in French on the subject. You can learn a lot more on the guided tours.

The **Carnac alignments** were probably erected around 3000 BC. Whatever their purpose, the effort involved in setting them up must have been enormous. According to the archaeologist Charles T. LeRoux, they may have taken some 500,000 to one million days in total to construct. Four alignments run in a row northeastwards from the top of Carnac-Ville, spanning around four kilometres. They still include thousands of standing stones, although many have gone missing and a good number that had fallen down had to be set back upright by order of specialist archaeologists. The individual blocks are very diverse in shape and size and tend to be much rougher in look than the caringly shaped menhirs common across Brittany.

These deeply complex monuments are unique in the world, although there are other lesser alignments in Brittany and elsewhere. Two plausible, related theories offer the most likely explanation for their creation: first, it's said that they marked out a religious site; second, that they relate to astronomical calculations and the seasons. The alignments might have been connected with fertility, funeral rites and imaginings of an afterworld, especially given the density of tombs scattered in the vicinity.

The **Alignements du Ménec**, the most southwesterly of Carnac's four alignments, count the largest number of stones still standing – more than 1,000 in up to a dozen rows, with a cromlech (or stone circle) at either end. To make out the western circle you need to search around homes on Carnac's outskirts – these neolithic wonders haven't always been treated with respect.

Things get chaotic in summer around the **Alignements de Kermario**, the most impressive of all the alignments. These are of roughly the same dimensions as those of Le Ménec, the standing stones almost as numerous, the 10 lines stretching over one kilometre. However, the Kermario alignments have suffered greater indignities: the enclosure of menhirs that once finished off the western end was destroyed some time ago; and by the mid-19th century, only around 200 of the stones had been left upright – hundreds have been put back up since then. From certain viewpoints, the rows look almost like rough stone stitching across the ground, and their great length along the undulating terrain becomes clearer.

Just before you arrive at the Kerlescan alignments, a tree-shaded path leads into woods and towards the **Grand Quadrilatère du Manio** and **Géant du Manio**. It's a fair walk to these two, but this only adds to their mystery. Those looking for worship of the fertile phallus in the neolithic should be relatively satisfied with the big menhir's shape. It's said that in past centuries, infertile women would come here to rub themselves against the stone in the hope that it might bring on conception. Otherwise, you might see a resemblance with the polished axes so beloved of neolithic civilization.

The **Kerlescan alignments** only consist of around 240 standing stones now, and many of them are quite small. But you should be able to make out some 13 parallel rows of them, extending over roughly 400 metres. There's also a dolmen here. Some visitors miss the **Petit Ménec alignments** east again, but eight rows are still standing here, despite the fact that numerous blocks were filched by builders to form the foundations for the lighthouse on Belle-Ile.

Note that if you speak French, there are interesting **special tours** you can sign up for in high season. Certain visits are followed by an *atelier*, when you might learn about prehistoric techniques of making fire, or weapons, for example; and there are themed visits, including night-time walks through the rows of standing stones on which you're regaled with tales and legends inspired by the alignments.

A Few Further Carnac Neolithic Tombs

The most impressive burial mound left in the area is the **Tumulus St-Michel** (*closed for restoration*) on the eastern edge of Carnac-Ville. Though the bracken and the chapel on top can obscure the fact that this is an artificial hillock, this turns out to be a massive piece of neolithic architecture. It conceals a series of tombs, probably dating from around 6,000 years ago. The burial chambers were covered with a layer of stones about eight metres thick; then a dome of sea mud was applied to seal the mound before a further 80 centimetres or more of stones were piled on top. The whole construction is an impressive 120 metres long, 58 metres wide and 10 metres high; originally it stood still taller.

The **Kercado tumulus** lies just south of the Carnac alignments, between Kermario and Le Manio. It stands in the grounds of a château that remains even better hidden than many a neolithic monument in these parts. This tumulus is surrounded by a rough ring of stones, and has a curious little menhir topping its mound. The entrance to the burial corridor has one of the most comical touches of any neolithic site – a light switch. Turn it on, then you can advance, squatting, through the corridor to the squarish chamber. The great table stone of the ceiling is engraved with a double axe, and some shield shapes, or possibly stylized mother goddesses, can also be made out. Around 150 beads discovered here can now be seen in the Carnac prehistory museum.

Carnac-Ville

Carnac town has its own quite amazing, Christian-era stone structure – the church of **St-Cornély**. A remarkable, colourful, naive scene on the outside represents the well-named saint, protector of horned cattle, with his charges. The church exterior otherwise looks sternly Breton, except for its extravagant baldaquin-porch, added in the 17th century, the top tied together with what look like ribbons of granite.

Within, you'll find a riot of decoration. The ceiling paintings, added in the 18th century, portray four cycles, depicting the life of Christ, the life of John the Baptist, the Mysteries of the Rosary, and the life of St Cornély, the last the most entertaining. Other extraordinary features include ornate altarpieces and the riches in the treasury.

Unearth some tempting shops and restaurants in the very pretty lanes around the church.

A Tour of the Carnac Coast

Many people don't visit Carnac to stare at ancient stones or visit the old town or church, but to enjoy the fabulous beaches. This beautiful coastal tour turns its back on the megaliths and the old town of Carnac, concentrating instead on the oyster beds of the Pô, moving round to the old village of St-Colomban, and then going along the beaches of Carnac-Plage.

Out west, at low tide, the flat sands of the **Pô estuary** lead your gaze to the low peninsula of Quiberon. The flat-bottomed oyster boats are left lying like beached sea creatures on the firm bed, though the scene quickly changes with the rising waters. Follow the coast down to the peninsula of **St-Colomban**. Beyond the cross you pass en route, a large old Breton fountain has been cleaned up; one section was apparently reserved for the village women to do their washing, the other for cattle to drink at. The substantial old village houses huddle round the rustic Flamboyant Gothic church that you can visit in summer. The St-Colomban beach is popular with windsurfers year round. The walk all the way round the coastal edge of the St-Colomban peninsula, via the Pointe St-Colomban and the Pointe Ty Bihas, is uplifting.

Carnac yacht club
www.yccarnac.com,
t 02 97 52 10 98

Nautic Sport
www.nautic-sport.com,
t 02 97 52 88 02

Carnac Evasion
www.carnac-evasion.com,
t 02 97 52 63 30

Centre de Thalassothérapie de Carnac
www.thalasso-carnac.com,
t 02 97 52 53 54

Pine-backed beaches, with their lifeguards' ladders planted in the sands, follow along **Carnac-Plage**. The **Carnac yacht club** is tucked in beside the artificial **harbour**, the Port en Drô, on the western end of this central resort. It offers courses through the year, as well as organizing regattas. **Nautic Sport** opposite it proposes further possibilities. As to **Carnac Evasion**, it specializes in the extreme sport of kite-surfing.

Curious big, brash modern buildings are set beside the inner waters of **Les Salines du Bréno** just behind the port. Here you'll find the **Centre de Thalassothérapie**, where you can enjoy all manner of pamperings, the large hotels that surround it, and the **Casino Barrière**.

Carnac-Plage's extensive **main beach** presents a gentle, genteel curve of sand much appreciated for family holidays. Behind the beach, a number of hotels mix with the villas looking out to sea at the little islands of Houat and Hoëdic. The centre of the resort turns into a hive of activity in summer, all manner of bars and restaurants competing for custom in the shaded streets just behind the beach. Carnac-Plage is bound to the east by the Pointe Churchill. The other side of this spit, residential quarters overlook further beaches, and in the middle of the bay, the Ile de Stuhan is joined to the mainland at low tide by a spit of sand.

La Trinité-sur-Mer and St-Philibert

You cross two thin peninsulas to get from Carnac to another of Brittany's neolithic highlights, Locmariaquer. On the way, explore La Trinité-sur-Mer and St-Philibert, separated by the River Crac'h's estuary.

The name of **La Trinité-sur-Mer** means yachts to French people, as this port attracts the finest sailors in the country. Three of the greatest sailors in the world at present, Francis Joyon, Loïc Perron and Marc Guillemot are based here. The place also has a certain notoriety as the home of extreme right-wing politician Jean-Marie Le Pen. Through spring and summer, La Trinité seems to be in a permanent state of regatta, packed with state-of-the-art yachts. This port's name turns out to be slightly misleading, however; La Trinité doesn't lie next to the sea, but along the estuary of the River Crac'h. The long street that parallels the vast, swanky **marina** is lined with alluring cafés, restaurants and boutiques, many of the last specializing in sea gear. Look out also for spectacular Breton photos and posters at the Plisson gallery. The harbourside remains vibrant for much of the year. Up among the quaint, quieter lanes of the slopeside old town, the main **church** contains paintings depicting La Trinité's quay in times gone by. Heading to the back of the estuary, past the **casino**, where new hotels are being built, **oyster boats** busy themselves harvesting shellfish; the view of the Crac'h from up on the **Kerisper Bridge** is memorable.

If you're itching to get out on the waters from La Trinité, the first obvious port of call is the yacht club, **La Société Nautique de la Trinité (SNT)**, which offers a whole range of possibilities, including sailing lessons and sea kayaking. To enjoy a short trip out to sea on board a skippered boat, choices include **Akéla Croisières** and **Exode II**. For diving, try **Made in Blue**. A gentler option is to hire an electric boat on the Crac'h River via **Ruban Vert**. Down La Trinité's peninsula, passing via Kerbihan, go in search of some excellent **beaches**. The **Pointe de Kerbihan** juts out into the Bay of Quiberon. From here you can enjoy a good view onto yachts sailing in and out of La Trinité and the Crac'h estuary on regatta days.

The Kerisper Bridge takes you to the **St-Philibert Peninsula**, a pine-covered spit sheltered from the hordes. A coast road goes down the edge of the River Crac'h then up the other, mud-edged side of the peninsula to **St-Philibert** itself, a quiet, old-fashioned village with a tiny **mariners' chapel** and typical old fountain overlooking another oystery river estuary.

Up from St-Philibert, **Crac'h** is known for its huge Breton biscuit outlet, **La Trinitaine**. Beside it, the **Plisson photography gallery** shows and sells the works of the brilliant Philip Plisson and his son. They have taken many of the most iconic images of Brittany and the sea in recent decades.

La Société Nautique de la Trinité (SNT)
www.snt-voile.org,
t 02 97 55 73 48

Akéla Croisières
www.akelacroisiere.com, *m 06 60 91 01 93*

Exode II
m 06 11 30 08 97

Made in Blue
t 02 97 30 16 06

Locmariaquer's Neolithic Peninsula

At the western entrance to the wonderful Golfe du Morbihan, Locmariaquer's peninsula contains one of France's most famous megalithic sites after Carnac. Like Carnac, Locmariaquer is also a sprawling, highly popular and deeply attractive summer resort.

Locmariaquer's Main Neolithic Monuments

Locmariaquer's
Main Neolithic
Monuments
*locmariaquer.monum
ents-nationaux.fr, t 02
97 57 37 59; open daily
May–June 10–6,
July–Aug 10–7, April and
Sept 10–12.30 and 2–5*

Locmariaquer's major neolithic monuments are clustered together outside of town. Excavations in the late 1980s and early 1990s around the three impressively large construstions here led to interesting discoveries. Since then, they've been fenced in together to form one tourist site. You enter via the helpful **Centre d'Informations Archéologiques**. The connection between the two tumuli and the great menhir remains unclear, but what is evident is that this site held enormous importance.

Weighing in at some 350 tonnes, the **Grand Menhir Brisé** must have been awe-inspiring when it stood upright, some 18 metres in height. Even looking at it now, prostrate and split into four sections on the ground, you wonder how the neoltihic engineers could have organized the lifting of such a mammoth piece of stone. This huge granite block went up some time between 5000 BC and 4000 BC. Its stone was not excavated at Locmariaquer; experts are convinced that it was brought from around 10 to 15 kilometres away, from the Rhuys peninsula on the other side of the Golfe du Morbihan.

In 1989, it was discovered that the menhir hadn't always stood on its own. Excavations revealed the roots of an alignment stretching out from it. Until the recent digs, it was said the great menhir fell as a result of an earthquake or of a lightning strike. Now it's thought that all the menhirs here were deliberately uprooted by later neolithic generations, who may even have cut the Grand Menhir into pieces, by means unknown. There's speculation that the dismantling of the standing stones may indicate old customs being overthrown in a radical shift in beliefs or thought.

It may be that both of the large tumuli close to the Grand Menhir date from a later phase of occupation on this site, roughly between 4000 and 3500 BC. The **Er-Grah tumulus** has been vaguely dated to around 4000 BC. Much reduced from its original height, it consists of a tomb on its northern end, covered by part of an enormous trapezoid barrow. This massive man-made mound wasn't built all in one go. A single tomb was first built, then covered by a larger one, around 40 metres in length, which sealed the original tomb off from the outside world. Later, the building was much extended to north and south, creating a stepped tumulus some 170 metres long and between 15 and 30 metres wide. Excavations under the tumulus revealed neolithic hearths and ditches below, as well as the remains of two heads of cattle, perhaps sacrificed on the spot.

The **Table des Marchand**, possibly constructed between 3700 and 3500 BC, looked like a vast table when it still stood exposed as an uncovered dolmen in the last century, hence the name. During this time, it featured in countless period representations of neolithic Brittany. However, following archaeological research carried out during the 1930s, the dolmen was covered over once again with a mass of stones to form a cairn similar to the one that would have been constructed over it originally. Further signs of an earlier settlement have recently been found under this cairn.

Quite intriguingly, once inside the tomb, you can make out a small, broken portion of the carving of a bull on the roof slab of the dolmen, as well as an axe and two buckles; extraordinarily, the other half of this engraving has been found some way off, in the dolmen on the island of Gavrinis (*see* p.429). However, the most remarkable carving here covers the ogival end stone, decorated with four rows of almost symmetrically positioned crooks; this recurring symbol inside Morbihan neolithic tombs has often been read as a sign of power or authority.

Around Locmariaquer

Locmariaquer fairly ignores its other neolithic vestiges. However, another reputed neolithic burial chamber hides in the northern outskirts of the village. Entering **Mané-Lud** you can make out a few engravings. At nearby **Mané Retual**, axes are engraved on the dolmen's massive covering stone. South of the village, towards Kerpenhir, the tumulus of **Mané-er-Hroëck** yielded a substantial treasure of axe heads and beads when it was opened up in 1863.

Locmariaquer itself has sprawled down this western side of the Golfe du Morbihan. The 11th-century church of **Notre-Dame de Kerdro** contains some Romanesque carved capitals. The views onto the calm, flat inland gulf, dotted with headlands and islands, are totally enchanting, and the many oyster boats reveal how a fair number of the locals make their living. You can visit **oyster beds** here from June to September.

Oyster beds
book via the tourist office on t 02 97 57 33 05

Amazingly neglected on the beach south of Locmariaquer, looking out on to the Bay of Quiberon and the ocean, stands the dolmen of **Les Pierres Plates**. Several of the stones in this tumulus have interesting carvings, including embossed shields said to be representations of the mother god, and an illustration of what may be a stylized boat with oars hinting that these neolithic men could have been early mariners – but you may need your own torch to appreciate them. The **Pointe de Kerpenhir** at the southeastern tip of the Locmariaquer peninsula marks the western entrance to the fabulous Golfe du Morbihan.

Market Days in Megalith Country

Erdeven: Saturday

Carnac: Wednesday and Sunday
La Trinité-sur-Mer: Tuesday and Friday
Locmariaquer: Tuesday and Saturday

(i) **Carnac >**
74 Ave des Druides,
B.P. 65, **t** *02 97 52 13 52,*
www.ot-carnac.fr

(i) **La Trinité-**
sur-Mer >>
30 Cours des Quais,
t *02 97 55 72 21,*
www.ot-trinite-
sur-mer.fr

(★) **Le Lodge**
Kerisper >>

(★) **Les Chambres**
Marines >>

(★) **Le Tumulus >**

(i) **Erdeven**
7 Rue de l'Abbé Le
Barth, **t** *02 97 55 64 60,*
www.ot-erdeven.fr

(★) **Rivages à**
Carnac B&B >

Where to Stay and Eat in Megalith Country

Carnac-Plage ✉ 56340

****Le Diana**, 21 Blvd de la Plage,
t 02 97 52 05 38, *www.lediana.com*
(€€€€–€€€). The most luxurious of the
modern seafront hotels, in need of
renovation at time of writing, but
with scenic views, restaurant, heated
pool and tennis court. *Closed mid-
Nov–Easter.*

***Novotel**, Ave de l'Atlantique, **t** 02
97 52 53 00, *www.thalasso-carnac.
com*, and **Ibis**, 6 Allée Fleur de Sel,
t 02 97 52 54 00, (€€€€–€€€). Rather
out-of-place, slightly pretentious, large
twin establishments overlooking a
lake on the western side of Carnac-
Plage, but they offer specialist
thalassotherapy pamperings, as
well as restaurants and pool.

***Best Western Celtique**, 82 Ave des
Druides, **t** 02 97 52 14 15, *www.hotel-
celtique.com* (€€€€–€€). Probably the
best-kept hotel in the beach resort,
though back from the seafront.

Carnac Old Town ✉ 56340

***Le Tumulus**, 31 Rue du Tumulus,
t 02 97 52 08 21, *www.hotel-tumulus.
com* (€€€–€€). Set apart from the
other hotels, in an extraordinary
location by the Tumulus St-Michel,
the place and its rooms have recently
been given a very smart make-over.
Attractions include pool and
pamperings.

Rivages à Carnac B&B, 23 Rue de
Courdiec, **m** 06 60 65 86 12 (€€€–€€€).
Upliftingly stylish, colourful,
contemporary rooms in a quiet home.

Le Râtelier, 4 Chemin du Douët, **t** 02
97 52 05 04, *www.le-ratelier.com* (€). A
wonderful ivy-covered hotel down a
quiet side street. Rooms may be old-
fashioned, but the restaurant serves
very good-quality cuisine.

Crêperie Chez Marie, **t** 02 97 52 83 05
(€). An excellent crêpe house by the
church.

Outskirts of Carnac ✉ 56340

Les Ajoncs d'Or, Kerbachique,
between Carnac and Plouharnel, **t** 02
97 52 32 02, *www.lesajoncsdor.com*
(€€). A characterful old stone family

house with really nice rooms in a
beautifully tended, walled, shaded
garden. *Closed mid-Oct–mid-March.*

La Côte, Kermario, **t** 02 97 52 02 80
(€€€). Refined cuisine including such
delicacies as roasted langoustine with
potato pancake. *Closed Mon, and Tues
lunch; out of season Mon, Sat lunch
and Sun eve.*

La Calypso, 158 Le Pô (down by the
river), **t** 02 97 52 06 14, *www.calypso-
carnac.com* (€€). A restaurant with
a fine reputation, in an old
whitewashed house close to the
superb sandscapes of the estuary.
Serves lobster grilled on an open fire.
Closed Sun eve and Mon.

La Trinité-sur-Mer ✉ 56470

***Le Lodge Kerisper**, 4 Rue du Latz,
t 02 97 52 88 56, *www.lodge-kerisper.
com* (€€€€€–€€€€). Set in the heart of
the old town, this very stylish new
little hotel has suites packed full of
charm, and charming objects, plus a
little garden and pool.

Les Chambres Marines, 1 Rue du
Men Du, **t** 02 97 30 17 00, *www.les-
chambres-marines.com* (€€€–€€). Six
high-quality rooms and a restaurant
with a splendid terrace overlooking
the port, offering excellent food at
reasonable prices.

L'Ostréa, Cours des Quais, **t** 02 97 55
73 23, *www.hotel-ostrea.com* (€€–€). A
small number of rooms looking onto
the port, perched above the
restaurant, **Le Bistrot du Marin**, with
its tempting terrace, where you can
enjoy really good food, including
copious seafood platters (€€€–€€).

L'Etage, Cours des Quais, **t** 02 97 59 56
12. Trendy spot to eat, restaurant on
pillars, with magnificent views.

St-Philibert ✉ 56470

***Le Galet**, Le Congre, **t** 02 97 55 00
56, *www.legalet.fr* (€€€€–€€). A
modern cube of a hotel, its rooms
done out in really refined
contemporary style. Heated
pool and tennis court.

Lann Kermané B&B, **t** 02 97 55 03 75
(€€). Charming little rooms within a
Breton stone house.

La Ferme de Kérino, Kérino, **t** 02 97 55
06 10, *www.kerino.com* (€€). Rooms in
a rambling cottage covered with vines.

(i) **Locmariaquer >**
*1 Rue de la Victoire,
t 02 97 57 33 05,
www.ot-loc
mariaquer.com*

Locmariaquer ✉ 56740

***Les Trois Fontaines, Route d'Auray, **t** 02 97 57 42 70, *www.hotel-trois fontaines.com* (€€€–€€). The most comfortable hotel in town, a smart modern building set back from the road, its rooms chicly done up in a marine style. *Closed mid-Nov–mid-Feb.*

L'Escale, 2 Place Dariorigum, **t 02 97 57 32 51 (€€). An unpretentious modern hotel beautifully located close by the water, some rooms with mesmerizing views, though check if renovated. The restaurant has the great views, plus a terrace. *Closed winter.*

Lautram, Place de l'Eglise, **t 02 97 57 31 32, *www.hotel-lautram.fr* (€€–€). Opposite the church, near the port, traditional rooms in a pretty building with charming garden.

Crac'h ✉ 56950

La Suite, 5 Rue de la Fontaine, **t** 02 97 55 17 45 (€€–€). Stylish new contemporary restaurant serving good classic fare.

The Western Golfe du Morbihan

 Golfe du Morbihan

The river of Auray runs down into the western side of the exquisite Golfe du Morbihan, past the historic town of Auray and the prettiest picture postcard of an inland port below it, St-Goustan. Ste-Anne d'Auray, a short way north, is one of the most venerated places in Brittany, and includes the major memorial to the Breton soldiers who perished in the First World War. Heading south beyond the hidden delights of Le Bono, dozens of little roads south of Baden lead down to the glorious coastal path along the Golfe du Morbihan. Brittany doesn't get much more serenely beautiful than this. The cairn of Gavrinis, the best of all the Breton neolithic sites, lies just a stone"s throw from the bank, on a private island.

Auray and Around

The port of St-Goustan, down in **Auray's** steep valley, outdoes the pretty upper town in utter quaintness. But through the Middle Ages the hill settlement dominating the Loch River was of great

---

The Magical Golfe du Morbihan

'As many islands as there are days in the year,' the saying goes about the fabulous Golfe du Morbihan. There are in fact a little over 40 islands strewn around this massive inland saltwater sea; all but two are privately owned, the Ile aux Moines and the Ile d'Arz. Measuring some 25 kilometres north to south from Vannes to Port-Navalo and around 20 kilometres from east to west, at its narrow opening to the ocean between Locmariaquer and Port-Navalo the Golfe du Morbihan is subject to some of the strongest currents in Europe. As a result, the coastline behind this opening changes substantially as the tide goes in and out; in the west, however, around the main two islands, you feel the effects of the tides less than in the east.

Facts and statistics count for little when you arrive at the Golfe du Morbihan. Its peppering of islands, along with the countless wooded tentacles of land dipping their tips gently into the waters, help to create an exquisite confusion of land and sea that quite turns the head. Out on the waters, you quickly lose any clear notion of what is mainland and what is island. This is one of Brittany's most magical places. In summer, crisscrossing vessels churn the waters in all directions and the traditional fishing and oyster boats are greatly outnumbered by yachts, motor boats, canoes and sailboards.

Getting around the Western Golfe du Morbihan

Auray and Vannes have **railway** stations well served by the rapid TGV line linking Paris with Quimper. Otherwise, **buses** from Auray or Vannes serve this area, under the umbrella network of the Transports Interurbains Morbihan. Details on going out on the Golfe du Morbihan are given on p.431.

importance in this part of Brittany. The major event in Auray's history took place in 1364, when the battle that sealed the Breton War of Succession took place outside the town.

This Battle of Auray, fought in the marshlands of Kerzo, brought to an end one of the most terrible wars Brittany has ever known. Charles de Blois and his troops, pitted against Jean de Montfort and his army, had adopted a poor position overlooked by de Montfort's men, but he decided to attack, against the better judgement of his great commander, Bertrand du Guesclin. The de Blois side was massacred, Charles dying in the battle, while du Guesclin was captured. Jean de Montfort apparently rued the death of his cousin Charles and saw to it that de Blois was given a grand funeral. The area of Auray, however, was left to suffer the consequences of pillaging armies. Jean de Montfort assumed the title of Duke Jean IV of Brittany after this battle, and built a church on the site of the decisive victory, which later became the Chartreuse d'Auray. Most of this monastery's buildings still standing date from the 17th and 18th centuries.

During the Ancien Régime, Auray merchants prospered from fishing and trade. You can see the results of their successes both in the upper town and in the gorgeously restored port of St-Goustan. In 1776, bad weather forced Benjamin Franklin to land in this safe harbour while on his way to discuss with King Louis XVI how France might assist in the American War of Independence against Britain.

The memory of the anti-Revolutionary royalist and Catholic Chouannerie also lingers around Auray. One of Brittany's most determined anti-Revolutionary, and anti-Napoleonic, figures, Georges Cadoudal, was born in the Kerléano district in 1771. He spent his short life battling for the restoration of the French monarchy, and in 1795 played an important part in the failed attempted invasion by royalist émigrés via the Quiberon Peninsula. Cadoudal survived, but 950 émigrés and Chouans who were captured during the disastrous landing were brought to a place outside Auray, since known grimly as the Champ des Martyrs. There, they were shot dead by the Republicans. At the Chartreuse d'Auray, a mausoleum in white marble in the funerary chapel was commissioned in the 19th century to commemorate the event. Another 19th-century chapel at the Champ des Martyrs itself also marks this massacre.

In 1796, at the tender age of 25, Cadoudal was made lieutenant-general of the royalist army in the Morbihan, but after a fierce battle in 1800 he signed a treaty with the enemy. Soon, however, he was off to Britain to rally troops there. He then became involved in a plot to try and bring about Napoleon's downfall, but was caught and sentenced to death.

Touring Auray, the lively **upper town** has retained a good number of grand houses, both in timberframe and granite, and boasts the substantial church of **St-Gildas**. The architecture of the latter is a typically Breton hotch-potch of styles, with Gothic, Renaissance and Baroque features all rolled into one. The stylish 19th-century Hôtel de Ville occupies the centre of Auray's main square, **Place de la République**, while **Rue Barré** leading off the square is the main shopping artery. The **Commanderie du St-Esprit**, with its enormous Gothic arches, recalls medieval Auray. Around the upper town, you can find a good choice of shops and eateries.

However, the most unmissable part of Auray is the port of **St-Goustan**, down in the valley. Tourist success means that almost every house here has been turned into a restaurant. Number 8 along the quay is where Benjamin Franklin stayed in 1776. On the river, the miniature **Musée La Goélette** is housed in a permanently moored schooner; its displays recall sailors' lives at the start of the 20th century. **Canoeing** on the river is a possibility. A steep little climb takes you to the two **churches** standing almost next to each other above the port. That dedicated to St-Goustan, with its slate helmet, contains vivid tales from the New Testament told in 19th-century stained glass.

Musée La Goélette
open daily in summer 10–7

A Pilgrimage to Ste-Anne d'Auray

C'est un peu le Lourdes breton. (It's a bit like Brittany's Lourdes.)
Le Guide du Routard

A handful of kilometres north of Auray, Ste-Anne d'Auray is one of the holiest Catholic shrines in Brittany. In fact, it has probably become the most venerated spot in the whole province, eclipsing the traditional seven cathedral stops along the Tro Breizh pilgrimage route. It helps that the biggest memorial to the Bretons who died in the First World War was also erected here.

Ste-Anne d'Auray arose out of a confusion of superstition and piety. In 1623, one Yves Nicolazic, a local peasant, witnessed the recurring apparition of a woman dressed all in white, coming to him carrying a candle. He took her to be none other than Anne, mother of the Virgin Mary, considered the patron saint of Brittany. She supposedly revealed to him that a chapel dedicated to her had once stood in one of the fields where he worked, though it had been destroyed in the year 701. She asked him to tell his priest that she wished for a chapel to be rebuilt in her honour. At first the peasant was dismissed as mad, but in March 1625, so the story goes, the apparition told him to start digging in a precise place. Nicolazic went with some friends and there unearthed a statue of Ste Anne, supposedly dating – guess what – from the early 8th century. Whatever the machinations behind this 'miracle', the Breton Church quickly exploited it, building a chapel on the spot.

This was replaced by the enormous neo-Renaissance **basilica** you now see, built in the mid-19th century, when the Church wanted so badly to reassert its power after the mayhem caused to it by Revolution and Napoleon. The imposing structure was built to plans by Edouard Deperthes, best known for designing the Paris Hôtel de Ville with Théodore Ballu. The bulky church tower is topped by an enormous statue... not the Ste Anne discovered by Nicolazic.

Inside, the stained-glass windows tell the life of Ste Anne and the miraculous local story. Nicolazic is portrayed as a clueless simpleton. His body rests in the first right-hand side chapel. The Church's persecution by the Revolution also features, along with the Breton determination to stick to the faith. The statue of Ste Anne that Nicolazic 'unearthed' was actually burned by rabid Republicans. There is, though, a lot more to see in the basilica, including an altar to the Virgin incorporating five 15th-century alabaster panels depicting Christ's Passion, and the main altar donated by Pope Pius IX.

Parts of the **cloisters** are sometimes used for art or photography **exhibitions**, on religious themes. On the south side of the church, the **Maison de Nicolazic** is the house where Ste Anne supposedly appeared to the Breton peasant. Also close to the church, the 19th-century **Scala Sancta**, or Holy Staircase, cuts a dash. The most fanatical pilgrims climb these stairs on their knees. Less showily, people can go and pray at the simple little **oratory to Ste Anne**, containing a dignified Breton statue showing mother and daughter reading. The *pardon* of Ste-Anne d'Auray draws tens of thousands of people every year on 25 and 26 July.

The extensive **First World War memorial enclosure** demands a visit too. This is one of the most moving spots in Brittany, commemorating the vast number of Bretons who died in the First World War. The names of tens of thousands of these victims of war are engraved on the enclosure's walls. Some historians estimate that up to a quarter of a million Bretons were wiped out in the Great War – an enormous percentage of the population, which inevitably left huge numbers of families devastated.

Museum of Breton dolls
t 02 97 57 58 50; open May–Sept Tues–Sun 10.30–12 and 3–6

A separate area commemorates Pope John Paul II's visit in 1996, in particular with the 'paving stones of faith'. There's also a **museum of Breton dolls** in costume, adding a lighter note to this sobering site.

Ecomusée de St-Degan-en-Brech
www.ecomusee-st-degan.fr, **t** *02 97 57 66 00; open July–Aug daily 10–7, March–June and Sept–Nov Sun–Fri 2–5.30*

A few kilometres west, the **Ecomusée de St-Degan-en-Brech** presents a gorgeous, somewhat sanitized image of how Breton country people lived in times past. Their daily customs are evoked in the enchanting cottages in this hamlet. Look out for special events in season.

Le Bono to Gavrinis

Just south of Auray, beside the Bono River, **Ste-Avoye** offers the double attraction of its thatched houses and a Renaissance chapel boasting a beautifully restored 16th-century rood screen, which shows the apostles on one side and a depiction of saintly Breton lawyer, St Yves, as well as the virtues, on the other.

The enchantingly shy port of **Le Bono** is tucked away on the steep slopes where the Bono and Auray Rivers meet. This inland harbour rivals the port of St-Goustan for quaintness, but is much less touristy. A waterside path takes you along a trail marked by the oyster-rearing activities of the past, while another way leads you high over the water to the wooded bank opposite the village. In the southern outskirts of Le Bono, seek out one of the most beautiful but least-known megalithic sites in Brittany, **Kernourz**. The series of **tumuli** here are delightfully shaded by pine trees that appear to bow inwards to pay homage to the central tomb. Some of the neolithic burial chambers may date from around 3000 BC; you can make out further prehistoric ones from the first millennium BC, described as Iron Age *tombelles*.

Around **Baden**, beautiful country lanes can lead you down a **series of peninsulas** with mesmerizing views onto the Golfe du Morbihan. You'll encounter oyster farms on the water's edge. There's also a glorious **golf course** with views onto the gulf here.

On the western side of Larmor-Baden a road leads down to the delightful **Pointe de Berchis** and **Le Paludo**, but signs spell out *baignade interdite* ('bathing forbidden') warning people off swimming. **Larmor-Baden**, a popular small-scale resort, has magical views out over the gulf from its broad waterfront. There are some exceptional islands you can make for from here. Sometimes at low tide you can explore on foot the edges of **L'Ile Berder**, in its magnificent setting.

Ile de Gavrinis
for boat trips, which run roughly every 30mins daily Easter–Sept 10–11.30 and 2–5, Oct–All Saints 2–5; call Vedettes Blanches Armor, **t** *02 97 57 15 27*

Larmor-Baden is also the port from which to get a ferry out to the cairn of Gavrinis. Having to take a little boat to get to **Ile de Gavrinis** certainly adds to the excitement of going to see France's most magical and artistic neolithic monument. You head to it past beautiful pine-covered headlands. The island of Gavrinis is privately owned, but the tumulus on the southern end is open to the public.

The **Cairn de Gavrinis** is roughly reckoned to date from the 4th millennium BC. The wealth of decorative designs engraved on its stones distinguishes it from all the other neolithic sites in Brittany. Many of these engravings resemble magnified fingerprints. It has been claimed that they represent a mother goddess linking the world of the living with the world of the dead. Axe-heads stand out too, as do crooks, described as symbols of authority. Serpentine shapes writhe below, while further designs appear to mimic birds' feathers. It's all too mysterious for words, defying our understanding. The tomb's entrance apparently lines up to coincide with the winter solstice.

A short distance from the island of Gavrinis, the much smaller **island of Er Lannic** boasts a cromlech in a figure of eight that's half submerged by the sea – a clear sign of how much the oceans have risen since neolithic times, in which period experts believe that this whole area would have been a large marshland.

To L'Ile aux Moines

East of Larmor-Baden, the next peninsula is that of lively **Port-Blanc**. The main reason hordes come here is to take the boats for tours of the gulf or trips out to the Ile aux Moines or Ile d'Arz.

L'Ile aux Moines, the most important island in the gulf, lies just a stone's throw from the mainland. Called the Monks' Island in French, this place apparently never saw any men in habits toil and pray here – they simply managed the place from a distance and exacted their dues. Nowadays, the **port** quays crawl with tourists throughout the summer. Apart from the crowds, L'Ile aux Moines is a little Breton paradise, with creeks and beaches, fishermen's cottages and luxuriant walled gardens. Pick up a free map from the tourist office at the island's port before you set out to discover the place. Bicycles provide the easiest way of discovering the island, but you can't take them on the coastal path that hugs the shore.

The north end of the island is the most crowded part. Many of the slightly grander 19th-century houses here were built for Vannes ships' captains, who made up the 'aristocracy' of the island. It's a fair walk from the port to the island's most **northerly tip**, complete with its 19th-century **calvary**. You go through the busy centre of **Le Bourg**, as the main village is named, where you'll find a selection of restaurants and bars. Down from the northern tip, the whitewashed 19th-century **church of Locmiquel** makes a cheerful sight. Along the eastern arm of the island, the views open up onto the Ile d'Arz. Along here stands the late-18th-century Château du Guéric.

Head southwards from Le Bourg and the crowds quickly thin. Sloe bushes proliferate and you get lovely views across the gulf. Around a kilometre from the bourg you come to **Kergonan**, a kind of second village. See if you can follow the full shape of the neolithic **cromlech** known as Er Anke, broken up by houses built in the midst of it; in its entirety it would be the largest stone circle in France.

Getting around the Golfe du Morbihan

The main Golfe du Morbihan port is the **Gare Maritime de Vannes**. Contact **Navix Atlantique, t** 02 97 46 60 00, *www.navix.fr*, the **Compagnie des Iles, t** 02 97 46 18 19, *www.compagniedesiles.com*, or **Izenah Crosières, t** 02 97 26 31 45, *www.izenah-croisieres.com*, for ferries from here. These companies also operate services from Locmariaquer and Port-Navalo and, in summer, Auray and Le Bono. The simplest way to get onto the Ile aux Moines is to take the very short, regular ferry from Port-Blanc run by Izenah Croisières. The **Passeur des Iles, t** 06 22 01 67 72, *www.passeurdesiles.com*, crosses from Kerners and Port Navalo to the Iles aux Moines and Gavrinis. The **Compagnie du Golfe, t** 02 97 01 22 80, *www.compagnie-du-golfe.fr*, operates ferries from Séné to the Ile d'Arz.

Ask at local tourist offices about hiring a motorboat or sailing boat to cruise around the gulf, or even a flight over the gulf. Vannes tourist office can inform you about trips aboard a *sinagot*, an old-fashioned gulf boat, departing from Séné.

As you reach the **southern tip** of L'Ile aux Moines, a solitary dolmen, Pen Hap, lies fully exposed on a bare patch of ground. An impressive top slab covers the main burial chamber. The most southerly point on the island, Pen Nioul, is in private hands, but it's worth cycling up as far as you can go to enjoy the views. Make for a couple of slithers of beaches just to the east, where you can take a breather and watch the boats busily chugging around the gulf.

L'Ile d'Arz

Arz, a bit further out in the gulf, is much flatter, less wooded and less popular than L'Ile aux Moines, and not quite as accessible. When you're dropped off here, there's just a single jetty and a few isolated modern buildings to greet you, one with a booth where you can pick up a free map. A sturdy 17th-century restored windmill also marks this northern **Pointe de Beluré**. Consider hiring a bike by the jetty as it's quite a walk to the main centre, and the island does measure *c*.3km in length. Arz's thin strips of beach fill up quickly with families in summer.

The village, again simply known as **Le Bourg**, is delightful, its belt of houses spanning the island's girth. The lanes have a nice open feel to them. The church is topped by a typical slate-helmeted Romanesque spire, the edifice below, dedicated to Our Lady, dating back in good part to the 12th century. The southern end of the island, **Pen Liouse**, has the vestiges of several neolithic dolmens, while from the eastern shore you get views on to the quieter half of the gulf. Here, **Pennéro** has some particularly smart old houses.

Port-Blanc to Arradon

There's really only one way to appreciate the full beauty of the north coast of the Golfe du Morbihan from Port-Blanc to Arradon – walk the fabulous **coastal path**. The views of the pine-covered islands out in the gulf accompany you all the way past Arradon and the peninsula to the east. You then pass the wonderful properties around **Penboch** and **Raguédas**, Penboch standing out with the top-heavy pyramidal steeple on its church.

At **Kerguen** you arrive opposite the tiny Chapelle de St-Antoine on the tip of the Ile du Petit Bois. Towards Vannes you come to a pretty faded pink house on the water's edge; the owners aren't allowed to change the colour, as the property is marked out for its colour on navigational maps. North from here, the substantial, lively town of Vannes, capital of the Morbihan, hides out at the back of the Golfe.

Market Days in the Western Golfe du Morbihan

ⓘ Golfe du Morbihan
www.golfedu morbihan.fr

Auray: Monday
Larmor-Baden: Sunday
Arradon: Friday

Where to Stay and Eat in the Western Golfe du Morbihan

ⓘ Ste-Anne-d'Auray >>
26 Rue de Vannes, t 02 97 57 69 16, www.sainte-anne-auray.com

ⓘ Auray >
20 Rue du Lait, t 02 97 24 09 75, www.auray-tourisme.com.

ⓘ Le Bono >>
Place Joseph le Clanche, t 02 97 57 88 98, accueil.lebono @wanadoo.fr.

ⓘ Brec'h
6 Rue Georges Cadoudal, t 02 97 17 79 90, www.brec'h.fr

Auray ✉ 56400

Le Marin, 1 Place du Rolland, t 02 97 24 14 58, *www.hotel-lemarin.com* (€€). Simple hotel very well located at the enchanting port. Canoes available.

*Le Celtic, 38 Rue Georges Clemenceau, t 02 97 24 05 37, *www.hotel-leceltic.com* (€€–€) Really decent refurbished little hotel up in the town centre.

La Closerie de Kerdrain, 20 Rue Louis Billet, t 02 97 56 61 27 (€€€€–€€). Upscale restaurant in an elegantly restored 18th-century *hôtel particulier* set in a walled garden, where culinary herbs are grown. Chef's specials include oysters in green apple and cucumber jus. *Closed Mon and Tues.*

La Table des Marées, 16 Rue du Jeu de Paume, t 02 97 56 63 60 (€€€–€€). High-quality cuisine, especially fish with spices, up in the town centre.

L'Eglantine, Place St-Sauveur, Port de St-Goustan, t 02 97 56 46 55 (€€€). Smart old-school style, with excellent seafood and pictures of royalist Chouan leaders on the walls. It's on the extraordinarily picturesque square down beside the port. *Closed Wed.*

Crêperie-Restaurant Capucine, 6 Rue St-Sauveur, t 02 97 56 35 53 (€). Just above the main tourist fray, simple family-run crêperie-restaurant with a snug pocket of a dining room, plus a small, colourful terrace.

Crêperie Féerie de la Soupière, 18 Rue du Lait, t 02 97 55 46 39 (€). A good cheap choice. *Pommes flambées* in caramel a speciality.

There are plenty of tempting touristy addresses with terraces beside the gorgeous port of St-Goustan.

Ste-Anne-d'Auray ✉ 56400

L'Auberge, 56 Route de Vannes, t 02 97 57 61 55, *www.lauberge-larvoir.com* (€€). Stylishly refurbished rooms in a Breton-style modern hotel, with a beamed dining room offering elaborate cuisine (€€€€–€€).

La Croix Blanche, 25 Route de Vannes, t 02 97 57 64 44, *www.hotel-lacroixblanche.com* (€). With decent rooms, a garden and a pleasant restaurant.

Le Bono ✉ 56400

Hostellerie Abbatiale, Manoir de Kerdréan, t 02 97 57 84 00, *www.manoirdekerdrean.com* (€€€€–€€€). A Best Western hotel in a Breton manor, offering comfortable rooms in a modern annexe, a pool, a tennis court and a golf course.

Hôtel Alicia, 1 Rue du Général de Gaulle, t 02 97 57 88 65, *www.hotel-alicia.com* (€€–€). Friendly little modern hotel, rooms with pretty river views from up above the valley. Really appealing restaurant serving inventive cuisine.

Le Vieux Pont, 23 Rue Pasteur, t 02 97 57 87 71 (€). A bar-cum-crêperie that's about as simple as they come, set on the delightful little port.

Baden ✉ 56870

Le Gavrinis, 1 Rue de l'Ile Gavrinis (2km east of Baden), t 02 97 57 00 82,

(i) **Ile d'Arz >>**
www.iledarz.fr

(i) **Larmor-Baden >**
24 Quai Pen Lannic,
t 02 97 58 01 26

(i) **Arradon >>**
Rue Bonnet Aubertot,
t 02 97 44 01 56,
www.arradon.com

(i) **Ile aux Moines >**
Le Port, t 02 97 26 32
45 (Easter–Sept only)

(★) **Le Logis de Parc er Gréo >>**

www.gavrinis.com (€€€–€€). A very cheerful hotel with flowers galore, some bright, modern guest rooms and its own garden. The cuisine (€€€–€€) is excellent refined Breton fare.

Larmor-Baden ✉ 56870

**Auberge Parc Fetan, 17 Rue du Berder, t 02 97 57 04 38, *www.hotel-parcfetan.com* (€€–€). A very good gulf-side hotel, with pool and restaurant, and a handy option for the ferry. *Closed mid-Nov–mid-Feb.*

Ile aux Moines ✉ 56780

Le San Francisco, 15 Rue Bénoni Praud, Le Port, t 02 97 26 31 52, *www.le-sanfrancisco.com* (€€). A hotel set in a former Franciscan convent, offering much sought-after cosy rooms. Great place to eat, both for views and food. *Closed Nov-mid-Feb.*

Le Clos B&B, Rue Neuve, Le Lério, t 02 97 26 34 29 (€€–€). Rooms in a typical rustic old fisherman's cottage with delightful garden.

Le Chemin des Iles B&B, Rue des Escaliers, t 02 97 42 63 45, *www.lechemindesiles.com* (€€). Fresh, bright rooms in a renovated Breton stone house with charming garden.

Les Embruns, Rue du Commerce, Le Bourg, t 02 97 26 30 86 (€€). An appealing restaurant. *Closed Wed.*

Ile d'Arz ✉ 56840

**L'Escale d'en Arz, Le Beluré, t 02 97 44 32 15 (€€€–€). Simple rooms on the island.

Arradon ✉ 56610

***Les Venètes, La Pointe d'Arradon, t 02 97 44 85 85, *www.lesvenetes.com* (€€€–€€). A modern hotel in a truly splendid location overlooking the gulf, with very comfortable rooms enjoying the views. Also fine waterside spot to dine.

***Le Logis de Parc er Gréo, Le Gréo, t 02 97 44 73 03, *www.parcergreo.com* (€€). Delightful maritime villa with a fisherman's cottage at the bottom of its scented garden, and a heated pool. *Closed mid-Nov–mid-March.*

L'Arlequin, 3 Allée Papin, t 02 97 40 41 41 . Stylish round restaurant in green setting, serving fine dishes.

L'Auberge d'Arradon, 2 Rue Bouruet Aubertot, t 02 97 44 02 20. In a lovely typical Breton house in the village, traditional provincial setting for really good Breton fare.

Vannes

A croissant of cafés curves out from the major gateway leading from Vannes's marina into the old town on its hill; this row of establishments offers an excellent place from which to contemplate how to spend a day or two in and around this buzzing city. Behind you, through that religious-looking gateway into town, you have the old paved streets leading to the cathedral on its sloping ground, the museums of Vannes (which include an important archaeological museum and a fine arts one), the bourgeois shops set in splendid timberframe buildings, and the medieval ramparts. In front of you, the quays lead to the town's outer port, serving the Golfe du Morbihan, beside which you'll find a batch of small, fun, modern museums.

History

Vannes has a superb, naturally protected port, as it lies hidden right at the back of the Golfe du Morbihan. Classical historians have speculated as to whether this might have been the main location of the settlement of the Venetes, the reputed Celtic tribe of

Getting to Vannes

Vannes' **railway** station is on the TGV line linking Paris to Quimper, and also at the end of the line crossing central Brittany north to south from St-Brieuc to Vannes. The station lies well north of the historic centre. South of town, Vannes's Gare Maritime is the principal port from which **ferries** leave for the islands of the Golfe du Morbihan (*see* p.431 for further details).

the region when the Romans attacked. A Gallo–Roman town called Darioritum certainly grew up northeast of medieval Vannes, where remnants of a forum and a fortified castrum have been found.

With the collapse of the Roman Empire, the Armorican peninsula would gradually turn into Brittany. Franks from the east advanced this far, while at approximately the same period, immigrants from Britain were arriving in western Armorica. In fact, Saint Patern, one of the seven Celtic Christian founding fathers of the province, thought all to have come over from Wales, appears to have made Vannes into his spiritual centre.

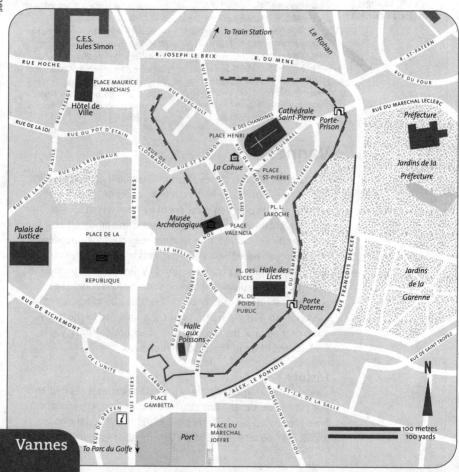

Around the middle of the 6th century, a Breton chief, Waroc'h, took control of the Vannetais by force. The great Frankish historian of the period, Gregory of Tours, details some of the brutal violence involved in the campaign, and one Bishop Regalis rued the fact that his people were put under what he called the 'Breton yoke'.

A still more powerful figure than Waroc'h in Brittany's history, Nomenoë, was a Breton who rose through Charlemagne's ranks in the early 9th century and was made Comte de Vannes as a reward. Charlemagne's successor, Louis le Pieux, conferred on him the important function of *missus* to Brittany in 826. However, once Louis had died, Nomenoë fell out with the Frankish monarchy and embarked on his project to make Brittany independent from the Carolingians, extending the Breton frontiers. Within 10 years he had succeeded, uniting the Bretons under him. For a short time, Vannes became capital of the Kingdom of Brittany. Vikings then wrought destruction in the region.

Remnants from medieval Vannes include impressive sections of its ramparts, which were put to much use in the Breton War of Succession in the mid 14th century, when Vannes was bitterly fought over by the opposing sides, its people forced to switch allegiance with head-spinning frequency. The city was occupied by English troops backing the de Montfort side for some time; when they won, Duke Jean IV of Brittany had the fortifications extended.

Duke Jean V of Brittany confirmed Vannes as one of the main centres of his duchy in the early 15th century. A few of the fine half-timbered houses date as far back as this. The massive Tour du Connétable also went up along the ramparts at this time, the lodgings for the head of the ducal army, as did Vannes's imposing cathedral. The citizens had continued to support the cult of St Patern down the centuries, much to the annoyance of the Church of Rome, which didn't recognize such Breton saints. A brilliant Spanish Catholic propagandist, Vincent Ferrier, was shipped in from 1418 to 1419 to bring a bit of Roman Catholic discipline to the people.

Brittany came much more directly under the control of the French monarchy once the last duchess, Anne de Bretagne, was forced into marriage to the French royal family late in the 15th century. However, it still held meetings of its own Estates, which gathered on several occasions at Vannes. Brittany's Act of Union with France of 13 August 1532, 'the perpetual union of the land and duchy of Brittany with the kingdom and crown of France', was signed in the city.

In the French Wars of Religion in the second half of the 16th century, Spanish troops supporting the ultra-Catholic side came briefly to occupy the town and Vannes lost the ducal administrative importance it had known during the 15th century.

In 1675, prosperity returned to the town, however. Louis XIV's administration punished the Rennes Parlement for the violent tax riots known as the Révolte du Papier Timbré that had taken place there, and the Breton Parlement was moved to Vannes for 15 years. During the Revolution, support in Vannes was mainly for the royalist, conservative, Catholic side; this caused the Revolutionaries in Paris to send the ruthless Republican General Hoche to do his persuasive worst in the region.

This conservative centre stagnated somewhat in the 20th century, and the neglected port even began to smell rather rank. Things have become distinctly more fragrant in the last few decades. Smart yachts have replaced merchant shipping, posh shops have taken up residence in many of the finest houses, the cultural scene has blossomed, and, even if one scarcely thinks of students being next to cleanliness, the new university has helped stir things up, making this a vibrant, very appealing contemporary city.

A Tour of the Town

From the café-lined crescent of **Place Gambetta,** head into the old town passing under the **Porte St-Vincent**. This 18th-century gate looks like a great portal into a church; and on it stands a statue of Vincent Ferrier, a colourful finger-pointing figure. **Rue St-Vincent** has retained many of the houses built for the Breton parliamentarians who moved here in 1675; the Revolution's henchman General Hoche also took lodgings here later. Now, tempting touristy shops beckon you in to most of the houses. Branching off at the start of Rue St-Vincent, a lane leads immediately to the **Halle aux Poissons**, the covered fishmarket.

Continue up Rue St-Vincent and you come to the first in a series of connecting, sloping squares. **Place du Poids Public** lies to the left, while **Place des Lices** takes you up the incline and joins with **Place Laroche**. Several characterful buildings from different periods stand out, including the particularly striking Hôtel de Francheville, with its 17th-century turret made out of tender tufa limestone. The 1900 neo-Moorish building, decorated with patterns in yellow bricks and green ermine tails, transforms itself into a food market on certain days of the week. Off on the eastern side, you can climb little sections of ramparts for fine views down onto the public gardens down below.

Musée d'Histoire de Vannes

t 02 97 01 63 00, musee@mairie-vannes.fr; open mid-May–mid-June daily 1.30–6; mid-June–Sept daily 10–6; Feb, Easter and All Saints hols 1.30–6

Just west of the interconnecting squares, the **Château-Gaillard** is a very smart town house that dates from the 15th century. It was built for Jean de Malestroit, one-time chancellor to the duke of Brittany. In 1912 it was bought by the Société Polymathique of Vannes, which turned it into the **Musée d'Histoire de Vannes**, concentrating on prehistory. It contains many of the finest finds from the excavations of Morbihan's neolithic sites: polished axes, the design and finish of which make them look like admirable, modern works of craftsmanship; rougher jewellery, in the form of necklaces, pendants and bangles, some in rare stone such as callais, a kind of turquoise; and fragments of tools, weapons and pottery.

Among other small collections you can view an Egyptian mummy, and Gallo–Roman coins and colourful rings. Upstairs, you stumble upon a room full of unintentionally comical 17th-century painted panels, the Cabinet des Pères du Désert. Medieval religious objects, tapestries and other ornate objects from Vannes's past lie more soberly on display in the room beyond it.

The Cathedral Quarter

The stocky **Cathédrale St-Pierre** sits somewhat uncomfortably on top of Vannes's hill. The slopes around it give its architecture some originality, but it's hemmed in by old streets on all sides, so you can't get any grand perspectives onto it. Take a walk all the way round the outside, though, to appreciate its varied architectural features, which go from the 12th to the 19th centuries. Heading down the south side, the very pretty timberframe façades of houses on the **Rue St-Guenhaël** may distract you more than the religious building. Several features will capture your attention along the north side on **Rue des Chanoines**: a crudely carved little calvary; the vestiges of a cloister; and a classical, round chapel from 1537, which holds Vincent Ferrier's remains.

The interior is remarkably wide and sombre, with a Gothic tracery balustrade running along above the low-pointed Gothic arches, and an elaborate old organ with a clock incorporated in the middle of it. Behind the sobriety of the main part of the cathedral, the wildly carved chapel at the east end comes as a shock; the place is a rococo orgy of decoration, where stone fruit pours out of a cornucopia above the figures of the Virgin and Baby Jesus.

Opposite the main entrance to the cathedral, on **Place St-Pierre**, the Act of Union between Brittany and France was signed in 1532 behind the thick walls of **La Cohue**. This building has served several purposes in its lifetime. In medieval times the covered market was held under its arches, while the local court met above. Occasionally, the Estates of Brittany gathered here. Now La Cohue contains Vannes's **Musée des Beaux-Arts**. Delacroix's *Crucifixion* is the most famous work in the collection of this intelligently presented fine arts museum. It's not one of the 19th-century prodigy's best pieces, however, showing a generously-busted Mary Magdalene in the Rubens mould. Painted wooden statues of Breton saints have been gathered around the enormous canvas. One room features Breton landscapes by Jean Frélaut (1879–1954), including a view of Vannes in a darkly grey but attractive light, with a tall ship at anchor at the

Musée des Beaux-Arts de Vannes

t 02 97 01 63 00; museums open daily 15 June–Sept 10–6, rest of year 1.30–6

10 Morbihan | Vannes

very gates of the town. There are also displays of work by Jean-François Boucher (1853–1937), a Parisian who captured the spirit of local markets and processions. Jules Noël, best known as a master of Breton seascapes, also features here. The museum has acquired a collection of royal portraits by Van Loo, showing Louis XV and family. The massive chambers downstairs hold exhibitions from the museum's fine collections of engravings as well as contemporary art exhibitions.

The square diagonally **north of the cathedral** and La Cohue, **Place Henri IV**, looks particularly striking with its amazingly colourful display of timberframe houses. Off it, **Rue St-Salomon** is one of the major shopping arteries in Vannes and leads out to some of the grand 19th-century buildings on the western edge of the old town and the upper part of **Rue Thiers** – the **Hôtel de Ville,** or town hall, counts among the architectural extravaganzas on this street that leads back down to the tourist office and port.

From the other, **choir end of the cathedral**, enchanting **Place Brûlée**, surrounded by tempting shops, leads down to the imposing **Porte Prison**, one of the best-preserved medieval gates. It once served as a prison, and narrowly avoided annihilation at the turn of the 19th century.

The streets beyond the Porte Prison contain a lively array of more studenty boutiques, bars and restaurants, set behind yet more colourful timberframe façades. The **church of St Patern** stands out on **Rue St-Patern** in this quarter.

Close by, the imposing Préfecture dominating **Rue du Maréchal Leclerc** is backed by smart **gardens**. Opposite them stand the best-preserved of the city's **ramparts**, the broad ditch below them now planted with immaculate formal flowerbeds. The most impressive of the many rampart towers is the Tour du Connétable, while the Tour du Bourreau (Executioner's Tower) was where the town hangman lived.

As you head back down to the port below the ramparts, you pass the grand 19th-century **Château de l'Hermine**. It was on this site that Pierre de Bretagne, later Duke Jean V of Brittany, was born; now law students study within. Very humble by comparison, the little roofed structure almost at the feet of the château was the town wash-house. Further well-tended gardens, the **Jardins de la Garenne** climb the slope above.

The Tourist Attractions of the Parc du Golfe

Looking south from **Place Gambetta**, you can see the long, straight, narrow channel of water and the modern shaded quays leading out to the Golfe du Morbihan. Restoration work carried out here in the mid-1970s completely transformed this neglected part of town. You may spot the *Corbeau des mers* on display close to

Place Gambetta; this langoustine-fishing boat has been declared an historic monument – it formed part of the fleet of small boats in which the exceptionally loyal men of the island of Sein sailed off from Brittany to Britain immediately on hearing Général de Gaulle's call from London to join the French Resistance on 26 June 1940.

The shaded quayside walk out from Place Gambetta and along the **Promenade de la Rabine** leads to the commercial port and the site from which you can take a **boat out onto the Golfe du Morbihan** (*see* p.431). A couple of modern tourist attractions have set up shop here, amid the large dull car parks. The least unsuccessful building holds a good **aquarium** with pools containing sharks, turtles, dangerous fish such as stone fish and the electric eel, and the less threatening polka-dot-marked fish known affectionately as the Grace Kelly. At the **Jardin aux Papillons** you can learn about the stages in a butterfly's life. The architecture is uninspiring, but the interior houses a humid tropical zone full of bright flowers, with butterflies flying around your face.

Walk on beyond this port area and you can join the lovely **coastal path** along the Golfe du Morbihan, finding tranquillity not far from the centre of town, although keen Vannetais joggers particularly appreciate pounding along the flat, pine-shaded route.

Aquarium
*t 02 97 40 67 40,
www.aquarium-du-golfe.com; open
April–June and Sept
10–12 and 2–6,
July–Aug 9–7.30,
Oct–Mar 2–6, hols
also 10–12*

**Jardin aux
Papillons**
*t 02 97 40 40 39,
. www.jardinaux
papillons.com; open
April–June and Sept
10–12 and 2–6;
July–Aug 10–7*

(i) **Vannes >**
*1 Rue Thiers, t 08 25 13
56 10, www.tourisme-
vannes.com*

(★) **La Villa
Kerasy >**

Market Days

Wednesday and Saturday

Where to Stay in Vannes

Vannes ✉ 56000

★★★★**La Villa Kerasy**, 20 Ave Favrel et Lincy, **t** 02 97 68 36 83, *www.villa kerasy.com* (€€€€–€€). Charming hotel by the station, with decor inspired by the oriental travels of the Compagnie des Indes.

★★★**Le Roof**, Presqu'île de Conleau, **t** 02 97 63 47 47, *www.le-roof.com* (€€€). In an exclusive position on the water's edge south of the centre, offering wonderful views onto the Golfe du Morbihan. With restaurant.

★★★**La Marébaudière**, 4 Rue Aristide Briand, **t** 02 97 47 34 29, *www. marebaudiere.com* (€€€€–€€€). Just a bit east of the centre, with more character than most of the hotels around the historic town.

★★**de France**, 57 Ave Victor Hugo, **t** 02 97 47 27 57, *www.hotelfrance-vannes.*

com (€€–€). Good choice with nicely decorated rooms just north of the old town.

★★**Au Relais du Golfe**, 10 Place du Général de Gaulle, **t** 02 97 47 14 74 (€). Situated above a locals' bar close to the ramparts.

Eating Out in Vannes

Regis Mahé, 24 Place de la Gare, **t** 02 97 42 61 41 (€€€€–€€€). Exotic, exciting restaurant by the station, mixing Breton and international flavours. *Closed Sun and Mon.*

Roscanvec, 17 Rue des Halles, **t** 02 97 47 15 96, *www.roscanvec.com* (€€€). Reputed haute cuisine, including surprising dishes such as spiced turbot in mango juice or langoustine with courgette flowers. *Closed Sun eve and Mon in low season.*

La Table des Gourmets, 6 Rue Le Pontois, **t** 02 97 47 52 44 (€€€). Tasty gastronomic Breton fare such as pan-fried red mullet fillets stuffed with tapenade, plus views on to the ramparts from opposite Vannes's ramparts. *Closed low season Mon lunch, Wed and Sun eves.*

Le Grain de Sel, 13 Rue des Halles, **t** 02 97 54 37 41, *www.legraindesel56.com* (€€). A restaurant in an old, beamed house on an atmospheric street, serving fresh, simple Breton produce. A good place to sample frogs' legs.

A l'Aise Breizh Café, Port de Plaisance, **t** 02 97 68 15 89 (€). With large terrace making the most of the location beside the port, serving salads and Breton dishes.

Au Pont Vert, at the Golfe end of the Avenue du Maréchal de Lattre de Tassigny, **t** 02 97 40 80 13, *restaurant-au-pont-vert@wanadoo.fr* (€). A good-value place on the tree-lined road following the port out to the sea, extremely popular with local workers for its unpretentious but copious lunches.

(★) Crêperie La Métairie de Kérozer >>

Crêperie La Cave St Gwenaël, 23 Rue St-Guenhaël, **t** 02 97 47 47 94 (€). In one of the oldest, most beautiful houses in Vannes, on the south side of the cathedral. *Closed Sun and Mon.*

Crêperie La Taupinière, 9 Place des Lices, **t** 02 97 42 57 82 (€). A sweet crêperie; you'll see why it's called the mole's house. *Closed Mon.*

St-Avé ✉ 56890

Le Pressoir, 7 Rue de l'Hôpital, **t** 02 97 60 87 63, *www.le-pressoir-st-ave.com* (€€€). Former station bistrot turned gastronomic haunt just northeast of Vannes. *Closed Mon and Tues.*

Crêperie La Métairie de Kérozer, Allée de Kerozer, **t** 02 97 61 88 45 (€). Splendid crêperie in every way.

The Eastern and Southern Golfe du Morbihan

The eastern shore of the Golfe proves more difficult to explore than the rest. What's more, a large portion of the eastern waters of the gulf is given over to oyster farming and to a bird reserve, and in addition is greatly affected by the tides. Large expanses of mud are revealed as the water recedes. The gulf remains as beautiful as ever, though, and the best way to see it is once again by foot. The Presqu'île de Rhuys is the name for the long spit of land that forms the protective southern barrier protecting the whole Golfe du Morbihan from the ocean.

From Vannes down the Eastern Side of the Golfe du Morbihan

South from Vannes via built-up Séné, signs lead to the **Réserve Ornithologique de Falguérec**, a 400-hectare bird reserve covering former salt pans. A secretive peninsula heads back in the direction of Arradon; go there to be rewarded with superb views onto the gulf at the **Pointe de Moustérian**, or, on the western tip of the peninsula, at **Port-Anna** – this delightful miniature port, set in a creek looking across to Conleau, is home to a *sinagot*, a traditional oyster boat with a ruddy sail. A little east, past Theix, the Château du Plessis-Josso presents a pleasing image of a defensive medieval manor and some interesting interiors.

Château du Plessis-Josso
t 02 97 43 16 16, *www.plessis-josso.com*; open July–Aug daily 2–7

Château de Kerlévenan
t 02 97 26 46 79; open Sat–Thurs July–Aug 1.30–5.30, Sept 2.30–5.30

For a glimpse of a grand Ancien Régime home, continue east for the **Château de Kerlévenan**, where you can go on a guided tour of the grounds with their follies. Among the beautiful spots to stop at before the Rhuys peninsula, the port of **Le Logeo** stands out.

The end of the **Rhuys peninsula** has become heavily built up with holiday blocks and suffers from massive overpopularity in summer. Arzon is the town by the point, but visitors focus on its two protected ports in their separate little inlets: the older one, **Port-Navalo**, which used to be known for its fishing fleet; and the more modern, suburban-looking **Le Crouesty**, which has a packed-out **marina**, the buildings around it resembling a modern shopping precinct. There are all manner of opportunities for getting out on boats from these twin harbours.

Two of the best places from which to appreciate the natural beauty of the tip of the Rhuys peninsula are its two neolithic tumuli. The **Petit Mont**, the more westerly, is one of the most substantial, memorable neolithic burial chambers you can visit in Brittany. It also has the dubious distinction of having served as a large Nazi bunker in the Second World War. As you arrive, you're greeted by the surprising, saddening and yet also slightly comical sight of sections of German blockhouse cement appearing out of the dry stone sides of the tumulus. More respectful digs carried out during the 1980s have allowed for an interesting visit within, and the interlocking tombs, dated to different periods, contain some well-preserved engraved stones.

Petit Mont
*t 06 03 95 90 78;
open April–June and
Sept Thurs–Tues
2.30–6.30; July–Aug
daily 10–1 and
2.30–6.30*

The **Butte de César** or **Tumiac tumulu**s just outside Arzon is much less interesting to visit. The way this circular tumulus was excavated makes it impossible to see the fascinating engraved stones within, though precious finds were transferred to the local museums. Traditionally, it was said that this tumulus was where Caesar watched the fatal naval battle that brought about the downfall of the Celtic Veneti tribe (*see* box below).

After the succession of **beaches east of Arzon**, you come to **St-Gildas-de-Rhuys**, once home to an important religious community. The **church** of St-Gildas-de-Rhuys appears none too welcoming from the outside, but its Romanesque apse and extravagant 17th-century stone retable must have filled medieval pilgrims with awe. The church is dedicated to Gildas – *see* box, overleaf.

10 Morbihan | The Eastern and Southern Golfe du Morbihan

A Thrashing from Caesar

Caesar's description of the Roman naval campaign against the Veneti in 56 BC counts as one of the most informative and evocative pieces on Armorica to have come down to us from history. Caesar had conquered Gaul the year before, and the local Celtic tribe, the Veneti, were the first to foolishly revolt in defiance of Caesar's troops. The great Roman commander led the campaign against them himself and, having written of the Veneti's strength, recognized how his army managed to defeat them through luck as much as good judgement, when the unfortunate Veneti found themselves cruelly becalmed in their excellent, swift sailing vessels. The Romans caught and massacred the seamen and Caesar sold the rest of the population as slaves. Read the famous passage in Caesar's *Conquest of Gaul* to get a fuller picture of this extraordinary event. Gallo–Roman fragments found at Le Petit Mont indicate that the site may have become a sanctuary where the Roman victory was remembered and celebrated.

Gildas, a Zealous Celtic Christian

Gildas would be one of the most important British religious figures to play a part in turning the Armorican peninsula into Celtic Christian Brittany. He may have been born by the Clyde at the start of the 6th century, but certainly developed into one of the most influential figures in the 6th-century Celtic Church. He went off to become a monk at Llaniltud in south Wales, and also built strong ties with many notable Irish monks of the period, visiting the Emerald Isle. Gildas is also thought to have gone to live for a time on the island of Flat Holm in the Bristol Channel, but he sailed off to spend his latter years in Brittany. Breton tradition says he settled on the island of Houat, then, around 536, at St-Gildas-de-Rhuys, where he founded a religious community of note.

Gildas is credited with composing *De Excidio Britanniae*, a work deeply critical of the secular rulers and clerics of the British Isles, in around 540. He blamed them for their lack of moral fibre, claiming that this was the reason for the success of the Anglo-Saxons' supremacy.

One legend has it that on his arrival on mainland Brittany, he encountered the devil disguised as a terrifying serpent. The saintly man made the creature swallow a ball of wool in which he had hidden a needle. The needle perforated the serpent's intestine and the triumphant Gildas attached the agonized beast to his horse and dragged it to the sea to drown it.

The Château de Suscinio

The Château de Suscinio
t 02 97 41 91 91, www.suscinio.info; open daily Nov–Jan 10–12 and 2–5, Feb–Mar and Oct 10–12 and 2–6, April–Sept 10–7

It's really rather extraordinary to see a medieval castle plonked by itself right on a beach like this. In fact, the attraction of Suscinio for the medieval dukes of Brittany who ordered this seaside château wasn't the bathing, but hunting, as the lands of the peninsula were covered with forests during the Middle Ages. An Act of 1218 mentions a castle here, but little is left of that early construction. However, massive walls and towers do survive aplenty from the 14th-century building campaigns.

In the second half of the 15th century, the château fell into decline, though the dowager duchess Isabel of Scotland, widow of Breton Duke François I, did stay on at Suscinio from 1450 to 1487. In 1488, Duke François II gave the property to Jean de Châlon, Prince of Orange, and the Château de Suscinio was then neglected by its absent owners, the powerful Conti family. At the Revolution a Lorient property speculator took away large quantities of its stone to sell on to builders, hence the much-damaged building you now see.

The *département* of the Morbihan bought the château ruins in 1965 and has been slowly mending them. The heavily restored apartments do give an indication of the sumptuousness of Breton ducal life in the Middle Ages. Some original medieval flooring stands out, with its richly varied patterns of tiles that lay hidden for centuries just outside the castle walls; they originally decorated a chapel.

Musée Régional des Arts et des Métiers
www.musee-arts-metiers.com, t 02 97 53 68 25; open Sept–June Tues–Sun 2–7; July–Aug Mon–Sat 10–12 and 2–7, Sun 2–7

A little way inland, the old stone **Manoir de Kerguet** may have been the château commander's home. It now contains the **Musée Régional des Arts et des Métiers**, run by a compulsive collector who has crammed it with displays of traditional items, from *coiffes* and clogs to old school desks.

The Atlantic pounds the long **stretches of beach at Suscinio and Penvins**. The Presqu'île de Rhuys officially comes to an end at **Le Tour-du-Parc**, where the area's former salt pans have been turned into a mass of modern oyster farms.

On the eastern side of the Penerf River, the six-kilometre stretch of sandy **beach** along the **Bay of Damgan** has clear seaside holiday potential, despite the uninspiring housing that forms the backdrop.

Market Days in the Eastern and Southern Golfe du Morbihan

Sarzeau: Thursday
Arzon: Tuesday
Le Crouesty: Monday in summer
Port-Navalo: Friday in summer
St-Gildas-de-Rhuys: Sunday, plus daily in July and August

Where to Stay and Eat in the Eastern and Southern Golfe du Morbihan

Sarzeau ✉ 56370
Auberge du Kerstephany, Route du Roallguen, t 02 97 41 72 41, *www.auberge-kerstephany.com* (€€). Once a farm, then the home of defrocked monks and later a herbalist. Eat on a terrace covered in climbing roses or by a fire inside, where meat and fish are grilled. *Closed Sun eve, Tues eve and Wed.*

Hôtel Lesage. With good restaurant.

St-Colombier ✉ 56370
Le Tournepierre, 4km east of Sarzeau, t 02 97 26 42 19 (€€€–€€). An excellent restaurant serving tasty fish and seafood in a village on the edge of the Golfe du Morbihan.

Le Crouesty ✉ 56640
****Miramar**, Port Crouesty, t 02 97 53 49 00, *www.miramar crouesty.com* (€€€€€–€€€€). A big fake liner of a modern building, anchored in an artificial round pond

by the sea, with smart, balconied rooms, restaurants with good views, a piano bar, a heated seawater pool, a tennis court, a sauna, a gym, a thalassotherapy centre (specialist treatments include post-natal anti-cellulite) and a beauty salon. *Closed Dec.*

Port-Navalo ✉ 56640
****Glann Ar Mor**, 27 Rue des Fontaines, t 02 97 53 88 30, *www.glannarmor.fr* (€€). Recently renovated rooms in a 1930s hotel with a restaurant.

Le Grand Largue, 1 Rue du Phare, t 02 97 53 71 58 (€€€). Great views, carefully cooked seafood such as lobster in a coral sauce and a good wine cellar. *Closed Mon and Tues in low season.*

Damgan ✉ 56750
****Hotel de la Plage**, 38 Blvd de l'Océan, t 02 97 41 10 07, *www.hotel-morbihan.com* (€€€–€). Right by the beach, with many rooms with excellent sea views. *Closed mid-Nov–mid-Feb.*

****L'Albatros**, 1 Blvd de l'Océan, t 02 97 41 16 85, *www.hotel-albatros-damgan.com* (€€–€). Many rooms with sea views too, though the decent restaurant looks on to the car park. *Closed Nov–mid-March.*

Le Café Pêcheur, 26 Rue du Port, t 02 97 41 10 38 (€€). With sunny terrace looking over Pénerf port west of Damgan, serving really good fish. *Closed Sun eve and Mon.*

Le Bistrot de la Mer, 17 Rue du Port, t 02 97 41 00 97 (€€). Near neighbour of above also doing good seafood dishes. *Closed Mon eve and Tues.*

Kervoyal
Crêperie L'Écurie, t 02 97 41 03 29 (€). A cheerful crêpe house at the eastern end of Damgan's bay, with terrace.

Around the Vilaine Estuary

The beautiful section of the Vilaine Valley from Rennes to Redon is described in the Ille-et-Vilaine chapter, but the river ends in style in the Morbihan. Don't miss the fine riverside village of La Roche-Bernard. Several charming sights lie close by. Beyond Tréhiguier, the Morbihan coast comes to a dramatic end with the golden cliffs of Pénestin.

Either Side of the Vilaine Estuary

The **Pointe de Penn Lann** just below Billiers marks the northern entrance to the beautiful Vilaine estuary, often referred to as La Vilaine Maritime. There's a lighthouse at the headland, while a little port nestles in the northern tip of the point.

Slightly inland, close to Muzillac and by the emerald-green waters of a lovely lake, the **Etang de Pen-Mur**, you come to the **Moulin de Pen-Mur**, a restored old watermill. The *papetiers* here use cloth to make paper, and on a guided tour they show you how.

Moulin de Pen-Mur
t 02 97 41 43 79, www.moulin-pen-mur.com; open July–Aug Mon–Sat 10–12.30 and 2.30–7, Sun 2.30–7

The well-regarded **Parc Zoologique de Branféré** northeast of Muzillac, spreads out around a handsome 19th-century manor house. The lovely lawns around it are often covered with scores of hopping maras, hare-like creatures that originated in Patagonia and have marsupial manners. The Buddhist creator of Branféré, Paul Jourde, and his wife, Hélène, were passionate zoological collectors, and Hélène, a well-known painter, featured many of their animals on her atmospheric canvases. The Fondation de France has run and developed this highly regarded zoological park along the lines of its creators since they died. In total, the place looks after 1,000 animals in its 60 hectares, plus there's a children's farm. Pygmy hippos are the latest addition to the menagerie.

Parc Zoologique de Branféré
t 02 97 42 94 66, www.branfere.com; open Feb–Mar and Oct–Nov daily 1.30–4, April–June and Sept 10–5, July–Aug 10–6

The **Barrage d'Arzal** is a funky modern dam across the Vilaine estuary, behind which lies a large **marina**. The best way to appreciate the beauty of the Vilaine Valley east of this *barrage* is to take a cruise up it. In the dam itself, you can go down to an **observation room** with a glass wall that allows you to see fish migrating up- or downstream according to the season.

The area of Pénestin is associated with *la mytiliculture*, mussel-rearing. The comical lighthouse at **Tréhiguier** has been turned into a bright little **Maison de la Mytiliculture** explaining the cultivation of both mussels and cockles – the Vilaine estuary is the largest site for cockles in France. The place can also help you sort out your netted dogwhelks from your piddocks, should you be having problems telling them apart.

Maison de la Mytiliculture
t 02 23 10 03 00; open Easter and All Saints and May–June Sat–Sun 3–6, July–Aug 10.30–12.30 and 3–6

The dramatic **Pénestin peninsula beach** is backed by impressively high cliffs, not made of rock, but of hardened, ochre-coloured sand, eroded into a picturesque arc by the elements. At sunset, the cliffs light up a lustrous golden colour, and you can well understand how the place got its nickname of *La Mine d'Or*, 'the Gold Mine'.

Up the Vilaine to La Roche-Bernard

Tucked out of sight of the N165 dual carriageway rushing past high over the Vilaine, La Roche-Bernard's narrow streets tumble prettily down the very steep hillside to the river. Up in the flatter part of the village, a number of good restaurants congregate around a series of little squares lined with atmospheric houses.

Musée de la Vilaine Maritime
t 02 99 90 83 47; open April–Oct, ask at tourist office for hours

The **Château des Basses-Fosses**, containing the **Musée de la Vilaine Maritime**, demonstrates the dramatic geography of the village – from the upper entrance the place seems like an elegant, low 16th-century house, but look at it from down by the river and you'll realize it descends a full five floors to the water. La Roche-Bernard's stormy history is retold inside. Going by the origins of the name, it would seem clear that a Viking founded a settlement here in the course of the 10th-century raids – the Norse term Bern-Hart means 'strong as a bear'. Since then, several successive castles built for the medieval lords of La Roche-Bernard have come and gone. In the Breton War of Succession, the local baron backed the losing side and lost his house. Subsequent barons then moved away to the splendid Château de la Bretesche some way southeast. In the 16th century, La Roche-Bernard became for a time one of the most important enclaves of the Protestant Huguenots in ultra-Catholic Brittany.

Thanks to its protected location along the deep Vilaine River, the place proved excellent for shipbuilding, developing into a major construction yard in the Ancien Régime. The first three-decked ship in France, *La Couronne*, was completed here in 1638. In 1644, the queen of England, Catholic Henrietta-Maria, daughter of King Henri IV of France and wife of beleaguered Charles I of England, came briefly to the Maison des Basses-Fosses, having fled the civil war across the Channel.

However, much of this beautifully presented museum focuses not on royalty or celebrity, but on the life of the ordinary people of La Roche-Bernard and especially on traditional types of fishing along the Vilaine, with models, nets and ephemera. Particular attention is also paid to the major bridges built here since the 19th century in order to span the wide chasm of the Vilaine Valley.

Market Days around the Vilaine Estuary

Muzillac: Friday
Questembert: Monday
Pénestin: Wednesday and Sunday
La Roche-Bernard: Thursday

★ **Domaine de Rochevilaine** >>

Where to Stay and Eat around the Vilaine Estuary

Billiers ✉ 56190
★★★★Domaine de Rochevilaine, Pointe de Pen Lann, **t** 02 97 41 61 61, *www.*

**ⓘ Maison du
Tourisme du
Pays de Redon**
*www.tourisme-pays-
redon.com, for general
information on
this area*

ⓘ Questembert ›
*15 Rue des Halles,
t 02 97 26 56 00,
www.questembert.com*

ⓘ Muzillac
*Place de l'Hôtel de
Ville, t 02 97 41 53 04,
www.tourisme-
muzillac.com*

ⓘ Pénestin ›
*Allée du Grand Pré,
B.P. 7, t 02 99 90 37 74,
www.penestin.com*

**★ Domaine de
Bodeuc ››**

**ⓘ La Roche-
Bernard ›**
*14 Rue Docteur
Cornudet, t 02 99 90 67
98, www.cc-pays-la-
roche-bernard.fr*

**★ Manoir du
Rodoir ››**

**🅭 La Roche-
Bernard, Josselin
and Rochefort-
en-Terre**

domainederochevilaine.com
(€€€€€–€€€). A very exclusive hotel
set on its own peninsula, with
saltwater pools, one covered, plus
well-tended gardens. Themed rooms
in buildings of 13th-century origin.
Enjoy splendid seafood dishes in the
dining room with its panoramic views.

Questembert ✉ 56230

★★★★Le Bretagne, 13 Rue St-Michel, t 02
97 26 11 12, *www.residence-le-bretagne.
com* (€€€–€€). Crisp, clean rooms lie
behind the sober ivy-covered front;
but it's known above all for its
superlative restaurant (€€€€), serving
inventive food, such as guinea fowl in
coconut mik and hibiscus ice cream.

Tréhiguier

La Visnonia, t 02 99 90 31 58 (€€).
Named after the ancient word for the
Vilaine, its lively first-floor seafood
restaurant overlooking the quayside.
Closed Sun eve and Mon.

Pénestin ✉ 56760

★★★Loscolo, Pointe de Loscolo, around
3km south of Pénestin, t 02 99 90 31
90, *hotelloscolo.com* (€€). Practical
modern rooms with views onto a
wildish section of the Pénestin coast
and direct access to a beach. The food
is good.

La Roche-Bernard ✉ 56130

★★★Auberge Bretonne, 2 Place
Duguesclin, t 02 99 90 60 28,
www.auberge-bretonne.fr (€€€). A
very highly regarded inn in the upper
village, with attractive rooms and the
reputation for containing one of the
best restaurants in Brittany with a
stupendous wine list. *Closed Thurs
and lunch Mon, Tues and Fri.*

★★Auberge des Deux Magots, 1 Place
du Bouffay, t 02 99 90 60 75, *www.
auberge-les2magots.com* (€). In the
upper village, distinguished by the
two sculpted monkeys emerging from
its walls. The rooms are comfortable
in the old-fashioned French manner,
as is the popular restaurant. *Closed
Sun eve and Mon lunch out of season.*

L'Auberge Rochoise, 42 Rue de Nantes,
t 02 99 90 77 37. Good restaurant *du
terroir.*

Le Petit Marin, Quai de la Douane,
t 02 99 90 79 41 (€€). A crêperie-cum-
moulerie down by the river, with an
extensive menu of creative dishes.

Les Copains d'à Bord, moored
alongside Quai Saint Antoine, t 02 99
90 81 03 (€). A boat-restaurant
offering ordinary food in a fun
setting. *Closed Wed out of season.*

Crêperie de la Roche, 14 Rue de la
Saulnerie, t 02 99 90 63 60 (€). An
atmospheric crêperie in an historic
house in the upper village. *Closed Mon
eve–Thurs outside school hols.*

Nivillac ✉ 56130

★★★Domaine de Bodeuc, Route de
Saint Dolay, t 02 99 90 89 63,
www.hotel-bodeuc.com (€€€). A smart
19th-century country home set in its
own lovely garden, offering a high
degree of comfort. Heated pool and
billiards table.

★★★Manoir du Rodoir, Route de
Nantes, t 02 99 90 82 68, *www.
lemanoirdurodoir.com* (€€€). The ivy-
clad exterior of this 19th-century
manor house conceals a chic
contemporary interior. Large gardens
and heated outdoor pool.

Northeastern Morbihan

This section takes you into the Morbihan countryside northeast
of Vannes, up via the startling art at the Château de Kerguéhennec
to Josselin, one of the grandest little inland towns of southern
Brittany. Josselin is also a boating town, as the Oust here doubles
as the Canal de Nantes à Brest. Several other delightful historic
spots grew up on or not far from the Oust, including Malestroit,
Rochefort-en-Terre and La Gacilly, the last now the fief of Breton
cosmetics magnate, Yves Rocher.

To Josselin via the Château de Kerguéhennec

Château de Kerguéhennec www.art-kergue hennec.com, **t** 02 97 00 44 44; open daily 11–6, July–Aug until 7

The wonderful **Centre d'Art Contemporain** at the Château de Kerguéhennec lies some 10 kilometres to the east of Locminé, almost 30 kilometres north up the D767 from Vannes. Brittany, a region that thrives on tradition, isn't generally associated with contemporary art. Here, though, the directors have gone for an uncompromising display, placed defiantly in, on and around that most traditional image of French Ancien Régime conservatism, an 18th-century château. The château itself, designed by Olivier Delourmeis, is a pleasingly well-ordered classical piece. But when the temporary exhibitions take it over, they create a riot. Scattered around the park is the permanent collection of discreetly or not so discreetly outrageous sculptures – pick up a map detailing their locations. One outbuilding has been converted into a very fashionable, extremely comfortable café-cum-library.

Some 10 kilometres north, by the rather messy public lake at **Réguiny**, stands a curious war museum, the **Musée Les Sanglots Longs**, which recalls the importance of the wireless during the Second World War and for the French Résistance. The museum's name refers to the coded message that announced the imminence of D-Day, taken from a very famous, beautifully melancholic poem by Verlaine.

Musée Les Sanglots Longs t 02 97 38 61 11; open May–Sept daily 10–7, rest of year Wed– Mon 2–6

Guéhenno lies about 10 kilometres east of Kerguéhennec. The attraction of this sleepy village is the 16th-century **calvary**, almost unique in the Morbihan, as these elaborately carved structures are really typical of the Finistère. Its figures were badly damaged at the Revolution, and much restored and added to in the 19th century. The ossuary for the bones of the dead also makes quite an impression.

Josselin

One of the sturdiest castles in Brittany dominates the Oust at Josselin, built on a solid rocky outcrop above the river. This is one of the rare great feudal Breton châteaux still to be owned by descendants of a great feudal Breton family, the Rohans. The town is also associated with Olivier IV de Clisson, one of the most power-hungry, violent and successful lords in Brittany in the Middle Ages. Today, this is a truly delightful, restful old riverside town, long retired from military service, its old quarters quietly resting against both banks of the Oust.

History

The early medieval story starts with Guéthenoc, lord of Porhoët, the area in which Josselin lies. He was supposedly attracted to this site above the Oust in AD 1000 by a statue of a Virgin found in the brambles here. His son was named Josselin, and would give his name to the new settlement. The lords of Porhoët continued to rule Josselin until they sided against Henri Plantagenet, alias King Henry II of England, who, in 1168, had much of Josselin and its castle destroyed.

The area round Josselin became a major battle zone in the Breton War of Succession. In 1351 the fort was commanded by Jean de Beaumanoir, supporter of Charles de Blois, who was backed by the French monarch. At neighbouring Ploërmel, the de Montfortist Bretons were supported by English troops under Robert Bemborough, or Bembro. On 26 March, Beaumanoir successfully took on Bembro, halfway between Josselin and Ploërmel, in an epic chivalric clash that took the form of a select battle between the 30 best knights from the opposing sides. The famed 14th-century chronicler Froissart gave a highly memorable, if wholly fictionalized, account of the spectacularly violent encounter known in French history as Le Combat des Trente.

In the medieval period of incessant warring between French and English royals, the Breton dukes would often switch allegiance to suit their best interests. The lords at Josselin would, by contrast, most often remain loyal to the French king. One man who become lord of Josselin in 1370 did, however, change sides, in most notorious fashion. Olivier IV de Clisson, from a noble family whose lands lay just south of the Loire, was brought up at the English court – his father had been killed by order of the French king. Nursing this terrible grievance, when Olivier returned to Brittany in the course of the Breton War of Succession he understandably took the side of the English-backed Jean de Montfort. A brilliant military man, Olivier helped win the Battle of Auray for de Montfort in 1364 (*see* p.426), enabling Jean de Montfort to become Duke Jean IV of Brittany.

But Olivier de Clisson was an opportunist; he soon saw what he could gain from serving the French and switched sides. By 1380, he would even succeed the famed Bertrand du Guesclin as Connétable de France, or head of the French army. Olivier, who had bought the lordships of Josselin and neighbouring Ploërmel in 1370, even decided to challenge the ducal power of Jean IV. In this period, he had Josselin mightily fortified on the outside, erecting 13 towers along the castle's ramparts, only a few of which remain standing today.

Olivier de Clisson had taken Marguerite de Rohan as his second wife. He died in 1407 and his great estates were left to his daughter Béatrice, who had been married to Alain VIII de Rohan, allowing the Rohans to become lords of Josselin – a position they had held in the past. Peace between the lords of Josselin and the dukes of Brittany would be shortlived, as Alain IX's son Jean II de Rohan married into the ducal line and fought for power with his brother-in-law, soon to become Duke François II de Bretagne. Jean II de Rohan had to flee to the French court for a while, while Duke François II had a part of Josselin castle brought down in 1488.

Time was fast running out, though, for the dukes of Brittany. François II died and his daughter, the young Anne de Bretagne, succeeded him. The French king Charles VIII imposed his authority on Brittany, taking Anne as his bride. Jean II de Rohan played an important part in brokering this crucial wedding, yoking the once-indepedent province to France. Jean II was rewarded for his work, enabling him to finance the lavish new decoration of the château.

Later, in the course of the French Wars of Religion during the second half of the 16th century, the Rohans famously supported the Reformation and the Château de Josselin became a Protestant stronghold in strongly Catholic Brittany. In the course of the first half of the next century, the centralizing, Catholicizing state imposed its will under Cardinal Richelieu's instructions. Josselin's castle keep was brought tumbling down, as were most of the outer towers. Although large portions of the castle did stay standing, for the remainder of the Ancien Régime, life for the Rohan lords centred around the French court in the Ile de France.

Château de Josselin

Château de Josselin www.chateaujosselin. fr, **t** 02 97 22 36 45; open April–June and Sept 2–6, July–Aug daily 10–6, Oct Sat–Sun 2–6.

It still makes a particularly formidable sight, arriving in view of Josselin castle along the Oust. The cliff-like walls and three of the many towers built for Olivier de Clisson rise almost sheer from the river bank, their forms reflected in the calm waters. By contrast, approaching the castle from the town side, it's hard to get any sense of the massive extent of the fortifications. The **chapel** to one side of the gateway scarcely hints at the major military structures beyond; now, this building is devoted to seasonal art exhibitions.

Through the gateway, you're greeted by a fabulous riot of decoration on the **castle's inner façade**. Late Gothic adornment was often exuberant, but this is late Gothic gone wild. How much of it is entirely original is hard to say, but the variety of motifs is staggering. Symbolism runs all over the building, along the roof balustrade, with its lozenges (a device adopted by the Rohans), its stylized ermine tails paying homage to the duchy, and its capital 'A's recognizing Anne de Bretagne. Coats of arms decorate the dormers, while monstrous dragons and beasts carved in stone rush round the masonry.

The **tour** inside the castle is quite short, covering five extravagantly decorated rooms on the main floor. The craftsmanship, from floor to ceiling, is a fine example of revivalist 19th-century art. Some elaborate portraits and pieces of furniture also stand out. The late-19th-century stables were converted by the present duchess into a **Musée de la Poupée**, with its extensive collection of antique dolls.

Josselin Beyond the Château

The fine **church of Notre-Dame du Roncier** dominates the centre of town outside the castle walls. This building's comical name, Our Lady of the Bramble Patch, refers to the tale of Guéthenoc's miraculous find of an effigy of the Virgin Mary. Amusing beasts adorn the church as well as the château; they include a pair of rabbits being chased down the façade by a pair of dogs above the main west entrance, and a crude, hairy-bodied gargoyle, which sticks out obscenely from one side of the façade.

Although the look of the church is late Gothic, the building actually consists of an amalgam of pieces from different periods. In fact, the belltower and the soaring steeple date from as recently as the early 20th century. You can climb the church tower to get fine views onto the pretty town below.

On the right-hand side of the choir, the 14th-century Chapelle Ste-Marguerite was built to hold the tomb of Olivier de Clisson and his second wife. To the left, the Chapelle Notre-Dame-du-Roncier has many features that recall the story of the discovery of the bramble-covered statue of the Virgin. In 1728, three children who suffered from a condition referred to as 'barking epilepsy' were said to have been cured here. Since that time, the Josselin *pardon*, which takes place on 8 September every year, has drawn many epileptics and their families in search of a miracle.

There are some pleasing historic shopping streets to discover in the vicinity of the church, but do go down to the **riverside**, where you can enjoy the great views of the castle, and embark on fine walks as well as a trip out on the water – choose from caneos, with the **Association Du Roncier**, or electric boats and pedal boats with **Nico Nautic**.

Association Du Roncier
m 06 73 50 62 82

Nico Nautic
m 06 25 26 82 29

Don't miss the quieter quarter of town up the **other bank of the Oust**. Climbing the steep lanes, you're rewarded with further surprising vistas of the castle before reaching the adorable **Chapelle Ste-Croix**. Set in the midst of an uplifting cemetery, this building has been given a new lease of life, serving occasionally for contemporary art exhibitions.

Just northeast, at the village of **La Grée St-Laurent**, a British couple have recently opened the **Musée Vélo Cyclo Moteur** where they show off fine collections of old bicycles and motorbikes.

Musée Vélo Cyclo Moteur
t 02 97 75 56 27; open April–Sept daily 2–6

From Josselin down the Oust to Redon

The Oust River runs down from Josselin to Redon, where it joins up with the Vilaine. It doubles as the Canal de Nantes à Brest for this particular stretch. Charming places such as Malestroit, Rochefort-en-Terre and La Gacilly lie on or close to the river. St-Marcel may be less attractive, but it has a fascinating museum on Brittany and the Second World War.

Lizio to St-Marcel

Lizio, a village of solid old granite houses some 20 kilometres south of Josselin has gained a bit of a reputation not just for its quaintness but also for its quirkiness. It's home to a curious collection of museums. At the **Univers du Poète Ferrailleur** eccentricity and amusement reign, including in a collection of mechanical scenes constructed from scrap objects. The mad-cap inventor here has also made an ecological house. The **Ecomusée de la Ferme et des Vieux Métiers** recalls the traditional trades of the past with its vast collections of objects. The modern **Insectarium** catalogues the lives and loves of insects and is a good option for children. In the neighbourhood, the **Manoir de Guermahia** produces seriously good Breton beer, or *cervoise*.

Returning to the Oust, continue downstream to **Malestroit**, a favourite stop for those cruising along the Canal de Nantes à Brest. The town celebrated its millennium in 1987. In medieval times it had the distinction of being capital of one of the nine baronies of Brittany. It also became home to three different religious orders. In the Breton Wars of Religion, an important treaty was signed here. The heart of town somehow lacks a bit of soul today, but it's still a very pleasant place.

The **church of St-Gilles** is the main focus of attention. It was built in a curious mix of a dried-blood-red blocks and light stone that looks as though it may have been shipped up from the Loire. A few vestiges of the original 12th-century structure have survived on the choir end, and above the main porch entrance, the Romanesque symbols of the evangelists stand out. Off the church square, **Place du Bouffay**, look out for several houses decorated with charming carved figures, including an animal playing bagpipes and a pig spinning. A little museum recalls the importance of inland navigation in these parts.

Some way northeast of Malestroit, outside **Monteneuf**, the fine array of megaliths of **Les Pierres Droites** is one of the most important of inland Brittany, if little known – perhaps because they were only properly rediscovered in 1989. An impressive trio of standing stones was still intact; but the archaeological digs

Univers du Poète Ferrailleur
www.poeteferailleur. com, t 02 97 74 97 94; check opening times

Ecomusée de la Ferme et des Vieux Métiers
www.ecomuseelizio. com, t 02 97 74 93 01; open April–Sept daily 10–12 and 2–7; March, Oct and school hols daily 2–6

Insectarium
www.insectarium delizio.com, t 02 97 74 99 12

unearthed more than 400 further ones. Extraordinarily, it seems that the stones were actually buried in the medieval period by Christians who wanted to eradicate these extraordinary symbols of a very powerful past religion.

St-Marcel's Musée de la Résistance

www.resistance-bretonne.com; open daily 10–12 and 2–6, mid-June–mid-Sept 'til 7

St-Marcel's Musée de la Résistance is a complex, moving museum on the Second World War, set a few kilometres west of Malestroit. Once you've penetrated into the dark, bunker-like rooms you'll fast become engrossed in the mass of painful detail accumulated here. It would take a whole morning to do any justice to the place. The best way to begin is by watching the film, which explains the importance of this location in the Second World War, with interesting accompanying footage. Basically, the area was very well suited for parachute expeditions by the Allies and the French Resistance, with places to land and woods in which to hide men and weapons. Already in 1943, it was used for one landing, but the more important battle fought here in 1944 is recalled hour by hour.

Rochefort-en-Terre

This utterly gorgeous old village steeped in Breton history was only made more beautiful when its streets were given new cobbles in recent times, but in summer you'll probably find the tourists as numerous as the cobblestones, and packed almost as close together.

The first lord of Rochefort goes back to the start of the 12th century, when his territories were split off from the massive Elven lordship of Argoët. The first castle was built on a spur of rock overlooking what was once an important trade route, and that was possibly settled by much older civilizations. It looks down over the Gueuzon Valley and across to the Landes de Lanvaux, a great length of rocky moorland that stretches east–west across much of central Morbihan.

Below the castle, a community developed, and a priory was founded on the back of the family fortune. But the Rochefort lords would by no means limit themselves to local issues. In the 14th century, Thébaud III de Rochefort gained the fief of Ancenis by the Loire through marriage, and became a *chevalier* in the king of France's service. He died in 1374 and left an heiress who married Jean II de Rieux, who took on the name of Rochefort so that the family became the Rieux-Rocheforts. This clan grew increasingly powerful in Breton politics and French affairs, playing a major role in the Hundred Years War.

Jean IV de Rieux-Rochefort probably eclipses all the family in terms of his importance. He was appointed tutor to the young Duchess Anne de Bretagne by her father François II de Bretagne shortly before the duke passed away in 1488. Jean IV had fought alongside the duke against King Charles VIII of France at the Battle of St-Aubin-du-Cormier earlier in that year, in the defeat that spelled the end of Breton ducal autonomy. Though Charles VIII had Jean IV's properties destroyed, including the castles of Rochefort-en-Terre, Rieux and Elven, Jean IV later received the sum of 100,000 gold *écus* from the French Crown for his part in organizing Anne de Bretagne's marriage to Charles VIII, leaving him the money he needed to reconstruct his homes.

Jean IV's granddaughter Claude married into the powerful Protestant family of the Colignys. During the bitter, mad French Wars of Religion, the Catholic side burned down the castle. Coligny descendants held on to Rochefort-en-Terre, however, until they sold it off in 1658 to Vincent Exupère de Larlan, the president of the Breton Parlement and a counsellor to King Louis XIV. The Larlans rebuilt a castle here, and their wealth spilled over into the village below. At the Revolution, though, the family fled, and the castle was eventually destroyed by Republican forces as a symbol of the old order.

Deprived of the influence of a lordly family, Rochefort-en-Terre lost much of its prosperity. But the village pulled through thanks to its sheer beauty. A colony of artists came and fell in love with the place at the end of the 19th century.

An American artist, Alfred Klots, arrived at the start of the 20th century; he liked the place so much he bought what remained of the **Château de Rochefort en Terre** and built up a fantasy home comprising sections of fine old houses collected from around the region. The composite reconstruction looks quite a picture.

Château de Rochefort en Terre
www.rochefort-en-terre.com; open July and Aug daily 10–6.30; June and Sept daily 2–6.30; April and May Sat, Sun and public hols 2–7

Having climbed the slope from the village, you enter the old château's fortifications to find yourself in an utterly enchanting courtyard. Only the 14th-century well is an original feature here. The few rooms you can visit have been described as being in the 'Americano–Hispanic–Italiano–Breton' style... which gives you a good indication of the confusion of styles within. The rooms in the **museum** to the side of the castle have been more carefully and thematically arranged. Temporary art exhibitions are held here, but at all times you can see the painted panels taken from Anastasie Lecadre's auberge and other works of the school of painters who came to Rochefort-en-Terre. Further rooms are devoted to typical Breton furnishings and Breton *coiffes*.

Down in the village, the **church of Notre-Dame de la Tronchaye**, rather than being the focal point as you might expect, was built to one side, down a slope. Now reading this chapter, you may be getting wise to any church in the Morbihan with Notre-Dame in the name – yes, here we go with yet another story of a hidden Virgin giving birth to a new church. The Morbihannais clearly liked their Virgin Marys very much, and the *département* remains to this day one of the most staunchly Catholic in France. The tale here takes us back to the time of the Viking invasions. With the marauding heathens venturing further inland, the locals' precious statue of Our Lady was concealed in a tree trunk (hence the name 'Tronchaye') to save it from destruction. Its secret location, however, would only be rediscovered by a shepherdess a couple of hundred years later. To celebrate the find, it was decided to build the church on the very spot. The 12th-century edifice was subsequently much adapted in Flamboyant Gothic style, and given its lovely window tracery.

One stained-glass window represents the scene of the shepherdess's discovery of the statue, but the multi-coloured sheep steal the show. Look up at the nave's ceiling, where the stringbeams have been carved with creatures and men, as well as family coats of arms. The finest statue in the church, the black-stained figure of the Virgin, heavily robed, can be found on the gallery at the west end. Also look out for what appears to be a lumberjack trying to carry home a whole tree trunk.

The main attraction for visitors to Rochefort-en-Terre is the principal village street, packed with craft shops, and picturesque **Place du Puits**. If you've always wanted an engraved bellows, this is certainly the place to come, as one boutique sells nothing else. Amid all the quaint beauty, look out for a rude gargoyle of a man bearing his bottom at passers-by, no doubt reflecting what some villagers think about the invasions of tourists.

A short way south of Rochefort-en-Terre, outside **Malansac**, the Parc de Préhistoire de Bretagne attracts families with its impressively sized models of dinosaurs but it also covers human evolution in Brittany.

Parc de Préhistoire de Bretagne
www.prehistoire.com, t 02 97 43 34 17; open April–mid-Oct daily 10–7.30, Easter and mid-Oct–All Saints hols Sun 1.30–6

La Gacilly

The village of La Gacilly stands *c*.20km northeast of Rochefort-en-Terre. The place may not be as obviously beautiful, but it is prettily located on the slopes of the Aff, a tributary of the Oust.

Yves Rocher, the internationally renowned Breton cosmetics magnate, hails from here. He apparently built the foundations of his glamorous empire on haemorrhoid cream, made to a recipe handed down to him by his grandmother. The **Yves Rocher cosmetics factory** at the bottom of the village is an extremely popular place with visitors: loads of lotions and potions, not many concerned with piles, are for sale to customers reassured about how naturally the cosmetics are produced.

Above the factory, the old houses have been taken over by many **craftspeople**, encouraged to settle here over the course of the last 30 years or so. You can usually watch several of them at work on any given day, with the most popular probably being the

Yves Rocher cosmetics factory
www.yves-rocher.fr, t 02 99 08 35 84; Jardin Botanique open mid-June–mid-Sept daily 10–7; Végétarium open April–mid-June Tues–Sun 2–6, mid-June–Sept daily 10–7; enquire at either about factory tours

blacksmith and the costume makers of Claymore. The latter are a couple who create all kinds of extravagant historical outfits, so if you've ever yearned for a Viking helmet, a Celtic cape or a chain-mail suit, you can order them here.

Not so long ago, a joint project between Yves Rocher and the Muséum National d'Histoire Naturelle brought about the the **Végétarium**, or museum of the vegetable. Way better than it sounds and a good bet for kids, it consists of an enjoyable exploration of the world of plants.

You can also go on a pleasant **cruise on the Aff** from La Gacilly to view the **Marais de Glénac**, a marshland to the south, with reedy expanses looking on to the rocks opposite. Further south, a few kilometres from Redon, the area around **L'Ile aux Pies** counts as one of the prettiest and quietest spots along the whole Oust Valley.

ⓘ **Pays Touristique de l'Oust à Brocéliande**
www.oust-broceliande-vacances.com

ⓘ **Locminé**
30 Rue du Général de Gaulle, **t** 02 97 60 00 37, www.pays-locmine.com

ⓘ **Malestroit >>**
17 Place du Bouffay, **t** 02 97 75 14 57 www.malestroit.com

ⓘ **Josselin >**
Place de la Congrégation, **t** 02 97 22 36 43, www.paysde josselin-tourisme.com

ⓘ **Rochefort-en-Terre >>**
7 Place du Puits, **t** 02 97 43 33 57, www.rochefort-en-terre.com

⭐ **Château de Talhouët >>**

Market Days in Northeastern Morbihan

Locminé: Thursday
Josselin: Saturday
Malestroit: Thursday
Rochefort-en-Terre: Saturday in July and August
La Gacilly: Saturday

Where to Stay and Eat in Northeastern Morbihan

Buléon ✉ 56420

***Domaine de la Ferrière, La Ferrière, **t** 02 97 75 30 00, www.domainedela ferriere.fr (€€€–€€). Glamorous little property west of Josselin, with very nice rooms, grounds and pool. Restaurant serving grills and crêpes.

Josselin ✉ 56120

du Château, 1 Rue du Général de Gaulle, **t 02 97 22 20 11, www.hotel-chateau.com (€€–€). A big, stolid traditional hotel with great views across the river to the château. The restaurant serves good traditional fare.

Le Clos des Devins B&B, Rue des Devins, **t** 02 97 75 67 48. Smart rooms in a fine stone house in the town centre.

La Table d'O, Rue Glatinier, **t** 02 97 70 61 39. Josselin's gastronomic restaurant, overlooking the canal.

La Duchesse Anne, 8 Place de la Duchesse Anne, **t** 02 97 22 22 37 (€€). Rustic fare in typical country town inn that has received a new lease of life recently.

There are a couple of tempting crêperies up in the centre and two by the canal.

Malestroit ✉ 56140

Le Canotier, 11bis Place du Docteur Queinnec, **t** 02 97 75 08 69 (€€). Offers a variety of good-quality regional dishes. Closed Sun eve and Mon.

Crêperie La Riveraine, 35 Faubourg de la Madeleine, **t** 02 97 75 22 22 (€). A decent, well-run budget option close to the ruins of the 12th-century church of La Madeleine. Closed Mon out of season.

Rochefort-en-Terre ✉ 56220

Château de Talhouët, outside Rochefort (head briefly north towards Pleucadeuc then west for Talhouët), **t** 02 97 43 34 72, www.chateaude talhouet.com (€€€€). A stunning manor-sized castle surrounded by greenery, with extremely comfortable rooms and luxurious bathrooms. Table d'hôte possible.

ⓘ **La Gacilly ➤➤**
Le Bout du Pont,
t 02 99 08 21 75, www.
paysdelagacilly.com

⭐ **Auberge du**
Castellan ➤

**Le Pelican, Place des Halles,
t 02 97 43 38 48, *www.hotel-pelican-rochefort.com* (€€€–€€). A small hotel set in Ancien Régime buildings.

St-Martin-sur-Oust ✉ 56200

Auberge du Castellan, a couple of km outside the village (signposted), **t** 02 99 91 51 69 (€€€–€€). A handful of light, spacious B&B rooms set in the grounds of a grand 18th-century building. *Table d'hôte* available.

La Gacilly ✉ 56200

**de France, 15 Rue Montauban,
t 02 99 08 11 15, *www.hoteldefrance lagacilly.com* (€). A reasonable option, where you can save your euros for Yves Rocher cosmetics – but note that the cosmetics company will soon open a swanky new green hotel in town.

Loire Atlantique

The name of the département could hardly put it more clearly. Here the Loire finally reaches the Atlantic, after its 1,000-kilometre journey from southeastern France. The massive tidal estuary of France's greatest river stretches over 50 kilometres from St-Nazaire back to Nantes. The latter, the historic capital of the Breton duchy, was shifted into the separate region of Pays de la Loire after the war, along with its surrounding département. However, this fast-changing, culture-mad city definitely merits its inclusion here. We also focus closely on the ports and resorts north of the Loire, which retain a distinctly Breton look, apart from La Baule, which makes up for that with one of the finest beaches in the land. As to gorgeous granite-ramparted Guérande, it stands aloof between the contrasting Pays Blanc and Pays Noir, extensive salt pans to one side, and to the other, the reedy, thatched-cottagey Brière marsh, where dark peat used to be extracted. Inland, the famous vineyards of Muscadet scarcely need an introduction.

11

Don't miss

⭐ **A salty city**
Guérande **p.463**

⭐ **A bustling group of resorts**
La Baule **p.466**

⭐ **Ocean-going surprises**
St-Nazaire **p.473**

⭐ **A truly cosmopolitan city**
Nantes **p.478**

⭐ **Rolling vineyards and the spot where Brittany meets Italy**
Muscadet and Clisson **p.497**

See map overleaf

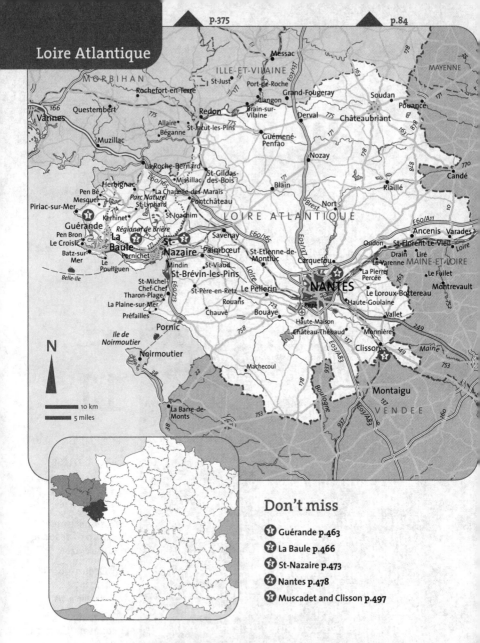

Loire Atlantique

Don't miss

Guérande **p.463**

La Baule **p.466**

St-Nazaire **p.473**

Nantes **p.478**

Muscadet and Clisson **p.497**

Nantes should count as by far the largest Breton city, being one of the largest towns in France. But in administrative fact, Nantes and the Loire Atlantique no longer form part of Brittany. In a stroke of questionable regional reorganization in the 1960s, this southern section of Brittany was shifted into the Pays de la Loire region.

Before the Act of Union formally joining Brittany to France in 1532, Nantes served for a long period as capital of the fiercely

ⓘ Comité
Départemental du
Tourisme de Loire-
Atlantique
*11 Rue du Château de
l'Erandière, 44306
Nantes cedex, t 02 51 72
95 40, www.loire-
atlantique-tourisme.
com/www.ohlaloire
atlantique.com; for up-
to-date information on
the public transport
network around the
département, consult
the Lila section on
www.cg44.fr*

independent duchy. The massive Château des Ducs de Bretagne still stands in the city, while the cathedral contains the tomb of the last Breton duke. After the union, Nantes would develop into the capital of the French slave trade, not edifying in historical terms, although it brought the town masses of colonial commerce and wealth, and many grand edifices.

Today, although many Nantais may feel indifferent to questions of regional identity – the city is large enough to feel self-confident and independent – many other inhabitants of the Loire Atlantique do retain a sense of belonging to Brittany, particularly those north of the Loire. However, most of the Loire Atlantique was never traditionally a Breton-speaking area. The Dark Ages immigration from Britain appears to have left few marks on the area, to go by the few Breton place names in the *département*.

Old châteaux and château ruins across the Loire Atlantique do still recall the Breton frontiers of medieval times, though. West of St-Nazaire, the granite ramparts of Guérande stand guard above the coastal salt pans. East of Nantes along the Loire, Ancenis served as one of Brittany's frontier towns next to Anjou. So too did Châteaubriant to the north of Ancenis, and Clisson to the south of it.

The magnificent Loire estuary divides the *département* in two. The look changes markedly from north to south of the river. To the north, the architecture certainly reflects Breton traditions, with typical whitewashed or granite houses with slate roofs. This northern Loire Atlantique is very quietly rural, with plentiful rivers and woods, its centuries-old tradition of iron production discreetly remembered. As you cross the Loire, suddenly features associated with southern France start to emerge. Orange-tiled roofs begin to replace the slate ones, and vines appear. The gorgeous gently rolling vineyards of Muscadet stretch from Nantes to Italianate Clisson.

Concentrating on the Loire Atlantique coast, as so many tourists do, along the stretch north of the Loire, you still feel strongly in Brittany, with the string of pretty ports around Guérande. But the most popular of all the Loire Atlantique's resorts, La Baule, doesn't look in the least Breton, with cloned blocks of apartments looking on to the massive beach, while the villas behind were built in a whole range of styles. However, La Baule boasts one of the best-organzied, longest beaches in Europe, and Batz and Le Croisic just to the west can provide a strong dose of Breton feel.

Nearby, two quite contrasting marshes lie either side of La Baule and Guérande. To the west, the salty white Marais Salants are supplied by ocean waters. To the east, the waterways running through the black peat bogs of the Brière were traditionally replenished by the flood waters of the Loire. Both the salty Pays Blanc, with its salt-farms, and the Pays Noir, with its reedy canals to boat through and its villages packed with thatched cottages, have an

11

Loire Atlantique

intriguing atmosphere well worth exploring. The Brière, incidentally, is the second-largest marsh in France after the Camargue.

The Loire Atlantique's coast south of the great river's mouth feels much less Breton than the coast to the north, although Pornic, with its rocky coves and megaliths, might be considered a last outpost of Brittany. We've come to the end of the Loire Atlantique, and to the southern end of Brittany here... or rather, what used to be Brittany.

Northern Loire Atlantique

The band of land running across the northern Loire Atlantique is one of the least touristy parts of Brittany, but it offers a pretty, rural tranquillity. Rivers, lakes, patches of forest and undulating fields lead to provincial Châteaubriant, significant among a chain of defences that marked the region's eastern frontier in medieval times.

Châteaubriant

To the gastronomic world, this town's name is synonymous with the finest of steaks. To the French, the name also evokes the country's most famous Romantic writer, François René de Chateaubriand; note the difference in spelling, though. Actually it was one Brient who gave this place its name, a Breton lord called upon to fortify these parts in the 11th century, in the aftermath of Viking incursions. He had a fortress erected on the promontory above the Chère River. This fortress gave way to mighty medieval defences, some of which still stand. A succession of important families then held sway over Châteaubriant down the centuries.

The barony came into the hands of the Dinan family at one stage. Françoise de Dinan, who inherited it in the late medieval period, served as governess to the young Breton duchess, Anne de Bretagne. In 1488 the troops of the French king Charles VIII, whom Anne would be forced to marry, destroyed much of this Breton frontier town. When Brittany was finally annexed to the French kingdom by King François I in 1532, Châteaubriant played a small part in the proceedings, the king staying here a while. Jean de Laval, the lord of the castle, had been made governor of Brittany, while his wife, Françoise de Foix, had earlier served as the French king's mistress.

The castle is the main reason for visiting Châteaubriant, although it also boasts a grand **covered market** and a sober **Romanesque church**, St-Jean-de-Béré, while some charming houses line the shopping streets in the historic centre.

Châteaubriant's Château

www.culture.cg44.fr, t 02 40 28 20 20; open for guided tours May–Sept Wed–Mon 2.30 and 4.30, June–mid-Sept Wed 3 in English; park open daily May–Sept daily 8–8, Oct–Mar 7.30–6

Châteaubriant's Château

This château, though relatively unknown and with little to show inside, presents an enchanting confusion of architectural styles,

Getting around the Northern Loire Atlantique

Châteaubriant is at the end of a minor **train** line from Rennes. **Bus** services reach Châteaubriant from Rennes, Angers and St Nazaire.

with examples of good and bad building. Passing under the towering entrance gateway, you enter the outer courtyard. In front stands the 13th- to 14th-century keep, still imposing, though now too dangerous to visit. Although the Renaissance castle grabs your attention to the right, you're first shown round the substantial ruins of the medieval fortifications. You can walk along a small portion of the ramparts. The area by the medieval chapel is particularly attractive: look out for the amazing variety of colours of the stone above the chapel doorway. The most striking feature of the architectural decoration of this château is in fact the way that beautiful blue schist has been used to pick out many details.

Going through to the Renaissance château, you can admire a whole colonnade of blue columns. They are of a rare beauty, contrasting with the brick building above them. Jean de Laval had this arcade and the end pavilion with its loggias added in the 1530s. This was relatively soon after Renaissance styles had been brought back from Italy to France. But this work is not so much pure Renaissance architecture as poor Renaissance. While Jean de Laval may have wished to be fashionable, his masons weren't up to the task; they got the symmetry, so vital to the harmony of Renaissance architecture, slightly wrong.

The other Renaissance wing is less eccentric, with lovely dormer windows typical of Loire Valley châteaux. The blue stone again adds greatly to the decorative effects inside and out. Some of the rooms serve for temporary, often contemporary, art shows. A separate staircase leads to the so-called room of Françoise de Foix, an early 17th-century extravaganza of a suite restored to its original vulgarity.

Market Days in the Northern Loire Atlantique

Châteaubriant: Wednesday morning

Where to Stay and Eat in the Northern Loire Atlantique

(i) Châteaubriant >
22 Rue du Couëré,
t 02 40 28 20 90,
www.tourisme-
chateaubriant.fr

Châteaubriant ✉ 44110

***La Ferrière, Route de Moisdon-La-Rivière, t 02 40 28 00 28, *www.hotel laferriere.fr* (€€). The most exclusive option, in wooded grounds 2km south of town. Charming, mid-sized château.

Les Marches de Bretagne B&B, La Boissière, Soudan, t 02 40 28 60 00, *www.lesmarchesdebretagne.com* (€). Rooms in an attractive property in a nice village, with good facilities such as a large pool. *Table d'hôte* possible.

Le Poêlon d'Or, 30 bis Rue du 11 Novembre, t 02 40 81 43 33 (€€€). Restaurant next to the central 3-star Le Châteaubriant hotel, slightly cluttered and with fussy décor, serving elaborate and refined cuisine. The Châteaubriant beef special is richly dressed *en croûte* and in foie gras. *Closed Sun eve and Mon.*

The Coast from La Vilaine to La Baule

We arrive back at major Breton tourist beach territory here.

From Pen Bé to Pen Bron

The most northerly stretch of the Loire Atlantique's coast is known above all for its oysters. Go to the headland of **Pen Bé** for a first taste of the Loire Atlantique's shores and seafood. This point marks the northern entrance to the **Mès estuary**, clogged with oyster beds and saltpans. Another excellent place to see how oysters are treated and sold is the *port ostréicole* of **Kercabellec**, opposite Pen Bé.

You then come to the popular resort of **Quimiac**, its stretches of beaches packed out in summer. For aquatic pursuits, from sailing and windsurfing to sea kayaking, this resort has one of the branches of **Nautisme en Pays Blanc** which also has schools at Piriac-sur-Mer and La Turballe. The spectacular coast road to Piriac passes just above a series of small cliffs and creeks where more intrepid families go scrambling down the sides of the sharp, low black rocks in search of precious private corners of sand.

Piriac-sur-Mer has the feel of a traditional Breton port and resort, but has been going much longer still. The Phoenicians are supposed to have come trading here way before the Romans arrived in Gaul.

Nautisme en Pays Blanc
www.npb,
t 02 40 23 53 84

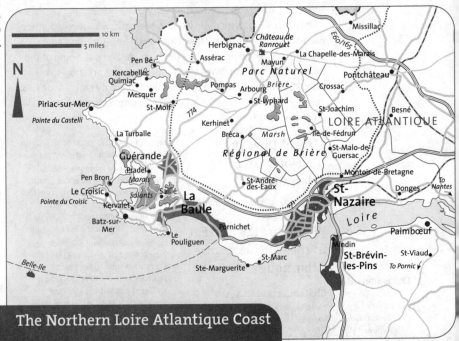

The Northern Loire Atlantique Coast

Close to the **Pointe du Castelli**, the 6th-century Breton chief Waroc'h may have built one of his most southerly fortifications. In the 19th century, writers such as Flaubert, Zola and Daudet discovered the place. The village has plenty of charm, especially as traffic is discouraged from entering, while the little port has a pleasant simple hotel bar that attracts some life, along with the sailing club. The **coastal path** around the Pointe de Castelli offers an elating route along the top of golden little cliffs, with small beaches framed by pierced rocks, but the picturesque erosion means that sometimes the coastal path itself is eaten away by the elements.

La Turballe, a short distance south along the rugged coast road, is grittier and more exposed, with a large working harbour. The port took off in the 19th century, tinning sardines its speciality. It is now the largest fishing port in the Loire Atlantique and one of the biggest in Brittany. Climb on to the roof of the large, ugly fishmarket to visit the **Maison de la Pêche**. A row of waterside cafés allows you to view proceedings in relaxed manner. Of course tourism fights it out with fishing now, and there are several options for practising watersports here.

A long stretch of beach known as **La Grande Falaise** reaches down to the headland of **Pen Bron**. Windsurfers congregate in large numbers here, while the unspoilt southern end attracts nudists or those in search of quieter sands, as it's a relatively long walk through pine woods to reach it. This long coastal spit of Pen Bron protects the salt marshes of Guérande behind from the ocean.

Guérande

🕦 Guérande

The name Guérande derives from the Breton for 'White Land'. White gold, alias salt, made this smart town's fortune. It was long a very precious commodity, its sale highly regulated and taxed. Guérande's wealth in the Middle Ages was largely built on the precious white crystals, and the place maintained a thriving port at the foot of its slopes through medieval times to export its salt. Magnificent, partly moated granite ramparts still protect Guérande's fine streets with their substantial granite houses.

This was clearly a Breton town of some importance, especially before Brittany's union with France. Back in the 9th century, when a separate Breton state was created, the town even became, if briefly, home to a bishopric, Bishop Gislard backed by the Breton chief Nomenoë in opposition to the Frankish bishop of Nantes. Then, once the Viking terror had abated, a Romanesque church went up in town, vestiges of which remain in the Collégiale St-Aubin, the impressive main church.

Inevitably Guérande was fought over by opposing sides during the 14th-century Breton War of Succession. The inhabitants lent their support to Jean de Montfort, backed by the English, but early in the conflict the enemy came and pillaged the place, massacring many. By the Treaty of Guérande of 1381, however, Jean IV of Brittany's position as duke was recognized by the French monarchy. Guérande could also celebrate in 1386 when the duke decided to get married to Jeanne de Navarre at the church of Saillé just outside town.

Subsequent dukes had the fortifications adapted to the warfare of the 15th century, and the ramparts with the four gateways and 11 towers you can still see today date mainly from that period. The collegiate church was also enlarged in fashionable Flamboyant Gothic style.

Distressingly, Guérande's port began to silt up more and more. In the centuries that followed, the harbours at nearby Le Croisic and Le Pouliguen grew at its expense. However, the grand town houses from the 17th and 18th centuries show that Guérande merchants knew how to defend their interests. Salt continued to bring large rewards until the Revolution. The place fared less well in the 19th century, increasingly isolated, bypassed by industrialization along the Loire estuary.

Four grand gateways lead you through the almost intact ramparts into town. The most impressive entrance is the **Porte St-Michel,** built in the second half of the 15th century. It looks more like a portion of castle than a mere gateway, and it did serve as home to the town governors in centuries past. It now houses the

Musée du Pays de Guérande
www.ville-guerande. fr, **t***02 28 55 05 05; open April–Sept 10–12.30 and 2.30–7, Oct 10–12 and 2–6; closed Mon am*

Musée du Pays de Guérande. The various displays are devoted to local history and local themes. Pieces of typical old Guérande furniture, painted in ox-blood red, stand out, as do the treasures from the main church, and the mannequins dressed in local costumes, as well as flowers made from shells. You can walk out on to a portion of the ramparts from here. Close to another gateway,

Musée de la Poupée et du Jouet Ancien
t *02 40 15 69 13; open April–Oct 10–1 and 2.30–7, Nov–March 2–6*

the Porte de Saillé, the **Musée de la Poupée et du Jouet Ancien** draws in the crowds with its collections of dolls and old toys, displayed against period backgrounds.

The streets of Guérande are packed with craft shops, gift shops and restaurants. In summer you have to fight your way through the tourist hordes to reach the **Collégiale St-Aubin**. This sombre mix of Gothic and Romanesque architecture was heavily restored in the 19th century. Inside, though, the columns' capitals teem with Romanesque carvings. Much of the stained glass with its amazing blue backgrounds dates from the 19th century. Look out too for the remarkable tomb effigy of Tristan Carné. The man served as *maître d'hôtel* to Anne de Bretagne and her second royal husband, Louis XII, clearly a lucrative position at court. Fine organ concerts are now held in the church.

Guérande's White Gold

It's hard to imagine these days just what a precious commodity salt was in bygone times, in the era before the refrigerator, when it was used to preserve so many foods, as well as being a vital ingredient in other ways. A complex, skilled, laborious process developed down the centuries to harvest the sea salt efficiently, and in the impressive patchwork of the Guérande salt marshes, a few salt farmers continue the old tradition, even if the monetary rewards may not be quite so great nowadays.

The seawater that enters the Guérande marshes is carefully regulated by a system of canals and gates. The salt harvest happens through the summer. When the time is right, the gates are opened to allow the water into the *vasières*, the pools that supply the *salines*, the network of smaller pools. In the *vasières*, some of the water evaporates and the salt settles. The salt water may then go through an intermediary set of pools, the *corbiers*, before heading down the extremely gentle slopes to the *salines* themselves. These *salines* are divided up into three kinds of pools. The water goes through the *fares*, then the *adernes*, and finally into the *oeillets*. Slate divides regulate the flow. More and more water evaporates at each stage. The wind and the sun help in this process of creating increasingly saline waters. It's in the *oeillets*, rectangular basins around seven by ten metres, that the salt is finally farmed.

The salt farmers are known as *paludiers*. They use special implements to harvest two types of salt, going about their business barefoot. Around 100 of them still work in the saltpans. Of the two types of salt they gather, the *fleur de sel* is much the finer. This salt collects in crystals on the surface of the pools. How much can be harvested depends on how clement the weather is. The *fleur de sel* has a particularly sparkling white colour, as it never enters into contact with the murkier bottom of the salt pools. It's especially rich in magnesium and other elements. The crystals of the *gros sel* settle on the bottom of the pools.

The salt, once gathered, is piled high on the banks of the pools and left to drain overnight on small round patches of land known as *ladures*. Then it's transported by wheelbarrow to the *trémets*, the sides of the *salines*, where it's left in pyramids before being taken to the *salorges*, the salt houses. Here it's dried and stocked for a year, then sieved and sorted before it goes on sale. The farmers don't use any chemical treatments or add anything; Guérande salt is regarded as particularly pure.

The Marais Salants or Pays Blanc

Terre de Sel, Espace et Nature at Pradel
www.seldeguerande. com, t 02 40 62 08 80; open daily winter 10–12.30 and 2–5, spring and autumn 10–6, July–Aug 9.30–8; call for times of walks, which vary in duration from 45mins to 2hrs

Maison des Paludiers
www.maisondes paludiers.fr, t 02 40 62 21 96; open Nov–Feb Sat 2.30–5, Feb–Oct 10–12 and 2–5

The intriguingly dour landscapes of the salt marshes below Guérande and the eccentric geometry of the saltpans have been declared a Grand Site National. The Marais Salants of Guérande-Batz combined cover some 2,000 hectares. The inland sea that supplies these marshes is known as Le Traict. The mounds of salt piled high on the sides of the saltpans make quite a sight. And in the holiday season, many farmers leave bags of Guérande salt outside their homes for visitors to buy.

The best way to appreciate the salt marshes and the work of its *paludiers* is to go on a guided walking tour. These are run from Terre de Sel, Espace et Nature at Pradel. You'll also find an exhibition on the flora and fauna of the Marais Salants here. The Maison des Paludiers at Saillé offers similar small attractions and activities.

La Baule to Le Croisic

Nine kilometres of unbroken fine sands have helped make the Bay of La Baule one of the most sought-after tourist spots in southern Brittany. La Baule, with its sister resorts of Pornichet and Le Pouliguen holding its hand to either side, is extremely lively, rather upmarket, and with more than a hint of kitsch. These places don't look very Breton. Just head a tad west along the long, thin peninsula, however, and Batz and Le Croisic do look the real Breton thing – be prepared for a lot of tourists, though, especially at the aquarium.

La Baule, Pornichet and Le Pouliguen

⑫ La Baule

You don't come to La Baule for history or museums. In fact, when you first arrive on the **waterfront** of its splendid south-facing sandy bay, the row of countless postwar apartment blocks disappearing into the distance might make you think you've arrived at Brittany's answer to Benidorm. However, this resort proves posh rather than brash. And it was born with pretensions. Created by 19th-century property developers, who first planted large numbers of pines along the coast to stabilize the dunes, by the 1920s, La Baule had gained an international reputation as one of France's grand new seaside towns. The splendid station from the 1930s, renovated in 1990 with the arrival of the TGV, is a listed historic building. However, the postwar developers got rid of most of the earlier seafront villas for more lucrative apartment blocks.

With their innumerable balconies, they look over what is a somewhat plain bay by Brittany's highly picturesque standards, but the glory of the place stretches out at the feet of the blocks of balconied flats. The **great expanses of sand**, described as one of nature's most generous playgrounds, allow for all manner of beach activity, from volley-ball to sandyachting (the latter only allowed out of season). A series of **sailing schools** are placed at regular intervals along the beach. Despite all the sporting pursuits, there's plenty of space for lazy lounging, and you may even be able to rent out one of the hundreds of stripy tents put up daily in the main summer season. The **Bureau de la Plage** at the level of Avenue de Gaulle is the place to go for all manner of matters concerning the beach, which is given a thorough clean every second night in high season.

Bureau de la Plage
*t 02 40 60 25 45;
open April–mid-Sept*

The luxury sea treatment market has found an easy home here; there are now three thalassotherapy centres along the bay. The competing ones at La Baule itself are **Thalassothérapie Thalgo La Baule** and **Relais Thalasso La Baule**. The first, on Avenue Marie-Louise, is the grander of the two; attached to the unmissable extravaganza of the Royal Barrière hotel lording it over the central section of La Baule's beach, it has three heated seawater pools as well as offering all manner of luxury treatments. You may find the second thalassotherapy centre, at 28 Boulevard de l'Océan, slightly more affordable, but it's very smart too.

**Thalassothérapie
Thalgo La Baule**
*t 02 40 11 99 99,
www.thalasso-
thermale.com*

**Relais Thalasso
La Baule**
*t 02 40 11 33 11,
www.thalasso-
labaule.com*

On the main street parallel to the seafront, a good many stylish **art galleries** stand out, offering a mixed bag of work. As to the **Chapelle Ste-Anne**, it serves for both concerts and temporary art exhibitions. The Eglise Notre-Dame is reserved for mass. Heading inland, you can enjoy the full panoply of La Baule's **villas**. Fantasy reigns. Behind the neat fences and hedges, their gardens deeply shaded by pines, these holiday homes were built in a variety of mock styles, not all in the best possible taste. Normandy beamed houses, Basque-type chalets, modern thatched homes, the odd Arabic folly and many other styles vie with each other for your attention. You may even spot the odd Breton-looking villa if you're lucky. L'Allée Cavalière is one of the best streets along which to admire La Baule's pre-war architecture; the name of this thoroughfare derives from the narrow horse track going down the centre of the road. The **Parc des Dryades** public gardens at the eastern end are very well tended, full of flowers and rare trees.

Pornichet is the loud easterly extension of La Baule, with its own thalassotherapy centre, casino and railway station to match. The **Centre de Thalassothérapie Daniel Jouvence** is at 66 Boulevard des Océanides, with heated seawater pool among its many attractions. Pornichet also has a huge **marina**, one of the largest along France's Atlantic coast, although it's a wholly artificial harbour, completed in the 1970s.

At the La Baule aerodrome behind Pornichet, the **Musée Aéronautique de la Presqu'île Côte d'Amour** preserves and restores classic aeroplanes. There's also the **Tropicarium Bonsaï** nearby; it's much more than a simple garden centre, with the exotic plant trail through its greenhouses. A bit further inland, near **St-André-les-Eaux**, the very large, posh **Golf International Barrière-La Baule complex** with accompanying hotel is run by the same luxury group that dominates the scene in central La Baule.

Just west of La Baule, **Le Pouliguen** stands slightly aloof, a more old-fashioned resort. It too has a **marina**, while its fishing port is still going. The old village has kept some of its winding fishermen's lanes.

Heading further east along the coast, things quieten down at more traditional **Ste-Marguerite** and **St-Marc**. Little cliffs begin to rise, the beaches set in small creeks. The resort of St-Marc was made famous by Jacques Tati's classic movie, *Les Vacances de Monsieur Hulot*. A beautifully shot film, *Presque Rien*, directed by Sébastien Lifschitz in 1999, presents another memorable view of this stretch of coast. It doesn't depict a classic holiday romance; instead, it's an extremely sensitive story of young gay love.

Le Croisic Peninsula and Batz-sur-Mer

In summer this beautiful peninsula is blighted by traffic, as the rocky southern coast road along it counts as a favourite drive for the hordes of holidaymakers from La Baule. This **Côte Sauvage**, picturesque, but not conducive to swimming, is bordered by small cliffs that diminish in size as you head west. Breton legend ascribes the grottoes along here to the Breton fairies, the *korrigans*.

Centre de Thalassothérapie Daniel Jouvence t 02 40 61 89 98

Musée Aéronautique de la Presqu'île Côte d'Amour www.mapica.or, t 02 51 75 10 43; open Mon and Wed–Fri 2–5; free

Tropicarium Bonsaï www.raphy.fr/ tropicarium, t 02 40 61 20 30

Golf International Barrière-La Baule complex t 02 40 60 46 18

Batz-sur-Mer, straddling the peninsula, has a traditional Breton feel to it with its cluster of whitewashed houses. Apparently, Breton continued to be spoken here up until the last century, and you can still buy Breton clogs at the Maison du Sabot. The church that dominates the centre of town is dedicated to a revered Breton saint of the Dark Ages, Guénolé (*see* p.313). Climb the narrowing stairs to the top of the steeple for magnificent views. Batz's **Musée des Marais Salants** is one of the oldest traditional local museums in France. It was started in 1887 by Adèle Pichon, a nun who was the daughter of a local *paludier* (*see* box p.465). She realized that the traditional ways of life would rapidly disappear, so she early set about preserving what she could.

Musée des Marais Salants
www.museedesmarai ssalants@wanadoo.fr, t 02 40 23 82 79; open June–Sept 10–12.30 and 2.30–7

Less quaint, the **Grand Blockhaus** was the biggest German bunker built for Hitler's Atlantic Wall. At a whopping 2,000 square metres, they made some attempt to conceal it between the villas of Batz. Today it houses a Second World War museum, the **Musée de la Poche de Saint Nazaire**, focusing on the St Nazaire Pocket, where hardened German soldiers held on well into 1945, causing the area to be the last to be liberated in France. Inside this chilling monstrosity, you can see dormitories, the radio post and the weapons room.

Grand Blockhaus
www.grand-blockhaus.com; open Feb and Easter school hols and April–All Saints 10–7

The port of **Le Croisic** stands sheltered on the north side of the peninsula. It looks out across the **inland sea of Le Traict** to the salt flats of Guérande. Only a narrow channel of water allows the boats in and out of its highly picturesque harbour. Like Batz, Le Croisic has retained its historic Breton feel. The port has even kept some of its 16th-century buildings. The Flamboyant Gothic granite church of Notre-Dame-de-Pitié was consecrated in 1507. Roughly from that time on, the Le Croisic fleet went off to fish for cod and whales off North America. Corsairs also set sail from here. Now, with its **marina**, it's much more geared to tourists.

Briefly rechristened Port Liberté during the Revolution, Le Croisic became one of the first successful Breton tourist destinations in the mid-19th century. The old **fish auctioning hall** from the late 19th century stands on Place Boston. The modern Criée went up on the Mont Lénigo, an artificial hillock built from ballast that the ships left at Le Croisic in times past as they loaded up with salt.

Océarium
www.ocearium-croisic.fr, t 02 40 23 02 44; open Feb and Easter hols 10–12 and 2–6, mid-April–mid-May 10–6, mid-May–June and Sept–Oct 10–12 and 2–6, July–Aug 10–7, mid-Nov–Dec 2–6

Beyond the port and the seafront restaurants and boutiques, the ultramodern **Océarium** is the major tourist attraction. This starfish of an aquarium has been set down amid the town's rampant modern suburbs. Its most impressive feature is a transparent-sided tunnel through which visitors can walk, looking at sharks, groupers and rays swimming around them. The southern hemisphere penguins were actually brought here from London Zoo.

(i) Guérande >>
1 Place du Marché au Bois, t 02 40 24 96 71, www.ot-guerande.fr

Market Days on the Coast from La Vilaine to La Baule

Mesquer-Quimiac: large Tue and Fri markets between 15 June and 15 Sept
Piriac-sur-Mer: Mon, Wed and Sat 15 June–15 Sept; rest of year Tue morning only
La Turballe: fishmarket generally Mon–Sat
Guérande: Wed am and Sat am, plus Sun at Pradel in July and Aug
La Baule: a superb covered market every morning April–Sept, plus various other markets held mornings on Mon, Tue, Thurs and Sat
Pornichet: fishmarket generally Mon–Sat, plus Wed and Sat morning markets
Le Pouliguen: large markets Tue, Fri and Sun
Batz-sur-Mer: Mon am year round, plus Fri am in summer
Le Croisic: Thurs and Sat am in covered market, plus Tues am and Fri am in July and Aug

Where to Stay and Eat on the Coast from La Vilaine to La Baule

(i) La Baule >>
8 Place de la Victoire, t 02 40 24 34 44, www.labaule.fr

(★) Castel Marie-Louise >>

(i) Mesquer-Quimiac >
Place du Marché, t 02 40 42 64 37, www.mesquer-quimiac.com

(i) Piriac-sur-Mer >
7 Rue des Cap-Horniers, t 02 40 23 51 42, www.piriac.net

(i) La Turballe >
Place du Général de Gaulle, t 02 40 23 39 87, www.laturballe.info

(★) Manoir des Quatres Saisons >

Mesquer ✉ 44420
Clos de Botelo, 249 Rue des Cap Horniers, t 02 40 42 50 20 (€). A pleasant B&B looking out over the Mesquer marshes.
La Vieille Forge, t 02 49 42 62 68 (€€€€–€€). Interesting restaurant in Ancien Régime forge, with terrace, offering French cuisine with Asian touches.

Piriac-sur-Mer ✉ 44420
**La Poste, 29 Rue de la Plage, t 02 40 23 50 90, www.piriac-hoteldelaposte.com (€€–€). A sweet, nicely located villa with decent rooms and restaurant.

La Turballe ✉ 44420
Manoir des Quatres Saisons, 744 Blvd Auvergnac (towards Piriac), t 02 40 11 76 16, www.manoir-des-quatre-saisons.com (€€). Splendid rooms in a very appealing old Breton home, with pool.

Terminus, 18 Quai St-Paul, t 02 40 23 30 29 (€). A pleasant seafood bistrot opposite the fishing port. *Closed Sun and Tues eves and Wed out of season.*

Guérande ✉ 44350
B&B La Guérandière, 5 Rue Vannetaise, t 02 40 62 17 15, www.guerande.fr (€€–€). A fine 19th-century house with garden next to the Porte Vannetaise, with ornately decorated rooms.
**Les Remparts, 14–15 Blvd du Nord, t 02 40 24 90 69 (€). Comfortable, traditional rooms and good food.
**Roc Maria, 1 Rue du Vieux Marché aux Grains, t 02 40 24 90 51, www.hotelcreperierocmaria.com (€). Simple rooms in very quaint old stone house in the centre, with one of the town's many crêperies attached.
**Les Voyageurs, Place du 8 Mai, t 02 40 24 90 13 (€). A solidly reliable, traditional French hotel with decent rooms, some with views onto the ramparts from just outside the gates, and a good restaurant (€€).
Le Vieux Logis, 1 Place de la Psalette, t 02 40 02 09 73. Good wood-fire grills served at a former town dignitary's home, with pleasant courtyard.

La Baule ✉ 44500
****Castel Marie-Louise, 1 Ave Andrieu, t 02 40 11 48 38, www.castel-marie-louise.com (€€€€€–€€€). A fine neo-Gothic mansion with a large pine-shaded garden in the heart of the resort. The rooms are plush to sumptuous. The restaurant (€€€€) offers cuisine full of interesting touches. Cookery courses in low season. Tennis court.
****Hermitage-Barrière, 5 Esplanade Lucien Barrière, t 02 40 11 46 46, www.lucienbarriere.com (€€€€€–€€€€). An enormous grand hotel with more than 200 swanky rooms standing out behind the beach – it's what the French call a 'palace'. Les Evens is its more luxurious restaurant, serving extremely inventive cuisine; the Eden Beach is cheaper, more relaxed and more popular with customers from outside the hotel. There's also a casino, a heated seawater swimming pool, beauty treatments and gym facilities.

(i) **Pornichet** >>
*3 Blvd de la
République, t 02 40 61
33 33, www.pornichet.fr*

(★) Sud
Bretagne >>

(★) **Le St-
Christophe** >

(★) **Villa
Flornoy** >>

(★) **Villa Cap
d'Ail** >

(i) **Le
Pouliguen** >>
*Port Sterwitz,
t 02 40 42 31 05,
www.lepouliguen.fr*

(i) **Batz-
sur-Mer** >>
*25 Rue de la Plage,
t 02 40 23 92 36,
www.mairie-
batzsurmer.fr*

****Royal Thalasso-Barrière**, 6 Ave Pierre Loti, **t** 02 40 11 48 48, *www.lucienbarriere.com* (€€€€€–€€€). In the same style as the above, not quite its neighbouring rival, as owned by the same group, but the important thing here is that this one is centred on the luxury seawater treatment centre attached.

***Bellevue Plage**, 27 Blvd de l'Océan, **t** 02 40 60 28 55, *www.hotel-bellevue-plage.fr* (€€€). One of the most stylish sea-view 3-stars, with contemporary styling and a roof terrace.

***Le Christina**, 26 Blvd Hennecart, **t** 02 40 60 22 44, *www.hotel-le-christina.com* (€€€–€€). Good rooms with balconies making the most of the views right along the beach.

****Le St-Christophe**, Place Notre-Dame, **t** 02 40 62 40 00, *www.st-christophe.com* (€€€€). Several family villas just behind the seafront have been joined together to form this charming hotel with its relaxed family feel and lovely mix of rooms. The restaurant (€€) is appealing too, giving onto the garden.

****Villa Cap d'Ail**, 145 Ave de Lattre de Tassigny, **t** 02 40 60 29 30, *www.villacapdail.com* (€€€–€€). A villa with charming rooms, at the heart of the action, a hundred metres from the beach.

****La Palmeraie**, 7 Allée des Cormorans, **t** 02 40 60 24 41, *www.hotel-lapalmeraie-labaule.com* (€€). A hotel with a lovely flower garden shaded by pines.

****Le Lutétia and Rossini Restaurant**, 13 Ave Olivier Guichard, **t** 02 40 60 25 81, *www.lutetia-rossini.com* (€€). Among the best, smartest 2-stars in town, set on one of the chic streets behind the beach. It has an elegant, highly regarded restaurant. (€€€).

La Véranda, 27 Blvd de l'Océan, **t** 02 40 60 57 77 (€€€€–€€). One of the best sea-front restaurants with dining rooms on two floors to make the most of the beach views.

La Barbade, on the beach (level of 31 Blvd Darlu), **t** 02 40 42 01 01. A classic restaurant actually down on the central stretch of beach.

Le Ponton, on beach near Le Pouliguen, **t** 02 40 60 52 05. Relaxed option on the westerly end of the great beach.

Ferme du Grand Clos, 52 Ave du Maréchal de Lattre de Tassigny, **t** 02 40 60 03 30 (€€). Rare old farm, turned into one of the most sought-after crêperies in town, with garden. *Closed Tues and Wed Sept–June.*

Le Loft, 277 Ave du Maréchal de Lattre de Tassigny, **t** 02 40 24 51 14 (€€). After an elegant redesign, Loft offers innovative cuisine.

La Villa, 18 Ave de Gaulle, **t** 02 40 23 06 00 (€€). Relaxed brasserie-style ambience.

Pornichet ✉ 44380

****Sud Bretagne**, 42 Blvd de la République, **t** 02 40 11 65 00, *www.hotelsudbretagne.com* (€€). A romantic choice, its chic rooms set in an old villa. Pools and restaurant (€€).

****Le Régent**, 150 Boulevard des Océanides, **t** 02 40 61 04 04, *www.le-regent.fr* (€). The best of the cheaper seafront options, with a stylish restaurant.

****Villa Flornoy**, 7 Avenue Flornoy, **t** 02 40 11 60 00, *www.villa-flornoy.com* (€€€). A very comfortable choice close to the beach, with nice restaurant open in season.

Le Pouliguen ✉ 44510

Le Garde Côte, 1 Jetée du Port, **t** 02 40 42 31 20 (€€). A dining room on the beach, done out like a 1930s boat and offering an unbeatable view on to the port and the bay of La Baule.

Batz-sur-Mer ✉ 44740

Le Fort de l'Hermione, 22 Route de la Gouelle, **t** 02 40 23 91 40 (€€). Batz's smartest restaurant, with a beachfront terrace and a stylish dining room.

La Marcanderie, 5 Rue Poulgot, Batz-sur-Mer, **t** 02 40 24 03 12 (€€). The best-known seafood place in town, with pretty décor.

Fleur de Sel, 42 Rue de la Chapelle (in Kervalet village), **t** 02 40 23 90 73 (€). One of the best crêperies in the area, where you can also enjoy *kig ha farz*, a Breton meat stew.

Le Café de la Plage, 3 Plage St-Michel, **t** 02 40 23 88 90 (€€–€). Smack bang on the beach, serving fresh, light meals.

ⓘ Le Croisic >
*Place du 18 Juin 1940,
t 02 40 23 00 70,
www.ot-lecroisic.com;
see also www.pays
blanc.fr for tourist
information along this
stretch of coast*

**★ Le Fort de
l'Océan >**

Le Croisic ✉ 44490

★★★★Le Fort de l'Océan, Pointe du Croisic, t 02 40 15 77 77, *www.fort-ocean.com* (€€€€€–€€€€). Superbly located big villa built on a coastal fort above the ocean, with amazing rooms with sea views and an excellent seafood restaurant. Heated pool in garden.

★★★L'Océan, Port Lin, t 02 40 62 90 03 (€€€). In another splendid coastal location, at the port, with colourful maritime rooms and a smart restaurant making the most of the setting.

★★Le Castel Moor, Baie du Castouillet, t 02 40 23 24 18, *www.castel-moor.com* (€€). A good mid-budget option in modern coastal villa, most rooms with balcony.

La Bouillabaisse Bretonne, 12 Quai de la Petite Chambre, t 02 40 23 06 74 (€€). A good seafood option, with sea views, but there are plenty of other very Breton crêperies and the like at the port.

St-Marc-sur-Mer ✉ 44600

★★★La Plage, 37 Rue du Commandant Charcot, t 02 40 91 99 01, *www.best western.fr* (€€€–€€). A beautifully located film star of a seaside hotel – it featured in one of the most famous comedies in French cinema, Jacques Tati's *Les Vacances de Monsieur Hulot*. It has recently been fully modernized. The restaurant serves local seafood dishes, and has a delightful terrace above the beach for summer dining.

The Brière, St-Nazaire and the Loire Estuary

The Brière

The second largest marsh in France after the Camargue, the Brière is a secretive, reed-hidden waterland few have heard of outside France. In 1970 it was declared a regional natural park to protect its environment and traditions. The whole park covers 40,000 hectares. The marsh stretches north to south from just below La Roche-Bernard on the Vilaine to the outskirts of St-Nazaire on the Loire. Its marshy heart measures 7,000 hectares. It's crisscrossed by a network of canals (*curées*) linking some of its many lakes (*piardes* or *copis*). St-Joachim, diminutive capital of the Brière, lies roughly in the centre of the marshes, along the only main road through them.

With all those reeds to hand, it isn't entirely surprising that the Brière can boast of having the greatest density of thatched houses left standing in France. They are a pleasure to see. The best way to discover the marshlands themselves is in a punt, with a local Briéron guide. There are also various nature trails to follow and local museums that explain more about the Brière and Briéron ways. The Brière is an important natural site, in particular for migrating birds, who find the reed beds most restful.

As ever in Brittany, the odd vestige of neolithic civilization stands out, for example the Dolmen de la Barbière at Crossac, or the Dolmen de Kerbourg at St-Lyphard. The people of the Brière, the Briérons, have long been an independent bunch. As far back as the

Getting to and around St-Nazaire and the Brière

St-Nazaire and La Baule have good **rail** connections. To find recommended places to go on a **boat** tour around the Brière, consult the listings on the website of the Parc Naturel Régional de la Brière (*www.parc-naturel-briere.fr* – look under *balades en chalands*. The site also provides details on getting round by canoe, horse or bike).

15th century, the Breton duke François II granted them the right to exploit the main section of the marshes, the Grande Brière Mottière. It was, exceptionally, declared an indivisible possession of the community.

The Briéron independence was only radically altered with the growth of St-Nazaire in the first half of the 20th century. The marshlands became increasingly neglected as many of the locals left their subsistence living to go and work in the major shipbuilding yards, and the traditional marshland activities of reed-cutting and peat-extraction quickly dwindled. But it was the gathering of the black peat that gave this little country apart its nickname Pays Noir.

Touring the Brière

If you're arriving in the Brière from the north along the main N165 dual carriageway, take the Missillac exit for a look at the magnificent **Château de la Bretesche**, a castle built for the barons of La Roche-Bernard from the late 14th century, and a splendid Gothic vision reflected in its lake. The château is now divided into flats, but you can pay a small fee to wander round the grounds, while the outbuildings have been converted into a stylish hotel with very fine **golf course** attached (*see* p.477).

La Chapelle-des-Marais, southwest of Missillac, brings you to the Brière proper. Its tourist office is the main one serving the park. The **Chaumière du Patrimoine** presents some of the old professions of the Brière. **Mayun**, just south of La Chapelle-des-Marais, has preserved a fair number of its thatched cottages. The place was long known for its basket-weaving, and a few locals continue the tradition. For families seeking diversion, the **Chaumière des Marionnettes** is an Aladdin's cave, or rather cottage, of hand-crafted puppets. The place runs workshops, for children and adults, where you can make your own. The nearby **Miellerie de la Brière** is housed in an interesting interpretation of a futuristic-looking *chaumière*. Here you can get an insight into all aspects of honey and the ecology of bees. West of Mayun, the ruins of the medieval **Château du Ranrouet** still impress.

Heading down the western side of the Brière, off the road from Mayun to St-Lyphard, the **Port des Fossés Blancs** is one of the places where you can take a boat out on the waterways of the Brière. Those of you interested in gardening might visit the small **Jardins du Marais**, an experimental ornamental kitchen garden.

Chaumière du Patrimoine
*t 02 40 66 85 01;
open daily 2–7*

Chaumière des Marionnettes
*t 02 40 53 27 40;
open daily 2–7*

Jardins du Marais
open mid-May–mid-Sept daily 2–6

On the north side of St-Lyphard, at the **Port des Prises du Coin**, there's a beautiful area for walking. In **St-Lyphard** itself, the church tower may not be architecturally inspiring, but you can climb it (small fee) to get the best of views down on to the Brière. The prettiest thatched villages in the park lie close by. **Arbourg**, just northwest of St-Lyphard, has a typical huddle of lovely thatched cottages.

A whole string of delightful thatched villages lie southwest of St-Lyphard. **Kerhinet** is by far the best known. The park authorities have taken this hamlet under their wing and made it into the Brière's main showcase. Cars are banned, craftspeople encouraged, and flowers proliferate. The **Musée du Chaume** explains the principal features of the traditional Briéron home. Nearby at Nezyl, you'll find the **Brasserie de la Brière**, brewing some fine beers. East of Kerhinet, **Bréca** is another Brière port from which you can take a punt out on the waterways.

St-André-des-Eaux lies in the southwestern corner of the park, with a luxury golf course nearby (*see* p.467). Duck enthusiasts can head east out of St-André for **Ker Anas**, the 'duck village', presenting some 90 species from around the world.

The real **heart of the Brière** marsh is the group of semi-islands around **St-Joachim**, north of St-Nazaire. **Ile de Fédrun** is where the tourist action is concentrated. It's an excellent place to go on a guided punt trip out on the Brière waterways. Two cottages here are open to the public, the presentations inside focusing on women's lives in the Brière. **La Maison de la Mariée** recalls in particular the 19th-century tradition of making false orange-blossom crowns for French brides, while the other cottage covers more general issues.

Rozé, just south of St-Joachim, was once one of the most important traditional ports in the Brière. Here, **La Maison de l'Eclusier**, a former lock-keeper's house, has been done up by the park authorities. The displays present the Brière's geology and history, and focus in on the tradition of peat extraction, as well as the boats used in that business. The place also introduces the Brière's flora and fauna. To appreciate these to the full, head on to the nearby **Réserve Ornithologique Pierre Constant** to enjoy the natural environment of the Brière for yourself, in particular from its bird-watching hides.

St-Nazaire

Hard-hit by war bombs, hard-hit by guidebooks in the past, the ship-building port of St-Nazaire was turned into a major Nazi submarine base in the Second World War and hence smashed to smithereens by Allied bombers. But the place does in fact have plenty of character. It stands in a mesmerizing location, where the

---

Musée du Chaume
open April–Sept daily 2–6

Brasserie de la Brière
open daily 9–12 and 2–5; closed Sun in low season

Ker Anas
www.keranas.fr, t 02 40 01 27 48; open Feb and Easter hols 2–6, Mar Sat–Sun 2–6, April–Sept 2.30–6.30, July–Aug 10–8, Oct Sat–Sun and All Saints hols 2.30–6.30

La Maison de la Mariée
open April–June and Sept 2.30–6.30, July–Aug 10.30–1 and 2.30–6.30

La Maison de l'Eclusier
open April–June and Sept 2.30–6.30, July–Aug 10.30–1 and 2.30–6.30

Réserve Ornithologique Pierre Constant
t 02 40 66 85 01; open April–June and Sept 2.30–6.30, July–Aug 10.30–1 and 2.30–6.30

🚉 St-Nazaire

great Loire River merges with the Atlantic. Industry may dominate along the river mouth, but turning the corner onto the coast, you come to a string of really appealing beaches and coves. However, with such widely known, highly successful seaside resorts close by, St-Nazaire finds it hard to compete in that field; very cleverly, it has turned its attentions to tourism in recent years, and transformed the terrible poisoned legacy left by the Nazis to very good effect.

St-Nazaire was a simple, innocent little fishing village until its exceptionally practical location was chosen for a major new shipbuilding port in the mid-19th century. The industrial facilities developed rapidly, at first in association with the Scottish company of John Scott. Penhoët, in the east of town, was chosen as the site for the shipyards. The vessel *L'Impératrice Eugénie* was the first to be built here, during the French Second Empire. St-Nazaire grew into one of the major European ports to operate transatlantic services. Many sailed off from here for good to start a new life in the Americas. During the First World War, though, thousands of North American soldiers arrived here before being sent out to the front, making an invaluable contribution to the victory in that conflict, many never returning home.

Between the two world wars, the most famous of France's massive ocean liners were built here, notably the *Paris*, the *Ile-de-France*, the *Champlain* and, most impressive of the lot, the misleadingly named *Normandie*, launched in 1932. But this was also a time of major global economic turmoil. The shipyard workers suffered terribly from the cyclical nature of their work, and in 1933 went on an important hunger march to Nantes.

Notoriously, when the Nazis occupied France, they turned St-Nazaire into one of their most important naval bases. Not only was a huge fleet of submarines sheltered here; it was also the only French Atlantic port large enough to take German battleships. The town became a crucial target for the British air force to wipe out. Operation Chariot in 1942 wrought much damage, with 600 British commandoes on HMS *Cambelltown* wrecking the docks, closing it to German battleships. There's a monument remembering this feat on Boulevard Verdun. Several of the major St-Nazaire ocean liners were destroyed in the war. While most of France was liberated in the summer of 1944, St-Nazaire was one of the pockets of territory which bitterly stubborn German soldiers defended right through to May 1945. By then, the town lay in ruins.

It was rapidly reconstructed along a grid plan in the 1950s, and naval and aeronautical construction took off again, although the work has been unstable, coming in waves. In recent times, though, Airbus has opened a major factory here, while the shipyards have been putting together some of the largest cruise liners in the world at a rate of knots, including the *Queen Mary II*.

St-Nazaire's Docks

A sinister, long building stretches along one side of the first, **outer dock** of St-Nazaire's vast estuary port. This is the dreaded **Nazi submarine base**. Built on such a massive scale, its concrete walls are so thick that it isn't feasible for the town to pay to destroy them. So instead, the St-Nazaire authorities took the bold step, in recent times, of turning the place into a tourist attraction. It's been a clever gamble that has paid off. For starters, the grim outside walls have been decorated here and there with colourful posters from a Tintin adventure that features the port of St-Nazaire. In addition, the odd shop and café has been opened in the very shadows of the U-Boot pens.

Inside one portion of the vast edifice, you can go on a highly enjoyable tour of **Escal'Atlantique**, a museum dedicated to the ocean-liner-building traditions of St-Nazaire. Dispensing with the tradition of inhabiting a crabby old authentic vessel, this is an entirely re-created *paquebot*, made with the aid of top architects and theatre set-designers. The project was 17 years in the planning; the appearance of the film *Titanic* around the time of its opening was a simple coincidence.

Every conceivable part of a liner is represented, including the hair salon, the emigrants' quarters and the engine room, and everywhere are bits of movie footage (including excerpts from the classics of the ocean liner's golden age) on porthole screens. You get a good idea of the cabins of each era, including the 1860s Jules Verne model, complete with *vomitoire*. There's also a cinema, where shows will entertain you. At the end of your tour, you can enjoy the rather glamorous setting of the café and restaurant, where at certain times of day, even the plates come to life.

It's possible to wander freely over the roofs of the submarine base, from which you get extensive views over town. Up in this curious setting, panels tell of St-Nazaire's history. The curiously shaped **Radôme** placed up here is a more recent gift from Germany to the town, a disused radar installation from Berlin airport. It looks like a strange piece of contemporary art.

As part of the outer dock has been turned into a **marina**, yachts now moor in the water right outside the pens, making a nice contrast with the past. On other sides of the dock, you can look at the colourful vessels of the St-Nazaire **fishing fleet**.

Across the waters, you'll spot another submarine pen, which holds a French submarine you can visit. It forms part of the local history museum, the **Ecomusée** (*open same times as Escal'Atlantic*). In front of the museum's main building, beside rather derelict ground on the edge of the Loire estuary, a moving sculptural group of life-sized figures draws your attention. Created by the sculptor Mayo, put up in 1991, it's called **A l'Abolition de l'Esclavage** and

Escal'Atlantique
open Feb–Mar and Oct–Dec Wed–Sat 2–6 Sun 10–12.30 and 2–6; school hols daily and April–Sept 10–12.30 and 2–6; mid-July–Aug 10–7

recalls the terrible slave trade that brought such wealth to the Loire estuary in the 18th century (*see* p.482), and such suffering to the appallingly exploited black Africans.

Inside, the Ecomusée tells the history of St-Nazaire in engrossing detail. Not only is its tradition of liner-building covered, but also that of aeronautics. As to a tour around the submarine *Espadon*, it makes for a memorable experience. It was donated to the town in 1986, having served the French navy for 25 years. Built in Le Havre in 1957, it became the first French submarine to cross the North Pole under the ice fields, back in 1964. Some 60 sailors lived in it for up to 45 days at a time – just a half-hour visit can make you feel claustrophobic.

Chantiers Navals
2hr tours Wed, Sat and Sun, reservation via tourist office obligatory

Definitely consider a guided tour of the **Chantiers Navals** at the **inner dock**, where the latest cruise liner built in St-Nazaire often marks the skyline. No photography is allowed on the bus tour, but it's memorable seeing how today's vast cruise liners are assembled, like vast toy models. Further industrial terrain is explored at the nearby **Airbus factory**, essentially a massive aircraft factory, where you can see St-Nazaire's other major technological industry in action.

Airbus factory
2hr guided tours on Wed; reserve via tourist office

From the Town Centre Along the Coast

St-Nazaire's town centre has improved radically in the last few years, with the development of two slick new **shopping areas**. **Le Ruban Bleu** is the most recent, extending up the slope from the submarine base. Nearby, on duller **Place du Dolmen**, you can go and see the surprising sight of a neolithic dolmen sat in the middle of a modern square. A bit further north, **Le Paqueot shopping quarter** has been designed in very appealing manner, its main set of airy buildings built to mimic the forms of an ocean liner.

West of the centre, St-Nazaire has a long **seafront** that turns its back on the docks and looks out to the ocean. It makes an interesting stretch of coast. You can start at the outer **fishing harbour**, with its comical row of square fishing nets, known as *carrelets*, left suspended in the air over the jetty while not in action. The big **main beach** curves round to a major statue on a rock, representing an American soldier perched on an eagle, a memorial in honour of the US soldiers who landed in St-Nazaire to then go and fight in the First World War. Just behind the strand, there's a pretty **public garden** with café, while along Boulevard Président Wilson, some 19th-century villas survived the bombs. Further west is a string of beaches that prove comfortably wide at low tide.

Looking south, an amazing serpent of a **bridge** crosses the Loire estuary, providing a spectacular ending to the River Loire. To the south, the resorts and flat beaches are more typical of the Vendéen coast, but they're relaxingly appealing, too.

Sidebar (left column)

(★) Auberge de Kerbourg >>

(i) Parc Naturel Régional de la Brière
The website for the Parc Naturel Régional de la Brière, www.parc-naturel-briere.fr, contains lots of useful information to get started with

(i) Maison du Tourisme de la Brière
38 Rue de la Brière, La Chapelle-des-Marais, t 02 40 66 85 01, www.parc-naturel-briere.fr

(i) Herbignac >
1 Rue de la Monneraye, t 02 40 88 90 01, www.herbignac.com

(★) Château Coëtcaret >

(i) St-André-des-Eaux >>
7 Place de l'Eglise t 02 40 91 53 53, www.saint-andre-des-eaux.com

(i) St-Nazaire >>
Blvd de la Légion d'Honneur, t 02 40 22 40 65, www.saint-nazaire-tourisme.com

(★) de la Bretesche >

(i) La Chapelle-des-Marais
38 Rue de la Brière, t 02 40 66 85 01

(i) St-Lyphard >
Place de l'Eglise, t 02 40 91 41 34, www.saint-lyphard.com

Market Days in the Brière and St-Nazaire

Herbignac-Missillac: Wednesday morning
Kerhinet: late June–early September, all day Thursday
St-Joachim: Saturday morning
St-Malo-de-Guersac: Thursday morning
St-Nazaire: Tuesday–Sunday

Where to Stay and Eat in St-Nazaire and the Brière

Herbignac ✉ 44410

Château Coëtcaret, off the D47, 4km south of Herbignac towards St-Lyphard, t 02 40 91 41 20, *www.coetcaret.com* (€€€). A smart little 19th-century manor on a large estate of some 200 hectares. Its B&B rooms are calm and comfortable.

M.& Mme Fresne, 12 Rue Jean de Rieux, Marlais, 6km from Herbignac, t 02 40 91 40 83 (€€–€). A B&B in a typical *longère*.

La Chaumière des Marais, Ker Moureau, t 02 40 91 32 36 (€€€–€€). A typical Briéron thatched cottage, with a good reputation for gutsy dishes such as duck with oysters and asparagus. *Closed Mon eve, and Tues out of season.*

Missillac ✉ 44780

★★★★de la Bretesche, t 02 51 76 86 71, *www.bretesche.com* (€€€€). Splendid hotel in the outbuildings of a fabulous Gothic, lake-side castle. The rooms have been impeccably done up. **Le Green**, the restaurant (€€€), counts among the finest in the area, with great views. Pool and tennis court. The grounds have been turned into one of the finest golf courses in France.

St-Lyphard ✉ 44410

★★Les Chaumières du Lac, Rue du Vigonnet, t 02 40 91 32 32, *www.leschaumieresdulac.com* (€€). A modern cluster of upmarket, purpose-built thatched cottages. The restaurant, **Les Typhas** (€€€), serves refined food. *Closed Sun eve, and Mon out of season.*

Auberge de Kerbourg, t 02 40 61 95 15, (€€€). The most memorable Briéron setting in which to eat. The cuisine is extremely refined and inventive, and sometimes uses produce from the beautifully tended garden. *Closed Tues lunch, Sun eve and Mon.*

Auberge du Nézil, on the D47, t 02 40 91 41 41, *www.aubergelenezil.com* (€€). A modern rendering of the Briéron thatched cottage. The cuisine is in the classic French tradition.

Kerhinet ✉ 44410

★★L'Auberge de Kerhinet, t 02 40 61 91 46 (€€). In beautiful thatched houses in the most touristy spot in the Brière; if you manage to book one of the 7 rooms you'll be able to appreciate the village when the tourist hordes have gone home. The restaurant serves local food (€€), including eels and frogs' legs. *Closed Tues and Wed.*

Ile de Fédrun ✉ 44720

La Mare aux Oiseaux, t 02 40 88 53 01 (€€€). This restaurant offers original presentations of classic *produits du terroir* such as *poisson bleu en tempura*.

St-André-des-Eaux ✉ 44117

Auberge du Haut-Marland, t 02 40 01 29 00 (€€€–€€). Renowned for its gourmet cuisine, plus a highly picturesque location by the marshes. *Closed Sun and Thurs eves, and Mon.*

St-Nazaire ✉ 44600

My Suit Appart Hôtel, 47 Blvd de Libération, Place de la Gare, t 02 40 00 64, *www.mysuitapparthotels.com* (€€–€). Big white contemporary block in the centre, with well-equipped apartments. Pool.

Au Bon Accueil, 39 Rue Marceau, t 02 40 22 07 05, *www.au-bon-accueil44.com*. A pleasant option on a smaller scale.

Le Berry, Place Sémard, t 02 40 22 42 61, *www.hotel-du-berry.fr*. Opposite the station, with comfortable rooms and decent restaurant.

Le Skipper, 1 Blvd René Coty, t 02 40 22 20 03 (€€). Showing the trendy new side of St-Nazaire, stylish contemporary restaurant serving succulent dishes at the sea end of the outer dock.

Nantes

Nantes has an ocean feel to it – even if the Atlantic lies some 50 kilometres away, and much of the shipping trade that brought the place such riches in the Ancien Régime moved west quite some time ago to be closer to the sea. Bombs rained down on the city during the Second World War. Despite the destruction, large portions of historic Nantes survived, including the massive castle of the late medieval dukes of Brittany, the medieval cathedral where the last Breton duke was buried, and some of the grand Ancien Régime streets and squares that the young Jules Verne would have known in his 19th-century childhood.

However, a huge historical shadow casts its darkness over the place – the vast wealth of the 18th-century merchants of Nantes, from which the city so benefited, was built on the slave trade. Clusters of ornate town houses are the most obvious legacy. The finest are typically decorated with *mascarons*, somehow appropriately grotesque stylized masks. Up until recently, the city mostly ignored its slave-trading past, which was particularly ironic as, in French history, Nantes is best known for an edict of tolerance signed here by King Henri IV of France in 1598, putting an end to the terrible French Wars of Religion in which Protestants and Catholics had torn each other apart. However, with the recent remodelling of the history museum in the Château de Nantes, the amnesia has been somewhat remedied.

Nantes has been changing a lot in the last decade. In the centre, there's a feeling of self-confidence and sassiness. The cultural scene is vibrant. In term time, the place teems with students. The town has its Breton features, but it also feels cosmopolitan, and it has regularly topped the charts for the best big French provincial city in which to live.

History

The Gaulish tribe of the Namnetes had a port at the spot where the Erdre River joins the Loire. The Pictones, meanwhile, favoured the south bank. Few signs have been found of their times, or even of Gallo-Roman Nantes for that matter. It is reckoned though that Christianity came early to the place, with its usual tales of cruel martyrdom. **Donatien** and **Rogatien** were the children of Aurlien, a Gallo-Roman governor of the town, who converted to the new faith. Donatien had already been baptized, Rogatien had not, when their persecutors hounded them down at the start of the 4th century. The imprisoned Rogatien is said to have uttered the tender words: 'If my brother, who is baptized, will deign to kiss me, his kiss will serve as a baptism for me', before the two of them were viciously tortured and had their heads cut off. Christianity soon got the upper hand, however, the bishops of Nantes becoming powerful figures.

Getting to and around Nantes

The **airport**, Nantes Atlantique, *www.nantes.aeroport.fr*, t 02 40 84 80 00, lies just southwest of the centre. Easyjet and Ryanair operate flights to and from London Gatwick, London Stansted, Nottingham East Midlands, Bournemouth, Cardiff and Liverpool, Dublin, Cork and Shannon. Nantes can be reached by **train** in a mere 2hrs from Paris on a TGV, and just 4hrs from Lille; in fact, you can get here by train from London in just under 6hrs. Tram lines crisscross the centre of town, complementing the bus service (call t 02 40 29 39 39 for information on both).

During much of the Dark Ages, the county of Nantes was fought over by Franks and Bretons. By Merovingian times, this county formed a part of the Frankish Marches. **Nomenoë**, appointed leader of Brittany by one Frankish king, made his successful bid for Breton independence under another. He conquered Nantes and its territories. But soon the Vikings sailed up the Loire to wreak havoc. After the turmoil, Nantes developed into the most significant town in Brittany.

In the **Breton War of Succession** in the mid 14th century, the city switched hands several times between the two sides, involved in such a vicious inheritance dispute. Under the powerful de Montfort dukes who won the conflict, Nantes maintained the upper hand over its rival Rennes – it was essentially the capital of Brittany.

In the chaotic, war-torn, superstition-riddled first half of the 15th century, **Gilles de Rais**, or **de Retz**, owner of large estates south of Nantes and a major player at the French court under King Charles VII, became one of the most notorious Frenchmen of his age. Having been fêted for fighting alongside Joan of Arc, he was later accused of raping and murdering scores of boys in his castles, and using them in satanic rituals. He may have been framed, but was certainly hanged and burnt in Nantes in 1440.

Under **Duke François II**, to be the last duke of Brittany, Nantes was thriving as capital of the province. A prestigious university had been inaugurated here in 1460, with the papacy's blessing. Duke François II's extraordinary daughter, **Duchess Anne de Bretagne**, was born at the Château de Nantes (*see* p.484) in 1477. Nantes would remain a city close to her heart for all her life – and after it was over. She married two French kings in a row; the first, Charles VIII, she was wedded to at the Château de Langeais up the Loire; the second, Louis XII, she married in the chapel of the Château de Nantes in 1499. Anne died at another château on the Loire, Blois, in 1514. While most of her mortal remains were taken to the French royal resting place of the Abbey of St-Denis, outside Paris, she specifically asked for her heart to be returned to Nantes to be buried. Anne's daughter Claude would marry King François I, who arranged Brittany's official union with France in 1532.

In the mid-16th century, with the creation of regional Parlements around France, Nantes lost out to Rennes. Then, during the **French Wars of Religion** in the second half of that century, Nantes fell under the control of the ultra-Catholic governor of Brittany, the

RUE FELIBIEN

PLACE VIARME

Market

RUE PAUL BELLAMY

QUAI DE VERSAILLES

RUE J. D'ARC

P

300 metres
300 yards

N

RUE J. CASSEGRAIN

RUE DE STRASBOURG

ALLÉE DES TANNEURS

RUE L. BIJUM

RUE SIMEON FOUCAULT

RUE JEAN JAURÈS

RUE HAROUYS

PLACE A. BRIAND

RUE MERCŒUR

PLACE DE BRETAGNE

P P

ALLÉE DUQUESNE

RUE A. BROSSARD

Hôtel de Ville

RUE DESHOULIÈRES

P

RUE LAFAYETTE

Tour Bretagne

COURS DES 50 OTAGES

ALLÉE D

RUE ST-LÉONARD

RUE DU MOULIN

RUE MARCEAU

RUE PARÉ

ALLÉE D

ORLEANS

RUE DE LA MARNE

RUE COPERNIC

PLACE DELORME

RUE DU CALVAIRE

RUE DU CHAPEAU ROUGE

RUE CONTRESCARPE

St-Nicolas

RUE D'ORLÉANS

RUE DE LA BARILLERIE

PLACE DU CHANGE

Ste-Croix

RUE KLÉBER

RUE DE LA ROSIÈRE D'ARTHOIS

RUE RACINE

RUE SCRIBE

P

PLACE ROYALE

RUE DU COUEDIC

RUE STE-CATHERINE

BOUFFAY

RUE CRÉBILLON

PASSAGE POMMERAYE

RUE DE LA FOSSE

PLACE DU COMMERCE

COURS FRANKLIN ROOSEVELT

Musée Thomas Dobrée

Museum d'Histoire Naturelle

PLACE GRASLIN

RUE VOLTAIRE

RUE GRESSET

RUE J.J. ROUSSEAU

i

P

ALLÉE DUGUAY-TROUIN

RUE KERVÉGAN

ILE FEYDEAU

ALLÉE TURENNE

COURS CAMBRONNE

RUE DE L'HÉRONNIÈRE

RUE MARÉCHAL DE LATTRE DE TASSIGNY

RUE FOURCROY

PLACE DE LA PETITE HOLLANDE

Mediathèque

P

P

QUAI DE LA FOSSE

ALLÉE DE L'ILE GLORIETTE

RUE DE LA VERRERIE

To Musée Naval, Maillé Brézé & Musée Jules Verne

QUAI DE TOURVILLE

QUAI MONCOUSU

PONT HAUDAUDINE

Bras de la Madelaine

PONT ANNE DE BRETAGNE

QUAI F. CROUAN

QUAI ANDRÉ RHUYS

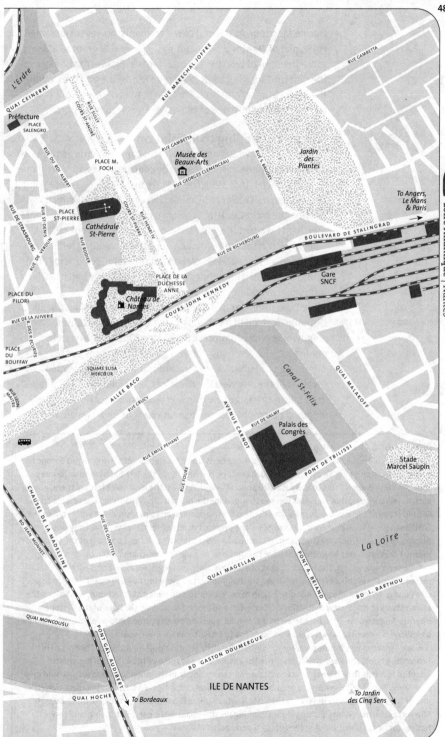

Duc de Mercœur. At the end of the torments, however, the famed 1598 **Edict of Nantes** worked out by King Henri IV granted at least some freedom of worship to Protestants in France. At the close of the 17th century, King Louis XIV would revoke the edict, rekindling the persecution of the Huguenots. In between times, Nantes was rapidly growing into one of the major French colonial ports.

From Slave Trading to Revolution

The most prosperous times for Nantes came with the acquisition of France's Caribbean colonies. By 1633, Guadeloupe and Martinique were in French hands. With the 1697 Treaty of Ryswick, France gained the western half of Santo Domingo (present-day Haiti), which became the most lucrative of all of France's colonies, and the Nantes merchants secured the lion's share of the action (*see* box below).

Before and after the Revolution, new town planning reflecting civic pride and wealth was carried out on a large scale across the centre of Nantes, the architects Ceineray and Crucy particularly influential in adding grand streets and squares.

The Revolution banned the slave trade. When the slaves of Santo Domingo rose up in revolt in 1791, the conservative Nantes shipowners wrote in protest to the king. Once the monarchy eradicated, the terrifying Carrier was sent to Nantes by the Committee of Public Safety to make some of the pig-headed royalists of the city wed the cause of the Revolution. The so-called 'republican marriages' he oversaw were cruel mockeries of the wedding ceremony: the un-Revolutionary offenders were tied in

Nantes and the Triangular Slave Trade

Historians have calculated that Nantes may have been the most significant slaving city in Europe for some time, outstripping all others in the 18th century. The first leg of the terrible triangular journey took the ships from Nantes to the east African coast. Working with the local slave traders there, goods such as jewellery, alcohol and guns were exchanged for the human cargo that filled the vessels on the second stage of the journey. Many slaves died on these appalling crossings; survivors were sold to the Caribbean plantation owners in exchange for the precious goods other slaves were already busily helping to produce, notably sugar, coffee, cotton and indigo. On the third and final leg of the triangular journey, these luxuries were brought back to Europe to be sold. The merchants often made a killing.

Between 1715 and 1775, the return to port of 787 slave ships was registered in Nantes – half the total recorded for the whole of France. However, the bulging vessels grew too large to travel right up to the city's quays. Much of the merchandise began to be loaded and unloaded at Paimbœuf, west along the Loire. However, major new industries developed in and around Nantes on the back of the Caribbean imports. Sugar was refined here to be sold across Europe. Cotton was turned into printed calico, known as *indiennes*... much of which went back to Africa to be bartered for more slaves.

Black African slaves became a common sight in wealthy Nantes households. Hugh Thomas, in his fascinating book, *The Slave Trade*, describes the casual attitude some of the city's rich merchants adopted towards their human chattels: 'Slave merchants, living in their fine townhouses ... would give such "négrillons" or "négrittes" to members of their household as tips.' As business boomed, from the end of the 17th century to the end of the 18th, Nantes's population doubled, from 40,000 to 80,000. The successful merchants, putting their sickening wealth to aesthetic use, built their grand town houses (or *hôtels particuliers*) in the Louis XV and Louis XVI styles.

pairs and bundled on to a boat with a hole in the bottom. The boat sank and the 'couples' drowned in the Loire.

François-Athanase Charette, a nobleman from the Loire Atlantique and one of the main leaders of the anti-Revolutionary, pro-Catholic and royalist Vendée uprising, led a desperate attack on Nantes in 1793, but it failed. Jacques Cathelineau, another hero of the anti-Revolutionary cause, was mortally wounded in the battle. Charette was eventually executed in Nantes in 1796.

The 19th and 20th Centuries

Napoleon reintroduced slavery, giving in to pressure from colonial interests. It would only be finally abolished in France in 1848, to the chagrin of many Nantes merchants. On a much lighter note, Turner came to paint here and along the Loire in 1828, the year that saw Jules Verne's birth in Nantes.

Rather less glamorously, but more importantly for the economy, the modern techniques of canning fish were developed in town at this time. Canning became a big industry in Brittany as a consequence. In spite of the end of the slave trade, Nantes's prosperity didn't drain away, as you can see for example in the extravagance of the mid-19th-century shopping arcade of the Passage Pommeraye. Trams started operating in the town as early as 1874 and have recently been revived.

Aristide Briand, one of the major French political figures of the early 20th century, came from Nantes. He became general secretary of the French Socialist Party in 1901 and framed the extremely important bill separating the Church from the French State in 1905. In the turbulent times at the start of the 20th century, he also served as prime minister no fewer than 11 times.

After the First World War, as part of the German war reparations, most of the seven channels of the Loire that had stagnated insalubriously in the city centre for so long were filled in by German workers. Briand continued to be a major political force. With Jean Jaurès he founded the left-wing newspaper *L'Humanité*. From 1925 to 1932, he served as French foreign minister and worked hard for reconciliation and disarmament, proposing a form of United States of Europe. In 1926 he and German foreign minister Gustav Stresemann were even awarded the Nobel Peace Prize. Unfortunately their efforts would prove tragically premature, although Briand can be considered one of the forefathers of the peaceable cooperation fostered by the European Union.

The Allied bombing raids on Nazi-occupied Nantes that took place during the Second World War have left their scars. As to the wide modern road artery through the centre known as the Cour des 50 Otages, it commemorates the execution of 50 French hostages in the Loire Atlantique in 1942, after Resistance fighters had killed the German commander in the region.

Postwar, several figures from the French art world paid homage to Nantes, including the much-respected film-maker Jacques Demy, whose movie *Lola* was shot here, and the writer Julien Gracq, whose work *La Forme d'une ville* is wholly devoted to the city. The university, closed at the Revolution, was reinstated in 1962, and hi-tech industries settled here. As to the Caribbean connection, sugar still arrives here in large quantities, in part to make some of France's best-known biscuits, produced by the local firm Lu, familiar to all French children. Interestingly, the biscuit industry originally grew up to cater for the shipping expeditions.

In the last few years, Nantes has turned into one of the trendiest cultural hotspots in France. The old Lu factory, for example, has been turned into one of the funkiest cultural spaces, Le Lieu Unique. The city has also spawned several figures who've been following in the footsteps of Jules Verne, creating extraordinary new creatures. The town is home to the ground-breaking Royal Deluxe theatre company that wowed London with its mammoth mechanical elephant. As to the dynamic duo of François Delarozière and Pierre Orefice, they've set about creating further vast moving models with their Machines de L'Ile, on the island just south of the historic centre; this Ile de Nantes, once devoted to shipping, is now being boldly converted into a major new quarter. For a long time, the city had turned its back on the Loire, on which so much of its history is based, but now it's showing it the attention it deserves once again. The inventions of Nantes's exciting innovators, along with the excellent more traditional museums, and the great variety of fashionable eateries, help make Nantes an exceptionally tempting city-break destination today.

The Château des Ducs de Bretagne and its Museum

The Château des Ducs de Bretagne and its Museum
www.chateau-nantes.fr; open Wed–Mon Sept–June 10–7; July–Aug 9–8, Sat 'til 11

Nantes is one of those big cities that doesn't have an obvious heart, but that does have several quarters worth exploring. The most obvious place to start is at the massive château. You can appreciate it from many angles even if you don't visit its museum. For starters, you can follow the example of many Nantais dog owners, and take a very pleasant walk around the outside of it, in the garden with its watery moat set below the great ramparts – originally, the Loire lapped at the castle's walls, but the branch here was eradicated when the river was re-routed in the 20th century. Alternatively, contemplate the great fort from the comfort of one of the restaurant terraces on the cobbled streets outside the castle. You'll spot a statue of a woman in medieval garb rushing towards the entrance – that'll be Anne of Brittany, the most famous historical figure associated with the place.

Seen from the exterior, Nantes's château is massive and forbidding, seven huge artillery towers sticking out from its sides. But enter the huge castle **courtyard**, which you can do for free, and a completely different aspect awaits, of sheer Loire elegance. Once within the courtyard, you can walk along a section of the **ramparts**, or go to the café. On an energetic walk up on the walls, you get good views of Nantes; sitting at the café's terrace, you can take in the extraordinary architecture at more leisurely pace. What you see today, known as the Château des Ducs de Bretagne, was in fact built in the main for the last duke of Brittany and his daughter Anne, although their forebears did have a home on the spot.

Contemplating the huge inner courtyard, the attention focuses on the blindingly bright white **two main wings, the Grand Gouvernement and Grand Logis**, which illustrate quite well the gradual shift from French late-Gothic architecture to French Renaissance forms so characteristic of the famed Loire castles of the late 15th and early 16th centuries. In fact, this castle might be regarded as the most westerly of the châteaux of the Loire. The soaring vertical lines, the slight lack of symmetry in the windows, and the ornate *lucarnes*, or dormer windows, fit the bill. In the angle between the two wings rises the **Tower of the Golden Crown**, lightened by Renaissance loggias high up. The name of the tower refers to the elaborate covering on top of the well in front; this crown in wrought iron was once gilded and was meant to represent the crown of the kings of Brittany of the Dark Ages.

The **Petit Gouvernement** is the small 16th-century building added for King François I and covered with restored French Renaissance detail, such as the shells in the dormers and the slate inlaid in the chimneys. The large rectangular block sticking out of one end of the courtyard like a bit like an architectural sore thumb is the 18th-century **Bâtiment du Harnachement**. It acts as a reminder of the fact that the château served as an army camp from the beginning of the 18th century to the start of the 20th. During that time, in 1800, the military managed to blow up a whole section of the castle by accident, including the chapel.

Until recent times, the whole inner courtyard looked jaded and messy. However, following some 15 years of restoration work, it looks spectacular. Not only has it undergone a glistening renaissance, the interiors of the main wings now house a 32-room museum, the **Musée d'Histoire de Nantes**, focusing on the history of the city and its close connections with the Loire. If that sounds daunting enough to send you scampering back out through the portcullis before it clangs shut behind you, be reassured: it's a contemporary museum where the presentations are pared down rather than cluttered, and where you'll find many interactive displays at which to pause. In fact, the Cadogan recommendation, as always with museums that offer the possibility these days, is to take the audioguide, because otherwise you may feel that there isn't always enough explanatory material provided to get your teeth into the subjects covered.

The seven sections cover themes from history and the port's development to folk, religious and decorative arts, plus Nantes as portrayed by artists; you can even listen to the classic French *chanson* set in the city, Barbara's *Il Pleut sur Nantes*, a painful weepy. Of much more painful historical significance, slavery hasn't been ignored. One of the key exhibits is the *Code Noir*, a little book, but one that laid down regulations for keeping slaves. There are more light-hearted moments touring the chambers, including a very silly video-trawl through Nantes's history at the end of the visit. There's plenty of room at the château to stage temporary exhibitions and cultural events, so look out for the programme.

South across the broad, confusing thoroughfare where a branch of the Loire used to flow, the **Tour Lu** marks the central spot where Nantes's hugely well-known biscuits used to be made; now the trendy flock to the exhibitions at the **Lieu Unique** which has taken the factory's place. You can not only pass judgement on the art shows here, there's also a theatre, and even a hammam in this very wide-ranging venue. You can also climb the iconic Tour Lu for views across town, while a video explains the importance of Lu biscuits in Nantes history. The boutique sells contemporary pieces.

To the Cathedral of St-Pierre

From the château you might take **Rue Rodier** (named after the man who planned the castle for Duke François II) straight up to the front of the cathedral on Place St-Pierre. Or if you prefer a grander route, opt for the wide, mid-18th-century boulevard of the **Cours St-Pierre**, running up from Place de la Duchesse Anne to the choir end of the cathedral. This *cours* is of Parisian proportions and elegance. It takes you to the imposing **Place Maréchal Foch**, where a rare statue commemorating beheaded King Louis XVI stands in the centre. The **Hôtel Montaudoin**, built for an infamously wealthy Nantes slave-trading family, stands out, the family arms proudly showing. Back close to the cathedral, clashing with the careful classical planning of the rest of Place St-Pierre, the massive **Porte St-Pierre** is a remnant of Nantes's 15th-century town walls, built on much earlier Gallo–Roman vestiges.

The **Cathédrale St-Pierre et St-Paul** is one of the cleanest cathedrals you're likely to see, and one of the emptiest. The interior had to be restored and cleaned after a terrible fire in 1972. Some of the uncluttered monuments appear even whiter than the Loire limestone used in the building's construction. Work began on it in 1434, financed by Jean V Duc de Bretagne and Bishop Jean de Malestroit. It went up on the site of the previous Romanesque cathedral, and possibly of Bishop Félix's 6th-century church. Only the Romanesque crypt under the choir was kept from the previous structures. The 15th-century architects were Guillaume de Dommartin-sur-Yèvre and Mathelin Rodier. The work proved laborious and lengthy, but the façade was completed before the end of the 15th century and the towers added by 1508. The nave and the aisles arose slowly through the 16th century, worship in the building only starting in 1577.

The major artistic interest within consists of the **tomb of François II Duc de Bretagne** and his two wives. This moving, gloriously crafted work is thought to have been executed in the Tours workshops of sculptor Michel Colombe between 1502 and 1507, though an Italian artist of great ability may have carried out some of the work. The two main effigies represent the duke and his second wife, Marguerite de Foix, mother of Anne de Bretagne. The large corner statues show personifications of Justice (thought to be a portrait of Anne de Bretagne), Fortitude, Temperance and Prudence, the last an amazingly refined piece, with its double-faced head, the one of a young woman, the other of an old man. This tomb was commissioned by Anne de Bretagne, who asked for her heart to be placed in it after her death; her wish was granted.

Another remarkably fine tomb in the cathedral dates from the 19th century. It was made by Paul Dubois in 1879, in honour of the formidably moustached military commander General Lamoricière. A Nantais by birth, he was celebrated in his day for his role in the French taking of Algeria, and in particular for his capturing of the Algerian leader Abd-el-Kader. Almost all of the cathedral's original stained-glass windows have been destroyed by explosions and fire. Some striking modern ones have replaced them.

Musée des Beaux-Arts and Jardin des Plantes

Musée des Beaux Arts de Nantes
*open Wed–Mon
10–8, Thurs 'til 8*

Back in the heart of town, the dignified Nantes Musée des Beaux Arts, or fine arts museum, stands on the other side of the Cours St-Pierre from the cathedral. The museum building, constructed in 1900 for the elevating educational purposes of the French Third Republic is a cleanly planned work. The founding collection was donated to the town a century earlier, in 1801, or the Year IX as it was known under the Consulate; this was one of 15 major provincial museums established around France after the Revolution.

Some of the works came from war booty. Another large haul arrived in 1810 from the collections of the Cacault brothers and their lovely Italianate villa in Clisson, which lies to the southeast of Nantes (*see* p.499). The brothers had been away on a wild art-shopping spree in Italy in the late 18th century. Further generous 19th-century donations and the 20th-century legacy of the French industrialist Gildas Fardel added to the riches on display. If you want a crash course in the history of western art from 13th-century religious works to present-day conceptual projects, this place does it pretty well. The 19th- and 20th-century collections are exceptionally good.

11

Loire Atlantique | Nantes

Among the highlights is Georges de La Tours' magnificent *St Joseph et l'ange*, showing his subtle candlelit style to best effect. Fine pieces from the 18th century include a typical Watteau inspired by *commedia dell'arte – Arlequin, Empereur de la Lune –* several Greuzes, and a whole series of portraits of rich families by Tournières. Gros' work *Le Combat de Nazareth* was an early 19th-century piece viewed as a precursor of the Romantic movement. The same room contains two exceptional sculptures, one by Canova of Pope Clement XIII, the other, by Ceracchi, of Washington.

Courbet's *Les Cribleuses de blé* counts among the most important works in the wide-ranging 19th-century collections. There's a fair representation of wildly over-the-top, sickly French Romanticism to revolt you, too. You might view with some irony, given Nantes's history, *L'Esclave blanche* ('The White Slave') by Lecomte du Nouy. *Le Sorcier Noir* by Herbert Ward shows a typical European vision of the black man as witch. On another artistic level, while Monet takes you off to Venice and the otherwordly visions of his *Nymphéas*, Emile Bernard's *Le Gaulage des pommes* depicts a forceful Breton landscape in the style of the Pont-Aven School. Local artist Metzinger gives a Pointilliste interpretation of the Château de Clisson. A whole room is devoted to Kandinsky's abstract work, while Chagall's *Le Cheval Rouge* is a typical piece by that great artist.

Many Nantais artists are represented in the later collections. Raymond Hains, a well-known conceptual artist, pays homage to the thriving Nantes biscuit industry with a barcode. But the contemporary art collection is huge, and, as ever, a mixed bag of very varying quality.

The very pretty **Jardin des Plantes** lies at the eastern end of Rue Georges Clemenceau beyond the museum. Among its collections, the magnolias stand out, one of the trees brought back from the colonies that the Nantais most came to love. The ornate **greenhouses** are sometimes open for visits.

Up the Erdre River

Rue du Roi Albert leads north from the cathedral square up to the **Préfecture**, Ceineray's classical masterpiece. On the cathedral side, the arms of France feature on the pediment, on the Erdre side, the arms of Brittany.

Another stylish boulevard by which to reach the Erdre is the grand **Cours St-André**. Following the quays north, you pass the **Ile de Versailles**, where the public garden isn't in classic French style, as you might expect, but Japanese. From here you can hire **canoes** or **electric boats** to go on **Erdre**, or just beyond, **Bateaux Nantais** run sight-seeing tours (including meals) on slick modern boats departing from the **Gare Fluviale de l'Erdre**.

Although modern suburban and business quarters come up close to the **Erdre River**, its banks have been quite well protected,

Canoes
t 06 62 28 60 48

Electric boats
t 02 51 81 04 24

Bateaux Nantais
t 02 40 14 51 14

and look beautifully Breton, with their indented, wooded creeks. Many grand houses have bagged great positions looking out over the waters. One or two of Nantes's many fine public gardens lie close to the water, and the **FRAC**, the region's collections of contemporary art, are displayed in a striking building in one of the biggest green spaces up this way.

FRAC
www.fracdespaysdela
loire.com, t 02 28 01 50
00; open July–Aug daily
2–6, Sept–June
Wed–Sun 2–6

**Nantes Erdre
Golf Club**
t 02 40 59 21 21

**Carquefou
Golf Club**
t 02 40 52 73 74

**La Beaujoire
football stadium**
t 02 51 88 91 91 for
tickets to games

A couple of the many **golf courses** around Nantes are located in pretty spots close to the Erdre too – contact the **Nantes Erdre Golf Club** or the **Carquefou Golf Club**. As to **La Beaujoire football stadium**, another big specialist attraction in this area, it's home to the Canaries, the high-profile, yellow-striped Nantes football team – the tourist office even organizes guided tours to its hallowed turf.

Quarters West of the Château

Back with the centre of historic Nantes, west of the castle, you first come to the **Bouffay quarter**. The tightly packed network of old streets makes this the liveliest and most charming part of old Nantes, the area mainly pedestrian. Several street names recall the activities carried out along them in medieval times, but only a few timberframe houses remain going as far back as the 15th and 16th centuries. In the Ancien Régime, grander houses were built here in what became the lawyers' quarter in particular. Nowadays, this is a neighbourhood of chic boutiques and often rather touristy restaurants, cafés and very many crêperies.

Wandering around you'll come across several intriguing little squares. **Place du Pilori** served for executions and other public punishments until **Place du Bouffay** took over that role. Place du Bouffay now hosts a lively fishmarket most mornings. The former town belfry has been affixed to the **church of Ste-Croix** in charming **Place Ste-Croix** nearby. The church is a quirky mix of architectural styles. Angels trumpet out the Christian message from the top of the ornate tower.

North of **Rue de la Marne** and **Rue de la Barillerie**, the main shopping arteries, several further elegant streets lead up to the town hall, for instance those going north from **Place du Change**, once the hub of historic Nantes. The **Hôtel de Ville** is a mix of 17th-century mansions and modernity.

On the opposite side of the Allées from Place du Bouffay, **L'Île Feydeau** was once an exclusive residential island on the Loire. It now stands somewhat sadly isolated by wide roads. This is where some of the very grandest Nantes shipowners had their town houses and offices from the mid-18th century on. You can only really get a good impression of their wealth by wandering along the central **Rue Kervégan**. The finest features on the façades are the grotesque Baroque masks, or *mascarons*, carved above the windows, each one showing a different grimacing face. Today, the place presents a strange mix of nice restaurants and sex shops.

Sleek trams running quietly up the broad curving **Cours des 50 Otages** make it slightly dangerous to cross into the smart quarter further west. Make it over for the chicest shopping streets as well as many elegant squares and streets from the late 18th and early 19th centuries. Rue d'Orléans leads to **Place Royale**. This sober-sided square was quite discreetly restored after suffering bomb damage. The original was planned by the architect Mathurin Crucy. Personifications of the some of the Loire's tributaries adorn the major fountain at the heart of this square, which often serves for big outdoor events.

Just northeast of Place Royale, beside **Place Fournier**, the huge steeple of the **Basilique St-Nicolas** soars skywards. The church is a neo-Gothic edifice of the mid-19th century which still attracts many faithful to mass. A fair way further north rises the still taller **Tour Bretagne**, Nantes's isolated central skyscraper, visible from afar as you approach the city. A modern precinct surrounds it.

Off fashionable **Rue Crébillon**, lined with up-market clothes shops, the **Passage Pommeraye**, Nantes's kitschly romantic 19th-century shopping arcade, trips town to Rue de la Fosse with its extravagant sweeps of stairs. Flaubert, on his tour of Brittany, found the boutiques here crammed with exotica from the colonies. Now, they sell trendy modern items of all sorts. You emerge at the bottom next to the tempting new Larnicol chocolate and cake shop, although the more old-fashioned Gautier-Débotté close by is its older rival, particularly, it would seem, in exotic macaroon displays to make Alan Bennett swoon.

You're now stood beside the **Bourse** on **Place du Commerce**. This former exchange building, with its impressive row of monumental Ionic columns, was once again planned by Crucy and completed in 1812. The commerce may have changed, as this is now a major FNAC, a temple to books, CDs and games, but a few of the building's original statues of renowned Breton sailors (some notorious corsairs in fact) remain in place. The Loire used to flow by here and the quay was reserved for the Nantais wine trade. Now, it's a magnet for students and young people, with a big cinema complex behind.

Back up on Rue Crébillon, this street links Place Royale with the more serious **Place Graslin** to the west. This square was yet again planned by Crucy. It's dominated by the **theatre**, the statues of muses atop their Corinthian columns making the building's purpose clear. The place saw its first performance in 1788. Up one side of the theatre, the Katorza cinema complex shows an excellent range of foreign films. The **Cours Cambronne**, off the southwest corner of Place Graslin, could hardly be more refined, if a little cold and aloof – the gates are shut at night to stop hoi polloi passing through.

Western Museums

A string of further intriguing museums lie west of the main shopping quarters. The golden reliquary for the heart of Anne de Bretagne stands on public display in the **Musée Thomas Dobrée**. Little can the last duchess of Brittany have imagined that it would one day be on view for all to see. It's the most striking piece of fine craftsmanship in a museum crammed with the finest stonework, woodwork and enamel work. Thomas Dobrée was a dedicated collector through the 19th century, the son of an extremely wealthy industrialist and shipowner. Among other objects, he amassed sculptures, paintings, furniture, art objects, plus manuscripts and letters from royals, nobles and literary figures in an obsessive manner.

Musée Thomas Dobrée
t 02 40 71 03 50; open Tues–Fri 1.30–5.30, Sat–Sun 2.30–5.30

He decided to build a grand house in which to install these collections, next to the **Manoir de la Touche**, and even oversaw much of the construction work on the building, with its neo-Romanesque look. It was built in brown-bear coloured stone, with figures of carved bears added on to the corners. Dobrée also had the Manoir de la Touche restored. This manor had been constructed for Bishop Jean de Malestroit as his retreat outside the city walls at the start of the 15th century. It later served as a Huguenot hospital in the Wars of Religion and from 1695 until the Revolution as a religious refuge for Irish priests who had been driven out of their country.

The museum collections include religious sculptures of great beauty. You can observe close up several huge statues originally made for Nantes's cathedral front, carved in Loire tufa, and a collection of Romanesque capitals with weird grotesque faces. A magnificent length of wooden stringbeam shows a bizarre mix of particularly graceful faces and crudely gesturing figures. Among the exquisite medieval church ceremonial objects on display, the collection of enamelled pyxides from the Limousin stands out, plus various encrusted altar crosses.

The Manoir de la Touche contains a mixed bag. The ground floor is devoted to Nantes at the time of the Revolution. Upstairs are archaeological finds from around the Loire Atlantique, including some interesting Bronze Age, Celtic, Gallo–Roman and Merovingian pieces.

Muséum d'Histoire Naturelle
t 02 40 99 26 20; open daily exc Tues 10–6

While in this quarter, it's hard to miss the imposing **Muséum d'Histoire Naturelle**, a major natural history museum, among whose more extraordinary exhibits are a whale skeleton, and the skin of a man.

Musée de l'Imprimerie
24 Quai de la Fosse, musee.imprimerie.free. fr, t 02 40 73 26 51; open Sept–June Mon–Sat 10–12 and 2–5.30, July–Aug Mon–Fri 10–12 and 2–5.30

Nantes has a clutch of further, smaller museums to visit if you continue further west along the Loire. Down close to the river, on **Quai de la Fosse**, beside the modern if slightly jaded-looking Médiathèque, the **Musée de l'Imprimerie** explores the development of printing in the region through an impressive collection of old printing presses.

The next major sight on the same quay, the massive-domed 19th-century **Notre-Dame du Bon Port**, makes a bold show of Christian strength beside the fickle-natured Loire. The church boasts ornate decorations both inside and out. Nearby, it's also hard to miss the **Maillé Brézé**, a decommissioned naval squadron escort vessel converted into a naval museum, part of the attraction being to clamber up and down the decks. From beside it, you can make a delightful short ferry trip with the **Navibus** to get across to the old fishermen's quarter of Trentemoult on the Loire's south bank (*see* below).

Sticking to north bank, and heading further west again, you reach the smart **Ste-Anne quarter** on its hill, with impressive views down across the Loire onto southern Nantes. In one of the area's grandest mansions, the **Musée Jules Verne** pays its respects to the great French visionary 19th-century science-fiction writer from Nantes, author of such worldwide classics as *Around the World in Eighty Days*, *Journey to the Centre of the Earth* and *Twenty Thousand Leagues Under the Sea*. In fact, he is one of the biggest-selling authors of all time, anywhere in the world. His works remain highly popular, and the museum was redesigned recently to make it more appealing to today's audience. You can easily imagine what an inspiration cosmopolitan Nantes must have been to the young Jules, even if it hardly features in his writing. A big statue featuring him as a child, with Captain Nemo, was put up with the re-opening of the museum. But for the most inspiration, read his books. People from the US might particularly enjoy his *De la terre à la lune* (*From the Earth to the Moon Direct in 97 Hours 20 Minutes*), a hilarious story about Americans competing with the Europeans to become the first men on the moon – but back in the 19th century!

It seems appropriate enough that the **Planétarium** should stand close by.

South across the Loire via the Ile de Nantes

The **Ile de Nantes** just south of the historic centre has been undergoing huge transformations in recent times. The western tip was known in centuries past as the shipbuilding quarter of the city. This activity gradually died out, leaving this once intensely bustling area semi-derelict. Since the beginning of the new millennium, it's been coming rapidly back to life. To get over to it, you can take the new pedestrian bridge, the **Passerelle Victor Schoelcher**, connecting the large open car parks stretching west of L'Ile Feydeau with the area. You arrive in front of **Jean Nouvel**'s sleek, slightly sinister new dark **Palais de Justice**.

Hopefully not many readers will be required to pay a visit to these law courts unless they want to admire the straight-lined architecture, but a bit west, you come to the Parc des Chantiers,

Maillé Brézé
*www.maillebreze.
com, t 09 79 18 33 51;
open daily June–Sept
2–6; Oct–May 2–5*

Navibus
*run by Marine et
Loire Croisières –
www.marineetloire.fr*

Musée Jules Verne
*3 Rue de l'Hermitage,
t 02 40 69 72 52; open
Mon and Wed–Sat
10–12 and 2–6, Sun 2–6*

Planétarium
*8 Rue des Acadiens,
t 02 40 73 99 23;
showings Mon–Fri
10.30, 2.15 and 3.45,
Sun 3 and 4.30*

once at the heart of Nantes's shipbuilding. Today, you may may be surprised to encounter a giant elephant lolloping slowly across the cleared land by the river... with some 40 people on board.

Galerie des Machines de l'Ile
www.lesmachines-nantes.fr, **t** 08 10 12 12 25; open July–Aug daily 10–8, April–June and Sept–Oct Tues–Sun 10–6, Nov–Dec and mid-Feb–March 2–6

Go to the **Galerie des Machines de l'Ile** to learn what this extraordinary entertainment is all about. Two locals, François Delarozière and Pierre Orefice, have been inspired by Jules Verne to bring to life some extraordinary vast mechanical creatures they've drawn up. Their next projects will be the Mondes Marins carousel, where you'll be able to step inside giant crabs, squid and other sea creatures, and the even more ambitious Arbre aux Hérons. At the gallery, you can see not just the drawings for these new creations, but you can actually watch the craftsmen at work making them at certain times. Because the tours on the **Grand Eléphant** are popular, try to book well ahead to be sure of a ticket. It makes for an exhilarating ride on the 12-metre-high animal, which can trumpet and spray passers-by with its trunk, although the creature hardly charges round; it moves at a leisurely 4kmph maximum. The **Mondes Marins** is scheduled to open from 2010.

You can continue walking westwards to the tip of the island. Following the quayside, the huge yellow crane, the **Grue Titan**, is a listed monument, a telling reminder of the river commerce once carried out here. You'll then walk alongside **Les Anneaux de Buren**, the huge rings punctuating the riverside walk, a sculptural series by the leading French contemporary artist Daniel Buren, vibrantly lit up at night. Buren made this work for an extraordinary art exhibition that stretched along the Loire from Nantes to St-Nazaire, Loire Estuaire. This experience was so positive that the event is going to be repeated uneven years – look out for the programmes for 2009 and 2011. Most of the works are just temporary installations, but Buren's have been kept on.

You reach the trendy new area of the **Pointe de l'Ile**, centred around the old **Hangar à Bananes**, where bananas imported from the French colonies used to be ripened. The building has been given a very contemporary make-over, making it a fashionable place to come, both by day, for the cafés and restaurants with their broad terraces and for the art galllery, and by night, with a nightclub among the additional attractions.

The other, **eastern end of the Ile de Nantes** has grown into a major new residential and administrative quarter, but there's a green park towards that tip much appreciated by the Nantais.

Cross the Loire **south from the Ile de Nantes** to reach **Rezé**, which has roots going back to Gallo–Roman times, but which is known nowadays for its modern architecture. The most famous piece in town is **Le Corbusier**'s bold experiment in new urban living, the **Cité Radieuse**, rising on its stilts, putting into practice his egalitarian *unité d'habitation de grandeur conforme*. Built in the mid-1950s to provide a new concept in council housing, it has now been restored. The striking curve of Rezé's modern **town hall** was conceived by Alessandro Anselmi. West along the river, **Trentemoult** has preserved its old villagey atmosphere and memories of the sea captains who used to retire here, planting exotic trees in their gardens to remind them of their far-flung travels – take the Navibus here from the centre for an enjoyable tour, especially of the Saturday morning organic market, or to enjoy a riverside meal.

Bateaux Nantais
www.bateaux-nantais.fr

While on the subject of river travel, the **Bateaux Nantais** run boat cruises on the imposing Loire (May–Oct) as well as on the Erdre.

Market Days in Nantes

Talensac: Tuesday–Sunday
Place du Bouffay: Food market Tues–Sun
Place du Commerce: Flower market, daily
Place de la Petite Hollande: Saturday
Place Viarme: Flea market, Saturday

Festivals in Nantes

Many of Nantes's festivals have a distinctly cosmopolitan flavour. La Folle Journée, first weekend in February, concentrates on honouring the works of a school of composers. There's a big carnival 'Mi carême' every March. Le Printemps des Arts celebrates Baroque music and dance in venues across the region in April, May and June. Cultural events such as dance, theatre, music and street entertainment take place under various umbrella associations through summer. All manner of boats and jazz musicians gather in Nantes for the Rendez-Vous de l'Erdre, the last weekend in August or first weekend in September.

Where to Stay in Nantes

ⓘ **Nantes ›**
3 Cours Olivier de Clisson and 2 Place St Pierre, *t 08 92 46 40 44 (premium rate)*, *www.nantes-tourisme.com*

Nantes ✉ 44000

★★★La Pérouse, 3 Allée Duquesne, t 02 40 89 75 00, *www.hotel-laperouse.fr* (€€–€). Ultra trendy contemporary hotel in historic Nantes.
★★★Graslin, 1 Rue Piron, t 02 40 69 72 91, *www.hotelgraslin.com*. Stylishly contemporary rooms close to a major

square in the heart of the best shopping district.
★★★L'Hôtel, 6 Rue Henri IV, t 02 40 29 30 31, *www.nanteshotelcom* (€€€–€€). Opposite the château, in a modern building, neat, comfortable rooms.
★★★de France, 24 Rue Crébillon, t 02 40 73 57 91, *www.oceaniahotels.com* (€€€€–€). The grandiose old-style option up above Passage Pommeraye, with a mix of elegant rooms that should be redone soon.
★★Pommeraye, 2 Rue Boileau, t 02 40 48 78 79, *www.hotel-pommeraye.com* (€€). Nice, friendly option in the heart of the best westerly shopping quarter.
★★Les Colonies, 5 Rue du Chapeau Rouge, t 02 40 48 79 76, *www.hotel descolonies.fr* (€€–€). Quiet rooms in quite characterful option with colonial theme, not far from the above.
★★Amiral, 26 bis Rue Scribe, t 02 40 69 20 21, *www.hotel–nantes.fr* (€€–€). Also well located close to Place Graslin, pleasant, good-value rooms.

Eating Out in Nantes

L'Atlantide, 16 Quai Ernest-Renaud, at the end of the Quai de la Fosse, t 02 40 73 23 23 (€€€€–€€€). Excellent, exclusive restaurant north of the centre up the Erdre quays, with roof-top view over the river and Nantes. *Closed Sat lunch, Sun and hols.*
Manoir de la Frégate, on east bank up the Erdre, just above ring road, t 02 40 18 02 97 (€€€€–€€). Lovingly restored riverside house with two smart dining rooms and a terrace overlooking the water, a great setting for an excellent, elegant out-of-town lunch or dinner. *Closed Mon.*

Les Enfants Terribles, 4 Rue Fénelon, t 02 40 47 00 38. Stylish contemporary restaurant serving refined French dishes.

La Cigale, 4 Place Graslin, t 02 51 84 94 94 (€€–€). A Nantes classic, a French brasserie worth visiting just for its extravagant Art Nouveau décor, set on one of an elegant squares. Decent food.

Un Coin en Ville, 2 Place de la Bourse (€€€). Hidden away behind the FNAC store, almost a secret cavern of a trendy little restaurant, serving Breton specialities with hints of spices.

La Vie de Château, 5 Place de la Duchesse Anne, t 02 40 74 31 85 (€€). A warm, intimate little restaurant opposite the massive castle, offering classic Nantes food.

La Poissonnerie, 4 Rue Léon Maître, t 02 49 47 79 50 (€€). A fine fish restaurant on the eastern end of L'Ile Feydeau, with a light, nautical look. Closed Sat lunch, Sun and Mon.

Chez l'Huître, 5 Rue des Petites Ecuries, t 02 51 82 02 02 (€€–€). A tiny brasserie with fresh and fast seafood specialities served by an eccentric host. Terrace too. Closed Sun.

Crêperie Heb Ken, 5 Rue de Guérande, t 02 40 48 79 03. Close to the Passage Pommeraye. The decor may be basic, but a lot of attention goes into the fine crêpes.

Crêperie L'Ile Mystérieuse, 13 Rue Kervégan, t 02 40 47 42 83. Bang in the middle of L'Ile Feydeau, a warm crêperie with stone interior encrusted with coins.

Crêperie des Délices, 19 Rue Paul Bellamy, t 02 40 48 15 20 (€). Almost a pastiche of a traditional Breton crêperie, near the Talensac market.

Café du Passage (€), Stylish new café with a literary bent, looking over to St-Pierre's steeple, serving traditional meals and good wines.

Ile Verte, 3 Rue Siméon Foucault, t 02 40 48 01 26 (€). A vegetarian option.

East from Nantes: the Loire and Muscadet

Along the Loire to the Old Breton Border

Turner found inspiration along this stretch of the Loire, though it isn't particularly well known. By contrast with the generally flat, dull and in parts heavily industrial estuary banks from Nantes to the mouth of the Loire, east of the former Breton capital the Loire Valley becomes much more dramatic.

You can enjoy dreamy glimpses of the Loire from around Le Cellier, near which the Château de Clermont boasts the finest views of all. This mid-17th-century castle built in brick, and an archetypal Louis XIII construction, was once owned by one of France's most famous comedians, Louis de Funès. There is an impressive panorama of the Loire from the vantage point of the abbey of St-Méen at St-Cléen, too, as well as a towpath edging the river all the way to Nantes. A many-sided keep rises high above the village of Oudon, a landmark along this stretch of the Loire. It formed part of a medieval castle built here for the Malestroit family under Duke Jean IV of Brittany. You can climb the tower at certain times of year to appreciate the superb views.

Getting around the Loire and Muscadet

Ancenis has a **railway** station at which fast TGVs from Paris to Nantes sometimes stop.

Ancenis is most appealing for its huge traditional market, which brings a good deal of life to its renovated heart. Here, you can try the local roast pork delicacy, *rillaud*, or buy some works of the local poet, who looks as if he's had a stall here for almost as long as the market has existed. In medieval times, this was an important Breton frontier post. The castle grew to substantial proportions in that period, although it has long lain in ruins. For centuries, boats passing this way paid tolls to cross the frontier between Brittany and Anjou. As well as the Maison des Vins, wine-lovers who like to browse a cellar or two would be expertly advised to visit the Épicerie-Cave of Jean-Pierre Bournigault near the market square on Rue de l'Abbé-Fresneau.

Palais Briau

Palais Briau
www.palais-briau.
com, t 02 40 83 45 00;
grounds open April–Oct
daily 2–6; house open
April–July and Sept–Oct
Sat and public hols, Aug
daily 2–6

Close to Varade, this sumptuous brick and limestone château of the 19th century has been open to the public since its relatively recent restoration. François Briau, a model of a 19th-century engineer, commissioned the construction. He had made his fortune planning the railway lines from Tours to Nantes and from Nantes to Pornic. But he had also worked in Italy. When he returned to the Loire, he decided to build his own *palazzo* along Italianate lines. The architect Edouard Moll planned the stocky building in 1854, following Palladian models. Inside, money was lavished on the stucco decoration, the elaborate wall coverings, the odd fresco and the monumental staircase. A tour of the beautifully proportioned interiors gives an excellent feel for life at the cutting edge of design and engineering in the Second Empire.

After visiting the house, you can wander freely through the restored terraced grounds. You can also go in search of the meagre

Ancenis Wines

The cliffs of the Loire begin to rise to some height around Mauves-sur-Loire. Vineyards slope down to the river, producing Coteaux d'Ancenis ('slopes of Ancenis') wines. The wide local range includes VDQS wines made from Cabernet, Gamay, Pinot or Gros Plant. The Coteaux d'Ancenis Malvoisie VDQS is a rare sweet white made from either Pinot Beurot or Pinot Gris. The one wine given the added distinction of its own *appellation* in this area is the Coteaux de la Loire Muscadet. Ancenis has a *Maison des Vins*, t 02 40 96 14 92, where you can learn about, taste and buy local wines. It also hosts blindfolded wine-tasting competitions where anyone willing and foolish enough can pit their taste-buds against the knowledge of the locals. You can organize vineyard visits from there. One recommendation is the **Domaine des Génaudières**, belonging to Brigitte Augustin (*open Mon–Sat 8–12.30 and 2.30–7*) and idyllically located on the hillside overlooking the Loire.

ruins of a medieval fort that was destroyed in 1599. This fort of Varades long guarded the north bank of the Loire.

The pretty village of **Varades** stands on the slope of the Loire's bank. On a round trip, head back to Nantes by crossing the Loire to the dramatically sited small town of **St-Florent-le-Vieil**, then follow the splendid **south bank** to the city. The Loire in these parts is covered further in the separate *Cadogan Guide to the Loire*.

Muscadet Country from Nantes to Clisson

😊 **Muscadet and Clisson**

The undulating, vine-covered countryside producing the well-known Muscadet de Sèvre et Maine *appellation* wines fans out from the southeastern suburbs of Nantes to the border with Anjou. You can visit wineries and the wine museum in this area, the latter also paying tribute to that passionate medieval theologian and lover, Pierre Abélard, born around here. Don't miss the little town of Clisson, which looks confusingly Italian. You might even follow the **Loire Valley Wine Route** through this area.

Muscadet Vineyards

Maison des Vins de Nantes at La Haie-Fouassière
t 02 40 36 90 10, open Mon–Fri 8.30–12.30 and 2–5.45, summer also Sat 11–5

A good place to start touring the Muscadet vineyards is the Maison des Vins de Nantes at La Haie-Fouassière, overlooking hectare upon hectare of vines. Or if you want to head straight out to a winery or two, one of the best ways of seeking out properties well used to receiving visitors is to consult the official website for wines from the Loire, *www.vinsdeloire.fr* – look under Caves Touristiques, Entre l'Océan et Champtoceaux. For other properties, it's well worth ringing in advance to check if they're open and whether someone might be there to greet you. Also look out for the most up-to-date booklets published on the vineyards.

Château de Goulaine
chateau.goulaine. online.fr; open late-Mar–July and Nov Sat, Sun and hols, July–Sept Wed–Mon 2–6

If you're looking for a spectacular property, you might try the Château de Goulaine, located just east of Haute-Goulaine, close to Nantes's southeastern suburbs. It's both a reputed Muscadet-producing estate and an historic castle that you can visit. The history of the Goulaine family goes back almost 1,000 years. The strong vertical lines of the main façade leading to decorated Loire *lucarnes* look archetypal Loire Valley stuff. Inside the château, you only see a small number of rooms, but they are sumptuously decorated. The tour includes a visit to the butterfly house. You also get the opportunity to buy the estate's wine.

Getting around Muscadet Country

There's a **railway** line down through the Muscadet de Sèvre et Maine area to Clisson.

Château du Coing
t 02 40 54 81 15, open Mon–Fri 8.30–12.30 and 2–5.45, summer also Sat 11–5

More discreet is the **Château du Coing**, close to **St-Fiacre-sur-Maine**. The vineyards lie on some of the prettiest slopes in the Muscadet area. The place, a true château, has impressive cellars where you can sample the wines. The winemaker is Véronique Günther Chéreau, a member of a well-known Muscadet-making family.

Château de la Galissonnière
t 02 40 80 45 83, www.chateau galissoniere.com; open Mon–Fri 8.30–12.30 and 2–5.45, summer also Sat 11–5; themed evenings in summer

Back with a more touristy grand Muscadet vineyard, the **Château de la Galissonnière**, close to **Le Pallet**, is well used to hosting visitors with a song and dance.

Musée du Vignoble Nantais
www.pays-vignoble-nantais.org, open mid-June–mid-Sept Tues–Sun 10–6, rest of year 2–6

For those of you accustomed to traditional, unreformed French local history museums, the newfangled approach of the **Musée du Vignoble Nantais**, also beside **Le Pallet**, will come as a bit of a surprise. The museum is startlingly slick, although it might be mistaken for a modern office comlex. It offers a good, if clinical, introduction to Nantais wines going back to Roman times and later developed by monks and noblemen. In modern times, Muscadet benefited greatly when the Breton coastal resorts nearby took off in the 20th century. Tourists grew accustomed to drinking the zingy, refreshing white wine with their seafood, and the fashion spread to Paris. The visit here includes a tasting of medal-winning wines from the region. This being a museum devoted to Pierre Abélard as well as the Pays Nantais vineyards, there's an interesting video presenting the history of the lives of Abélard and Héloïse, and engravings inspired by their famously tormented love story.

Clisson

Clisson, southeast along the Sèvre Nantaise where it's joined by the Moine River, is the highly picturesque town where Brittany and Italy meet. The darkly romantic feudal ruins of its medieval château stand out dramatically to one side of town. The vestiges look classically French. Several medieval masters of Clisson became feared warlords. In the 13th century, when Olivier I de Clisson returned from crusading, he's believed to have ordered the start of work on a castle based on the model of the fort of Caesarea in the Holy Land. Some of his successors became famously embroiled in the Breton War of Succession in the mid-14th century. The Clissons supported the English-backed Jean de Montfort against the French king's candidate, Charles de Blois. The awkward Olivier III de Clisson was duped into accepting an invitation to Paris from the first French Valois king, Philippe VI. The Valois had the courtesy of having his guest's head chopped off, sending it back to Nantes by way of example.

Olivier IV de Clisson was brought up by his mother with an understandable hatred of the French and was sent for a time to the English court to be educated with Jean de Montfort the younger. Once of age, Olivier IV joined the fighting, taking part in the decisive Battle of Auray, in which Charles de Blois was killed and Bertrand du Guesclin captured. But after the de Montfort victory, Olivier IV was deeply disappointed by his rewards. He fell out with Duke Jean IV de Montfort and joined the French army. Ironically, he became so successful that he succeeded the Breton du Guesclin as Constable of France, or head of the French army, gaining the honoured title of Boucher des Anglais ('Butcher of the English'). In the course of his life, he amassed substantial territories in Brittany, for example the Château de Josselin and its estates.

Château de Clisson
www.culture.cg44.fr,
t 02 40 54 02 22, open
Wed–Mon May–Sept
11–6.30, Oct–April
2–5.30.

You can visit the impressive carcass of the **Château de Clisson**. Important additions were made to it in the 15th century for the last duke of Brittany, François II, trying desperately to strengthen his region's frontier castles in response to pressure from the French king Louis XI. In the 16th-century Wars of Religion, further defensive bastions were built. But Jean-Baptiste Kléber, a Revolutionary leader sent to quash the Vendéen uprising in these parts, had the château burned down in 1793 in revenge for his defeat at Torfou. The vestiges have been secured, and in the odd chamber not open to the skies, you can watch short videos on Clisson's history.

Although the magnificent timberframe **Halles**, or covered market near the castle survived the Revolutionary torching, as did a couple of enchanting **medieval bridges**, and one or two **medieval churches**, the last now used as temporary art venues, most of the rest of the old town of Clisson was wiped out by the vengeful Republican troops. The new town that arose afterwards, from 1798, was inspired by artistic, wealthy local brothers Pierre and François Cacault of Nantes, and their friend, sculptor Frédéric Lemot, who had spent a great deal of time in Italy. They deliberately decided to build Roman-style homes that influenced the whole new town.

The church of **Notre-Dame** sets the tone, offering a fine example of Clisson's Italianate style, a campanile rising next to its colonnaded apse, a couple of umbrella pines framing the edifice. Inside, homage is paid to the local people sacrificed in revolutionary times. Around the church and covered market, you'll find some charming shops – Clisson is a bit of a magnet for wealthy Nantais at weekends. There's also a Muscadet producers' tasting shop beside the tourist office.

Head down the steep slope to the **river**, and you can enjoy fabulous views of the whole Italian effect, making an enchanting picture. Across the main bridge, shops, galleries and restaurants occupy some of the finest houses, while punts line the shaded riverbank up to the magnificent 19th-century **viaduct**.

Across the viaduct, you come to **La Garenne Lemot**. This Italianate villa and its grounds are a delight. Ironically, it was anti-republican riots in Rome that forced Frédéric Lemot to return to France. He bought La Garenne ('The Warren' – of the castle) in 1805. Lemot was a sculptor and his most famous works were of royalty; he executed the casting of the equestrian statue of Henri IV on Paris's Pont-Neuf. He was also a man of great taste and great passion for Italy.

La Garenne Lemot
t 02 40 54 75 85; park open daily May–Sept 9–8, Oct–April 9.30–6.30; villa Tues–Sun May–Sept 11–6.30, Oct–April 2–5.30

The **Maison du Jardinier** near the entrance to the estate was built in rustic Italian style. It houses a very well-presented permanent exhibition on Clisson and the Italian influence on French artistic circles. The graceful symmetrical **villa** is reached by a garden lined with statues. The interior is now used to host contemporary art exhibitions, but also displays Lemot's prize-winning sculpture of the Judgement of Solomon as well as retaining many of its original decorative details. The **grounds** offer a treasure hunt of **follies**. You can go in search of the fake antique columns and tomb, or the temple of Vesta, or simply enjoy the picturesque river walk. From the other bank, you can embark on a canoeing trip.

Market Days in the Loire and Muscadet

Ancenis: Thursday morning
Varades: Saturday morning
Vertou: Saturday and Sunday
Le Loroux-Bottereau: Sunday
Vallet: Sunday
Clisson: Friday

ⓘ **Oudon**
11 Rue du Pont Levis, t 02 40 83 80 04, www.ville-oudon.fr

Where to Stay and Eat in the Loire and Muscadet

ⓘ **Varades >>**
Place Jeanne d'Arc, t 02 40 83 41 88, www.varades.fr

⭐ **Palais Briau B&B >>**

ⓘ **Ancenis >**
27 Rue du Château, t 02 40 83 07 44, www.pays-ancenis-tourisme.fr

Le Cellier ✉ 44850

Auberge Le Vieux Cellier, t 02 40 25 40 07, *www.aubergelevieuxcellier.com* (€€€). Solid establishment serving traditional well-cooked food.

Ancenis ✉ 44150

Les Terrasses de Bel Air, Bel Air, along the N23 towards Angers, t 02 40 83 02 87 (€€€–€). Top-notch Loire Valley food accompanied by views of the river itself. *Closed Mon, Sat and Sun lunch.*

La Charbonnière, t 02 40 83 25 17 (€€€). A restaurant perched over the river, with lots of glass windows and terrace seating, offering good local river fish dishes. *Closed Sun and Wed eves, and Sat lunch out of season.*

La Toile à Beurre, Rue St-Pierre, t 02 40 98 89 64 (€€). A good traditional restaurant by the church, with terrace. *Closed Sun and Mon.*

Varades ✉ 44370

Palais Briau B&B, t 02 40 83 45 00, *www.palais-briau.com* (€€€€–€€). Four sumptuous rooms in this 19th-century extravaganza, with blissful views over the countryside.

Closerie des Roses, 455 Haute Meilleraie (beside the river), t 02 40 98 33 30 (€€€). Seasonal takes on river specialities by a young chef, plus the local wines. *Closed Tues eve, Wed, Sun eve, and Tue and Wed in July and Aug.*

⍟ Abbaye de
Villeneuve >

⍟ Château de la
Sébinière B&B >>

ⓘ Pays de
Vignoble Nantais
www.pays-vignoble-
nantais.org

ⓘ Vallet >>
1 Place Charles de
Gaulle, t 02 40 36 35 87,
www.cc-vallet.fr

ⓘ Vertou
Place Beauverger,
t 02 40 34 12 22,
www.vertou.fr

ⓘ Clisson >>
Place du Minage,
t 02 40 54 02 95,
www.valleedeclisson.fr

ⓘ Le Loroux-
Bottereau
12 Place Rosmadec,
t 02 40 03 79 76,
www.loire-divatte.fr

Les Sorinières ✉ 44840
****Abbaye de Villeneuve, Route
de la Roche-sur-Yon, t 02 40 04 40
25, www. abbayedevilleneuve.com
(€€€€–€€). Formerly part of Cistercian
abbey, now a charming hotel just
south of Nantes, with some great
beamed rooms. Grand restaurant
serving traditional regional cuisine.
Pool.

La Haie-Fouassière ✉ 44690
Le Cep de Vigne, Place de la Gare, t 02
40 36 93 90 (€€€–€€). Classic French
cuisine and home-grown Loire wines.
Closed Sun eve and Wed.

Château-Thébaud ✉ 44690
Gérard & Annick Bousseau B&B
Domaine de La Pénissière, t 02 40 06
51 22 (€€). A working wine estate with
smart accommodation and fine
vineyard views.
Chez Valentine Barjolle B&B,
8 Brairon, t 02 40 03 81 35, hotes-
brasseau@wanadoo.fr (€). A decent,
competitively priced option.

Monnières ✉ 44690
Château de Plessis-Brézot, t 02
40 54 63 24 (€€). A reputed wine
domaine and stylish B&B choice
within a little 17th-century property
situated above the Sèvre Nantaise
river. Pool.

Le Pallet ✉ 44330
Château de la Sébinière B&B, t 02 40
80 49 25, www.chateausebiniere.com
(€€€–€€). Outstanding rooms in a
lovely 18th-century home run with
exceptional charm.

Vallet ✉ 44330
**Don Quichotte, 35 Route de Clisson,
t 02 40 33 99 67 (€€). Simple rooms
and a restaurant (€€) where you can
try such regional specialities as hot
oysters in Muscadet, located close to a
windmill. Closed Sun and Fri eves.

Le Landreau ✉ 44430
Auberge du Vignoble, 4 Rue Aubert,
t 02 40 06 42 94 (€). A very appealing,
rustic-looking, good-value inn with
hearty country cooking. Closed Mon.

Clisson ✉ 44190
Le Cèdre de la Trinité, 9 Rue du
Couvent des Dames, t 02 28 21 58 85
(€€). Lovely, spacious, quiet rooms in a
charming typical town building.
La Bonne Auberge, 1 Rue Olivier de
Clisson, t 02 40 54 01 90 (€€). A stylish
gastronomic restaurant near the
centre. Closed Mon, Tues and Wed
lunch, Sun eve.
Restaurant de la Vallée, 1 Rue de la
Vallée, t 02 40 54 36 23 (€€€–€€).
Delightfully located by the river, with a
summer dining terrace. Good food too.

The Southern Loire Atlantique Coast

Here you enter Bluebeard country, the Pays de Retz. Arriving from
the west, once you've made your way around the enormous lake of
Grand-Lieu, you soon come to a string of coastal resorts. They feel
much more southern than those to the north of the Loire, with the
exception of Pornic.

Via the Lac de Grand-Lieu

Heading southwest from Nantes towards the coast, you pass
the enormous but well-hidden, slowly dwindling **Lac de Grand-
Lieu**, a major pull for hundreds of species of birds, and for keen
ornithologists. The natural reserve here covers some 7,000
hectares. If you go north of the lake, the road takes you past the
Safari Africain, a popular game park by Port-St-Père that you can
tour round in your car. Head down the eastern side of the lake and
make a detour to **Passay**, a sleepy little port with fine views on to

Getting around the Southern Coast

A **rail** service links Nantes with Préfailles. There are stops along the coast at Bourgneuf-en-Retz, Les Moutiers-en-Retz, La Bernerie-en-Retz, Pornic and Ste-Marie-sur-Mer.

the lake itself. **La Maison des Pêcheurs** presents the life of the local fishermen. An observatory has been posted in this strategic position to help visitors spot the rich bird life of the area.

St-Philbert-de-Grand-Lieu, south of the lake, has very sound Christian credentials and the distinction of a well-preserved **Carolingian church.** It is very rare to find such an edifice, dating in good part from the 9th and 10th centuries, that has survived down the centuries. St Philibert was a zealous 7th-century religious man who founded numerous monasteries in France, most famously those of Jumièges in Normandy and Noirmoutier, the latter, to the south, in the Vendée. He was buried at the monastery on the island of Noirmoutier. Muscadet is produced all around the lake of Grand-Lieu, although the wine is less highly regarded generally.

To the west, you arrive in Bluebeard country. The frightening figure of Gilles de Retz (*see* p.479) had one of his most important castles at Machecoul, now a sad ruin. At **Bourgneuf-en-Retz** nearby, the old-fashioned local history museum recalls the more innocent country ways of the area in centuries past.

The coast of the Pays de Retz, known poetically in the tourist literature as the Côte de Jade, doesn't feel particularly Breton. The big resorts of **St-Brévin** and **St-Michel-Chef-Chef** are hugely popular and very lively, fronted by long stretches of sand, but they resemble the long, flat Vendée strands. However, the coast around Pornic can put in a good claim to possessing the most southerly of Brittany's rocks.

Pornic

If Pornic was good enough for Lenin it should do everyone else nicely. The Russian revolutionary enjoyed a short break in this delightful, utterly bourgeois retreat, the most southerly historic Breton port.

At the back of the estuary lies the **old fishing port**. You can go on boat trips out to sea from here. The south quay leads you into the smart residential areas of Gourmalon. On the north side, **Quai Leray** is at the centre of the action. The western end of it leads to the castle of Gilles de Retz, a medieval **fort** somehow transformed in the 19th century into a pleasure villa; it's still privately owned. Up above, the **old village** and its picturesque network of lanes are sometimes somewhat quieter than the quays, although there are plenty of seaside boutiques up here. Pornic has its own **pottery works**; to visit, ask at the tourist office.

The unmissable **estuary path**, the boardwalk circling the castle ramparts and passing below grand villas, takes you out to the **Port** de Plaisance de Noëveillard, this major modern marina well protected from the ocean. One end is reserved for the dwindling number of traditional fishing boats. Their most profitable catch is of *civelles*, highly prized, astronomically priced baby eels.

On the southern side of the resort, a swanky modern complex offers both **thalassotherapy sea-water pamperings** and casino. For a plain, old-fashioned treatment, walk the beautiful **coastal paths** in either direction from Pornic. You stumble upon the odd neolithic remain and Nazi blockhouse along the way. The most famous neolithic monument in Pornic is the **Tumulus des Mousseaux** to the north, a cairn from around 3500 BC, but the **Tumulus de la Joselière** along the southern coastal path has far more atmosphere.

Ever-present in the distance lies Noirmoutier, a mirage of an island with gorgeous beaches. A boat service links Pornic and Noirmoutier in July and August– contact **Les Vedettes de la Presqu'île**. Closer to home, you can learn to sail with the **Club Nautique de Pornic**, or enjoy a trip on a skippered boat with the **Corsaires de Retz** or **Le Shamra**. Electric boats, diving, sea-kayaking, and sea-rowing count among many other sporting possibilities; or to get away and relax, explore the small creek beaches away from the main crowds.

Les Vedettes de la Presqu'île
m 06 33 56 52 36

Club Nautique de Pornic
t 02 40 82 34 72

Corsaires de Retz
m 06 72 17 90 32

Le Shamra
m 06 71 17 12 65

Market Days on the Coast South of the Loire

Pornic: Thursday and Sunday

Where to Stay and Eat on the Coast South of the Loire

La Plaine-sur-Mer ✉ 44770
***Anne de Bretagne**, 163 Blvd de la Tara, Port de la Gravette, north of Pointe St-Gildas, **t** 02 40 21 54 72, *www.annedebretagne.com* (€€€€–€€€). An extremely comfortable modern seaside hotel on the dunes in front of the Loire's mouth. Very stylish contemporary rooms, some with balcony. The cooking is top-notch, and there's a pool and a tennis court in the garden. *Restaurant closed Tues, Sun eve and Mon.*

Pornic ✉ 44210
***L'Alliance**, Plage de la Source, **t** 02 40 82 21 21, *www.thalassopornic.* com (€€€€€–€€€€). A posh modern hotel attached to the Pornic thalassotherapy centre, on the sea on the south side of town. Large rooms with balconies. Stylish restaurant in a rotunda making the most of the views.

Beau Soleil, 70 Quai Leray, Place du Petit Nice, **t 02 40 82 34 58, *www. annedebretagne.com* (€€€–€€). A modern wedge of a building on the quay just north of the castle, in the centre of the action. It has bright, neat rooms.

Auberge La Fontaine aux Bretons, Chemin des Noëlles, **t** 02 51 74 07 07 or **t** 02 51 74 08 08 (restaurant), *www.auberge-la-fontaine.com* (€€€–€€). Charming rustic rooms and restaurant in old farm buildings set around a courtyard, with own *potager*, vineyard, farm animals and a flower garden with a pool.

Beau Rivage, Plage de la Birochère, **t** 02 40 82 03 08 (€€€€). A superb location in which to enjoy splendid seafood cuisine. *Closed Mon and Tues.*

ⓘ **Pornic** >
Place de la Gare,
t 02 40 82 04 40,
www.ot-pornic.fr

Language

Use *monsieur, madame* or *mademoiselle* when speaking to everyone (and never *garçon* in restaurants!), from your first *bonjour* to your last *au revoir*.
For Food vocabulary, *see p.58*.

Pronunciation

Vowels

a/à/â between a in 'bat' and 'part'
é/er/ez at end of word as *a* in 'plate' but a bit shorter
e/è/ê as e in 'bet'
e at end of word not pronounced
e at end of syllable or in one-syllable word pronounced weakly, like *er* in 'mother'
i as *ee* in 'bee'
o as o in 'pot'
ô as o in 'go'
u/û between *oo* in 'boot' and *ee* in 'bee'

Vowel Combinations

ai as *a* in 'plate'
aî as e in 'bet'
ail as *i* in 'kite'
au/eau as o in 'go'
ei as e in 'bet'
eu/œu as *er* in 'mother'
oi between *wa* in 'swam' and *wu* in 'swum'
oy as 'why'
ui as *wee* in 'twee'

Nasal Vowels

Vowels followed by an **n** or **m** have a nasal sound.
an/en as o in 'pot' + nasal sound
ain/ein/in as *a* in 'bat' + nasal sound
on as *aw* in 'paw' + nasal sound
un as *u* in 'nut' + nasal sound

Consonants

Many French consonants are pronounced as in English, but there are some exceptions:

c followed by *e, i* or *y*, and *ç* as *s* in 'sit'
c followed by *a, o, u* as *c* in 'cat'
g followed by *e, i* or *y* as *s* in 'pleasure'
g followed by *a, o, u* as *g* in 'good'
gn as *ni* in 'opinion'
j as *s* in 'pleasure'
ll as *y* in 'yes'
qu as *k* in 'kite'
s **between vowels** as *z* in 'zebra'
s **otherwise** as *s* in 'sit'
w **except in English words** as *v* in 'vest'
x **at end of word** as *s* in 'sit'
x **otherwise** as *x* in 'six'

Stress

The stress usually falls on the last syllable except when the word ends with an unaccented **e**.

Useful Phrases

hello *bonjour*
good evening *bonsoir*
good night *bonne nuit*
goodbye *au revoir*
please *s'il vous plaît*
thank you (very much) *merci (beaucoup)*
yes *oui*
no *non*
good *bon (bonne)*
bad *mauvais*
excuse me *pardon, excusez-moi*
Can you help me? *Pourriez-vous m'aider?*
My name is... *Je m'appelle...*
What is your name?
   Comment t'appelles-tu? (informal)
   Comment vous appelez-vous? (formal)
How are you? *Comment allez-vous?*
Fine *Ça va bien*
I don't understand *Je ne comprend pas*
I don't know *Je ne sais pas*
Speak more slowly
   Pourriez-vous parler plus lentement?

How do you say ... in French?
Comment dit-on ... en français?
Help! *Au secours!*

WC *les toilettes*
men *hommes*
ladies *dames or femmes*

doctor *le médecin*
hospital *un hôpital*
emergency room *la salle des urgences*
police station *le commissariat de police*
No smoking *Défense de fumer*

Shopping and Sightseeing
Do you have...? *Est-ce que vous avez...?*
I would like... *J'aimerais...*
Where is/are...? *Où est/sont...*
How much is it? *C'est combien?*
It's too expensive *C'est trop cher*

entrance *l'entrée*
exit *la sortie*
open *ouvert*
closed *fermé*
push *poussez*
pull *tirez*

bank *une banque*
money *l'argent*
traveller's cheque *un chèque de voyage*
post office *la poste*
stamp *un timbre*
phone card *une télécarte*
postcard *une carte postale*
public phone *une cabine téléphonique*
Do you have any change?
Avez-vous de la monnaie?
shop *un magasin*
central food market *les halles*
tobacconist *un tabac*
pharmacy *une pharmacie*
aspirin *l'aspirine*
condoms *les préservatifs*
insect repellent *l'anti-insecte*
sun cream *la crème solaire*
tampons *les tampons hygiéniques*

beach *la plage*
booking/box office *le bureau de location*
church *l'église*
museum *le musée*

sea *la mer*
theatre *le théâtre*

Accommodation
Do you have a room?
Avez-vous une chambre?
Can I look at the room?
Puis-je voir la chambre?
How much is the room per day/week?
C'est combien la chambre par jour/semaine?
single room *une chambre pour une personne*
twin room *une chambre à deux lits*
double room
une chambre pour deux personnes
... with a shower/bath
... avec douche/salle de bains
... for one night/one week
... pour une nuit/une semaine

bed *un lit*
blanket *une couverture*
cot (child's bed) *un lit d'enfant*
pillow *un oreiller*
soap *du savon*
towel *une serviette*

Directions
Where is...? *Où se trouve...?*
left *à gauche*
right *à droite*
straight on *tout droit*
here *ici*
there *là*
close *proche*
far *loin*
forwards *en avant*
backwards *en arrière*
up *en haut*
down *en bas*
corner *le coin*
square *la place*
street *la rue*

Transport
I want to go to... *Je voudrais aller à...*
How can I get to...?
Comment puis-je aller à...?
When is the next...? *Quel est le prochain...?*
What time does it leave (arrive)?
A quelle heure part-il (arrive-t-il)?
From where does it leave? *D'où part-il?*
Do you stop at...? *Passez-vous par...?*

12 Language

How long does the trip take?
Combien de temps dure le voyage?
A (single/return) ticket to...
un aller or aller simple/aller et retour) pour...
How much is the fare?
Combien coûte le billet?
Have a good trip! *Bon voyage!*

airport *l'aéroport*
aeroplane *l'avion*
berth *la couchette*
bicycle *la bicyclette/le vélo*
mountain bike *le vélo tout terrain, le VTT*
bus *l'autobus*
bus stop *l'arrêt d'autobus*
car *la voiture*
coach *l'autocar*
coach station *la gare routière*
flight *le vol*
on foot *à pied*
port *le port*
railway station *la gare*
ship *le bateau*
subway *le métro*
taxi *le taxi*
train *le train*

delayed *en retard*
on time *à l'heure*
platform *le quai*
date-stamp machine *le composteur*
timetable *l'horaire*
left-luggage locker *la consigne automatique*
ticket office *le guichet*
ticket *le billet*
customs *la douane*
seat *la place*

Driving

breakdown *la panne*
car *la voiture*
danger *le danger*
driver *le chauffeur*
entrance *l'entrée*
exit *la sortie*
give way/yield *céder le passage*
hire *louer*
(international) driving licence
un permis de conduire (international)
motorbike/moped
la moto/le vélomoteur
no parking *stationnement interdit*
petrol (unleaded) *l'essence (sans plomb)*

road *la route*
roadworks *les travaux*
This doesn't work
Ça ne marche pas
Is the road good?
Est-ce que la route est bonne?

Numbers

one *un*
two *deux*
three *trois*
four *quatre*
five *cinq*
six *six*
seven *sept*
eight *huit*
nine *neuf*
ten *dix*

eleven *onze*
twelve *douze*
thirteen *treize*
fourteen *quatorze*
fifteen *quinze*
sixteen *seize*
seventeen *dix-sept*
eighteen *dix-huit*
nineteen *dix-neuf*

twenty *vingt*
twenty-one *vingt et un*
twenty-two *vingt-deux*
thirty *trente*
forty *quarante*
fifty *cinquante*
sixty *soixante*
seventy *soixante-dix*
seventy-one *soixante et onze*
eighty *quatre-vingts*
eighty-one *quatre-vingt-un*
ninety *quatre-vingt-dix*

one hundred *cent*
two hundred *deux cents*
one thousand *mille*

Months

January *janvier*
February *février*
March *mars*
April *avril*
May *mai*
June *juin*

July *juillet*
August *août*
September *septembre*
October *octobre*
November *novembre*
December *décembre*

Days

Monday *lundi*
Tuesday *mardi*
Wednesday *mercredi*
Thursday *jeudi*
Friday *vendredi*
Saturday *samedi*
Sunday *dimanche*

Time

What time is it? *Quelle heure est-il?*
It's 2 o'clock (am/pm) *Il est deux heures (du matin/de l'après-midi)*

...half past 2 ...*deux heures et demie*
...a quarter past 2 ...*deux heures et quart*
...a quarter to 3 ...*trois heures moins le quart*
it is early *il est tôt*
it is late *il est tard*

month *un mois*
week *une semaine*
day *un jour/une journée*
morning *le matin*
afternoon *l'après-midi*
evening *le soir*
night *la nuit*
today *aujourd'hui*
yesterday *hier*
tomorrow *demain*
day before yesterday *avant-hier*
day after tomorrow *après-demain*
soon *bientôt*

Glossary of Breton Words

You may recognize many of these words in western Brittany, but do note that Breton words beginning with a consonant often change the first consonant according to preceding article and case and if in the plural.

aber: river estuary
amzer fall: bad weather
amzer gaer: excellent weather
an: the (form used before words beginning with vowels and d, h, n or t)
ankou: sudden death, the Grim Reaper
aod: coast, strand
ar: the (form used before words beginning with most consonants)
arvor: coastal region
avel: wind
aven: river estuary
bag (bag pesketa): boat (fishing boat)
bagad: Breton band
banal: broom
bara: bread
ar bed: the earth
beg: headland
beuzec: boxwood
bez: tomb
bihan: small
bili: pebbles
biniou: bagpipes
bloavez mad: Happy New Year
bombarde: Breton oboe
bot: bush
braz: big
Breizh: Brittany
bro: region
brug: heather
bugel: child
buoc'h: cow
coat: woods
coz: old
cosquer: old village

croas: cross
de mad: hello
digemer mad: welcome
dol: table
douar: earth, ground
dour: water
drennec: bramble patch
du: black
enez: island
erenn: dune
faou: beech
fest noz: night festival
feunteun: fountain
frout: stream
Gallaou: French person
gast: one of the most common Breton swearwords, literally meaning whore
gast amzer: bloody awful weather
glaw (bezo glaw): rain (it is raining)
glaz: green or blue
gwele: bed
gwenn, guenn: white
gwern: marsh
gwez: trees
gwiler: hamlet, village
gwin: wine
gwreg: spouse
ha: and
hent: road
heol: sun
hir: long
huel: high
iliz: church
izel: the bottom, the lowest
kador: chair
karreg: rock or reef
kastell: castle
kenavo: goodbye
kenkiz (or quenquis): summer home
ker, quer, or **guer**: hamlet, village or town

ki: dog
killi (or quilly): hedged fields
konk (or conq): cove, creek:
kouer: peasant
krampouz: crêpes
kreiz: centre, middle
krogen: shell
lan: monastery, religious place
lann: moor or gorse
loc: hermitage, isolated place
lost: the end, tip or tail
louarn: fox
mad: good
mamm: mother
mamm goz: grandmother
marc'h: horse
men: rock
menez: rounded hill
mez: big
meur: large, important
mor: sea
moraer: seaman
mor braz: the big sea, i.e. the ocean
Mor Breizh: the Breton Sea or Channel
morzen: mermaid
nevez: new
nouz vad: good night
penty: cottage
penn: head, tip or start
pesk: fish
plou: parish
porz: cove, port
poul: pond, pool, creek
roc'h: crest, schist rock

roue: king
roz: mound, hillock
ruz: red
Saoz: English person
so or zo: is
stang: lake
ster: river or stream
tad: father
tad koz: grandfather
tal: opposite
taol: table (see also dol)
toul: place or hole
tref: part of a parish
ty: house
yer mat: cheers

Some Numbers in Breton

unan: one
daou: two
tri: three
pevar: four
pemp: five
c'hwec'h: six
seizh: seven
eizh: eight
nav: nine
dek: ten
ugent: twenty
tregant: thirty
daou-ugent: forty
hanter-kant: fifty
kant: one hundred

13

Glossary

Index

Main page references are in **bold**. Page references to maps are in *italics*.

About the Updaters

Original author **Philippe Barbour** was heavily involved in the updating of this new edition. He was greatly helped in his research by his Breton family, notably his beloved grandmother, Ninan, and his Breton aunt and uncle, Dine and René, not forgetting his very patient parents. As ever, in the full updating of this edition, the staff of the Breton *départements*, *pays* and *offices du tourisme* have been very helpful and enthusiastic.

Georgina Palffy now lives in New Zealand, but before leaving the UK she worked as a travel editor for Cadogan Guides, a political and media analyst for an intelligence organization, a foreign affairs journalist at *The Guardian* and *Daily Telegraph* newspapers and an art reviewer for a London listings magazine. She also lived and worked in Rome for several years.

4th edition published 2009

Cadogan Guides is an imprint of
New Holland Publishers (UK) Ltd
London • Cape Town • Sydney • Auckland

New Holland Publishers (UK) Ltd	80 McKenzie Street	Unit 1, 66 Gibbes Street	218 Lake Road
Garfield House	Cape Town 8001	Chatswood, NSW 2067	Northcote
86–88 Edgware Road	South Africa	Australia	Auckland
London W2 2EA			New Zealand

cadogan@nhpub.co.uk
www.cadoganguides.com
t +44 (0) 20 7724 7773

Distributed in the United States by Interlink

Text copyright © Philippe Barbour 1998, 2002, 2005, 2009
Copyright © 2009 New Holland Publishers (UK) Ltd

Cover photographs: Front: © Doug Pearson/JAI/Corbis; Back: © Philippe Barbour
Photo essay photographs: © Philippe Barbour
Maps © Cadogan Guides, drawn by Maidenhead Cartographic Services Ltd
Cover design: Jason Hopper
Photo essay design: Sarah Gardner
Editor: Sarah Greaney
Proofreading: Susannah Wright
Indexing: Isobel McLean

Printed and bound in Italy by Legoprint
A catalogue record for this book is available from the British Library

ISBN: 978-1-86011-417-5

Brittany touring atlas

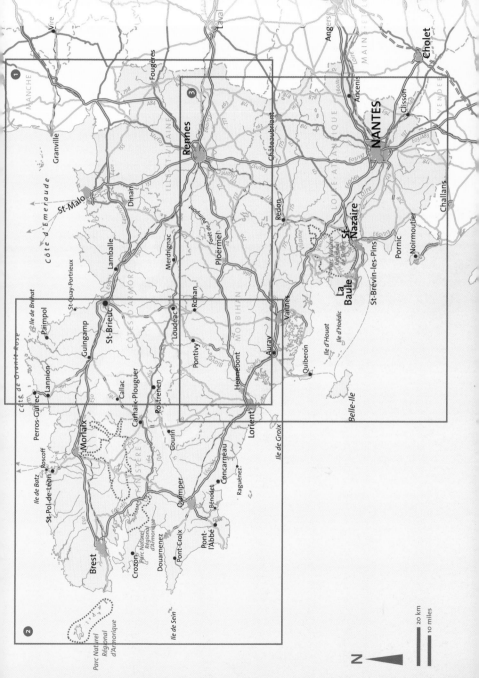

N

20 km
10 miles

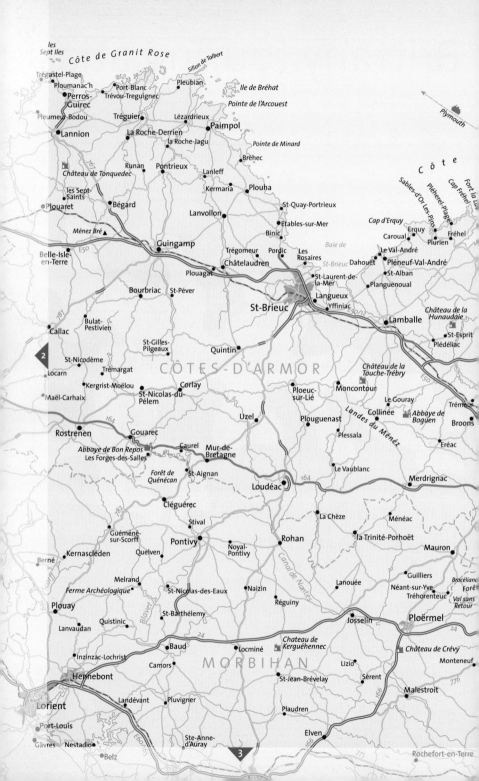

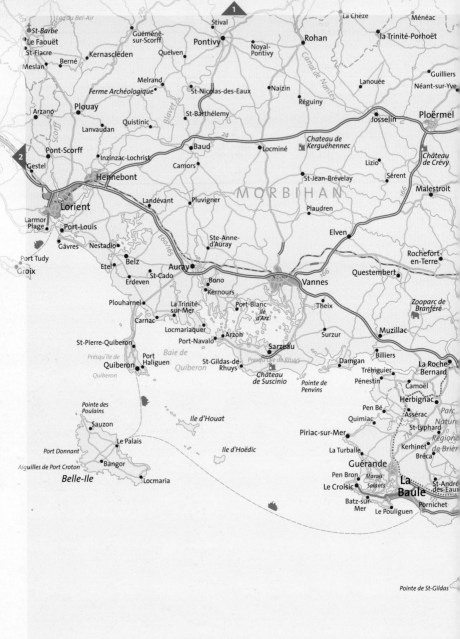

CADOGANguides

Working
and Living

'Impressively
comprehensiv

Wanderlust Magazine

Working and Living Australia • *Working and Living* Canada • *Working and Living* France • *Working and Living* Italy • *Working and Living* New Zealand • *Working and Living* Spain • *Working and Living* USA